The American South

A HISTORY

Volume II / Third Edition

❖

WILLIAM J. COOPER, JR.
Louisiana State University

THOMAS E. TERRILL
University of South Carolina

Boston   Burr Ridge, IL   Dubuque, IA   Madison, WI   New York
San Francisco   St. Louis   Bangkok   Bogotá   Caracas   Kuala Lumpur
Lisbon   London   Madrid   Mexico City   Milan   Montreal   New Delhi
Santiago   Seoul   Singapore   Sydney   Taipei   Toronto

McGraw-Hill Higher Education

A Division of The **McGraw-Hill** Companies

THE AMERICAN SOUTH
A History
Volume II

This book is printed on acid-free paper.

2 3 4 5 6 7 8 9 0 DOC/DOC 0 9 8 7 6 5 4 3 2

ISBN 0-07-246088-1

Editorial director: *Jane Karpacz*
Executive editor: *Lyn Uhl*
Developmental editor: *Kristen Mellitt*
Marketing manager: *Janise Fry*
Associate project manager: *Catherine R. Schultz*
Production supervisor: *Carol A. Bielski*
Coordinator freelance design: *Mary L. Christianson*
Photo research coordinator: *Jeremy Cheshareck*
Photo researcher: *Connie Gardner*
Cover design: *Jamie O'Neal*
Cover image: *© 1966 by Jerry Howard, commissioned by the International Bluegrass Music Association to celebrate its annual "World of Bluegrass" event in 1996.*
Typeface: *10/12 Palatino*
Compositor: *Carlisle Communications, Ltd.*
Printer: *R. R. Donnelley & Sons Company*

Library of Congress Cataloging-in-Publication Data
Cooper, William J. (William James), 1940–
    The American South: a history / William J. Cooper, Jr. [and] Thomas E. Terrill.—3rd ed.
        p. cm.
    Includes bibliographical references and index.
    ISBN 0-07-246059-8 (v. 1 : acid-free paper)—ISBN 0-07-246088-1 (v. 2 : acid-free paper)
    1. Southern States—History. I. Terill, Tom E. II. Title.
F209.C64 2001
975—dc21   2001044088

www.mhhe.com

About the Authors

❖

William J. Cooper, Jr., is a Boyd Professor at Louisiana State University. He received his A.B. degree from Princeton University and his Ph.D. from Johns Hopkins University. Professor Cooper has spent his entire professional career on the faculty at Louisiana State University, where he also served as dean of the Graduate School from 1982 to 1989. He has held fellowships from the Institute of Southern History at Johns Hopkins, from the Charles Warren Center at Harvard, from the Guggenheim Foundation, and from the National Endowment for the Humanities.

He is the author of *The Conservative Regime: South Carolina, 1877–1890* (1968); *The South and the Politics of Slavery, 1828–1856* (1978); *Liberty and Slavery: Southern Politics to 1860* (1983); and *Jefferson Davis American* (2000). He has also edited three books and written numerous articles.

Thomas E. Terrill, Professor of History at the University of South Carolina, received his B.A. degree from Westminster College, his M. Div. from Princeton Theological Seminary, and his M.A. and Ph.D. from the University of Wisconsin. He received fellowships from the National Endowment for the Humanities and the Rockefeller Foundation and was a Fulbright Senior Lecturer at the University of Genoa, Italy. As result of ties he developed there, more than a dozen young Italian scholars have come to the University of South Carolina to work on Southern history; this sponsorship has now been formalized by the Italian government. He is an affiliate of the Centro Studi Euro-Atlantici at the University of Genoa.

He is the author of *The Tariff, Politics and American Foreign Policy, 1874-1901* (1973), co-editor of *Such As Us: Southern Voices of the Thirties* (1978) and co-author of *The American South Comes of Age* (1986) and has many publications in journals and proceedings. He is currently writing a book on labor in the American South. He helped produce a Southern-based feature film (*The Gardener's Son,* screen play by: Cormac McCarthy) for national television, an award-winning documentary film on the General Textile Strike of 1934 ("The Uprising of '34"), and a television course on the modern South for undergraduate and graduate students.

For
William Cooper and Holmes Cooper
and
Andrea Terrill and Mitchell Terrill

Contents

❖

$\mathcal{P}$reface

———— ❖ ————

This is the third edition of *The American South: A History*. That this edition is appearing means that over the past decade many people have found the first and second editions of the book useful. We are pleased and grateful.

In this new edition we have held to our basic themes and structure, including the chronological framework. *The American South* continues to reflect our fundamental assumption that the South is thoroughly American in its life and culture, yet is a distinctive region even today. The complex tension between being both like the rest of the country but distinctive has been continuous, though the tension has been expressed differently at different times, from a superpatriotism during the Mexican War and the Cold War to a sense of profound alienation that underlay secession and the bloodiest American war, the Civil War.

In addition, our book still evinces our conviction that blacks and whites together created and shaped the South. In our judgment it is impossible to understand southern history without comprehending the constant, complex interaction between the races. Yet for the sake of convenience, we follow the convention that "southerners" are white, though we explicitly deviate from that convention at several critical points. The dynamism of black-white relations from slavery to the civil rights revolution and thereafter is a central theme in these pages, as are class and gender roles. Although the southern lady may be a regional icon, women, black and white, have been vigorous participants and catalysts throughout the history of the South.

We have also retained basic changes made for the second edition. We present the South chiefly as proactive, not reactive. Dubbed "Uncle Sam's Other Province," the South has often been perceived as American, but equally often, it has been perceived as so dissimilar as to be an exotic dependent, peopled at various times by slaves and masters, southern ladies, shoeless dirt farmers, passive ex-slaves and their progeny, religious xenophobes, and paunchy courthouse politicians. But that image hardly correlates with the region's dynamism. Among other contributions, the South had a leading role in the American Revolution, had great influence on the making of the Constitution and on the creation of political parties, precipitated the Civil War, figured prominently in both Populism and

Progressivism, and provided the setting and the principal leaders for one of the most important movements in American history, the civil rights revolution. Moreover, post–World War II politics in America has been profoundly molded by developments and politicians in the South.

Throughout the book we have tried to incorporate the newer scholarship on the South. And scholarly interest in southern history has been intense. The product of that interest is remarkable and has transformed how historians understand traditional subjects such as political leadership, plantation economics, and Reconstruction. At the same time historians have given previously neglected topics, such as the slave family, postemancipation blacks, industrial workers, women, and gender relationships, a great deal more attention. The scope of the scholarship on the history of the South is revealed in the comprehensiveness of the bibliographical essay, including the section on biographies, which is intended to be a guide to the major literature on southern history.

Although our fundamental perspective remains unchanged, as does the basic narrative, we have added new material. Most obviously, the chronology has been extended through 2000, with particular coverage given to the presidential election of 2000, which underscores the increasing importance of the South in national affairs. Additional topics that have been substantially revised or expanded include colonial slavery, the role and influence of George C. Wallace, and religious fundamentalism in the twentieth century. Additionally, we have brought the bibliographical essay, including the section on biographies, up to date. There are also some new illustrations. Finally, we have striven to correct factual errors and to clarify the text.

Our story is set within the context of forces that recognized neither national nor regional boundaries: European overseas expansion and empires, plantation economies and involuntary labor, racial prejudice, the western expansion of the new nation, industrialization along with the revolutionary social and economic changes it brought, urbanization, the postindustrial revolution, and new directions in cultural and intellectual currents.

We start with the colonial era, with emphasis on British colonialism because it was so formative in the American South. The first half of the book covers the more than 250 years from European contact with the native peoples in the South and the following successful European settlements to the Civil War, in which the South, as the Confederate States of America, unsuccessfully attempted to establish its independence. The second part focuses on recovery from defeat in the Civil War to the New South and then to our own time, the Modern South.

Our debts to others remain large, and indeed have grown. Our wives, Patricia and Sarah, still stand as steadfast supporters of our commitment to this book.

The extent of our obligations to fellow scholars is indicated in the bibliographical essay. Former graduate students at Louisiana State University helped a great deal: Bradley Bond, Ralph Eckert, Kenneth Startup, Eric Walther, and Kevin Yeager. At the University of South Carolina James A. Dunlap III, Luther Faggart, Janet Hudson, and James Tidd did likewise. An LSU undergraduate, Amanda Gustavson, assisted with preparing the bibliography for this edition. Previous editions have been reviewed by Walter Buenger, David L. Carlton, Willard Gatewood, John Inscoe, and Bertram Wyatt-Brown. We especially appreciate the comments from the five anonymous reviewers who provided our publisher with a critical assessment of the second edition. Although we did not agree with every point they made and constraints of space precluded incorporating all suggestions, their views informed our work. Additional friends and colleagues who over the years generously read portions of the manuscript or gave other invaluable advice and assistance include: Robert A. Becker, Keen Butterworth, Lacy K. Ford, Jr., Gaines M. Foster, Benjamin Franklin V, Michael F. Holt, David Katzman, Daniel Littlefield, David W. Murphy, Sydney Nathans, Paul F. Paskoff, George Rable, Charles Royster, W. Lynn Shirley, Allen H. Stokes, Jr., Robert M. Weir, John Scott Wilson, and R. Jackson Wilson. Three Italian colleagues provided valuable perspectives: Valeria Gennaro Lerda, Fernando Fasce, and Giovanni Fabbi.

We have had good luck with our editors. For the first edition, support came from Niels Aaboe, Jane Garrett, Jack Wilson, and especially David Follmer and Christopher Rogers. Peter Labella initiated the second edition; Lyn Uhl and Jane Vaicunas took up that effort and supervised its completion. In the rapidly changing world of publishing, we are fortunate that Lyn is still with us and remains a stalwart. For this edition, Kristen Mellitt has also been enormously helpful, as has Catherine Schultz, who oversaw production. Still, this book is ours, and we accept full responsibility for it.

William J. Cooper, Jr.
Thomas E. Terrill

Prologue

The Enduring South

— ❖ —

T he South, Wilbur Cash wrote in his celebrated book *The Mind of the South* (1941), is "not quite a nation within a nation but the next thing to it." The sources of that enduring distinctiveness are many and complex. As early as 1750, a generation before Americans went to war against Great Britain to secure their political independence, clear differences distinguished the southern colonies from the northeastern and middle Atlantic colonies. Those differences persisted after the American Revolution and intensified during the first half of the nineteenth century. By 1860, though the similarities among the states remained powerful, the gap between the South and the rest of the country had grown into a chasm that seemingly could not be bridged by any compromise. The American South had become synonymous, though not entirely identical, with plantations, cotton, and black slavery—with places such as Davis Bend, Mississippi.

Thirty-odd miles south of Vicksburg, Mississippi, Davis Bend was a fertile peninsula formed by a large horseshoe curve of the Mississippi River. Today, more than four generations since the flood tides of war swept over it, Davis Bend and the people who lived there in 1860 provide important clues to southern identity before that time and since. The bend got its name from Joseph Davis, a large landholder in the area and the eldest brother of Jefferson Davis, president of the Confederacy. Joseph Davis had prospered as a lawyer in Natchez, Mississippi, a booming cotton and commercial center that served as the capital of Mississippi until 1817, when the territory became a state. He was intensely interested in politics, and when his youngest brother, Jefferson, developed an interest in a political career, Jefferson frequently turned to Joseph for advice.

Joseph Davis bought most of the 11,000 acres of Davis Bend from the federal government in 1818 and obtained the rest from several frontier farmers who had been the first whites to settle and clear the area. Davis sold off 6,000 acres of the bend to friends. Then in 1827, when he was forty-two, he left his law practice and with his sixteen-year-old, three daughters, and a few slaves he had inherited from his father established a plantation at the bend. Eight years later, Jefferson Davis started a plantation of his own on 900 acres that Joseph had given him.

During the next three decades, Joseph Davis became a very wealthy man. In 1860 he was one of only nine planters in Mississippi with more than 300 slaves. He had a spacious mansion and almost a village of outbuildings, which included a cluster of slave cottages. To protect his holdings from flooding by the great river that almost encircled it, Davis and the other leading planters at Davis Bend built a mile-and-a-half-long levee that was six to eighteen feet high. Davis's twenty-five-acre flower garden was so spectacular that passengers disembarked from river steamboats to tour it. No doubt the tourists knew they were in the American South and that their host was a southerner. Neither Davis nor his plantation was typical of the South, though both were typical of what many southerners aspired to.

Davis's background did resemble that of a majority of antebellum southerners. His grandfather, son of a Welsh immigrant, was born in Philadelphia around 1730 and moved as a young man to the colonial South, first to South Carolina, then to Georgia. Joseph's father, Samuel, fought in the American Revolution, married a South Carolina woman he met while serving in the military, and took up farming near Augusta, Georgia, on land the state had given him for his military

DAVIS BEND, MISSISSIPPI (New York Public Library, Schaumberg Collection)

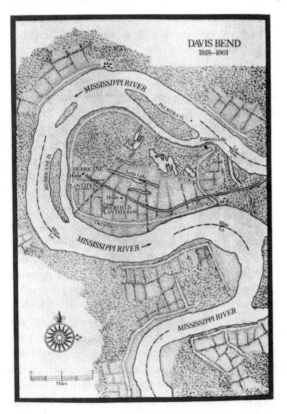

service. The family moved to Kentucky in 1793, a year after the territory had become a state, and there they produced two of that region's principal products: tobacco and horses. In 1810 the Davis family moved again, still pursuing the frontier; eventually they settled in southwestern Mississippi, an area that only nine
years earlier had been ceded by the Choctaws. Settlers such as the Davises kept
continual pressure on Indians to vacate western land so that whites could safely
settle there. In the 1830s the Choctaws and Chickasaws gave up the last of their
holdings in Mississippi and moved west beyond Arkansas to what was called Indian Territory. Whites later followed the Indians, took over most of their land, and
created the state of Oklahoma; the name means "home of the Indian."

On their newly acquired land in Mississippi the Davises cultivated cotton as
their major cash crop. To clear the land and plant, cultivate, and harvest the cotton, they relied on their own labor and the handful of slaves Samuel owned. Improving fortunes allowed them to build a substantial home graced by a veranda—
a large step up from the four-room log cabin the family had occupied in Kentucky.
The family of Samuel Davis strongly resembled the great majority of whites who
populated the South from its earliest years to the Civil War: yeoman farmers who
pushed south and west for more than a century and a half in search of cheap, fertile soil, frequently acquiring a few slaves, always bending their backs as they
tried to improve their lot and station.

Their pursuit of the southern version of the American dream propelled such
families from Virginia into the Carolinas and Georgia, southward into Florida,
and westward as far as Texas before 1860. These pioneering farmers often settled
in areas very different from the great plantation regions of which Davis Bend was
a part. They made up the great majority of farmers in the mountains of Appalachia and the Ozarks and were predominant in the valleys and rolling hills of
the piedmont and along the vast coastal plain that ran from the Chesapeake
through Florida and on to the Texas gulf coast. Other southerners made their
places in the cities and towns of the overwhelmingly agricultural South. Such
places were sites for commercial enterprise and some manufacturing. Urban areas
also afforded desired refinements for their residents and for the surrounding
countryside.

Joseph Davis found Natchez a good place for an ambitious attorney, and Jefferson Davis attended a private academy near there as well as one in Kentucky.
Like many ambitious Americans at the time, the youngest Davis believed that advanced education could improve his prospects. Thus, Jefferson graduated from
academies to Transylvania University in Lexington, Kentucky, where he spent a
year. Founded in 1780, Transylvania developed into the first center of learning
west of the Appalachians and south of the Ohio River. Jefferson Davis completed
his formal education at West Point. After an unexceptional academic career, he
spent most of his seven-year army career at frontier posts in Wisconsin, Illinois,
and Oklahoma.

Jefferson Davis briefly returned to the military in the 1840s, where he fought
with distinction in the Mexican War. After 1835, however, he devoted most of his
energies to his plantation and to his highly successful political career. Despite ill
health, Davis drove himself to build first an impressive plantation estate and then
an impressive political career. The latter pursuit required innumerable stump

JOSEPH DAVIS (Eleanor S.
Brockenbrough Library,
Museum of the Confederacy,
Richmond, Virginia)

speeches, interminable rounds of political meetings, and mountains of correspon-
dence with constituents and fellow politicians. Several heated disputes stopped
just short of duels. Davis survived horrible weather, dirt roads, mud roads, carts,
wagons, carriages, lurching spark-spewing trains, steamboats, inns, hotels, good
food, bad food, and tobacco-spitting, importuning, and sometimes sweaty constituents from Mississippi to Washington and back. Davis represented his state in
the U.S. House of Representatives and the Senate and served as a highly competent, dedicated secretary of war in the administration of President Franklin Pierce.
Like other southerners in his day and later, Jefferson Davis was an American in
his efforts to succeed and in his national loyalties. Indeed, Davis was convinced
that as a leader first of the South in Congress and later of the Confederate States of
America he was risking civil war and his life and fortune to preserve the Constitution, which he saw as the bulwark of liberty.

    To Davis, the election of Abraham Lincoln posed a revolutionary threat; Lin-
coln's election meant the triumph of the antislavery movement—a movement
dedicated to destroying southern rights. Announcing his resignation from the
Senate in January 1861, Davis told his fellow senators and the nation that the
southern states had been forced to secede from the Union because the Republicans who were coming to power "denie[d] us equality . . . refuse[d] to recognize
our domestic institutions which preexisted the formation of the Union, our property which was guarded by the Constitution." He accused Lincoln of making "a
distinct declaration of war upon our institutions." Davis asked that the states that
chose to secede be allowed to do so peacefully, but if the North insisted that the
South "remain as subjects to you, then, gentlemen of the North, a war is to be inaugurated the like of which men have not seen."

In 1860 and 1861 the southern states seceded from the Union to prevent the federal government from intruding on their rights and abolishing slavery, the cornerstone of white southern society. To preserve the society the South took up arms against the Union. As a consequence, the Union intruded massively in the South—and with devastating impact—from 1861 until the end of Reconstruction in 1877. After the Civil War, the South erected a defense to ward off unwelcome outside intrusions in its race relations and other aspects of its life. The most concrete form of that defense was the "Solid South," or the thorough dominance of the South by the Democratic party. Fashioning itself as "the party of white supremacy," the Democratic party grounded its appeal on maintaining white unity in the South, keeping southern blacks subordinate ("in their place"), and preventing interference with that arrangement.

Erected during the 1870s and 1880s, the Solid South remained in place until after World War II. Breaches in the one-party politics of the Democratic South appeared earlier, however, under the federal government's efforts to combat the depression of the 1930s. The Solid South cracked during the 1948 presidential election, then shattered during the Civil Rights revolution of the 1950s and 1960s. Propelled by America's post-1940 economic boom and by massive federal spending in the region, a more prosperous, two-party South found a comfortable place in the Sunbelt and in national politics and became a much greater force in the nation than it had been at any previous time since the 1860s.

The South's failed attempt to reshape America by leaving the Union in 1860 defined the region and its people for all the generations that have followed. The South and southerners can be defined as the states that seceded and the people who supported secession and identified themselves then and later with what they believed was its noble cause. But defining the South and southerners only in terms of the Civil War is too narrow. Though that definition has the advantage of clarity, it seriously distorts the past and even the present. In this book, the southern states are defined as the eleven Confederate states plus Kentucky, Maryland, and, after the Civil War, Oklahoma, the creation of latter-day pioneers who erected a Dixie on the plains. Kentucky and Maryland nearly seceded. Both provided troops for the Confederacy, as did Missouri, a state deeply divided by the Civil War. This state-based definition of the South is hardly free of ambiguities. Parts of West Virginia, for instance, are more southern than west Texas, southern Florida, and parts of Kentucky and Oklahoma ever were, and substantial numbers of West Virginians served in the Confederate armed forces.

Using the Civil War as a reference point to define southerners is even more misleading. Not all southerners in the 1860s supported secession or identified with its cause, though they often suffered from the defeat of the Confederacy. Unionist sentiment was strongest in the South among mountain whites. Depredations during the war reinforced the Unionist feelings of many people, particularly in Appalachia. Black southerners celebrated the defeat of the Confederacy for obvious reasons. African Americans lived all over the South in 1860, but usually on plantations such as those at Davis Bend, and they had interacted with whites since the seventeenth century to create much of what made the South. Without that interaction there would have been no "South" as the term and the region are commonly understood. Moreover, southern blacks and whites had and have striking cultural similarities and strikingly similar historical experiences. Both have experienced economic inferiority, and both have been disdained as cultural and moral inferiors. The labor, skills, and ideas of blacks have been critical to the development and evolution of the South. For the sake of convenience and clarity, however, southerners are white in this book unless we explicitly state otherwise or unless the context implies a different interpretation.

The Davises, especially Joseph Davis, certainly knew how important blacks were to them. They acknowledged the importance of blacks to their lives, in part by being humane masters. Some local whites disparaged Joseph Davis's slaves as "Mr. Davis's free negroes." The neighbors may have had Benjamin Thornton Montgomery in mind when they said such things. Born into slavery in northern Virginia in 1819, Montgomery grew up as the companion of his young master. He moved westward involuntarily to Natchez in 1836 when, without notice or explanation, he was sold to a slave trader. The trader took Montgomery with a gang of other recently purchased slaves to the booming slave markets of Mississippi's black belt. There Joseph Davis bought Montgomery, but the young slave soon ran away. Unfamiliar with his new surroundings, Montgomery was caught almost immediately. When Davis questioned Montgomery about his attempted escape, he quickly realized Montgomery's considerable capacities and encouraged them. Montgomery, who had learned to read and write from his former master in Virginia, eventually became a mechanic, inventor, surveyor, builder, and merchant. He and his wife, Mary Lewis Montgomery, who was also literate, arranged, with Davis's approval, for the schooling of their children. Montgomery played a major role in the life of Davis Bend before and after the war reached the peninsula.

In January 1861, Jefferson Davis left Washington and returned home. In February he left Davis Bend to be inaugurated as president of the Confederacy. In April 1862, Joseph Davis took his family and about a hundred slaves and fled his river home to escape the advance of Union forces. Most of their slaves deserted during the hasty retreat, and some of them later descended upon the mansion to pillage clothing and furniture. Union troops did even more damage when they arrived. Not long afterward, Benjamin Montgomery reasserted his leadership. Eventually, after the war, he bought the plantation from Joseph Davis, with whom he had maintained regular communication. For several years Montgomery struggled, but forces beyond his control doomed his efforts. Eventually the community at Davis Bend dissolved. Even the river took its toll: in 1867 the main channel of the Mississippi swept across the neck of the peninsula and turned Davis Bend into Davis Island.

The war destroyed the slave-based plantation society of the antebellum South: the South of planters, slaves, and highly profitable cash crops, which once was so easily identifiable, faded. Within a generation another, also easily identifiable South emerged: a region of chronic underdevelopment, poverty, one-party politics, and Jim Crow, a rigid racial caste system. Once again, to the rest of Americans the South was the deviant region. And it seemed not to change at all until World War II. That perception was wrong, however, just as was the perception that the antebellum South had been unchanging.

The South did not stand still from 1865 to 1940. The New South, a more urban, industrial South, began to appear soon after the Civil War, but it did not emerge fully until the 1920s. Still, low incomes persisted, race relations remained frozen, and one-party politics and impotence on the national scene seemed permanent conditions. But before World War II, each of these fundamental characteristics of the South after the Civil War began to change. The depression of the 1930s and the New Deal of President Franklin Roosevelt hastened change, and World War II accelerated the process by which the Sunbelt South emerged.

In the years since 1945, the economics, politics, and race relations of the South have changed so much that the South of the twenty-first century, the Sunbelt South, seems to have almost no connection with the South of Jefferson Davis or the South after the Civil War, even with the South of the 1930s. The South is now more prosperous than it has been since the 1850s. Unlike the antebellum South, however, the Sunbelt South resembles the rest of the country in its politics and its race relations. Though vestiges of poverty, one-party politics, and Jim Crow remain, the picture of the poor, backward South has dissolved into an image of prosperity.

Defining southerner or southern identity is not so easy as it once was. One of the region's loyal sons and keen observers declared in 1973 that "the South is just about over as a separate . . . place." But a decade later another perceptive student of the South said that he "knows when he is in the South." The South may have lost some of its distinctiveness, but much remains. The South remains the United States' most obviously distinctive region in ways that are still very important: in culture and religion, in ethnic composition, in its sense of having a unique past, and in its sense of place. Southerners have deep attachments to their region. Those attachments have been expressed, among other ways, in the determination

BENJAMIN THORNTON
MONTGOMERY (Library of
Congress)

of southerners to remain Americans with a special regional identity even in the homogenized culture of the early twenty-first century. That determination helps explain why the South has endured as the United States' most distinctive region for more than two hundred years and why the history of the South continues to fascinate so many people.

This book tries to answer two questions: What was and is the American South? What was and is a southerner? The answers to these questions depend largely on where and when they are asked. The answers are easier and clearer at some times than at others. The answer to the question about southern identity is harder and less clear now than at any time since the mid-eighteenth century. Still, the South endures. It endures in part because not even a flood of changes has washed away critical connections between the past and the present in the South.

Map Essay

The Geography of the Civil War

— ❖ —

*T*hese maps emphasize the critical events leading up to the Civil War and outline the most important military engagements of the conflict. The first two focus on the two crucial political events of 1860 and 1861: the presidential election and secession. The former delineates the sectionalism that dominated the presidential contest while the latter illustrates the range of reactions in the slave states to the outcome of that election. The third map depicts the harbor of Charleston, South Carolina, where the first shots of the war were fired. The final five maps are designed to help clarify the campaigns of the war. They identify the key army movements and specify the locations of the major battles in both the eastern and western theaters.

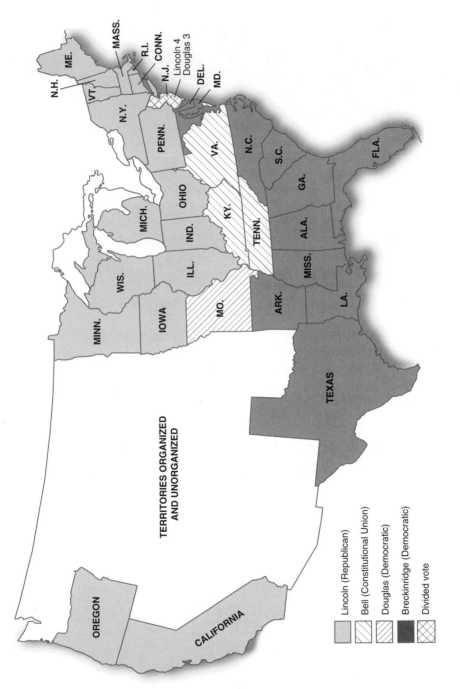

THE ELECTION OF 1860

Lincoln (Republican)
Bell (Constitutional Union)
Douglas (Democratic)
Breckinridge (Democratic)
Divided vote

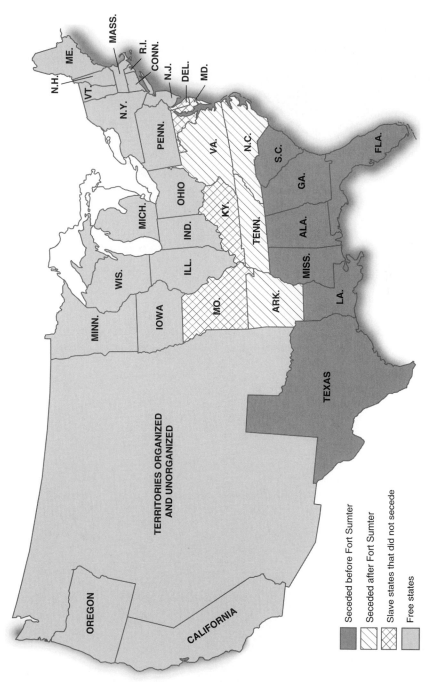

THE PATTERN OF SECESSION

Seceded before Fort Sumter

Seceded after Fort Sumter

Slave states that did not secede

Free states

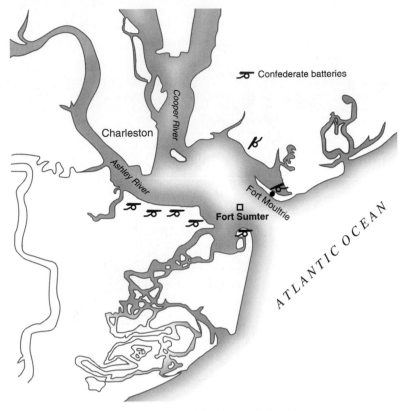

Confederate batteries

Charleston

Cooper River

Ashley River

Fort Moultrie

Fort Sumter

ATLANTIC OCEAN

CHARLESTON HARBOR, 1861

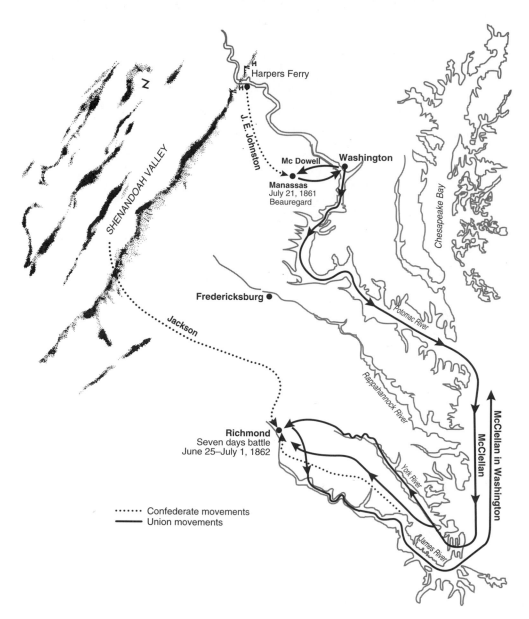

MAJOR CAMPAIGNS IN THE EAST, 1861–JULY 1862

333

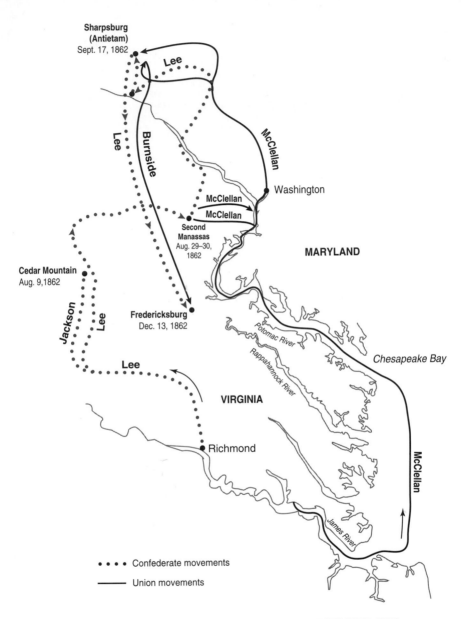

Sharpsburg
(Antietam)
Sept. 17, 1862

Lee

Lee

Burnside

McClellan

Washington

McClellan

McClellan

Second
Manassas
Aug. 29–30,
1862

MARYLAND

Cedar Mountain
Aug. 9,1862

Jackson

Lee

Fredericksburg
Dec. 13, 1862

Potomac River

Rappahannock River

Chesapeake Bay

Lee

VIRGINIA

Richmond

McClellan

James River

• • • • Confederate movements

——— Union movements

MAJOR CAMPAIGNS IN THE EAST, JULY–DECEMBER 1862

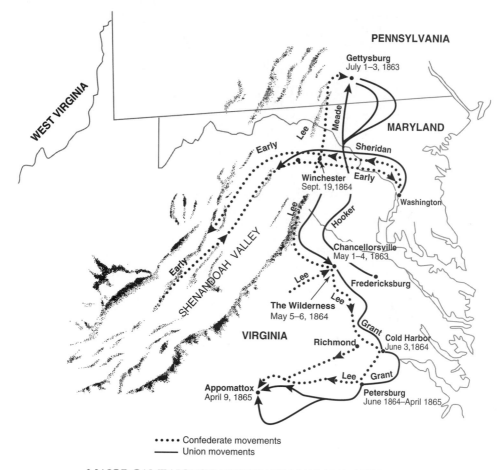

MAJOR CAMPAIGNS IN THE EAST, MAY–1863–APRIL 1865

335

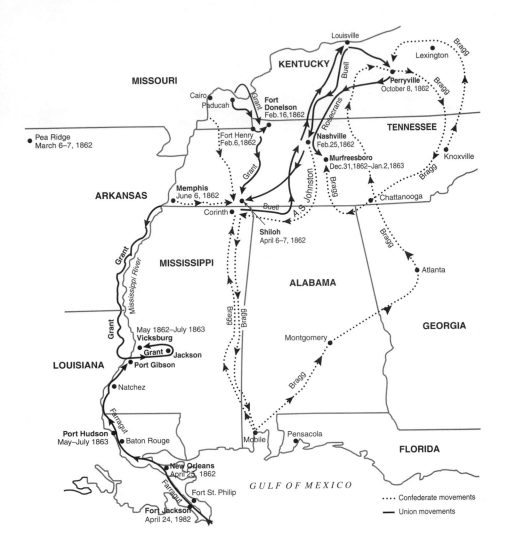

MISSOURI

KENTUCKY

TENNESSEE

ARKANSAS

MISSISSIPPI

ALABAMA

GEORGIA

LOUISIANA

FLORIDA

Pea Ridge
March 6–7, 1862

Cairo

Paducah

Fort Henry
Feb.6,1862

Fort
Donelson
Feb.16,1862

Louisville

Lexington

Perryville
October 8, 1862

Knoxville

Nashville
Feb.25,1862

Murfreesboro
Dec.31,1862–Jan.2,1863

Chattanooga

Memphis
June 6, 1862

Corinth

Shiloh
April 6–7, 1862

Atlanta

Mississippi River

Vicksburg

May 1862–July 1863

Jackson

Port Gibson

Natchez

Montgomery

Port Hudson
May–July 1863

Baton Rouge

Mobile

Pensacola

New Orleans
April 25, 1862

Fort St. Philip

GULF OF MEXICO

Fort Jackson
April 24, 1982

Grant

Buell

Rosecrans

A.S. Johnston

Bragg

Farragut

····· Confederate movements
——— Union movements

MAJOR CAMPAIGNS IN THE WEST, 1861–SUMMER 1863

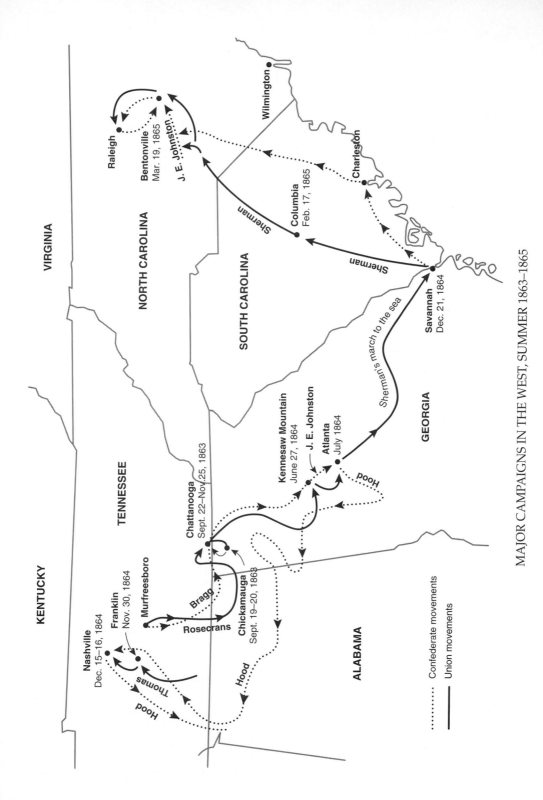

MAJOR CAMPAIGNS IN THE WEST, SUMMER 1863–1865

KENTUCKY

VIRGINIA

TENNESSEE

NORTH CAROLINA

SOUTH CAROLINA

GEORGIA

ALABAMA

Nashville
Dec. 15–16, 1864

Franklin
Nov. 30, 1864

Murfreesboro

Chattanooga
Sept. 22–Nov. 25, 1863

Chickamauga
Sept. 19–20, 1863

Kennesaw Mountain
June 27, 1864

Atlanta
July 1864

Savannah
Dec. 21, 1864

Columbia
Feb. 17, 1865

Charleston

Wilmington

Raleigh

Bentonville
Mar. 19, 1865

Wilmington

Bragg

Rosecrans

Thomas

Hood

Hood

Hood

J. E. Johnston

J. E. Johnston

Sherman

Sherman

Sherman's march to the sea

········ Confederate movements
——— Union movements

337

15

The Confederate Experience

———— ❖ ————

ort Sumter stands three miles from Charleston, at the point where the harbor meets the Atlantic Ocean. Construction on it had begun in the late 1820s, as part of a plan devised after the War of 1812 by Secretary of War John C. Calhoun to defend the nation's seacoast from attack. Still unfinished in the spring of 1861, Fort Sumter had become the most visible symbol of the divided nation. Even though the fort lay entirely within the borders of South Carolina, and thus of the Confederate States of America, the Stars and Stripes still flew over the masonry structure. Manned by eighty-five men under the command of Major Robert Anderson, Fort Sumter gave force to President Abraham Lincoln's cry that the Union remained inviolable while it challenged the Confederacy's claim to independence.

Fort Sumter became the prize in the first great contest between the Union and Abraham Lincoln and the Confederacy and Jefferson Davis. The stakes were more political than military, for the Sumter garrison, massively outnumbered and outgunned by Confederate troops and artillery, could not hope to win a fight. On the political front, however, the potential rewards and dangers were much greater. Some of Lincoln's advisers, including military leaders, recommended withdrawal from Fort Sumter, but the president rejected their advice. To his mind, to pull out was to concede the Confederacy's independence and possibly to end his cherished dream of keeping the Union whole. Even so, Lincoln realized that a straightforward military reinforcement not only would require a Confederate counteraction but might push both the upper South and the border states into the Confederacy, which would then have fifteen states instead of the seven Deep South states it now had. To double the Confederacy's base was to court disaster for the Union. Rejecting reinforcement as well as withdrawal, Lincoln decided on a master stroke. He announced that he would resupply Fort Sumter. He would send in no new soldiers or guns, only food and medicine for the troops already there. This action, Lincoln proclaimed, would leave unchanged the calculus of power in Charleston Harbor. This masterful maneuver provided a clear sign of the political genius that would make Lincoln such a great president and war leader.

While Lincoln made his momentous decision, President Jefferson Davis and his advisers also pondered the problem of Fort Sumter. Powerful arguments supported the contention that the Confederates should take the fort. The first was that the Union's occupation of Fort Sumter mocked the Confederacy's independence. According to this thinking, the Confederate States of America could not stand as an independent nation so long as another power maintained an uninvited military force within the Confederacy's borders. Second, some Confederates feared, with justification, that hotheads in South Carolina might strike against the fort on their own initiative. Any such action would undermine the authority of the Confederate government and commit it to a course it had not decided upon. Some Confederate leaders also maintained that a Confederate move against Fort Sumter would mobilize the citizenry behind the government and, equally important, bring the upper South within the Confederate fold. Those who opposed direct action stressed the harm that could come from a first strike. Such an attack, they argued, would lose the Confederacy numerous friends in the North and at the same time strengthen Lincoln's hand. But these arguments did not prevail. President Davis decided to demand the surrender of Sumter, and if it were not forthcoming, he would attack.

CONFEDERATE PRESIDENT
JEFFERSON DAVIS (Mississippi
Department of Archives and
History)

From Montgomery orders went to General Pierre G. T. Beauregard of Louisiana, in command of all Confederate forces at Charleston, to demand the surrender of Fort Sumter. If Major Anderson refused, Beauregard was to take the fort. Presented with this alternative, Anderson told the Confederates that he would have to evacuate the fort unless new supplies reached him. Beauregard, aware of the criticalness of the situation in Charleston Harbor, informed his government in Montgomery of Anderson's response. The new directive issued to Beauregard gave him some latitude. If Anderson would provide a specific date for his evacuation, Beauregard was not to open fire. Once again Beauregard contacted Anderson, who did specify a date for withdrawal but added a qualification: he would evacuate Fort Sumter unless controlling instructions from his government directed a different course of action. Beauregard now knew he had no choice; his orders had been explicit. At 4:30 A.M. on Sunday, April 12, the Confederate batteries aimed at Fort Sumter opened fire. After thirty-three hours of bombardment Anderson surrendered. War had begun.

PLANS AND POLICY FOR WAR

With the onset of hostilities, the Confederate government suddenly found itself a war government. Thus almost from its birth the chief mission of the Confederate government became the fighting of a great war.

Jefferson Davis and his advisers faced a formidable task. They led a country that had just been created. This new country had no armed forces, no treasury, no economic or fiscal policy, no foreign policy or diplomatic missions. It did not even have that most popular scourge of all governments, a bureaucracy. The Confederate leaders had to confront problems in all these areas simultaneously. They could not address one, solve it, then move to the next. All had to be coped with at once, for all were crucial; none could be postponed. Moreover, all interacted with one another.

The Confederate government began its operations in Montgomery, Alabama. In the center of the Deep South, Montgomery was a logical place for the convening of the delegates from the states that created the Confederate States of America, wrote the Constitution, and selected the first president and vice president. But after Fort Sumter and the secession of Virginia, a movement commenced to move the capital from Montgomery to Richmond. Numerous reasons prompted this pressure. A small town, Montgomery had neither the facilities nor the services to house conveniently either the apparatus or the personnel of the government. Richmond, though no metropolis, offered considerably more. In addition, Richmond was the most important industrial center in the Confederacy. To guarantee its protection, some Confederates argued, it should be made the capital.

Motives other than size and industry also worked in favor of Richmond. Confederates were thrilled when Virginia, the ancient mother and leader of the South, finally sided with them. Many of them believed it only appropriate that their capital be located in the native state of George Washington and other founders who had led the colonies to victory in the American Revolution. In his inaugural address in Montgomery, President Jefferson Davis proudly equated the Confederates of 1861 with their Revolutionary War ancestors. Southerners, in Davis's mind, "labored to preserve the government of our fathers in its spirit." Accordingly, in May 1861 the entire Confederate government was transferred to Richmond, which remained the capital of the Confederate States of America for the new nation's lifetime.

After April 12 all the tasks confronting the Confederate leadership co-alesced into one immense undertaking—the conduct of war. An army had to be raised. Even before Fort Sumter the Confederate Congress had authorized the recruitment of 100,000 volunteers for the Confederate States Army. In May the Congress provided for 400,000 more; by July 1861 the Confederacy, with a white population only one-quarter the size of the Union's, had nearly two-thirds as many men under arms. Although southerners did respond enthusiastically to the colors, the Confederate War Department had difficulty arming them. Some 150,000 muskets were available from captured U.S. arsenals in the seceded states, but most were obsolete. The first Confederates who joined up brought their own firearms— hunting rifles, shotguns, even ancient flintlock muskets. In 1861 each regiment in the Confederate Army wore its own uniform. Although the government designated the famous cadet gray as the official color, in fact an enormous variety of outfits colored Confederate units. Never did all Confederate soldiers wear a regulation uniform.

At the same time that Confederate authorities strove to find ways to equip their fighting men with the tools of war, they had to make critical decisions about the methods of financing the war. With an overwhelmingly agricultural economy and a tradition of low taxes, the South was not financially ready for a major modern war. Southern leaders believed that the economic power of their cotton would force France and especially Great Britain to intervene on their behalf. No one was quite sure what form such intervention would take, but most envisioned a variety of measures, including financial assistance. With that utterly erroneous faith in European aid and with a massive hostility to taxation, the Confederate Congress at the outset rebuffed the argument of Secretary of the Treasury Christopher Memminger that secure financial support for the war required a levy of taxes.

Denied tax revenue, the Confederate government turned to borrowing. Early in 1861 the government issued $15 million in bonds, which took up most of the available specie in the Confederate states. Then in May a produce loan authorized farmers and planters to pledge a portion of their crop income in return for bonds equal in value to the market price of their pledge. This tactic produced little revenue, because the income from the pledged crops never kept up with the depreciation of Confederate currency. Efforts to raise money in Europe met with no more success, though in late 1862 a loan was negotiated with a French banking house. The Erlanger loan, so called after the banking house, eventually provided between $6 million and $8.5 million to the Confederacy for the purchase of war goods and the repayment of old debts. It was far from enough.

The chief source of revenue was the treasury notes issued by the Confederate government. The introduction into the Confederate economy of large amounts of paper money backed by nothing but hope set off an inflationary spark that soon became a conflagration. In 1864, after three years of this avalanche of paper money, it took $46 to buy what $1 had bought in 1861. From a base of 100 at the beginning of 1861 the price index shot upward to 762 by 1865. This inflationary surge, the result of a reckless fiscal policy, wrecked the economy. Inflation grew so intolerable that popular pressure pushed Congress to enact taxes in an effort to curb it. In 1863 Congress responded by instituting a variety of taxes—excise taxes, license taxes, a 5 percent tax on land and slaves, even an income tax. But the package was too little too late. Lax enforcement and active evasion combined to make the new laws largely ineffective.

Misplaced faith in the omnipotence of cotton governed Confederate diplomatic strategy as well. The Davis administration set one overriding diplomatic goal: to win recognition from the European powers, chiefly France and Great Britain. In cotton the Confederate government thought it had the lever that would force Great Britain to recognize the Confederacy as an independent nation and possibly even intervene in the war on the Confederate side. And when Great Britain adopted a pro-Confederate stance, France would not be far behind.

Confederate authorities might have built up credits in Europe by exporting as much cotton as possible. Instead, to make sure that Great Britain would follow the path they intended, they embargoed all the cotton remaining within their borders. In their view, the British economy could not withstand the absence of Confederate cotton. They made a grave miscalculation. In the first place, cotton was not so central to the British economy as they assumed. Then, to undermine their plans even further, the great crop of 1859 had enabled British merchants and manufacturers to stockpile huge quantities of cotton. Finally, Great Britain had two other sources of cotton within its own empire: Egypt and India. Cotton never forced Great Britain or anyone else to recognize the Confederacy. In short, the cotton the Confederates considered their ace turned out to be a joker.

Even so, the act of a zealous Union naval officer made it appear, at least momentarily, that the Confederacy might get its wish. In November 1861 a Union warship stopped and boarded a British mail packet, the *Trent,* which carried two Confederate diplomats: the Virginian James Mason, traveling to London, and John Slidell of Louisiana, bound for Paris. Mason and Slidell were removed from the *Trent* and taken to a prison in Boston. Huzzahs greeted the news in the North, but London was enraged by the lack of respect shown to the British flag. Tension grew between the two governments, but cool heads and moderation prevailed. The British demanded an apology and the release of the diplomats, and the French sent a supporting note. The Lincoln administration replied that the action had occurred without authorization and ordered the diplomats released. Britain accepted that explanation. Mason and Slidell went on to their posts in Europe; neither succeeded in gaining recognition for the Confederacy.

At home the Confederate leaders had to wrestle with the problems of fighting a war. The Davis administration never developed any written war plans. In a fundamental sense, Davis and his advisers settled on a basic strategy that under the circumstances appeared both logical and reasonable. They had one chief goal, to be let alone. Thus they decided not to go on the strategic offensive; they would not try to secure their independence by attacking the North. This decision resulted in large part from a realistic appraisal of the Confederacy's resources. President Davis wanted to strike at the North, but he realized that he just did not have the means to do so. To a friend he wrote in 1862, "My early . . . hope was to feed upon the enemy and teach them the blessings of peace by making them feel in its most tangible form the evils of war. The time and place for invasion has been a question not of will but of power." And though in three instances Davis was able to carry the war into enemy territory, he never commanded the sustained power for an offensive strategy.

Instead his troops would stand on the defensive and guard their own territory. From Virginia in the east to the Mississippi River and beyond, the Confederate frontier covered more than 1,000 miles. And the coastline stretching from Virginia on the Atlantic around Florida and across the Gulf of Mexico all the way to the Rio Grande was much longer. If the Union was to subdue the Confederacy, it would have to attack this immense domain. When the Union forces moved into various portions of their territory, the Confederates would strike them at points of opportunity. Thus the Confederates would combine selected offensives with their basic defensive posture. This strategy also included an unstated or undeveloped intention—to wear down the enemy. By luring the Union armies to invade their land—an operation that would require huge numbers of troops and enormous sums to maintain them, and one that was bound to result in substantial casualties—the Confederates hoped to make the North pay a higher price in men, money, and matériel than it could afford. In this view, the Union had neither the will nor the substance to pay the terrible cost necessary to subjugate the Confederacy.

To manage the war the Confederacy had no general staff in the modern sense, with overall command responsibility. Early on the Confederates implemented a departmental command structure: the country was divided into various departments, the commander of each department reporting to the War Department in Richmond. This structure, which seemed rational but worked against cooperation and concentration, remained in place until almost the end of the war. President Davis had a military adviser, but the adviser had no command responsibility. The president acted not only as the constitutional commander in chief but also often as a general in chief, transmitting his orders through the secretary of war. If the numerous departments were to be coordinated in any way, he would have to do the coordinating. To command the major departments Davis assigned the senior generals of the Confederate States Army, most of whom had been professionals in the prewar United States Army. When their states had seceded and formed the Confederacy, they had resigned their commissions in one army to become officers in another.

*T*HE *NAVAL WAR*

On the water the Confederates found a different problem. The Confederacy had an immense seacoast and a vast river system, but no navy at all. President Davis gave the task of creating one to former U.S. Senator Stephen Mallory of Florida. Mallory's job as secretary of the navy was complicated by the Union's decision to impose a blockade on the entire coast for the purpose of impeding both exports such as cotton and imports of war matériel. While Mallory pondered how best to deal with the blockade, he also had to think about protecting the rivers that provided avenues of invasion into the Confederate interior.

Mallory and other officials knew that they could never match the United States Navy ship for ship. To counter the Union's overwhelming numerical superiority, the Confederates turned to technology. As early as May 1861 Secretary Mallory began talking about building a navy of ironclads that could destroy the blockade. Upon investigation, however, Mallory found that because of technological deficiencies and the production of other war matériel, Confederate ironworks could not provide the necessary iron sheeting. To obtain the desired vessels the Confederates entered into contracts with European companies, but Union diplomacy and financial difficulties impeded deliveries. Though the Confederates managed to get some ironclads in the water, their fleet of oceangoing ironclads never materialized.

Their first serious effort resulted in naval history. In 1861 and early 1862 Confederates at Norfolk, Virginia, overhauled the captured Union ship *Merrimac*, clad it in iron, and renamed it the *Virginia*. With this armored vessel, equipped with guns mounted on all sides, the Confederates aimed to smash the blockade. On March 2, 1862, the *Virginia* steamed to the mouth of the Chesapeake Bay to challenge blockading Union ships. The first day was a rousing success. As the *Virginia* sank two ships and forced three others aground, the shots from the Union navy just bounced off its iron coat. On the second day, however, the *Virginia* was met not by wooden ships but by another ironclad. The Union's *Monitor* did not look at all like its southern opponent. A revolving turret with two guns sat on a hull low in the water; observers called the ship "a tin can on a shingle." On March 9 the first battle in history between two ironclads took place. After three hours of hard fighting, neither had substantially damaged the other. But that draw ended the Confederates' dream that ironclads could end the blockade. As for the *Virginia*, when Union forces captured Norfolk in May 1862, the Confederates wrecked the ship. The North went on to build dozens of ironclads based on the design of the *Monitor*.

Because the *Virginia* could not overcome the *Monitor*, the Confederate navy never seriously challenged the Union navy on the high seas. Instead the Confederates sent raiders or cruisers to disrupt Union commerce, a strategy that proved quite successful. Confederate raiders or cruisers captured or destroyed more than 250 merchant ships flying the Stars and Stripes. The most famous of all the raiders, the *Alabama*, built in England and commanded by Captain Raphael Semmes, sank sixty-two merchant vessels and one warship between its commissioning in 1862 and its destruction by the United States Navy in 1864, off the coast of France.

Although Mallory never realized his dream of defeating the blockade with ironclads, the Confederates did construct other iron-coated vessels. Generally smaller than the *Virginia*, they were designed to stop Union gunboats on southern rivers. Despite enormous technical and manufacturing difficulties, the Confederate navy managed to place ironclads on the Mississippi and at other strategic spots, such as Mobile Bay. Yet technological shortcomings hampered the effective use of these vessels. Maneuverability on the narrow waterways was always a problem. Most of these ships had short careers. Mechanical shortcomings, chiefly engine failure, caused as many casualties among the ironclads as enemy shot. Many ended up scuttled by their own crews.

THE EASTERN THEATER, 1861–1862

On the ground serious military conflict began in the summer of 1861. The first major battle took place in Virginia, between Richmond and Washington, the corridor that would provide more battlefields than anywhere else during the war. When the Confederate capital was moved to Richmond, a clamor arose in Washington for Union troops to march on the city. Many Washingtonians seemed to regard the coming confrontation as an opportunity for a holiday outing. Confederates, for their part, were confident that they could block any Union advance. Many Confederates, in fact, believed that the South's manliness and fighting skills were so superior that any Confederate force could whip a considerably larger Yankee force.

Americans commenced killing and maiming each other in significant numbers on July 21, 1861, no more than twenty-five miles south of Washington, along a small stream called Bull Run. The First Battle of Manassas, the name given the carnage by the Confederates, provided a foretaste of what this war would be like. First Manassas was no holiday. The congressmen and other picnickers who followed the Union army to watch the gala affair were to have no counterparts at later contests. At First Manassas the roughly 70,000 men in the two armies, fairly evenly divided, demonstrated that both sides could fight and that each would demand a heavy price in suffering and blood from the other. More than 2,700 Union troops were killed, wounded, or missing; the Confederates lost almost 2,000.

First Manassas introduced commanders to real battle. General Pierre G. T. Beauregard, the conqueror of Fort Sumter, found the direction of thousands of soldiers in the turmoil of battle considerably more complicated than aiming artillery at a fixed position. His colleague General Joseph E. Johnston, whose army from the Shenandoah Valley joined Beauregard's on the battlefield, proved that the new mobility provided by the railroad would enable commanders to concentrate troops rapidly at critical points. If not for the movement of Johnston's 12,000 men from fifty miles away to reinforce Beauregard, the Union army under Brigadier General Irvin McDowell would probably have claimed the first victory. But the combination of Beauregard and Johnston overwhelmed the Federals. On the field many Confederate officers who later had important roles in the war gained their first experience commanding soldiers in battle. They included Jubal A. Early, Edmund Kirby-Smith, and Thomas J. Jackson, who received his famous nickname, Stonewall, for a stalwart stand against charging Union units.

The Confederate victory at Manassas taught a hard lesson. Though the Confederates won on that hot July day, their army was too bloodied and too exhausted to take full advantage of its tactical triumph. Those who called for the victorious Confederates to hurry to Washington and end the war had little understanding of the hard blow the battle had dealt the Confederate army. Beauregard and Johnston had blunted the Union advance, but they could neither destroy their enemy nor promptly take the offensive. A similar pattern would appear often over the next four years, on both sides.

After First Manassas the two armies, almost as if suffering from shock, went into practically permanent quarters facing each other. Not until the beginning of 1862 did they begin to stir. A new commander of the Union army fresh from early victories in western Virginia, Major General George B. McClellan, took charge. McClellan planned to use the Union's superiority on the water to move his army from the environs of Washington around the Confederate army to a point below Richmond, on the peninsula between the York and James rivers, where Virginia had first been settled and where George Washington had defeated the British at Yorktown. With the advent of McClellan the main Union army in the East, which became known as the Army of the Potomac, swelled massively, to some 100,000 soldiers.

In the face of this threat, the Confederates struck back with the audacity and imagination that were to be their trademarks in the Virginia theater. Both of these characteristics were intimately associated with two men who became captains of the first rank. General Robert E. Lee, fifty-five years old and serving that spring as military adviser to President Davis, had been born into one of the great Virginia families. But the Lees had lost their economic and political leadership by the time Robert came to maturity. Now that the Lees were no longer great planters, Robert took another road. After graduating from West Point in 1829, he served as a professional soldier. During his more than thirty years as an army officer Lee distinguished himself in the Mexican War and enjoyed a sterling reputation among senior officers. A colonel in 1861, he refused the offer to command the Union field army and, upon the secession of Virginia, resigned his commission. When Virginia joined the Confederacy, he became a full general in its army. In the spring of 1862 Lee was still an unproven general; in fact, in his first combat assignment, in western Virginia, he had lost to George McClellan. Major General Thomas J. "Stonewall" Jackson, only thirty-eight years old, was also a Virginian, but from the transmontane region of the state, not the tidewater. Although he lacked Lee's pedigree, Jackson, too, had graduated from West Point, had been in the regular army, and had participated in the Mexican War. But he had given up his army career, and the 1850s found him on the faculty of the Virginia Military Institute in Lexington.

Together Lee and Jackson derailed McClellan's plan. In order to make Lincoln and his advisers divert units intended for McClellan, Lee urged Jackson stationed in the Shenandoah Valley to advance down the valley toward the Potomac River. In a series of dazzling marches and attacks, the stern, taciturn Jackson confused and defeated several Union generals in the Shenandoah. Jackson's victories worked precisely as Lee had hoped. Because of Jackson's success, the Federals were not able to concentrate as many troops below Richmond as McClellan had hoped.

Because Joseph Johnston had been wounded, Lee now commanded the major Confederate field army, the Army of Northern Virginia. He ordered Jackson to move rapidly and secretly from the Shenandoah Valley to Richmond. When Jackson joined him, Lee intended to take the offensive and destroy McClellan. During the last week in June, in a series of bitter fights known as the Seven Days Battle, Lee did stop McClellan's advance on Richmond, but at a terrible price. During the week's fighting the Federals suffered almost 16,000 casualties out of 100,000 in their army. The Confederates, usually on the attack, took even heavier casual-

ROBERT E. LEE, THE GREAT
CONFEDERATE WARRIOR
(Cook Collection, Valentine
Museum, Richmond, Va.)

ties—more than 20,000, practically one-fourth of their army. These casualty figures meant that with Lee in command ferocity would have to be added to audacity and imagination.

Lee and other Confederate leaders had little time to savor the turning back of
McClellan. When information arrived that a new force had started south from
Washington, Lee dispatched Stonewall Jackson to counter it. Then, convinced that
Jackson was facing a major threat, Lee hurried north from Richmond to join forces
with his subordinate. In a daring move that sent Jackson around and deep in the
rear of the Federal army, commanded by Major General John Pope, Lee struck and

punished the Federals on the same ground where the first great battle had been fought. With the success of the Second Battle of Manassas, Lee and the Confederates had the initiative and the power of decision.

Lee and President Davis decided to go north, to carry the war out of the Confederacy into the Union. Various motives prompted this decision. Without question the general and the president wanted to relieve the pressure on Virginia. They thought of the food available in Maryland and anticipated new recruits for the Army of Northern Virginia. And they hoped that the presence of a major Confederate army in the eastern states, especially a victorious one, would convince the North that the South could not be defeated. When Lee crossed the Potomac, the Confederates had one eye cocked toward England. A triumph on enemy soil might just persuade the British to intervene on behalf of the Confederacy.

But events turned out otherwise. Marylanders did not flock to the Confederate colors. Even more important, a set of Lee's confidential orders fell into the hands of McClellan, once again leading the Army of the Potomac against the Confederates. With that information McClellan moved more rapidly than Lee expected. Confronting this new development, Lee altered his plan of rapid movement through Maryland toward Pennsylvania in favor of regrouping to face McClellan. The two old foes joined battle again along Antietam Creek at Sharpsburg, Maryland. By attacking the Confederates piecemeal instead of in sustained fashion, McClellan frittered away his substantial numerical advantage of 35,000 men. Even though Lee's thin lines held and the Confederates could claim that the Federals had not driven them from the field, Sharpsburg smashed the Confederates' great expectations for this advance into enemy country. McClellan suffered

THE PRICE OF BATTLE: CONFEDERATE DEAD AT SHARPSBURG (Library of Congress)

more than 11,000 casualties, but Lee sustained almost 12,000. The combined casualties—about four times as many as the Americans suffered on D-Day in World War II—made this the single bloodiest day of the war. Lee had no choice but to retreat into Virginia. Strategically the Union won a decisive victory at Sharpsburg.

THE WAR IN THE WEST, 1861–1862

While cries of "On to Richmond!" reverberated in the East, critical developments took place in the West. The initial crucial question involved the fate of Kentucky. Of the border states it had the greatest percentage of slaves and the largest number of Confederate sympathizers. The Confederacy hoped that Kentucky would secede and join the new nation, but many Kentuckians remained loyal to the Union. For Kentucky any North-South conflict would literally become a war of brother against brother. That deep division can be seen in the family of Senator John J. Crittenden, whose attempt at compromise failed in the winter of 1860–1861. One of his sons became a general in the Confederate army, the other a general in the Union army. To escape that horror, Kentucky attempted to remain neutral. Despite an official state proclamation of neutrality, both sides pressed Kentucky, and both took recruits and supplies. For several months, however, neither sent organized forces across the Kentucky border. But in September 1861, to thwart an expected Federal advance, Confederate soldiers entered the state. Technically the Confederacy was the first to violate neutral borders, but Union troops crossed the Ohio River promptly thereafter. Thus the Confederates, commanded by General Albert Sidney Johnston, a stalwart of the prewar United States Army who had a glowing though unproven reputation as a great soldier, occupied a line stretching from east to west through the center of the state. With both sides there in force, the state threatened to become the first great western battleground.

Confederates and Yankees did not, however, fight a major battle for Kentucky. Because of the insight and determination of an unimpressive-looking Union general who chewed on cigars, the Confederates had to pull out of Kentucky without much fighting at all. At the beginning of 1862, Ulysses S. Grant was still a relatively obscure officer, but he would not remain unknown much longer. Grant recognized that the two rivers flowing northward through Tennessee and Kentucky into the Ohio offered an opportunity both to flush Johnston out of Kentucky and to invade the Confederate heartland. The Cumberland River went to Nashville; the Tennessee River cut through the entire state whose name it bore. Grant planned to send a combined navy-army force up the rivers to blast the Confederates by sea and land.

The Confederates were also aware that the Cumberland and the Tennessee provided a watery highway into their interior. To block any Union advance, the Confederates constructed two forts on the Kentucky-Tennessee border where only fifteen miles separated the two rivers. Fort Henry, on the eastern bank of the Tennessee, and Fort Donelson, on the western bank of the Cumberland, guarded the water routes. They proved no match, however, for Grant's land-sea attack. Poorly situated, Fort Henry had to contend with the rising waters of the Tennessee as well as the advancing Federals. It did neither successfully and fell on

February 6. Ten days later Fort Donelson, plagued by command problems, capitulated to Grant's infantry.

Grant's victory meant disaster for the Confederacy. With his Kentucky line fatally breached and a Federal army in his rear, Johnston pulled out of Kentucky. With Grant astride the two rivers, Tennessee offered no haven, so Johnston retreated southwestward across the state. Not only Kentucky came under Union control; so did central Tennessee, with its important supply point at Nashville and the ironworks of the Cumberland River valley.

Grant did not rest on his laurels. He pushed on up the Tennessee with the goal of inflicting a crippling blow on the Confederate war effort in the West. Flung back across hundreds of miles and two states, Johnston stopped to regroup in northeastern Mississippi. At some point he had to stand and fight, and Sidney Johnston decided the time was now. His army had been strengthened by bringing in every available soldier; he even got General Beauregard as second in command. Moreover, his opponents had temporarily divided their forces. Grant was coming up the Tennessee with the main body, but Federal units sent to Nashville had not yet rejoined him. Grant's army of around 40,000 was encamped on the western bank of the Tennessee just inside the state at Pittsburg Landing, near a small country place of worship called Shiloh Church.

Johnston and Beauregard planned to drive Grant into the Tennessee River before any reinforcements could reach him. At daylight on April 6 the Confederates, 40,000 strong, stormed out of the woods into a generally surprised Union army. Neither Grant nor his generals had expected an attack. During the day the soldiers in gray and blue fought with a ferociousness never before seen on the continent. The bloodletting was appalling. Among the casualties was General Johnston, mortally wounded while urging his men forward. For a time a Confederate victory seemed inevitable, but vigorous stands by individual Federal units kept Grant's line intact. Nightfall found the Confederates short of their goal, and Grant prepared to take the offensive the next day with the reinforcements that arrived during the night. When Beauregard was unable to hold Grant back, he withdrew into Mississippi. The casualties shocked everyone; each side suffered more than 1,700 killed and 8,000 wounded. Though at terrible cost, the Confederates served notice at Shiloh that the western war had not yet ended.

The frightful carnage on Civil War battlefields resulted in large part from technological improvements in weaponry. Chief among these advances was the rifling—the cutting of spiral grooves within barrels—of both infantry and artillery weapons. Rifling imparted a spin to a bullet that greatly increased the range and accuracy of a weapon. The effective range of the basic infantry musket went from 100 yards to 300 or 400 yards. In the face of this enhanced firepower, the traditional infantry charge, widely relied on by most commanders, usually led to disaster. A participant in a Confederate charge described the attack as the "work of death." "Volley after volley of musket balls sweep through the line and mow us down like wheat before the scythe." Witnessing such devastation, a junior officer wailed, "Down! down! go the boys."

After the shooting stopped, grisly sights surrounded the survivors. A Confederate veteran of Chancellorsville described the dead everywhere, some with their heads shot off, some with their brains oozing out, some pierced through the head with musket balls, some with their noses shot away, some with their mouths smashed, some wounded in the neck, some with broken arms or legs, some shot through the breast and some cut in two with shells.

Being killed outright, however, was often preferable to being wounded. Because both medical knowledge and sanitary conditions were primitive, many of the wounded eventually died or survived severely maimed. Military hospitals were appalling places. A Confederate soldier observed:

> The sorriest sights . . . are in those dreadful field-hospitals, established in barns, under large tents, and in houses. The screams and groans of the poor fellows undergoing amputation are sometimes dreadful—and then the sight of arms and legs surrounding those places, as they are thrown into great piles is something one that has seen the results of battle can never forget.

Farther west, beyond the Mississippi, the conflict also raged. In 1861 both sides struggled over control of Missouri, like Kentucky a slave state that had not seceded. For a time in mid-year the Confederates controlled most of the southern half of the state, but by early 1862 Confederate forces had been pushed back into Arkansas. In March 1862 a key battle took place in northwestern Arkansas, at Pea Ridge, where a decisive Union victory ended any serious Confederate threat to Missouri. The remainder of the war in this vast area, including Arkansas, northern Louisiana, and Texas—the Confederacy's Trans-Mississippi Department—was not of primary importance. Few troops, long distances, and poor transportation made military operations difficult. Trans-Mississippi's chief contribution to the war effort was as a supplier of such critical items as horses. When Union victories in 1863 closed the Mississippi, eastward traffic slowed and the entire Trans-Mississippi came under military command. With the closure of the great river, President Davis gave the departmental commander, General Edmund Kirby-Smith, the right to exercise civil as well as military authority. Kirby-Smith remained in charge of the Trans-Mississippi for the duration of the war.

The bloodbath at Shiloh had not paralyzed the Confederate leadership. On the contrary, standing and fighting seemed to rejuvenate the Confederates. The shocking loss of New Orleans, the major port of the Confederacy and the guardian of the lower Mississippi, had somehow to be overcome. Only three weeks after Shiloh, New Orleans had fallen to a Union naval task force under David G. Farragut, which had run past the downriver forts defending the city. Determined to turn events around, President Davis replaced Beauregard, who had fallen back deeper into Mississippi, with General Braxton Bragg, an organizer and a disciplinarian. Initially this seemed a wise move, for Bragg determined to take the offensive. By a roundabout rail route he took the bulk of his army to Chattanooga to assist the Confederates defending eastern Tennessee. But once he arrived there, Davis ordered Bragg to invade Kentucky with the combined force of around 50,000 troops.

Such an advance offered enormous potential for the Confederates. With their major western field army in Kentucky, much of the territory lost since Forts Henry and Donelson would seem once again to be within their grasp. Nashville and central

Tennessee were still in Federal hands, but the Union forces would evacuate them if the Confederates prevailed in Kentucky. The Confederates hoped not only to recruit Kentucky volunteers and replenish their supplies but to add Kentucky to the roster of Confederate states—a major political triumph. Then the front line would be the Ohio River, not the Tennessee. Strategically, politically, and psychologically the Confederates could gain enormously. But of course this outcome depended on the Confederates' success on the battlefield.

Bragg, who took his army from Mississippi to Kentucky with confidence and decisiveness, lost those characteristics in Kentucky. Once in the state, he did not promptly effect the concentration of all Confederate troops in order to fight the Union forces on ground favorable to him. Nor could he decide on priorities between an aggressive political policy aimed at inaugurating a Confederate governor and a military plan designed to end in Confederate triumph. The campaign that began with such anticipation ended in a muddle. The political goals went nowhere, and the major fight on October 8, 1862, at Perryville in the central part of the state, found Bragg outnumbered by Federal forces commanded by Major General Don Carlos Buell. With less than half his army on the field, Bragg pulled away after a day of fighting. His hopes shattered, Bragg retreated to Tennessee.

A CHANGING WAR

Decisive military victories in Maryland and Kentucky could have put the Confederate States of America in an almost unassailable position. Such triumphs would have put immense pressure on Lincoln to work out some plan for peace. But Lincoln never felt that pressure; it was Jefferson Davis who had to contend with fundamentally altered circumstances.

The strategic reverses suffered by the Confederates in the autumn of 1862 settled the basic international question. Defeat in Kentucky and especially in Maryland exploded the Confederates' dream that Great Britain and perhaps other European powers would intervene on their behalf. Because of Britain's naval power, no one else in Europe would act unless Great Britain led the way. And serious discussions had occurred in England about the proper policy toward the United States and the Confederate States. A weakened United States would certainly be in Britain's interest. And though cotton from Egypt and India had made the loss of the South's cotton less serious than it would have been otherwise, a guaranteed supply from the South would boost Britain's textile industry and general economy. But the foreign policy of the Lincoln administration made clear to the British government that any action to benefit the Confederacy would probably mean war with the United States. Thus England was not going to get involved unless the evidence clearly pointed toward a Confederate victory. And after Sharpsburg and Perryville, the signs indicated confusion at best and the South's defeat at worst. So if the Confederacy were to prevail, it would have to do so without help from England.

The Confederate retreat from Maryland also provided an opportunity for Lincoln to claim the moral high ground. At the outset the Confederacy estab-

lished independence as its chief war aim, while Lincoln claimed he fought to preserve the Union. As for slavery, Lincoln stated, he would take any stand that
would aid preservation of the Union. But after Sharpsburg, Lincoln issued his
Emancipation Proclamation, and the elimination of slavery became a second
major goal of the war. The proclamation made a decision to help the South even
more difficult for England and France because both opposed slavery. Even
though the Emancipation Proclamation could not and did not even attempt to
free all slaves, it was a significant document. Claiming that his war powers gave
him the required authority, Lincoln announced that all slaves held in states still
in rebellion on January 1, 1863, would become free. The proclamation did not
free slaves in the states of the Union or in those areas of the Confederacy occupied by Union forces. Despite its limitations, it did alter in a basic way the moral
calculus of the war.

The Confederates reacted angrily. In a message to the Confederate Congress,
President Davis denounced the proclamation as "the most execrable measure in
the history of guilty man." He even threatened to treat captured Federal officers
as "criminals engaged in inciting servile insurrection." The Union's warning that
it would hold Confederate officers for similar treatment guaranteed that Davis's
threat would never be carried out. Despite the outcries of the Confederate leaders,
many of them recognized that the Emancipation Proclamation put them on the
moral as well as the military defensive.

Although disappointed by the refusal of the European powers to intervene
and outraged by the Emancipation Proclamation, the Confederate government
moved forthrightly to strengthen its ability to carry on the war. The first necessity
was manpower. Even before Shiloh and the Seven Days, Confederate authorities
recognized that volunteers alone could never meet the requirements for soldiers.
On April 1, 1862, the Confederate Congress enacted the first conscription law in
American history; it made all white men between the ages of eighteen and thirty-
five eligible for military service, though it permitted substitutes and exempted the
clergy and men in critical occupations, such as ironworkers, teachers, and state
employees. In the fall Congress extended the upper age limit to forty-five and
established an exemption for owners and overseers of twenty or more slaves. As
troop requirements grew more desperate, Congress continued to respond. In February 1864 it broadened the age brackets to include ages seventeen to fifty and
curtailed exemptions.

Though conscription was not popular, it helped fill Confederate ranks. Some
state officials opposed conscription as an invasion of local and states rights by the
central government. The provision permitting owners and overseers of more than
twenty slaves to escape the draft brought forth cries that this conflict was a rich
man's war and a poor man's fight. Despite the problems, the statistics demonstrate the overall effectiveness of the various conscription bills. The Confederate
population included approximately 1 million white males between seventeen and
forty-five; some 750,000 served in the Confederate military. When the men who
worked in vital civilian positions are taken into account, it becomes clear that
most of those million men directly aided the Confederate war effort. With the help
of conscription the Confederate government kept sizable armies in the field until
the final months of the war.

Fighting men could accomplish nothing, however, without the materials of war. At the commencement of hostilities the Confederate government had no ready supply of arms; its inventory consisted solely of armaments captured from federal arsenals. But because of the efforts of one of the true geniuses of the Confederacy, Confederate soldiers usually had weapons and ammunition. In April 1861 an obscure captain in the old United States Army accepted a commission as major and assignment as chief of the Confederate Ordnance Department. A native Pennsylvanian, a graduate of West Point, and the son-in-law of a former governor of Alabama, Josiah Gorgas set about arming the defenders of the Confederacy. With immense organizational gifts and astonishing enterprise, Gorgas turned plowshares into swords. At the outset he sent an agent to Europe to buy arms and ammunition, which entered the Confederacy through the blockade. Then Gorgas created a munitions industry. He built powder mills; the largest, at Augusta, produced 1 million pounds of gunpowder in 1863 alone. To obtain the essential ingredient, potassium nitrate, or niter, Gorgas mined saltpeter in caves, created niter beds from carcasses of dead animals, and collected the contents of chamber pots. The Tredegar ironworks in Richmond made a wide variety of essential items, such as propeller shafts and plate for ironclads. New foundries to cast cannon were established at Augusta, Columbus, and Macon, in Georgia; a naval gunworks was built at Selma, Alabama. Looking back from the spring of 1864, Gorgas accurately observed in his diary: "Where three years ago we were not making a gun, a pistol nor a sabre, no shot nor shell (except at the Tredegar Works)—a pound of powder—we now make all these in quantities to meet the demands of our large armies." While many men were promoted to high rank because of their performance on the battlefield, Gorgas advanced only to brigadier general, but without him the combat generals would never have been able to lead armies in battle for four years.

The government agencies in charge of procuring and supplying food and clothing had no Josiah Gorgas. Armies often drew from the areas in which they operated for clothing and especially for food. Most soldiers provided most of what they wore, and it was never abundant. Footwear was particularly shoddy and in short supply, though by 1864 shoe factories in Richmond were turning out 800 pairs a day. To feed its troops the government called on planters and farmers to shift from cotton to foodstuffs. The production of cotton declined dramatically, from just under 4 million bales in 1860 to around 300,000 in 1864. The spread of the territory occupied by Union troops surely accounted for some of this decrease, as did the difficulty of marketing the crop; but just as certainly support for the government's efforts contributed significantly. Corn and wheat shipments from farms and plantations to armies crisscrossed the South. Most field armies used nearby food sources as much as possible; the Shenandoah Valley, for example, served as the granary for Lee's Army of Northern Virginia.

HOPE BECOMES DESPAIR

After the Confederate setbacks in Maryland and Kentucky, the war returned southward for the winter. But in neither East nor West did hibernation set in. In

Tennessee, at Murfreesboro or Stones River, and in Virginia, at Fredericksburg, armies fought bloody December battles, neither of which had any significant strategic importance. In mid-December at Fredericksburg, Lee pummeled a new opponent, Major General Ambrose Burnside, from a strong defensive position. At the end of the month, in an uncoordinated attack, Bragg failed in an effort to defeat the Federal army commanded by Major General William S. Rosecrans and to open the road to Nashville, only thirty miles beyond Murfreesboro. After these two inconclusive fights the armies waited for spring.

The spring and summer of 1863 brought two great offensives. In the East Robert E. Lee mounted his second campaign north of the Potomac, while in the West Ulysses Grant struck vigorously at the great Confederate stronghold on the Mississippi, Vicksburg. In May at Chancellorsville, just west of Fredericksburg, Lee in a brilliant battle whipped Major General Joseph Hooker and turned back another Union drive for Richmond. Although Chancellorsville stood as a notable Confederate victory, it demanded a high price. Wounded by fire from his own men, Stonewall Jackson contracted pneumonia and died on May 10. Despite that blow, Lee retained enormous confidence in his officers and men. Having reorganized the Army of Northern Virginia, he once again aimed it at the North. Although Confederate officials no longer seriously contemplated European intervention, President Davis and Lee wanted the war in enemy country. The food, fodder, and other supplies available in Maryland and Pennsylvania would lessen the demand on Virginia. But also the Confederate leadership wanted northerners to experience the presence of armies, troops, and battle. A resounding victory on Union territory could put enormous pressure on Lincoln to recognize the Confederacy and negotiate with the Davis administration. It was not to be, however. Lee's offensive ended in early July in a small Pennsylvania town, Gettysburg. There, after three days of desperate fighting, Lee failed to overcome a Union army commanded by Major General George G. Meade. Having lost more than 25,000 men—over one-third of his troops—Lee once again led his bleeding army back into Virginia.

While Lee was marching northward toward his fateful rendezvous at Gettysburg, Grant was menacing Vicksburg. Vicksburg was of critical importance to the Confederates because along with Port Hudson, just over a hundred miles to the south in Louisiana, it kept the Mississippi open for communication with the Trans-Mississippi area, which provided horses and other critical items. Jefferson Davis ordered the commander at Vicksburg, Lieutenant General John C. Pemberton, a northerner who had sided with the Confederacy, to hold at all costs. After failing to capture Vicksburg from the North, Grant conducted one of the most brilliant campaigns of the war. On the western bank of the Mississippi he moved his army overland; south of Vicksburg he transported his troops to the eastern bank. Then he moved rapidly northeastward toward Jackson before turning back to the west and driving toward Vicksburg. Knocked off balance by Grant's daring and his rapid movements, the Confederates responded ineffectively. By late May, Grant had Pemberton cooped up in Vicksburg; the siege lasted some six weeks. On July 4, 1863, one day after Lee's defeat at Gettysburg, Vicksburg capitulated. With Port Hudson falling to the Union on July 8, the entire length of the Mississippi came under Federal control.

The losses at Gettysburg and Vicksburg were major blows. In the East the Union forces inflicted heavy casualties on the main Confederate field army and forced it to retreat into Virginia. In the West President Lincoln finally realized a major strategic goal, command of the Mississippi. The bagging of the 30,000 troops in the Vicksburg garrison did nothing to help the Confederate war effort, either. In the Washington-Richmond corridor as well as the Mississippi Valley the Federals had the upper hand and the initiative.

Despite the Confederate disaster at Vicksburg, Bragg's Army of Tennessee remained whole and in the field, though after Murfreesboro he had eventually retreated all the way to Georgia. In September, however, Bragg struck the Union army under Rosecrans in a bitter contest known as the Battle of Chickamauga. Reinforced by 12,000 men from Lee's army, transported by rail to northern Georgia, Bragg overwhelmed his foes and drove them back into Chattanooga. Bragg occupied the heights surrounding the city and attempted to force a surrender, but Chattanooga was still holding out in October, when Grant arrived to take command of the besieged Union forces. Immediately he reopened the Union supply line as a prelude to breaking Bragg's hold on the city. In late November he launched attacks that broke through Bragg's lines; once again the Confederates withdrew into Georgia.

The year 1864 opened with the Confederates on the defensive across the South. In Virginia, on ground just west of his triumphs at Fredericksburg and Chancellorsville, Lee awaited still another march on Richmond. This time his antagonist would be Grant, the conqueror of Vicksburg and Chattanooga, now a lieutenant general in command of all Union armies. While Grant prepared to hurl his troops against Lee, his chief subordinate in the West, Major General William T. Sherman, moved out of Chattanooga and pointed his divisions toward Atlanta and the Army of Tennessee, now under Joseph Johnston, who had replaced the oft-defeated and oft-criticized Bragg.

Grant and Sherman gave Lee and Johnston more than they could handle. The two Confederate generals waged quite different campaigns. From the moment Grant crossed his front in early May, Lee assaulted him on every possible occasion. In a series of bloody engagements—the Wilderness, Spotsylvania Courthouse, the North Anna—Lee delivered fierce blows that would have stopped and probably turned back his previous foes, but Grant kept driving ahead despite horrendous losses. Finally on June 3 at Cold Harbor, only ten miles from Richmond, Grant launched a frontal assault that resulted in 7,000 Union soldiers killed or wounded, most in the first few minutes. In a month of bitter fighting Lee had inflicted on the Union army casualties about equal to the 60,000 men with whom Lee started the campaign. And still Grant remained in his front. Lee despaired of what would happen if Grant pinned him in a static position where he could not maneuver. To one of his commanders he predicted with terrible accuracy that if the contest between him and Grant ever "bec[a]me a siege, . . . then it [would] be a mere question of time."

Joe Johnston in Georgia never attacked Sherman. By superb handling of his troops in a succession of flanking moves, Sherman thoroughly confused Johnston, who did not seem to understand what his canny opponent was about. After six weeks Sherman had maneuvered Johnston out of mountainous north Georgia to the banks of the Chattahoochee River, with Atlanta in sight and the plains of central and south Georgia beyond. An understandably upset Jefferson Davis could get no plan from Johnston, who informed the president that Sherman's actions would determine his own. Believing he had no choice, Davis relieved Johnston and replaced him with General John B. Hood, a ferocious combat leader who had had an arm maimed at Gettysburg and a leg amputated at Chickamauga but was untested as an army commander. Hood did his president's bidding and fought vigorously, albeit unsuccessfully, for Atlanta. After six weeks and several hard fights, the city fell to Sherman on September 1.

In the fall of 1864 the Confederates faced a bleak military situation. Lee found himself in trenches at Petersburg with overextended lines and his maneuverability gone. Even so, he tried to recreate the circumstances of 1862 by using the Shenandoah Valley to alarm Washington and lessen the pressure on his beleaguered army. Back in the summer he had dispatched Lieutenant General Jubal A. Early with 10,000 troops he could not really spare to stop a Federal incursion in the Shenandoah. After doing so, Early headed down the valley toward the Potomac. He crossed the Potomac and in mid-July came up to the fortifications guarding the northwestern approach to Washington. Lee's hopes were realized when Grant sent an entire corps, more than 15,000 men, up from Petersburg to counter Early. But 1864 was not 1862; the numerical disparity was too great. Even without that corps, Grant maintained inexorable pressure on Lee. At the same time superior Federal numbers forced Early back into Virginia. There he could not contend with the Federal force under Major General Philip Sheridan. By October Sheridan had both decimated Early's little army and laid waste to the Shenandoah. In the trenches at Petersburg, as Grant kept moving southward, Lee could only watch the thin gray line of defenders becoming thinner.

In the West, General Hood received permission from President Davis to strike at Sherman's rear and his supply lines. As a result, the two major armies marched away from each other. While Hood headed for Tennessee with visions of a dazzling victory, Sherman started for Savannah and the sea with his veteran army and without substantive opposition. Christmas brought vastly different tidings to the two sides. Hood made it to Tennessee, but his gross tactical errors and the Union's numerical superiority wrecked the Army of Tennessee. Battles at Franklin and Nashville claimed more than half his infantry. After a superior Union army under Major General George H. Thomas smashed the Confederates at Nashville, a battered Army of Tennessee limped back into Mississippi, where for all practical purposes it ceased to exist. Simultaneously Sherman was cutting a wide swath through central and south Georgia on his march to the sea. He gave President Lincoln a special Christmas present, the city of Savannah.

THE IMPACT OF THE WAR

The Confederate military effort did not take place in a vacuum. As the battlefield contests began consistently to go against the gray armies, other areas also experienced severe dislocations and setbacks. The economy went out of control. Inflation, inevitable in the absence of a realistic fiscal policy, seemed propelled by gunpowder.

Between midsummer and the early fall of 1863 prices rose by 58 percent. Between October 1863 and February 1864 the cost of a barrel of flour in Richmond leaped from $70 to $250. The tightening blockade made any item from abroad difficult to obtain and therefore precious. As advancing Union armies overran more and more Confederate territory, less land was available to produce foodstuffs for fighting men and civilians alike.

The fate of coffee, a favorite drink of southerners regardless of social standing, indicates the deprivations caused by the war and how southerners attempted to cope with them. Few southerners could contemplate a world without coffee. But by 1862 real coffee practically disappeared for all but the wealthiest, and even they could not count on obtaining it. Southerners never quit struggling to concoct a replacement. Almost every imaginable item was substituted for the unavailable coffee bean. Parched corn, rye, wheat, okra seed, sweet potatoes, and blends of them all ended up in Confederates' coffee cups. No one mistook any of these concoctions for real coffee, however.

Confederate reverses also affected politics. Confederate politics became chiefly the politics of personality. In the spring of 1861 southerners had united behind a cause and a president to lead them. Past political loyalties and divisions over secession dissolved in the cheering moment of the birth of the Confederate States of America. Old parties did not survive as identifiable entities, and no new ones were created. Involvement with parties would somehow have seemed unpatriotic. Because the government was not identified with a party, its opponents could not band together in a party of loyal opposition. When natural and normal opposition to administration policies arose, it had no institutional outlet. Without such a forum, opposition to the Davis administration, as well as support of it, became a matter of vituperation.

Consumed by the cause of the Confederacy and determined to take any step he believed necessary to gain its independence, Jefferson Davis did not envision the presidency as just another political office. He did, after all, face a monumental task. Like George Washington, he had to create a nation where none had existed, but unlike Washington, he did not have the shared experience of a successful revolution as a foundation for his building. Davis's revolution consisted of current events. When Davis supported conscription and other measures that increased the power of the central government, he knew that he was going against the South's tradition of limited government and local power. But to Davis ultimate victory, in his mind the only legitimate goal, required such measures. And anyone who opposed one of his policies, including Vice President Alexander Stephens and strong-minded governors, became not just a political opponent on that issue but an enemy of the cause. In a similar manner Confederates who honestly feared a powerful central government condemned the president as a power-mad despot who did not care about the principles on which the Confederacy was founded. As personal attacks, even vendettas, became commonplace, the Confederate Congress often resembled little more than a shouting hall.

Davis as war leader was unquestionably committed to securing independence for the Confederate States of America. He tried valiantly to rouse the people to carry on the fight. In both 1863 and 1864 he traveled into the Deep South to call on citizens for sacrifice, courage, and determination. His overall view of the

Confederate war effort was certainly reasonable, but he permitted personal squabbles to influence command and professional decisions. His bitter conflict with both Joe Johnston and Beauregard did not help the prosecution of the war. Although both military men must share the blame for their bad relations with the president, Davis did not rise above their pettiness. His commitment to Braxton Bragg, by contrast, lasted long after Bragg, who had lost the confidence of senior commanders, could function effectively as commanding general of the Army of Tennessee. It is easy to criticize Davis's management of the war, but he confronted an increasingly horrendous situation.

Southern society also felt the impact of war. At the outset whites expressed great enthusiasm for the Confederate enterprise. They saw themselves as the true sons and daughters of the American Revolution and as the only faithful constitutionalists. Moreover, their ministers proclaimed the Confederate enterprise as blessed by God and under His care. From pulpits across the Confederacy the message boomed loud and clear: God was on the side of the South; the Confederates were His chosen people. Cheers supported the political leadership; volunteers populated the military. But the seemingly unstoppable Union advances and the hardships of total war eroded both unity and enthusiasm. Class antagonism surfaced when rich men were permitted to hire substitutes to do their duty for them, and the exemption from conscription for owners and overseers of twenty or more slaves especially rankled. Increasing numbers of men began to avoid military service; desertion came to occupy the attention of almost every Confederate commander. Most deserters did not come from the upper orders of society. Some scholars have argued that desertion did at least as much as battle casualties to undermine the strength of Confederate armies. That claim is extreme, though undoubtedly desertion hurt and hurt severely.

Avoidance of service and desertion had concrete causes. Most Confederate men had gone into the military to defend their homes and their families from invasion. They wanted to protect their liberty. But the tide of the war, particularly after 1863, raised questions of how best to carry out what most Confederate soldiers considered their most sacred mission. By 1864 Union armies were pouring into almost every state. The invading bluecoats were threatening the social organization the Confederacy was formed to preserve. To some men, defense of home and family required them to return to protect their loved ones and property. Confederate defeats spurred desertion. As the situation on the battle lines and the home front became increasingly desperate, the cries from home became louder and louder.

The cries underscored the plight of people on the home front. Trying to obtain his son's release from the army, a father informed the War Department, "If you dount send him home I am bound to louse my crop and cum to suffer. I am eiaghty one years of adge." In her effort to bring her husband back a desperate wife made a forceful case. "Thare is no use," she declared, "in keeping a man thare to kill him and leave widows and poore little orphen children to suffer. . . . My poor children have no home nor no Father." Many soldiers could have but one response to such pleas. One Confederate civilian went straight to the heart of the issue: "What man is there that would stay in the armey and no that his family is sufring at home?" By the last winter of the war thousands of soldiers disappeared from the ranks. To their minds their fundamental duty lay at home, not in the army.

Four years of war did affect the status of southern women. When so many men from every social and economic class went off to fight, women had to assume many of their duties. In far greater numbers than before 1861 women began to manage farms, plantations, and slaves. The wounding and killing of fathers, husbands, brothers, and sons often turned temporary management into what seemed like a permanent condition. Women worked in factories, engaged in charitable activities, and even commented on political matters. Those endeavors surely differed sharply from the experience of the vast majority of women during the prewar years. Even so, very few tried to make any fundamental alterations in their position in southern society. Most were too busy trying to survive to view their activities as somehow permanently changing conventional definitions of female propriety. As a result, what appeared to be a striking transformation in the economic and social roles of southern women had mostly short-term effects. When the war ended, most women resumed their traditional roles, and old definitions of the proper relations between the sexes prevailed once more. The war did not create a new southern woman.

THE WAR AND SLAVERY

Although the war did not transform the place of women, it had a momentous impact on black southerners. The South's black slaves contributed immensely to the Confederate war effort. On farms and plantations they produced the food that fed the soldiers. Their labor enabled tens of thousands of whites to enter the ranks. An Alabama newspaper underscored this relationship when it observed that slavery permitted the South "to place in the field a force so much larger in proportion to her white population than the North."

Slaves did a lot more, however, than toil in fields. They made up a substantial percentage of the industrial labor force in mines, ironworks, ordnance plants, and other enterprises. Blacks also helped on specific military projects, such as fortifications—work that their owners did not always volunteer. From the beginning the Confederate government recognized the enormous value of slaves. Accordingly, Congress passed legislation permitting the impressment of slaves for military necessity.

Though most slaves remained faithful to their masters through most of the war, new circumstances strained the old relationship and eventually broke it down. When masters marched off to war they left ultimate control of slaves with others, usually overseers or other family members. Then impressment carried slaves off farms and plantations and put them under the control of government officials. Though disruptive, neither of these situations endangered the system. The advance of Union armies, however, did pose a mortal threat to it. Many slaves took the first opportunity that presented itself to escape to Union lines. To prevent such occurrences, numerous owners transferred their slaves to remote locations in the hope of evading Union forces. Even slaves who had been loyal to masters or the surrogates of masters departed at the approach of blue-clad soldiers, for loyalty to a master stopped when a realistic chance for freedom presented itself.

Developments at Brokenburn Plantation in northeastern Louisiana illustrate just what the war did to slaves and slaveholders. In the spring of 1861 the men went to war with body servants and the public blessings of the house servants and the field hands. In that initial summer Kate Stone, twenty-year-old daughter of the plantation mistress, confided to her diary that "the house servants have been giving a lot of trouble lately—lazy and disobedient. . . . I suppose the excitement in the air has infected them." When the Yankees moved against Vicksburg, just to the east of Brokenburn, during the summer of 1862, Kate worried that they would come and take the family's slaves. Her mother told all the male slaves to hide from the Yankee soldiers. "We think they will," she consoled herself. But in early July, Kate admitted, "Generally when told to run away from the soldiers, they go right to them." In the spring of 1863: "All the Negroes are running away now." By this time many of the Brokenburn slaves had been moved to rented property in the western part of the state. During the summer the remaining whites and blacks headed west. Brokenburn had become a casualty of the war.

By the spring of 1865 the Confederate States of America itself was succumbing. The hungry, ragged veterans in Lee's army and the broken corporal's guard that remained from the Army of Tennessee could no longer hold against the powerful armies of Grant and Sherman. From the trenches at Petersburg, Lee told Davis that he would soon be forced to give up Petersburg, and that move would require the evacuation of Richmond. Called back to command the skeleton of the Army of Tennessee in North Carolina, Joe Johnston could hardly even slow down Sherman, who in the winter had laid waste to South Carolina on his way from Savannah to link up with Grant in Virginia.

Jefferson Davis did not want to contemplate surrender. In a last desperate effort to gain Confederate independence he severed the powerful cultural forces that had given the antebellum South its basic identity and had brought about the creation of the Confederate States of America. At least since the Revolution white southerners had been unable to separate their liberty from their institution of black slavery. Slavery governed the definition of liberty. But in that final, anguished winter Davis split what previously had been unsplittable; he separated liberty from slavery. He reluctantly concluded that to secure liberty the Confederacy must jettison slavery. In this last lunge Davis reached in two directions at once. He dispatched a confidential agent to Europe with instructions to offer Britain and France emancipation in turn for their recognition of the Confederacy. England said never. It was too late. To arrest the disintegration of his armies, Davis simultaneously advocated the enlistment of slaves as soldiers. When one of his generals had broached the idea a year earlier, he had rebuffed it. But in March, with Lee's support, Davis prevailed on a reluctant Congress to enact a law that would permit black slaves to don gray uniforms. The bill did not, however, offer emancipation in exchange for military service. Whether or not slaves would have fought for their masters will never be known. The war ended before the formation of any black regiments.

THE END

The end came in April and May. On April 9, 1865, Palm Sunday, at Appomattox Courthouse, eighty-five miles southwest of Richmond, Lee surrendered the Army

COLUMBIA DESTROYED (Kean Archives, Philadelphia)

of Northern Virginia to Grant. Some two weeks later, just outside Durham, North Carolina, Joe Johnston capitulated to Sherman. By May 4 all Confederate forces east of the Mississippi had surrendered. Still President Davis refused to give up. Calling for continued resistance, he retreated through the Carolinas in the hope of getting to the Trans-Mississippi and carrying on the war from there. But in south Georgia on May 10 a Union cavalry detachment captured Davis and his party. Finally on May 26 General Edmund Kirby-Smith surrendered his Trans-Mississippi army. The Confederate States of America ceased to exist.

Although arguments about whether or not the Confederacy could win abound, its defeat was not foreordained. At least three possibilities offered a chance for a different result. The first two would have involved European intervention. Help could have come at the very beginning of the war if Great Britain had refused to permit the Union to blockade Confederate ports. More likely, Great Britain would have acted in the autumn of 1862 had the Confederates won on the battlefield in Kentucky and Maryland. Had Lee triumphed at Antietam, Great Britain might have moved in such a way as to impel Lincoln to make peace with an independent Confederacy. The third chance occurred in the hot, bloody summer of 1864. If Grant had concluded that enough Union blood had soaked the Virginia ground and had followed his predecessors in retreat, or if Sherman had been stopped before Atlanta, then a political shift could easily have occurred in the North that would have forced Lincoln out of office in favor of a peace government. That none of those possibilities turned out to favor the Confederacy does not mean they did not exist. The proper conclusion to draw is that the results on specific battlefields and the character and ability of particular generals and leaders had an enormous impact on the outcome.

RICHMOND IN RUINS (Library of Congress)

Many reasons explain the Union victory and the Confederate defeat. The North enjoyed a substantial advantage in two critical areas—a significantly larger population and a vastly more powerful industrial machine. Neither of them, not even both together, guarantees military success or failure. During both the American Revolution and the Vietnam war the greater power lost. In the 1770s and 1780s America prevailed over Great Britain, then the leading military and industrial power in the world. Almost 200 years later in the 1960s and 1970s the United States, with almost unlimited military and industrial strength, failed to subdue North Vietnam. The critical difference in war is not material superiority alone but the will to use that superiority. In neither the American Revolution nor the Vietnam war did the stronger side throw all its might against the weaker with absolute determination to win. But that is precisely what Abraham Lincoln did. He never wavered; he would never relent or hold back. He was willing to use his advantage to the fullest. And he stayed in the fight until he found commanders who had a resoluteness that matched his own. With that kind of leadership the side with the stronger battalions and the larger factories prevailed.

Defeated in open battle, the Confederates did not try to keep their cause alive through guerilla warfare. Having experienced the brute force of the Union military juggernaut, which had blasted their armies and destroyed their land, they believed they had made their stand and had nothing left to prove. Moreover, they thought guerilla activities might very well lead to anarchy and the social disintegration of their homeland. Without question racial considerations were critical in this assessment. Although no one knew where the elimination of slavery might lead race relations, anxiety about the racial situation worked mightily against any cause that could end in lawless marauding in the South.

The South in the spring of 1865 was a broken land. The Confederate experience had cost the South dearly. Slavery and the several billion dollars invested in it disappeared with the Confederacy. Physical destruction marred the southern landscape like an ugly scar. Two-thirds of the railroads, the bulk of the industrial plants, countless bridges and buildings, thousands of homes, a huge quantity of livestock—all were destroyed during the war. The human price staggers the imagination. With 260,000 men killed and at least that many more wounded, few white families did not know the grief of a dead or maimed father, husband, brother, or son. Confederate casualties accounted for almost 9 percent of the southern white population. Though the Union suffered 360,000 dead, its casualties did not quite reach 3 percent of the population. In World War II American casualties amounted to only a fraction over one-half of 1 percent of the population. Trying to cope with an uncharted racial course and with massive physical and human devastation, southerners, black and white, faced an uncertain future.

16
After the War

───────── ❖ ─────────

The Civil War reached its climax in <u>April 1865, at Appomattox Courthouse</u>. The Confederacy sputtered on until the end of May, but the surrender at the Virginia courthouse was the end of the Confederate States of America, and of much else.

Ham Chamberlayne, a Virginia officer, did not wait for the formal surrender. He wrote his family:

> I am by no means conquered yet. . . . We refused to take part in the funeral at Appomattox C.H. & cut or crept our way out. . . . I am off for Miss. No notion of laying down my arms—Probably make Texas during the Summer. . . . I cant stay here. Twould kill me by inches. I am going off with what I have on. I shall make it, never fear.

Ben Davis, a former slave, remembered another battle and another surrender.

> I saw a big white flag going up toward the skies, like a big white-robed angel, going to heaven. I was too startled at first to grasp what it meant or what it was but, as I got my senses back, I saw it was surrender, surrender, surrender. . . . "We is free, we is free. . . ." We stood there looking up to heaven, thanking God. . . . I stood there after I come to myself and shouted, clapped my hands for joy and shouted and shouted, as if the Holy Spirit was coming down. White folks set their guns down and shouted, "I'm glad of it, I'm glad of it!" And right there midst all that joy and shouting, men were digging graves and others were putting in the bodies, just piling three or four in one grave, like dogs, one on top of the other. . . . It was sad, sad!

Those bodies were among the 260,000 Confederates and 364,000 Federals, including 38,000 blacks, who died along the dreadful, bloody way to Appomattox. One-tenth of all southern white adult males died during the war. Another 282,000 Union troops sustained wounds; Confederate wounded numbered at least half as many. No one counted the permanently disabled or other human costs that are difficult to calculate but no less real. Those costs included mental disability, for combatants and noncombatants alike; reduced opportunities for women to marry and have a family; and increased chances for poverty. How many disillusioned men moved west, as Ham Chamberlayne did, and unlike him, never returned?

Other Americans did, of course, migrate to the South after the war, but for years their numbers were exceeded by those moving out of the South. Only after World War II did in-migration begin consistently to exceed out-migration.

The grisly total of the Civil War dead was greater than the sum of all the Americans killed in every war from the American War for Independence up to World War II. Bill Holmes, sometime preacher, sometime farmer from Tennessee, recalled the madness of the bloody battle of Shiloh and his dead friend. "The firing got hot, so I fell down . . . flat on my belly. I looked and see Burl coming, falling as he come . . . his heart was shot all to pieces."

Survivors in the South confronted devastation on a scale unprecedented in American history. Major cities and important towns—Atlanta, Charleston, Richmond, Columbia, Selma—lay in ruins. So did two-thirds of southern shipping and most of the 9,000 miles of the southern rail system. Rolling stock, roadbeds, and rails were in shambles, as were warehouses, depots, bridges, shops, water tanks, trestles, and switches. The small but important industrial sector of the South suffered from wear and tear, neglect, and destruction by the military. Worthless Confederate currency and bonds were bitter reminders of past hopes and present despair. Almost all other paper forms of exchange—banknotes, personal notes, state and local bonds—had little value. Not much more could be expected from rail and industrial stocks and bonds. The intricate credit system erected during the antebellum years had collapsed. Personal belongings and real property had in many cases been destroyed. The average value of all real property declined 50 percent, farm property 70 percent. One-third of all livestock was gone, and $3 billion invested in slaves had been transferred from slaveholders to the

REMAINS OF PLANTATION HOUSE, FREDERICKSBURG, VIRGINIA
(Library of Congress)

former slaves, the largest single confiscation and transfer of private property in American history. Production of the principal southern crop, cotton, did not return to prewar levels until 1879. The South's share of the nation's wealth fell from 30 to 12 percent in the 1860s.

> A set of forks with whole tines . . . is a curiosity. Clocks and watches have nearly all stopped. Hair brushes and tooth brushes have all worn out, combs are broken. . . . Pins, needles and thread, and a thousand such articles, which seem indispensable to house-keeping, are very hard to find.

After the war the South pursued economic recovery and growth vigorously, envisioning a New South, a South with more industry and cities and fewer farms. The pursuit lasted a long time, is continuing, and has been largely successful, yet even today the South trails the rest of the nation in per capita income and in other important measures of economic welfare.

Estimates of the *direct* costs of the war run as high as $6.6 billion, or about $206 for every person living in the North and South in 1861. Those costs, which include expenditures by the Union, the Confederacy, and the states, the costs of running conscription systems, losses in human capital resulting from the deaths and wounds to the soldiers, and the price of wartime destruction, virtually equaled the gross national product of the United States in 1869 ($7.4 billion). The $206-per-person cost is nearly twice what Americans averaged in individual consumption in 1860. The $6.6 billion expended could have been used to buy the slaves from their owners, pay the freed slaves 100 years of back wages ($3.5 billion), and give each freed family forty acres and a mule. But hindsight cannot undo the tragedy of the Civil War, and figures cannot measure all the costs. Nor does there exist a humane calculus to measure the toll that slavery had taken or that its continuation could have taken on blacks, or on whites. Would slavery have died without the massive defeat of the South? Was the road to emancipation unavoidably strewn with rotting bodies, severed limbs, and destruction? Ben Davis sensed this terrible irony when he shouted that he was free, free at last, and then gasped at the crude burial of the fallen.

The Civil War took an enormous toll in blood and treasure. The conflict also sharpened and magnified sectionalism in the United States even as it abetted the forces of nationalism. The war rendered secession a dead option and greatly enhanced the powers of the federal government even as it underscored the divisions of the country into oversimplified terms, "the North" and "the South." The North became the equivalent of the non-South, or anything that was not the South. The Civil War also made the prewar South the Old South, because the war destroyed the main engine of the prewar South, slave-based plantation agriculture. The war effectively ended the dominance the plantation world had had over almost all of the South before 1865, even in areas remote from plantation agriculture.

The war did not, however, settle the terms on which the former Confederate states would be restored to the Union. Nor did the results of the war clearly determine the place of blacks in American society. Those matters reached some resolution only during Reconstruction and thereafter.

The war left an even more immediate, pressing issue in its wake—survival. The economy of the South had to be made to function again; people had to make a living.

Probably neither Ham Chamberlayne nor Ben Davis nor Parson Bill Holmes gave much thought to anything else in 1865. Chamberlayne never made it to Texas, though he did get as far as his uncle's plantation in Mississippi before he returned to Virginia in November. The 1858 graduate of the University of Virginia nearly ruined his health trying to run his family's farm. Then he clerked for a railroad and later edited newspapers. Chamberlayne came to terms with Appomattox. As founder and editor of *The State* in Richmond, he became a leading spokesman for reconciliation between the once warring sections and for the economic diversification of the South.

Ben Davis walked seventy-five miles to Atlanta, joining the people who more than doubled the city's population between 1865 and 1870. But he enjoyed little of the prosperity of the city that showed such remarkable powers of recovery. At first a generous white family gave him food and shelter. Then he scrambled for a living the rest of his life—as a day laborer, factory worker, and preacher. At one point he left his wife and children behind while he worked in Indiana and mailed home his meager savings. In 1938 Davis rocked on his daughter's porch in Athens, Georgia, dispensed potions, advice, and folk medicine, told his life story to an interviewer from a federally funded history project, and awaited his end.

Parson Bill Holmes did likewise. Weary and a bit befuddled, Holmes wandered from past to present and back as he talked about himself to a government interviewer in 1938. At eighteen years of age, Holmes went to war. "We was fighting to keep the slaves. But it's a good thing they's freed. Still, they sure would have hit the nail square on the head if they'd colonized them niggers. It ain't best to have two races of God's children mixed. One is going to boss the other every time that happens." After the war he proposed to Emma. "I told her I wanted to make one crop before we was married. And she says, 'And I want to make some quilts and things.' " Holmes farmed some and then preached as a Primitive Baptist after he "felt a call." He survived three wives and one son lost to drink, gambling, and a barroom brawl, left a "large Holmes family in its several branches," and looked forward to "Heaven, sweet heaven."

In 1938, time and the tumultuous events of World War II had not yet pushed the Civil War from the center of memory in the South. Reconstruction also remained a vivid memory. Debates about why the South lost the Civil War raged in 1938. Only a few historians debated Reconstruction. Everyone else *knew* Reconstruction was bad, that it was an era of unprecedented corruption presided over by vengeful, self-serving, often incompetent politicians. In collective memory Reconstruction had become a morality play between good and evil. But Reconstruction was not that simple or clear-cut.

RECONSTRUCTION

Reconstruction actually began before the defeat of the Confederacy and at a relatively obscure place in the South Carolina tidelands in the fall of 1861. On November 7, Admiral Francis Du Pont led his forces into Port Royal and began to bombard the Confederate defenses there. Sam Mitchell fled what he thought was a violent storm and ran to the safety of his mother, Tyra. "That ain't no thunder," she told him, "that Yankee come to give you Freedom." The next day, Federal

FORMER SLAVES NEAR HOME OF SAM MITCHELL, BEAUFORT DISTRICT, SOUTH
CAROLINA, 1862 (Library of Congress)

troops occupied the area, including Beaufort, the only town of any size on the
sound. Overnight the Federals became an army of occupation with responsibilities for defending Port Royal and the one white man—too drunk to flee—and the
10,000 slaves they found there.

Provisions had to be made for these people immediately. Only slightly less
pressing was the need to determine the legal status of the slaves. Obviously, what
had begun as only a military mission became more than that. The Lincoln administration, especially because it still shied away from any suggestion that the abolition of slavery was one of its war aims, was poorly prepared to deal with the
questions raised by the victory at Port Royal.

The story that unfolded at Port Royal in the succeeding months was a rehearsal for Reconstruction. Thus events at Beaufort revealed something of the
way blacks and whites would deal with one another after the war. Moreover, as
the diverse groups clustered around Port Royal discovered, distant events and
people had enormous impact on their lives. Policies formulated in Washington
shaped life and labor on the sound. Equally important was the return of the local
whites and the struggles to determine who would have dominance in South Carolina after the war ended.

A critically important fact became very obvious in Port Royal soon after Du
Pont's victory: the blacks were not passive lumps of dark clay waiting to be

molded by others. The Port Royal blacks, or "contrabands of war" (a politically expedient term employed by the Union government to describe slaves who came within Union lines before emancipation was proclaimed in 1862), mystified, exasperated, and pleased the newly arrived northern whites. They had done the same to their departed owners. The contrabands demonstrated abject dependency, some of which was calculated and some of which was real—a product of their slave experience and their present condition. This dependency confused observers, then and since, and tended to disguise how assertive the former slaves could be. Most had spent their entire lives as slaves. Few had skills as leaders. Even fewer could read and write. Most had worked only as farm hands.

Yet the blacks at Port Royal asserted themselves in ways that belied the guise of dependency. Many had acted to secure their own liberty. When Tyra Mitchell's husband told her that their master had ordered him to take the master to Charleston to avoid capture by the Federals, she exploded. "You ain't gonna row no boat to Charleston, you go out that back door and keep a-going." Mitchell fled. He returned when Du Pont's victory was certain, worked as a carpenter for the Union army, and eventually bought himself a ten-acre farm nearby. Other blacks along the coast took the first opportunity to join the Port Royal blacks, though the Federals' intentions toward slaves were often unknown and despite warnings from southern whites that the Union forces sold runaways to Cuba.

Blacks were determined to escape slavery and to control their own lives. The contrabands at Port Royal, like the millions of other slaves freed during and after the Civil War, had been hurt but not crushed by the terrible burden of bondage. In fact, they acted a lot like other Americans. They moved quickly to formalize their marriages and to collect their scattered families. They eagerly sought work, education for themselves and especially for their children, and land of their own. The number of blacks who sought schooling overwhelmed the teachers and facilities at Port Royal after Du Pont's victory. The blacks grasped at the American dream of self-improvement, self-employment, and upward mobility. Accordingly, they often resisted working for wages and planting cotton, a crop that had not benefited slaves directly in the past. They preferred to plant food crops and to raise livestock. A number of adult male contrabands fought with distinction in the Union army. The blacks at Port Royal especially wanted land of their own.

The prospects for land remained unclear for long, anxiety-filled months, as did the legal status of slaves and the prospects for Union victory. The outcome of these issues depended very largely on events, forces, and decisions beyond Port Royal. In September 1862 President Lincoln committed the Union to emancipation, which was later made effective by the Union's victory in the war. But ownership of the land at Port Royal remained unresolved at the end of the war. That became a critical issue as local whites began to return. Their return raised another pressing question: How would former masters and slaves deal with one another?

By 1865, ownership of the land around Beaufort had become a complex matter. Federal authorities had seized some land for unpaid taxes and sold it at auction. Buyers included whites recently arrived from the North and a few former slaves, who bought small parcels. The great majority of the blacks, however, simply occupied deserted plantations. The ranks of the squatters swelled as the war went on, especially after General Sherman's march to the sea and his Field Order

15, which set aside coastal lands between Charleston and Savannah for use by the refugees. But ownership of these squatter lands was unclear, which became a critical matter in mid-1865 when the former planters returned.

Most returning planters were welcomed. Some received gifts, loans, and help from their former slaves. But there was a coolness to the welcome. One graciously received planter was "firmly and respectfully informed . . . : 'We own this land now. Put it out of your head that it will ever be yours again.' " Another planter had his land but found that not one of his old hands would work for him, not even "Old Gib," his former trusted driver.

Land and labor were *the* issues, as they had been before the war. They were necessary for survival, for social position, and for self-respect. In an agrarian world where most people earned their living from the land and nonfarm work was scarce, landlessness and dependency on wages meant uncertain todays and blank tomorrows.

Whatever Old Gib and other freedmen thought and wanted, most of the prewar white landowners soon regained their land, and most of the freedmen remained landless and had no choice but to work the land for others. Less than a year after the planters came back to Port Royal, they received full pardons from President Andrew Johnson, and they were allowed to reclaim most of their land when Federal troops drove the squatters off. Blacks protested to no avail. "Why do you take away our lands? You take them from us who have always been true, always true to the Government! You give them to our all-time enemies! That is not right!" Landless blacks then reluctantly signed work contracts with the planters because when spring came "nature called men, white or black, to plant or starve." As before, decisions made elsewhere—in this case, in Washington—shaped life in Port Royal and throughout the South.

PRESIDENTIAL RECONSTRUCTION

President Andrew Johnson, whose Reconstruction policies profoundly affected Port Royal in particular and the South in general, began to outline and implement those policies in May 1865. Like his predecessor, Lincoln, Johnson stressed reconciliation between the Union and the defeated Confederacy and restoration of civil government in the South. In December 1863 Lincoln had issued a "Proclamation for Amnesty and Reconstruction." He had promised a "full pardon" and restitution of all property, save for slaves, to those who had rebelled against the Union and who would take an oath of allegiance to the Union. Some were excluded: officials of the Confederacy, ranking military officers, and some other prominent Confederates. When the numbers of people who took the oath reached at least 10 percent of those who had voted in 1860, they could form a state government, which Lincoln promised to recognize. Lincoln applied his Reconstruction formula in Arkansas and Louisiana in 1864. Both established governments, he recognized them, and they then conducted elections for state and national offices. Both of these new governments accepted abolition. Neither, however, gave the vote to any blacks, though Lincoln had especially urged Louisiana to do so because of the substantial number of propertied, well-educated blacks in New Orleans. Congress refused to admit the newly elected congressional delegations from Arkansas and Louisiana. Nor would Congress count the electoral votes of either state or those of Tennessee, which had a federally sanctioned provisional government, in the 1864 presidential election.

Clearly the Republican Congress had balked at Lincoln's Reconstruction plan. Most congressional Republicans believed that more than the restoration of political control of the South to loyal citizens was required. They believed Reconstruction had to include a clear renunciation of secession; assurances to southern Unionists of personal safety and a political voice; guarantees that slavery had been abolished forever and that blacks had secured civil rights; and at least for a while, restrictions on the rights of former Confederate leaders to vote and to hold public office. Many congressional Republicans favored some form of suffrage for blacks. In July 1864 Congress passed its own Reconstruction plan: the Wade-Davis Bill (named after its sponsors, Congressman Henry Winter Davis of Maryland and Senator Benjamin Wade of Ohio). Congress gave greater stress to the creation of southern state governments that were loyal to the Union than to sectional reconciliation and the rapid restoration of civil government in the South. The Wade-Davis Bill required that a majority of the voters in each of the former Confederate states take a loyalty oath; it stipulated that only those who could swear they had not willingly supported the Confederacy could vote for delegates to the state constitutional conventions that were charged with establishing new governments; and it created some legal protection, which the federal courts would enforce, for blacks. The Wade-Davis Bill did not, however, enfranchise any blacks.

Although Congress passed the bill by nearly a unanimous vote, Lincoln vetoed it. Congress could not act further on the measure until it returned for a new session. Wade and Davis reacted promptly, however, with a bitter public attack on Lincoln's veto. It was extraordinary for an incumbent president to be so severely criticized during a presidential campaign by leaders of his own party. Clearly the issues dividing the president and Congress were quite serious.

The Republicans had not resolved their differences over Reconstruction policy when Lincoln was assassinated and Andrew Johnson succeeded him in April 1865. Johnson chose to ignore these wide differences and moved quickly on Reconstruction. On May 29, 1865, President Johnson granted a broad amnesty and pardon to southerners who had rebelled and a "restoration of all rights of property, except as to slaves," provided those who had been in rebellion take an oath of future allegiance. Some southerners would require special pardons from the president, including all the categories of exceptions Lincoln had established earlier plus all those with taxable property worth $20,000 or more. Johnson's addition suggested that he intended to humble the planter elite, a group he had often attacked. If it encouraged the Republicans to believe that the new president was going to be firmer toward the South than Lincoln had been, they soon learned better.

The same day that he issued his proclamation of amnesty and pardon, Johnson appointed William H. Holden as provisional governor of North Carolina and charged him to arrange a convention to draft a new state constitution, abolish slavery, and repudiate secession and the state's war debt. Those who voted for delegates to the convention and the delegates themselves had to be white adult males who had sworn their allegiance to the United States and who had received amnesty or pardons. Shortly thereafter, Johnson made similar arrangements for South Carolina, Florida, Georgia, Alabama, Mississippi, and Texas. Six of these seven states (distance caused delays until April 1866 in Texas) held elections and conventions that met Johnson's stipulations before December 1865. He also accepted Francis H. Pierpoint's government in exile, which the Union had previously supported, as the provisional government of Virginia, and he accepted the governments in Tennessee, Louisiana, and Arkansas, which Lincoln had recognized. The president then declared the Union restored in his first State of the Union message, which he sent to Congress as it was opening a new congressional session and as representatives of the former Confederate states waited to be seated in Congress.

By the time the Senate and the House of Representatives reconvened in December 1865, Johnson had officially welcomed all the former Confederate states except Texas back into the Union. They had met his terms. They had elected new state governments, had repudiated or annulled secession and the Confederate debts, and had abolished slavery, and the required proportion of their voters had sworn allegiance to the Union. Johnson's lenient pardon policy amounted in practice virtually to a general amnesty. About 15,000 applied for special pardons; Johnson granted 13,500 in 1865 alone. Johnson's policies allowed for the restoration to southerners of property that had not already been sold or lost or destroyed—except, of course, slaves. As southerners celebrated the restoration of statehood and civilian government in late 1865, few had any sense that their new state governments might be rejected in the North.

SOUTHERN DEFIANCE: UNCONQUERED REBELS?

Southerners praised President Johnson, for obvious reasons. They had received far better terms than they had expected, including the assurance that they had not lost their lands. They had gotten back some of their lost dignity and had received succor for their war-caused trauma. Their trauma was compounded of many elements: exhaustion, great losses of blood and treasure, four years of wartime sacrifices and disruptions—destroyed, damaged, or neglected plantations, farms, railroads, industries, towns, and cities—genuine suffering and deprivation that continued long months after surrender, and the abolition of slavery, the cornerstone of the southern world. Southerners experienced a shattering decline of position, status, and prospects. Save for American Indians and possibly the Revolutionary War loyalists, no group in American history has experienced a decline so severe as that suffered by the planter elite.

Southern honor had been massively assaulted. The deeply religious South confronted a terrifying question: Had the God they believed had ordained and sanctioned their society and its slave foundation found them wanting? Was not the defeat of the South its day of judgment? William Henry Ravenel, South Carolina planter and scientist, felt he could not "avoid the conviction that a righteous

God had designed this punishment for our sins.""This is the bitter end of four years of toil and sacrifices," General Josiah Gorgas, chief of ordnance for the Confederacy, confided to his diary in August 1865.

> What an end to our great hopes. Is it possible that we were wrong? Is it right after all that one set of men can force their opinion on another set? It seems so, and that self government is a mocking before the Almighty. He permits it or refuses it as seems good to him. Let us bow in submission and learn to curb our bitter thoughts.

Leaving what had been an enormously profitable rice plantation, William H. Heyward sought refuge in a Charleston hotel, where for a time he lived in virtual solitary confinement in his room. "I am sometimes on the verge of self-destruction. . . . When I go to rest at night, my wish and great desire is that I may never open my eyes another day." Some southerners fled the country, many never to return. Many southerners believed themselves to have been massively wronged, that secession was legal, that the South had followed the revolutionary tradition of 1776, and that the Confederacy had defended republicanism, the American sine qua non, against a power-mad Union. Atrocity stories—real or imagined and heavily embellished—about the conduct of Union armed forces during combat and occupation were widespread and widely believed.

Perhaps worst of all, blacks were out of control. Thousands had fled during the war, more afterward. Former masters worried about how former slaves would react to them, about who would provide critically needed farm labor if blacks did not, about whether blacks would seek revenge. Rumors of planned Christmastime rebellions and massacres by blacks swirled. Visions of postemancipation Haiti and Jamaica rose as nightfall came to the thinly populated stretches of the rural South. Actually, physical attacks on the persons of former masters were remarkably rare. Assaults on the property of former slaveholders were more common, though perhaps as often former slaves defended the property of their former masters.

Much more usual was the widespread tendency of blacks to distance themselves from southern whites. Blacks usually greeted former masters warmly, even gave them aid, but refused to work for them. Many former slaves agreed to live in what had been slave quarters only if they could drag the houses to new, dispersed locations away from the old slave compounds. Finally, blacks rejected second-class status in white-dominated churches. They formed black-only congregations within white-majority denominations, usually Baptist or Methodist, or they joined black denominations, such as the African Methodist Episcopal church, which had been founded before 1860.

This distancing of themselves from southern whites puzzled and angered former masters who had treated their slaves paternalistically. Despite its limitations and its frequent violations, paternalism had permeated black-white relations before the defeat of the Confederacy. Paternalism rested on a bond of affection and mutual obligation. Former masters seemed to need an acknowledgment from blacks that that bond had been genuine and that it had not entirely disappeared. Former slaveholders thus complained bitterly about "ungrateful" former slaves and gloated over signs of affection and dependence. Mary Boykin Chesnut seemed genuinely pleased when an elderly nurse came back from a brief flight away with Union troops. She "knew well on which side her bread ʼ and she knew too, or found out, where her real friends were."

Whites genuinely feared anarchy and bloodshed. Their fears were strongest in areas where blacks were most numerous. Whites desperately wanted order restored to what seemed like chaos. They also anguished about how they would obtain critically needed labor. Convinced that blacks would not work without coercion, whites sought ways to force blacks to labor for them. Strengthened by President Johnson's policies and once again in control of the state and local governments, southern leaders moved quickly in 1865 to assert control over the life and labor of southern blacks. None of the restored southern legislatures gave the vote to any blacks. Most of the new state governments and many local governments revised their vagrancy laws to address the largely illusory problem of idleness among blacks. The result was a legal net to snare the presumably idle and dump them back into the fields. Several states made these changes part of more comprehensive statutes, the infamous Black Codes. Mississippi's Black Code defined a vagrant as anyone who was guilty of theft, had run away, was drunk, was wanton in conduct or speech, had neglected job or family, handled money carelessly, and lest anyone escape, "all other idle and disorderly persons."

The Mississippi code defined a Negro as anyone who was one-eighth or more Negro (anyone who had at least one black great-grandparent). The code recognized slave marriages as permanent and allowed blacks to make contracts, hold property, sue and be sued, and be witnesses in cases to which blacks were parties. Interracial cohabitation and marriage were forbidden, and blacks were not permitted to vote, hold public office, serve on juries, or bear arms. Other measures of control included exclusion from many occupations, restrictions on conducting certain businesses, limitations on where blacks could own land, and apprenticeship laws. The last allowed indigent young blacks to be apprenticed involuntarily to whites, with former slavemasters receiving preference when apprentices were assigned. The codes also attempted to prevent "enticement" of labor from one employer to another and circumscribed the right of blacks to assemble.

> Any freedman, free negro or mulatto, committing riots, routs, affrays, trespasses, malicious mischief, cruel treatment to animals, seditious speeches, insulting gestures, language, or acts, assaults on any person, disturbance of the peace, exercising the function of a minister of the Gospel, without a license from some regularly organized church, vending spirituous or intoxicating liquors, or committing any other misdemeanor, the punishment of which is not specifically provided for by law, shall, upon conviction thereof . . . be fined not less than ten dollars, and not more than one hundred dollars, and may be imprisoned . . . [up to] thirty days.

The code also required blacks to be courteous, dutiful, and diligent employees. Unlike white lawbreakers, convicted blacks could be whipped and pilloried. Local ordinances, such as curfew laws, added to the burdens of blacks. South Carolina and Louisiana adopted comparable Black Codes, others had less harsh laws, and several states did not pass such comprehensive measures.

Most states started leasing convicts to planters, coal mine operators, railroad construction companies, and others. Often brutal in practice, the system passed a substantial portion of the costs of the states' penal systems to the private contractors, and states even made profits from the leases. In turn, the contractors got cheap (primarily black) workers to whose welfare they could be indifferent. The resulting punishment was often worse than blacks had experienced during slavery. Moreover, Johnson's suggestion, echoing Lincoln's, that a stringently qualified franchise for blacks might have a desirable effect on the North fell on deaf ears. The adoption of the Black Codes proved to be a serious political mistake.

Racial fear and prejudice and a crisis mentality fueled these actions. So did a distorted paternalism and legal precedent. Blacks, it was assumed, were permanently children. Thus blacks needed permanent protection. Conversely, white southerners also insisted that these supposedly perpetual children posed a massive threat. Whether or not such assumptions were genuinely believed, and they probably were in many cases, they contained blatantly logical flaws. Finally, white paternalism squared too neatly with white self-interest. Not too surprisingly, many northern Republicans believed that blacks needed protection from, not by, southern whites.

Southern legislatures did not act in a legal vacuum. They found precedents in the slave codes, which had been voided by emancipation; in vagrancy statutes, north and south; in the northern and southern laws that applied to antebellum free blacks; in the legal codes that had been enacted in the British West Indies after the abolition of slavery there; and even in some of the regulations of the Freedmen's Bureau, the agency created by the federal government to aid blacks in their transition from bondage. Panic reinforced harshness. The most severe legislation was passed before the end of 1865, when anxieties about securing a workforce for the next farm season and fears about a black rebellion reached fever pitch. Visions of ruin, starvation, and massacre haunted white lawmakers.

The hopes of the newly freed slaves complicated matters. They did not immediately return to the fields when the war ended, and they did leave plantations in large numbers and move about a great deal. Blacks wanted to explore the boundaries of their new status—to escape reminders of their past, to search for members of their families who had been dispersed by the vagaries of slavery or the war, or merely to see places that had been denied them during their bondage. Cities had a particular attraction. Blacks also waited to see if the federal government would give them the homesteads they believed they had earned by their labor as slaves and thought they had been promised by the Union, especially those who had served in the Union army. Unfortunately and tragically, those promises never had a real chance of becoming reality for the great majority. Finally, former slaves hardly looked forward to returning to someone else's land. By 1866, most did. Necessity prevailed. Southern legislatures had not, however, waited for the invisible hand of economic forces to ease the farm-labor crisis.

These efforts of southern whites to develop a new system of race relations to replace the one that had prevailed during slavery, to establish their superior position in a slaveless South, and to assure themselves of a steady supply of docile black labor bore strong resemblances to slavery itself. The Black Codes in particular were strongly criticized in the North and were prime catalysts for the undoing of the restored state governments that Lincoln and Johnson had created. Northern critics saw these laws as blatant attempts to reestablish slavery. Southern defenders of the vagrancy laws and Black Codes were puzzled, then outraged by what they saw as a double standard. They believed that they had followed precedents in dealing with pressing problems. Their attitude and behavior toward blacks did not differ markedly from what they had heard and seen in their encounters with northern white troops and agents of the Freedmen's Bureau, and they certainly knew that blacks faced serious legal disabilities, flagrant discrimination, and even physical abuse in the North.

Southerners, however, did not realize that in their drive to secure a stable agricultural workforce and white dominance they had overreached themselves and now ran the risk of offending northern opinion, which had become closely attuned to southern behavior and attitudes. Northern Republicans began to have grave doubts about the willingness of the southern states to do what the northern Republicans thought was absolutely necessary before the South could rejoin the Union. Northern Republicans began to come to the unsettling conclusion that southerners had not accepted the verdict of the battlefield, that secession and slavery were not dead, that the South was not going to be loyal to the federal government, and that blacks, southern Unionists, and northern immigrants would not be secure and fairly treated in the South. In sum, the South appeared to be a land of defiant, unconquered rebels.

Efforts to determine the mood of the former Confederate states and the conditions there turned pulse-taking into an industry. Journalists sent daily dispatches northward from all over the South, reporting interviews and overheard conversations, pleasant encounters and hostile receptions. Letters and reports flowed northward from travelers and from southerners themselves. These writings reflected the expectations of the writers and their intended readers. President Johnson, for instance, was told that southerners had embraced his restoration program and were loyal to the Union. Congressional Republicans heard otherwise, especially from southern Unionists.

Carl Schurz penned perhaps the most accurate report on conditions and feelings in the South. Schurz was a German-American leader, a Union general, and later an excellent secretary of the interior who was noted for his fairness. Schurz debunked several unsettling rumors. The South was defeated, knew it, and was not planning more armed resistance against the Union. As Schurz pointed out, most southerners were working to reestablish state governments according to Johnson's policies. But Schurz found too little Unionist feeling in the South and too much firm belief that the South had done no wrong. Southerners despised northerners recently arrived in the South, southern Unionists, and most of all, black troops. Southerners longed for the good old days of slavery and expected blacks to accept something that approximated it, for their own good. Schurz was convinced that southern blacks and southern Unionists urgently needed protection.

What southern political leaders were doing substantiated Schurz's conclusions. First, there were the new laws that applied to freed slaves. Then, not all the southern states repudiated secession and slavery; they just declared them null and void. Some accepted emancipation only reluctantly. Mississippi and Texas refused to ratify the Thirteenth Amendment (making slavery unconstitutional), and Mississippi and South Carolina declined to repudiate state debts incurred during the war. Mississippi even revived its state militia and manned it with Confederate

s. Several state constitutional conventions would not fly the Union flag. Confederates dominated the restored state governments, although many of these leaders had been reluctant Unionists before the Civil War. The newly elected southern congressional delegations included Confederate cabinet officers, congressmen, generals, and colonels. Georgia even sent the former vice president of the Confederacy to Congress. The fact that Alexander H. Stephens had voted against secession in Georgia's secession convention in 1861 was not enough to offset the stigma he bore in the North as the second-highest official of the Confederacy. Loyalty to proven, beloved leaders was understandable, but sending Stephens to the Senate was worse than foolish.

Several factors may account for these miscalculations. Southern leaders mistakenly believed President Johnson accurately reflected the views of the North and the federal government. Johnson should have been more firm when he advised southern leaders about what was expected of the South. Perhaps Johnson missed the opportunity to demand more of the South in 1865 while the South was still in shock and might have been more accommodating. Yet he and most southern leaders no doubt felt the South was not being defiant and had already paid a high price. The South generally repudiated secession and its Confederate debts, had accepted emancipation and granted some civil rights to the blacks, and had sworn allegiance to the Union and formed new state governments. They had, in fact, met the president's terms. But they had not met those of the Republicans, who, after all, controlled Congress. It became clear in late 1865 that neither Johnson nor most southern leaders paid sufficient attention to what had occurred between Lincoln and Congress over the Wade-Davis Bill or to other issues the Republicans had been raising about Reconstruction.

THE REPUBLICANS AND JOHNSON'S RECONSTRUCTION POLICIES

When Congress reconvened in December 1865, the Republican majority immediately registered its reaction to Johnson's policies, the politics and legislation of restoration in the South, and reports it had received of southern sentiments and behavior. The majority first refused to seat any newly elected southerners in the Senate or the House. (Congress has the constitutional authority to "be the Judge of the Elections, Returns and Qualifications of its own Members.") In taking this action, Congress also raised serious doubts about the future of the new state governments, putting them in a political and constitutional limbo.

Congress subsequently extended the life of the Freedmen's Bureau, which was near expiration, and expanded its duties to include oversight of labor relations between blacks and white employers, provision of impartial courts for blacks in the defeated Confederacy, and supervision of abandoned and confiscated lands in the South. (Johnson's quick restoration of property in the South negated most of the last responsibility.) Congress passed the Civil Rights Bill of 1866 to counter the Black Codes and to negate the Dred Scott decision (1857), which held that blacks could never become citizens. The bill represented a constitutional shift of immense importance in American history. It was the first attempt ever by the federal government to define American citizenship. Also for the first time in federal law, the civil rights of citizens were defined and attempts were made to protect those rights. Congress stated that

> all persons born in the United States and not subject to any foreign power, excluding Indians not taxed, are hereby declared to be citizens of the United States; such citizens, of every race and color, without regard to any previous condition of slavery or involuntary servitude . . . shall have the right in every State and Territory in the United States, to make and enforce contracts, to sue, be parties, and give evidence, to inherit, purchase, lease, sell, hold and convey real and personal property, and to full and equal benefit of all laws and proceedings for the security of person and property, as is enjoyed by white citizens, and shall be subject to like punishment, pains and penalties, and to none other, any law, statute, ordinance, regulation, or custom, to the contrary notwithstanding.

Federal courts had exclusive jurisdiction over the law. The president was explicitly authorized to act to get speedy trials, and could use army, navy, or militia to enforce the law. President Johnson vetoed both the Freedmen's Bureau Bill and the Civil Rights Bill, and Congress overrode both vetoes to make them law. Never before had Congress overridden a presidential veto of a major bill. The gap between the president and the Republican Congress over Reconstruction had become all but unbridgeable.

Congress soon took another major step in keeping with the Republican approach to Reconstruction. It wrote and passed the Fourteenth Amendment to ensure the constitutionality and permanence of the Civil Rights Act of 1866. The first section of the amendment has had lasting, critical importance in American history. Its derivation from the Civil Rights Act is obvious.

> All persons born or naturalized in the United States, and subject to the jurisdiction thereof, are citizens of the United States and of the State wherein they reside. No State shall make or enforce any law which shall abridge the privileges or immunities of citizens of the United States; nor shall any State deprive any person of life, liberty, or property, without due process of law; nor deny any person within its jurisdiction the equal protection of the laws.

The amendment also provided for a reduction in congressional representation if any state prevented adult male citizens from voting. Despite later massive and blatant violations of this provision, it has never been enforced. Other parts of the amendment declared Federal Civil War debts valid, voided all Confederate debts, and disqualified all former state or federal officials who served the Confederacy during the Civil War from holding office again unless Congress pardoned them. The Republicans made ratification of the amendment a prerequisite for readmission of any Confederate state to the Union. The amendment constituted Congress's plan for Reconstruction. When the South continued to resist that plan, Congress imposed it by passing the Reconstruction Acts in 1867 and 1868.

A complex set of motives prompted these actions. Congress wanted to assert itself against the executive branch, which during the Civil War had greatly enhanced its powers at the expense of Congress and the courts. Northern Republicans feared a revived Democratic party in the South and the North. Only part of this fear sprang from purely selfish partisanship. Republicans also genuinely believed that the Democrats had led the nation into a disastrous civil war and that the views of most Democrats on such major issues as the tariff, banking, excise taxes, and internal improvements were wrongheaded and could hurt the nation. Another major factor in the northern Republicans' determination to create and implement their Reconstruction plan was their conviction that they had to protect what the Union had won in battle from a seemingly unbowed South. Republicans also felt compelled to do something to protect Unionists and blacks in the South.

Events in Memphis in the spring of 1866 indicated that these concerns were well founded. When two carriages, one driven by a white and the other by a black, collided on a Memphis street, the collision ignited the powder keg that the city had become. The city's population had doubled in only two years. Irish immigrants and former slaves had poured in. A wave of crime beset the Irish-run city government and police. Former Confederates in Memphis, newly bereft of political power and of much of their wealth, were full of contempt for "damn yankees," whose presence at nearby Fort Pickering was all too apparent. Matters became acute when four regiments of the 4,000 black troops at Pickering were released without pay by the army. Some of them clashed with the Memphis police on April 30. The minor incident involving the carriage drivers grew into three days of riot, arson, rape, and looting that left forty-six blacks and two whites dead.

Such violent outbursts fed the antisouthern feeling already strong in the North. Angry memories of the war, of great sacrifices, required more than a "make up and forget" policy. The reaction of the Chicago *Tribune* to the Mississippi Black Code reflected those feelings. "We tell the white men of Mississippi that the men of the North will convert the state of Mississippi into a frog pond before they will allow such laws to disgrace one foot of soil in which the bones of our soldiers sleep and over which the flag of freedom waves." The charge of being "too soft" on the South was a political liability for Republican politicians, whose constituents had lost family and friends in combat, had had their lives disrupted for four years, and had watched prices, taxes, and the federal debt soar.

Republicans' fears that the Democrats would regain their antebellum political dominance were not fantasies. The dominance of the Republican party was not assured in 1865 and would not be until the 1890s. Only then were the Republicans able to control the White House and both houses of Congress consistently. Divisions among Democrats in 1860 and the secessions that followed had given the Republicans an unusual political opportunity but not a secure upper hand during the Civil War. When the South rejoined the Union, it would be more politically powerful than it had been before the war because emancipation voided the three-fifths rule (by which each slave was counted as three-fifths of a person for apportionment of members of the House of Representatives and of the electoral college). One ironic result of abolition was an increase in the South's strength in Congress and in the electoral college. Moreover, Republicans correctly suspected that President Johnson, a Tennessee Democrat, was attempting to build a new coalition, perhaps a new political party, whose future was tied to the quick restoration of the South. Not incidentally, he hoped that this coalition might get him reelected in 1868. In fact, during the 1866 congressional election, Johnson worked toward those goals by participating in the National Union political movement, a coalition of Democrats and a few prominent Republicans who generally agreed with Johnson on Reconstruction.

THE 1866 ELECTION AND THE FOURTEENTH AMENDMENT

Relations between Johnson and Congress reached an impasse before the 1866 congressional election. In less than twelve months, the good feeling that had prevailed when Johnson succeeded Lincoln evaporated. Johnson failed a basic test of political leadership—he was unwilling and unable to compromise. He did succeed at something else: he forced the Republicans to settle the differences among themselves. Thus the Freedmen's Bureau Act, the Civil Rights Act, and the Fourteenth Amendment were compromise measures for which moderate Republicans were primarily responsible. Contrary to what is often believed, the Radical Republicans, such as Thaddeus Stevens of Pennsylvania and Charles Sumner of Massachusetts, who wanted more sweeping measures, did not control Congress and did not dictate the writing of Reconstruction legislation. Johnson, often portrayed as the victim of a vengeful Congress, thwarted compromise by his political and constitutional rigidity and compounded the difficulty by his fiery rhetoric. In February 1866, for instance, speaking to a group celebrating the birthday of George Washington, Johnson likened opponents of his Reconstruction policy to Judas and himself to Christ: he was willing, he said, for his "blood . . . to be shed . . . on an altar to the Union."

The conflict between Johnson and Congress spilled over to the 1866 congressional election, in which the Fourteenth Amendment was the focal issue. Then came a riot in New Orleans which took thirty-eight lives—thirty-four blacks, three white Republicans, and one white rioter. The New Orleans clash was more explicitly political than the riot in Memphis, and it had a major impact on the election. It developed out of attempts by Republicans in Louisiana to protect themselves against a state government controlled by former Confederates whose intentions were all too clear. The Louisiana state Democratic party declared in its 1865 platform:

> *Resolved,* That we hold this to be a Government of white people, made and to be perpetuated for the exclusive benefit of the white race; . . . that the people of African descent cannot be considered as citizens of the United States, and that there can, in no event, nor under any circumstances, be any equality between the white and other races.

Republican proposals in 1866 to reopen the Louisiana state constitutional convention in order to enfranchise blacks and disfranchise former Confederates alarmed local whites. Democratic politicians harangued. Newspapers circulated rumors of the worst. Local whites, led by the police, refused to wait for the courts to rule on the doubtful legality of reopening the constitutional convention, which had been officially closed. They confronted blacks who were joyously marching to the proposed convention site. The confrontation turned into riot, murderous pursuit, and gunning down. Whites besieged the convention hall, assaulting and killing defenseless blacks and their white allies while ignoring three separate attempts by the assailed to surrender. The *New Orleans Daily Picayune* regretted "the bloody details of yesterday. . . . It was horrifying; but there seemed to be no alternative." President Johnson neither decried the massacre nor expressed sympathy for its victims. Instead, he accused Louisiana Republicans of provoking the rioters.

The New Orleans riot, along with that in Memphis and similar incidents at Chattanooga, Louisville, and Vicksburg, had an electric effect on the northern public and northern Republicans. Given a choice between Johnson's Reconstruction program, which suggested that the South ought to be allowed to reconstruct itself, whatever the consequences, and the Republican program, which was expressed in the Fourteenth Amendment, northern voters overwhelmingly endorsed the Republicans. The Republican party gained the upper hand in every northern state and in West Virginia, Tennessee, and Missouri, and the party held on to its 3-to-1 margin in Congress. But only one former Confederate state, Tennessee, ratified the Fourteenth Amendment. Ten southern legislatures, many unanimously and with Johnson's encouragement, refused to adopt the amendment. "If we are to be degraded," the governors of North and South Carolina declared, "we will retain some self-esteem by not making it self-abasement." Southern honor, the elemental glue of southern society, had to be defended. In this case, the South may have defended its honor, but it squandered an opportunity to be restored to the Union on the mildest terms the Republicans could or would offer. The spurned opportunity set the stage first for Military Reconstruction and then for Radical Reconstruction.

The predominantly Republican Congress reconvened in December 1866, and the Republicans—still divided into conservative, moderate, and radical wings—hammered out a compromise program designed to create a different system of politics in the postwar South. Johnson's ineptitude, the South's intransigence, and the results of the 1866 election caused moderate and even some conservative Republicans to embrace a fundamental position of the Radical Republicans: the South could not be reconstructed unless blacks were given the vote. Congress passed legislation that effectively unhorsed the Johnson state governments, created a series of interim military governors (Military Reconstruction), and laid the basis for Republican control of the former Confederacy (Radical Reconstruction, or the so-called Black Reconstruction).

Southern whites were confused, embittered, and outraged. They felt they had met Johnson's requirements for the restoration of self-government. Now they confronted different terms. They were bitter because the new policy rested on the wholly unacceptable assumption that secession was treasonous, that the South had to bear the burden of war guilt. The North had claimed that the Union was indissoluble and had gone to war in support of that claim. Now Congress was telling the South it had to seek readmission to the Union that the North had claimed was indissoluble. It was monstrously hypocritical, maddening.

Southerners were outraged because Congress was using suffrage requirements and disqualifications for public office to cause a political revolution in the South. Congress stepped into areas traditionally reserved for state action. Congress committed the greatest villainy of all when it gave black adult males the vote.

RECONSTRUCTION: MYTH AND REALITY

Southerners came to view Reconstruction as the Tragic Era. Radical or Black Reconstruction became one of the enduring myths of the South. It was canonized in hundreds of speeches, writings, and even sermons; it was written into textbooks, north and south; and today it is still widely accepted as dreadful fact. Myths combine and blur fact and fiction. They become "truth" and last because they bear some resemblance to reality and have meaning and utility. The myth of a horrific Radical Reconstruction does violence to historical fact. Contrary to the myth, Radical Reconstruction was not interminable, was not uniquely corrupt, was not black—if that means that blacks dominated the South during Reconstruction— and was not imposed at the point of a bayonet by a large army of occupation. Moreover, Radical Reconstruction left some notable achievements.

Virginia experienced Military Reconstruction but never had an elected Republican government. Tennessee was specifically excluded from the Reconstruction Acts and was readmitted to the Union in 1866 after it ratified the Fourteenth Amendment. By 1869, coalitions of local white Democrats and former Whigs took control of Tennessee. The state did, however, have to endure the excesses of its Republican governor, William G. "Parson" Brownlow, whose contempt for blacks and former Confederates came in equal parts. North Carolina Conservatives overwhelmed William W. Holden, the Republican governor and a North Carolina native. Then they expelled him on specious grounds, making him the first governor in American history to be thrown out of office. Republican power waxed and waned elsewhere. Only Louisiana, Florida, and South Carolina had Reconstruction governments as late as 1877, and moderate Republicans held sway throughout the period in Florida. Political strife was so intense in Louisiana that the state virtually had no government when Reconstruction ended. And by the last months of 1876, white resistance had reduced Daniel H. Chamberlain, a Republican, to governor of South Carolina in name only.

Corruption in South Carolina reached heights that were not achieved elsewhere, save possibly in Louisiana. Henry Clay Warmoth, onetime Republican governor of Louisiana, declared that members of the state legislature were "as good as the people they represent. Why, damn it, everybody down here is demoralized. Corruption is the fashion." Mississippi Republicans, by contrast, had a remarkably honest record. In some places native whites, both Democrats and Conservatives (the name former Whigs gave themselves after 1865), showed a talent for theft from public treasuries that supposedly was unique to southern Republicans. In Alabama and North Carolina, for instance, native Democrats joined forces with homegrown and immigrant Republicans in scandalous transactions involving state bonds issued for urgently needed but financially questionable railroad schemes. The wretchedly corrupt Louisiana Lottery benefited Republicans and Democrats alike. Finally, corruption, to whatever degree it occurred in the South,

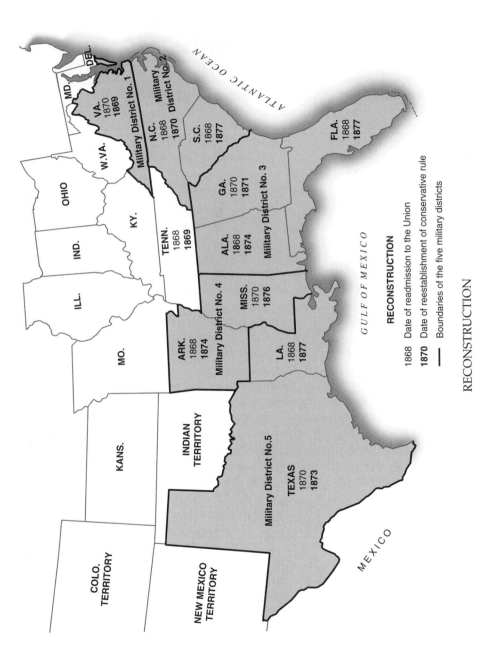

RECONSTRUCTION

RECONSTRUCTION

1868 Date of readmission to the Union

1870 Date of reestablishment of conservative rule

—— Boundaries of the five military districts

was not introduced to the South during Reconstruction. Antebellum southern leaders had not always been above helping themselves to public funds.

Southern states during the era of Reconstruction did incur large debts, which became a serious burden. When some states later repudiated them, they were left with tainted credit records. Critics have too readily assumed that those debts were a clear index of public thievery by Republican officials. Some debts were—those of North Carolina, South Carolina, and Georgia in particular. The Republican government in North Carolina in 1868–1869, for instance, committed that state to spend $27.8 million to support railroad construction. More than $17.6 million of that sum was actually spent, but a large portion of it went into politicians' pockets rather than into railroads.

Other debts reflected poor financial judgment—which is lamentable but not illegal or immoral. Moreover, the increase of government debt began before Radical Reconstruction and continued afterward in some cases. Throughout the period, Conservatives and Democrats lent a hand in deficit spending. Almost all of the state governments created under Johnson's plan subsidized efforts to rebuild and expand railroads, and several created immigration agencies to attract white workers to replace blacks. Legislatures assisted railroads with corporate charters, land grants, and endorsements of bonds. Repairs and construction of other internal improvements—levees, roads, ports, and harbors—received some help also. In these actions southern legislators were following antebellum precedents. Most of the governments created under the Johnson plan also attempted to deal with the pressing problem of private indebtedness. Banks, whose restoration was crucial to economic recovery, received legal authority to scale down war-inflated debts. Individual debtors also got some relief.

Republican state governments often followed the lead of their predecessors. When Republicans in Alabama implemented their very generous program of aid to railroads, for instance, they did so under legislation passed by Alabama's provisional legislatures in 1866 and 1867. Finally, most of the growth of these debts resulted from needed expenditures for postwar recovery and from the states' assumption of responsibility for new services, such as provision of public schools, which had been almost nonexistent before the war. Aid to railroad construction absorbed by far the greatest portion of the increased expenditures of the southern state governments. This spending pattern continued into the 1870s before necessary budget reductions ended almost all state efforts to assist railroads.

Southern state governments had to increase taxes to get the money they were spending, and those taxes were extracted from a badly weakened economy. The increased tax burden fell especially hard on small landowners. In the past, their tax load had been light because government provided few services and because taxes on slaves had been a major source of state revenue. Emancipation, of course, ended the latter tax. Now almost all public revenue came from taxes on real property, and coincidentally, the rate of taxation had increased. Thus, ironically, small landowners, who elsewhere in the United States were staunch Republicans, were the most adversely affected by the tax policies of the Republican state governments in the South.

Also contrary to another widely held notion, blacks did not dominate the South during Radical Reconstruction, even numerically. Although black voters

outnumbered white voters (735,000 registrants to 635,000 in 1867 in the ten unreconstructed states) and had majorities in Louisiana, Mississippi, Alabama,
Florida, and South Carolina, only sixteen blacks served in Congress, fourteen in
the House and two in the Senate. Several won election as lieutenant governors,
and a few others held high state offices. Blacks had a majority in only one southern state legislative body, the lower house in South Carolina.

Black politicians varied in competence and quality of service, just as American politicians have always done. The image of ignorant, arrogant blacks suddenly come to power is grossly unfair. John R. Lynch, a largely self-taught former
slave in Mississippi, rose to be speaker of his state's House of Representatives and
won the praises even of southern whites. He later served as an officer in the
United States Army and then spent the remainder of his life in Chicago, where he
practiced law and tried his hand in real estate. After helping rewrite the constitution of his native state, Francis L. Cardozo was elected secretary of the treasury in
South Carolina, a position in which he showed considerable ability and a strong
distaste for dishonesty in government. When he died, he was a school administrator in the District of Columbia.

Factors other than their native abilities prevented blacks from achieving political power commensurate with their numbers. Poverty left blacks vulnerable and
with more urgent concerns than public office, political organizing, and elections.
Slavery had left them with limited experience as organizers and with a tendency
to defer to whites. Blacks and their presumed supporters often differed. White
Republicans in Georgia even joined with Conservatives in 1870 to deprive black
legislators of their seats. Blacks sometimes broke with their white allies, feeling,
for instance, that they were not receiving the leadership roles due them. Blacks
also divided among themselves. South Carolina black leaders divided along color
lines, black versus mulatto, and along antebellum lines, former slaves versus
blacks who had not been slaves before the Civil War. Divisions among black Republicans, between black and white Republicans, and between southern- and
northern-born Republicans hindered the party and hastened its demise in the
South. Those divisions also make a mockery of one of the persistent images of the
"Tragic Era" legend—that Republicans marched like Roman phalanxes across a
helpless South. The South was not that helpless, and the Republicans were not
that unified in the South or in Washington.

Those who wished to build and maintain a strong Republican party in the
South faced enormous odds. To most southern whites, the Republicans symbolized war, invasion, defeat, and abolition. Thus the most economically and politically powerful elements in the South were the most hostile to the party. On the
other hand, southern blacks flocked to the Republicans, and understandably so.
About 80 percent of the party's supporters were blacks, the least powerful elements in the region. The mountain and upland regions of Alabama, Georgia, Tennessee, North Carolina, and Virginia became centers of Republican support
among whites. So did the Ozarks in Arkansas and the "German" counties in central Texas. But these voters were too few to have much impact beyond their immediate areas. Also, the Republican party had no historical roots in the South; it was
an import, not the product of evolutionary growth that successful political parties
have been in the United States. Moreover, northern Republicans favored eco-

nomic policies—high tariffs, restricted banks, and excise taxes on tobacco and alcohol—that most southerners believed hurt their interests. Finally, sharp factional divisions plagued the Republicans in the South throughout Reconstruction. The seriousness of the difficulties the Republican party encountered in the South is indicated by the failure of the Republicans to sink firm roots in southern soil until after World War II.

White Republicans tried to attract southern whites by various means. One of the most important of these tactics was their championing of the New South, or the idea that the South had to distance itself from its antebellum past, industrialize and urbanize, and diversify and modernize its agriculture, and that to achieve these things government had to aid private enterprise. State aid to railroads was the most obvious and substantial expression of that policy and was based on the belief that recovery and expansion of the South's rail system was necessary for economic development. The cause of the New South appealed particularly to southern Whigs and similar elements among the southern Democrats. Business and political leaders in Atlanta, in northern Alabama, and in Charleston and Richmond joined the New South crusade. White Republicans in the South also tried to appeal to native white leaders through political patronage and by sometimes tempering their commitment to public education. The latter policies, however, risked alienating blacks, who were the principal source of Republican support in the South.

Southern Republicans might have enjoyed greater power after 1865 had they put greater restrictions on voting or officeholding by southern whites. They chose not to do so in part because southern blacks who served as representatives in the conventions that drafted new constitutions for the southern states and who served in southern state legislatures usually opposed such steps. Such actions indicated that Reconstruction often lacked the vindictiveness ascribed to it, even on the part of most blacks, who had the greatest justification for vindictiveness. The reluctance to proscribe southern whites also reflected good sense. Preventing large numbers of southern whites from voting or holding office would very likely have worsened the political turmoil that already existed. Moreover, black leaders understood that blacks were going to live in the South after Reconstruction and were going to have to coexist with southern whites, whose economic power alone gave them enormous leverage over blacks.

Nor was Reconstruction enforced by a massive army of occupation. When the Civil War ended, the United States Army rapidly reduced its forces, and much of what remained was stationed on the western frontier and on the Mexican border. Fewer than 18,000 troops remained in the South in 1866, and only some 6,000 were there in 1876. Immediately after the war, the army helped maintain order in the South and distributed relief. During Military Reconstruction, the army supervised the establishment of Reconstruction governments, but southern whites often found that the army was a valuable ally, as in Florida, where the military governor threw his weight behind moderate Republicans and against the more radical Republicans. The army could only occasionally exert force to deter southern whites from excesses. It did so when it was ordered to suppress the Ku Klux Klan. Blacks continued to have mixed feelings about the men in blue, who were often hostile and sometimes used force to make blacks sign contracts and work as wage laborers and sharecroppers. Southern whites resented the army most when black troops were stationed nearby.

Reconstruction can also be credited with important positive achievements. Southern Republicans drafted state constitutions that recognized blacks' political and civil rights, though they generally left social segregation intact. The Reconstruction constitutions also granted women greater control over their property. Constitutional conventions apportioned legislatures more equitably, expanded the number of elective offices, eliminated property qualifications for officeholding, and checked the power of county political machines. The South eventually accepted many of these constitutional changes. Their permanence despite the numerous revisions of state constitutions since Reconstruction testifies to the merits of the work of the southern Republicans. The South became permanently committed to public education, probably the greatest accomplishment of Reconstruction policy in the South. Other expanded public services included institutions for the poor, the mentally ill, and the physically handicapped. During Reconstruction, Auburn University and the University of Arkansas were created, the University of Alabama and Louisiana State University were reopened, and South Carolina College became the University of South Carolina, with a highly innovative curriculum.

The South began its economic recovery during Reconstruction. The region's rail system was largely restored and was expanded by nearly 7,300 miles. That expansion greatly increased penetration of southern Appalachia. The Freedmen's Bureau spent $1 million on relief for southern blacks and whites and $5 million for education. Working with or alongside teachers from such groups as the American Missionary Association, the New England Freedmen's Aid Society, and the Freedmen's Relief Association, the bureau made significant though modest beginnings toward schooling for blacks. Literacy rose impressively among blacks. Other reminders of these educational efforts remain: Fisk, Hampton, Howard, Atlanta, Talladega, Dillard universities, and others. By 1876 more than half of the white children and two-fifths of the black children in the South were enrolled in school.

The myth of Reconstruction also obscures what did not happen—mass arrests and executions or long imprisonment or deportation of Confederate leaders. Very few southern whites suffered prolonged disfranchisement or disqualification for public office, and the southern states did not suffer extended terms as territories that ended only after a stringent list of requirements was met. One Confederate officer was tried and hanged for war crimes: Captain Henry Wirtz, who had been commander of Andersonville prison, was undoubtedly the victim of a political trial. Jefferson Davis, the former president of the Confederacy, did suffer somewhat humiliating treatment, though briefly. After 1872, when Congress passed the Amnesty Act, only a handful of former Confederate leaders still had to apply for special pardons before they could hold public office. Such pardons were routinely granted.

Southerners did, of course, suffer after the war, but far more as a result of the war itself than as a result of Reconstruction, and blacks suffered far more than whites. Blacks experienced more stark poverty and genuine hunger, and far more of them were the targets of murder, assault, and intimidation. They were deserted by a federal government that was unwilling and unable to secure their political and civil rights and give them a reasonable chance to escape peonage.

The myth that Reconstruction was the Tragic Era persisted because it met an urgent need. Southern whites salved wounds of defeat and feelings of massive wrong with this and other legends: the Lost Cause (the war for southern independence was a noble cause—ignore slavery as the root cause), the Great Alibi (the war made the South economically backward), and the Old South (the antebellum South was an idyllic world peopled by genteel masters, gracious ladies, and happy slaves). A thicket of fact and fiction grew and thrived with nurturing into a mass that still defies comprehension.

The myth that Reconstruction was the Tragic Era also served to justify efforts of Southern whites to regain and maintain political and economic control. Political "outs"—southern Democrats and Conservatives—found the legends useful for attacking the political "ins." Like northern politicians who waved the Bloody Shirt and shouted "Johnny Reb" and "traitor," southern politicians fulminated about "scalawags" and "carpetbaggers" and Radical and Black Reconstruction. As is often the case, historical reality and political rhetoric parted company. Reconstruction was neither black nor radical. It was not dominated by blacks, and except for the proposal to give blacks full and equal citizenship, it was not a program of revolutionary change. Nor were southern whites a monolithic mass. While they had much in common, they were divided by politics, interests, and geography. The secessionist versus Unionist divisions of the antebellum and war years persisted and were exacerbated by the crushing defeat in the Civil War and the turmoil that followed. Whigs and Democrats continued their long-standing feud. Small farmers often differed with planters, and both usually felt uneasy with the urban South, with manufacturers, merchants, and railroad leaders. Old geographically based differences persisted: upcountry versus low country, mountain versus piedmont, western versus middle versus mountain in Tennessee, hill country versus delta in Mississippi.

The negative image associated with carpetbaggers and scalawags also persists in spite of historical fact. Some carpetbaggers did fit the stereotype: they did throw a good portion of their worldly belongings into their carpetbags and head south in pursuit of what they could get. Most, however, were former Union officers and were at least as honest and able as their southern Democratic opponents, and many were more idealistic. Most carpetbaggers had some capital to invest in the South, which they believed had great economic potential, and most had a good deal of training and education. Carpetbaggers taught in or administered schools for freedmen, worked for the Freedmen's Bureau, and served as lawyers, physicians, and engineers. Those carpetbaggers who entered politics, one scholar has concluded, "may have been the best educated group of Americans in politics, North or South. . . . They also invested human capital—themselves—in a drive to modernize the region's social structure, revive its crippled economy, and democratize its politics."

Southern Democrats labeled the Republicans' southern white allies *scalawags*, a term for scrub horses or cattle. Drawn from the ranks of former Whigs in the urban South and the black belt and of Unionists in the upland South and the German counties of Texas, scalawags joined the Republicans, at least temporarily. They had mixed motives. Some scalawags were simply political opportunists. Some carried over hostility toward the Democrats from antebellum years. Others loathed the planters and the old planter regimes, and some of them had fought against the Confederacy. Scalawags often embraced the Republican party as the party of "progress, of education, of development"; "good roads . . . free bridges"; "free schools and the advantages of education for your children." The scalawags found that the Republican party—the party that promised a modern South—provided them with the means to pursue concerns that they had had before the Civil War.

Even as southern Democrats decried carpetbaggers, scalawags, and Black Reconstruction, they whitewashed the Ku Klux Klan, the Knights of the White Camellia, and other vigilante groups. Terrorists murdered, maimed, intimidated, whipped, and burned. The toll in lives reached the hundreds. Restoration of the Democrats' political dominance was their prime aim. First blacks, then white teachers and Republican leaders were their prime targets. The vigilantes left a wide trail that began in Tennessee in 1866, nearly brought civil war to North Carolina in 1869, and reached a climax in South Carolina in 1871, when President Ulysses S. Grant had to declare virtual martial law in nine South Carolina counties. Yet no southern jury ever convicted one vigilante during the Reconstruction era. And prominent southerners acquiesced in, supported, and even led the terrorists. Only in the early 1870s, when this means to achieve control became too risky—when vigilantism triggered federal intervention or threatened to devolve into widespread turmoil—did southern leaders cease secret organized Klan terror. Later in the 1870s, more open and somewhat less violent means were employed by organized local rifle clubs and "Red Shirts," groups that were important in the overthrow of the last of the Reconstruction governments. Thus the myth of Reconstruction as the Tragic Era salved wounds and consciences, excused the fraud and violence that attended the fall of Reconstruction, and justified the subordination of blacks. Eventually the myth of Reconstruction came to be accepted as fact.

THE EMERGENCE OF THE ONE-PARTY SOUTH

The high tide of northern support for Reconstruction passed in 1867, receding almost as quickly as it had risen. Increasingly the South was left to its own devices, and increasingly, southern opposition to Reconstruction asserted itself in various ways. The Republicans in Washington lacked public support to do more than they had done. They went as far as circumstances and their ideology would allow when they passed the Fourteenth Amendment, the Reconstruction Acts, and the Fifteenth Amendment. The last, which was proposed by Congress in 1869 and ratified in 1870, forbade any state to deny or abridge the right to vote "on account of race, color, or previous condition of servitude." (Ominously for the future, Congress failed to take a more positive position and specifically give blacks the vote. Thus legislatures could, and later did, disfranchise people on nonracial grounds: literacy, poll taxes, "understanding" the Constitution, and so forth.) Having passed this last amendment and no longer needing the unity they had developed to oppose the now departed President Johnson, the Republicans fell back into their conservative, moderate, and radical divisions.

"Hang, curs, hang! * * * * *   *Their* complexion is perfect gallows. Stand fast, good
fate, to *their* hanging! * * * * * If they be not born to be hanged, our case is miserable."

The above cut represents the fate in store for those great pests of Southern society—
the carpet-bagger and scallawag—if found in Dixie's Land after the break of day on
the 4th of March next.

KKK WARNING (Collection of the Alabama State Department of Archives and History)

That Republican Reconstruction had passed its climax became very clear during the Grant administration (1869–1877), when the federal government adopted
a generally passive attitude toward the South. Neither Congress nor the administration acted to stop the depredations of the Ku Klux Klan, for instance, until they
reached epidemic proportions in the 1870s. Finally Congress held extensive hearings and left a voluminous record of murderous outrages and willful disregard of
the law that showed that the Klansmen were not noble defenders of virtue and
honor, though many Klansmen were of the "better" sort. Congress then passed
the Ku Klux Klan Act of 1871, which allowed the federal government to act to prevent interference with voting rights. To enforce the law, the president could sus-
pend the writ of habeas corpus and order the army in, and federal courts had the
power to expel Klansmen from juries and inflict heavy penalties for perjury. The
Grant administration hesitated, then acted with vigor to enforce the law. Federal
agents infiltrated the Klan, the administration suspended habeas corpus in nine
South Carolina counties, and thousands of suspected Klansmen were arrested.
Some sixty eventually received federal sentences of up to five years, more exchanged guilty pleas for reduced charges, and charges were dropped against perhaps 2,000 who had been indicted for lesser offenses. The worst excesses of the
Klan stopped, and the organization became moribund. The strong actions of Congress and the Grant administration and the persistence of Republican strength in
the early 1870s helped make the 1872 election the freest and the most democratic
presidential election in the South until 1968.

The federal government had to intervene with force in Louisiana in 1873 after elections there produced two legislatures and two governors, products of regular Republicans on the one hand and of an alliance of Democrats and dissident Republicans on the other. President Grant finally had to send troops to enforce a federal court order that supported the regular Republicans. Factional and partisan battles continued, however. So did violence, and it got worse. Black militiamen and local whites fought at Colfax, Louisiana, in April 1873. Two whites and seventy blacks died; about half the dead militiamen were slaughtered after they had surrendered. The White League, a vigilante group, killed six Republican public officials near Shreveport in August. The following month, White Leaguers routed police and state militiamen in New Orleans: the clash left thirty killed and a hundred wounded. Grant sent troops, again. Their presence calmed matters, but the Democrats continued their ascendancy. And the "bayonet rule" issue surfaced again. In Arkansas, Republican factional strife deteriorated into the Brooks-Baxter "war," while in South Carolina and Florida, Republicans were bitterly divided. By 1874 southern whites controlled the governments of Virginia, North Carolina, Georgia, Tennessee, Alabama, and Texas, and they presented growing challenges in South Carolina, Florida, Mississippi, Arkansas, and Louisiana.

That year the Republicans faced severe challenges nationally. Grant and the Republicans were increasingly unpopular. Scandals in the administration, Grant's poor political judgment, weariness after so many years of Republican control of the White House and Congress and the turmoil associated with Reconstruction, and most important, the long depression that began in 1873 took a heavy toll. The Democrats got control of the House of Representatives after gaining seventy-seven seats in the congressional election of 1874, one of the most sweeping victories in American electoral history. For the first time since 1860, the Democrats had a majority in one chamber of Congress, and they had solid grounds for their hope that they could take the Senate and the White House in 1876.

Even as Democrats were savoring their 1874 victories, Mississippi Democrats launched their Mississippi Plan for the 1875 Mississippi state elections. They routed Republicans with appeals to white unity and racial fears, with economic force to intimidate poor dependent black workers and sharecroppers, with rifle clubs and "riots" that they themselves provoked. Dozens died. Voters seemed to vanish. The Republicans got a *total* of 25 votes in 1875 in five counties that previously had had large black voting majorities. The Democrats swept the election and began a long era of white-supremacy politics and one-party rule in Mississippi.

Similar political developments occurred elsewhere in the South. White-supremacy politics and one-party rule became the norm, a norm that persisted until after World War II. The Republican party was driven to the margins of political life while the Democrats achieved overwhelming dominance by making white supremacy the cornerstone of their party. White-supremacy politics had internal and external dimensions. Internally, or within the South, the Democrats argued that whites must unite to exclude blacks from the political process and ensure their own dominance. Any split among whites—if whites divided between the Republican party and the Democratic party, for instance—would allow blacks to play whites against each other and thus escape their subordinate place. The preservation of white supremacy required the success of the Democratic party. At

NORTHERN DISILLUSION (American Antiquarian Society)

the same time, the Democrats trumpeted themselves as the party best suited to prevent interference from external or nonsouthern forces in southern race relations, interference that might disrupt what was becoming a rigid racial caste system.

During the early days of Reconstruction, southern Democrats had not adopted such a consistently white-supremacist position. When Republicans first took office in the former Confederate states, some Democrats acquiesced in the new Reconstruction policies, cooperated more or less openly with southern Republican leaders, and even accepted the proposal to give some blacks the vote and some civil rights. Concern for political survival and for recognition of their legitimacy by the North figured heavily in their political calculations. Most of these "New Departure" Democrats were in the urban South, in banking, manufacturing, railroading, and commercial enterprises. Some had once been Whigs or had been allied with the Whigs. Almost all the New Departure Democrats embraced the idea of the New South. Benjamin H. Hill, for instance, began his political career in Georgia as a Whig. A persistent Unionist through the 1850s, Hill left the crumbling ranks of the Whigs and then joined the secessionists. After the Civil War, during which he was a Confederate senator, he denounced Reconstruction and the enfranchisement of blacks. By 1869 he had reversed himself on black suffrage, joined the Democrats, and participated in their revival. He urged his fellow southerners to imitate the North and "go to work to build our own fortunes, get possession of our own affairs": "our material prosperity must now begin."

Practitioners of the politics of moderation, New Departure Democrats frequently worked with Republicans, especially in efforts to obtain state aid for railroads, and they sometimes made serious efforts to attract black voters to the Democratic party, though they assumed that black Democrats would have only a subordinate place in the party. Democrats in Virginia joined a bipartisan coalition to elect a moderate Republican governor in 1870. By electing northern-born Gilbert C. Walker, banker, manufacturer, and railroad man, Virginia managed to be the only former Confederate state not to have a Radical Republican government. A similar coalition in Tennessee elected De Witt Senter governor and opened the way to a constitutional convention that adopted universal manhood suffrage. This broad franchise speeded the return of the Tennessee Democrats to dominance in the state.

"Straight-out" or "straight" Democrats spurned cooperation with Republicans or efforts to appeal to blacks. Instead, following a policy of racial exclusion, or "the white line," they rallied southern whites, many of whom had been politically apathetic, with mass-oriented political tactics. They created grassroots organizations and mobilized voters with parades, barbecues, and paramilitary organizations or rifle clubs, which, unlike the KKK and the White League, operated openly and publicized their activities.

Angered by rising taxes and growing state debts and wrenched by the depression of the 1870s, the straight Democrats demanded lower taxes and severe budget cuts. To reach these goals they created highly effective nonpartisan pressure groups called taxpayer unions. These organizations usually evolved into more openly partisan political groups. The straight Democrats drew upon their Jacksonian roots in their efforts to reject most forms of state aid to private enterprise. Believing that public schooling had little value and, worse, benefited blacks more than whites, they sought to end or drastically reduce public spending for education.

Led by the straight Democrats, most southern states in the 1870s stopped or revoked land grants to railroads, state purchases or endorsements of railroad bonds, and tax exemptions for corporations. Thus they largely gave up any attempt to use their taxing and spending powers to expand and diversify the economy of the South. Several southern states passed measures to regulate railroad rates. Moreover, the Democrats cut expenditures and taxes by shrinking the size and role of government through very direct means. The Alabama constitution of

1875 limited the legislature to biennial sessions, limited its members' pay to $4 a day, and reduced its powers. The executive branch did not escape the attention of the frugal: the number of officials in that branch was reduced, and those that remained took a 25 percent pay cut.

The straight Democrats did not completely reverse the policy of state aid to private enterprise, however. Consisting as they did almost entirely of planters and farmers, they gave their blessings to publicly funded agricultural experiment stations, geological surveys, and even—in Virginia, the Carolinas, and Mississippi—agricultural and mechanical colleges. The straight Democrats also favored measures to ease farm debt and crop-lien laws designed to secure landowners' control of farm labor. The latter became crucially important in the economy of the South.

The triumph of the straight Democrats in the 1870s represented a climax in southern history. Their policies became the accepted policies of the Democratic party, and that party became the only one that had a realistic chance of winning the great majority of offices in the South. Southern whites had clearly reestablished their supremacy over blacks—though they continued to believe that maintaining their position required constant vigilance. Landowners had obtained much stronger legal means of controlling their labor. The crop-lien system, which applied to whites as well as blacks, was not the same as slavery, though it seemed to be, since it kept landless farmers in endless debt. Finally, the Democrats had secured self-perpetuity: they had created the one-party Democratic South. Grounded on white unity, the Democratic party stood ready (and sometimes armed) to protect the racial hierarchy of the South against internal enemies and external threats. About the same time, developments in the border states added to the power of the Democrats in the region and the nation. Relying heavily on appeals to white racism, Democrats enjoyed a resurgence of power in Missouri, West Virginia, Delaware, and Maryland.

The federal government did little after 1872 to oppose these developments. Probably it could have done little that would have had lasting effect. The Grant administration did consider intervening in the 1874 election in Mississippi, but did not do so. Ohio Republicans convinced President Grant that if he sent troops to Mississippi, the Republicans might lose the approaching state elections in Ohio to the Democrats, who would make political capital of the issue of "government by bayonet" in Mississippi. "The whole public are tired out with these annual autumnal outbreaks in the South," the president told the besieged Republican governor of Mississippi, "and the great majority are now ready to condemn any interference on the part of the government." Political considerations and realities outside the South had again shaped the political options available to those developing and implementing policies with respect to the region.

Congress tacitly acknowledged as much when it passed the Civil Rights Act of 1875, the last major Reconstruction law enacted by Congress. Senator Charles Sumner proposed a law to prohibit racial segregation in public schools, in selection of juries, on all forms of public transportation, and in public accommodations. Southern Republicans, especially the factions in which blacks were prominent, gave the bill strong support. But many members of Congress had reservations as to the proposed measure's constitutionality, doubts about its enforceability, and fears of the voters' reaction to it. The death in 1874 of Sumner, one of the keepers of the Republican conscience, may have provided the necessary impetus to secure the act's passage, after removal of the provision applying to public schools. Congress may have believed that the law would have little impact and even less of a future when it was reviewed by the courts. In 1883 the Supreme Court ruled the act unconstitutional. The Court held that though governmental bodies could not legally discriminate by race, individuals could not be prevented by law from doing so.

THE COMPROMISE OF 1877

A year after the Civil Rights Act became law, the 1876 presidential election took place. It ended without a clear victor in the electoral college. The deadlock centered on South Carolina, Louisiana, Florida, and Oregon, where the presidential election results were hotly disputed. Congress took up the dispute in early 1877, exercising its constitutional duty to resolve the undecided election. But the Constitution contained no provision as to how Congress should resolve an inconclusive presidential election. The impasse evolved into a lengthy acrimonious dispute, which was resolved only hours before the Grant administration ended.

Congress created an electoral commission to investigate the disputed state results and to recommend a resolution to Congress. The commission soon found itself in a hopeless thicket when it tried to sort out the election mess in South Carolina, Louisiana, and Florida. So bad was the situation that the governor of Louisiana reportedly offered that state's electoral votes for $200,000. The commission heard testimony that revealed that fraud, violence, and intimidation were common. It was obvious that the Democrats had cast the most ballots in each of the states. Equally obviously, they had also prevented large numbers of blacks from voting. In South Carolina, for instance, the campaign organization put together by Wade Hampton, Confederate hero and future governor, included rifle clubs and Red Shirts. One of his supporters later recalled that some whites voted ten times each at three polling places, that whites paid blacks for their votes, that dead people voted, and that election officials cleverly arranged the tally sheets. Her brother, a bank official and manufacturer, "was an expert at all such manipulations, and I am sure God has forgiven him for all such chicanery with the purpose we all had in view." She did not, however, recall any violence during the election. Others did, and even celebrated it. South Carolina erected a monument to commemorate the Hamburg riot. Two hundred local whites battled a black militia unit at Hamburg, South Carolina, in July 1876; then they killed five militiamen they had captured. After Hamburg and at the request of the Republican governor, Daniel H. Chamberlain, Grant increased the number of troops stationed in South Carolina. Their presence reduced the instances of violence during the election, but only somewhat. Intimidation, violence, and outright fraud played lesser roles in the results in Florida in 1876 than they had done earlier or would do later. In 1876 other factors had greater impact on the election in Florida. White voters slightly outnumbered black voters, the Republicans suffered from bitter factional fights, and the Democrats' campaign was much better organized.

Historians have attempted to determine whether Samuel Tilden, the Democrat, or Rutherford B. Hayes, the Republican, won in the three southern states whose elections were disputed. The generally accepted conclusion, based on careful examination of historical records and elaborate calculations, is that if the elections held in South Carolina, Louisiana, and Florida had been fair, Hayes would have gotten majorities in the first two but Tilden would have taken Florida, and thus the election. The electoral commission did not, however, attempt such a thorough process of sifting and winnowing. The commission had a Republican bias and was operating under severe time constraints. The commission decided by 8 (Republican) to 7 (Democratic) votes to accept the election results as reported by the Republican officials in South Carolina, Louisiana, and Florida. The commission also declared the Republicans the winners in Oregon. The action of the commission made Hayes the victor: he had 185 electoral votes, Tilden 184.

The Democrats countered by threatening to prolong the impasse, perhaps by a filibuster, and maybe get Tilden elected. But the Democrats had serious handicaps. The Republicans had the presidency (at least until March 4), the Senate, the armed forces, and the enormous advantage of being the party of national patriotism, the party that had defended the Union. The commission's action could not realistically be set aside, because Congress had stipulated that the commission's rulings could be vetoed only by both houses of Congress. The Republican Senate was hardly going to reject the commission's decision. Filibustering to delay action beyond March 4, the date for a new administration to begin, required more unity than the Democrats probably had, in light of their own sectional divisions and mounting pressure from the public and from important business interests to settle the election. Democrats, especially in the North, could not risk being again labeled the party of disunion. Northern Democrats showed far less tenacity on Tilden's behalf than did their southern counterparts. These circumstances cast considerable doubt on the assertion that Hayes struck a clear bargain with southern Democrats in order to ensure his election. If Hayes and the southern Democrats had had a firm, explicit bargain, they should not have been the most persistent opponents to the electoral commission's report.

Hayes's representatives did engage in negotiations with the southern Democrats, which laid the groundwork for the Compromise of 1877. They concluded a series of "understandings," which were not entirely clear at the time and still are not. Hayes indicated that he would remove federal troops from the South and that he would not attempt to prop up feeble Republican governments in South Carolina and Louisiana, where both Democrats and Republicans claimed that they had captured the governorships and the legislatures in 1876. In this instance, Hayes was not making big concessions. The Democrats had so much power in both states that the great majority of whites paid taxes to the Democratic governments, not to the Republican governments that still claimed to exist officially. In Louisiana, the Democrats controlled the state courts and the New Orleans police. Hayes could have done little to alter the situation in either state, even from the White House. The Democratic-controlled House of Representatives simply could have refused, as it said it would do, to appropriate funds for the armed forces that would have been required to keep the Republicans in office in South Carolina and

Louisiana. Moreover, it is highly doubtful that Hayes could have gotten enough public support to use the army in the South.

Hayes also agreed to appoint a southerner to the cabinet and to give some patronage to moderate southern Democrats. And he did so. Hayes also indicated that he favored the use of more federal funds for internal improvements in the South, such as levees for the Mississippi River and a rail link to connect the South directly with the Pacific Coast, something southerners had long wished for. If, as some historians believe, he committed himself to supporting government subsidies for Tom Scott's Texas and Pacific Railroad, he later changed his mind. Subsequently, as president, Hayes gave government encouragement, but not funds, to Collis P. Huntington's Southern Pacific Railroad to complete a southern transcontinental road. (Completion came in 1882.) Hayes's support for internal improvements struck strong responsive chords in the South, and the South did receive more federal money for internal improvements during the Hayes administration than it had received earlier.

In seeking these understandings, Hayes may have been as concerned about running the country after the election was settled as he was about getting elected. How could any president function effectively and how could there be domestic peace if he had to keep sending troops to one region of the country? Hayes believed that moderation and conciliation might be more productive than a more aggressive approach and would have broad support in the North. Hayes and his advisers also hoped that a conciliatory strategy might help the Republican party gain strength in the South. They thought that many white southerners, such as former Whigs, shared the Republicans' commitment to economic development and public education. Many did, but few were inclined to seek those goals from within the Republican party in the 1870s or for many years thereafter. Also the vast majority of southern whites believed that white supremacy must be the cornerstone of postbellum southern life. Southern white leaders may have led Hayes to think that blacks and Republicans would receive fair treatment in the South, but they were quite prepared to disappoint him on both points. As Hayes quickly discovered after he was in the White House, southern whites would go to great lengths to secure their supremacy and that of the Democratic party. A disillusioned Hayes also found that he could do little to stop them.

Though the Republicans got the main prize, the presidency, they did not do as well as they had thought they would in the House. Hayes Republicans thought they had assurances from southern Democrats that a few of them would break ranks with their party and help the Republicans organize the House. No such break occurred. The Democrats thus kept control of the House. They also triumphed in South Carolina and Louisiana, ending the last Republican governments in the South. Thus the Democracts now had control of the governments of all the states of the former Confederacy and the border South.

Reconstruction had ended.

Five times during the nineteenth century sectional divisions took the United States to the brink of a bloody conflict. Four times, as C. Vann Woodward, distinguished historian of the American South, has noted, compromise prevailed—in the Missouri Compromise of 1820, at the end of the nullification crisis in the 1830s, in the Compromise of 1850, and in the Compromise of 1877. Compromise failed once, and civil war resulted. "The Compromise of 1877," Woodward writes,

✗ marked the abandonment of principles and of force and a return to the traditional ways of expediency and concession. The compromise laid the political foundation for reunion. It established a new sectional truce that proved more enduring than any previous one and provided a settlement for an issue that had troubled American politics for more than a generation. It wrote an end to Reconstruction and recognized a new regime in the South. More profoundly than Constitutional amendments and wordy statutes it shaped the future of four million freedmen and their progeny for generations to come. . . . The settlement was not ideal from any point of view, nor was it very logical either. But that is the way of compromises.

The blacks at Port Royal certainly understood such matters. Tyra and Moses Mitchell, their son Sam, and other blacks discovered the limits of the freedom the Yankee had come to give them, a freedom they had worked hard to earn. Southern whites kept or regained ownership of most of the land and, sooner or later, political dominance. Blacks had to accept peonage—sometimes worse—and second-class citizenship. The federal government deserted the blacks when they evicted the squatters at Port Royal. Then the federal government deserted blacks elsewhere in the South and in other ways. If it was ever intended to do so, Reconstruction fell dismally short of bringing sweeping change to the South. That result can be traced largely to the constraints imposed on the federal government by elemental American institutions, beliefs, and traditions.

Redistribution of land from former slaveholders to former slaves fell afoul of the cardinal American principle of the sanctity of private property. Any comprehensive, long-term aid program for blacks or the South conflicted with the nineteenth-century belief that government's responsibilities for the economic welfare of its citizens were severely limited. Congress revered the Constitution and felt the limitations it set acutely. The war may have made the Union supreme, but it was still a union of states to which certain powers were reserved. Blacks were given the vote, a revolutionary step, and then left to work out their future in a hostile South—to, in the words of one contemporary, "root, hog, or die." And the South was left to elevate itself by its own bootstraps.

The United States also lacked the institutional means to carry out broad domestic changes.

Without the tradition, the means of communication, the legal framework, or the administrative apparatus—in effect, without anything beyond an army and the tenuous cooperation of some local citizens to implement a detailed public policy—reconstruction had guaranteed confusion, disappointment, and recrimination.

The Freedmen's Bureau, for instance, had a budget too niggardly ($5 million), a staff too small (900 people at its peak), and tenure too short (five years) to do much. Even the number of federal troops was reduced to 17,700 by 1868 and to 6,000 by 1876, and one-third to one-half of them served in Texas, where the army patrolled the Mexican border.

Racism, which abounded in the halls of Congress as it did among most white Americans, north and south, severely limited northern whites' willingness to exert themselves on behalf of the former slaves. After all, the North only reluctantly embraced emancipation, then tardily enlisted blacks in the armed forces, and finally, swayed by the valor of blacks in the field and by the excesses of southern whites after the war, gave blacks the vote. The concern and sympathy of northern whites reached their limits there. Other things mattered more: a deep, understandable yearning for peace, for reconciliation with the white South and reunification of the nation, and for steps to bolster the faltering national economy.

Reconstruction left a flawed record, a record that belies both its professed ideals and the myth of the Tragic Era. That record included the happenings at Washington, Atlanta, Montgomery, and other political centers and wherever blacks seized their chance—"You ain't gonna row no boat to Charleston, you go out that back door and keep a-going"—to build new lives in the New South.

17

Economic Reconstruction,

1865–1880

❖

T hey were driving stakes into the ground when Bryant Watkins found them on his plantation near Greensboro, Alabama. They said that "Yankees" told them half the land belonged to them. "Listen, niggers," replied the planter, according to one of his former slaves,

> "what's mine is mine, and what's yours is yours. You are just as free as I and the missus, but don't go foolin' around my land. I've tried to be a good master to you. I have never been unfair. Now if you wants to stay, you are welcome to work for me. I'll pay you one third the crops you raise. But if you wants to go, you sees the gate."

Thus economic reconstruction began on Bryant Watkins's plantation, as it did on thousands of plantations and farms and in cities and towns in the South as soon as the fighting ended. Economic reconstruction began before Republican Reconstruction, lasted longer, and had a far more lasting impact on the South. Southern whites and blacks had to replace the social and economic organization that slavery had provided. The critically important southern railway network had to be rehabilitated. So did commerce, industry, and cities and towns. Growth came later, occasionally faster than was anticipated. The contours that emerged during economic reconstruction were determined by a blend of past and present. The South's antebellum heritage, the circumstances of the South in 1865 and the several decades thereafter, the limits of human imagination in nineteenth-century America, and national and international forces and events set the patterns for economic reconstruction. Those contours lasted a long time and became basic elements of the postbellum South.

Economic reconstruction left King Cotton on his throne. The fortunes of cotton and of the South were virtually identical for a long time, though cotton did not grow everywhere in the South and not everyone was part of the vast network associated with it. But growing and marketing cotton were the principal activities and sources of income for southerners as late as 1930. Cotton lay at the nucleus of southern social, political, and economic life: the ownership and use of land, obtaining and controlling labor, the rise and fall of individual fortunes as measured by pocketbooks and places in society, and how far the South would distance itself from its antebellum roots and the destruction of war and defeat.

LANDLORDS, SHARECROPPERS, AND TENANTS

Bryant Watkins probably was not thinking so abstractly about the role of cotton in the South's economy that morning. He still had land despite the Civil War, but he no longer controlled his workforce as he had during slavery. His former slaves owned their labor but no land. The requirements of survival compelled them (and Watkins) to strike a bargain. Watkins's former slaves could use some of his plantation for a portion of the crop they produced. Or they could leave. Watkins and his former slaves made an "arrangement," in this case what came to be called sharecropping. Along with tenancy (land renting), it became a fixture of postbellum southern agriculture. Sharecroppers and tenants were the products of an antebellum culture shaped by wartime destruction and upheaval. Their situations were also defined by the policies of the federal and state governments and by the growing commitment of southern farmers to cash crops, cotton in particular.

Most of the land remained in white hands, often in large parcels. Many whites lost their landholdings, but apparently not nearly so many as family legends suggest. Recent studies indicate that most landowners survived the Civil War in better shape than was once believed. Blacks, of course, had owned little real estate before the war, and most remained landless afterward. Slavery had provided the means for obtaining and organizing black labor in exchange for food, clothing, shelter, other assorted necessities, and an occasional "luxury." Emancipation destroyed that means, and sharecropping and tenancy evolved as the principal ways to obtain farm labor.

The story about the Watkins plantation, as told years later by Simon Phillips, an elderly former slave, suggests a speedy transition from slavery to these new means. Whatever the experience of Watkins and his former slaves was, most southern landlords learned that much of the control they had previously enjoyed as slaveholders could be restored by necessity (hunger), the realities of the marketplace, the power of contracts enforced by laws and the courts, and occasional violence and intimidation.

Immediately after the war, most former slaveholders despaired of finding adequate labor. Sidney Andrews, a northern reporter, concluded after a trip to Georgia and the Carolinas in 1865 that three-fourths of the whites "assume that the negro will not labor except on compulsion." Only the heartiest of dreamers believed that slavery would be reestablished. Many more thought blacks could not survive as free people, that they would "perish by hunger and disease and melt away as snow before the rising sun," that "being in contact and competition with a superior race," they were "destined to die out" as the Indians apparently had. Others saw visions of boatloads of immigrants coming to the now slaveless Dixie. Almost all the southern states created commissions and appropriated funds to attract immigrants to the South. These efforts achieved little. In fact, the South had fewer foreign-born residents in 1880 than it did in 1860. Nor did the blacks vanish. If they had done so, the economy of the South would have collapsed completely. Blacks were absolutely essential to the South.

New ways of obtaining labor in the slaveless South actually began to develop before the Civil War ended. The transition began wherever the Union army captured southern farmlands and where there were blacks. That conjunction occurred before 1864 at Port Royal in South Carolina, along the Mississippi, and in southern Louisiana. The methods employed by the army sometimes violated the concept of free labor. In the occupied parts of Louisiana, Union soldiers began in 1863 to seize and transport unemployed former slaves to plantations where their labor was needed. The army arranged labor contracts that stipulated terms of employment and obligations between employer and employee. Louisiana planters were delighted and called for more troops. Eventually the Freedmen's Bureau took over this responsibility in Louisiana and then everywhere in the defeated South. The army and bureau also gave the former slaves and many whites emergency relief, and they made some effort to ensure that laborers got fair treatment. The extent of these efforts may be measured by the frequency and intensity of planters' complaints of interference with their labor. Planters wanted help in obtaining workers but not questions about how workers were treated.

The concept of annual contracts for the labor of former slaves soon caught on. By 1867, the role of the bureau as negotiator of labor contracts had shrunk; landowners and tenants preferred to make their own arrangements. Marked improvement in southern farm output by 1868 suggests that the southern farm labor market had overcome the disorganization of the immediate postwar period and that whites had learned that blacks would work in the absence of slavery.

Government policies usually strengthened the hands of the landholders and creditors and did little to help blacks become farm owners. Shortly after the Civil War, southern legislatures passed stringent vagrancy laws, some of which were part of the more comprehensive Black Codes. Republican Reconstruction policies did not include provision of land for former slaves; the "forty acres and a mule" so many blacks thought they had been promised did not materialize. Some blacks did manage to purchase land around Beaufort, South Carolina, and other blacks in that state bought land in small parcels and on favorable terms from the South Carolina Land Commission. But this state agency was the only one of its kind during Reconstruction. Elsewhere, a few blacks took advantage of the Southern Homestead Act of 1866. But the slow implementation of the act and the inability of most blacks to meet even the rather small costs of starting a homestead seriously limited the impact of the law. Poverty was and remained the greatest obstacle to blacks in their efforts to join the ranks of the landed, even on a modest scale. Most blacks became tenants or sharecroppers, like those on the Watkins plantation.

Cropping and tenancy evolved into a pattern that unfolded in the course of a year. Landlords and tenants made oral or written contracts or "arrangements" in January or February. Planting began in April, then came cultivation in the summer months, and harvest and "settling up" in the fall. The types of arrangements and the amounts paid depended on the bargaining power of the landlord and that of the prospective tenants or workers. Labor-short landlords offered better terms. Less advantaged tenants—those with few able-bodied workers in their families, with little or no equipment and few or no work animals—had to accept less favorable arrangements. Equal or one-half shares became most common in sharecropping. Farm employers also paid wages in cash.

Landlords disliked cash wages and renting because most had little cash for wages and because rental agreements lessened their control over the crops. Landless farmers, though, preferred to rent. Rental had a higher social status than other arrangements—renters were known to have at least some means, perhaps farm equipment, tools, even a mule. Tenants, moreover, worked without the unwelcome supervision that sharecroppers and laborers experienced, which must have brought unpleasant reminders of slavery for many. Finally, unlike sharecroppers and farm laborers, tenants owned and controlled their crops until they were sold.

Blacks and the Limits to Freedom

Although the poverty of the former slaves left them few options, they actively probed the limits of their new freedom. They successfully resisted landowners' attempts to work them in gangs, another reminder of slavery. Blacks, most of whom lacked the means to become renters, preferred sharecropping to working for wages. Their persistence on this point helped make sharecropping a basic institution in the agricultural South. Blacks turned to sharecropping because they believed it allowed them a place in the decision making on the farm and hence greater personal freedom. But southern courts in the 1870s ruled that croppers were simply laborers and had no control over the crops they grew.

Whether they rented, sharecropped, or worked as wage laborers, blacks—especially women and children—worked less than they had as slaves. According to careful estimates, blacks reduced the amount of work they had done as slaves by more than a third. Landlords complained bitterly. A cotton merchandising company surveyed a number of southern planters and concluded that one of the "chief needs" of the planters was "Laborers, laborers, reliable laborers." The planters raised "an almost universal cry for emigrants! emigrants!!" A Georgia planter reported that it was "harder, much harder to get laborers," that many had gone to work on railroad construction or had taken

> to little rude cabins and patches in poor lands, where they set up for themselves. . . . White labor was diminished by the war, and fifty per cent, more than fifty per cent, of black labor had disappeared from the *fields*. The negroes are not dead, nor gone, as elections show; but they very much quit the fields. . . . Give us cash capital and labor; *certainty* of labor, and its *control*.

Blacks also objected to living in what had been slave quarters. They often moved old slave houses out of the quarters area, creating a new geography of housing on plantations. In this and in other ways, such as their determination to create and operate their own religious institutions, blacks attempted to distance themselves from whites, to limit the intervention of whites in their lives. Thus blacks initiated some of the forms of postwar racial segregation in order to assert at least a portion of the freedom that emancipation afforded them.

Blacks also distanced themselves from whites and their former slave lives by leaving their masters. Initially blacks left to follow the Union army, for a while their preferred protector and provider. Or they went in search of dispersed families, to see places heard of but never before seen, and to seek nonfarm employment. Simon Phillips remembered being "treated good" as a slave, but he left the plantation in 1866 to work in Tuscaloosa (for 17 cents a day). Planters in the less settled areas of the South—Arkansas, Louisiana, Mississippi, and Texas—urgently needed labor, and they offered better terms than those available in the more settled areas. According to an 1866 report to Washington, "every railroad train during this winter has been loaded with negroes going to the west under the promise of increased wages."

Southern legislatures attempted to restrict this movement, to lessen if not destroy the freedom of the labor market. Immediately after the Civil War, for example, they enacted antienticement laws that made it a criminal offense to hire or entice away any laborer under contract. Though most of these laws were set aside during Reconstruction, they reappeared in other forms and remained part of the statutes of most southern states well into the twentieth century. It is uncertain whether such laws prevented laborers from seeking and finding the best pay available to them. The limited economic opportunities for former slaves anywhere in the United States long after Appomattox probably had far greater effect than the actions of state legislatures. In any event, by 1919 most blacks lived about where they had when the Civil War ended, in the black belt. This persistence was a physical expression of the limits to the freedom blacks had secured at emancipation. Too few escaped the seemingly endless cycle of poverty that ensnarled too many southern farmers after the Civil War in the "vast pawnshop" that postbellum southern agriculture became.

"FURNISH," CROP LIENS, AND COUNTRY MERCHANTS

Simon Phillips's narrative slighted some important details about the transaction on the Watkins plantation. The land rental undoubtedly included housing, but Phillips did not explain how the former slaves obtained "furnish," or provisions (food, clothing, and medicine), and supplies, equipment, and work animals to begin farming and to carry them through the year until they could harvest and sell their crops. Eventually southerners devised a means to meet those needs and to finance the production and marketing of their crops. Local merchants and the better-off landowners advanced "furnish" against future crops, secured by crop liens. The holder of a crop lien had a legal claim, second only to that of the landholder against his rented land, to the proceeds of the crop of the indebted farmer. In other words, tenants and croppers were legally bound to settle their debts for land rentals and then for "furnish" before they paid other debts or bought anything for themselves.

Renters got better terms than sharecroppers because they usually had some work animals and equipment of their own, even some money. Renters had a good deal of autonomy in making decisions about the farming they did: they controlled the crops that they produced, and they worked without the close supervision that

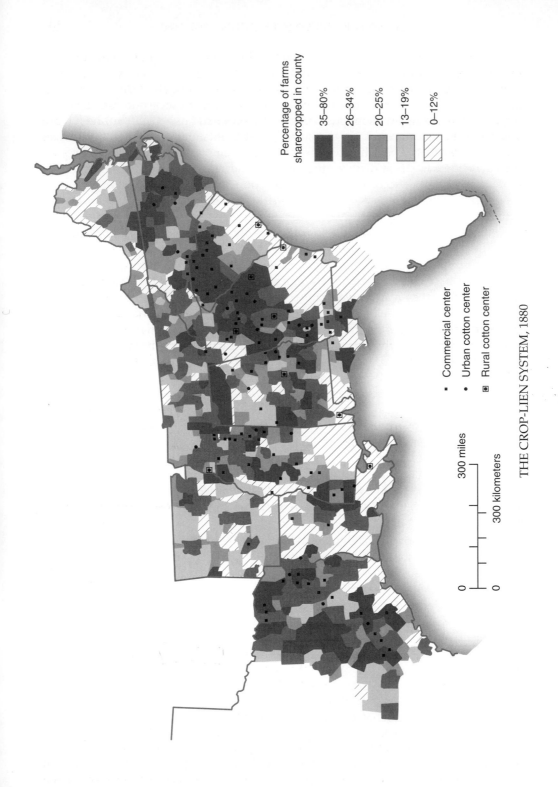

Percentage of farms
sharecropped in county

35–80%

26–34%

20–25%

13–19%

0–12%

■ Commercial center

● Urban cotton center

◉ Rural cotton center

0 ____ 300 miles

0 ____ 300 kilometers

THE CROP-LIEN SYSTEM, 1880

sharecroppers frequently had to accept. Renting was more common in some regions of the South than sharecropping was. Renting was also more common among whites than among blacks, because blacks had fewer assets. As the map on page 000 indicates, sharecropping tended to become concentrated in the black belt regions of the South where slavery had been concentrated and in the Mississippi and the Arkansas deltas. Extensive farming of the delta regions developed after the Civil War. Late in the nineteenth century, landowners there relied heavily on the labor of black sharecroppers, who had migrated to the area. These sharecroppers usually worked in closely supervised groups.

Tenants, sharecroppers, and landlords, "furnish" and crop liens, country stores and country merchants evolved into staples of the rural South and in time involved small landholders as well as tenants, whites as well as blacks. When railroads penetrated previously isolated areas and brought greater access to distant markets for sales and purchases, farmers with small landholdings increased their cash-crop farming and became a part of the expanding cotton South. Country merchants proliferated, another product of the growth of the southern railway network and cash-crop farming and crop liens. The roles of the landlords and merchants intermingled. Landlords sometimes opened their own stores, and certainly many supplied their own sharecroppers directly. Many merchants acquired substantial landholdings as a result of land foreclosures when debts went unpaid too long.

Merchants became community and political leaders who challenged the power of the planters. They became pillars of churches, stalwarts of local school boards, community boosters, investors in railroads and industry, and bosses of rural politics. Linked by railroads to such trade centers as Louisville, Nashville, Atlanta, Memphis, Dallas, and New Orleans, country stores spread the values associated with modern urbanization and industrialization into the rural South.

Country merchants and their stores brought consumerism and the physical artifacts of modern life: ready-made clothes and shoes, kerosene (for everything from illumination to cleaning privies), prepared foods, Pear's and Fels Naphtha soaps, Hoyt's cologne, tobacco (including the most modern form of the noxious weed, cigarettes), *McGuffey's Readers* and other school supplies, corsets and petticoats when they became fashionable, contraceptives, ready-made caskets (for as little as $5), furniture, tableware, eyeglasses, toothbrushes, sporting goods, musical instruments, playing cards, patent medicines. The Chattanooga Medicine Company used mass marketing techniques, such as almanacs and calendars, to sell Wine of Cardui, a mixture of alcohol and herbs that supposedly relieved "female troubles," and Black Draught, a blend of plant extracts and herbs for constipation, which may have been common given the diet of the day. Country stores offered other forms of relief—liquor and, before federal laws restricted their trade, laudanum, opium, calomel, morphine, and paregoric. Some stores had lunch counters that offered sardines, sausages, crackers, oysters, salmon, and other favorites. Most stores had some fancy merchandise. Apparently all sold pistols, a requirement for the suitably attired male. At Christmas they offered oranges and coconut for coconut cake, once-a-year delicacies. Country stores provided postal services, news and gossip, courting places for persons so inclined, sites for magistrates' courts, and focal points for local politics.

Many merchants also had cotton gins and grinding mills for grains, services that were vital to southern farmers. They functioned as middlemen in the produce and egg trade, provided informal legal and small banking services, and tendered advice. But, above all, they controlled local credit. Sometimes known simply as "the Man," they dispensed monthly "draws" or "rations" (food, clothing, fertilizer, and so forth) and "toted up" what by the end of the year was a farmer's "run." Successful merchants and landlords supervised their debtors closely. What and when to plant? When to cultivate or harvest, repair fences, dig ditches, cut wood? How to manage animals? What and how much to buy at the store? There were lots of questions about purchases of tobacco, liquor, or other "luxuries," about whether children went to school or to the fields. These questions reminded black and white renters and croppers repeatedly what their station was, that they were not far from slavery. In sickness and death, the Man was there, arranging for the physician or undertaker. The Man was, of course, not invincible. Even Will Varner lost first place in the county to Flem Snopes, his son-in-law.

William Faulkner described Varner in *The Hamlet* as the

> owner of the Old Frenchman place . . . chief man of the country. He was the largest landholder and beat supervisor in one county and Justice of the Peace in the next and election commissioner in both, and hence the fountainhead if not of law at least of advice and suggestion to a countryside which would have repudiated the term constituency if they had ever heard it. He was a farmer, a usurer, a veterinarian; Judge Benbow of Jefferson once said of him that a milder-mannered man never bled a mule or stuffed a ballot box. He owned most of the good land in the country and held mortgages on most of the rest. He owned the store and the cotton gin and the combined grist mill and blacksmith shop in the village proper and it was considered, to put it mildly, bad luck for a man of the neighborhood to do his trading or gin his cotton or grind his meal or shoe his stock anywhere else.

Will Varner was the looming presence of Frenchman's Bend, Faulkner's fictional hamlet. Country merchants were not creatures of the imagination. They occupied the crossroads of the rural South, literally and figuratively. They were envied for their real and imagined wealth, feared for their power to reduce landowner to tenant, tenant to sharecropper, and suspected of and despised for seemingly hard-fisted ways. Critics denounced them for what were perceived to be extortionate interest rates and prices. Merchants, commentators charged, forced farmers to give first place to cash crops and were partly responsible for the calamitous consequences. Southern farmers failed to diversify, bought food that they could have produced themselves, and grew more cotton than they could sell at a reasonable profit. "The merchants . . . ," lamented one critic, "have replaced the former masters and have made peons of them and their former slaves."

Such strong feelings are understandable in light of the erratic fortunes of southern farmers from 1865 to World War II and the enormous human toll that resulted. Southern agriculture did have good years, and some farmers did do well, but most did not. Over the years, tenancy spread and the ranks of landowners shrank. In 1880, somewhat more than one-third of southern farmers were tenants or sharecroppers. Twenty years later one-half were, and more than half of those were white.

Merchants often stood out as the prosperous amid the deprived, as parasites living off a dead or chronically ill body, as Will Varners waiting to foreclose and take the farm and home place away. Merchants held potentially profitable though precarious positions. They supplied farmers whose few assets made them poor credit risks and whose crops had not yet been planted, might never be harvested, and if harvested might not sell for as much as the debt owed. Merchants had legal protection through the crop-lien laws, the first of which was passed in 1866 in Georgia, and more generally through the power they held in relation to borrowers in negotiating contracts. A merchant sometimes "furnished" a sharecropper, for instance, only after the landowner agreed to waive his prior claim to what the sharecropper produced. But collecting debts could be very difficult and, given the resources of many debtors, often not worth the costs involved. Moreover, croppers and renters tended to move on after a year or two, frequently leaving with debts unpaid. Merchants who pressed defaulters could alienate other customers. Still, foreclosed mortgage notices littered courthouse squares.

STORE LEDGER (South Caroliniana Library)

Merchants reduced their risks by careful supervision of borrowers and their accounts and by charging high interest rates and high prices. They used a two-price system, one price for cash purchases and a considerably higher price for credit purchases. Merchants charged as much as 50 percent interest and even more. In part, they were passing on the costs they incurred by making loans that were not repaid and passing on the costs for their own borrowing, which could be quite high. They bought on credit from manufacturers and wholesalers and borrowed from what local banks there were. These banks borrowed in turn from banks in larger cities.

Country merchants had risks and costs that justified substantial interest rates, but probably not so high as those they charged. Clearly the business was profitable and very attractive. Though no one knows just how country merchants fared, studies suggest that they had satisfactory rates of success and that their numbers grew significantly. Country stores offered solid opportunities. "Clerking" in them became an important avenue for advancement for ambitious young men in the postbellum South. Merchants could go far, apparently without tampering with farmers' accounts. Still, the suspicion lingered that merchants and clerks cheated their customers. The inability of too many farmers to read or to do simple arithmetic complicated matters and fed their bitterness.

MONEY AND INTEREST

The interest rates charged by country merchants reflected the acute shortage of capital in the South after 1865. Neither was a new economic factor. The antebellum South had lacked adequate banking facilities and depended heavily on the factorage system and other outside sources for capital. In 1860 the future Confederate states—exclusive of Texas and Arkansas, for which we have no reports—had 104 banks, including branch banks, with capital of $92 million. That same year, New York, Massachusetts, and Pennsylvania had 567 banks, including branch banks, with $301.5 million in capital.

The Civil War, federal legislation and policy, and general economic trends made matters worse. When the shooting stopped in 1865, southern banking was in shambles, Confederate bonds and money were worthless, and U.S. greenbacks were almost impossible to find. The elaborate structure for the financing and marketing of southern farm products lay in ruins. The value of southern assets that could be used to secure loans had declined so drastically that loans were hard to obtain and very costly. The value of southern farms and farm implements, for instance, dropped almost 50 percent, that of livestock 25 percent. The average value of southern farms remained about one-half the national average as late as 1900, and the southern average did not improve much in the next twenty-five years. When emancipation took effect, it liberated what had been one of the principal forms of collateral that slaveholders had.

Federal banking laws affected southern banking adversely. In an effort to increase federal revenues during the Civil War and to make the banking system more stable and less subject to panics, Congress passed the Banking Act of 1863. Banks in towns with fewer than 3,000 people were required to have $50,000 capital to get a national charter, $100,000 in towns with 6,000 to 50,000 people, and $200,000 in larger cities—requirements that were difficult to meet in the postbellum South. Congress also put a 10 percent tax on banknotes issued by state-chartered banks in an effort to force them to join the national bank system. National banks could not make mortgage loans; therefore they could not meet an especially important need of farmers. Other parts of the banking laws and a sectional bias in the granting of national bank charters also inhibited the growth of national banks in the South. In 1900, when the United States had 1,737 national banks with $417.6 million in capital—252 of them, with capital of $75.9 million, were in New York— the eleven former Confederate states had a total of 125 banks with $26 million. Not too surprisingly, southern congressmen and senators figured prominently in the successful efforts to change federal banking laws and create the Federal Reserve System in 1913. Other, now conventional means for raising capital for investment and lending—such as insurance companies and mutual savings banks—were extremely limited in the postbellum South. In 1900 there were only six class A life insurance companies (companies that had at least $10 million in assets) in the entire South. And only after 1890 did the United States have the truly national financial institutions necessary to move capital easily from one region to another, say from the Northeast to the South or the West. The shortage of banks and the lack of development of other financial institutions increased the costs of borrowing in the South.

Moreover, the money supply (the sum total of all forms of money) grew at an unusually slow pace from 1865 to 1879, and in fact contracted severely during the depression of the 1870s. That contraction of the money supply is still noted for its severity; only one other such occurrence compares with it, the Great Depression of the 1930s. The reduction of the money supply pushed interest rates up. (Those who recall more recent American experiences with increases in the money supply and interest rates must bear in mind that the circumstances that prevailed in the late nineteenth century differed radically from those of more recent times.) Though not the most severe economic crisis in American history, the depression of the 1870s was the longest and was quite serious.

The government generally practiced deflationary policies in the late nineteenth century—passing the Resumption Act of 1875; fending off efforts of greenbackers and silverites, who favored a looser monetary policy; passing the Gold Standard Act of 1898; and of course, spending little, balancing the federal budget, and even paying off the debt the federal government had incurred during the Civil War. This policy may have been virtuous, and certainly it was what most "right-thinking people" believed must be done, but it favored lenders and hurt borrowers.

Banking, money, and monetary policy were part of a larger whole, the longest deflationary trend in American history. Prices fell by one-half between 1865 and 1898. Unfortunately for cotton farmers, the price of cotton fell faster than other prices while credit costs rose, and the Republican policy of protectionism increased the costs of the manufactured goods that southern farmers purchased. Save among the Louisiana sugar growers, a small but politically powerful group, protectionism found little favor with southern farmers. They added high tariffs to their list of grievances, which by the late 1880s had become as long as their patience was short.

By then southern farmers were finding common cause with western wheat farmers, who had similar experiences, and they were laying the base for a major political upheaval. But that is a story for a later chapter.

The interest rates southern farmers paid were obviously not simply the product of willful, greedy merchants or other local creditors. Merchants hardly had a
free hand with respect to interest rates. "Merchants . . . were only functional parts
of the whole ineffective scheme of production and credit." Nor did they have the
power over time to force farmers to produce certain crops, such as cotton, or to
buy their food from country stores instead of producing it. But they were widely
criticized for supposedly doing these things.

Though motivated by genuine and understandable alarm about the state of
farming and the plight of farmers in the South, this criticism rested on dubious assumptions and ignored certain factors. The interests of merchants and their
farmer customers were not always in conflict. Merchants had reason to want their
borrowers and customers to succeed. For one thing, collecting defaulted debts
could be difficult, sometimes not worth the costs of collection. Moreover, farmers
who prospered bought more than farmers who did not. Land acquisitions by for-
feiture for debts could reach the point of diminishing returns, where the value of
land had fallen so far as to make further acquisitions pointless or even costly.
Falling land values could also have an adverse effect on land the merchant already owned. Finally, in small communities, merchants and farmers might be
friends or relatives, even across color lines.

It is doubtful that merchants had the monopolistic control that critics and
some scholars have inferred. They could not prevent others from entering the
mercantile business or effectively stem the constant movement of tenants and
sharecroppers from one farm to another, from one community to the next. Itinerant peddlers, drummers, fertilizer salesmen, and buyers of cotton and tobacco
also traded directly with farmers. Last, the patterns of commodity prices and the
response of farmers to those prices did not conform to the notion of a merchant
monopoly. Commodity prices were determined by international markets, far
beyond the will or the whim of a Will Varner. Southern farmers also watched
prices carefully and shifted their crop selections accordingly.

Farmers were not mindlessly attached to cotton. In comparison with other
production choices open to farmers at any given time, cotton had an advantage
and kept it well into the twentieth century. Demand for raw cotton was strong
throughout most of the late nineteenth century, though demand increased more
slowly than it had before 1860. Start-up costs were low: to begin cotton farming, a
family needed little equipment and few work animals. Southerners knew how to
grow cotton. Land was readily available through purchase, rent, or working on
shares, and the climate of the South and much of its soil were suitable for cotton.

Farmers had few realistic alternatives to cotton as a cash crop in the postbellum South. Diversification may have sounded good, especially when cotton
prices fell, but it was not possible for many farmers. Most of them lacked the required capital. The dearth of cities and the slowness of railroad development
made for constricted markets and inadequate transportation for would-be truck
farmers. Climate, soil types, pests such as the cattle tick, and the undeveloped
state of agricultural science precluded the evolution of a more complex farm mix

of staple crops, forage, and quality livestock in the cotton South. Farmers there may have wanted to imitate the diversified agriculture of farmers in the North and in the upper South, but even if they had had the money to invest in such pursuits, it would not have been possible to do so until at least 1920. Farmers in the South did practice mixed agriculture when and where they could, especially in the Shenandoah Valley in Virginia.

Almost all farmers grew food for their own tables. Corn was grown virtually everywhere in the South, primarily for food for the family and for livestock. Pigs, usually of poor quality, provided the staple meat. Farmers (outside of Texas) raised little beef cattle and even less poultry. Homegrown potatoes, sweet potatoes, beans, peas, and other vegetables lent some diversity to diets, as did a variety of fruits and berries. Many berries grew wild. Farms in the South produced small amounts of hay, oats, wheat, and nuts. Peanut growing was centered in Alabama, Georgia, and Virginia.

Two important antebellum cash crops—sugar and tobacco—revived after the Civil War. Sugarcane remained in the limited areas of the South where it could be grown and recovered only slowly from the extensive damage it suffered during the Civil War. Cane farming evolved into three basic patterns. Plantations employing large numbers of wage laborers and having large milling facilities produced most of the sugar. Many planters and large farmers also used black and white sharecroppers. Finally, some farmers owned or rented small farms where they grew sugarcane along with other crops.

Kentucky remained the leading tobacco state in the South, followed by Virginia and Tennessee. That situation changed after 1890, when demand for bright-leaf flue-cured tobacco soared to meet the demand of the cigarette manufacturers. Paddy-grown rice, which had long been concentrated along the coasts of South Carolina and Georgia, enjoyed only a modest restoration after 1865. It never again attained its previous prosperity and would eventually lose out to field-grown rice in Texas, Louisiana, and Arkansas. Cattle ranching flourished in Texas. It rivaled cotton in importance to the state. The legendary cattle kingdom with its longhorns (durable in the field but tough to eat), mavericks, open ranges, long drive, and gun-toting cowboys free to roam where they pleased had a brief reign after 1865. By 1880, it was giving way to barbed-wire fences and systematic beef production.

Breeding for better stock and transporting livestock by rail to better grasslands, then to feedlots at meat packers, produced the better meat that consumers came to demand. After the railroad network penetrated farther south and west, meat-packing companies opened new plants. By 1890, Dallas and Fort Worth had become the leading meatpacking centers in Texas and the nearby region. Less than a decade later, the Swift and Armour companies, principals in the "beef trust," were well established there. The beef trust processed and sold a large portion of the meat Americans then consumed. The power of the beef trust touched virtually every cattle raiser. It financed much of the industry while establishing parameters on price and shaping consumer tastes. Beef was becoming the meat of choice in America.

The cattle industry survived wild speculative schemes that attracted the gullible from as far away as New York and Great Britain, fence wars and range wars, overgrazing, erosion, droughts, and several economic depressions. Even the cattle tick, long a scourge in the Southwest, was in retreat, the victim of chemical dips.

At the same time, in large areas of the South—Appalachia, the Ozarks, and the piney woods of Georgia, Alabama, and Mississippi—thousands farmed and lived in a world with little or no cash and few cash crops. They met their needs by scrambling to raise some corn and a few vegetables on parcels of begrudging land, letting their livestock run the woods, and supplying large portions of their diets by hunting, fishing, and picking berries. These small farmers and others like them elsewhere in the South got a good deal of public notice in the late nineteenth century because of their opposition to fencing laws. Designed to fence in livestock in order to protect crops, these laws met stiff opposition from many small farmers who believed these laws would harm them and their way of life. Disputes over these laws revealed class conflicts between the traditional small farmers and the newer, larger commercial farmers and their allies in the banks and mercantile establishments in the towns. Well into the twentieth century, large areas of the South had no effective fence laws.

For too many southern farmers, black and white, the result of hard effort was poverty compounded by isolation. Trips to town, church, revival meetings, and political and agricultural gatherings helped. So did fairs and holiday celebrations. Still, the feeling of isolation remained. Years after he went to Congress and rose to become speaker of the House of Representatives, Sam Rayburn recalled the loneliness of life on his father's Texas farm. As a boy, Rayburn used to go down and sit by the road that passed the farm and wait to see if someone, anyone, would come by.

Women had it even worse. They bore the greatest burden of responsibilities inside and outside the house. They gave birth to and raised large families at a time when maternal and infant deaths were common. Unless a woman was married to one of the relatively few well-fixed planters or farmers, she did a lot of fieldwork. She also gardened, and she cooked, washed, sewed, ironed, and cleaned long hours without electricity, running water, or indoor plumbing. She had fewer social and recreational opportunities than her husband had. Many women, usually widows, ran farms on their own. Most, widowed or not, aged quickly.

Understandably, many southerners tried to find a living and a life away from the farm. Unfortunately, nonfarm options in the South were not plentiful and seldom attractive. Some urban areas expanded rapidly after 1865, and many people hastened to take advantage of the opportunities of Richmond, Charlotte, Atlanta, Nashville, Little Rock, Houston, and New Orleans. But southern cities were too few, too small, and too poor to act as truly effective safety valves. As late as 1910, only about one in five southerners lived in an urban area, compared with a national rate of nearly one in two. The same, of course, was true of southern industry. Southern manufacturers employed less than 10 percent of the working people of the South in 1910. Nor did northern cities and industries provide effective avenues of escape for most southerners. Rapidly expanding northern industries and cities received ample supplies of cheap, unskilled labor from the tide of European immigration between the end of the Civil War and World War I. Lack of skills also circumscribed the choices open to most southern blacks and whites, and the former faced racial discrimination in various forms everywhere in America. Finally, southerners, black and white, demonstrated a strong attachment to the land and to the South. The modest but significant gains blacks made in landholding from 1865 to 1900 may have encouraged them to remain in Dixie.

PUPPET MONARCH

The burden of southern welfare thus fell on cotton. It could not bear the burden. Cotton culture spread anyway, throughout the lower South and into the lower reaches of the upper South, following the expanding railroad network and its companion system of dirt roads into the Mississippi delta after the restoration and expansion of the levee system in the late 1880s, and increasingly beyond the Mississippi. "Cotton was king, but he was a puppet monarch."

The boom that the cotton South experienced in the 1850s did not recur. The demand for cotton rose faster in the antebellum era and particularly in the 1850s than it ever would do again. Also during the 1850s some of the richest cotton-growing soil in the South had come into production. This cotton bonanza was not repeated. As figures for per capita income indicate, King Cotton was not able to bring prosperity to his subjects. Still, the postbellum economy was not stagnate.

For twenty years after the South recovered from the Civil War, when personal incomes declined sharply, the economy kept pace with the rest of the nation, which was enjoying strong growth. After 1910, incomes rose significantly in

PERSONAL INCOME PER CAPITA AS A PERCENTAGE OF THE U.S. AVERAGE, 1840–1950, BY REGION

Region	1840	1860	1880	1900	1920	1930	1940	1950
United States	100%	100%	100%	100%	100%	100%	100%	100%
Northeast	135	139	141	137	132	138	124	115
New England	132	143	141	134	124	129	121	109
Middle Atlantic	136	137	141	139	134	140	124	116
North-central	68	68	98	103	100	101	103	106
East	67	69	102	106	108	111	112	112
West	75	66	90	97	87	82	84	94
South	76	72	51	51	62	55	65	73
South Atlantic	70	65	45	45	59	56	69	74
East south-central	73	68	51	49	52	48	55	62
West south-central	144	115	60	61	72	61	70	80
West	—	—	190	163	122	115	125	114
Mountain	—	—	168	139	100	83	92	96
Pacific	—	—	204	163	135	130	138	121

SOURCE: Richard A. Easterlin, "Regional Income Trends, 1840–1950," in Seymour E. Harris, ed., *American Economic History* (New York: McGraw-Hill, 1961), p. 28. Reprinted by permission of McGraw-Hill, Inc.

COTTON PRODUCTION IN THE SOUTH, 1850–1987 (THOUSANDS OF BALES)

State	1850[a]	1860[a]	1870[b]	1880[b]	1890[b]	1900[c]	1910
Ala.	564	990	429	670	915	1,094	1,130
Ark.	65	367	248	608	617	706	777
Fla.	45	65	39	55	58	54	65
Ga.	499	702	474	814	1,192	1,233	1,992
Ky.	1		1	1	1	1	3
La.	179	778	351	509	659	700	269
Miss.	484	1,203	565	963	1,155	1,287	1,127
Mo.		41	1	20	16	26	54
N.C.	74	146	145	390	336	433	665
Okla.							923
S.C.	301	353	225	523	747	844	1,280
Tenn.	195	296	182	331	191	235	265
Tex.	58	431	351	805	1,471	2,584	2,455
Va. & W.Va.	4	13		20	5	10	10
Totals for South	2,469	5,385	3,011	5,709	7,363	9,207	11,015

[a]av. 400 lbs.
[b]av. 450 lbs.
[c]av. 500 lbs.
[d]av. 480 lbs.

SOURCE: James C. Bonner, "Cotton," *The Encyclopedia of Southern History*, David C. Roller and Robert W. Twyman, eds. (Baton Rouge, La., 1979), p. 301; U. S. Bureau of the Census, *Agricultural Statistics, 1981* (Washington, D.C., 1982), p. 63; U.S. Bureau of the Census, *1987 Census of Agriculture* (Washington, D.C., 1987), Vol. I, Table 25.

Texas, Louisiana, and Oklahoma, probably because of oil, and in the Southeast, probably because of industrial growth. Then military spending during World War I gave a strong stimulus to the Southeast. Unlike most Americans, however, southerners saw their incomes drop during the 1920s, before the Great Depression engulfed the country. The failures of King Cotton were widely acknowledged even before 1938, when President Franklin Roosevelt declared that the South was "the nation's No. 1 economic problem."

The cotton South had structural flaws that made it peculiarly vulnerable, and that vulnerability helped explain much of what lay behind those figures on per capita income. Year after year, farmers in the cotton South acted on virtually the only option they had. They gambled each year that this year they would "pay out"—have enough money from the sale of their crop to pay their debts—and perhaps have some money left over. They went to their creditors again and again. Too many planted cotton in soil that was too thin for repeated cotton plantings, that was too subject to erosion, and that required large amounts of fertilizer. In the Southeast especially, erosion reached crisis levels and undermined the land, the single most important farm asset. Mechanization also came more slowly to cotton farming than to wheat and corn farming. Productivity in cotton grew less than

COTTON PRODUCTION IN THE SOUTH, 1850–1987 (THOUSANDS OF BALES) *(Cont.)*

1920	1930	1940	1950	1959	1969	1980[d]	1987
718	1,313	773	824	683	498	275	382
869	1,398	1,351	1,584	1,484	1,150	444	817
20	34	11	18	14	10	7.5	33
1,682	1,344	905	610	521	311	86	286
3	9	16	13	11	5		
307	799	718	607	479	516	460	922
958	1,875	1,533	1,497	1,561	1,383	1,143	1,655
64	225	433	472	482	332	177	306
858	764	458	472	319	115	52	94
1,336	854	802	242	458	193	205	306
1,477	836	850	544	411	236	77	102
307	504	436	617	620	428	200	567
2,972	3,793	2,724	5,550	4,156	3,041	3,320	4,072
25	52	13	19	12	3	.2	15
11,596	13,800	11,023	13,069	11,211	8,221	6,447	9,557

productivity in any other major American farm commodity. Without greater increases in productivity, too many cotton farmers played a losing game against cotton prices. Too many cotton farmers experienced the "annual defeat of the crop market . . . , the weekly defeat of the town market and mounting debt, and the small gnawing daily defeats of crumbling barn and fence, encroaching sagebrush and erosion, and one's children growing up in illiteracy."

The cotton South was a land of landlords, tenants, sharecroppers, and country merchants for nearly fourscore years. They seemed fixed, permanent. They stood as specters that could be little softened by nostalgia or ties of kin and friendship and remembered kindnesses. Then, sometime around 1940, no one can say just when, these fixtures of the South began almost magically to vanish. An age had ended and now seems so distant as to be foreign.

SOUTHERN RAILWAYS

Even as the postbellum agricultural system was evolving, southerners were rebuilding and expanding their railways. The Confederacy and the border states of Kentucky and Maryland had more than 9,000 miles of track in 1860. That figure compared well with those of the Northeast (10,000) and the Middle West (11,000), but comparisons with respect to quality of roadbed and facilities (such as stations) and quantity of rolling stock (engines and cars) were not so favorable. Dispersed population and limited industrialization made railways less profitable in the South than were railways in more populous, more industrialized areas.

The Civil War sharpened these contrasts. Four years of combat destroyed or crippled more than half the South's railroads at a cost of at least $28 million. A South Carolinian observed that "one week we had passably good roads, . . . the next week they were all gone." "Sherman hairpins"—rails that Union troops had ripped up, fired, and bent double—indicated what the massive conflict had done to most of the southern rail system. The only major railway in the South to escape serious damage was the Louisville and Nashville. It had thrived. The L&N moved quickly after 1865 to build one of the largest rail empires in the nation, anchoring itself in the booming commerce of its urban namesakes and the coal and iron of northern Alabama.

Coincidentally, the badly damaged railways of the South recovered with remarkable speed to approximate the antebellum status quo by 1870. Southern railroads obviously had considerable resilience, vigorous leadership, and more. For its military purposes, the Union army had rebuilt some of the southern railways—one of the few benefits the South received from the war. The L&N was a major beneficiary, having been captured early in the war, then operated and maintained by Union forces. The L&N also enjoyed the continuing leadership of James Guthrie. Southern rail companies still owned their rights of way and their roadbeds, though of course, many of the roadbeds needed repairs. Some railways had the foresight to bank in London during the war or to have stockpiled cotton, which they sold for substantial profits. Even Sherman hairpins were not complete losses: they could be straightened and reused or, if beyond reclamation, sold for scrap.

Most important, southern railroads enjoyed a very strong demand for their services. Government officials and business leaders alike saw the close connection between the railroads and the South's recovery and growth, and they supported efforts to restore and expand the southern rail system. Private creditors and investors postponed settlement of debts. The U.S. Military Railway Department quickly restored the railroads it had seized to their former owners and subsequently declined to collect more than half the money owed it for the postwar sales of government-owned rolling stock to southern railways.

Southern state governments, like their antebellum predecessors, lent their support to the restoration of the railways as early as 1866 and before any Radical Reconstruction government was in power. Before the war, southern states had joined the nationwide trend of subsidizing railroads. They had employed a variety of the usual means for doing so: land grants, state guarantees for bonds issued to raise money for railroads, purchases of railroad stock, and even state ownership of railways. Virginia had substantial holdings in stock, including three-fourths of the important Richmond and Danville. North Carolina had a similar amount of North Carolina Railroad stock. Prewar Tennessee made direct loans of state bonds to railroads and incurred a debt of $14 million to do so. Georgia owned the Western and Atlantic, which connected Atlanta and Chattanooga. Many smaller communities, too, had subsidized railroads. Continuing the subsidies made sense, given the need to rehabilitate and expand the southern rail system in 1865. Major trade routes that lacked railroads included the intercoastal regions of the South, northern connections for the piedmont through Appalachia, and north-south routes in Mississippi. The more that postwar state and local governments subsidized railroads to meet these needs, the more they increased the amount of track they got—and increased the opportunities for political and financial fraud. Paper railroads and theft from the public treasury became synonymous with Reconstruction. The machinations of General Milton S. Littlefield of New York and of George W. Swepson, Tarheel native, nearly doubled the state debt of North Carolina, to over $28 million—an outrageous cost to incur in order to obtain the 136 miles of track laid from 1868 through 1870. South Carolina had a comparable experience. Its debt rose to $25 million, much of it the result of fraudulent railroad schemes involving three Republican governors, at least two black political leaders, and perhaps James L. Orr, provisional governor under President Andrew Johnson and reluctant secessionist Democrat. Under Republican Governor Rufus B. Bullock, new railroad schemes proliferated in Georgia. Political cronies became managers of companies whose workings mystified them. A special relationship with the governor and a satchel of money with which to ply the legislature proved useful in efforts to secure state aid for proposed railroads.

Railroad swindles added significantly to Alabama's horrendous $30 million state debt—swindles perpetrated by Democrats and Republicans alike. Railroads were decisive political forces in Alabama during Reconstruction and remained so afterward. There, Reconstruction was closely related to and shaped by the struggle between the Louisville and Nashville and the Alabama and Chattanooga for access to the coal and iron regions of Alabama. The Reconstruction government in Mississippi mandated that state aid for such internal improvements as railways was unconstitutional. Thus Mississippi escaped the railroad swindles that were all too common elsewhere; it also had few miles of track laid from 1865 to 1880.

Usually the states that aided railroads the most got the most track laid and were the most swindled. Alabama, Georgia, Arkansas, and Texas led the South in state aid and in new railroad construction from 1865 to 1875. Texas used its vast public landholdings for large grants to the Texas and Pacific and the Southern Pacific, which laid major lines across Texas and finally achieved the antebellum dream of a southern rail connection to the Pacific. The president of the important Little Rock and Fort Smith Railroad recognized that "without . . . state aid the road could not have been accomplished by our company."

By 1880, railroad mileage in the South (including, in this instance, Maryland, Kentucky, West Virginia, and the District of Columbia, because their figures were included in census reports) reached 19,430 miles, more than double the 1860 total. Nationally, railroad mileage almost tripled between 1860 and 1880, to 87,800. (These figures include the South. They are somewhat misleading because figures for the nonsouthern states include the recently built transcontinental lines.) These disparities reflected the South's need to spend much of its money and energy on postwar rehabilitation of its railroads and the general disruption of the region that southern railroads had to serve. Construction and maintenance costs were lower in the South than elsewhere, but not enough lower to offset these disadvantages. The doubling of the rail system in the South increased access from farm to market, provided urgently needed transportation for industry, and laid or reinforced the foundations for cities, towns, and villages. Railroads also speeded the nationalization of the southern market. Southern consumers could find Standard Oil kerosene, Iowa corn, and New England woolens on the shelves of even small merchants by 1880.

Labor troubles also rode the rails. The Great Strike of 1877 was one of the first and, certainly, one of the most dramatic indications that American labor relations had entered an era of stormy confrontation between the power of industrial capitalism and the anger and desperation of industrial workers whose only future was wage work. In July 1877 the bloodiest strike in American history began after the Baltimore and Ohio Railroad announced wage cuts for its already underpaid and overworked trainmen. The strike swept across the country, the first nationwide strike in American history. At least forty persons were killed and perhaps $10 million in property was destroyed. The strike largely bypassed the South. Little Rock and New Orleans had minor disturbances. Workers withdrew a strike threat against the Georgia Central after the railroad made some concessions. Black male workers in Galveston, Texas, marched, organized, and successfully allied themselves with white male workers to get a minimum wage of $2 a day. Black laundrywomen in Galveston then demanded and got $1.50 a day. Louisville fared worst. During a one-day riot a black and white mob stoned streetlights, stores, houses, the Louisville and Nashville's depot, and the home of its president. Working people in Louisville subsequently elected Workingmen's party candidates to five of the seven seats on the city council. The *Little Rock Arkansas Gazette* congratulated the South "that nearly all of the mob violence . . . occurred north of the Ohio River." The *Raleigh Observer* chimed in: "Southern people are not as . . . Northern people, . . . person and property, life and liberty are alike safe where Southern men hold sway." This observation was a curious one in light of the only recently ended Reconstruction, and it was not the first time or the last that the South would claim too much for its supposedly harmonious employer-employee relations. As events in the 1880s and 1890s showed, the South experienced widespread industrial conflict.

More important were the actions of the federal government. President Rutherford B. Hayes took the unprecedented step of sending federal troops to quell domestic disturbances during peacetime. The federal courts acted with dispatch against strikers and real or alleged rioters. The lesson was clear: the federal government would more readily defend the interests of capital than those of labor, *or* those of blacks and Republicans in the South.

*B*ANKRUPTCY, CONSOLIDATION, AND REGULATION

The depression of the 1870s brought more than labor problems to southern railroads. It interrupted expansion and caused about one-half of the southern railroads either to default on their debt payments or to go bankrupt. The failure rate of southern companies was twice the national rate. Railways in the South were more financially vulnerable than those in other regions.

The defaults and bankruptcies opened many southern railways to takeovers and consolidations. The new owners and managers were more likely to be from outside the South, and much more significant, they differed in type and orientation from their predecessors. They speculated in railroads more than they ran them. They made more money by constructing railways, manipulating stocks, and investing in land, timber, and mineral schemes than by actually operating railroads. Railways in the postwar South, as elsewhere in the United States, began to be dominated by large companies that had large assets and potentially great economic and political power. Because railroads needed so much capital to operate, control of them generally shifted to financial centers like New York. The president of the Louisville and Nashville, for instance, was called a "railway emperor," but by 1880 the company's finances were increasingly controlled from New York.

Faced with hard times and railroad wars, southern railway leaders developed the first successful railroad pool (a form of business merger) in the country. Under the leadership of Albert Fink, an L&N executive, the Southern Railway and Steamboat Association was formed in 1875 to represent the interests of railroads east of the Mississippi River and south of the Ohio and Potomac. It lasted until 1887, when the federal Interstate Commerce Act made railroad pools illegal. The association's twenty-seven member corporations divided markets, settled disputes among members, and tried to make rates stable and uniform. The organization may have been a factor in the steady decline of freight rates in the South.

But the association reinforced the fears of monopoly that railroads aroused. As economic conditions worsened in the 1870s, these fears became important politically. Several southern states created railroad commissions, most of which initially had only advisory powers. Presumably encouraged by the Supreme Court's decision in *Munn* v. *Illinois* (1877) and prompted by continuing protests, the legislature of Georgia gave its commission power to set rates, and the Georgia commission became a model for others. The presence of the Grange—a farm movement that engaged in education and lobbying—and the rumblings of such independent political movements as the Greenbackers may have unsettled state governments in the South. Most southern states in 1880 also placed severe constitutional limits on the ways states could subsidize private enterprise. Overindulgence in state-aided railway projects and mounting state debts made sobriety attractive, indeed necessary.

CITIES, TOWNS, AND INDUSTRY

Railroads and their leaders had played and would continue to play a critical and ever larger role in the South. Atlanta, the creature of railroads, formed the political and economic nucleus of postbellum Georgia and eventually became the leading metropolis of the Southeast. As early as November 1865, an observer reported, out of

> ruin and devastation a new city is springing up with marvelous rapidity. The narrow and irregular and numerous streets are alive from morning till night . . . with a never-ending throng of pushing and crowding and scrambling and eager and excited and enterprising men, all bent on building and trading and swift fortune-making. . . . The four railroads centering here groan with the freight and passenger traffic. . . . Where all this eagerness and excitement will end no one seems to care to inquire. The one sole idea in every man's mind is to make money.

Atlanta was just one of the interior cities of the South to prosper at the hand of the railroads after 1865. So did Richmond, Nashville, Louisville, and Memphis, and such smaller ones as Augusta, Macon, Little Rock, Chattanooga, Montgomery, Greensboro, Charlotte, and Columbia. Far to the west, Dallas, Houston, Fort Worth, and Shreveport were becoming more than small towns. New Orleans was still the largest city in the South, but it grew little. Charleston, Savannah, Mobile, and Alexandria, all seaport cities, declined relatively. This pattern of growth reflected old and continuing migratory habits, a general movement to urban areas and westward.

But the depression, then disease, slowed urbanization in the 1870s. Hard times slowed urban growth to a crawl and created fiscal crises in many cities and towns. To make matters worse, yellow fever struck Montgomery and New Orleans in 1873. New Orleans lost nearly 4,000 of its 191,000 residents. Cholera afflicted Nashville the same year. Then, five years later, a yellow fever epidemic killed 5,800 of perhaps 45,000 people in Memphis; about half the victims were Irish. The scourge drove Memphis Germans to St. Louis, where they stayed. The killing fever left Memphis temporarily demoralized and permanently changed its ethnic makeup.

Southern cities remained primarily centers for railways, for financial, governmental, and legal services, for merchandising, and for the marketing of farm products. Industrial Birmingham and nearby Bessemer and Sheffield grew little in the 1870s. Anniston was only starting up. The Alabama iron industry had not yet lived up to the expectations of its boosters. The cotton textile industry, which had entered the first stage of its postbellum growth, built its own villages in rural areas and on the edges of small cities and towns, such as Danville in Virginia, Greensboro, Winston-Salem, and Charlotte in North Carolina, Spartanburg and Greenville in South Carolina, and Columbus and Macon in Georgia. Urbanization in the South increased less than a tenth of a percent in the 1870s, well below the approximately 2 percent increase of the 1860s. In 1880, the percentage of urbanized southerners (8.7) was far short of the national rate of 28.2 percent.

Industry in general developed slowly in the decade and a half after Appomattox. Although the former Confederate states and Kentucky had nearly 30 percent of the nation's people, they produced only about 6 percent of the nation's industrial output in 1879. That output did not, however, include domestic manufacturers. Southerners still did a lot of processing of cotton, corn (into meal and, illicitly, liquor), meats, and leathers at home. Virginians still made linen from locally grown flax. Southern manufacturing usually involved first-stage processing of raw materials and agricultural products—ginning, turpentining, lumbering, making of pig iron, spinning and weaving of cotton, pressing of cottonseed oil, making of cigars and plug tobacco, distilling, sugar refining, and flour milling. These industries added little value to their raw materials, required many unskilled workers and few highly skilled ones, paid low wages, and did not generate extensive or related industries in the South.

Cotton textiles are a case in point. Textiles were the only southern industry to grow significantly in the 1870s, and that growth was modest. Investment by southern cotton manufacturers was about 10 percent of that by companies in New England and about half that by those in the Middle Atlantic states. Still, southern

MORGAN SQUARE, SPARTANBURG, SOUTH CAROLINA, 1884 (Courtesy of the
Spartanburg Chamber of Commerce)

boosters were cheered by reports of the opening of the Eagle and Phoenix factory
at Columbus, Georgia, in 1868, only three years after Union troops burned the
Eagle Manufacturing Company to the ground. Columbus, looking northward to
Massachusetts's most famous mill town, claimed to be the "Lowell of the South";
Augusta and other towns disputed Columbus's claim to the title. Local capital,
much of it earned during the Civil War and Reconstruction, built these southern
Lowells. But they failed to generate related industries, such as machine tool manufacturing. For years southern textile companies bought their machinery from
New England manufacturers. Southern textile companies usually produced
coarse "gray" goods, which were shipped elsewhere for dyeing and other final
processing steps. Only after 1900 did southern textiles begin to compete effectively in the market for fine cottons. In the textile industry's early stages, north
and south, women and children made up over half of the modestly skilled, low-
wage workforce. Southern companies excluded blacks from all but the most menial jobs. Since most of the textile companies were located on the edges of cities
and towns or in rural areas, southern textile workers lived in a racially segregated
and hierarchically ordered world that was unusual even for its day.

This isolation did not, however, assure companies of the control over workers
that nineteenth-century manufacturers thought was essential. Across the Savannah River from Augusta and twelve miles away, in the Horse Creek valley in
South Carolina, workers struck in late 1875 after the Graniteville Manufacturing

Company announced a wage cut. The strike was the first of its kind, and it occurred even as South Carolina whites were uniting in a mass movement to expel the Republicans from state office in 1876. The strike lasted a month, and before it was over the superintendent of the company had been shot and the factory sabotaged. The company did not rescind the wage cut, but neither did it discipline the strike leaders. The strike clearly indicated that southern white elites were not immune to challenge by other whites and that divisions among whites were serious and could not be erased by simplistic appeals to white solidarity against blacks and other presumed threats. If the economy faltered, divisions among whites could become sharp and even threatening to those who had assumed leadership in the South after Reconstruction.

When the long depression of the 1870s ended in 1879, southerners celebrated its passing. The editor of the *New Orleans Times-Democrat* rejoiced: "The stagnation of despair has given . . . place to . . . hope, . . . courage, . . . resolve." Then, in his understandable excitement, he claimed too much: "We are a new people. Our land has had a new birth."

Southern railroads had recovered from the Civil War, had expanded, and were ready to expand even faster. The South's cities and industries remained small but portended better times. But the reign of King Cotton was as powerful in 1880 as it had been in 1865, and it was spreading. So were sharecropping, tenancy, crop liens, and country merchants. The evolution of a South in which cotton was no longer monarch would be slow and painful. Change and changelessness seemed to coexist in the South of the 1870s.

18

The Redeemers and the New South, 1865–1890

❖

The funeral train left Miami, moved up the east coast of Florida, angled north-west through the pines and sand of southeastern Georgia, and finally climbed through rolling hills into Atlanta. Mourners and the curious gathered all along the way. At one place where the train stopped, an old man took his jacket off, laid it on the coffin, and then took it back. "Now thousands couldn't buy . . . the jacket from me." President Theodore Roosevelt telegraphed his respects. Legislatures, city councils, and dozens of organizations memorialized the deceased. Flags hung at half-staff. Businesses closed. Governors, senators, congressmen, and former soldiers of all ranks, the United Confederate Veterans, the Sons of the Confederate Veterans, and the United Daughters of the Confederacy were in attendance. Railroads charged reduced rates to people who wanted to go to the final services and burial.

On January 15, 1904, they laid to rest the mortal remains of Lieutenant General John Brown Gordon, the "very embodiment of the Lost Cause." Gordon had been with General Robert E. Lee at the surrender at Appomattox and was one of the last surviving Confederate generals and the first commander of the United Confederate Veterans. The *Atlanta Constitution* eulogized the general: "Gordon, who found his Calvary at Appomattox, his Gethsemane in the days of reconstruction, has gone beyond to reap the harvest he has so richly earned—on to his immortal Lee, his beloved Jackson and so many of his old command."

In its magnitude and its display of emotion and sentiment, the commemoration of Gordon's death compares with the outpourings of grief at the deaths of Abraham Lincoln, Franklin D. Roosevelt, John F. Kennedy, and Martin Luther King, Jr. The vast display of feeling in 1904 suggested that the South remained fixated on the War for Southern Independence, the Lost Cause. Had the South changed so little since 1865? People who observed Gordon's funeral from a distance must have wondered.

JOHN BROWN GORDON (Hargrett Rare Book and Manuscript Library, University of Georgia Libraries)

The more reflective, more informed smiled. They knew better. They probably savored the irony of having Gordon's last rites in Atlanta, the very embodiment of the New South. Nor, as many were aware, had Gordon himself spent the years since Appomattox merely telling war stories. He had been very busy and sometimes successful in politics and business. Gordon, in fact, had taken an active part as a Redeemer in shaping the New South. The Redeemers were the southern Democrats who presided over the end of Reconstruction, the restoration of native white supremacy and black subordination, the evolution of the one-party South, and the emergence of the New South. The Redeemers did not, however, necessarily encourage or even endorse the New South. Indeed, they were divided among themselves about it, though they did little to oppose it.

Opponents of the Redeemers often called them Bourbon Democrats. The label was borrowed from Napoleonic France. The French Bourbons supposedly represented those who wanted to restore prerevolutionary France, reactionaries who their opponents said could forget nothing old and learn nothing new. Given the Redeemers' habit of referring to one another in public by military titles—general, brigadier, colonel—their frequent appearances in their old gray uniforms, and their endless talk of "the War," the label seemed appropriate.

Opponents of the Redeemers used the Bourbon label effectively, especially in the 1880s and the 1890s, but the name distorted reality. The Redeemers were not an easily definable group with a fixed set of positions on public issues. Historians still debate about the origins of the Redeemers. Were they antebellum planters who lived into the postbellum South with most of their property and their agrarian ideas intact and a determination to retain as much of the Old South as possible? Or were they urban businessmen and landed farmers who wanted a modernized South, one that differed greatly from the antebellum South? Or were they something between these two extremes, people who wanted a more industrialized, urbanized South but one that retained the hierarchical social and economic structures of the Old South?

Rhetoric contributed to the confusion. Postbellum boosters who urged the South to make a strong commitment to industrialization, urbanization, and diversified agriculture drew sharp contrasts between the South they envisioned—the New South, as they called it—and the South before the Civil War, the Old South. The South before 1865 and the one that came after clearly differed in at least two ways. First, any attempt to create a separate nation or federation of southern states was dead as a viable political option. The South after 1865 had to resolve its problems within the framework of the Union. Reconciliation of North and South thus became a primary concern. Second, slavery was also dead. As bad as conditions were for blacks after the war and for many years thereafter, blacks were not chattel anymore. That was an enormous difference, for blacks especially but also for whites.

New South boosters in their enthusiasm wrongly pictured the Old South as too little concerned with economic growth and personal profit, disinclined to work hard, and indifferent and even hostile to industrialization and urbanization. Large-scale planters, the dominant personages of the Old South, supposedly had a leisurely lifestyle, a satisfied indifference to their personal incomes, and a distaste for cities and factories. Such portrayals of the Old South and the planters made for effective public imagery, but they were woefully inaccurate. Most of the antebellum planters worked hard, energetically pursued profits and assets, and made investment decisions in accordance with anticipated returns and risks. They invested most of their money in slaves and land, which were good investments at the time. They also invested in other things, including manufacturing plants. Jefferson Davis, for one, hardly fit into the picture of the Old South drawn by New South boosters. Nor did such influential cities as New Orleans, Memphis, Nashville, Louisville, Savannah, Charleston, and Richmond, to name only the most obvious urban centers of the antebellum South. Nor did the railroads and the hardly insignificant, though small, iron, textile, forest products, and tobacco industries of the South before 1865, industries that were generally hailed by southern leaders.

The Redeemers in South Carolina, for instance, defied easy labeling or description. Like their leader, Wade Hampton, most came from planter backgrounds. They preferred to retain as much of the past as possible, yet they welcomed industry to their desperately poor state. They were eager to expand the textile industry, which had enjoyed modest but significant growth in their state before the Civil War. In this instance, the Redeemers imitated the antebellum South Carolina leaders who had supported the development of railroads and of cotton manufacturing in their state and who had felt comfortable in Charleston. Unlike some Redeemers in other states, South Carolina Redeemers did not become agents for outside investors at the expense of their state and its citizens. Once in office, they avoided some of the more reprehensible policies that Redeemer Democrats in other states followed. The South Carolina Redeemers did not, for instance, desert the public schools. Moreover, they supported black schools and white schools about equally. They also avoided the worst abuses of the convict lease system, which became a scandal in Georgia and Tennessee.

Though the Redeemers everywhere in the South, including South Carolina, revered the Old South that existed as much in their minds as in reality, they did not seek to restore it: they did not oppose change, want to keep sectional hostilities alive, or believe that they could revive slavery. Many Redeemers in fact championed the New South; others spurned it or approached it warily. Very probably all defended the Lost Cause, but it was subject to various interpretations. Some saw a conflict between the Lost Cause and the New South, but not General Gordon. Indeed, he embraced the New South creed.

The commemoration of Gordon's death could also mislead observers in another way. It suggested that southern whites had a cohesive bond forged in combat, a bond that superseded all divisions among whites. In reality, southern whites were divided during the Civil War and during Reconstruction. They continued to disagree after they returned to power. Gordon's political career, in fact, ended amid the massive political turmoil that swept the South as well as the rest of the nation in the 1890s. In the South, that turmoil reflected deep divisions over the direction economic and political change had taken. Disappointment festered to become deep bitterness. The New South promised more than it produced, and the New South creed seemed hollow indeed in the midst of the depression of the 1890s, America's worst economic crisis before 1929.

*T*HE NEW SOUTH CREED

The assumptions and ideas that underlay the New South—the modernizing of the postbellum South—evolved by the 1880s, if not earlier, into a creed, the New South creed. The creed became so much a part of the South after 1865 that it seemed inborn. The creed was a simple set of beliefs with a powerful shaping force. It can be expressed in the form of a catechism, a statement of religious beliefs that is intended to be memorized and recited:

QUESTION: Why did the North defeat the South?

ANSWER: The South could not compete with the North because the South relied too much on cotton and slave-based agriculture. The South failed to develop industries and cities and towns. Southern leaders were too interested in politics and too uninterested in work and making money.

QUESTION: What should the South do?

ANSWER: The South must change its attitudes toward work and what is worthwhile. Work is good and is necessary for success. Financial success is more important than success in politics.

QUESTION: Then what must the South do?

ANSWER: The South must build factories and cities. Its farmers must grow a wider range of crops and use the best methods and tools for farming.

QUESTION: What kind of relationship should the South have with the rest of the nation?

ANSWER: Harmonious. Disharmony wastes energy and, more important, discourages people who might invest in the New South.

QUESTION: What about relations between blacks and whites?

ANSWER: Those must also be harmonious.

QUESTION: Does that mean racial equality?

ANSWER: No! Southern whites must dominate the South. Whites are naturally superior and more civilized, and they know what is best for the blacks. Blacks may have certain civil and political rights, but they cannot have power in proportion to their numbers. Social equality is unacceptable. Miscegenation and interracial marriage are abhorrent.

The New South creed had its apostles. Many of them had newspapers for pulpits. In fact, several of the most prominent were distinguished journalists who improved southern newspapers significantly even as they preached salvation through economic uplift. Francis Warrington Dawson, who immigrated from England in 1861 to join the Confederate army, founded the *Charleston News and Courier*. Henry Watterson made the *Louisville Courier-Journal* his personal vehicle and it became second only to the *Atlanta Constitution* as a voice for the New South. Richard H. Edmunds's *Manufacturer's Record* was a business journal that reported economic and financial news and beat the drum for the New South. Daniel Augustus Tompkins published the *Charlotte Observer* and the *Greenville (S.C.) News*. A trained engineer and an ambitious entrepreneur, Tompkins also owned several cotton textile mills in the South. Walter Hines Page spread the New South gospel in the pages of the *Atlantic Monthly*, then in his own magazine, *World's Work*.

Among New South evangels the first rank belonged to Henry Grady, editor of the *Atlanta Constitution*. A Georgian whose father was a successful businessman in antebellum Athens, Grady got an undergraduate degree from the University of Georgia and then did graduate work at the University of Virginia. He began his career in journalism in the 1870s. He started work for the *Constitution* in 1880, and when he was just thirty years of age he became part owner and editor of the paper. Grady used the *Constitution* to pronounce and propagate the New South creed, which Atlanta seemed to embody.

Recognition of Grady's stature and abilities brought him an invitation to speak at the annual banquet of the New England Club of New York in 1886. Grady needed his skill and his considerable boldness. The New England Club had never before issued such an invitation to a southerner. Before Grady spoke, other speakers rhapsodized about New England and the Puritan heritage and told again the Union version of the Civil War. General William Tecumseh Sherman, an old favorite in Atlanta and several other places in the South, spoke just before Grady did. The general told a war story. He expressed regret that wars necessitated bloodshed and destruction, blamed the war on the "bad ambitions" of antebellum politicians, and asked that bygones be bygones. Then Sherman returned to his seat at the head table to listen to the young Georgian.

Grady opened by declaring a truce and disarming his listeners. "There was a South of slavery and secession—that South, thank God, is dead. There is a South of union and freedom—that South, thank God, is living, breathing, growing every hour." He lauded Abraham Lincoln as the symbol of national unity, "the first typical American" who had "within himself all the strength and gentleness of this republic . . . the sum of Puritan and Cavalier." Even Sherman got some praise, lightened with humor. "[He] is considered an able man in our parts, though some think he is . . . careless . . . about fire."

Having pacified the gathering, Grady went on to other essentials. Southerners had not given in to "sullenness and despair" after their defeat. They had gone to work and rebuilt the South. Atlantans, for instance, had taken the "ashes" Sherman "left . . . in 1864 . . . and raised a brave and beautiful city. . . . We have fallen in love with work" and "have challenged your spinners in Massachusetts and your iron-makers in Pennsylvania." The South, he claimed, now knew that slavery was wrong. It accepted and even welcomed emancipation. The South had committed itself to public education for black and white alike. "The relations of the Southern people are close and cordial." He anticipated that blacks would continue to improve their lot, but they must do so under the tutelage of "those among whom [their] lot is cast." He did not specify when or whether that tutelage would end. Grady departed momentarily from his roseate tones and put a hard edge on his words when he warned against intervention in southern race relations from outside the region.

The South, Grady concluded, had kept its "faith with" the North by accepting defeat and pledging allegiance to the Union. The war had freed blacks and the whole South.

> The old South rested everything on slavery and agriculture, unconscious that these could neither give nor maintain healthy growth. The new South presents a perfect democracy, the oligarchs leading in the popular movement . . . a hundred farms for every plantation, fifty homes for every palace—and a diversified industry that meets the complex needs of this complex age. The new South . . . is stirred with the breath of a new life . . . she understands that her emancipation came because through the inscrutable wisdom of God her honest purpose was crossed, and her brave armies beaten.

But the "South had nothing for which to apologize." He recited the Lost Cause article of faith: the South "believes that the late struggle between the States was war and not rebellion; revolution and not conspiracy, and that her convictions were as honest as yours." Grady recalled his father, who was killed during the Civil War.

> But . . . the cause in which he suffered and for which he gave his life was adjudged by higher and fuller wisdom than his or mine, and I am glad that the omniscient God held the balance of battle in His Almighty hand and that human slavery was swept forever from American soil—the American Union was saved from the wreck of war. . . .
> Now what answer has New England to this message? . . . Will she make Lincoln's vision of a restored and happy people . . . a cheat and delusion?

The audience jumped to its feet and cheered. A band played "Dixie." The speech made Grady famous; it was printed over and over again. Grady's favorable reception resulted from more than momentary things—toasts, fine foods, displays of fellowship, and his artful presentation. Grady succeeded in large part because his speech, like the New South creed he was expounding, fitted the national mood and trends and seemed to suit the needs of the South. Americans wanted reconciliation. They wanted to put the Civil War and Reconstruction behind them. Grady spoke to these desires. He also carefully avoided divisive sectional issues, except for race relations. Even there he was on rather safe ground. Few whites in America in 1886 questioned white supremacy. Most believed race relations in the South were strictly a southern affair, beyond either the duty or the capacity of the federal government to alter or influence.

Grady virtually celebrated the victory of the Union, and he glowed with pleasure at the South's embrace of the supposedly northern virtues of hard work and money getting. Yet southern sensibilities were not neglected as he recited basic tenets of the Lost Cause. Thus Grady defended the Confederate version of the causes of the Civil War and declared that Confederate efforts and sacrifices had been noble. He reassured the South about its past, and his bubbling optimism gave assurance about the present and the future of the region.

Most important, the New South creed and Grady's remarks fit the predominant American mentality of the day—a blend of religion (or religiosity) and materialism. People nearly everywhere in the United States saw and most experienced the economic boom of the late nineteenth century. The surge of growth was so strong in the 1880s that even the sober-minded got giddy. The economist David Ames Wells wrote in 1889 that the "economic changes that have occurred during the last quarter of the century . . . have unquestionably been more important and varied than during any former corresponding period in the world's history." Americans read one Horatio Alger rags-to-riches story after another, no matter how prosaically written or how familiar the plots. Americans vulgarized Darwinian theory into a cliché: "survival of the fittest." They apparently never tired of hearing the Reverend Russell Conwell declare that making money was a Christian duty. At least 6,000 audiences heard him deliver his famous sermon, "Acres of Diamonds." The Southern Methodists were not to be outdone by a Baptist. In 1885 they published William S. Speer's *Law of Success,* "a summary of business methods deduced from the crystallized experiences of twelve hundred successful men on public station and private life." In fact, just before Grady spoke to the New England Society, General Sherman expressed the popular ideology of the day when he told the audience that after the Civil War and emancipation, "all men in America, north and south and east and west, stand free before the tribunal of the Almighty, each to work out his own destiny according to his ability, and according to his virtue, and according to his manhood."

Grady was a political kingmaker as well as the principal apostle of the New South. He enjoyed his greatest success with General Gordon and the Georgia gubernatorial election of 1886. When the campaign began, Augustus Bacon seemed assured of the Democratic nomination. In the solid South, that nomination was tantamount to election. Bacon, however, had not anticipated Grady's capacity for selling a candidate. Modern image-makers would have been impressed by what the editor of the *Constitution* accomplished.

Grady got the aged Jefferson Davis to come to Georgia to unveil a monument to Benjamin H. Hill, former Confederate and U.S. senator from Georgia. General Gordon escorted Davis from Montgomery, Alabama, to Atlanta. Everywhere large crowds cheered the former president of the Confederacy, and the praise spilled over and onto Gordon, the alleged hero of Appomattox. Skillfully molded by Grady, the praise became a gubernatorial nomination forced upon a supposedly reluctant Gordon.

Gordon's campaign and election were highly appropriate expressions of the ambiguities of the Redeemer South. Gordon may have embodied the Lost Cause; he certainly embodied the New South. Shortly after the Civil War, he took steps then common to the ambitious in the Southeast: he ended a short career in farming and moved to Atlanta. In 1867 he ran unsuccessfully on the Democratic ticket for governor. Coincidentally, he joined the Ku Klux Klan and apparently served for a short time as the Grand Dragon of Georgia. By the early 1870s, the Democrats had defeated the Republicans and ended Reconstruction in Georgia. In the process, Georgia became a one-party state with whites in control. Gordon, Alfred H. Colquitt, and Joseph E. Brown rotated so smoothly between the U.S. Senate and the governor's mansion that they were called "the Georgia triumvirate."

Gordon sought his personal fortune in insurance, book publishing, law, and land speculation. Only the last endeavor proved very profitable. He served as the broker for an English company that purchased 1.3 million acres of Yazoo delta land in Mississippi. He kept company with the likes of Collis P. Huntington and Henry W. Flagler, railroad magnates. Flagler, once a partner of John D. Rockefeller, provided special cars for Gordon's funeral train.

Both Gordon and the Redeemer South depended heavily on imagery, and both differed significantly from the images they projected. The Redeemers did not create "a perfect democracy" or even a rough approximation of one. Nor had southern manufacturers or the southern economy developed sufficiently to challenge those of the Northeast or the Midwest. Nor had family farmers replaced planters. Nor had race relations in any broad sense become (or ever been) "close and cordial." Still, the Redeemers had presided over the early years of the New South. That was the greatest legacy of the Redeemer years. Ironically, another major legacy of those years was the Lost Cause.

THE LOST CAUSE

Even as southerners moved, sometimes ambivalently, toward the New South, they kept memories of the Confederacy alive as the Lost Cause. The term may be derived from *The Lost Cause,* an 1866 book by Edward S. Pollard that defended the constitutionality of secession. The Lost Cause evolved into a set of commonly held ideas that were ritualized, institutionalized, and often expressed in religious terms. The Lost Cause was the way in which southerners of the Civil War generation and their children understood the war and coped with crushing defeat, and it was the means they chose to convey that understanding to succeeding generations. Variants of the Lost Cause developed, reflecting changes over time. Individuals and groups often gave the Lost Cause their own particular meaning. Clergymen, for instance, often gave the Lost Cause an intensely religious interpretation.

In the first decade or so after the Civil War, mourning was the predominant theme of the Lost Cause. Later, as southerners were more and more divided by the changes occurring in the New South, unity became the major theme. Interest in the Lost Cause was particularly strong during the divided decade of the 1890s. The Lost Cause, with its celebration of the mythologized Old South and Confederacy, also provided a shield against the assaults of "outsiders" and a vehicle for expressing defiance toward a wide assortment of enemies, including the federal government.

Monuments—most memorably Monument Avenue in Richmond and Stone Mountain, Georgia—and Confederate cemeteries virtually everywhere lent permanence to the Lost Cause. Local memorial associations sprang up soon after the war. Their activities included annual observances of Confederate Memorial Day. Southern state governments declared Robert E. Lee's birthday a holiday. Regional organizations—most important among them the Southern Historical Society (founded in 1869), the United Confederate Veterans (1889), the United Daughters of the Confederacy (1895), and the Sons of the Confederacy (1896)— spread the word of the Lost Cause. So did magazines and periodicals: *The Land We Love, The Southern Review, The Southern Bivouac, The Southern Historical Society Papers, Confederate Veteran;* so did books: Jefferson Davis's *Rise and Fall of the Confederate Government* and the less measured *U.S. "History" as the Yankee Makes It and Takes It,* by John Coussens, a Confederate veteran. Episcopal High School at Alexandria, Virginia, the University of the South at Sewanee, Tennessee, and Washington and Lee University at Lexington, Virginia, became citadels of the Lost Cause. The name of Washington and Lee contained an irony. Lee, who served Washington College from 1865 until his death in 1870 and probably saved it from collapse, forcefully modernized the school's curriculum during his brief presidency. In renaming the college to honor him, the trustees looked as much to the future as to the past.

Groups, in particular the United Daughters of the Confederacy, also watched to see that textbooks were not "Yankeeized," that the right, or southern, version of history was told. Katherine Du Pré Lumpkin, Georgia-born sociologist and educator, recalled that her father and his friends repeatedly said, "We were never conquered," and sneered at Reconstruction by proclaiming that they were "unreconstructed rebels." In lighter moments they sang:

> I've not been reconstructed,
> Nor took the oath of allegiance.
> I'm the same old red-hot rebel,
> And that's good enough for me!

Her father carefully instructed his children in the Lost Cause. Institutionalized and ritualized into a civil religion, the Lost Cause also had a political impact by reinforcing the solid South.

J. E. B. STUART MONUMENT UNVEILING, RICHMOND, VIRGINIA, 1907
(Cook Collection, Valentine Museum)

The Lost Cause rested on several tenaciously defended beliefs. First, the Confederacy had been founded on the fundamental, correct constitutional principle that sovereign states may make and unmake associations, that secession was constitutional, and that the Confederacy had fought nobly for that principle. Second, the South had not been defeated. It had been exhausted by overwhelming numbers and greater resources, not by superior armed forces and military leaders. Third, the Confederacy was a Christian society and better than its adversary, which was too given to money making and was disorderly, insufficiently Protestant, and a jumble of ethnic groups. The Old South, by contrast, according to Lost Cause doctrine, had been an orderly, hierarchical, moral society based on evangelical Protestantism, less concerned with financial success than with honor and duty. Slavery was part of this good orderly society and had elevated blacks by Christianizing and civilizing them.

Though slavery as an institution fit neatly into the Lost Cause, the end of the Confederacy did not. Had not southerners believed and received assurances from men of the cloth that God was on their side? The result of the Civil War defied easy explanation. Some lost their faith. Most found other solutions. In some way the South had sinned or erred grievously, and God had punished it to prepare it for another mission, perhaps to provide moral leadership for a reunited America. Those who stressed the religious aspects of the Lost Cause warned against the materialism of the New South, decrying Yankee "mammonism."

The Lost Cause had its martyrs, among whom Robert E. Lee, "Stonewall" Jackson, and Jefferson Davis were the most important. Lee the man was lost in the portrait of him as a faultless Christian knight and a noble aristocrat of the kind many southerners wanted to believe peopled the antebellum South. Jackson was the common man who rose to high station to serve a great cause. Davis represented abiding uncompromising commitment to correct constitutional principles and a willingness to suffer for them. Blacks also had their place in the Lost Cause—as faithful slaves. Women received their due, too. Women were praised for their heroism and sacrifice during the Civil War and lauded as symbols of home and family, preservers of moral purity and virtue. Such attitudes may help account for the great stress put on the Southern Lady and the South's resistance to coeducation after the Civil War. Subtle but important differences in attitudes among and toward women found expression in the Lost Cause. When the Confederate Veterans, the Daughters of the Confederate Veterans, and the Sons of the Confederacy decided in 1906 to erect a monument to Confederate women, their ideas of an appropriate memorial differed significantly. The men favored a monument that celebrated the Confederate woman as subordinate helpmate, while the women wanted a monument that stressed the dignity and strong spirit of the women of the war.

A WOMAN OF THE NEW SOUTH

The debate over how to memorialize Confederate women suggested that the place of women in the postbellum South was changing, or at least that women's attitudes toward themselves and their roles in society were changing, though the changes were gradual and were less obvious than similar developments in the North.

The Civil War had obvious consequences for southern women. During the war itself, many women assumed new responsibilities. What long-range effect these new responsibilities had on women, or on men, is not known. Nor do scholars know much about the effects of the deaths or disabling of so many men during the war. Presumably young women had fewer opportunities to marry and to have families. Some things are clear, however. The defeat of the South greatly improved the lives of women who had been slaves. The experience of most white women was the reverse. Incomes and living standards among whites suffered a general decline and recovered only slowly. Families in reduced circumstances had less to spend on education, for example. If families had the money to educate only one child, a son would be favored over a daughter. The economic circumstances of the postbellum South put great pressures on poorer whites. Many poorer white women—particularly those who were widowed or single—had to seek employment outside their homes or off the farm. Domestic work offered them little opportunity: that was usually but not always considered to be black work and was very poorly paid. Industrial work—in cotton mills and tobacco manufacturing particularly—afforded limited but growing opportunities. Domestic manufacturing (production performed at home) and services (like sewing) performed in the home remained important sources of income for women.

Opportunities for middle-class women increased after the Civil War. Teaching— an almost exclusively male preserve in the South before 1860—offered women a new source of income, and possibly a career. So did office work or clerking in stores in larger urban areas, opportunities enhanced by urban growth and economic expansion. In some cases, women became proprietors of shops, especially of those that catered to women. Race, of course, was a factor here. White women found teaching and office and store work more readily than black women did, and white women found the doors to proprietorships more open than did black women. Black women got only the worst jobs in tobacco manufacturing and, like black men, were virtually excluded from textile manufacturing. Canneries, especially in areas like Mobile or New Orleans that had large black populations, readily hired black women. They paid poorly, however, and offered only seasonal work.

The changing place of women in the postbellum South was reflected in the life of Rebecca Latimer Felton. Born in 1835 into the family of a Georgia planter and slave owner, she graduated from Madison (Georgia) Female College at eighteen and married Dr. William H. Felton, a thirty-year-old widower, in 1853. A physician and then a minister, Felton was active in politics and reform. The Feltons soon established a school in which both taught on the site of their modest northern Georgia plantation. It was the first of many joint activities.

The Civil War years left deep scars on the Feltons. One of their small sons died of measles during the war, another of malaria immediately after the war. Another son, born in 1869, lived until 1926. Their last child, born in 1871, lived only two years. (Their only daughter had died before the war.) Rebecca Felton's deeply felt evangelical Protestant faith must have been severely tested by these personal tragedies. The Feltons saw the war firsthand. They cared for wounded and dying soldiers, fled their home to escape Sherman's march to the sea, and returned to their plantation after the war without slaves or much else. Soon they reopened their school, whose operations they had suspended during the conflict.

Rebecca Felton subsequently went from being wife, mother, and educator to political campaign manager, author, newspaper editor and columnist, businesswoman, and suffragist. She was an advocate of women's rights, of temperance, and of education and penal reform. She became the first woman member of the U.S. Senate, having received a token appointment in 1922. She was also a firm religious fundamentalist and a strong racial segregationist.

A self-conscious pioneer who was never shy, Felton became openly and heavily involved in politics, a most unusual occurrence in her day. She took advanced positions on many issues: women's suffrage, equal rights for women in churches, public funding for maternal and child care and sex education, compulsory school attendance; she opposed convict leasing. She believed that secession had been wrong and that the South had fought the war in order to preserve slavery. She defended white women workers in cotton mills and their employers, asserting that the women, some of whom were Civil War widows, had to work, and that the mills were among the few places where they could find employment. She tended to ignore the callous exploitation and the poor working and living conditions in many mills and mill villages. A member of the Woman's Christian Temperance Union, she used her fiery pen to preach against drinking, smoking, and gambling. An active participant in the United Daughters of the Confederacy, she joined other Daughters in their efforts to obtain pensions and retirement homes for Confederate veterans and their widows.

Women, Felton argued, should be admitted to the University of Georgia on an equal basis with men, and the university should be better supported by the legislature because it offered people of modest means an opportunity for a college education. The Georgia legislature approved coeducation at the university in 1889, but the trustees of the university did not admit women students until 1919. Rebecca Felton was also a major supporter of the Georgia Normal and Industrial College (now Georgia State College for Women), which opened in 1889, and the Georgia Training School for Girls, which opened in 1913. Speaking of the former, Felton took a clearly feminist position: "Don't make it a man's college, patterned after man's ideas and based upon what man had done or can do." In a similar vein, she declared that men should help women with work around the house.

Felton passionately defended the racial caste system of the South. She had a pathological mind-set about race and the purity of white women. The defense of white women against "raving beasts" required drastic measures, even lynchings "a thousand times a week if necessary." Apparently Felton never probed the possible inner psychological sources of her rage, nor did she show comparable concern for black women.

Church leaders, bankers, railroad presidents, and political opponents were targets for a pen that was still active in 1929. Disinclined to forget or forgive, she relished fights and could sling mud with the best. Felton particularly disliked John Brown Gordon, whom she accused of flipflopping on so many political issues that he was a "political gymnast."

As the 1920s drew to a close, Rebecca Felton, unwilling to trust to others or to fate, supervised construction of her own mausoleum and arranged to have her papers, with newly added marginal notes, deposited where scholars and others could use them. She could not stop the highway department from building a sidewalk and paving the road in front of her house, and she could not avoid the higher taxes that resulted. She lived to see the stock market crash in 1929 and the Depression begin. Momentarily forgetting her Protestant piety, she allowed that "things are in a hell of a shape." Yet at her death in January 1930 she left an estate of $250,000. A person of "well defined and firmly fixed opinions upon social, moral and political questions," one observer declared, she "was always ready to defend them."

Felton stood out among women—and men, for that matter—but she was not a solitary figure. Black and white women first used women's groups in their churches and then created reform organizations to provide the means for protest and action against a whole range of social ills, including the abuses of alcohol, public health problems, the inadequacies of public education, prostitution, child labor, and the exploitation of workers, especially female workers. Particularly concerned about extending their realm of domestic responsibility for the family, women stressed family issues in their reformism. It was no accident that women were actively involved in and often leaders of the most important reform movements from the 1880s through the progressive era.

Women had to tread carefully in the South, where ladies were not supposed to "unsex" themselves by stepping into the masculine world of politics, work,

FLOAT FOR CONFEDERATE VETERANS *(Confederate Veteran)*

saloons, and such. Color, of course, muted the reform efforts of black women and removed them almost entirely from the struggle for women's suffrage that developed at the end of the nineteenth century. That struggle revealed very clearly how different the South was from the rest of the nation. No region resisted extending the franchise to women more persistently than the South.

On several occasions, the writer Elizabeth Meriwether Gilmer publicly brushed aside the demure veil of the Southern Lady. The creator and author of "Dorothy Dix Talks," the first women's advice column published in the United States, wrote in the *New Orleans Picayune* in 1898 that "everything in the world had been written about women and for women, except the truth." "They had been celebrated as angels . . . pitied as martyrs . . . advised to be human doormats." They "were fed up with fulsome flattery and weary of suffering and being strong. So I began writing for my sex the truth, as I have seen it, about the relationship between men and women." Women had as much "right [as men] to be as ugly as nature made them, and to look as old as they really are." Marriage should not resemble a "vaudeville show" where the wife continually performed for an audience of one—her husband. "There comes a time in the life of every woman when she has to choose between a species of slavery and freedom, and when, if she ever expects to enjoy any future liberty, she must hoist the red flag of revolt and make a stand for her rights. . . . That our jailer happens to love us does not offer adequate compensation for being in prison."

POLITICAL INDEPENDENTS CHALLENGE THE REDEEMERS

In the 1870s the Redeemers faced more immediate threats from political independents than they did from southern women, even Rebecca Felton. Of these threats, one of the most formidable was her husband, William H. Felton. He led the Independent Democrats in Georgia and was a force to be reckoned with until the 1890s. Running against the Georgia triumvirate, Felton enjoyed his greatest electoral successes in the 1870s, when he won a seat in Congress three times beginning in 1874. Other independents won congressional elections in Georgia, Alabama, and Texas in 1878. In 1880 Tennessee Republicans regained the governorship of the state when the Democrats divided over whether and how to reduce the state debt. Two years later the national Republican party threw its support behind the successful effort of a Mississippi Independent Democrat to win a seat in Congress. Alarmed, the Redeemers talked about the dangers the independents represented because they split white voters and thus risked "Africanizing" the politics of the South. They claimed that "Mahoneism" was on the loose and was a great peril. "Mahoneism" referred to political developments in Virginia. It was there, in the most tradition-bound state in the South, that the most serious challenge to Redeemer policies came in the late 1870s.

After Reconstruction and before the Populist upheaval of the 1890s, Virginia was the scene of the most divisive political conflict in the South. The dispute focused on whether the state should repay (or fund) its debt in full or at a reduced (or readjusted) level. This dispute developed into two factions, the Readjusters and the Funders. The Readjusters challenged the Funders in the 1870s, overwhelmed them for a time, and appeared to be developing a permanent political party. Then, like similar efforts in the South after 1865, this attempt to develop a political movement or party independent of the Democratic party failed. The conflict between the two factions had elements that were peculiar to Virginia and others that revealed much about the South as a whole after Reconstruction.

The Readjusters and the Funders were offspring of the Virginia Conservatives who came to power after Union occupation forces left in 1870. The origins of the Conservatives lay in a coalition of moderate Republicans, Democrats, and Whigs. This three-part coalition outflanked Radical Republicans and kept Radical Reconstruction out of the Old Dominion. Then the Democrats and the Whigs, who called themselves Conservatives in order to bridge the pre-1865 divisions among them, outmaneuvered the moderate Republicans and became preeminent in Virginia politics. The Conservatives strongly resembled the Redeemers of other southern states, though Virginia had no Radical Republican government from which to be "redeemed."

The Virginia Conservatives generally were members of the white elite and served the interests of that elite, often at the expense of other groups. The state debt crisis demonstrated how narrow their vision could be. Virginia had entered the Civil War with a $33 million debt, the result of state subsidies for the construction of railroads, canals, and turnpikes. (State assets in these internal improvements totaled $43 million in 1860.) After four years of war, the debt (the amount of outstanding bonds) had increased to $45 million. None of this sum, it should be noted, was the result of Reconstruction. In 1871 the Conservative-controlled state government passed the Funding Act and committed the state to pay the debt in full. No other southern postwar government funded its debt at such a high rate. The honor of Virginia, said the Conservatives, was at stake. They probably believed what they said, but what they said was at least partially self-serving. Some Conservatives may have owned state bonds, and some served as legal and business representatives of bondholders. Most of the bondholders were from the Northeast and Europe, and many bought the bonds at considerably less than half their face value. The Conservatives also sold the state's holdings in valuable railroad stocks at suspiciously low prices. Apparently some prominent Conservatives profited from these transactions, among them William Mahone, future leader of the Readjusters.

Payment of the debt hobbled the state. Interest payments alone exhausted state revenues. Virginia was chronically in debt in the 1870s, had to borrow just to keep the government operating at all, and virtually eliminated expenditures for social services. Ignoring constitutional requirements that the legislature bear much of the cost of the newly established public school system, Conservative leaders simply stood by while half the public schools closed and 100,000 students were turned away. Some Conservatives thought school closings were a regrettable but necessary consequence of preserving the honor of the state. Rather than readjust the debt, close the schools. The governor thought public schools were "a luxury . . . to be paid for . . . by the people who wish their benefits." As they would soon discover, the Funders were out of touch with public sentiment.

"Kill the public schools, will you?" a Virginia farmer reportedly warned his representative in the legislature. "Do it and this will be your last winter in Richmond." The warning reflected a widespread sentiment. By the 1870s most Virginians and most other southerners had rejected the long-held idea that public education was for paupers only. But the Conservatives in Virginia persisted. They also acquired a new name, Funders. The Funders put themselves in the politically absurd position of defending the interests of the bondholders, most of whom were not Virginians and who were making very substantial profits on their bonds, against the interests of Virginians. Reports of bribery, theft, and forgery clouded the Conservatives' claim to be defenders of Virginia's honor. Cash payments to high officials apparently had speeded passage of the Funding Act. Consequently, the Readjusters became a major force in Virginia politics by the late 1870s.

William Mahone, the principal leader of the Readjusters, puzzled his contemporaries then and historians since. How much did he mix self-interest with his politics?

Was he prompted by conscience or by opportunism? Was he the leader of what might have been a significantly different politics in Virginia and in the South? How responsible was he for the successes of the Readjusters? Their failures? Mahone was the grandson of an eighteenth-century Irish immigrant to Virginia, son of a moderately prosperous innkeeper, graduate of Virginia Military Institute, railroad engineer and then president of his own line, slaveholder, Democrat, secessionist, member of the state legislature of Confederate Virginia, major general in the Confederate army, hero of the Battle of the Crater, and highly influential Conservative leader; he hardly seemed the type to break ranks with his fellow Conservatives.

But by 1877 the general sought another battle. The depression of the 1870s had cost him his nascent railroad empire (suggestively named the Atlantic, Mississippi, and Ohio Railroad Company). He may have wanted to revive his railroad through what was then the accepted means, the state legislature. If Mahone could lead the Readjusters to a successful conquest of the legislature, the legislature might look favorably on the state railroad charter he had to have. Whatever his motives, Mahone sided with efforts to reduce the state debt and declared himself "the friend of the public school system of Virginia." He quickly took command of the Readjusters.

Led by Mahone and using the debt issue as an entering wedge, the Readjusters won control of the legislature in 1879 and the governor's office in 1881. They reduced the debt by a third and the interest rate on it from 6 to 3 percent.

VIRGINIA DEMOCRATS USED RACIST ATTACK ON WILLIAM MAHONE AND THE READJUSTERS, 1881. (The Library of Virginia)

Virginia's creditors, they argued, should bear some of the costs of Virginia's war-reduced economy and of the revenue losses associated with the secession of West Virginia. The Readjusters' rhetoric had a distinctly modern ring. They decried the flow of capital to the state's creditors rather than to industry and agriculture. Harrison H. Riddleberger, Readjuster chieftain and future U.S. senator, wanted to "combine manufactures with agriculture." The *Staunton Valley Virginian* hailed Virginians as "a new people, living under new conditions, looking to new pursuits, new methods, and new results." In other words, slavery and secession were dead, and Virginia wanted to end its dependence on agriculture.

The Readjusters reformed the tax system by reducing taxes on farmland and small businesses, by ending the policy of self-assessment by the railroads for tax purposes, and by collecting delinquent taxes. At the same time, the Readjusters spent more on social services—on hospitals, asylums, the penitentiary, higher education, and the public schools. The number of schools, teachers, and students more than doubled. Yet Virginia had a budget surplus of $1.5 million in 1883. The Readjusters embraced other activist ideas about the role of government. Some wanted to enact maximum hours laws, restrict child labor, and give aid to the needy. In another break with southern tradition, the Readjusters formally declared their support for protective tariffs. The Readjuster legislature enacted laws to ensure the quality of agricultural fertilizers and to regulate the activities of life insurance companies—but only those based outside the state. Influenced perhaps by Mahone, the Readjusters did not respond positively to pressures to regulate railroads more vigorously.

The humanitarian reform and public school movements and the activist notions of the proper role of government, found elsewhere in nineteenth-century America, had reached the Old Dominion. As elsewhere, self-interest and the urge to impose social control were factors. The Readjusters defended public schools as an asset for economic growth and as a stimulant to "a general ambition" for "prosperity." Keenly aware of their dependence on black voters, the Readjusters made voting easier for blacks and passed other measures designed to appeal to them. Thus they repealed the Conservative law that made the poll tax a requirement for voting and the law that disfranchised men convicted of petty larceny. These measures also broadened the franchise for low-income whites. Ironically, those whites might then vote against their benefactors if they believed the Readjusters had failed to defend white supremacy adequately. The Readjusters abolished the whipping post (hated vestige of slave times), increased patronage for blacks, created a college for blacks (now Virginia State University), and supported a state mental hospital for blacks. Black legislators, whose numbers grew during the Readjuster years, figured prominently in these efforts.

REPUBLICANS AND DEMOCRATS IN VIRGINIA

Mahone attempted to transform the Readjusters into a permanent political party by joining forces with the Republicans. The general cast his lot with the Republicans in 1881, when he went to the U.S. Senate. His vote allowed the Republicans to organize the Senate and thus to elect its officers and control its committees. In return, the general got command of federal patronage in Virginia, essential for political party building. But the Readjusters and Republicans could not overcome the problems that for nearly a century after 1865 plagued challengers of southern Democrats. Circumstances and Mahone's own failings undermined the efforts to make a strong Republican party out of the Readjusters.

The Funders, who formally declared themselves to be Democrats in 1883, had enormous political assets. Self-proclaimed defenders of the South, they stood opposed to the party of Lincoln, which symbolized the Civil War, emancipation, and Reconstruction. Cloaked in Confederate gray and surrounded by the Stars and Bars, they recalled past glories and bitter memories. They promised to maintain a South rooted in tradition, white supremacy, and black subordination. Democrats also drew their leaders from those who were politically active and able to assure the Democrats of ample funds.

The Virginia Democrats also made some timely changes in their course. They distanced themselves momentarily from their Funder past. They adopted the programs of the opposition and imitated Mahone's statewide organization. They declared the debt issue settled and committed themselves to keeping the public school system and most other Readjuster reforms. Ironically, the Readjusters' victory on the debt deprived the insurgents of the issue that had been the glue of the Readjuster coalition of blacks and nonelite whites.

Mahone himself weakened the coalition. His imperial style bred harmful divisions among Readjuster and Republican leaders. He perceived other Readjuster and Republican leaders as rivals. He demanded oaths of loyalty—to himself—and used patronage like a bludgeon. Opponents effectively equated Mahoneism with bossism. Mahone's decision to join forces with the Republicans was a calculated risk in the South, where the party was abhorrent to most voters. That bold step, however, offered the Readjusters the only realistic chance to develop a permanent political party that could challenge the Democrats.

More than anything else, however, the race issue doomed the Readjusters, even though they approached the color line discreetly. The white Readjuster leaders, including Mahone, were white supremacists. They supported racial segregation in schools, handled race and access to public facilities gingerly, and flatly rejected miscegenation and racial intermarriage. "Our party . . . encourages each race to develop its own sociology separately and apart from unlawful contamination with each other, but under a government which recognizes and protects the civil rights of all." Still, their constituency left them exposed to racist attacks.

The Democrats could win elections without black votes. Their opponents could not—unless an unusual circumstance should arise, such as the crisis over the state debt. Anyone who wished to build a permanent political party that could present a continuous challenge to the Democrats in Virginia had to have strong support from blacks. As the Readjusters metamorphosed into Republicans, they were gored on the horns of a dilemma not of their making. They had to court black leaders and black voters, who understandably and often rightly suspected that white politicians only wanted to use them. But every concession to blacks, born of self-interest or of good conscience, and every black candidate, elected official, or appointee darkened the Readjusters and Republicans in white Virginia. Blacks, understandably, wanted to see more blacks in office, and they used the number of black officeholders as an index for measuring the sincerity of the whites who sought their support. Also, at a time when blacks had very limited avenues for making a living and a public office was a fine prize to receive, blacks hungrily pursued nominations and appointments.

Conversely, the Democrats claimed to be "the white man's party." The *Richmond Daily Dispatch* put it simply in 1883: "Shall the whites rule . . . or shall the negroes?" "I am a Democrat," explained John W. Daniel, Democratic senator, "because I am a white man and a Virginian." These leaders were disposed to exploit race for political advantage even as they courted—usually covertly—black voters with promises of patronage and gifts of money. The last was very tempting for voters who probably realized that in most elections there was no viable candidate who was their friend. In some instances, of course, blacks genuinely believed that the Democrats were their best choice. One of the striking things about politics in the Gilded Age South was that voters, black and white, turned out in large numbers. That changed after the new election laws that, beginning in the 1890s, dramatically reduced the electorate in the South.

During the 1883 Virginia state elections, "the white man's party" cynically played the race issue. Leading Democrats were even willing to stage a serious public disturbance on the eve of an important election, or they might take advantage of opportunities such a disturbance might offer. Danville seemed a likely place. Located in Southside Virginia, an area where blacks made up about half the populace, Danville itself had a black majority, a white carpetbagger mayor, several blacks on the town council, a black judge, and several black policemen. The white minority in the town, according to the "merchants and manufacturers and mechanics" who signed the "Danville Circular" on the eve of the 1883 state election, deeply resented "the injustice and humiliation to which our white people have been subjected and are daily undergoing by the domination and misrule of the Radical or negro party." Danville supposedly hovered on the brink of economic collapse. Actually, it had a booming trade in tobacco, three railroads, and the recently started Riverside Cotton Mills. Another grievance was that Negro maids allegedly were uppity. How much of the circular was contrived, how much was factual, and how much was believed are impossible to discern. It probably did reflect the feelings of most local whites and the determination of the Democrats in Danville to win the state election and regain control of their town. The authors and signers of the circular warned that if the Democrats lost, *"we are doomed."* Whites also threatened to boycott businesses that did not support the Democrats and suggested that property owners not rent to blacks or Republicans. Three days before the polls opened, an argument of uncertain origin led to a shooting that left four blacks and one white dead. Inflated into a "riot" and broadcast by poster, telegraph, and mounted courier, the incident became the focal point of what was already a racially oriented campaign.

The resultant emotional upsurge helped the Democrats to a decisive electoral victory in the 1883 state election. They then quickly consolidated their gains. Using their newly won control of the legislature, the Democrats took over the election machinery of the state. That control helped them carry the state for Grover Cleveland in the 1884 presidential election and to recapture the governorship and Virginia's congressional delegation. Stuffed ballot boxes, falsified election returns, and intimidated opposition supporters became commonplace. The Democratic leader Hal Flood explained that once the polls closed, election judges, all of whom were Democrats, "changed the ballots to suit themselves." Gerrymandering also helped. The Democrats drew electoral lines for Danville so artfully that its black majority became a minority. So effective were these political practices that sweeping disfranchisement laws (Jim Crow election laws) were not enacted in Virginia until 1902. The Democrats did not need Jim Crow laws to stay in power.

A historian recalled that during his boyhood in eastern Virginia around World War I, people who remembered Mahone

> spoke of him with horror . . . He had threatened Virginia with Negro-Republican rule. His career had been an offense to Virginia's dignity and decency. In campaign after campaign such views were reiterated by the leaders of the ruling Democratic party. The worst charge that could be brought against an opposition candidate was that he had been associated in any way with Mahone and the Readjusters. . . . The prevailing opinion was that only the Democrats had served that state with honesty, dignity, and integrity.

Mahone had obvious shortcomings, but he deserved better. So did the Readjusters. At the very least, they offered black and nonelite white Virginians a better present and future and all Virginians a wider range of political options and a less racially skewed politics.

The attempt to build a viable opposition to the Redeemers-turned-Democrats failed even in Virginia, where it had considerable advantages, certainly greater advantages than those of similar efforts in other southern states. The debt crisis had been a catalyst for political dissent. In Virginia, unlike several Deep South states, blacks were numerically a minority and could not realistically threaten "black domination." Virginia had not experienced Radical Reconstruction. The Readjusters had able leaders who were natives of the state and relatively immune to the charges of outside intervention that were common during Reconstruction. Still they could not prevail against the postbellum Democrats in Virginia.

THE SOLID SOUTH

As events in Virginia revealed, any opposition to the Democrats faced almost insurmountable odds. Southern Democrats based their defense on the solid South: the South had to remain solidly Democratic because the Democratic party offered the best means of preventing the federal government from intervening in race relations in the South and the best means of keeping blacks in their place within the South. To maintain their two-front strategy of defense of white supremacy (and their own political fortunes and sometimes their own economic positions), southern Democrats were willing to go to great lengths, often well beyond the bounds of the truth and the law. Southern Democrats conjured up visions of past horrors—real, imagined, and embellished. Versions of the past served aims of the present. Particular interpretations of the past and events selectively remembered became fact. Thus the story of Mahone and the Readjusters went through the process that had turned Reconstruction into the Tragic Era. More critically, southern Democrats bludgeoned their opponents with Negrophobia. They exploited rumors, such as the supposed collapse of Danville, for their own gain. The Democrats succeeded in making the South a one-party region and in making that party a white man's party, although they often neglected the interests of many whites. The concern of the Virginia Democrats for the bondholders and their indifference to public education were all too typical of the Redeemers or the postbellum southern Democrats. On whom should the burden of taxes fall? What kind of services—schools, asylums, and so forth—should state and local governments provide? Should railroads and industrial corporations be regulated? Essential questions such as these tended to get obscured in a politics laden with race and memories of the Civil War and Reconstruction. Who was going to challenge heroes of the Lost Cause, General This, Colonel That, Captain Something Else?

The Democrats who triumphed in Virginia and in the rest of the South after Reconstruction dominated the politics of the region throughout the remainder of the century. They left a heritage that lingers even to the present. Their legacy included a one-party politics that became so fixed and persisted so long that the "solid South" or the "Democratic South" seemed to be divinely ordained. The Democrats assisted Providence. They thwarted whatever possibilities existed for the development of a strong two-party politics. To gain and keep power, the Democrats were willing to risk the "honesty, dignity, and integrity" for which they were noted in some quarters. Fraud and violence at elections did not cease when Reconstruction ended.

Southern Democrats also found bribery effective, as were calculated manipulations of state constitutions and laws. The Democratic legislature in North Carolina removed the threat of black power in areas of the state where blacks were the majority by simply vesting control of county and local governments in itself. The Redeemer constitution in Louisiana achieved a similar effect by expanding the governor's already considerable powers over the legislature and over county and local officials. South Carolina passed its notorious eight-box voting law in 1882. Voters then had to match ballots with boxes, with candidates in proper order, or have their ballots invalidated. Democratic election officials counseled bewildered voters selectively. Southern legislatures gerrymandered without pretense of subtlety. They did not blush to create pretzel-shaped congressional districts that diluted the power of black votes.

The southern Democrats succeeded politically to a remarkable degree. Blessed by the circumstances of the Civil War and Reconstruction and by whites' fear of blacks, the Democrats gave the South unprecedented one-party dominance. In time it became difficult to remember that the South had a two-party tradition, to remember when the South was not solid.

SOUTHERN DEMOCRATS AND BLACKS

Once the Democrats regained office they did not immediately disfranchise black voters. It was not in their interest to do so. Suitably contained and manipulated black voters served the needs of Democratic leaders within the South and without. By various means, fair or foul, the Democrats used ballots cast by blacks to frustrate their challengers. White minorities in black belt counties in Georgia, Alabama, and Mississippi used the ballots of black majorities to offset those cast by whites in white-majority counties. A Mississippi judge told that state's 1890 constitutional convention that

> it is no secret that there has not been a full vote and a fair count in Mississippi since 1875—that we have been preserving the ascendancy of the white people by revolutionary methods. In plain words, we have been stuffing ballot boxes, committing perjury, and here and there in the State carrying the elections by *fraud* and violence until the whole machinery for elections was about to rot down.

Outside the South, the Democrats found the presence of black voters useful for political and economic reasons. That presence was interpreted by the North and by potential investors as an indication that the slavocracy was dead and that the Democrats had rejected their grievous errors of the past and were enlightened. The strategy of racial accommodation—which was preached and sometimes practiced—also diminished the possibility that the federal government might intervene again, politically or militarily.

It is important, however, to remember the limits of this strategy. Its cornerstone was white supremacy and black subordination. As long as the cornerstone remained securely in place, blacks could continue to have certain political and civil rights: vote, hold office, serve on juries, testify in cases involving whites, and bear arms. They also had access to many public places and to public transit, and not always on a segregated basis.

Blacks voted in large numbers in the South until the late 1890s. But blacks hardly made their electoral decisions freely in many places. Though blacks often constituted a majority of potential voters, southern whites would not let that fact be translated into black majorities in state and local governments. Blacks served in Congress, in state legislatures, and on city councils and local boards of education in such places as Richmond, Jackson, and St. Augustine until the early twentieth century. Four blacks even served as delegates to the 1895 constitutional convention in South Carolina, which was called to disfranchise blacks. The black delegates dissented without effect. (Their remarks, which included a more accurate analysis of Reconstruction than the one that appeared in history textbooks for years, were excluded from the official minutes of the convention.)

Whatever the limits of the race relations policies of the postbellum Democrats, they were more favorable to blacks than were the rigid segregationist policies that came during the 1890s. Tragically, however, the policies and actions of the Democrats in pursuit of their own survival nurtured the racism and bloody violence that racked the South in the 1890s.

THE SOLID SOUTH AND NATIONAL POLITICS

The solid South equaled the Democratic South, of course, and that equation had political meaning beyond Dixie and long after the Civil War. The South ensured the Democrats of a substantial portion of any Congress and of the electoral votes in a presidential election. (The Republicans had similar bastions in many non-southern states.) The solid South helped create a nearly even balance of power between the two major parties in the late nineteenth century. The equipoise began as the 1870s started and it lasted until the mid-1890s. Then the Republicans became the dominant party, a position they held until 1930.

Between 1874 and 1894, the Democrats usually controlled the House of Representatives, the Republicans the Senate and the White House. Democrats ran well enough in parts of the North to elect a number of congressmen, who joined forces with southern Democrats to control the House. Democrats outside the South had less success in winning statewide elections and hence less success in capturing seats in the Senate or winning electoral votes in presidential elections. Making the White House Democratic depended on a simple, though not easily applied, formula. To the South add a reasonably attractive Democrat from a large eastern state in which the Democrats were strong, and hope for favorable circumstances. Governor Grover Cleveland of New York fit this description, and circumstances obliged during the 1884 and 1892 presidential elections when economic difficulties and serious intraparty dissension damaged the Republicans.

Southern Democrats enjoyed considerable success in Congress, even when the Republicans controlled the White House and the Senate. Democrats from the South provided leadership and a substantial vote for the passage of the Interstate Commerce Act in 1887. That law initiated federal regulation of railroads and created the first federal regulatory agency, the Interstate Commerce Commission. Before that, southern congressmen displayed their skills at securing federal funds for river and harbor improvements in the South by making timely bargains with Democrats from the West and Midwest and with Republicans. In 1879 they persuaded Congress to create the Mississippi River Commission. That move put federal money and organization into efforts to solve one of the chronic problems of the southern Mississippi region. The river prevented cultivation of much of the lowlands in the area, and periodic flooding often brought damage or destruction to the lands that were cultivated. Much of the area called the Yazoo delta, for instance, could not be farmed until the Mississippi was better controlled. Convinced that the costs of levee construction and flood control exceeded the capacity of private investors and the states along the lower Mississippi, leaders in the region had sought federal aid. In their successful quest for the Mississippi commission, these leaders cleverly broadened their appeal by claiming that the commission and its funding would ensure improved navigation along the river. Thus they obtained strong support among congressmen, senators, and others throughout the Mississippi Valley.

According to the conventional wisdom, the South loyally clung to states rights and small federal budgets. Conventional wisdom, in this instance, is inaccurate. Though wary of the federal government, especially in matters of race, southern Democrats did turn to the federal government for programs and funds they thought the South (and the nation) needed.

Those efforts revealed deep divisions in the Democratic party. Congressional Democrats from the South differed sharply among themselves about the advisability of using the federal government. Even more serious for the Democrats were the differences between southern Democrats and Democrats from other regions. These differences devastated the party in the 1890s. The attitudes of the eastern Democrats particularly galled southern Democrats. As they learned in the disputed Hayes-Tilden election and the struggle over the Compromise of 1877, eastern Democrats had little sympathy for efforts to spend federal funds for internal improvements. Eastern Democrats denounced such appropriations as "raids on the Treasury" and worse. Though those views had merit, most southern Democrats believed the easterners wished to stop these appropriations only after they had secured the funds the East had wanted. Southern Democrats also felt that the easterners were insensitive to the acutely needy South.

THE BLAIR BILL

The congressional fight over the Blair Education Bill in the 1880s demonstrated the sharpness of these sectional conflicts within the Democracy. Republican Senator Henry F. Blair of New Hampshire proposed in 1881 that Congress disperse surplus federal funds to the states for educational purposes.

By 1881 the government had retired much of its Civil War debt and was collecting more revenue than it was spending. The obvious remedy—cutting taxes—was not easily applied. There was no income tax to cut. Federal taxes on tobacco and liquor had already been cut, to the delight of the defenders of bourbon and tobacco, who were concentrated in Kentucky, Tennessee, Virginia, and the Carolinas. Tariffs—taxes on imports—produced most of the revenue the federal government collected. Logic pointed to tariff reduction as the best solution, but tariff reduction was a political porcupine best avoided. The Republicans, powerful economic interests, and a small, politically potent group of Democrats made tariff reduction almost impossible at that time. Therefore, the politically embarrassing budget surplus remained and grew. So did the popularity of the Blair Bill.

Blair wanted to apportion funds according to the number of illiterates in each state. Since the South had a higher rate of illiteracy than the rest of the country, it would be the major beneficiary of the Blair Bill. Southern and eastern Democrats generally split over the bill, even though the opponents used arguments that normally had strong appeal to southerners. The bill was denounced as a device to avoid tariff reduction and a dangerous precedent for federal intervention in affairs rightly belonging to the states. Alabama's Senator John Tyler Morgan worried that the Blair Bill would set a precedent for "national prohibition, pure food and drug laws, abolition of penitentiaries, requirements of higher wages for workers, and socialized medicine."

Most southerners in Congress had few such qualms and were little impressed even with arguments based on states rights. Southern Democrats supported the Blair Bill more consistently than any other group in Congress. Their allies on the issue were Republicans and western Democrats. Eastern Democrats provided the most consistent opposition of all groups. The Senate passed the bill twice, but it never came to a vote in the House because it was tied up in committee. Southern Democrats in the House backed unsuccessful efforts to vote the bill out of committee, but they could not overcome the power of the speaker of the House, who opposed the measure. John G. Carlisle, a Kentuckian, believed deeply that tariff reduction was critical and that the Blair Bill would hurt attempts to lower import duties. He was also intensely committed to the idea that good government is little government. Finally, when Grover Cleveland, who had similar ideas, was elected president in 1884, all hope for the Blair Bill died.

The debate over and the votes on the education bill suggested that the ideal of limited government was still strong among the Democrats but that it was fading, especially in the South. In any event, southern supporters of the Blair Bill saw an acute need that the federal government might relieve. The South's ability to provide public education, even of dubious quality, faced serious difficulties. The South had less income and wealth to tax than the rest of the country and a greater proportion of school-aged people. Moreover, the South bore the costs of a self-imposed dual school system.

THE LEGACY OF THE REDEEMERS

The fortunes of the southern Democrats became linked in the late nineteenth century with those of Grover Cleveland. It was a mixed blessing. Cleveland's success in the presidential elections of 1884 and 1892 meant more federal patronage for all Democrats. Cleveland appointed Senator L. Q. C. Lamar of Mississippi secretary of the interior and Senator A. H. Garland of Arkansas attorney general in 1885, and in 1893 he selected John G. Carlisle of Kentucky to be secretary of the treasury, Congressman Hilary A. Herbert of Alabama as secretary of the navy, and Hoke Smith of Georgia as secretary of the interior. A year later, Cleveland nominated Senator Edward D. White of Louisiana for a seat on the Supreme Court, replacing Lamar, whom Cleveland had appointed in 1888 and whose place on the Court became vacant at his death.

Equally important to the white South and the southern Democrats, Cleveland's victories lessened the possibility of federal intervention in the South's peculiar race relations. Cleveland, like most Democrats outside the South, acquiesced in the southern view of race relations. Even as southern race relations entered their most bloody and violent era, Cleveland showed little concern about beleaguered and murdered blacks and no inclination to dispatch troops to the South to defend them. Yet Cleveland took a lively interest in "law and order" in Chicago after the Haymarket Riot (1886), and he used federal troops during the Pullman strike in 1894.

Cleveland joined southern Democrats in calling for tariff reduction, and he even went along with southern Democrats when they insisted that the legislation lowering the tariff had to include an income tax. They saw the income tax as a way to make the wealthier eastern states pay a greater share of federal taxes. Cleveland accepted tariff reduction and the income tax even though many eastern Democrats resented them both.

Unfortunately for southern Democrats, Cleveland did not differ from his fellow eastern Democrats on banking or federal subsidies for internal improvements. Southern Democrats wanted to alter banking laws in order to increase the number of banks and to disperse them more widely. At the very least, they wanted to repeal the 10 percent tax on state-chartered banks. Cleveland and other eastern Democrats opposed any changes in the national banking acts. Most important, Cleveland stood firmly with the East on monetary policy.

The markedly deflationary monetary policy that the federal government followed after 1865 favored the East and hurt the South. Debtors were affected adversely because the costs of borrowing rose steadily. Most southerners were farmers and thus were borrowers, and the South as a section borrowed heavily because it was short of capital. Southern congressmen and senators, therefore, generally supported efforts to stem deflation, and they voted for mildly inflationary measures whenever possible. Cleveland and most of the eastern Democrats held to deflationary policies through the savage depression of the 1890s. For the Democrats, it was a disaster. The Republicans swept the 1894 congressional elections and the 1896 presidential election and became the dominant political party in the United States for a generation. The Democrats became the minority party in national politics in the 1890s, a position to which they were relegated until the 1930s. Consequently, after 1894 the solid South found itself excluded from national power. Southern Democrats were entrenched but often impotent.

Yet politically the Redeemers had accomplished much in the quarter century after 1865. They helped restore whites to political dominance in the South. They managed to handle race relations cleverly enough to ensure white supremacy and to avoid (with very few exceptions) federal intervention in black-white affairs. The Redeemers stood their ground but did not ignore northern sentiments, and so they eased sectional reconciliation. When Senator Charles Sumner died in 1874, for instance, Senator L. Q. C. Lamar of Mississippi eulogized his late Massachusetts colleague who had long been the scourge of the white South. Four years later, General Gordon told a Boston audience: "The causes that divided us are gone, and gone forever. The interests which now unite us will unite us forever."

The Redeemers were also largely responsible for the postbellum Democratic party and its overwhelming dominance in the South. Moreover, southern Democrats in Congress made astute alliances with people outside their section and even outside their party. In doing so, they revived the art of political compromise, which somehow southern leaders had lost during the 1850s. Part of the success of the southern Democrats rested on irony. Emancipation gave the South more seats in the House of Representatives and more votes in the electoral college. Slaves had been counted as three-fifths of a person in apportioning seats in the House and the electoral college. Emancipation converted the fractions to whole numbers, if not whole persons.

The Redeemers also presided over the emergence of the New South, something about which they had mixed feelings. Clearly they were not sure that the New South creed should be the creed of their South. Conversely, they were sure about the Lost Cause. One of their legacies to succeeding generations was a deep reverence for the Confederacy. The Lost Cause, like other Redeemer legacies, was based on and reinforced the bond among whites. That bond was severely tested in the 1890s.

Early death spared Henry Grady the experience of the depression of the 1890s, the accompanying Populist upheaval, and the near-destruction of the political structure the Redeemers had erected. Gordon was not so fortunate. He did not escape the turmoil of the 1890s that shook the foundations of the New South. When he died in 1904, it was probably too early to realize that the handiwork of the Redeemers remained largely intact.

Much of it still does.

19

A Different South Emerges

Rails, Mills, and Towns

—————— ❖ ——————

T he disputants paced off the required distance, turned, fired their pistols, missed, shook hands, and departed. For 1889, it was a peculiar way to conduct business, even in the South. The incident involved more than a momentary revival of the antebellum practice of dueling. The principals were J. D. Williamson, president of the Chattanooga, Rome, and Columbus Railroad, and Patrick Calhoun, senior legal counsel for the Richmond and West Point Terminal Railroad and grandson of John C. Calhoun. Calhoun wanted Williamson to sell his railroad to the Richmond Terminal. Williamson refused.

The issues involved more than the fate of two railway companies. They were part of a much larger story: the development of a modern transportation system in the region and the evolution of a South that was more urban and industrial. Railroads came first: they formed the superstructure of the economy of the New South. They were the elemental precondition to better times.

Railroad mileage in the South doubled between 1865 and 1880. Then it more than tripled between 1880 and 1900. The latter rate of expansion far exceeded that in the rest of the country. Obviously the New South had contracted the railroad mania of the nineteenth century, and for good reasons.

Railroads offered solutions to the geographical barriers that segmented the South and made economic development there difficult in many areas.

Mountain ranges. The Appalachians and the Ozarks are the major mountain ranges of the South. The southern Appalachians are composed of the Blue Ridge, Cumberland, and Great Smoky Mountains. They impose themselves between the Southeast and the Ohio Valley and fragment large areas of Kentucky, Tennessee, Virginia, North Carolina, and Georgia. The Ozarks separate much of Arkansas and Missouri.

Pine and sand barrens.   The piedmont is separated from the coastal plains and seaports by stretches of land so sandy that it will support little but pine and scrub oak, except where rivers have left deposits of rich soil.

The fall line.   Along a line stretching across the piedmont from Virginia to Mississippi, rivers fall to coastal plains. Above the fall line, few rivers are navigable.

The semiarid grasslands.   The most prominent geographical features of Texas and Oklahoma are semiarid grasslands. Beyond lies the desert of the Southwest, which southern commerce must traverse if it is to reach the West Coast and the Pacific.

The Florida peninsula.   The Florida land mass runs for more than 400 miles from north to south, reaches 150 miles at its widest point, and has few navigable waterways.

Railroads also supplemented navigable rivers and river systems. The most important of these rivers are those of the Chesapeake region; those of the southeastern coastal plain from Wilmington, North Carolina, to Savannah; the Ohio, Tennessee, and Cumberland rivers; and of course, the Mississippi and its tributaries, the Missouri, Arkansas, and Red rivers. Eventually, railroads reduced most of these and other navigable waterways to secondary, though not insignificant, roles in transportation. Railroads also traversed waterways, including the bayous of Louisiana and Mississippi.

Furthermore, railroads helped translate economic potential into economic reality. They hastened the spread of cotton culture into areas where cotton would not otherwise have been grown profitably because of inadequate transportation. Without railways, the development of most of the interior cities and towns of the South, the southern textile and lumber industries, the cattle industry, the coal and iron regions of Kentucky, Tennessee, Georgia, and Alabama, and the oil fields of Texas, Louisiana, Arkansas, and Oklahoma would have been much delayed. And this list could be much longer.

Railroads also expanded rapidly because they had clear advantages over the alternate means of transportation then available for great areas of the South that lacked ready access to usable waterways. Trains offered speed, flexibility as to location, and less vulnerability to droughts, floods, and other "acts of God." Over time, railroad freight rates declined markedly. Though freight rates on waterways were lower still, rail transportation often cost less in the long run because trains offered better services for most shippers. Rapid transit of people, products, and raw materials offered the cost advantages of speed and efficiency. Moreover, advances in the design and construction of rails, engines, cars, and terminal facilities increased railroad productivity. So did improvements in managerial and accounting techniques, air brakes, refrigerated cars, and the adoption of the standard gauge (the distance between rails). Fully implemented in the United States in the 1880s, the standard gauge made a national, interconnected rail system possible and facilitated the integration of the South into the then developing national market.

Given the advantages railroads offered, railroad mania was understandable. No one should be without a railroad—so thought legions of city fathers, town elders, county notables, farmers, manufacturers, and virtually everyone else. Communities lived in dread of being bypassed by the railroad, of being excluded from the Iron Age. Narrower interests, as usual, played their part, too. Hope of handsome profits from land sales to railroads quickened the pulse of landowners. Visions of fortunes to be made from developing land, timber, minerals, factories, and new markets had a similar effect. Other people could and often did make substantial sums by building railroads and by manipulating railway stocks and bonds.

The result was too much of a good thing. Railroads seemed to be everywhere in the South. By 1890 more than 300 companies operated in the South, though only about sixty of them owned as much as 100 miles of track. Steady profits or an acceptable return on invested capital proved elusive. Characteristically, railways had high fixed costs. Moreover, the South presented some peculiar vexations. It had fewer capital resources and a weaker economy than did other regions. The South also had a low population density. In 1900 Massachusetts had seven times, New York three times, and Ohio two times more people per square mile than Tennessee, the most densely populated southern state. The dominance of agriculture in the South hurt southern railroads. Farm products created highly seasonal demands on transportation that peaked at harvesttime and fell sharply thereafter. Farm products could not bear heavy transportation charges as easily as highly processed products, like machine tools. Neither could first-stage processed raw materials, such as timber, pig iron, and coarse textiles, which were the principal manufactured products of the New South. In comparison with other American railroads, those in the South had some cost advantages, such as lower prices for land and labor, but not enough to offset the regional disadvantages. Thus railways in the South experienced more financial crises than those elsewhere. Railways made critical contributions to the evolution of the New South, but they also increased its vulnerability to economic fluctuations. That weakness became especially apparent in the 1890s.

RAILROAD EMPIRES

No one should have been surprised when the financially fragile, overbuilt southern rail network nearly collapsed during the economically turbulent 1890s. Companies that controlled 13,000 miles of track (about half the total mileage in the South) went bankrupt. Hard times hastened the already ongoing process of consolidation of southern lines. By 1902, rail systems that owned more than three-fifths of the lines in the South were established: the Baltimore and Ohio; the Norfolk and Western; the Atlantic Coastline; the Seaboard Airline; the Southern Railway; the Louisville and Nashville, the Illinois Central; the Missouri Pacific; the Missouri, Kansas, and Texas; the Sante Fe; the Texas and Pacific; and the Southern Pacific. Still, rail mileage increased very substantially after 1900 in several southern states: Florida, Louisiana, Arkansas, Texas, and Oklahoma.

The emergence of extensive railroad empires introduced southerners, like other Americans, to the mixed blessings of the Gilded Age and its most important offspring, the corporation. Railroads "were the first American business to work

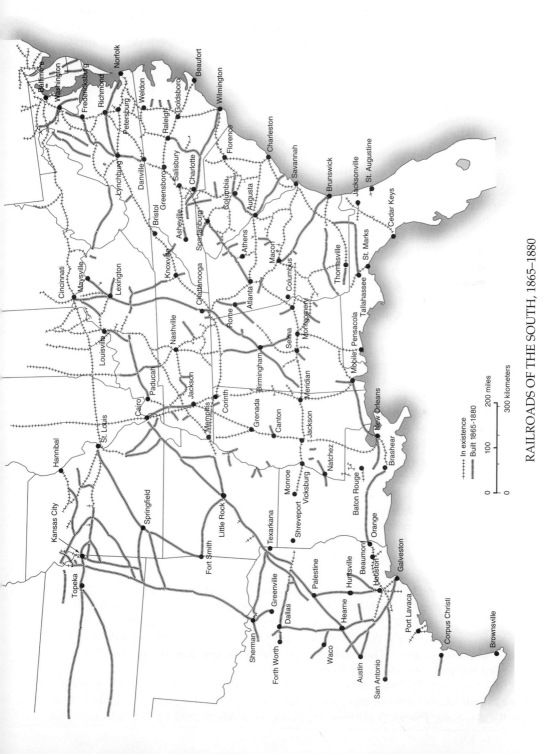

RAILROADS OF THE SOUTH, 1865–1880

out the modern ways of finance, management, labor relations, competition, and government regulation."

Their size alone troubled Americans. Big business, it ought to be remembered, was just making its appearance in the United States. Standard Oil and Carnegie Steel, for example, were young concerns. Railroad officials took on the appearance and some of the reality of emperors. They had command over critically needed services and enormous assets. They became heavily involved in politics, not always willingly. Given the nature of the business, they could hardly have done otherwise. The Illinois Central, for instance, became one of the major issues in Mississippi politics. So did the Louisville and Nashville in Kentucky and Alabama. Some saw the hand of the L&N in the notorious Goebel affair in Kentucky, where state elections resulted in two state governments, mountaineer vigilantes roamed the state capital, and the newly elected governor, William Goebel, was assassinated in 1899. In Alabama, regulation of railroads in general and of the L&N in particular dominated the political scene for years.

Railroad leaders were semipublic figures if not quite household names. Among the most notable and notorious were John Inman of the L&N and the Richmond Terminal, Henry W. Flagler of the Florida East Coast Line and pioneer of Florida's tourist industry, Jay Gould of the Missouri Pacific and the Texas and Pacific, Milton Hannibal Smith of the L&N, Collis P. Huntington of the Southern Pacific, and last but certainly not least, J. P. Morgan, who orchestrated the creation of the Southern Railway.

The name of Morgan suggests one of the profound changes that occurred in American railroading in the last years of the nineteenth century. Control passed to the men who were able to supply the capital needed by the increasingly large rail companies—northern, mainly New York, capitalists. The railroads' enormous need for capital helped centralize and institutionalize the nation's investment markets in New York.

Thus most southern railroads fell under the control of absentee capitalists. Their interests and those of the railroads and of the users of rail services were not necessarily the same. Jay Gould, to cite an extreme example, reputedly built a fortune of at least $75 million by manipulating railway stocks and bonds and by being indifferent to the sound construction, regular maintenance, and good service of the companies he controlled. A recent biography, however, paints a more positive picture of Gould as a businessman and entrepreneur.

More important, because of the company's size, were the games of high finance played by the Richmond Terminal. Richmond Terminal was a holding company—that is, a company that has a controlling interest in other companies but does not own their physical assets. Byzantine in its organization, Richmond Terminal involved plots within plots. Composed of 105 train lines, it had 8,500 miles of track in 1891, 27 executive committees, a $9 million debt, inadequate revenues, and such a tangle of accounting systems that statements of profit and loss had a fictional quality. The early shock waves of the depression of the 1890s knocked the tottering structure over.

The Southern Railway replaced the Richmond Terminal in 1894, embracing most of the components of the old Terminal company. The Southern launched itself by adopting the $375 million financing plan developed by J. P. Morgan and

Company, the nation's premier financial banking firm. Perhaps only Morgan's name and financial genius could have built what became a strong, stable company out of the chaos of the Richmond Terminal. The house of Morgan clearly thought highly of its services. It received $750,000 in stock for its work and $100,000 for expenses. Morgan also got effective control for some years over a railroad that extended from New York to New Orleans, from Jacksonville to Memphis and Cincinnati. Before 1900 the Southern began its very profitable career.

But size and the existence of powerful, often distant, sometimes irresponsible owners were not enough to explain the fear and anger railroads often aroused in the South. Railroads provided an essential service. Their customers were uncomfortably dependent on them, and many railroads had a monopolistic relationship with their customers. The opportunity to charge excessive rates was there. Undoubtedly that opportunity was seized. Shippers often asserted that they were defenseless victims of metallic monsters. Of the aggrieved parties, farmers had the best case. Studies suggest that farmers benefited the least from the lower transportation costs railways brought. Farmers operated very close to the margin during those years, so they were extremely sensitive to real and imagined grievances. Farmers repeatedly vented their anger at railroads and railroad officials, especially during hard times. When farm prices fell in the late 1880s, the Southern Farmers' Alliance demanded "the most rigid, honest, and just state and national control and supervision of public . . . transportation." If that did not work, then the Alliance called for public ownership of railroads. In 1892 the political legatees of the Alliance, the Populists, declared cogently: "We believe that the time has come when the railroad corporations will either own the people or the people must own the railroads." Farmers' discontent with railroads during the late nineteenth century helped make railroad rates one of the major political issues of the day. Whether and how to regulate railroads, monetary policy, banking, and the tariff were the most persistent political concerns of the time. The South had a vital stake in each.

Starting in the 1870s, every southern state passed legislation to create a railroad commission. And southerners played leading roles in writing and passing the Interstate Commerce Act of 1887. The act created the first federal regulatory agency, a landmark on the road America took in response to the modern corporate economy.

By 1900 the southern rail system was largely in place. Imposing physical expressions of the desire to transform the southern economy, railroads carried southerners into a world of corporations, captains of finance, and new forms of government support for and regulation of private enterprise. Rail systems allowed or encouraged the development of new areas, wove the South more tightly into national markets, and made the region and its inhabitants more susceptible to the good and bad fortunes of distant, faceless men and economic forces. J. D. Williamson resisted the persuasion and even the pistols of Patrick Calhoun that day in 1889. But bankruptcy got him and his company.

The Richmond Terminal bought out Williamson's Chattanooga, Rome, and Columbus Railroad in 1890. Four years later, the company regained its independence, but then sold out to the Central of Georgia in 1901. The railroads were full of the promise (and some of the reality) of better days and full of dangers (real and imagined) that seemed beyond the ability of individuals to understand or control. The railroad carried southerners into the Gilded Age, if belatedly. Most wanted to go even if they were not sure where the trip would end.

INDUSTRY IN THE NEW SOUTH

"The time was when the South was exclusively agricultural in its pursuits, but the past few years have seen factories spring up all over the section." It was not quite that way. It seldom is. But the editor of the *Americus (Georgia) Recorder* ought to be forgiven his hyperbole. He had succumbed to the exhilaration many southerners understandably felt as the South recovered first from the Civil War and its aftermath and then from the depression of the 1870s and began a period of substantial growth in the 1880s. Moreover, the editor had correctly sensed the emergence of a South very different from its antebellum predecessor. The South had adopted a new course since 1865; it no longer was willing to stake virtually everything on agriculture.

Just as important was the shape that industrial expansion took in the New South. The basic contours of the New South were molded by the fundamental characteristics of its industrialization. First, its industry was based primarily on the processing, often through only the first stages, of the raw materials of the region, materials from forests, mines, and farms. Second, such industries typically rely on low-skill, low-wage labor. The work is usually repetitive, exhausting, and sometimes unhealthy and dangerous. Third, resource-processing industries also are usually dispersed geographically. Consequently, while southern industrial development after 1880 did stimulate urbanization, that urbanization usually took the form of small towns and small cities. Last, southern manufacturing firms, especially those that needed large injections of capital, characteristically looked to sources outside the region. There were exceptions, of course. William Gregg, Edwin M. Holt, and Daniel Pratt, for instance, used their large profits from the Civil War to expand their cotton mills in South Carolina, North Carolina, and Alabama, respectively. In fact, much of the postbellum expansion of southern cotton manufacturing was financed within the region. More usual was the experience of Henry Fairchild de Bardeleben. He was an Alabamian and a stereotypical Gilded Age American businessman, given to uttering maxims about "the survival of the fittest." The son-in-law of Daniel Pratt and heir to his fortune, de Bardeleben envisioned an empire of coal and iron in northern Alabama. He, James W. Sloss, and Truman H. Aldrich—known later as the "captains of the Old Guard of Birmingham"—founded the Pratt Coal and Coke Company in 1878. Three years later they sold it, and in 1886 de Bardeleben built the de Bardeleben Coal and Iron Company with the assistance of capital from London and Baltimore. Within five years the Tennessee Coal, Iron, and Railroad Company (TCI) beat de Bardeleben in a financial war and took over his company. In 1907 United States Steel bought out TCI. Such chains of events illustrate the dependent nature of the industry and the economy of the South and fit with allegations that the North had imposed a "colonial economy" on the South. Here rhetoric parted with reality. (See page XXX for an analysis of the "colonial economy" as a concept.)

FOREST PRODUCTS

As they had done since earliest colonial settlement, southern forests provided materials for a variety of products. Pine trees were tapped for resin and burned for a residue of tar. Resin was distilled into turpentine and rosin. Forest products were used in paints, varnishes, medicines, chemicals, industrial processing, and soap- and papermaking. For many years farmers made tar from pine and "turpentined" as subsidiary activities. This form of domestic manufacturing gave way well before 1900 to larger, company-run operations. After that, turpentiners were usually black males whose existence often resembled serfdom or peonage. Also before 1900, North Carolina lost its leadership in the forest products industry, first to South Carolina, then to Florida. The industry was small in money terms. The value of its products was only $5.9 million in 1880 and $12.3 million in 1900.

Lumbering gained importance after 1800 and overshadowed the naval stores industry. By 1900 lumbering overshadowed all other industry in the South: it was the largest industry in the region. The demand for southern yellow pine exploded when northern white pine became scarce toward the end of the nineteenth century. Chauncey W. Depew, for one, saw the South as "the Bonanza of the future," with "vast forest untouched" and "enormous veins of coal and iron." The prominent New York Republican, chieftain in the Vanderbilt railway system, and favorite on the banquet circuit, declaimed: "Go south, young man."

Many went, especially after Congress opened federally owned lands in the South without restriction and on a cash basis. The Illinois Central ran special

SAWDUST EMPIRE (Stephen F. Austin, State University Library)

trains to Louisiana and Mississippi to accommodate the rush. When a decade of land speculation ended in 1888, almost 5.7 million acres of federal land in southern states had been sold. By then it must have been almost impossible to remember that Congress had originally intended that much of this land should go to former slaves. At the same time, Florida sold Hamilton Disston of Philadelphia 4 million acres for 25 cents an acre. The Florida legislature endorsed railroad grants with such enthusiasm and personal greed that its arithmetic did not add up. Out of a public domain of 15 million acres, the legislature made grants of 22 million acres. Texas was not to be outdone. It granted railroads 32.4 million acres of state lands, along the way squandering that part of the public domain that had been set aside for the benefit of public education. Groups of capitalists, especially from northern states and England, consumed enormous portions—196,000 acres went to some Chicagoans, 2 million acres to one English syndicate, 1.3 million acres of Mississippi's enormously fertile delta land to Phillips, Marshall, and Company of London. "The living embodiment of the Lost Cause," General John B. Gordon, served as broker for this last transaction. Warnings about environmental consequences were dismissed as "immeasurably stupid" while, in the opinion of one expert forester, "probably the most rapid and reckless destruction of forest known to history" took place. Southern forests provided approximately 1.5 billion board feet of yellow pine in 1869, 2.7 billion in 1879, and 9.7 billion in 1899. By 1910 Louisiana, Mississippi, Arkansas, Texas, and North Carolina had joined Washington and Oregon as the nation's leading lumber-producing states.

Lumber companies in the South followed the mobile, dispersed, and highly wasteful patterns so long practiced by the industry in the United States. Companies hacked their way through forests in a great arc from the Southeast to the Southwest. By 1916, production in the South rose to 20.5 billion board feet. Lumbering left vast stretches of cutover land throughout much of the South. Fragile soils and wildlife suffered devastating losses. Ecological systems were threatened. Yet by 1892 Gifford Pinchot, later a major figure in the American conservation movement, had begun the first application of scientific forestry in the United States. Working at Biltmore, the estate of George W. Vanderbilt near Asheville, North Carolina, Pinchot set out to demonstrate "the ability to produce favorable money results, while improving the forest. . . . In other words, forester and lumberman must be combined." Pinchot exhibited his North Carolina work at the Columbian Exposition in Chicago in 1894. Four years later the Biltmore Forest School opened, the first of its kind in the South and one of the earliest in the nation. Although the natives called it Vanderbilt's Folly, Biltmore "became a mecca for advocates of scientific forestry and forest preservation."

Timber companies and sawmills offered backbreaking, dangerous, unhealthy, seasonal, low-wage work that usually involved a minimum of skill. Pinchot's crews earned the lordly sum of 90 cents to $1 a day. (Mules earned 75 cents.) Logging and lumber companies usually hired young men, poor white and black, who lived in the available housing—often company-owned, isolated, and crude. Companies also generally owned the stores, virtually the sole source of supply for food and other necessities. Such circumstances invited abuse. So did the fact that half of the highly dependent labor force was black. In 1900 lumbering employed one-fifth of the industrial workers of the South.

Demand for and exploitation of southern hardwoods followed a course comparable to that of southern pines. Much of the hardwood became furniture. Southern furniture manufacturing reached a landmark in 1884 when it established itself at High Point, North Carolina, the future center of southern furniture making. The proximity of raw materials and low-cost labor played a familiar causal role in this development. Another forest-product industry, pulp and paper, did not become significant in the South until after 1920.

METALS AND MINERALS

The southern states possessed a number of important metals, but their utility depended on their profitability. That was determined by the quantity and quality of the minerals, accessibility to adequate, affordable transportation and technology, and market demands. Iron and coal contributed the most by far to southern incomes before 1900. After that, petroleum began to challenge their leadership. Other minerals—phosphates, clays, and salt, for example—played lesser roles.

Almost all the southern states had iron ore, and by 1860 most had small blast furnaces, bloomeries, and forges to convert the ore into pit, cast, and wrought iron. The last could be shaped into a wide range of useful items. In addition, there were rolling mills, rail mills, and naileries. On the eve of the Civil War, southern iron production accounted for 15 percent (125,000 tons) of the nation's total production. The war stimulated rapid expansion of the industry, in particular at the Tredegar Iron Works in Richmond and at ironworks in Selma and Shelby, Alabama. Those operations also attracted Union troops, who made a shambles of the southern iron industry. Tredegar made the most rapid recovery, but the future lay elsewhere.

The southern iron industry shifted to larger, more efficient operations and to western Virginia, eastern Tennessee, and especially, central Alabama after 1865. The Elyton (Alabama) Land Company declared itself to be in the business of city building in January 1871: "The city to be built . . . shall be called Birmingham," after Birmingham, England, center of the English iron industry. Other land developers joined in. They, too, knew about the rich iron ore, coal, and limestone deposits in central Alabama, which provided the material basis for "Magic City." An Alabamian remembered that when she first saw the site of Birmingham "there were only two . . . houses . . . nothing else. But my husband pointed up the long valley. 'There lies Birmingham,' he said; 'all that is going to be Birmingham some day.' And he spread his arms out to take in the whole country." "Colonel" James R. Powell, president of the Elyton company and first mayor of Birmingham, got the county seat relocated to Birmingham and reportedly got the New York Press Association to meet there before Birmingham was even listed on any map. A surprise awaited the New Yorkers: "Marshes and mud roads everywhere and yellow pine shacks and a box car for a depot, and gamblers and traders all over the globe. A man had to drink a full quart of whiskey before he could see what Powell said was there."

So valuable was the iron and coal region of northern Alabama that it ignited railroad and industrial wars. Struggles to gain rail access to the region shaped

Alabama politics from the end of the Civil War throughout much of Reconstruction. The Louisville and Nashville Railroad beat back the Alabama and Chattanooga and emerged as the principal railroad in the region. Then, guided by Albert Fink, one of the masterminds of American railroading, the L&N bought 500,000 acres of central Alabama to become the "great empire builder of the Alabama mineral region."

In 1881 John H. Inman, "a Southern carpetbagger in Wall Street" who was closely associated with the L&N, formed a group that bought the Tennessee Coal and Railroad Company, reorganized it, and renamed it the Tennessee Coal, Iron, and Railroad Company. TCI entered Alabama in 1886 and began buying up deposits of coal and iron, coking facilities, and blast furnaces. By 1891 it had captured first place in the region. Other companies pursued a similar course. By 1900, mergers created four large corporations—Sloss-Sheffield Iron and Steel Company, the Republic Iron and Steel Company, the Woodward Iron Company, and TCI—that dominated ironmaking in central Alabama. Absentee ownership was another sign of the times. More than 95 percent of TCI shares were owned by New Yorkers or New Englanders. Then in 1907 J. P. Morgan arranged for the purchase of TCI by U.S. Steel.

From 1880 to 1900, southern iron production grew from 397,000 tons to nearly 2 million tons, about 20 percent of total national production. Alabama accounted for more than 60 percent of southern production. By 1900 Birmingham was the largest exporter of pig iron in the United States and the third largest in the world. Southern ironmakers enjoyed lower costs, especially for iron ore and coke and labor. In some years TCI had a peculiar advantage in labor costs. Well connected with such leading Tennessee Redeemers as Governor John C. Brown and Arthur S. Colyar, editor of the Nashville *American,* the company got to lease the entire population of the state penitentiary for use in its coal mines. After visiting the mines in 1886, the U.S. Commissioner of Labor reported: "Wretched surroundings, bad management, appalling death rate. The prison system in all ways atrocious. . . . But the state makes a large profit from its convict labor."

Cheap labor—convict or not—may have been a mixed blessing. It may have reduced costs in some respects, but it slowed investment in new machinery and the adoption of new techniques. Transportation costs were also higher for the southern industry. Other problems were more important, however. The industry had a late start: it had to compete with more experienced, much stronger industries. The quality of the ore used by Alabama ironmakers was inferior to that found in the famed Mesabi Range in Minnesota and was more difficult to extract. Ironmakers in the South also confronted weaker demand for the products in their region than others had elsewhere.

The southern iron industry relied heavily upon technical and managerial expertise from outside the region and had heavy capital costs. Unlike lumbering and cotton manufacturing, two staples of the New South, the iron industry required large amounts of capital. Thus it lacked the capital necessary to adopt the latest technology or to expand enough to enjoy fully the economies of scale then achievable. Although TCI began to make steel in 1899, for instance, it did not have the resources to build the facilities that would have allowed it to make steady profits from steelmaking. Only after U.S. Steel took over TCI and made its capital resources available did steelmaking become a major industry in the South.

Federal banking and monetary policies compounded the difficulties of those borrowing capital. The protective tariff policies of the American government did aid industries that had international competitors. Given the problems the iron industry—and other developing industries—faced in the South, their success was notable, though it did not achieve all the magic that Birmingham boosters had envisioned.

Before 1860, coal was mined on a considerable scale in the border states of Maryland and Missouri and on a much smaller scale in several southern states. Post–Civil War industrial and urban growth in the United States stimulated demand for bituminous coal, of which southern Appalachia had a vast supply. That demand and the development of adequate transportation made mining in the region economically feasible. The New River coalfield in West Virginia opened when the Chesapeake and Ohio Railroad reached there in 1872. Some ten years later, the rich Pocahontas field along the Virginia–West Virginia border came into production after the Norfolk and Western Railroad penetrated the area. Only after 1900 was intensive coal mining introduced in eastern Tennessee and eastern Kentucky. Coal production in the southern states rose from about 7 million tons in 1880 to 52.8 million tons in 1900, or about one-fifth of the coal produced in the United States. Coal mining companies threw up company towns and hired blacks and whites. Most came from nearby, but some whites were immigrants from Europe. A crazy quilt of racial and ethnic patterns evolved, from segregation to a rough-hewn integration. Generally, though, blacks got the worst jobs and the least pay.

South Carolina enjoyed a short, small boom in minerals. Phospate mining grew rapidly in that state after 1880, reached its peak in 1890, and began to fade by 1900. By the last year Florida led the nation. It still does. Phosphate mining, however, never was a large industry. South Carolina, for example, earned only $2.9 million from phosphates in 1890; ten years later, those earnings had declined to a little more than $1 million. Thus, while phosphate was important to the economy of part of the South and was critical for agriculture, phosphate did not have the impact that iron ore had on Alabama or that oil was to have on Texas.

Work in phosphate was hazardous, though not so dangerous as coal mining. Workers, most of whom were black, had to clear the land, cut through to the phosphate, dig out the phosphate rock, convert the rock to liquid with water under high pressure, and then dry and process the mineral. Phosphate workers endured the rigors of heat, cold, and humidity and the dangers of chemical dust and emissions of toxic, potentially explosive gases.

Other mineral resources of the southern states became much more significant in the twentieth century. When cheap hydroelectric power became available and reduced the costs of making aluminum, the amount of bauxite being processed increased dramatically. However, commercial oil production had begun as early as the 1890s in Indian Territory (later Oklahoma), and interest in the Texas Gulf area was strong. Drillers hit an important field at Corsicana in 1894. People suspected there was more oil beneath the surface of the Gulf coast, but even the most optimistic oilmen had not imagined the likes of the Spindletop well near Beaumont. As the drill came closer and closer to the black underground lake in January 1901, the driller upped his production estimates. It might do better than the 50 barrels per day he originally predicted. It might reach 75 barrels. Then they struck oil. As a huge geyser sprayed them black, they celebrated a well that would produce 75,000 barrels a day. The year Spindletop came in, Ohio, Pennsylvania, West Virginia, California, and Indiana were the leading oil-producing states, and total oil production in the United States reached 210 million barrels. By 1920, it reached 443 million, and Texas, California, and Oklahoma led the nation in petroleum output.

The development of oil production in the Gulf coast quickly spread into Louisiana. Less than five years after Spindletop, major strikes in Oklahoma elevated the Mid-Continent (Oklahoma and Kansas) oil region into the nation's leadership position, at least for a while. Other major discoveries followed in succeeding years—West Texas, East Texas, Oklahoma City, El Dorado, Arkansas, and so forth. Fortunes were made and often lost. Personal incomes in the western region of the South improved significantly. Petroleum became the leading industry in Texas and Oklahoma. It helped lay the foundation for the economic and political power that pushed Texas to preeminence in the region and the nation.

The industry had a chaotic quality and ethos of its own. Prices rose and fell erratically as supply and demand seemed to be chronically disconnected. The "Wild West" of the cattle drives had vanished, but, to the delight or alarm of many, the "Wild West" reappeared in the oil boom towns that were thrown up overnight. Instant, haphazard towns of crude wooden structures and unpaved streets and crude "facilities" with hundreds of transient workers, "fancy" women, gamblers, and enterprising sorts proliferated. Law and order came later, sometimes with a style of its own. "You're interested in women?" Then the madam and former prostitute who worked oil towns told the interviewer from the Federal Writers' Project, "You should have been up in Three Sands [Oklahoma Territory] the day they cleaned us out. The U.S. [marshals] rounded up all of us and hired a train to ride us out on. They took us out in daytime. Three hundred whores hollering at every punk they'd seen and throwing their tails out the window when they'd pass through a town. They run us all over hell and dumped some out in Kansas and Arkansas and down in Texas."

Oil field work was done by men, was often dangerous, and was always dirty and exhausting. It lured the jobless and the adventurous, the skilled and the unskilled, despite its boom-bust cycles and considerable hazards. A longtime worker recalled that during the drilling of a well, a derrick fell and killed his father. "It mashed him and the other two men out like pancakes, killed 'em before they could even make a break and try to run out of the way of it. I wasn't but five at the time, but I remember we didn't get another look at him after he left home that morning; there wasn't enough left of him to show, so they nailed down the coffin before the funeral."

Oil fields attracted folks with a little money in hand and an urge to try their luck at drilling a well of their own. Most of them, sooner rather than later, were displaced by larger entrepreneurs. The latter included the familiar (and widely hated) Standard Oil Company and others that would become familiar—the Texas

Company (Texaco), Sun Oil, Gulf Oil, and Humble Oil (later known as Exxon). They had the large sums of money required to drill deep wells and to build pump stations, pipelines, and refineries. Their capital also obtained the means of shipping their products, including railroads, or at least railroad tank cars, and tanker ships.

Generally, the chemical industry grew little in the South before the middle of the twentieth century. One facet of the industry, however, developed early—patent medicine. Several factors encouraged the growth of the industry: poverty, the state of medical knowledge and practice, and a wide range of life-threatening and debilitating diseases for which there seemed to be no remedies. The all-too-common poverty of the South increased the hazards of birth, maternity, and childhood and forced people to have poor diets, to work and live in unhealthy and sometimes hazardous places, and to seek medical aid at the lowest cost. Given the state of medical knowledge and practice before 1900, people were probably wise to avoid most doctors and most hospitals. Yet where could they turn for relief from the ravages of tuberculosis, syphilis, typhoid, malaria, scarlet fever, diphtheria, whopping cough, hookworm, influenza and pneumonia, and cardiovascular diseases? In 1900, life expectancy at birth in the United States was 48.7 for white females, 46.6 for white males, 33.5 for nonwhite females, and 32.5 for nonwhite males. Presumably it was lower for all these groups in the South.

Under such circumstances, the promises of miracles from the makers of nostrums found a ready audience, and drug manufacturers spent large sums for advertising to reach that audience. Makers of patent medicines refined the art of consumer persuasion in the process. Newspaper readers could read almost daily about Berry's Creole Tea (naturally, a New Orleans product), "a perfect tonic" that "makes good blood and a beautiful complexion"; Duffy's Pure Malt Whiskey, which "cured" consumption (tuberculosis), depression, bronchitis, general debility, "La Grippe," malaria, colds, and exhaustion and weakness "from whatever causes"; and Dr. Williams's Pink Pills for Pale People. In addition to newspaper advertising, patent medicine companies churned out a flood of calendars and almanacs, sponsored traveling medicine shows, and papered and painted so many buildings, barns, fences, trees, and hillsides with posters and signs that they triggered a movement to save the landscape. No doubt the substantial quantities of alcohol, cocaine, and opium in these compounds helped sales. Many of the same newspapers that ran advertisements for nostrums also ran notices of private sanitariums that claimed they could cure addiction to alcohol, cocaine, and opium.

Such prominent Americans as Robert E. Lee, Ulysses S. Grant, and Mrs. Grover Cleveland endorsed products. A Mrs. L. L. Lindsay testified at length that Wine of Cardui, at $1 a bottle, had rid her of problems associated with menstruation. She also endorsed Thedford's Black Draught. The remedies so helpful to Mrs. Lindsay were the most profitable products of the most successful patent medicine company in the South, the Chattanooga Medicine Company, founded by two Union army veterans after the Civil War.

Farther to the south, Asa Griggs Candler joined the exodus from the farm to Atlanta, where in the 1880s he opened a wholesale and retail drug business and began some drug manufacturing. In 1891 he curtailed his drug business in order to concentrate on a new product: he had just purchased the rights to a newly formulated

CRUDE OIL PRODUCTION IN THE SOUTH, 1889–1997
(THOUSANDS OF BARRELS)

State	1889	1899	1909	1919	1929
Ark.					24,917
La.			3,060	17,188	20,554
Miss.					
Okla.			47,859	86,911	255,004
Tex.		669	9,534	79,306	296,876
United States	35,164	57,071	183,171	378,367	1,007,323

SOURCE: U.S. Bureau of the Census, *Statistical Abstracts, 1981* (Washington, D.C., 1981), p. 739; *Statistical Abstracts, 1992* (Washington, D.C., 1992), p. 697; *Statistical Abstracts, 1999* (Washington, D.C., 1999), p. 712; U.S. Department of Commerce, *Mineral Resources of the United States, 1929* (Washington, D.C., 1932), Pt. II, pp. 432–433; U.S. Department of the Interior, *Minerals Yearbook, 1940* (Washington, D.C., 1940), p. 954; U.S. Bureau of Mines, *Minerals Yearbook, 1949* (Washington, D.C., 1951), p. 874; U.S. Bureau of Mines, *Minerals Yearbook, 1959* (Washington, D.C., 1960), Vol. II, p. 352; U.S. Bureau of Mines, *Minerals Yearbook, 1969* (Washington, D.C., 1971), Vols. I–II, pp. 819–820.

headache remedy for $2,000. He soon transformed Coca-Cola, a carbonated beverage, into a drink that promised refreshment, not therapy, and laid down an advertising barrage behind the theme "Refreshingly delicious." Candler sold more than 35,000 gallons of Coca-Cola in 1892, a considerable improvement over the 25 gallons his predecessors had sold in 1886. By 1900, more than 370,000 gallons were sold, some as far away as the Pacific states. Forays into the European market had already begun. Such aggressiveness helps explain why the company sold more than 6.5 million gallons of the liquid refresher in 1912.

*P*ROCESSED FARM PRODUCTS

From 1880 to 1900, manufacturing of materials from southern forests and mines grew in output, but it was dwarfed by the output from processing of farm products. Cotton, of course, led the way, followed by tobacco, then rice and sugar.

The location and methods of rice cultivation and processing in the South changed dramatically after 1880. In that year South Carolina and Georgia led Louisiana in the production and processing of rice. Ten years later the situation was almost reversed. Seaman A. Knapp brought his pioneering ideas about agriculture to the South in the late 1880s. The Iowan, best known for the battle he led against the cotton boll weevil, persuaded farmers in southwestern Louisiana to plant field rice, which they irrigated with water from wells and nearby bayous. Field rice had greater resistance to insects and disease than paddy-grown rice. The soil in the area was better for rice than was the soil of the coastal Southeast, and it also allowed the introduction of heavier machinery than could be used in the coastal rice-growing areas. The use of heavy machinery was the most important of several factors in farmers' ability to increase production while reducing costs. This fortuitous combination helps explain the rapidity with which rice production shifted to Louisiana and then to adjacent areas in Texas and Arkansas. By

CRUDE OIL PRODUCTION IN THE SOUTH, 1889–1997
(THOUSANDS OF BARRELS) *(cont.)*

1939	1949	1959	1969	1979	1989	1997
21,143	29,936	26,329	18,049	19,000	11,000	8,000
93,869	19,715	354,611	844,603	494,000	154,000	134,000
	37,966	47,928	64,283	37,000	30,000	21,000
160,072	151,902	196,487	224,729	194,000	124,000	83,000
484,527	743,990	983,840	1,157,775	1,013,000	686,000	537,000
1,264,256	1,840,307	2,574,590	3,371,751	3,115,000	2,779,000	2,355,000

1900, Louisiana companies cleaned and polished about two-thirds, or $5.7 million of $8.7 million, of the rice grown in the United States.

Louisiana continued its long-held leadership in domestic sugar production, and by 1900 was second only to New York in sugar refining. Demand outstripped supply, however, even though southern sugar output increased from about 130,000 short tons in the 1880s to about 350,000 in 1900. Americans ate about 73 pounds of sugar per person per year. Because more than 80 percent of that sugar came from abroad, where costs were very low, Louisiana sugar growers operated with narrow profit margins. Low sugar prices and rising labor costs forced the growers to invest heavily in machinery, to rely increasingly on the railroads that penetrated the sugar regions after 1880, to search for and practice the best farming methods, and to form a tightly knit growers' association.

Among its several activities, the Louisiana Sugar Planters' Association effectively encouraged agricultural experiment stations and better refining and marketing techniques. Large-scale engine-powered, centrally located sugar milling and refining replaced the older pattern of widely dispersed, horse-powered operations. Around the turn of the century the association lost ground in its efforts to maintain protective tariffs against imported sugar. The annexation of Hawaii and Puerto Rico in 1898 and a 1903 trade treaty with newly independent Cuba meant that Louisiana sugar would face even stiffer competition.

Meatpacking, leather making, flour milling, and distilling in the South remained small and localized. But here, as in the processing of several other major farm products, such as dairy products, the output of the Midwest far exceeded that of the South. Georgia and Virginia manufactured a modest number of agricultural implements. Kentucky, however, established itself as the nation's leading producer of bourbon.

TOBACCO MANUFACTURING

The manufacture of tobacco and cotton products had a much greater impact on the South than did the processing of any other agricultural product. Americans in 1860 dipped, smoked, and mostly chewed tobacco. Smokers preferred cigars and

CHAPTER 19

TOBACCO PRODUCTION IN THE SOUTH, 1850–1997
(THOUSANDS OF POUNDS)

State	1850	1860	1870	1880	1890	1900	1910
Ala.	165	233	153	452	162	312	91
Ark.	219	990	595	970	955	832	316
Fla.	999	829	157	21	470	1,126	3,506
Ga.	424	919	289	229	264	1,106	1,486
Ky.	55,501	108,127	105,306	171,121	221,880	314,288	398,482
La.	27	40	16	56	47	102	172
Md.	21,407	38,411	15,785	26,082	12,357	24,589	17,845
Miss.	50	159	61	415	62	63	19
Mo.	17,114	25,086	12,320	12,016	9,425	3,042	5,373
N.C.	11,985	32,853	11,150	26,986	36,375	127,503	138,813
S.C.	74	104	35	46	223	19,896	25,583
Tenn.	20,149	43,448	21,465	29,365	36,368	49,158	68,757
Tex.	67	98	60	221	176	550	162
Va.	56,803	123,968	37,086	79,989	48,523	122,885	132,979
W. Va.	Incl. in Va.	Incl. in Va.	2,046	2,296	2,602	3,087	14,356
Totals	184,984	375,265	206,522	350,265	369,889	668,539	807,940

SOURCE: C. L. Gupton, "Tobacco," *The Encyclopedia of Southern History*, David C. Roller and Robert W. Twyman, eds. (Baton Rouge, La., 1979), p. 1237; U.S. Bureau of the Census, *Agricultural Statistics, 1981* (Washington, D.C., 1982), p. 99; U.S. Bureau of the Census, *1987 Census of Agriculture* (Washington, D.C., 1987), Vol. I, Table 25, *passim*. U.S. Bureau of the Census, *Census of Agriculture*, Vol. 1, Table 13, *passim*.

pipes, in that order. Cigarettes had only recently begun to gain popularity. Southern farmers produced nearly one-half of the more than 434 million pounds of tobacco grown in the country, much of it for export. Three border states (Kentucky, which alone provided one-fourth of the nation's output, Maryland, and Missouri) and the southern states accounted for 86 percent of the tobacco grown in the United States when Abraham Lincoln went to the White House. National output grew slightly in the next twenty years, but not in the South. There, output declined appreciably, as it did in Maryland and Missouri. Kentucky, however, increased its production by 60 percent, a clear indication that burley, a darker, stronger-tasting tobacco that grew well there, still dominated the market.

But a highly significant shift in the kinds of tobacco grown and consumed was occurring. That shift had a major impact on several areas in the South and in the border states and was a critical factor in the development of two major corporations with southern origins, American Tobacco and R. J. Reynolds. The shift had its beginnings in a Dixie version of a true-to-life Horatio Alger story. Reportedly, Union and Confederate troops, quartered in and around the railroad hamlet of Durham, North Carolina, when General Joseph E. Johnston surrendered to General William T. Sherman in 1865, "borrowed" some tobacco from local tobacco farmers and processors. They liked it. When they got home, they wanted more,

TOBACCO PRODUCTION IN THE SOUTH, 1850–1997
(THOUSANDS OF POUNDS) *(cont.)*

1920	1930	1940	1950	1959	1969	1980	1987	1997
2,031	357	296	356	492	815	826	665	541
267	95	82	34	23	2	0	0	NA
4,474	9,248	20,322	22,536	23,413	24,142	20,343	12,615	16,192
10,585	82,364	94,409	102,505	98,308	94,625	110,550	65,722	85,790
504,662	376,649	324,518	404,881	335,099	375,549	416,962	336,364	505,258
221	81	374	257	74	91	56	15	NA
17,337	21,624	28,209	35,533	32,568	24,771	22,035	13,752	11,987
726	5	17	0	3	1	0	0	NA
4,075	4,549	5,470	5,237	4,295	4,963	5,263	3,654	6,431
280,163	454,223	715,616	661,982	654,439	674,932	761,705	478,051	703,559
71,193	83,303	118,963	61,263	81,255	129,169	125,450	87,431	125,220
112,368	112,237	109,423	127,324	120,653	111,492	111,981	85,716	106,785
27	8	3	0	0	0	0	0	NA
102,391	115,826	136,754	124,904	127,706	117,548	106,791	80,583	115,735
7,587	5,362	2,166	3,756	2,976	3,109	2,250	2,159	2,737
1,118,107	1,265,931	1,556,622	1,550,568	1,481,304	1,561,209	1,684,212	1,166,727	1,680,685

and they wrote back to Durham for the bright leaf tobacco they savored. This inadvertent advertising made tobacco and Durham synonymous.

The William T. Blackwell Company of Durham seized the initiative, especially after Julian Shakespeare Carr joined the firm. Blackwell and Carr produced a quality product with a memorable trademark, Bull Durham (for the Durham bull, a breeding animal noted for its quality in what was then a predominantly rural America). Mechanizing whenever possible, defending its trademark whenever necessary, and pursuing customers whenever and wherever possible, the Blackwell company enjoyed great success. Like other tobacco manufacturers, it had to confront an oversupply of competitors and a lack of built-in demand. (Unlike food or petroleum, as John D. Rockefeller understood, tobacco is not a necessity, though it may seem that way.) Tobacco manufacturers had to persuade people to use tobacco and their particular products. To do so, Blackwell and Carr spent as much as $150,000 annually for advertising in newspapers. They gave clocks to customers, got testimonials from notables, and plastered pictures of the Durham bull throughout the United States and in parts of Europe and Asia. The Blackwell company built "the largest smoking-tobacco factory in the world," a physical expression of the dominance of the company.

Nearby, Washington Duke and his sons, Benjamin and James Buchanan "Buck" Duke, watched with fascination, envy, and mounting despair. Though their company, W. Duke and Sons, had done well, Buck Duke concluded that the Dukes "faced a stone wall," that they were overmatched by Bull Durham, and

JAMES B. DUKE (Courtesy Duke University Library)

that they had to find a new product. In 1881 they recruited about a hundred cigarette makers from New York, most of whom were European immigrants. Then,
three years later, Duke became the first company to use the Bonsack cigarette machine, the first practical machine for manufacturing cigarettes. The Bonsack immediately reduced the cost of production from 80 cents per thousand cigarettes to
30 cents. Within a year, most of the cigarette makers returned to New York. Within
two years, Duke's cigarette production jumped 600 percent. Possessed of intense
drive, a competitive urge that strained the bonds of civility, and most important,
nearly exclusive control of the Bonsack machine, Buck Duke, along with Ben
Duke and J. W. Watts, built an empire. William T. O'Brien, a machinist and mechanical genius in Duke's employ, contributed greatly to the firm's success by
perfecting the Bonsack. Duke marketed with fury and flourish. In the late 1880s
he spent as much as $800,000 a year on advertising, including packages embel-
lished by pictures of lovely ladies and sponsorship of touring hockey teams that
competed on roller skates. Duke's success, however, may have been attributable
primarily to the fact that he was the first tobacco manufacturer to adopt the centralized, departmentalized structure of the modern corporation. In 1890 Duke

joined its four other major competitors to form the American Tobacco Company, the "cigarette trust." Assuming that competition was bad for profits, the American Tobacco Company used the ample capital it amassed by the sale of cigarettes to make itself dominant in the manufacture of all tobacco products except cigars. American Tobacco also benefited from the fact that tobacco was virtually depression-proof. The company thrived during the 1890s despite the severe economic slump of 1893–1897.

Thorough mechanization of cigar making did not become possible until after 1920. Cigar making remained decentralized, carried on by a large number of small companies spread throughout the country. Several cigar factories opened in Tampa in the 1880s, when Spaniards who made cigars in Cuba moved their operations to Florida in order to escape the political and economic turmoil that resulted from Cuba's attempts to end Spanish colonial rule. Eager officials in Tampa subsidized these moves. Tampa had a favorable coastal location, recently acquired rail connections, and an expansive vision. But the heralded growth of the town's economy did not occur as rapidly as the heralds claimed it would. Tampa continued to look like the semitropical outpost it was. It had few houses and even fewer businesses, dirt streets, and alligators in the vicinity, some of whom were inclined to take nocturnal strolls through town. Understandably, the town fathers welcomed the cigar companies, even their Cuban workers. In time, Italian workers came, too. Tampa acquired an ethnic and religious diversity that was unusual in the South. That diversity found disharmonious expression on occasion, as when the Spanish-American War started, when labor and management had a series of bitter conflicts, and when native white Protestants tried to impose prohibition on the town. These disturbances did not, however, seriously hinder the rapid rise of Tampa as a cigar making center. By 1900 Florida led the South in this industry and ranked among the top ten states in the country in the production of America's favorite form of tobacco.

Before the 1880s, work in tobacco factories was seasonal; manufacturers usually suspended operations during the winter months. Most of the workers were black males. (Before 1865, slaves made up the majority of the workforce.) White men managed and supervised. Most of the tasks involved hand labor and a good deal of heavy lifting in hot, dirty, dusty workrooms. Sanitary facilities were crude, if they existed. Workers drank out of common ladles from open buckets and barrels. In *The Romance of a Plain Man* the novelist Ellen Glasgow caught the mood and atmosphere of the tobacco factory before it became heavily mechanized. Ben Starr, who worked as a messenger in a factory—doing, his boss said, "what a nigger can't do"—found the factory workroom intimidating.

At first the stagnant fumes of the dry lead mingling with the odours of so many tightly packed bodies caused me to turn suddenly dizzy, and the rows of shining black faces swam before my eyes in a blur with the brilliantly dyed turbans of the women. Then I gritted my teeth fiercely, the mist cleared, and I listened undisturbed to the melancholy chant which accompanied the rhythmic movements of the lithe brown fingers.

At either end of the room, which covered the entire length and breadth of the building, the windows were shut fast, and on the outside, close against the greenish panes, innumerable flies swarmed like a black curtain. Before the long troughs stretching waist high from wall to wall, hundreds of negroes stood ceaselessly stripping the dry leaves from the stems; and above the soft golden brown piles of tobacco, the blur of color separated into distinct and vivid splashes of red, blue, and orange. Back and forth in the obscurity these brilliantly colored turbans nodded like savage flowers amid a crowd of black faces, in which the eyes alone, very large, wide open, and with gleaming white circles around the pupils, appeared to me to be really alive and human. They were singing as we entered. . . . And it seemed to me as I stood there, half terrified by the close, hot smells and the savage colors, that something within me stirred and awakened like a secret that I had carried shut up in myself since birth. The music grew louder in my ears, as if I, too, were a part of it, and for the first time I heard clearly the words:—

> "Christ totes de young lambs in his bosom, bosom,
> Christ totes de young lambs in his bosom, bosom,
> Christ totes de young lambs in his bosom, bosom,
> Fa-ther, de ye-ar-ur Jubi-le-e! . . .
>
> "Christ leads de ole sheep by still watah, watah,
> Christ leads de ole sheep by still watah, watah,
> Christ leads de ole sheep by still watah, watah,
> Fa-ther, de ye-ar-ur Ju-bi-le-e!"

After the Civil War, tobacco manufacturers moved gradually to year-round operations as the industry grew, mechanized, and shifted its emphasis to smoking tobacco and cigarettes. Whites began to seek employment in the formerly black-dominated factories, and serious racial conflicts among workers followed. One such episode may have been the catalyst for the Danville "riot" of 1883. Blacks, however, continued to make up most of the workers in the older portions of the industry, and they filled the heaviest, dirtiest, and lowest-paying positions in the newer portions of the industry.

Clear race and gender patterns marked the cigarette plants as they became highly mechanized. White men supervised, and white men operated most of the newer, more complex machines. White women, most of them single, performed lighter, cleaner tasks. These jobs were highly repetitive, however, and the women were under a lot of pressure because their pay depended on meeting production quotas. Black women, most of whom were also single, had much less desirable tasks, such as stemming tobacco. Management went to considerable lengths to ensure that white female workers conducted themselves "properly" and were protected from sexual harassment. Employers did not show a comparable concern about black female workers. Black men performed menial and often very heavy work around the factories. Blacks and whites, particularly black men and white women, usually worked in different rooms.

Pay rates reflected these race and gender patterns. Wages for all were modest. Workers in North Carolina in 1879 averaged $101.25 for the year. Workers complained, individually and in groups. A skilled white male worker in Durham declared that his wages in 1887 were so small that he and his wife had trouble meeting their expenses. "We are not in as bad circumstances as some others in the locality," one of them said. "We do not expect to look for any heaven to lay up, but we want, when the time comes when one of our family is called away, to be able to go to the furniture store and purchase what we need to bury the dead."

Groups of workers registered protests in Richmond, Petersburg, and Durham in the 1880s and 1890s. The Knights of Labor attracted a following in these areas in the 1880s, and at the end of the 1890s the National Tobacco Workers Union had some success in the same areas. But racial divisions and economic vulnerability undermined unionization efforts and aborted most of the walkouts that occurred. Perhaps, as one longtime, black worker believed, scores would be evened by other means. Elviry Magee stemmed and graded tobacco for sixty years in Danville.

> I tell you one thing, I knows tobacco. I knows all de grades an' blends. I knows bright tobacco an' burley tobacco an' Kaintucky tobacco an' all de rest. You 'members Old Man Hughes what built all dese here schools an' horspitals in town? Well, I learnt Mister John how to grade tobacco when he first come in de factory. Yes, Jesus, I give Mister John his start. I'm po' now an' I was po' den but he come to be a rich man. But it didn't do him no good. De Lawd called him away wi' Bright's misery. I believes one reason was cause he didn't pay niggers nothin'. I was his best hand—he say so hisse'f—an' he didn't never pay me no mo'n fifty to sebenty-five cents a day.

Only cigar making had escaped the powerful hold of the American Tobacco Company when the Supreme Court dissolved the company in 1911. The attack on the American Tobacco Company was part of the larger war on "trusts" during the Progressive era. *Trusts* was a term loosely applied to various business structures devised to reduce or eliminate competition—pools, trusts, corporations. American Tobacco produced 85 percent of the plug tobacco, 76 percent of the pipe tobacco, and 86 percent of the cigarettes made in the United States. Moreover, it had cartel agreements with major foreign tobacco manufacturers. The nature of tobacco manufacturing lent itself to such a high degree of concentration. The Dukes, then the American Tobacco Company, built their power on the control of essential equipment. Virtually exclusive control of the Bonsack cigarette-making machine made a series of connections possible: from high profits to ample company-controlled capital to monopoly to even higher profits. Highly favorable returns on its investments allowed American Tobacco to advertise and mass market while undercutting its competitors. The monopoly came first in cigarette manufacturing, then in most other areas of tobacco manufacture. Great fortunes followed. From 1878 to 1908 the value of the Duke tobacco interests rose from $78,000 to $39 million.

Such success attracted a good deal of attention and vociferous criticism. More than envy accounted for the criticism. The American Tobacco Company attained its heights by means fair and foul. Competing manufacturing firms, wholesalers, and retailers had good reason to complain about the tactics of the American Tobacco Company. Tobacco farmers joined in, blaming the "tobacco trust" for what they believed were low prices for raw tobacco. Scholarship indicates, however, that the farmers may have been the only people in the tobacco business who had no real basis for their complaints against the Dukes and their associates.

Nor was the company helped by its attachment to the noxious weed. Opposition to tobacco had a long history. James I of England issued his *Counterblaste to Tobacco* in 1604, denouncing the "precious stink" as "loathsome to the eye, hatefull to the Nose, harmfull to the braine, dangerous to the Lungs," and a sin. In the 1890s the antitobacco movement revived itself and took particular aim at the cigarette. Centered in areas where bright leaf did not grow, the movement enlisted adults and children in singing, parading, sermonizing, and pamphleteering. City councils passed laws against selling cigarettes to minors and sometimes even to adults. A subsequent momentary decline in cigarette sales worried Buck Duke. But the antitobacco movement found the public no easier to persuade than had James I. Nor until possibly very recently has any antitobacco campaign enjoyed much success.

A more aggressive attack upon the tobacco trust occurred in the Black Patch, an area of prime tobacco-growing land in Kentucky and Tennessee near where the Tennessee and Ohio rivers join. Well-organized farmers and others from the area tried to raise the price farmers received by withholding their product from tobacco manufacturers. Those efforts took a violent turn in 1905 with the first of a series of arsons and dynamitings. Whippings and several murders followed. Noncooperating farmers and warehousemen and buyers for tobacco companies were prime targets, though in some instances, the vigilantism attracted new elements with a different agenda. Then blacks and those alleged to deviate from community standards of morality became targets.

Armed and organized and strongly supported in most of their communities, the vigilantes of the "Black Patch war" for some time survived the efforts of those law officers and courts that tried to stop them. Governor Augustus E. Willson, the second Republican to be elected governor of Kentucky since Reconstruction, declared that his state had "reached a stage of lawlessness where the constituted authorities were unable to make headway for the preservation of law and order." He recommended that individual citizens arm themselves against the Black Patch warriors. The wars reached a climax in 1908, going on only sporadically thereafter. The Black Patch war had little discernible effect upon the prices tobacco farmers received. In that respect, the wars were simply another failure of voluntary efforts to improve farm prices.

However, the attack on the tobacco trust in the federal courts was successful, or so it seemed. In 1911 the Supreme Court ordered the dissolution of the American Tobacco Company (and the Standard Oil Company of New Jersey) for being in violation of the Sherman Antitrust Act (1890). When the American Tobacco Company was dissolved by the Court, it was replaced by an oligopoly of companies that continued to dominate the industry. One of those firms, R. J. Reynolds, had an especially prosperous career after 1911.

The Dukes, who remained in control of the now smaller American Tobacco Company, had other interests by this time. They had started to invest in the development of hydroelectric power and in higher education in the South. They also put capital in banking, insurance, railroads, and textiles. Assured that money invested in cotton mills would earn "at the rate of 40% *net profits,*" the Dukes built the first of several large cotton mills in North Carolina in 1892.

COTTON MANUFACTURING

The tobacco barons, led in this case by Ben Duke, had again demonstrated their sense for finding lucrative opportunities. In doing so, they joined in a cotton-mill boom that had its origins in the late 1860s and reached fever pitch between 1880 and 1905. The number of active spindles rose from 11,898 to 32,266 to 110,000. (The spindle count is the most common, though admittedly crude, way of measuring the size of a textile industry. It is wise to note whether or not spindles are active in order to differentiate between active and idle industrial plants.) Between 1880 and 1900, consumption of raw cotton expanded sevenfold. The value of the southern cotton mills multiplied almost nine times, to a little more than $95 million; the amount of capital invested increased from $11.1 million to $124.6 million; and the number of workers rose from 16,714 to 97,494. These figures actually underestimate the growth in investment and output because they are expressed in current, not constant, dollars. Prices declined steadily and sometimes markedly in these years; consequently, the value of the dollar went up.

Cotton textiles dwarfed other major manufacturing industries in the South. Even when Maryland, West Virginia, and Missouri are included, the iron and steel industry of the South employed only 22,423 people and represented an investment of $44.7 million in 1900. At the same time, the tobacco industry employed a similar number of people and had an investment of $19.3 million. Cotton textiles required relatively small amounts of capital to start up and operate, especially in Gilded Age South, when cotton textile plants were usually small. Steel, by contrast, required a great deal more capital. That was a major reason the steel industry developed slowly in the South.

The U.S. Census Bureau noted in 1900 that the "growth of the [cotton textile] industry has been remarkably steady . . . , attended with not a little public excitement, . . . failures have been few, and upon the whole the return upon the investment in Southern cotton mills greatly exceeded that upon factories in the North."

Obviously, such growth reflected a substantial and growing demand for the coarse cottons the South manufactured. (Fabrics are calibrated, coarse to fine, according to the number of threads in a given unit of measure. Fine goods have more fibers per square inch and require more complex machinery and more skilled labor.) Southern mills made handsome profits while underselling domestic competitors. (High tariffs imposed by Congress prevented the import of fabrics except for very fine goods used only in luxury items.) Southern textile factories even did rather well during the severe depression of the 1890s, when northern textiles and most other industries faltered or collapsed. Southern mills sold most of their product domestically, but some had substantial foreign sales. Sixty percent of the cotton goods exported from the United States in 1900 came from southern factories. That year South Carolina exported over 45 percent of the production of its cotton mills. Government policies designed to expand foreign commerce received vigorous support from southern cotton manufacturers.

While strong, sustained demand was a great stimulant, advantages in critical items kept costs to southern cotton mills markedly lower than those of their older competitors to the north. Southern firms enjoyed a 7 to 8 percent differential in costs of materials and a 25 percent differential in labor costs. Using newer machinery and concentrating on coarse goods, southern mills employed less skilled labor, an especially important consideration in a labor-intensive industry such as textiles. Southern state and local governments also gave new cotton mills tax breaks. But since tax favors represented such a small portion of the costs of starting and running a cotton mill in those days, they were not very important.

COTTON TEXTILE INDUSTRY BY REGION, 1880–1900

	Capital invested and value of product			Number of spindles and looms		
	1880	1890	1900	1880	1890	1900
United States[a]	$208,280,346	$354,020,843	$467,240,157	10,653,435	14,188,103	19,050,952
	192,090,110	267,981,724	339,200,320	225,759	324,866	455,752
New England	156,754,690	243,153,249	276,089,821	8,632,087	10,836,155	12,891,787
	143,353,030	181,112,453	191,690,913	184,701	250,166	302,018
Middle Atlantic[b]	31,014,759	51,676,249	61,985,519	1,391,164	1,633,722	1,647,251
	29,389,286	40,664,476	48,961,806	27,318	35,074	38,060
Southern	17,375,897	53,827,303	124,596,874	542,048	1,554,000	4,299,988
	16,356,598	41,513,711	95,002,059	11,898	36,266	110,015

Average Number of wage earners

	1880	1890	1900
United States[a] Total	174,659	218,876	302,861
Men, 16+	61,760	88,837	135,721
Women, 16+	84,558	106,607	126,882
Under 16	28,341	23,432	40,258
New England Total	125,779	147,359	162,294
Men, 16+	45,521	63,749	78,217
Women, 16+	62,554	73,445	73,258
Under 16	17,704	10,165	10,819
Middle Atlantic[b] Total	28,118	31,841	34,843
Men, 16+	8,919	11,580	14,473
Women, 16+	13,185	16,240	16,056
Under 16	6,014	4,021	4,314
Southern Total	16,317	36,415	97,494
Men, 16+	4,633	12,517	40,528
Women, 16+	7,587	15,083	32,528
Under 16	4,097	8,815	24,438

[a]Includes states not in the three regions here.
[b]Includes Maryland.

SOURCE: U.S. Bureau of the Census, 1900, Manufactures (Washington, D.C., 1902), Pt. III, pp. 19–72.

Women and children under sixteen years of age made up a greater part of the industry's workforce in the South than elsewhere in the country. Factory hands in 1890 worked sixty hours a week for wages that varied from 15 cents to $1.25 a day and averaged 85 cents. The almost all-white workforce came from areas close to the mills. Mills limited blacks to the most menial, dirtiest, least desirable jobs. The Graniteville Manufacturing Company of South Carolina, for instance, drew nearly all its workers from that state, although the company was located only twelve miles from Augusta, Georgia. As Ben Duke explained to a Massachusetts textile executive and as most southern cotton manufacturers knew, there was an "abundance of cheap white labor." More than other factors, cheap labor accounted for the success of the textile industry in the South.

Southern textile companies also took advantage of current technological advances. The ring spindle, the power loom, and the humidifier allowed for greater speed, and the new spindles and looms required less skill on the part of the operators. Northern companies, by contrast, tended to continue to use the older machinery they had already paid for. The savings that southern cotton mills realized from material and labor costs and from advanced technology more than offset disadvantages in transportation and insurance costs, managerial inexperience, and start-up expenses. By 1900 southern textiles manufacturers surpassed northern factories in the production of the coarsest fabrics; then they got the upper hand in fine goods after 1920. Northern textiles never recovered.

The size, extent, and rapid growth of the southern textile industry explain why the industry made such a deep imprint on the South and why it shaped the way the South was perceived from within and without. Thus, if we are to understand the South since 1865, we have to understand the southern textile industry and its characteristics. Unlike iron- and steelmaking and most of tobacco manufacturing, textiles were not concentrated organizationally or geographically. Textiles lent themselves not to monopoly or oligopoly but to a scattering of small to medium-sized firms that usually engaged in only one or two stages of manufacture and that were highly competitive. This competitiveness had enormous influence on the way textile companies dealt with financial adversity and with organized labor.

Most southern companies produced yarn and "gray goods," or coarse fabrics. These goods were then shipped elsewhere, usually to the North, for weaving, bleaching, dyeing, printing, and other final processing. Only years later were extensive facilities for these processes developed in the South. The manufacture of textile machinery followed a similar history and arrived in the South even later. As a result, the textile industry did not have the same "multiplier effect" in the South as it did in the North, where the industry established itself earlier. Southern textiles therefore did not generate a large pool of skilled machinists and mechanics, a basic necessity for more sophisticated industrial growth.

Southern cotton mills generally grew up along the fall line in the piedmont, where the water power that the industry initially depended on could be found. Mills sprang up along an arc more than 700 miles long from Danville, Virginia, to eastern Alabama and away from that arc in eastern North Carolina, the midlands of South Carolina, middle and southern Georgia, eastern and middle Tennessee, and Mississippi. The Carolinas, Georgia, and Alabama were the leading textile states in the South; eventually they came to be leaders for the nation. Most of the plants' sites did

CARRYING LOOM TO MILLS BY CART (Courtesy of Mildred Gevin Andrews, Mercer University Press)

not afford enough power to support textile factories on the scale of Lowell or Fall River, Massachusetts, or Manchester, New Hampshire. Thus southern cotton mills contributed to the fundamental demographic patterns of the New South—a profusion of villages and small towns, some medium-sized cities, and several large cities. Steam engines, then the use of electrically powered motors, reinforced this dispersal. The textile industry also lent a powerful hand to the shift of economic activity and population growth in the South from the coast to the interior.

Unlike other major businesses in the South, such as railroads and iron and steel, southern cotton manufacturing relied heavily on local sources for capital— merchants, bankers, professionals, successful farmers. The relatively small size of textile firms facilitated this strategy. Efforts to raise capital for cotton mills often were cloaked in civic piety. An evangelist reportedly claimed that "the great morality in Salisbury [North Carolina] was to go to work," and that the "establishment of a cotton mill would be the most Christian act his hearers could perform." Chastened business leaders, so the story went, then built a cotton mill. The "cotton mill campaign," as such efforts have been called, took its basic themes from the ideology of the New South: the belief that "industrialization could cure the region's economic ills . . . that economic development was . . . a public service to help the region in general and poor whites in particular."

Southern cotton mills did, of course, provide jobs for families that desperately needed them. Children and women filled many of these jobs. As one textile executive said, "There was no thought . . . in those times [1880 to 1910] with regard to who should work or how many hours they should work." (His "who" did not include blacks.) The cotton mill provided the "instrumentalities" for "men, women, and children . . . [to] earn a livelihood, . . . [to obtain] the bare necessities of life, which could be gotten in the cotton mills of that period only by the combined toil of the whole family. . . . Literally, it was a question of 'bread and meat.' " One scholar and New South enthusiast went too far in 1920 when he asserted that "even machinery was wrapped with idealism and devotion." The *Wilmington,*

(N.C.), *Daily Review* came closer to reality in 1881 when it reported that cotton mills in the South averaged profits of 22 percent and then asked, "Where will philanthropy pay better?"

Undoubtedly cotton mill owners and managers felt some personal ties with their workers. The mills may have been closer to the communities where they were located than were other industries. Face-to-face dealings between labor and management were not uncommon. Nor should claims of concern about factory hands be dismissed out of hand. Caution, however, is urged. Provisions for such amenities as schools, health care, and better housing were closely tied to concern about profits. Mill managers may have felt some sense of noblesse oblige, but that did not preclude their adamant opposition to even the least militant labor unions or their willingness to put black labor in positions normally reserved for whites if their white workers overstepped themselves.

Finally, the southern textile industry became noted for the characteristics of its workforce, characteristics that reflected the nature of the industry and its particular chronological and geographical contexts. Most work in textiles was machine tending, which generally required few and readily learned skills. And this was especially the case in southern cotton mills in the late nineteenth century. Textile factories had very few highly skilled positions, such as mechanic, and they offered little prospect for promotion or for significant improvements in income and status. Cotton mills in the postbellum South relied heavily on women and children. Only in about 1900 did male workers begin to outnumber female workers. At the same time, one-fourth of the factory hands were less than sixteen years old. Coincidentally, the number of adult workers also increased, an indication that the industry's workforce was maturing and increasing its productivity.

Most employees worked under the family wage system. Working as families and pooling their wages, they earned more than they could on farms, virtually the only other significant occupational alternative open to whites in the Southeast for many years after the Civil War. Landless farmers faced especially poor prospects in agriculture. If people had not made better money in cotton mills than on farms, they would not have gone to the mills. They went, and in large numbers, for many years. For a family with a minuscule income and a preponderance of females, cotton mills had a particular attraction. The harsh physical requirements of agricultural work limited the value of females as farm labor. Nor could low-income white women turn easily to domestic work, which was thought to be appropriate for black women only. It also paid wretchedly. Only after the South became increasingly urbanized was there much demand for white women to work in offices and in retail stores.

Southern textile workers lived in a remarkably segregated world. They usually lived in company houses, often shopped in company stores, and frequently worshiped in churches built and maintained by the mills. Far more than most southerners at the time, mill workers worked and lived in a white world. Blacks were scarcer in a cotton mill than in any other industrial workplace in the South, and when they were allowed to live in a mill village, they were restricted to the most meager dwellings at the edge of the settlement. The textile industry in the South had even fewer immigrants among its workers than other southern industries had, and the others had very few. Thus the cotton mills reinforced a long-standing pattern: southern whites were native-born Anglo-Saxons.

But cotton mill hands were not safe from vicious pejoratives in their white sanctuaries. Their contemporaries labeled them "lintheads" and "mill hands." More polite circles preferred "mill people." These terms were fraught with meaning and innuendo. *Linthead* was an Industrial Age colloquialism for "poor white," that elusive label that meant anything from "that alleged Caucasian degenerate no-good who hasn't got any gumption" to "good folks who fell on hard times through no fault of their own." Bearers of the label were objects of scorn and pity. *Linthead* also suggested the existence of an industrial underclass. The term promised hoped-for social distance. *Lintheads* were what many people thought of when they thought of industrial workers in the South. Finally, the label stigmatized a large number of human beings who deserved much better.

Mill workers were not lumps of clay waiting passively to be molded by mill owners. Workers had a substantial role in shaping their work lives and even greater roles in creating and shaping the mill villages in which they lived. Workers restrained management prerogatives by demanding racial segregation in the mill and the village, by slowing the pace of work in the mill, by absenting themselves from work for limited periods of time, and by leaving work altogether. Mills had high absentee and turnover rates, especially when the industry was shorthanded. Workers also registered their dissent by walkouts, strikes, and occasional efforts at unionization. Despite intrusions by management, workers generally controlled their own churches and created their own forms of recreation. Some workers showed their independence by joining Holiness and Pentecostal churches. Connected by kinship, workers often policed the life of the village according to their own standards. Older workers set and enforced the rules of dating and courtship. Women practiced folk medicine, meeting medical needs. Some men became noted as musicians, others as athletes on mill baseball and basketball teams. Women carried particularly heavy burdens: they worked outside the home even while they functioned as wife, mother, and homemaker. By 1900 the southern cotton textile industry had grown so large that one long mill village ran along the southern piedmont from southern Virginia to northern Alabama. It was a world that was more firmly shaped by its inhabitants than the epithet *linthead* suggested.

Linthead did, however, suggest fierce hate and its opposite, elemental fear. The great dread of several generations of southern whites was that, like others before them, they might have to go to the mills, that their relatives and friends might quit speaking to them, that their children might be physically and verbally abused in school and on the streets, that they might become objects of derision and condescension in local stores and at church. Not much stood between many people and the mills. Failure in farming, a clear and seemingly always present danger for too many people in the New South, often meant going to the cotton mills.

Southerners developed a second, smaller but important industry based on the processing of cotton. Cottonseed mills ground the once neglected seed into cottonseed oil, which was used for salad oils, lard, margarine, and soap, and into meal, which made an excellent fertilizer and feed for cattle. Paper companies used the husks from the seed in fine grades of paper. Between 1880 and 1900 the number of cottonseed mills more than doubled, to about 300 companies with an output worth $30 million. Thus cotton provided the raw material for the New South's largest and most important manufacturing industry, textiles, and for an important smaller industry, cottonseed milling.

URBANIZATION IN THE NEW SOUTH

Cotton also powerfully influenced the contours of urbanization in the New South. Short-staple cotton could be and was grown over an enormous area that ran from Virginia to Oklahoma and covered more than 400,000 square miles. The more than 10 million bales of cotton harvested in 1900, for instance, had to be ginned to separate the seed from the fiber; then the seed was crushed at mills while the fiber was compressed into bales of 500 pounds each, weighed, tested for quality, stored, sold, and shipped and perhaps sold, shipped, and stored several more times. Banks, brokerage houses, and merchants provided the financing required for these processes; others sold insurance to buffer the risks involved in these complex, often lengthy transactions.

The people who provided these services clustered first at seaports and river ports, then more and more along the network of rails that covered the cotton belt as the southern rail system expanded rapidly in the late nineteenth century. These clusters followed a stair-step pattern of small towns to large towns to small cities to large cities. Logically, metropolises came next. But in 1900 the South had only one urban center of those dimensions, New Orleans. These small urban clusters grew rapidly after 1880. The number of urban places in the South went from 119 in 1880 to 320 in 1900, four-fifths of which had fewer than 10,000 people. Thus urbanization patterns in the South reflected changes in agriculture and the growth of rail systems more than industrialization. Again cotton demonstrated its power to mold the South.

Urban growth occurred more in the interior than at the once more populous seaports—at Richmond, Danville, Greensboro, Charlotte, Columbia, Atlanta, Nashville, Dallas, and Houston rather than at Wilmington, Charleston, Savannah, Mobile, or New Orleans. Norfolk was the most important exception. Most southern cities and towns continued their primary functions of serving commercial, legal, and governmental needs. Few relied heavily on manufacturing for jobs and incomes. Birmingham provided the most notable exception here. Manufacturing did dominate some smaller cities: tobacco in Durham and Winston after the center of tobacco manufacturing shifted from Richmond; cotton mills in Gastonia, Greenville, Spartanburg, Macon, Columbus; furniture in High Point; cigars in Tampa; and iron in Chattanooga and Birmingham's sister towns of Anniston, Bessemer, Gadsden, and Sheffield.

Urbanization provides a convenient device to measure the degree to which the South, a generation after its massive defeat and the demise of slavery, had begun to resemble the rest of the United States and yet remained distinctive. Urban areas in the South differed from those in the rest of the country in that they were fewer and smaller and had fewer assets. Southern urban areas, even the larger ones, had lower tax rates, lower public debts, and hence fewer services than those elsewhere in the nation. No southern city over 25,000, a Bureau of the Census study found, had a per capita tax levy in 1902 above the national average of $12.89; most were well below the average. Only a few southern cities exceeded the national average for debt per capita. Relatively lower per capita incomes explained most of these differentials. Tightfistedness and the dominance of businessmen may have been factors, too.

Southern towns and cities had made some effort to provide most, if not all, services expected or required of cities at that time: water, sanitation, street improvements, sewer systems, transportation, police and fire protection, schools, some health services, and in times of economic stress, a modicum of public assistance for the most needy. In the South, as elsewhere in the country, urban communities learned some critical lessons between 1880 and 1900. Firemen and policemen, for example, had to be paid and trained if they were to provide adequate protection, and that protection would be better if they were depoliticized. Unregulated, privately owned utility companies often delivered water, gas (made from coal), electricity, and transportation erratically and expensively. Epidemics threatened the lives of all citizens, not just the less fortunate, and cast shadows over the reputations of communities as places to live or invest. Some learned slowly. Only after yellow fever took 400 lives in New Orleans in the late 1890s did the city take over the defunct sewerage company and start laying sewer pipe. By 1900, southern urban leaders lent strong support to improvement of a wide range of services either through direct government action, such as municipal ownership of services and utilities, or through government regulation of privately owned agencies. Their concern also took the form of greater attention to public schools; they helped establish the first publicly financed high schools in the South. They also encouraged the development of urban parks. Thus these leaders formed the vanguard of progressivism and its kin, professionalism and bureaucracy, in the South.

Much remained to be done, however. In 1902 a federal census of American cities revealed that Memphis had 17 miles of paved roads and 140 unpaved miles; Atlanta, 63 and 137, respectively. New Orleans had paved only 200 of its 700 miles of roads. Business districts and the better residential areas received the great majority of these improvements. Atlanta called itself "the Chicago of the South" but in 1903 it had only 96,550 people in 11 square miles, whereas Chicago had nearly 2 million in 180 square miles. Chicago's financial institutions cleared nearly $7 billion in 1900, while Atlanta's cleared only $96.4 million.

Streetcars, most of which were electrically powered by 1900, did reach the majority of the citizenry. Richmond was the first American city to adopt the electric streetcar, a device that facilitated the evolution of central business districts and the commercial wonder of the age, the department store. Streetcars also hastened the emergence of a residential pattern deeply etched by class and race, and they hurried the growth of suburbs and the extension of the distance between work and residence.

Southern towns and cities had more blacks and fewer foreign-born residents than other communities in the United States. The Irish had an important political role in such places as Savannah, Charleston, and Memphis. Jewish merchants figured prominently in a number of southern communities. Small enclaves of recently arrived Greeks and Lebanese could be found in many cities and towns. Immigrants from Italy and Cuba left their mark on New Orleans and Tampa, as Mexican Americans were doing in the Southwest. But no southern city had the variety or numbers of immigrants to be found in most northern cities in those years. The so-called new immigration—the large wave of immigrants from eastern and southern Europe that came between 1880 and World War I—largely bypassed the South. Thus the South remained less ethnically and religiously diverse than the rest of the country.

The proportion of blacks in southern towns and cities varied from less than 10 percent in Houston to more than 50 percent in Charleston and Savannah, averaging about 25 percent. The proportion of blacks did not exceed 5 percent in any city outside the South or in the southern border states, save for Washington (31.1) and Indianapolis (9.4). Southern white urbanites believed that it was of critical importance to control the black populace, more critical than ever now that slavery had ended. Southern towns and cities led the way in the evolution of black-white relations in the South. Racial segregation, with its elaborate edifice of laws, customs, and taboos, had most of its origins in the urban South. Ironically, racial segregation often represented an advance for blacks. In numerous instances they were admitted on a segregated basis to places where previously they had been excluded altogether.

Southern cities thus formed the vanguard for the development of the South's rigid caste system and the progressive movement in the region. Southern cities also provided a number of major political figures during the era. Perhaps the most noteworthy were Hoke Smith of Atlanta, governor, senator, and secretary of the interior; Colonel Edward M. House of Houston, a close adviser to Woodrow Wilson; and Josephus Daniels of Raleigh, North Carolina, prominent newspaper editor and secretary of the navy. City-based editors—Francis W. Dawson, Henry Grady, Richard H. Edmonds, and Henry Watterson—played prominent roles in the formation of public opinion. Urbanization went arm in arm with the New South creed. Thus southern urbanites still had more influence on the South than their numbers warranted. Though only a small percentage of southerners lived in urban areas, city-based leaders had and would continue to have a disproportionate voice in the shaping of the South.

A DIFFERENT SOUTH:
AT THE TURN OF THE CENTURY

Thirty-five years after the guns of the Civil War fell silent and twenty years after the longest depression in American history, that of the 1870s, distinctive outlines of a different South had appeared. It was not the New South envisioned by the New South evangels—not yet, anyway—and it was not the antebellum plantation- and slave-based South, obviously, or simply an agrarian, racially divided society with a commercial fringe and a scattering of towns and villages suspended in rustic equilibrium. Though much of the plantation world of the antebellum South remained, it was receding. In its place was a town world or sometimes a city world that was closely tied to a farm world but that increasingly distanced it-self from the farm world.

Some figures do, however, suggest that the changes that had taken place were minimal. Six in ten gainfully employed southerners earned their living from farm-ing, about one in ten from manufacturing. These figures differed significantly from those elsewhere in the country. In 1900, according to the federal census, about 40 percent of Americans lived in urban areas. In the north Atlantic division of the census (Maine, Vermont, Massachusetts, Connecticut, Rhode Island, New York, New Jersey, and Pennsylvania) 68.2 percent of the population lived in urban areas, 35.8 percent in cities of more than 100,000. In the north-central division (Ohio, Indiana, Illinois, Michigan, Wisconsin, Minnesota, Iowa, Missouri, North Dakota, South Dakota, Nebraska, and Kansas) 38.5 percent lived in urban areas, and in the western division (Montana, Idaho, Wyoming, Colorado, New Mexico, Arizona, Utah, Nevada, Washington, Oregon, and California), 40.6 percent. In the south-central division (Kentucky, Tennessee, Alabama, Mississippi, Arkansas, Louisiana, Texas, Oklahoma, and the Indian Territory), by contrast, only 15.5 per-cent lived in urban areas, and in the south Atlantic division (West Virginia, Vir-ginia, North Carolina, South Carolina, Georgia, Florida, but not Maryland, Delaware, or the District of Columbia), 21.4 percent. These census divisions also differed markedly in the proportions of their populations in agriculture and man-ufacturing.

Cotton was still king; it still had a pervasive, elemental impact on the lives of southerners from Virginia to Texas. Despite considerable effort, the proportion of capital invested in manufacturing still hovered around 11 percent, where it had been for four decades. Southerners also remained overwhelmingly rural. Only Louisiana had as much as 25 percent of its population in urban areas. (Urban, ac-cording to the federal census, was any political subdivision of a county with as many as 2,500 souls.) Mississippi, Arkansas, and even North Carolina, one of the South's proudest examples of industrial growth, had less than 10 percent. Finally, in per capita income the South still trailed the nation by about 50 percent, a mar-gin that had not changed in twenty years.

But the South was hardly standing still. From 1880 to 1900 the American economy grew at an extraordinary rate, and the South kept pace with that growth even though it remained behind. The South held its own, for instance, in the growth of per capita income, in investment in industry, and in urban growth. The extension and consolidation of the southern rail system and the emergence of the cotton textile, iron and steel, tobacco, forest products, and coal industries clearly were benchmarks of a different South. Petroleum was only beginning to make its impact. Southern urbanites were forces for change far beyond their numbers and the attainments of their cities. Increasing numbers of southerners, like other Americans, were becoming part of an industrial workforce. By 1900 more than 343,000 southerners, many of whom had not yet seen their sixteenth birthday, tended machines in factories or worked in mines and forests. They en-tered a world where machines increasingly dictated the pace and location of work, where time was measured in minutes and hours rather than from sunup to sundown, where places of work and residence were increasingly distant, and where, most important, they had less individual autonomy on the job than they had had on the farm.

Finally, the South of 1900 was distinguished by more rails, factories, mines, and growing cities. It was distinguished also by Jim Crow and by the scars of the Populist upheaval and challenge to the New South. The South that evolved by 1900 had to pass through the cauldron of the 1890s.

20

The South and the Crisis of the 1890s

❖

The crowd and the dignitaries gathered and waited. Promptly at 10 A.M. on September 18, 1895, President Grover Cleveland pushed an electric signal at Buzzard's Bay, Massachusetts, and the Cotton States and International Exposition opened at Atlanta. Then the president turned to more pressing business, a national financial and economic crisis.

The crowd in Atlanta settled back for a reading of "The Exposition Ode" and the main event of the day, the inaugural address by Judge Emory Speer, who had been an Independent Democrat in the 1870s but had since become a regular Democrat with ties to leaders in Atlanta. Speer's oration was appropriately optimistic, reflecting the perspective of the Gilded Age urban boosters who sponsored such expositions. Predictably, Speer looked out and saw progress at every hand, and he poured syrupy praise over all the exhibitors.

But Speer's speech deserves serious attention if for no other reason than that it reflected the times and setting and, consequently, provides some significant insights into the American South at the turn of the century. Memories of the Civil War and its aftermath lingered. Sectionalism was very much alive. Accordingly, Speer paid particular attention to sectional reconciliation. He touched lightly on Reconstruction, praised the generosity of the North to the defeated South, applauded the demise of slavery (a "hindrance" to progress in the South), and declared that Confederate veterans would unite with Union veterans to fight if the nation went to war, a real possibility given America's growing imperial ambitions. The United States had already openly clashed with Great Britain over Venezuela. American officials were closely watching events in Cuba, where a rebellion against Spain had started.

Judge Speer also declared that "the so-called 'negro question' does not exist," that without resorting to force, whites, secure in this Anglo-Saxon stronghold, were firmly in control of the South. In fact, he gave special stress to Anglo-Saxonism, a form of nativism that flourished at the time almost everywhere in the United States. The desire for sectional harmony, however, did not prevent Speer from pointedly as-

486

serting that blacks had better job opportunities in the South than in the North. The judge advocated industrial education for blacks, a theme that Booker T. Washington, president of the Tuskegee Institute in Alabama, had expounded earlier in the day in a speech that became famous as "The Atlanta Compromise."

The judge claimed to see things that the New South evangels had preached: thriving commerce in cities and towns, new factories, and a diversified agriculture with burgeoning ranks of farmers who tilled their own land. With respect to commerce and industry, his vision was accurate if somewhat rose-tinted. With respect to agriculture, his vision was seriously blurred. Even the enormous cotton production he proudly advertised was not necessarily a cause for celebration. The vast sea of white fiber that covered much of the South suggested a dangerous overdependence on cotton. And the dangers of that dependency were painfully obvious in much of the South even as Speer spoke.

For the moment, however, the crowd had other things on its mind. It dispersed after the judge ended his oration on what by 1895 had become a standard note in the South: he thanked God for preventing the permanent division of the United States into North and South. The crowd was the first of the more than 1.3 million people to visit the displays sent by cities, states, nations, and associations and to amuse themselves on the midway. Visitors to the exposition could even examine a model jail, which had a gallows that could be "ready at the touch of a button" and a mobproof room. The model jail, unfortunately, was all too relevant for its day.

At the presidential retreat on the coast of Massachusetts, there would have been little tolerance for gallows humor or humor of any kind. The president and his closest advisers faced a grim prospect. In the midst of what was then the worst depression in American history, the federal government appeared to be running out of gold reserves. Since it was widely believed that the government had to have at least $100 million in gold in reserve if the nation's commercial system was to function, the depletion of the reserve represented a crisis. Working closely and quickly with major bankers, the Cleveland administration eventually resolved the crisis over gold. It could not, however, end the depression. Before the economy recovered, the very foundations of the postbellum South shook. More than a few of the people who reflected on the Cotton States Exposition may have wondered if it symbolized dreams more than realities.

Judge Speer had in fact hinted that his generally happy portrait of the South was distorted. Only the least informed would not have understood what he meant when he acknowledged that "of course there have been seasons of great political excitement when even good men lose the tolerance and mental equipoise which characterizes the majority." Great political excitement indeed swept the South in the 1890s, and economic distress lay at the root of the turmoil. Odes to the New South certainly seemed misguided.

THE DEPRESSION OF THE 1890S

The depression of the 1890s was the worst economic crisis in American history, save for the Great Depression. The economy faltered in early 1893, then began a sharp twelve-month decline in June of that year. Conditions improved markedly from June 1894 to December 1895, when a second sharp decline of about twelve months began. Although general prosperity returned by 1898, full recovery did not come until 1901–1902. The double-cycle depression of the 1890s took a heavy toll. Gross national product fell as much as 10 percent. More than 550 financial institutions closed their doors in 1893 alone; of the 158 national banks that failed, 153 were in the South and West. The rate of business failures in the South exceeded the national average by a wide margin. With the collapse of the byzantine Richmond Terminal, no trunk line in the southern states remained solvent. Among manufacturing industries in the South, cotton textiles alone prospered, and even textiles faltered during the economic crisis. The famed "mill boom" made its mark: between 1890 and 1900, the capital invested in southern cotton mills increased 131 percent, the number of plants 67 percent, and the number of spindles more than 100 percent. Most of that vigorous growth, however, occurred at the beginning and the end of the decade. In the middle of the decade, wages declined and cotton mill workers were not fully employed.

Still, cotton mill workers in the South were more fortunate than most workers during the depression. Nationwide, unemployment reached 20 percent of the workforce, or 3 million people. Distress spilled over into labor disputes, which were not limited to the more industrialized North. The Pullman strike of 1894, which began in Chicago and had its greatest effect in the North and West, riveted public attention at the time and has sustained historians' interest since. Richard H. Edmonds gloated in his *Manufacturer's Record*, "The South has fortunately demonstrated its freedom from labor riots and from anarchistic teachings." Edmonds either did not know about serious labor conflicts in the South in the early 1890s, or he chose to ignore them. Probably the first general strike in American history occurred in New Orleans in 1892 and involved black and white workers. Then, several months before Pullman, Alabama coal miners joined a national soft coal strike. They formed the nucleus of the more than 7,500 Alabamians who walked off their jobs that year. Black and white miners jointly confronted hostile mine owners, local law officers, troops sent in by the governor of Alabama, Pinkerton detectives, labor spies, and blacks who were sent in as strikebreakers. Some of these groups, however, may have been sympathetic to the strikers. The strike of the Alabama coal miners became entangled with a bitter state election and with the Pullman strike when Birmingham railroaders joined forces with Eugene V. Debs's American Railway Union. In late August 1894 the Alabama strikers acknowledged defeat and returned to work. At the same time, labor unrest broke out among miners in Virginia. In October, conflicts that began on the wharves of New Orleans led to riots, several deaths, and considerable property damage. Contrary to the biracial character of the general strike of 1892, blacks opposed whites in New Orleans in 1894. Considerable numbers of workers walked out that year in Georgia, Florida, and Texas; in Kentucky, 27,000 workers struck.

But the depression of the 1890s had its greatest impact in the South on farmers and their families. Two in three southerners earned their living in agriculture, and the majority of those farmers relied on cotton for a cash crop. Declining cotton prices thus had an especially devastating effect. Average at-the-farm prices for cotton fell from 8.4 cents per pound in 1892 to as low as 4.6 cents in 1894—well below what most farmers calculated was the break-even price of 10 cents a pound. At the New Orleans Cotton Exchange, one of the nation's largest, reported prices fell to fifty-year lows. A Louisianan worried that "if there is nothing done to alleviate the suffering among the people, . . . we will have a revolution." A Kentuckian claimed, "We have reached the stage where slow, reasoned arguments cannot any longer affect us. . . . It is a question of bread and meat, and we are ready to fight."

Nature compounded the difficulties. Floods in Mississippi in the early 1890s drove thousands of people from their homes and left many with virtually nothing to eat, destroyed livestock, and left hundreds of acres unusable for years. Then there was too little water. In 1895 and 1896, drought withered crops in Louisiana, Texas, Arkansas, and Mississippi. The winter of 1894–1895 brought the great freeze, which devastated Florida orange growers and caused many to suffer.

Southern farmers created their own storms in the 1890s. More than 3 million of them joined either the Southern Farmers' Alliance or the Colored Farmers' Alliance.* Many of them later swelled the ranks of the Populists, to make the People's party the most powerful independent party in American history. The Populists contributed to and reflected the political upheaval of the decade, which included two major Republican defeats, victories and then massive defeats for the Democrats, and finally, sweeping Republican triumphs that made the Republicans the dominant party in America for more than three decades. The Democrats retreated to several strongholds, chief of which was the South. Within the South, the Democrats, "the party of the white man," became even more secure than they had been in 1890. The party, however, underwent major internal changes during the decade. Amid the upheaval of the 1890s, the place of blacks in the South had become at least temporarily less certain than before. But by 1900 Jim Crow was in place, well defined, strongly supported by whites, and, from all appearances, permanent. Though the upheaval of the 1890s ended even before the decade did, the damage done by that upheaval affected life in the South long afterward.

That there was political turmoil in the South in the 1890s and that it had its origins and base in the rural areas of the region were hardly surprising. Most southerners lived and worked in rural areas, and southern agriculture was in trouble. That cotton farmers faced especially desperate times had particular significance, politically and otherwise. They numbered in the thousands and dwelled in all the states of the South, though in small numbers in Virginia and Florida. When their desperation became intense anger and was channeled into agitation and politics, they became a major force in southern and national politics.

Cotton farm families had much to be distressed about. They worked hard and often earned little more than subsistence. Effort did not lead to success. Instead, cotton prices fell, debts mounted, and tenancy grew. By contrast, the railroads, the banks, and the army of middlemen who serviced agriculture seemed to thrive.

---

*The official name of the Southern Farmers' Alliance was the National Farmers' Alliance and Industrial Union. But the more conventional name, Southern Farmers' Alliance, better reflects the origins and membership of the organization.

BLACK SHARECROPPER HOUSE, 1890s (Courtesy Georgia Department of Archives
and History)

Even the weather appeared to conspire against men and women of the soil. And
the boll weevil was coming. It crossed from Mexico to Texas in the early 1890s.
Like many other farmers, thousands of cotton growers felt victimized.

By 1890 American agriculture had become a highly complex, commercialized
business in which distant forces and persons seemed to control the destinies of
thousands. Cotton farmers sold their product for cash at prices determined by the
world market. They purchased much, sometimes all, that they ate, as well as manufactured goods, including much of their limited wardrobe; they bought seed,
fertilizer, implements, workstock, and livestock; and they made payments on
their debts. In sum, like the vast majority of American farmers, they were not self-
sufficient. Indeed, farmers in the United States and in much of the rest of the
world shared the experience of moving from self-sufficiency (or at least minimal
dependence on a cash crop) to commercialized agriculture.

"What a growing part of agriculture all over the world had in common," the
English historian E. J. Hobsbawm has written,

> was subjection to the industrial world economy. Its demands multiplied the commer-
> cial market for agricultural products—mostly foodstuffs and the raw materials of the
> textile industry, as well as some industrial crops of lesser importance—both domesti-
> cally, through the rapid growth of cities, and internationally. Its technology made it
> possible to bring hitherto unexploitable regions effectively within the range of the
> world market by means of the railway and the steamer. The social convulsions which
> followed the transfer of agriculture to a capitalist, or at least a large-scale commercial-
> ized pattern, loosened the traditional ties of men to the land of their forefathers, espe-
> cially when they found they owned none of it or too little to maintain their families. At
> the same time the insatiable demand of new industries and urban occupations for
> labor, the growing gap between the backward and "dark" country and the advancing
> city and industrial settlement attracted them away.

Luke Wadkins experienced these macrocosmic changes on a microcosmic level, at the farm he owned in Georgia's upper piedmont. Wadkins moved from near self-sufficiency to commercialized agriculture between 1860 and 1880. The Wadkins family (the sole source of labor on the farm) grew enough grain, tobacco, vegetables, and cotton (one bale) in 1860 to supply their needs and have something left over for barter or cash exchange. Twenty years later, Wadkins had a farm of ninety acres (worth about $400), of which twenty were in cotton, which produced nine bales. The money value of the cotton and other products of the farm—its *annual* product—was $369. Cash earnings, primarily from cotton, were now important, since the Wadkinses no longer produced adequate provisions for themselves. Also, Wadkins had to pay his $131 fertilizer bill and make payments on the credit he had received from merchants.

Wadkins was not unusual. Rupert Vance, a pioneer student of the rural South, concluded that the *average annual gross income* from twenty acres of cotton was (in constant dollars) $472 in 1880, $304 in 1890, and $332 in 1900. Vance and others also found that, at the same time, the proportion of farms in the cotton states owned by the people who farmed them shrank from 61 percent to 48 percent. "The mortgage," a Georgia farmer wrote, "stayed forever." Or until the bank foreclosed it.

Naturally, understandably, cotton farmers sought relief and redress, and they found many allies within and without the South. Like Americans before them, these dissidents resorted to voluntary associations and pressure groups, then to politics. They had substantial precedent when they did so. In fact, even before the depression of the 1890s had started, more than a million southern farmers had joined the Alliance movement, one of the largest grassroots movements in American history.

PRELUDE TO THE ALLIANCE MOVEMENT

The 1870s provided the lineal antecedents for the Alliance movement and then the Populist party: the Grange and the Greenbackers. The Grange, or the Order of the Patrons of Husbandry, was the largest and best known of these two organizations, and is the only one that still exists. Founded in 1867 by Oliver H. Kelley, an agent of the U.S. Department of Agriculture, the Grange reached its greatest strength in the mid-1870s, then faded. In 1875 it claimed 850,000 members, 350,000 of them in the South.

Convinced that improvement of farm life required better knowledge and more training, the Grange gave particular stress to informal and formal education. These efforts led to lasting institutions in the South: the Agricultural and Mechanical College of Louisiana, now part of Louisiana State University; Mississippi State University; and Texas Agricultural and Mechanical University.

The Grangers addressed themselves to other needs. Local Granges provided social opportunities for farm families—meetings, picnics, barbecues, and the like. Deliberately copying the Masons, the Grange had a secret, elaborate ritual. Unlike the Masons, they welcomed women as members (though not as officers), and some played important parts in the Grange. Some Granges organized buying and selling cooperatives or hired agents to run them. Among the southern states, Arkansas, Tennessee, Louisiana, and Mississippi had the strongest cooperatives.

Regional concerns and preoccupations shaped the Grange in the South. Only whites could join. Councils of Laborers were created for blacks. The separation and names of the councils spoke for themselves and pointed to two of the persistent problems faced by farm groups in the South. Could the all-important color line be maintained without fatal divisions in the ranks of farmers? Did farm groups include landed and landless farmers, farmers with ample means and those without? Which farmers should or could organizations represent? Grangers in the South had a very particular form of uplift in mind when they founded Councils of Laborers. A leading student of farm movements in the South concluded that the Grangers intended "to make the Negro a reliable farm hand, trusty, stable, and industrious." Coincidentally, the Grangers in the South also wanted publicly funded efforts to attract European immigrants in order to lessen their dependence on black labor and to reduce the potential political power of blacks. The Grange avoided one problem that later unsettled farm organizations in the South: it did not engage in partisan politics and thus did not challenge the primacy of the Democrats.

The Patrons of Husbandry in the South took up other regional causes. They lent support to efforts to obtain a southern transcontinental railway. They pleaded for greater diversity in farming and less dependence on cotton, and got involved in abortive attempts to limit cotton production. They lobbied for refunds of the federal tax imposed on cotton immediately after the Civil War, and they pressed for the repeal of the 10 percent federal levy on banknotes issued by state-chartered banks. The state banks, it was hoped, would lower interest rates and make loans more readily available.

Unlike Grangers elsewhere, those in the South did not become heavily involved in efforts to pass railroad regulatory legislation. That issue may have been preempted by the regulatory legislation passed by the Redeemer governments in the 1870s. Thus the legacy of the Grange in the South did not include anything comparable to the widely known, landmark Granger regulatory laws that were enacted in the Midwest in the 1870s. The Grange in the South did, however, provide a legacy on which other farm groups would build. The Grange might have been stronger and accomplished more in the South if Reconstruction and the depression of the 1870s had not imposed themselves. Restoring and maintaining native white political dominance took precedence in most of the southern states in the 1870s. The depression hurt Grange cooperatives and left farmers with even less money to pay the Grange's modest dues. Then currency contraction and deflation—monetary issues that the Grange had largely avoided—became major concerns in the late 1870s and would remain powerful forces in American politics for years to come.

These two monetary issues became ensnarled with partisan politics and sectionalism and with conflicts between interest groups. The Alliance movement, the Populists, the Democrats, and the Republicans became entangled in that snarl. The principal unknotting finally came in two major steps: the Gold Standard Act of 1898 and the Owen-Glass Act, which created the Federal Reserve System, in 1913.

The monetary issues had their roots in the Civil War. In order to ease an acute currency shortage in 1862, the federal government created treasury notes (known popularly as "greenbacks") and made them legal tender (acceptable for payments of debts and taxes). After the war, the secretary of the treasury began to retire greenbacks because it was believed that they destabilized money. Congress stopped him after he had called in about one-fourth of the greenbacks. It feared that the already rapid postwar deflation would get worse and would take the whole economy down with it. Thus greenbacks remained in circulation, and doubts about their value persisted. Was one greenback worth one gold dollar?

A related controversy involved the national banking system, which Congress created in 1863–1864. The country now had a more stable banking system, but it could issue no more than $300 million in banknotes. That limitation and the tendency of the banks to cluster in major urban centers in the Northeast resulted in serious maldistributions. The southern and western states wanted and needed easier access to national banknotes and banking services. Moreover, the economy as a whole needed currency expansion in keeping with its rapid post–Civil War growth.

A financial panic in 1873 and the depression that followed reopened the greenback and banking issues. Producers, primarily farmers, demanded relief from deflation, which lowered prices for what they produced (and, at a slower rate, for what they bought) while increasing the costs of borrowing. Farmers borrowed heavily to buy or rent the land they needed and to carry themselves over the months between planting and selling their products. They wanted to increase the number of greenbacks and national banknotes. Opponents of these measures decried these steps as leading to an unstable currency that would adversely affect the economy. These defenders of "sound" or "honest" money pointed to the damage done to the United States in the past by unstable currencies and attacked the so-called cheap-money measures as threats to lenders and investors and to America's critically important trade with foreign countries, especially Great Britain. Congress and the Grant administration passed compromise legislation, the Specie Resumption Act (1875), which put equal value on greenbacks and gold dollars and provided for an increase in the number of national banknotes. The new law ended uncertainties about the value of greenbacks. It did not, however, stimulate a significant expansion in national banknotes, because the reserve requirements of National Bank acts precluded more than minimal increases in notes. Thus the Resumption Act did not settle the monetary issues. They festered, then burst out from time to time when the economy faltered or when it became painfully obvious that the postwar deflationary trend was continuing.

Greenbackerism, or antiresumption, entered partisan politics in the 1870s. The Greenback party's presidential ticket drew a scant following in 1876. Two years later Greenbacker candidates under a new banner, the National Greenback-Labor party, won fourteen seats in Congress, though none in the South. Greenbackers in northern Alabama, however, lent vigorous support to the successful congressional candidacy of William M. Lowe. Greenbackers showed considerable electoral strength in Texas and Arkansas in 1880, but that year marked the high tide of the Greenback-Labor party in the South.

Greenbackers' ideas outlasted their electoral success. Greenbacker leaders and ideologues espoused a subtle, sophisticated policy that belied the accusations of simpleminded inflationism that their critics hurled at them. Greenbackers, who included politicians, farmers, manufacturers, theorists, and labor leaders, contended that the value of a nation's currency depended on the strength, real or perceived, of its economy. Hence Greenbackers attacked one of the cornerstones of the monetary theory and policy of their day: the belief that currency must be based on a metallic standard, preferably gold. The Coinage Act of 1873 drew special fire from the Greenbackers as well as others. With this legislation, Congress left the bimetallic (gold and silver) standard and joined the international movement toward a monometallic (gold) standard. The move had a deflationary effect and soon became known among its critics as the "Crime of '73." Greenbackers argued that deflationary policies, such as the Resumption Act and the Coinage Act, limited economic growth and rewarded creditors while punishing producers and debtors. These ideas became elemental in American politics for years to come.

Reacting to the sentiments on which Greenbackerism fed and keenly aware of an unsettled economy, Congress tried its hand at compromise again, this time with respect to the monetary standard. The Bland-Allison Act (1878) required the secretary of the treasury to purchase no less than $2 million and no more than $4 million of silver per month and coin it as standard dollars. This mildly inflationary legislation may have appeased some inflationists, but it fell far short of the unlimited silver coinage they had sought. The Treasury Department further restrained the impact of the law by electing to purchase the least amount required.

The return of prosperity in 1879 eased pressures on Congress to act on monetary issues. The struggles over monetary policy, however, had portents for the future. Both major parties, the Republican and the Democratic, discovered that the "money question" was explosive. It caused sharp internal divisions in both parties and threatened the coalitional foundations of both. Therefore, both parties sought to avoid the money question, and both sought a more serviceable issue, which they found: the tariff. Monetary issues also stoked the latent fires of sectionalism—not North versus South but Northeast versus West and South. Monetary policy evoked intense feeling and abrasive rhetoric: "sound," "honest," or "cheap" money, "the moneyed interests," "good" and "evil," and so forth. People could march in two different monetary armies and feel righteous. The money question touched the most sensitive American nerves: a sense that there were stark inequalities in income and wealth and well-being in America; suspicions that some people prospered by conspiracy, not effort; and fears that equality of opportunity did not exist. The money issue was one of those fairly rare issues in American history that polarized Americans. During the latter part of the nineteenth century, the erratic fortunes of too many American farmers and the sometimes chaotic American economy kept divisive monetary issues alive. They percolated to the surface throughout the 1880s. Then, in the 1890s, monetary policy became *the* issue in American politics, thanks in large part to the Alliance movement.

THE ALLIANCE MOVEMENT: TEXAS ROOTS

The Alliance movement had uncertain origins and a complex family tree. The Alliance began in Texas prairie country in 1877 or in 1879, but its growth dates from the latter year. The founders, cotton farmers and small ranchers, initially developed their voluntary association as a way to deal with stray cattle, cattle thieves, "land sharks," and big ranchers, who preempted large areas of land by fencing. The Texas Farmers' Alliance (its official name) had 144 lodges or suballiances by 1881 and 500 by 1885, a testament to the Alliance's ability to respond to the needs of many people and to its organizing capacities. Not all of those needs were economic. Like the fraternal orders then found everywhere in the United States, the Alliance had a secret ritual, hand grips, passwords, and regalia. "Throughout its career," one scholar has noted, "the Alliance, particularly at the local level, was a cohesive social institution as well as agency for political and economic action." The Alliance was steeped in the morality and revivalism of nineteenth-century rural Protestantism. "We held an old-fashioned experience meeting," an Alliance member recalled. "We all owned up like men, told our respective shortcomings, and made good resolutions for the future. In that meeting I saw brethren embrace each other in loving embrace, and to this day, the effects of that meeting are plainly visible in Navarro County." Alliance lodges limited their membership to rural whites of all occupations, except lawyers, merchants, bankers, and their ilk. Townsmen were not welcome. Local notables, however, could prompt a more inclusive spirit. General (later Senator) John Brown Gordon was readily initiated into the Alliance when it expanded into Georgia. Save for the poorest, the membership of the Alliance included the entire spectrum of farmers, though probably most members were small landowners.

The Alliance employed paid lecturer-organizers extensively—$1 for each lodge organized, later $3.35. Local officers carried on the work of the suballiances after the lecturer-organizer moved on. The itinerant teachers created an informal school system in which hundreds of "students" heard and, presumably, digested Alliance teachings. Drawing on events from the 1870s, from the Grange, and especially the Greenback movement, the Alliance emphasized Currency expansion or "soft money" and cooperatives. Cooperation was critical to the success of the Alliance. It founded a number of small cooperatives for buying and selling and some cooperative cotton gins and compresses, flour mills, and grain elevators.

Antimonopoly sentiments and ideas permeated Alliance thought. The fear of monopoly or economic concentration was pervasive in the United States at the time. Large combinations of industry, banking, merchandising, and transportation presumably had the power to dictate prices to consumers and producers, to make vassals of labor, to manipulate politicians at will, and to destroy small enterprises. These "moneyed" behemoths could trample the economy, basic freedoms, and people. They were "parasites" living off the substance created by the "real producers."

Defining "producers" and arriving at interests they had in common proved to be very difficult for the Alliance and for its successors. The Alliance thought of industrial workers as "producers" and tried to develop ties with the Knights of Labor, the major labor organization in the United States in the 1880s. The Knights, who wanted one union for all workers and whose ranks grew very rapidly in the mid-1880s, had local units in Texas. When the Knights forced Jay Gould's Texas and Pacific Railroad to rescind a wage reduction in 1885, membership multiplied all over the country. Almost half the nonfarm workers in Texas belonged to the union, and in some places suballiances and the Knights cooperated closely. Both were made up of "producers," and any railroad, but especially one of Jay Gould's, was an enemy they had in common. But did the interests of the Alliance members include support for longshoremen in Galveston, who, not incidentally, were black, or the Knights' boycotts of two Texas companies? More to the point, how would farmers react to the Knights' efforts to unionize farmworkers and make demands on their employers? Was a farm-labor coalition possible?

The issue remained unsettled into 1886, when the Knights and Gould clashed again. This time Gould won decisively. That defeat and the reactions against the Knights for allegedly precipitating the Haymarket riot in Chicago in June began the Knights' rapid decline. Many Alliance members, however, continued to be interested in some kind of coalition with organized labor. The Alliance had supported the Knights against Gould during the strikes in 1885 and 1886, even when the 1886 strike came close to being a pitched battle. Afterward, suballiances and local units of the Knights continued to work together in northern Texas, and 10,000 Alliancemen and Knights paraded in Dallas in August 1886. That year, an Alliance convention at Cleburne, Texas, endorsed several of the "demands" of the Knights of Labor, including the abolition of convict labor, state recognition of unions, and the creation of a national bureau of labor statistics.

Closely related to the debate over forming a coalition with organized labor was the debate about whether and how the Alliance ought to get involved in politics. The question of political involvement and the issue of a farm-labor coalition became so intense that they nearly split the Alliance permanently in 1886. The following year, the Alliance downplayed its divisions, plunged anew into cooperation, and expanded beyond the borders of Texas. Charles Macune led the way. A native midwesterner who had moved to Texas, Macune taught himself pharmacy, medicine, and law, all of which he practiced at one time or another. He joined the Alliance in 1886, became editor of an Alliance newspaper, and quickly rose in the organization's ranks. As acting president and then president of the Texas Alliance, he got the Alliance to unite behind his plan for a state cooperative exchange. The Texas State Exchange, which was headquartered at Dallas and for which Macune served as the elected business agent, was designed to bypass the middlemen by having members sell their cotton directly to northeastern and European buyers and by buying farm equipment and supplies directly from manufacturers. The Exchange soon realized that many Alliancemen could not use the Exchange because they had to mortgage their crops in order to obtain supplies and provisions to start and go through a crop year until they could sell their products. So the Exchange decided to make cash advances to Alliancemen provided they agreed to sell their cotton through the Exchange. A year later, the Exchange had to be liquidated. Macune and others blamed hostile bankers and intermediaries, who undoubtedly were not pleased to see such a competitor. But probably more important was the Exchange's lack of the capital reserves it needed to conduct such a large business and the inadequate backing of the promissory notes members signed when the Exchange furnished them with supplies.

The creation of the Exchange and the struggle to keep it going stimulated an extensive campaign in political education by the Alliance. Lecturer-organizers, Macune, other Alliance officials, Alliance newspapers, and newspapers sympathetic to the Alliance spread the gospel of cooperation, in Texas and then throughout the cotton belt and beyond. The failure of the Texas State Exchange was costly to the Alliance's members in Texas, and it never regained its earlier strength. The successful boycott conducted by cotton farmers against a combination of jute-bag manufacturers in 1888–1889 did, however, strengthen the Alliance. Cotton farmers forced manufacturers to cut prices on cloth the farmers used for bagging cotton. Cooperation and organization got a widespread, well-publicized demonstration of their potential effectiveness. By 1889 the Alliance had members in every state in the South, on the border, and beyond. Its growing power and mounting farm discontent were forcing the issue of the Alliance's stance toward partisan politics. More and more Alliancemen were coming to the conclusion that the Alliance would have to get into politics if it was going to be successful with its program.

The Alliance enjoyed spectacular growth after 1886 and became a major force in American politics. Its greatest strength lay in the South and West. In 1887 the Texas Farmers' Alliance merged with the Louisiana Farmers' Union to form the National Farmers' Alliance and the Co-operative Union, the largest farm group in the United States. A year later it joined forces with the Agricultural Wheel to form the Farmers' and Laborers' Union of America, which then took in the North Carolina Farmers' Association. These merged groups were what is generally called the Southern Farmers' Alliance or Southern Alliance. The Agricultural Wheel had begun in Arkansas in 1882, absorbed the Brothers of Freedom, spread through much of Arkansas, and grown strong in Tennessee, Kentucky, Missouri, and especially Alabama. Leonidas L. Polk founded and led the North Carolina Farmers' Association. An established farm leader, he was largely responsible for the creation of the North Carolina Department of Agriculture. He served as its first head, then left the department when he concluded that it was too reactionary, and in 1886 began a major farm periodical, *Progressive Farmer*.

Behind the rapid expansion of the Southern Alliance lay a strong sense of injustice and bitter feeling. Polk wrote in 1887:

> There is something radically wrong in our industrial system. There is a screw loose. The wheels have dropped out of balance. The railroads have never been so prosperous, and yet agriculture languishes. The banks have never done a better or more profitable business, and yet agriculture languishes. Manufacturing enterprises never made more money or were in a more flourishing condition, and yet agriculture languishes. Towns and cities flourish and "boom" and grow and "boom," and yet agriculture languishes.

In 1888 the Southern Alliance initiated efforts to unite several of the larger farm organizations into a confederation and to develop a working relationship with organized labor. The farm organizations included the National Farmers' Alliance (popularly known as the Northern Alliance), the Colored National Farmers' Alliance, and the Farmers' Mutual Benefit Association. Founded in Chicago in 1880 and financed largely by Milton George, editor of the *Western Rural,* the Northern Alliance had about 50,000 to 100,000 members in its loosely structured organization. The Colored Farmers' Alliance began in Texas in 1886. Though started by blacks as another of the many black self-help associations and officered largely by blacks, the Colored Alliance's most prominent public figure was Richard Manning Humphrey, a white Baptist minister and Confederate veteran. Though the claims of the Colored Alliance to a membership of 1 million were exaggerated, it did have an extensive following. The Farmers' Mutual Benefit Association had its base in Illinois, where it originated in the early 1880s; it had at least 150,000 members and concentrated its energies on marketing the grain of its members. It showed little interest in merging with other farm groups, but did agree to cooperate with them. The color barrier precluded a confederation between the Colored Alliance and the Southern Alliance.

Conflicting interests also divided them. Most of the members of the Colored Alliance were landless farmers or agricultural day workers whose interests clashed with the interests of the majority of the Southern Alliance, who owned land and hired labor. Whites in the Mississippi delta, some of whom were probably members of the Southern Alliance, became alarmed in 1889 about the growth of the Colored Alliance. Attempts to intimidate the blacks failed. Instead, a group of armed blacks marched into a Leflore County village and presented a letter of support for the Colored Alliance. They signed the letter, "Three Thousand Armed Men." The sheriff of Lefore County countered by creating a posse that went on a manhunt and left perhaps twenty-five black men dead. A similar fate occurred to cotton pickers in the Arkansas delta in 1891, when, encouraged by the Colored Alliance, they attempted to strike for higher wages.

The Southern Alliance was much more interested in a confederation with the Northern Alliance. To that end, the two alliances met separately in St. Louis in early 1889. The Southern Alliance drew delegations from all the southern and border states as well as Kansas, Nebraska, and Indiana. Delegates from eight midwestern and western states and territories attended the meeting of the Northern Alliance. Negotiations between the organizations failed to produce a merger. The Alliances remained separate. Sectionalism and partisan politics contributed to the failure of the merger; so did the self-interest of the officers and members of the Alliances. Given the size of the two organizations, the Northern Alliance would have been swallowed up by the Southern, and the newly formed confederation would have been dominated by southerners and Democrats and would have been more militant than the Northern Alliance was. Possibly those prospects plus the loss of offices and titles proved too much for the leaders of the Northern Alliance.

The collapse of the unification attempt also reflected the conflicts of self-interest that often divided farmers by region and product. The heated politics of butter, oleomargarine, and lard demonstrated these divisions. Dairy farmers, who were concentrated in the Northeast and Midwest, wanted federal protection for butter against oleomargarine ("bogus" butter), and midwestern hog farmers wanted the same thing for "pure," or pork, lard against "blended" lards. Manufacturers used cottonseed oil, fast developing as an important element in the cotton industry, in both oleomargarine and blended lard. They also used cattle fat in blended lard. Cotton farmers and cattle growers fought vigorously against federal legislation designed to protect butter and pure lard. Farmers also differed over tariff policy. Though most opposed tariffs in general as adding to the costs of the manufactured goods that they purchased, farmers modified their opposition to particular import duties on the basis of self-interest. Wheat farmers along the Canadian border, for example, favored high import duties on Canadian wheat.

Despite the failure of its negotiations with the Northern Alliance, the Southern Alliance did expand as a result of the St. Louis meeting. The Kansas Alliance and the South Dakota Alliance left the Northern Alliance and joined the Southern. In 1890 the North Dakota Alliance did likewise. Thus the Southern Alliance took on a more national character. At its peak the Southern Alliance had organizations in thirty-two states and had 1.5 million members, three-quarters of whom were southerners. In several southern states, more than half of those eligible to join became members of the Southern Alliance. It was a mass movement. The expanding, increasingly militant Southern Alliance also opened its doors to industrial labor. It changed its constitution in order to allow mechanics to be members. Along with the Knights of Labor, which had become highly politicized even as its ranks dwindled, the Southern Alliance issued a list of "demands." The list strongly resembled the "platform" that the Northern Alliance issued at the same time in St. Louis. Ideology did not keep the Alliances apart. The differences in tone between "demands" and "platform," however, did reflect differences in militancy.

Refined, sharpened, and added to in at least one significant way, the documents drafted at St. Louis appeared as the Ocala Demands of the Southern Alliance (officially, the National Farmers' Alliance and Industrial Union) in December 1890. Delegates came from as far away as California, North Dakota, and New York to Ocala, Florida, where the list of demands was drafted. It represented the distillation of nearly twenty years of thinking and agitating for change. The Alliance demanded "the abolition of national banks," currency expansion "to not less than $50 per capita," free silver (put the United States on a bimetallic standard), "laws prohibiting alien ownership of land," the surrender of "all lands now held by railroads and other corporations in excess of such as is actually used and needed," lower tariffs, a graduated income tax, and "government control and supervision of the public means of communication and transportation, [or] government ownership of such." The Ocala meeting also called for severe limits on government spending in order to keep taxes down and for the direct election of United States senators in place of the then prevailing system of election by state legislatures. The Ocala Demands were a frontal assault on what many people believed were monopolies in land, credit, money, transportation, and communications.

The most novel of the demands was the subtreasury plan. It would create subtreasuries to lend "money direct to the people" at low interest rates "on nonperishable products" and on real estate. The plan had first been introduced during the final hours of the meeting of the Southern Alliance in St. Louis. Charles Macune apparently was primarily responsible for the subtreasury scheme, which he may have derived in part from French and Russian precedents. Necessity also played a strong hand. Most of the Southern Alliance cooperatives had failed by 1889, and survivors faced grim prospects. The cooperatives could not raise enough capital to succeed; perhaps governments could. By 1889, moreover, the Southern Alliance had begun to give greater stress to currency expansion and an overhaul of the banking system.

The subtreasury appeared to meet these needs. According to the plan, the U.S. Department of the Treasury would open a branch (subtreasury) in every county in the nation that produced at least $500,000 worth of farm products. Every subtreasury would have facilities to store nonperishables such as cotton, wheat, sugar, corn, and tobacco. A farmer would be able to store products for up to one year and obtain a loan in subtreasury notes of up to 80 percent of the market value of the crop when it was stored. Costs to the farmer would be small: the subtreasury would charge a small fee for storage and handling and 1 percent interest on the loan, which could run up to twelve months.

The subtreasury plan had a multiple purpose. Farmers could end their dependence on local merchants, warehousers, and grain elevator operators, who often had local monopolies. Since they would have money from the subtreasuries, farmers would not have to sell their crops as soon as they harvested them; they could hold their crops in the hope of selling at better prices. Subtreasury notes would be legal tender and would displace national banknotes. Since subtreasury notes would be far more numerous than banknotes, the subtreasury plan also would substantially expand the amount of money in circulation. The subtreasury promised a way out of the "vast pawnshop" that entrapped so many farm families.

The subtreasury scheme was a new and certainly an ingenious proposal. Government had never remained aloof from the American economy; tariffs, subsidies to railroads, and tax revenues for education, to cite only a few examples, attested to that. But in 1890, despite such governmental activities, most Americans still believed that politics and economics occupied separate spheres, and they usually spurned government aid to the economy as "class legislation." Serious questions were raised about the constitutionality of the proposal, and there were also concerns that the plan was a step toward centralizing American government, something that the South had long feared and traditionally resisted. The subtreasury elicited those criticisms, and others, when it was proposed, and it probably never had much chance of passage in Washington.

To begin with, it was too innovative to gain quick acceptance. Governments (and people in general) tend to break new ground quickly only in extreme circumstances, in emergencies more serious even than the one posed by the American economy at the end of the nineteenth century. For instance, as its fortunes declined drastically after 1862, the government of the Confederate States became the first in North America to conscript troops and even built and operated war industries. The subtreasury also raised the specter of an unstable, expansive currency. Bankers and most intermediaries opposed the subtreasury for obvious reasons. The subtreasury had more than a hint of "class legislation" about it since it favored farmers, but not all of them, and would adversely affect many others by raising food and fiber prices.

Many farmers were either hostile to the subtreasury or indifferent to it. The subtreasury appealed primarily to cotton and wheat farmers, who confronted especially hard times and whose products could be stored easily and for long periods of time. Corn, hog, dairy, vegetable, and fruit producers had little use for the subtreasury plan. Most farmed in the north-central and north Atlantic states and were considerably more prosperous than wheat or cotton farmers. Those states accounted for 70 percent of the farm wealth in the United States in 1890; the north-central states alone accounted for one-half of national farm wealth. Inflation, or currency expansion, might lessen the value of what farmers owned in those states. And if the government was going to lend them money, they were more interested in mortgages on land than in loans on crops. That argument explained why the Southern Alliance at the Ocala meeting added real estate to its demand for a subtreasury.

THE ALLIANCE IN POLITICS

The issue of political activity also made itself felt during the Ocala meeting. Whether to be "in politics" was no longer the issue, as the Ocala Demands made clear. Now the question was how. The organization could lobby as a pressure group, work with and perhaps try to dominate the Democratic and Republican parties, or form a third party. The Ocala meeting indicated that the Alliance was leaning toward the last approach. It elected Leonidas L. Polk, who had third-party inclinations, to succeed Macune, who did not, to the presidency. Macune continued to function as editor of the *National Economist*, the official national newspaper of the Alliance; he used it to beat a steady drum for the subtreasury plan. A 1,000-member National Reform Press Association was also formed at Ocala.

But the Alliance wavered on its political tactics. The third-party strategy threatened to divide the organization permanently. The core of the Alliance, its southern white members, had a virtually patriotic commitment to the Democratic party. Memories, habits, and Negrophobia cemented the attachment. Moreover, some Democratic politicians had been receptive to the Alliance, and the Alliance became a force in several southern states by working with Democrats. The Republicans inadvertently reinforced that attachment. In 1890 the Republican House of Representatives passed the Lodge Election Bill, or the Force Bill as it was called by its mostly southern opponents and as it has since been known. Proposed in 1889 by Henry Cabot Lodge, then a Massachusetts congressman, the bill provided for federal supervision of elections to ensure that blacks could vote freely in the southern states. Attacks of conscience and partisan politics prompted the Republican action. Violations of the political and civil rights of blacks were flagrant and routine in the South. Republicans also had a strong interest in expanding their voter base, because in national politics they confronted an equally powerful Democratic party.

For years the Republicans sought ways to increase their following in the South. Convinced that blacks offered their best hope and equally convinced that election frauds had prevented Republican successes in many places in the South, the Republicans turned to the Lodge Bill. Though it had little chance to pass in the

Senate, the Lodge Bill set off alarms in the South and memories of resistance to Reconstruction. Recalling "that glorious era," the *Atlanta Constitution* opined that "what we did twenty years ago we can do again." Southern delegates to the Ocala meeting of the Alliance shouted their approval of a resolution protesting the bill. At the same time and at a separate meeting in Ocala, the Colored Alliance endorsed the Lodge Bill. Racial fears kept the Alliance close to the Democrats even as those same fears divided the Alliance movement along racial lines.

Election returns in 1890 gave the Alliance reason to hope that it could achieve its aims within Democratic ranks. In South Carolina, "Pitchfork Ben" Tillman used Alliance support to win the governorship as a Democrat while driving out his opponents in the Democratic party ("the aristocratic coterie") and establishing a personal political machine. James S. Hogg achieved a similar success in Texas with help from the Alliance, the Grange, and the Knights of Labor. Tennessee sent the president of the state Alliance to the governor's office, and more than a third of the state legislators had ties with the Alliance. In several states—North Carolina, Florida, Georgia, Alabama—the Alliance was a major force in legislative and congressional elections. An Alliance-supported candidate won the governorship of Georgia, and another nearly became governor of Alabama. The Alliance split in Arkansas, and a faction joined forces with the Union Labor party in a strong, though unsuccessful, third-party effort. In Virginia, Louisiana, and Kentucky, several congressmen pledged allegiance to the Alliance. Leonidas L. Polk celebrated the returns. "We are here to stay. . . .The people of this country are desperately in earnest. They will no longer put up with this nonsense. Old Party fossils have lost their grip." An Allianceman sounded a triumphant theme: "Being Democrats and in the majority, we took possession of the Democratic Party."

What politicians meant when they took the pledge of allegiance to the Alliance, however, was not clear. The Alliance discovered that the Democrats whom they helped elect and who had expressed sympathy with the organization behaved more like Democrats than like Alliance enthusiasts. Tillman in South Carolina and Hogg in Texas embraced only part of the Alliance program; Hogg never accepted the subtreasury, and Tillman did so only to get elected. Hogg even tried unsuccessfully to destroy the Alliance. In Georgia, a supposedly Alliance-dominated legislature elected elderly General Gordon, one of the state's Bourbon triumvirate, to the U.S. Senate and failed to act on railroad regulation or any antitrust legislation, but it did pass legislation to aid businesses.

Southern Democrats had an uneasy relationship with Alliancemen. Some disparaged the Alliancemen as country rubes with outrageous ideas and simple-minded solutions for complex problems, "continually harping," a Mississippi editor wrote, "on the evils of National Banks and the crushing power of Wall Street. Poor, pitiful, sinful cranks! Not one of them was ever inside a bank, and know as little as to how they are managed as a hog does about the holy writ of God."

Other critics were more analytical. They noted that most of what the Alliance wanted could not be obtained through state legislatures but had to come through federal action. Currency expansion, lower tariffs or import duties, and the creation of subtreasuries were matters for the federal government. Southern Democrats had well-founded reservations about the subtreasury plan, but their support for currency expansion was growing.

Southern Democrats also genuinely believed that lower tariffs would lead to expanded foreign markets for American farmers. They had long championed tariff reduction and had been instrumental in making it the major domestic policy of the national Democratic party versus the high tariff or protectionist policy of the national Republican party. That policy particularly galled southerners. Then, by the 1880s, it was well known that income from high tariffs was the primary reason there were growing surpluses in the national treasury.

Though the federal government had an embarrassment of riches, the Republicans resisted the obvious—tax reduction—because that meant tariff reduction. They increased spending instead. The leading and fastest-growing expenditures were for pensions for Union army veterans and their dependents. (Confederate veterans and their dependents did not, of course, qualify for federal pensions. Their much more modest pensions came from southern state funds.) One consequence of these policies was that for many years, the federal government took considerably more out of the South in taxes than it spent in the South.

THE MISSISSIPPI PLAN

Mississippi produced the most surprising and the most important outcome of the Alliance's involvement in politics in 1890. Exhorted by the Alliance, the state Grange, and others, the state legislature called a constitutional convention in order, according to James Z. George, U.S. senator and Mississippi's leading politician, "to devise such measures, consistent with the Constitution of the United States, as will enable us to maintain a home government, under the control of the white people of the state." The convention devised the "Mississippi Plan" as a legal mechanism to circumvent the Fourteenth and Fifteenth amendments and to preclude federal intervention—as the Force Bill called for—in Mississippi elections.

The Mississippi Plan was an important precursor to a Southwide movement to eliminate blacks and large numbers of poor whites from the political process. The new state constitution required voters to have resided in the state for at least two years and in their election districts for one, to have paid all their taxes for two years before registering to vote, and to register and pay a poll tax of $2, unless they qualified for one of the few exemptions. Voters had to "be able to understand" any part of the state constitution when it was read to them "or give a reasonable interpretation thereof." Drafters of the constitution had a general understanding that registrars would pass illiterate whites and fail blacks.

As soon became obvious, the constitutional interpretation or "understanding" clause did not, as had been promised, provide adequate insurance for the voting rights of poorer whites. The tax clauses, especially the poll tax, effectively disfranchised many whites and most blacks in a state where the average income produced by a farm was about $400 a year. Given the transience of lower-income groups, the residency requirement reinforced the class and race pattern of disfranchisement. The "understanding" clause invited fraud. Factions or machines in control of the electoral system could manipulate the clause for the desired effect, perhaps disfranchising some and enfranchising others, possibly blacks, in order to win elections.

After 1890, "the legal Negro voter, and consequently the Republican party," a student of Mississippi politics wrote, became "a negligible factor in state-wide elections." For instance, Republican vote totals in presidential elections plummeted from 43,000 in 1884 to 1,500 votes in 1892. Not until 1920 did a Republican presidential nominee again get as many as 6,000 votes. Political participation in general declined sharply, even among Democrats. Of the 120,000 whites who could vote in 1890, only 68,000 registered in 1892. That year some 40,000 Mississippians voted for Grover Cleveland; in 1888, more than 85,000 had done so.

Disfranchisement, as these figures indicate, secured the dominance of white people in Mississippi politics and determined which whites would have predominance. Mississippi politics, to simplify somewhat, reflected the divisions between the delta counties (those near the Mississippi and its principal tributaries) and the rest of the state. The delta, with its enormously rich riverine soil, had large, highly productive, profitable landholdings or plantations, which were owned by whites and most of which were worked by black sharecroppers and day laborers. Blacks in the delta outnumbered whites from 3 to as much as 15 to 1.

Northeastern Mississippi provided the delta planters with their strongest opposition. Whites in the northeast considerably outnumbered those in the delta, but they farmed inferior land and had much less income. The southeastern part of the state, the piney woods, afforded even fewer opportunities than were available in the northeast and was thinly populated. The lumber boom did not reach the southeast until the mid-1890s, and the primary beneficiaries of the boom were large lumber companies. Almost all of what industry Mississippi had was located in the southern part of the state. Only after new sources of energy were available to make up for the lack of coal and the absence of water power did industry spread elsewhere in Mississippi. A strip of counties along the eastern edge of the delta had considerable agricultural wealth and provided a transitional area between the delta and the rest of the state. Large landholders and successful farmers in this strip and in areas scattered throughout the state were political allies of the delta planters, as were railroad leaders and prominent lawyers, merchants, bankers, and manufacturers. Most of the latter groups centered their activities in Jackson.

Black disfranchisement threatened to cost the delta dearly. Delta planters and their allies in the state, often labeled Bourbons or Redeemers, used black votes to maintain their strong position in Mississippi politics. To get black votes, the Bourbons resorted to intimidation, unsubtle persuasion, fraud, and "fusion." "Fusion"— the division of local offices with blacks—was a tactic employed most frequently in the delta. Confronted by a restive agrarian movement in the state in the late 1880s, the Bourbons increasingly resorted to various fraudulent voting tactics. Such methods and the continuing insensitivity of the Bourbons to the needs of smaller farmers fueled demands by the Alliance and other radical agrarians for disfranchisement of blacks as a necessary first step to getting what the agrarians wanted from the legislature.

At the constitutional convention, the Bourbons countered with a scheme designed to shore up the power of the delta and its allies. The new constitution shifted some representation away from the delta, but it still allowed these elements very disproportionate power. The result was gross overrepresentation of the delta. This disproportion was also carried over to methods used for electing governors, who were given wide powers, such as responsibility for the appointment of all judges in the state.

Ironically, as a result of the plunge of the Alliance and the Grange into politics, thousands of whites (as well as blacks) were deprived of their votes, and for some years anti-Alliance forces were strengthened. Mississippi Democrats also embraced free silver in the early 1890s. That position and the Mississippi Plan may have been enough to keep the Democrats firmly in power and to account for the failure of the Populist party in Mississippi in the 1890s.

Equally unsettling for the Alliance was what occurred in Washington. Congressional Democrats allowed a bill to create the subtreasury to die in committee. Congress did pass a mildly inflationary currency measure, the Sherman Silver Purchase Act, in 1890, as well as the Sherman Antitrust Act, a landmark antimonopoly statute. For many members of the Alliance, these measures were not enough. Then in 1891, when the now heavily Democratic House of Representatives could not pass the more inflationary Bland Silver Bill, many Alliancemen in the South became embittered and consequently more interested in what the Alliance had done in Kansas. There it had formed an independent party, the People's (Populist) party, in 1890, and had won sweeping victories at the polls.

THE POPULISTS

During 1891 the Populist party became a national party with supporters in every southern state, especially in Texas, Alabama, Georgia, North Carolina, and Florida. Delegates gathered for the party's national nominating convention in Omaha in July 1892. They met, according to a party statement, "in the midst of a nation brought to the verge of moral, political, and material ruin." The convention chose a slate and wrote a sweeping, highly specific platform, unlike the platitude-filled platforms that usually emerged from national political conventions.

The Populists called for election reforms that included the Australian (secret) ballot system; a graduated income tax; currency expansion and the replacement of national banknotes by government-issued notes; "free and unlimited coinage of silver and gold" at a ratio of 16 to 1; the subtreasury; government ownership of railroads, telephone, and telegraph; and an attack on land monopolies and landowning by aliens. Endeavoring mightily to build a farm-labor coalition, the Populists expressed the hope "that the union of the labor forces of the United States this day consummated shall be permanent and perpetual. . . .Wealth belongs to him who creates it." The platform urged greater protection against immigrant labor, which "crowds out our wage-earners," and expressed its sympathies with the Knights of Labor and with workers' efforts to organize and to get shorter hours. The Populists favored free and open elections and had a strong interest in them, since the Democrats had so effectively used their control of the election machinery in several southern states for partisan ends. Yet the Populists opposed the Force Bill. Obviously southern sentiments prevailed on this issue.

The Populists had difficulty selecting their nominees for president and vice president. The strongest candidate from the South—an Alliance and Populist stronghold—had been lost when Leonidas L. Polk died suddenly in early 1892.

FAMILY REUNION, 1890s (Courtesy Georgia Department of Archives and History)

The convention chose General James B. Weaver of Iowa as its presidential nominee. Weaver had served in the Union Army during the Civil War, but he had ties and friends in all sections of the country and was an experienced campaigner and politician. He left the Republican party in the 1870s and, with Democratic support, gained a seat in Congress in 1878 as a Greenbacker. In 1880 he ran for president on the Greenback ticket, campaigning throughout much of the country. In the 1880s he returned to Congress as a Greenback-Democrat. Then he joined the Populists. For vice president the Populists picked General James G. Field, a Confederate veteran from Virginia. A colonel during the Civil War, Field may have been "promoted" for his service as attorney general in Virginia or in the Virginia militia. Such "promotions" were not uncommon.

The Populists left Omaha in high spirits and with a sense of mission and an immense task. In addition to the usual problems faced by new political parties, the Populists faced the enormous barriers presented by sectionalism, race, and a militant opposition that knew few scruples. As new parties usually did, the Populists lacked a reservoir of good candidates with established reputations, especially at the state and local levels, and they did not have an experienced campaign organization, substantial sums of money for electioneering, or patronage to offer party workers. As assailers of the status quo, the Populists unsettled many voters, and their fiery rhetoric reinforced those feelings. Conversely, the Populists could draw upon the ideas, the emotions, and sometimes the organizations that the Alliance had produced. Certainly, many potential voters found the rebellious spirit of the People's party attractive. Many farmers in the South, however, were not in a rebellious mood, because they were successful. Not all were on the verge of moral or material ruin. Many enjoyed at least middle-class status and incomes.

The Populists also had to persuade people to break old party loyalties, loyalties complicated by sectionalism and especially by race. Party loyalty, as analyses of American politics have shown repeatedly, is a powerful force. Party loyalty fell along ethnic and religious lines, strong factors everywhere in the United States in the late nineteenth century. Protestants and Catholics in the northern states, for instance, showed strong attachments to the Republicans and the Democrats, respectively. In the southern version of ethnic politics, Democrats drew a familiar and favorite equation: the Democratic party equaled white supremacy and sectional patriotism. That equation was an enormous asset for the Democrats. Furthermore, they enjoyed the considerable advantages of being the most entrenched party in the South and of having, in 1892, a likely victor in the presidential race, Grover Cleveland. The Democrats also took over some Populist issues. Governor Hogg of Texas, for example, succeeded in getting strong railroad regulatory legislation, while South Carolina's Tillman got approval for an agricultural school, Clemson College (now Clemson University).

Probably the greatest challenge faced by the Populists was to attract the black voters they had to have if they were to succeed. "The negro vote will be the balancing vote in Texas," a black delegate to the Texas state Populist convention declared. "If you are going to win, you will have to take the negro with you." Just how far the Populists were willing or able to "take the negro" with them was a matter of dispute in the 1890s and has been debated by historians since. In light of the sad history of black-white relations in the South especially, but also in the country as a whole, it is tempting to see the Populists as bolder innovators in race relations than they were. A desire to see the past as more heroic than it was is entirely understandable, but it may lead one to see a past that was not there.

The Populist approach to the blacks should be examined for motivation and for what the Populists did and did not do. The Populists included blacks in their meetings, usually on a segregated basis, and selected blacks for party offices, but not for candidates for public office. John B. Rayner, a black, served as an officer and very effective speaker for the Texas Populists. The Populists were acting from self-interest. Not only did they urgently need black voters, but they also assumed that they and the blacks, as the disinherited farmers of the South, had common interests. The Populists emphatically rejected social equality or anything that approached it, but they had enough vision and sense to spurn blatant Negrophobia, something the Democrats did not do. Tom Watson put the Populist appeal to blacks in cogent terms: "Once it appear[s] plainly that it is to the interest of a colored man to vote with the white man, . . . he will do it."

The Populists dared to breach one of the most formidable barriers of the South, the wall between blacks and poorer whites. Those breaches required mental and sometimes physical courage. Moreover, unlike the Democrats, the Populists did not exploit Negrophobia to advance their cause or advocate the disfranchisement of blacks. Later, however, many disappointed, embittered Populists, most notably Tom Watson, did look back on their defeats and hurl their pent-up fury at blacks.

MIDDLE-CLASS FARM HOME, 1890s (Courtesy Georgia Department of Archives and History)

Blacks responded variously to Populist appeals. Not all saw an identity of interests with the Populists. Black political leaders had a stake in the Republican party—status and possibly a desired appointment. Most blacks had strong emotional ties to "the party of Lincoln," the party of emancipation. The small urban black middle class had good reason to fear the Populist program. Thousands of blacks were sharecroppers and farm day laborers, and their interests often differed from those of their white employers, who might be Populists. Blacks had bitter experiences with the Southern Alliance, the spiritual father of the People's party, which had kept the Colored Farmers' Alliance at arm's length. The Southern Alliance in Georgia, for instance, had supported laws that required segregation by race on railroad cars and had favored the revival of the whipping post for some crimes. In Mississippi, the Alliance had been in the forefront of the movement to disfranchise blacks.

In some instances the Democrats tried to speak to black concerns. In Georgia, Governor William J. Northen advocated more money for black schools and an end to lynching. But Northen also verbalized a stark, self-serving paternalism in which blacks were perpetual children consigned permanently to farm labor. Understandably blacks wondered with which whites they should ally themselves, whom they could trust. Given the alternatives, many impoverished blacks probably acted rationally when they sold their votes. Money in hand was better than the promises of politicians. Some blacks undoubtedly voluntarily voted for Democrats. Many more did so involuntarily.

The Populists also represented a challenge to the established order—to among other things, the "right thinking" of the day on banking and currency, to men like Judge Emory Speer, and to those who built and promoted the Atlanta

Exposition. "The wellspring of Populism," a sympathetic scholar has concluded, was its efforts

> to overcome a concentrating system of finance capitalism that was rooted in Eastern commercial banks and which radiated outward through trunk-line railroad networks to link in a number of common purposes much of America's consolidated corporate community. [The Populists'] aim was structural reform of the American economic system.

That aim alone would have triggered a furious response by the more established elements. Then add the challenge Populism presented to the Democratic party and to white supremacy, and the fiery rhetoric with which they issued it. In Georgia the Populists told voters as they got ready to vote:

> The hand of God is in our movement and will be until we triumph.
> We are slaves now. It used to be only the colored people.
> Fellow citizens, our homes and our liberties are at stake, and in the name of Almighty God let us pledge ourselves and not give up the fight until we win the victory.

The *Augusta (Ga.) Chronicle* replied:

> Never has there been a time since the days of reconstruction, when it was so absolutely necessary for every southern man to do his duty at the ballot box to his God, his country and himself.
> In the triumph of democratic doctrines and policies is the perpetuity of our government and the prosperity of our country.
> The south and especially the tenth [congressional] district is threatened by anarchy and communism. The direful teaching of Thomas E. Watson, and the visionary promises of the demagogue have aroused the cupidity of the ignorant, and influenced the passions of intemperate men, who would sacrifice their country and their people to their own selfish desires.

A battlefield mentality permeated the South during the 1892 election. General Weaver received a hostile reception when he campaigned in the South. Earlier, as a Greenbacker, he had not, but in 1892 Weaver constituted a much greater threat. Weaver was shouted down, pelted with rocks, and egged until he "was made a walking omelet by the Southern chivalry of Georgia." Mary E. Lease, Kansas Populist spokeswoman, remembered for advising farmers in her home state "to raise more hell and less corn," got similar treatment. The Populists were prepared to see women take a more active part in politics, but much of the South was not. The *Greensboro (N.C.) Daily Record* felt that "the sight of a woman traveling around the country making political speeches . . . is simply disgusting," that "Southern manhood revolts at the idea of degrading womanhood to the level of politics."

The level of politics got very low in 1892 and probably unnecessarily so in the South. The Democrats won there easily. Weaver got one-third of his 1 million votes (out of 12 million cast in the nation) in the South, but none of his electoral votes. Only Alabama gave Weaver as much as a third of its votes (36.6 percent); Texas ranked second (23.6 percent).

A Populist-supported candidate did nearly win election as governor in Alabama. Reuben Kolb had developed a wide following among Alabama farmers, and he was probably the most popular politician in the state. Yet anti-Alliance Democrats controlled the nominating process and kept Kolb from getting the Democratic nomination in 1890 and 1892. After the second rebuff, Kolb and his followers formed a separate faction, the Jeffersonian-Democrats. They embraced much of the Populist program and joined forces with the Populists and the Republicans. They appealed to Republicans with a platform promise that declared, "We favor the protection of the colored race in their political rights."

The Democrats attacked that "nigger rights' section of the platform," but their hostility to it did not discourage them from using their control of the election machinery to marshal black votes to defeat independents in Alabama. Democrats favored black voting when they controlled that vote. The issue in Alabama was not whether or not blacks could vote; "the real question was *how* the Negro voted."

Kolb lost to the Democratic incumbent, Thomas G. Jones, in 1892 by 11,435 votes. Jones's strength lay in the black belt, where he had 30,217 more votes than Kolb and where most counties had more blacks than whites. It may have been the most fraudulent election in Alabama since Reconstruction. Desperate to stop Kolb, Jones's supporters threatened, intimidated, and bribed voters and stole ballot boxes. Such tactics were not exclusive to counties with black majorities, but the black belt provided the margin of victory for Jones. There, an Alabama wag noted, the planter, "by patience, perseverance and courage . . . has maintained his influence with the nigger and has neutralized nigger supremacy with nigger votes, which is the grandest political achievement of the century. He has knocked out the Republicans with the boomerang they hurled at him." The Democrat won with a formula that became an Alabama standard after the 1880s. The planters of the black belt combined forces with the Big Mules,* the commercial and industrial leaders of Birmingham and Mobile, to counter rural counties with white majorities.

Tom Watson met a similar fate in his congressional reelection campaign in Georgia. The former Democrat, now a Populist, ran into an urban version of Democratic election chicanery. Patrick Walsh, political boss of Augusta, led the way. Augusta reported twice as many votes in 1892 as there were legal voters in the city. Blacks reportedly were brought by wagonloads from South Carolina to vote for Watson's opponent. This action was an old tradition in the area. In earlier years, whites from the Augusta area had crossed the Savannah River to help South Carolina Democrats defeat Republicans.

*P*OLITICAL UPHEAVAL

The Democrats also won the presidential election in 1892, but that victory had the potential for disaster. Grover Cleveland, a militant gold-standard man, won. When the Democrats had renominated Cleveland, they had ignored the distressed farmers of the West and the South and gone for a winner, a former New York governor and former president who had failed to win reelection to the presidency in 1888 by a narrow margin. To the sure bloc of votes from the solid

*The term was first coined in the 1930s. It has since come to be used retrospectively.

TOM WATSON, POPULIST
LEADER, AT 48 (Culver
Pictures)

South, Cleveland added the votes of his home state and those of several other northern states and returned to the White House. Ironically, even as the Populists were asserting themselves and many Democrats in the South were drawing close to the positions of the Alliance and the Populists, the presidency became a gold-standard stronghold occupied by a Democrat. Moreover, the new president took particular pride in assuming forthright positions and defending them at all costs. Cleveland had little taste or gift for the art of compromise.

Confronted by the depression of the 1890s, the worst economic crisis in American history until 1929, Cleveland did what was expected of a president then—next to nothing. Cleveland expended his greatest efforts in defense of the gold standard, which he and many others thought was of critical importance to the economy. Cleveland waged a bitter, successful battle to repeal the Sherman Silver Purchase Act, and he moved with dispatch to preserve the government's gold reserves.

Cleveland's stand on the gold standard incensed the Populists and many Democrats in the South as well as in the West. They had embraced currency expansion and after 1892 had become committed to free silver as essential to the economic well-being of southern and western farmers and of the country as a whole. They saw these policies as fundamental to an effort to wrest power from the eastern "moneyed interests" so that a political and economic democracy might be "restored." Cleveland talked about "the cankering rust of national dishonesty" and "national bad faith," and warned that "popular discontent and passion [were being] stimulated by the art of designing partisans to a pitch perilously near to class hatred or sectional anger." He saw a "line of battle [being] drawn between the forces of safe currency and those of silver monometallism." Ben Tillman declared that "when Judas betrayed Christ his heart was not blacker than this scoundrel, Cleveland, in deceiving" the Democratic party. Tillman promised to attack the "old bag of beef . . . with a pitchfork."

Like the last Jacksonian Democrat in the White House, Andrew Johnson, Cleveland refused to compromise. Ironically for a Jacksonian, Cleveland relied on Wall Street for advice, and he turned again to Wall Street—to J. P. Morgan and other bankers—to shore up the declining gold reserves of the government even as the Atlanta Exposition was opening. As some people were celebrating the New South in Henry Grady's town with a blessing from the president, others saw no New South or did not like much of what they saw of it. They also believed that Cleveland's gold policies would lead to even harder times and greater disasters. In growing numbers they distanced themselves from the Cleveland Democrats by turning to Populism or to free silver within the Democratic party.

But Cleveland persisted and won, and in doing so contributed substantially to the near-destruction of the national Democratic party. The Republicans achieved something they had never been able to do: they became the majority party in the 1890s. Thereafter Republicans could largely ignore the South and still dominate national politics. That dominance lasted a generation, during which the solid South generally found itself excluded from national power.

The political turbulence occasioned by the depression of the 1890s gave the Populists their opportunity. Populism reached its electoral peak during the next major election year, 1894. It enjoyed greater success in the South than elsewhere in the nation and did best where Populists fused with Republicans or with dissident Democrats. In North Carolina the Populists joined ranks with the Republicans, who had strong support in both the eastern part of the state, which had a large black population, and in the largely white western part of the state. The Populists won control of the state senate and shared the state house of representatives with the Republicans. A Republican filled the unexpired term of the deceased senator Zebulon Vance, a Democrat who had been a fixture in North Carolina politics. The Populist Marion Butler won a six-year term to the U.S. Senate. Three Populists, two Republicans, and one Independent served North Carolina in the national House of Representatives. The Populist-Republican fusion in North Carolina owed much of its success to the Populists' moderation. They softened their appeal to class interests and retreated from open efforts to build a black-white coalition.

Alabama Populists followed a similar course. They joined forces with Jeffersonian Democrats rather than with Republicans. Fusionists in Alabama were awarded several congressional seats after they got disputed elections reversed by Congress. But Kolb lost the governorship again, probably for the same reasons he had lost in 1892. He and his followers staged their own "inaugural," but, faced by overwhelming police force, they dispersed after a brief informal ceremony. Kolb did attract more votes from the coal miners and ironworkers in and around Birmingham than he had earlier. Miners, 7,000 of whom went on strike in 1894, found Kolb particularly attractive. They thought he would be less inclined to use force and convict labor to break strikes than were the Democrats, who had used those tactics against the miners' strike. Thus a farm-labor coalition existed in Alabama, if briefly. Industrial labor would pay a significant role in Alabama politics thereafter. Tom Watson had an experience similar to Kolb's. He lost again in Georgia in his race for Congress, and again he may have been defrauded by unscrupulous Democrats.

In their search for electoral success, the Populists altered their positions on some issues, sometimes drastically. Populists in North Carolina and Alabama, for instance, dropped the Populist financial program and staked their entire economic appeal on free silver. Georgia Populists kept the faith on most economic issues, but like the Populists of North Carolina and Alabama, they muffled or completely altered their appeals to black voters. Only in Texas did the Populists refuse to endorse free silver as the key financial issue. There they adhered to class-interest politics. They kept the full Populist financial program, supported labor, and openly appealed to black voters.

Populist or fusion tickets got nearly 54 percent of the vote in North Carolina, 48 percent in Alabama, more than 36 percent in Texas, and, in 1895 and 1896 respectively, more than 25 percent in Mississippi and nearly 44 percent in Louisiana. Louisiana Populists joined antilottery Democrats to defeat an entrenched Democratic machine whose assets included $10 million in profits per year from a state lottery that cost them only $40,000 for an exclusive franchise. Under Bourbon rule, public services in Louisiana sank to their nadir. Though Louisiana had more wealth than its neighbor Arkansas, it devoted less than one-half of the amount of tax money Arkansas did for public schools. As one historian noted sardonically, on the basis of literacy rates Louisiana "climbed from fifth to first place in ignorance between 1880 and 1890."

The 1894 election had other implications, most of which were not happy ones for the Populists. Outside the South, the Populists suffered setbacks where they had been a majority or a near majority—in Kansas, Colorado, Idaho, the Dakotas, Nevada, and Wyoming. Much more important, the Republicans scored an enormous victory nationally in the congressional race. The 1894 election was a decisive factor in making the Republican party the dominant major party in the United States for more than three decades. The Republicans gained 117 seats in the House of Representatives and 5 seats in the Senate. They gained the upper hand for the 1896 presidential election while the Democrats counted casualties and fell into bitter divisions over whom to blame for their defeat and over policy, especially over gold versus silver. Eventually free silver triumphed among the Democrats. They nominated William Jennings Bryan for president in 1896. When the Republicans chose William McKinley as their nominee, the stage was set for one of the most dramatic and climactic elections in American history.

For the Populists, 1896 was also climactic. They faced hard choices. Fusion had been their most successful tactic, whether with the Democrats in Kansas or with the Republicans in North Carolina. But the national Republican party had rejected free silver and had adopted a moderate gold-standard plank in its platform.

Moreover, the Republican party hardly suited the antielitism of the Populists, and the Republicans remained repugnant in most of the South, where Populist strength now was centered.

The Democrats had more appeal for the Populists. They had endorsed free silver and nominated Bryan, a populistic candidate—someone who could legitimately claim to be "a man of the people." Bryan's candidacy also demonstrated that the Democratic party had been sensitive to distressed farmers and had shifted politically in the direction of the Populists. Prominent southern Democrats became converts to free silver: Senator John Tyler Morgan of Alabama, James Z. George of Mississippi, and James K. Jones of Arkansas were Bourbons and major figures in the Senate. Secretary of the Interior Hoke Smith supported Bryan after he was nominated; Cleveland forced the Georgian to resign from his cabinet.

But fusion with the Democrats involved high risks and heavy costs for Populists. After all, southern Populists had fought bitter struggles with the Democrats; the Democrats had a populistic nominee for president, but in the South the party still had a distinctly Bourbon or standpat flavor. Moreover, the Democrats had chosen Arthur Sewall of Maine, who had made a fortune in shipping, for vice president. Middle-of-the-road Populists believed that fusion with either Republicans or Democrats meant extinction. Tom Watson warned: "The [Democratic] idea of fusion [is that] we play Jonah while they play the whale." Moreover, these Populists thought that in endorsing free silver and then trumpeting the issue so vigorously that the 1896 campaign was becoming a single-issue campaign, silver versus gold, the Democrats were following a simpleminded course. Middle-of-the-road Populists believed Populism had a far more thorough and better program for the country, that free silver in Democratic hands was a fatally adulterated Populism.

The Populists could have chosen to nominate a candidate of their own or to endorse none at all. But the first alternative would ensure Republican victory in the presidential race because the anti-Republican vote would be split. The second alternative would be unacceptable for a party that claimed to be a national party; it would signal that the Populists could not even select a presidential ticket. The Populists were sharply divided and ended up with an awkward, though understandable, compromise. They first nominated Watson for vice president, then Bryan for president. Bryan never formally accepted the nomination nor did he reject Sewall, the Democratic nominee for vice president, as the Populists asked him to do. Bryan did not have to do either. He had, in effect, captured the Populists without making a concession. Whether, if he won, he would have appointed some Populists to positions in his administration is uncertain. Many of the Populist leaders who favored fusion with the Democrats in 1896 certainly anticipated such rewards. Those hopes may explain part of their motivation for supporting Bryan.

Bryan lost the presidency in 1896, and the Populists lost ground everywhere except in North Carolina. They did well in Georgia, Alabama, and Texas and might have won in those states if the elections had been fair. In North Carolina, where the elections were generally free and open, the Populists won decisively, fusing with the Republicans and helping elect Daniel L. Russell, the only Republican governor in North Carolina between 1877 and 1973.

In 1898 the white Democrats in North Carolina mounted a scurrilous Negrophobic campaign and routed the Populists and Republicans. The rout reached its bloody finale at Wilmington, North Carolina, in late 1898, when local Democrats overthrew the black-majority city government and installed themselves. At least eleven blacks were killed and more were injured.

Elsewhere in the South after 1896, Populism faded quickly, though more quietly in Alabama and Georgia than in Texas, where it held its own a little longer. In Mississippi, Florida, and Louisiana it was virtually nonexistent. In South Carolina, Tillmanism, a weak variant of Populism, held sway. The Democrats in Arkansas, who had adopted free silver, easily bested their Republican opponents and absorbed remnants of the Populists. The strong one-party tradition of that state prevailed. In Tennessee the Populists never became more than a vocal but small faction amid the highly factionalized politics of the state. Democrats were, however, forced to call upon former governor Robert Love "Our Bob" Taylor. A skilled compromiser, Taylor pulled the Democratic factions together to defeat the Populists and a strong Republican challenge in 1896. It did not hurt that Bob Taylor was adept at the fiddle and storytelling. Republicans, however, remained as a force in Tennessee politics, a greater force there than in other southern states. Virginia Democrats used their tightly organized party structure and their control of the state electoral apparatus to contain the Populists, who enjoyed limited success in the 1890s and then withered. Most members of Virginia's strong Alliance balked at joining the People's party. Democrats used fears of blacks and Mahoneism effectively. They claimed William Mahone was covertly supporting the Populists. Nationally, the Populists faced an equally bleak future. Populist numbers in Congress shrank by 1900. The same year, the Populists followed Bryan again in the presidential race, and Bryan lost again. Four years later, they chose Tom Watson, who got only 114,501 popular votes and no electoral votes.*

THE POPULIST LEGACY

Though the Populists faded fast, the breadth of their following and the extent of their legacy suggested that they were not a momentary phenomenon. Some of their proposals later became law. The Federal Farm Loan Act and the Warehouse Act of 1916 derived their assumptions from the subtreasury plan. More important, the Populists increased public pressures for major shifts in public policy. Government ownership of the transportation and communications systems of the nation never received broad acceptance, but Congress increased its regulatory powers over both. In 1913 Congress created the Federal Reserve System. In the same year the ratification of the Sixteenth Amendment made federal income taxes constitutional, and four years later, as the United States entered World War I, Congress passed a graduated income tax as part of the War Revenue Act. The national government and various state and local governments enacted measures that implemented the direct democracy that the Populists often called for: the Australian

---

*A splinter group of Populists nominated a bizarre slate in 1900. For their presidential candidate a rump of the party selected Wharton Baker, an aged Philadelphia banker and monetary theorist who had joined the Populists in 1896. For vice president they chose Ignatius Donnelly of Minnesota, a none-too-stable veteran of many reform campaigns.

ballot system, direct election of U.S. senators, primaries, initiative, referendum, and recall.

Monetary history also lent support to the position of the Populists. When gold discoveries in Alaska and South Africa markedly increased the supply of gold in the world and thus increased the amount of currency in circulation (inflation), the economy benefited. Moreover, the expanded supply of gold meant that when the United States passed the Gold Standard Act in 1898, the country could end the uncertainty about which monetary standard it would follow without contracting the currency (deflation).

The Populists obviously were not solely and perhaps not primarily responsible for the implementation of their ideas. Nor were all the ideas they espoused original. Even the Redeemers had called for a federal income tax and generally had supported railroad regulation. Still, the Populists left a remarkable legacy. They developed and articulated a wide range of ideas and proposals for a society that was in disarray. Their creativity and boldness stood in stark contrast to the timidity and vacuity of both the Democrats and Republicans. In challenging the color bar and in speaking for the dispossessed, they showed uncommon courage. A historian of Populism in Alabama concluded:

> To embrace Populism in the 1890s was an act of defiance. A man could not thereby increase his social prestige. . . . No one voted Populist from habit for the People's Party was new. Men who voted Populist were frequently plagued by social ostracism, loss of financial credit, and sometimes physical intimidation. If the charges of white Democrats were true, Populists were guilty of treason to party, race, religion, and sacred Jeffersonian principles.

The strength of the Populists' legacy indicated the extent of their debt to the deep currents of postbellum reform thought and agitation, currents that had their sources in urban and industrial America as well as in rural America. That legacy also indicated that increasing numbers of Americans shared the sentiments if not the particular ideas the Populists espoused. More than anything else, the Populists were part of and shapers of a growing feeling that the government and the economy could not exist in separate spheres if the United States was to have any hope of living up to its expressed dreams and ideals. Thus, through the Alliance first and then the People's party, the South contributed in an elemental way to altering the course of the nation that only a generation earlier it had tried to sunder.

As an institution, the Populist party failed. In its earlier years, it enjoyed amazing success for a new party at the polls. But the Populists could not overcome the limitations imposed on all new political parties in the United States or the severe problems specific to their time and place. Racial animosities and fears and sectionalism took heavy tolls.

The Populist party, like the Alliance before it, created some of its own difficulties. Try as they might, the Populists could not keep from sounding like a single-interest movement. Too much of what they wanted appeared primarily to serve the interest of southern cotton growers and western wheat farmers. Other farmers spurned them or ignored them. So did industrial workers, for the most part. The Populists defined "producers" too narrowly, thus discounting the positive role of bankers, investors, merchants, and other "nonproducers" in aiding and sustaining economic growth and activity. In fact, the Populists became so caught up in their praises of agrarianism that they often appeared to be reactionaries in search of the lost world of Thomas Jefferson.

That they were not. Their proposals alone ought to silence the notion that Populism equaled agrarian antiquarianism. The Populists sensed the threat that concentration of economic and political power posed for American life. Yet the Populists never went so far as to break with their attachment to the concept of private property. They blamed "monopolies" for the problems of American agriculture and shied away from blaming a market-oriented economic system.

Within the South, the Populists took dead aim at the foundations of the Lost Cause and the New South. As one historian wrote,

> Southern Populism collided full tilt with the whole edifice of Southern Politics; with the romantic attachment to images of the past; with the separation of politics and economics; with the entombing one-party system, with the [white] folk unity forged by Reconstruction. The Populists talked the language of economics and self-interest. They spoke of class consciousness and class legislation, of combining farmers and laborers in one party, of using government to solve economic problems. Most alarming of all, they said that economic self-interest transcended race. They proposed to fit the Negro in somewhere in their great combination.

Moreover, the Populists did enjoy some success with working-class Americans in the South and elsewhere. The Knights of Labor enjoyed a resurgence after 1890, allied themselves with Eugene V. Debs's American Railway Union, and joined forces with the Populists. Some of these workers and their leaders subsequently became a part of the Socialist party, which showed surprising strength in Texas, Arkansas, Louisiana, and Oklahoma in the early twentieth century.

No wonder the Populists excited such hostility.

DISFRANCHISEMENT: JIM CROW AND SOUTHERN POLITICS

The Democrats discovered in the 1890s that their best weapon to ensure their dominance was the law. Seeking legal means to limit the franchise, they forged the law into an ornate iron gate that effectively barred the way to undesirable voters. That iron gate included poll taxes, complicated registration laws, such mystifying election procedures as multiple ballot boxes and vague secret ballots, literacy and property tests, and understanding clauses and grandfather clauses.* Most

---

*"Understanding" clauses are discussed on p. 000. They were enacted in Mississippi, South Carolina, Georgia, and Virginia. North Carolina, Louisiana, and Oklahoma passed grandfather clauses, which exempted all men who could have voted before 1867 (before Republican governments came to power during Reconstruction) from property or literacy requirements. The exemptions sometimes applied to their descendants as well: the descendants of veterans could get exemptions in Alabama and Georgia under their "fighting grandfather" clauses.

These clauses provided only limited protection to poorer whites who could not meet other requirements for registering and voting, since the period of time during which these exemptions were available was limited. Only Mississippi put no time limit on its "understanding" clause. The small number of these clauses and the time limits imposed on them suggest that the men who designed them were concerned primarily to get the disfranchisement laws and constitutional changes past voters who might object to disfranchising low-income whites.

of these tortured statutes clearly discriminated against the poor and the less well educated. Most of these people were black, but many were white. Some efforts were made to lessen the impact on poorer whites, but not many. It is more than suggestive that of all the measures passed by the southern states to limit the franchise, only the poll tax was enacted in every state.

Only Mississippi, South Carolina, Louisiana, Alabama, and Virginia held constitutional conventions to constrict the franchise. Of those states, only Alabama submitted its revised constitution to the voters. Passage was secured by heavy majorities in the black belt. Either the result was fraudulent or Alabama blacks had taken the unusual step of voting to disfranchise themselves.

The disfranchisers overwhelmed white and black opponents, many of whom were Populists, in legislatures, in constitutional conventions, at the polls, and in the courts. In 1898, in *Williams* v. *Mississippi,* the U.S. Supreme Court upheld the constitutionality of the disfranchisement provisions of the Mississippi state constitution. The decision was the climactic moment for legal disfranchisement. Legal disfranchisement began modestly in the 1870s and early 1880s, accelerated and broadened dramatically after 1888, and reached its peak during the 1890s.

The decision of the Supreme Court meant that the federal government would not attempt to defend the political rights of blacks. In making its decision, the Court fell back from the bolder constitutional innovations of the Reconstruction era and retreated to the more familiar ground where states had traditionally had the power to set eligibility rules for voters, even in federal elections. Disfranchisement had racial and class motives and implications. In 1904 Mississippi Congressman Eaton J. Bowers explained that Mississippi had

> disfranchised not only the ignorant and vicious black, but the ignorant and vicious white as well, and the electorate in Mississippi is now confined to those, and to those alone, who are qualified by intelligence and character for the proper and patriotic exercise of this great franchise.

A disfranchisement leader in Louisiana assured

> the large class of the people of Louisiana who will be disfranchised under the proposed limitations of the suffrage [that] what we seek to do is undertaken in a spirit, not of hostility to any particular men or set of men, but in the belief that the State should see to the protection of the weaker classes; should guard them against the machinations of those who would use them only to further their own base ends; should see to it that they are not allowed to harm themselves. We owe it to the ignorant, we owe it to the weak, to protect them just as we would protect a little child.

Partisan aims were also served. Some Democrats wanted disfranchisement to protect the position of their party and to minimize competition. However, disentangling the motives of the disfranchisers in order to determine whether race, class, or partisanship played the biggest part is probably impossible. Most historians give primacy to race as a motive. Since blacks were poorer than whites and more likely to be Republicans, racial discrimination in registration and voting automatically involved class and partisan discrimination. But because many of the voting laws had a class bias—that is, they discriminated against people who were illiterate, did not have property, moved often, or could ill afford to pay the cumulative poll taxes—the voting laws adversely affected the political rights of the small white landowners who formed the base of the Populist party.

Disfranchisement had a major impact on southern politics. Declines of 50 percent in registration and voting were common. Blacks became nonentities as political participants. The Democrats became so entrenched that they had no effective political opposition except in some local elections and congressional races in eastern Tennessee, western North Carolina, southwestern Virginia, the Arkansas Ozarks, central Texas, and northeastern Oklahoma. (Oklahoma achieved statehood in 1907.) In 1895, Kentucky elected the first of several Republican governors, and Tennessee picked a Republican governor in 1900. For all practical purposes, the most important elections in the South were the Democratic primaries, and the Democrats limited their primaries to whites only. The South thus became a one-party region in which politicians did not have to appeal to the majority of the citizens.

The South reversed the long nineteenth-century trend of expanding the suffrage. Scholars see some comparable developments in the North, where politicians acted to limit the impact of the votes of the "new immigration" from eastern and southern Europe. Governments exist to solve problems that escape private solutions. Private efforts to create an electorate congenial to the southern Democrats had failed and had repeatedly raised charges of fraud and threats of federal intervention in elections; so the Democrats turned to government to get the kind of electorate they sought. Coincidentally, as we shall see in chapter 21, southern white governments erected an elaborate code of racial segregation governing virtually every facet of life in the South. Jim Crow, as the system of racial segregation was called, had been largely informal in the past. Now it was formalized.

THE FOUNDATION RESECURED

Disfranchisement probably ended any prospects the Populists might have had in the South. Then economic recovery eased anxieties and dampened ardor for reform. Farmers especially enjoyed better times. Coincidentally, Americans, north and south, joined in the war against Spain. Good times, "a splendid little war," new territorial acquisitions, and a heightened sense of the country's importance in the world caused memories of the depression and the political turmoil of the 1890s to fade. White supremacy at home and abroad seemed natural, indeed divinely ordained.

White supremacy was fixed in the South. So was the Democratic party. So was cotton. The *Little Rock Arkansas Gazette* declared in 1899: "Once more the South is getting up on its feet. . . . The wait has been a long one, but the hour of prosperity has come, and come to stay. Once more cotton is king."

Even if the Populists had gotten their subtreasury plan passed and had substantially changed the credit system, it is very doubtful that dependency on cotton would have been much altered or that the average southern farmer would have enjoyed sustained prosperity. Though much had changed in the South since 1865, as the Cotton States Exposition attested, most southerners were still overdependent on agriculture for their livelihood. The great majority of southerners no

THE PANTHEON, EXPOSITION IN NASHVILLE, 1897 (Tennessee State Library and Archives)

doubt correctly sensed that they had too few alternatives in the kingdom of cotton and that cotton was a miserly monarch. No doubt they resented those frequent homilies about diversified farming delivered by the likes of Judge Emory Speer. The judge told the inaugural audience at the exposition about a fruit and vegetable farm he had seen on a recent vacation trip to the Georgia mountains. He urged southern farmers to use such farms as models. Unfortunately, at the moment, that approach to farming was entirely inappropriate to and beyond the means of the vast number of southerners who toiled in the fields.

21
Jim Crow: Black and White South

--- ❖ ---

There were and (still are) many Souths. The two most obvious and most widely discussed are the black South and the white South. The distance between the two and the hostility between them became greater in the 1890s than it probably had ever been before and remained so for more than a generation. One man tried to bridge the gap.

THE ATLANTA COMPROMISE

In 1895 Booker T. Washington, who rose from slavery to become the founder and then president of Tuskegee Institute in Alabama, suggested terms for a truce or compromise between the black South and the white South in a speech he delivered at the Cotton States and International Exposition in Atlanta in September 1895. His remarks, which became known as "The Atlanta Compromise," fit the occasion like a glove and mirrored the times and the place with arresting precision.

Washington spoke to a racially segregated, predominantly white audience, which initially gave him a cool reception. But when he finished, the audience cheered him wildly. Washington succeeded by saying what southern whites wanted to hear, by making blacks feel proud, and by praising northern whites "for the constant help that has come to our educational life, . . . especially from Northern philanthropists." He spoke in biblical terms while embracing the rampant materialism of the times and the place. Blacks were delighted to have one of their own recognized by southern whites. Such recognition was rare, and

Washington did blacks proud by performing wonderfully. Initially few blacks dissented from his remarks; eventually many did.

Washington began his speech with an assertion that formed the foundation of his address: blacks and whites had mutual, entwined interests. "One-third of the population of the South is of the Negro race. No enterprise seeking the material, civil, or moral welfare of this section can disregard this element of our population and reach the highest success." He tacitly accepted the white version of the Reconstruction and post-Reconstruction eras and endorsed a gradualist approach to black participation in southern politics. In the 1860s, "ignorant and inexperienced" former slaves had made the mistake of trying to start "at the top instead of at the bottom . . . a seat in Congress or the state legislature was more sought than real estate or industrial skill. . . . It is at the bottom of life we must begin." Washington decried efforts to encourage blacks to emigrate to Africa or to encourage Europeans to swell the labor force in the New South. He adroitly blended the "faithful Negro" theme, a southern white staple, with allusions to labor conflicts in the immigrant-populated North. He could rely on his audience to recall Haymarket, Homestead, and Pullman, three long-remembered episodes of American industrial warfare that had occurred within the past decade.

> As we have proved our loyalty to you in the past, in nursing your children, watching by the sick-bed of your mothers and fathers, and often following them with tear-dimmed eyes to their graves, so in the future, in our humble way, we shall stand by you with devotion that no foreigner can approach, ready to lay down our lives, if need be, in defense of yours, interlacing our industrial, commercial, civil, and religious life with yours in a way that shall make the interest of both races one.

Then, raising his hand high, Washington electrified the audience with a memorable gesture and reassuring words: "In all things that are purely social, we can be separate as the fingers, yet one as the hand in all things essential to mutual progress." The "whole audience," a New York *World* reporter wrote, "was on its feet in a delirium of applause."

Washington accepted or acquiesced in the divisions between the black South and the white South. He dismissed "the agitation of questions of social equality" as "the extremest folly. . . . Progress in the enjoyment of all the privileges that will come to us must be the result of severe and constant struggle rather than of artificial forcing." He implicitly suggested that the securing of political rights for blacks could wait until another, unspecified day. Washington did, however, make an oblique call for civil rights: he hoped that there would be "a determination to administer absolute justice . . . [and] a willing obedience among all classes to the mandates of the law."

Throughout, Washington based his remarks on the assumption that material progress had transformative powers, that it promised a better day (someday) for patient, hard-working blacks and for the entire South. He also assumed that blacks would play a subordinate role in this process, principally as a critically needed source of labor, especially on the farm. Such assumptions reflected the pervasiveness of materialism at the time and fit neatly into white perceptions about the place of blacks in the nation.

BOOKER T. WASHINGTON STATUE (Tuskegee Institute, Alabama)

Jim Crow

Many blacks then and more since criticized Washington as an "Uncle Tom," or a toady to southern whites. They had a point, but Washington's remarks reflected the realities of his day. The great majority of blacks lived in the South, where whites were dominant in every facet of life and were determined to remain so. The great majority of northern whites offered little support or encouragement to blacks. Indeed, the attitudes of northern whites seemed to differ only slightly from those of southern whites. Blacks lacked the power and self-confidence at that time to put up more than token resistance.

In 1895 the Jim Crow system of de jure and de facto subordination of blacks in the South was beginning to reach its maturity. The Jim Crow system was a racial caste system. It was based on race in a starkly simple way. Anyone—from a pale-skinned mulatto to the very dark-skinned—who had Negroid physical characteristics was considered to be a Negro. Negroes were born into their caste and could not escape it by marriage or by personal achievement. They could never earn enough or achieve enough to escape their caste. Jim Crow was systematic. It involved the virtually total disfranchisement of blacks and sweeping racial segregation in social relations and, in many instances, in economic relations. The system grew out of white supremacy, or the idea that whites are inherently and culturally superior to "non-whites." In the American South, blacks were the prime target of white supremacy, and there white supremacy involved more than prejudice and discrimination against people who had a particular ancestry and certain physical characteristics. In the South, white supremacy "suggest[ed] systematic and self-conscious efforts to make race or color a qualification for membership in the civil community." Jim Crow involved formal codes, restrictions written into law, and informal codes, unwritten but understood forms of behavior. The informal codes, for instance, required that blacks use only the back door at the home of a white and that blacks address a white by title and last name while whites almost always used the first name or nickname of a black. By law, blacks were segregated or excluded altogether from virtually all public places: public transportation; schools; housing; libraries; restrooms; drinking fountains; barber and beauty shops; the offices of physicians, dentists, and lawyers; hospitals; institutions for the incapacitated and dependent; and cemeteries. Jim Crow also involved blatant economic discrimination.

By 1895, when Washington spoke, most of the southern states had taken significant legal steps to restrict the civil and political rights of blacks. These measures had been preceded by nonlegal measures. During Reconstruction, these measures first hampered and then undermined Republican state governments and Republican officeholders in the South and seemed to assure the Democrats of dominance. Legal disfranchisement measures began to appear after 1875, reached flood proportions in the 1890s, and continued to come until 1915. As blacks disappeared from the polls, they disappeared from public offices and from jury boxes. The last black congressman left office in 1901. There would not be another until 1928, and he was from Chicago.

Predictably, blacks did not receive equal protection of the law. Neither did their concerns command the attention of politicians and public officials. Blacks were three times as likely as whites to be incarcerated and received much harsher sentences for the same crime—a pattern that continued for many years. In South Carolina, 80 percent of the felons executed by the state from 1915 to 1962 were black. Blacks were also overrepresented in the convict lease system and on chain gangs, the most brutal manifestations of the penal system. By 1910, however, most of the southern states abandoned the convict lease system after a series of newspaper exposés and legislative hearings revealed that the system was too grotesque even for the Jim Crow era. Embarrassment may have been a more powerful force for change than a stricken conscience.

White governments developed penal systems and laws that resembled the infamous Black Codes. They were a means of obtaining menial labor and subordinating blacks. Although the convict lease systems were eventually abandoned by the states that had them, chain gangs remained. Local governments found chain gangs important sources of labor for services and projects. Vagrancy laws provided a useful means of obtaining labor when it appeared to be in short supply— short sometimes because employers conspired to create labor shortages by keeping wages low. In 1903 Alabama defined a vagrant as "any person wandering or strolling about in idleness, who is able to work, and has no property to support him; or any person leading an idle, immoral, profligate life, having no property to support him." The next year the *Atlanta Constitution* wryly notified the local police: "Cotton is ripening. See that the 'vags' get busy."

The number of blacks who were subjected to this form of involuntary servitude cannot be accurately calculated, nor can the number of those who worked in debt peonage (court-ordered hiring out to individuals to work off debts) or under surety contracts (court-ordered hiring out to individuals to work off fines and sentences). Debt peonage, which sometimes claimed white victims, was usually found in more remote areas, such as turpentining camps, where public attention was unlikely and where the work was harsh even without the brutalities that accompanied peonage. Peonage represented "the shadow of slavery," a shadow with real substance.

Southern white farmers and governments also continued their attempts to restrain the freedom of black farm laborers. To prevent blacks from leaving farms during the crop year, laws were passed making such departures criminal rather than civil offenses, and specifying fines both for the blacks who moved on and for the persons convicted of enticing them away. "Emigrant agents" who recruited black labor in the South faced stiff barriers. In 1891 the Carolinas passed laws that required such agents to buy a license in each county in which they operated, at $1,000 per county. Failure to do so could result in a fine of $5,000 and a sentence of two years. The "system of involuntary servitude was a unique blend of slavery and freedom which gave whites the option of limiting black movement while leaving Negroes otherwise free to come and go as they pleased"—and, it might be added, more responsible for their own survival than slaves had been. How successful these efforts to restrain the freedom of black farm laborers were is not clear. Very likely, the mobility of the laborers was constrained to a degree, but the size of black migrations from the South indicated that there were limits to the success of those constraints. The numbers of blacks leaving the rural South became so large in the late nineteenth century and remained so large for many years thereafter that the movement became known as the "Great Migration."

Blacks were also the primary targets of extralegal "court systems" that operated in all the southern states. Between 1882 and 1951, vigilante mobs in the United States "executed" or lynched—sometimes after a "trial" in which "evidence" was given to and assessed by a "jury"—more than 4,900 people, more than four-fifths of whom were blacks. Initially, lynching had been a phenomenon primarily of the American frontier. After the mid-1880s, however, it shifted to the South, where some 80 percent of lynchings were committed. The number of recorded lynchings also increased dramatically. Nearly three-fourths of the lynchings from 1882 to 1951 were committed in the quarter century after 1882. The worst year was 1892, when perhaps 235 died, and the numbers did not fall consistently below 100 until 1908.

Lynching was community-sanctioned murder. Crimes were alleged; trials were summary; death, often accompanied by torture and mutilation, came by hanging, shooting, burning, stabbing, dragging, and combinations thereof. Lynchings often attracted large crowds, which frequently included women and children. Lynchers were almost never arrested or convicted. Eventually, national and community pressures brought the barbarous ritual to an end. In only one-sixth of the lynchings in the South was rape of a white woman by a black man even alleged, though this "crime against white womanhood" was the primary justification given for lynchings, and such lynchings were even publicly defended by prominent public officials. Lynch victims were accused of everything from theft to arrogance toward whites to being "bad." Economic competition between blacks and low-income whites may have been the root cause in most instances.

Thomas Pearce Bailey, a South Carolina–born psychologist and distinguished educator, summarized the racial credo of southern whites in 1914:

1. "Blood will tell." 2. The white race must dominate. 3. The Teutonic peoples stand for race purity. 4. The Negro is inferior and will remain so. 5. "This is a white man's coun-

A LYNCHING (Library of Congress)

try." 6. No social equality. 7. No political equality. 8. In matters of civil rights and legal adjustments give the white man, as opposed to the colored man, the benefit of the doubt; and under no circumstances interfere with the prestige of the white race. 9. In educational policy let the Negro have the crumbs that fall from the white man's table. 10. Let there be such industrial education of the Negro as will best fit him to serve the white man. 11. Only Southerners understand the Negro question. 12. Let the South settle the Negro question. 13. The status of peasantry is all the Negro may hope for, if the races are to live together in peace. 14. Let the lowest white man count for more than the highest Negro. 15. The above statements indicate the leadings of Providence.

Bailey, however, had a more moderate, even advanced view: "The real problem is not the Negro, but the white man's attitude toward the Negro."

WHY JIM CROW?

Why Southern whites acted with such venom and so systematically is not clear. Nor can why they acted *when* they did be fully explained. But it may be helpful to examine four factors: the levels of confidence and fear among southern whites, the strengths and weaknesses of outside pressures, the shifting role of the federal government, and the power of blacks.

After the Civil War, southern whites developed a reasonably acceptable (at least, to them) pattern of racial dominance in which sweeping segregation laws seemed unnecessary and were not sought. In the later 1880s, however, whites were saying more and more often that the pattern was not working. They talked about troublesome blacks, in particular about the coming of age of the first generation of blacks who had not been reared in slavery and had not been taught the proper roles and spheres of blacks and whites. By 1905, articles on "the Negro problem" or "Negro question" appeared in many publications. Most authors saw gloomy, often threatening prospects for race relations. Whites' perceptions of blacks had some factual basis, both narrowly and broadly conceived. The first generation of postslavery blacks was in fact reaching adulthood. More important, economic change and urbanization unsettled the racial modus vivendi of the postbellum South. Competition between blacks and whites as farm laborers, in services and industry, and sometimes in skilled trades rubbed against exposed nerves. Competition for housing and public services in urban areas became intense as southern towns and cities shared in the explosive growth of Gilded Age America. Towns and cities raised other volatile issues. Were the taboos and the understood rules of racial etiquette of the rural South known and applied in the urban South? Was it not necessary, indeed urgent, that they be codified or written into law, especially since blacks made up to 40 to 50 percent, sometimes more, of the population of cities and towns in the South? Black successes in farming and business, of which there were many, also incited envy and fear among whites. "Uppity" blacks had to be taught their place. Blacks often wisely avoided public displays of success by building their homes back from roads or ordering clothes from catalogs rather than purchasing them in town.

The already fragile relationship between blacks and whites became much more intense when the economy collapsed in the 1890s. Democrats warred with one another, with the Populists, and with the Republicans in one of the most tumultuous decades in southern politics, and the political storm enveloped blacks. The dearth of jobs, the mounting debts and declining returns from farming, and the dwindling of money for the essentials of life fueled elemental fears. In turn, race relations suffered.

Fear also grew from less concrete sources than competition for jobs, housing, and public services. That fear had a phobic, irrational quality that had its sources in deep, tangled emotions. How else can the enormous anxiety of whites about the security of white women against sexual attacks by black men be explained? Or the firm belief of whites that efforts of blacks to secure their civil and political rights were an opening wedge for attempts to end social segregation and achieve some never-defined social equality? Or the fears of racial contamination that propelled white school officials to go so far as to keep school textbooks in racially segregated warehouses? Apparently thousands read *The Clansman* (1904), by the Reverend Thomas Dixon, Jr., despite its subtitle, *An Historical Romance of the Ku Klux Klan*. Part of its attraction was its lurid descriptions of blacks:

> He had the short, heavy-set neck of the lower order of animals. His skin was coal black, his lips so thick they curled both ways up and down with crooked blood-marks across them. His nose was flat, and its enormous nostrils seemed in perpetual dilation. The sinister bead eyes, with brown splotches in their whites, were set wide apart and gleamed ape-like under his scant brows. His enormous cheekbones and jaws seemed to protrude beyond the ears and almost hide them.

D. W. Griffith made this novel into a highly successful film, *The Birth of a Nation* (1915), which was widely popular with white audiences, in the North as well as the South. The movie ignited black protests. Some of those who protested had also participated in the founding of the National Association for the Advancement of Colored People (NAACP).

Conversely, whites in the South were confident that white peoples were by birth and achievement superior to all other peoples. Whites virtually everywhere in the world at the time believed that. Southern whites were confident because they had long established their power and their will to dominate blacks. Southern whites were also confident by the 1890s because they faced little outside pressure of any kind, including interference from the federal government, to slow the course of Jim Crow. Finally, whites could be confident that blacks had little power to oppose them.

The federal government had retreated since the 1860s from intervention on the part of blacks in the South. Confronted after 1865 by the resurgence of the Democrats outside the South and by the return of the South to the Union, the Republicans had initially tried to establish beachheads south of the Mason-Dixon line by enfranchising blacks and supporting those whites who had Union sentiments and were Republicans or presumably would join the Republican party. Reconstruction ended in defeat for this Republican strategy. The Republicans then experimented with other approaches, also without much success. They had conciliated the white South with the Compromise of 1877, which made it explicit and widely known that southern whites had virtually a free hand in race relations in the South. In 1883 the Supreme Court struck down the Civil Rights Act of 1875, which on paper had outlawed racial discrimination in public accommodations. The Court ruled that though governments could not legally discriminate in public accommodations, individuals could. The Republicans had sought alliances with independent political movements, most notably with the Readjusters in Virginia in the 1870s and 1880s. In the 1890s, some Republicans in the South joined forces with the Southern Farmers' Alliance and then with the Populist party.

In 1890 Republicans in Congress tried to return to their basic strength in the South, blacks. In doing so, Republicans made their last effort of any consequence to use federal power on behalf of blacks. The Republican-controlled House of Representatives narrowly passed the Lodge Election Bill, which was designed to counter election frauds in the South by providing federal supervision of congressional elections when citizens petitioned to protest returns in those elections. Proponents of the measure claimed that fraudulent election returns were depriving the Republicans of electoral victories in the South. Opponents—primarily Democrats in all sections, but especially in the South—countered with visions of Reconstruction revived and federal government tyranny. Borrowing from the traditions of the American Revolution, they denounced the bill as the Force Bill. The name stuck, an ironic twist to the intent of the bill. The measure died in the Senate and with it Congress's last attempt for many years to assure blacks of their voting rights in the South. The bill may have been an exercise in political cynicism. The Republicans probably knew the Force Bill had no chance in the Senate, but they pushed it anyway to embarrass the Democrats about election frauds in the South.

Political developments in the 1890s reinforced the Republican retreat on race. The national debacle of the Democratic party in the 1890s helped the Republicans become the majority party in the country even though they received no electoral votes from the South and were seldom factors in any statewide election there. The Republicans dominated American politics from the mid-1890s until 1930 with no more than a shadow of a party in the South. The Republicans' newly achieved power allowed them for the first time in their history largely to ignore the South—and blacks. The functions of the Republicans in the South shrank to those of a "post office" party. Republican presidential hopefuls exchanged promises of political appointments (postmasterships and so forth) for southern Republican votes at national nominating conventions. No longer in need of southern votes to win national elections, Republicans acquiesced in white supremacy in the South. The Democrats were hardly likely candidates at that time to become champions of black rights.

The Supreme Court acknowledged the completeness of the retreat of the federal government as defender of the rights of blacks when it made several landmark decisions that gave judicial sanction to Jim Crow. In *Plessy* v. *Ferguson* (1896) the Court enunciated its famous "separate but equal" doctrine in ruling that a Louisiana law requiring racial segregation in public transportation was constitutional. Only Justice John M. Harlan, a Kentuckian from a family of former slaveholders, dissented. The Constitution, he contended, was color-blind. Two years later the Court ruled that Mississippi could require literacy tests and poll taxes for voter registration. Southern political leaders correctly perceived that the Fourteenth and Fifteenth amendments could be legally evaded, that Jim Crow was not an outlaw.

American blacks also suffered setbacks outside the South. Though black men generally retained the right to vote in the North, blacks faced mounting hostility there. State laws against racial discrimination remained largely unenforced. Segregation, in schools and elsewhere, was common. The never substantial number of black officeholders in the North shrank. Support for the rights of blacks among organized labor declined. Though not always a consistent defender of black workers, the Knights of Labor treated them more fairly than virtually any other organization or institution in the United States at the time. But the American Federation of Labor (AFL), which in the 1880s displaced the Knights as the leading American labor union, tacitly accepted Jim Crow in the workplace. Two unions affiliated with the AFL, however, included many blacks among their ranks: the International Longshoremen's Association and the United Mine Workers. Moreover, scattered evidence suggests instances of racial cooperation in local trade unions. However, these instances were exceptions to the general pattern of growing hostility toward blacks, north and south.

Beyond the United States, pressures against Jim Crow were nonexistent. If anything, they reinforced Jim Crow. Ideologically and politically, white supremacy was attaining new heights. History, achievements in the arts, economic development, and gains in technology were believed to give indisputable proof that whites were superior. A particular subspecies of white supremacy flourished: Anglo-Saxonism. Politically, whites had demonstrated their capacity to shape the world. Europeans and Americans carried their money, products, and culture throughout the world. In a remarkably short time Europeans expanded or established political control over much of Africa and Asia. The United States followed with new footholds in the Caribbean, Central America, and the Pacific. History and contemporary events seemed to justify and reinforce white supremacy. White supremacy was not peculiar to the South, though the forms it took there and the intensity with which it was embraced were unusual even at that time.

Blacks did not retreat readily before these overwhelming odds. They continued to assert their rights as citizens and human beings. Black men exercised their franchise in spite of mounting discouragements and barriers until the Jim Crow system eliminated virtually any possibility of voting. As they had done earlier, blacks protested segregation on public transportation and did so effectively as late as 1894 in Atlanta. Other boycotts of streetcars in southern cities, however, proved more indicative of the direction of southern race relations. Not one of a dozen such boycotts between 1896 and 1908 succeeded. Atlanta fell into step, too. Jim Crow prevailed on the streetcars there after 1906, the year of a gruesome race riot in Atlanta. Blacks occasionally formed protest organizations, of which the Afro-American Council was the most important. Founded in 1890, the council stagnated by the middle of the 1890s and became extinct by 1908, testimony to black impotence against white power. Others sought a quieter form of protest; they moved. Moving offered more safety and greater prospects for oneself and one's family. It was an old story that dated back to the movements of free blacks within and out of the slave South, then to movements of blacks during and after the Civil War. Cities and towns offered refuge and hope—more safety from whites, greater personal freedom, better jobs, and greater opportunities for educa-tion. Newer farm regions inside and outside the South, as in Kansas in the 1870s, also beckoned.

Although large numbers of blacks moved outside the South in the late nine-teenth century, 89 percent of American blacks still lived in the South fifty years after the Civil War, a decline of only 3 percent in a half century. Significant shifts occurred in that half century, however. Migrations to Louisiana, Texas, Arkansas, and Oklahoma helped raise the black population in those states to nearly 2 mil-lion, almost one-fourth of the total number of blacks living in the South. At the same time, 1.5 million blacks moved to urban areas in the South.

After the Civil War some blacks left the United States entirely. Most signifi-cant of the few emigrants were those who chose exile in Africa. Henry McNeal Turner, a bishop in the African Methodist Episcopal church and a politician and activist in Georgia, became the principal spokesman of back-to-Africa interests, which had a brief but well-publicized life in the 1870s and periodically thereafter until 1900. The meager response to Turner's appeals and to similar appeals by others can, however, mislead us as to the importance of the back-to-Africa move-ment. Turner preached black pride—pride in black skin, in the achievements of blacks, and in their African heritage. He and others who had similar ideas thus presented a markedly distinctive message in a day of rampant Anglo-Saxonism and European ethnocentrism.

The fact that Turner commanded an audience but made few converts to emi-gration had profound implications. Few blacks had a realistic alternative to living in the United States. Moreover, despite all that had happened to them, blacks showed they were Americans with a deep attachment to America, though they had an African heritage and a historical experience that was strikingly different from that of other groups in the United States. W. E. B. Du Bois, the brilliant black scholar and activist, called this dichotomy the "twoness" of being "an American, a Negro; two souls, two thoughts, two unreconciled strivings." Du Bois believed, as he said in 1901, that the

history of the American Negro is the history of this strife . . . to merge his double self into a better and truer self. . . . He would not Africanize America, for America has too much to teach the world and Africa. He would not bleach his Negro soul in a flood of white Americanism, for he knows that Negro blood has a message for the world. He simply wishes to make it possible for a man to be a Negro and an American, without being cursed and spit upon by his fellows, without having the doors of Opportunity closed roughly in his face.

Du Bois openly criticized Booker T. Washington, something blacks rarely did at the time because Washington was the most powerful black leader in the country. Washington, Du Bois argued publicly, put too much blame on blacks for their poverty and lack of education and too little blame on whites. Du Bois believed that in accepting whites' demands that blacks stay out of politics, Washington had conceded too much and did not realize that political participation was a prime means for blacks to register dissent and gain attention for their concerns. Finally, Du Bois attacked the basic philosophy of Tuskegee Institute, which stressed a vocational education that he thought was inadequate to prepare its students for life in the twentieth century.

Questions about the origins of Jim Crow have stimulated an extraordinarily rich debate among scholars and have left some very perceptive insights into the past of the American South. The debate has focused on several questions: Why was Jim Crow so systematic? What mode of race relations did it displace or augment? Why did Jim Crow emerge when it did? What were the alternatives to Jim Crow? Did Jim Crow represent a major break with the older modes of race relations in the South? The debate has extended beyond the boundaries of the United States as scholars have turned to comparisons between race relations in the American South and in Latin America and South Africa. South Africa's system of rigid racial segregation, called *apartheid*, had close parallels to Jim Crow, yet the systems also had some striking differences.

Jim Crow displaced what has been called laissez-faire segregation: a patchwork pattern of political segregation, some self-segregation, segregated parallel institutions, and understood behavior. Well before 1900, southerners were divided by race. Most blacks voted Republican, most whites voted Democratic. Blacks and whites segregated themselves in churches, in many businesses and professions, and in social relations. Schools were racially divided also. Thus, parallel, racially segregated but similar structures evolved in the South. Blacks rode where they pleased on public transportation, sat where they pleased in theaters, ate in restaurants that they chose—in some places in the South but not in others. Whites employed random means to keep blacks "in their place"—lynchings and physical threats and abuse, discriminatory justice, intimidation. Paternalism and personal patronage softened the force of laissez-faire racism, although both reinforced the notion and reality of white dominance.

Sometime, perhaps in the late 1880s, race relations took a noticeably negative turn. Jim Crow subsequently displaced laissez-faire segregation. Clearly Jim Crow did not introduce racial segregation to the South, a fact underlined by the recent work of scholars. But Jim Crow did represent a sharp change in race relations because it was so thorough and sweeping and because it had the backing of the law, which was usually enforced. Jim Crow was put in place in the 1890s and the early twentieth century, not, as once was thought, when Reconstruction ended or when the North first showed it had little inclination to intervene on behalf of blacks. The economic and political turbulence of the 1890s stimulated Jim Crow

BLACK STUDENTS AT HAMPTON (Library of Congress)

enormously. Jim Crow then became entrenched and acquired the appearance of permanence, the appearance that it represented what had always been and what always would be.

Jim Crow examined reveals much more than that. Its creation was supported by the great majority of whites. That support came from upper- and middle-class whites, not just from poorer whites variously labeled "rednecks," "crackers," and "white trash." Southern white leaders found Jim Crow a useful means of building unity among whites and blurring class divisions among them. Jim Crow lay at the foundation of what has been called the "Herrenvolk democracy" of the South, a system of political democracy for whites only that ignored or obscured class divisions. Jim Crow brought order to race relations—a retrogressive, repressive order, but order. Once Jim Crow was in place, for instance, the number of lynchings declined. Elections became more orderly, though they were markedly less democratic, because so many adult males had been disfranchised. There were alternatives to Jim Crow; most were worse. Operative forces in the 1890s made a continuation of laissez-faire segregation highly unlikely. Far more unlikely would have been developments comparable to those that occurred after World War II, when segregation and disfranchisement of blacks were ended. Massive, forced deportation of blacks did not occur, nor did forced removal to specially created reservations, nor did genocide. Could such horrors have taken place? Certainly they had occurred before, and they have occurred since in human history. Such happened to Indians in America.

Why did not even worse happen? Perhaps the ties, including deep emotional attachment, between southern blacks and whites played a part. Blacks in America assimilated white culture to a much greater extent than Africans in South Africa. The degree of assimilation was reflected in the strong similarities between southern blacks and whites with respect to religion, family structure and roles, and commitment to materialism. After all, in an age of the self-made man, Booker T. Washington fit hand in glove with the dominant white culture. Blacks and whites shared a common citizenship, though they received widely disproportionate shares of the fruits of that citizenship. Unlike white South Africans, for example, American whites could not treat blacks as aliens without certain rights, such as the right to remain in the United States. Moreover, blacks could (and did) move to states outside the South, where they hardly received warm receptions but did get to vote and frequently were able to improve their lives and the lives of their families. The American tradition of adherence to the law, though often more honored in the breach than in the observance, must have had some influence here, as it has had throughout most of American history.

Probably the most important factor that precluded alternatives worse even than Jim Crow was the labor of blacks. As whites clearly understood, the economy of the South required large amounts of black labor. Agriculture, most of the extractive industries, some manufacturing, shipping, and services relied heavily on black workers. Moreover, competition between black and white labor tended to be blunted by chance or design. Unlike white workers in South Africa, those in the South were not faced by a mass of black workers whose numbers threatened to drive them from the labor market altogether. White South Africans faced such threats, and the government passed laws to exclude black Africans from most jobs. Southern states stopped short of wholesale legal exclusion.

Nor did employers in the South pay blacks far less than whites for the same work, as South African employers have done. Demographic patterns had a part in that. Population patterns in the South softened black-white competition in farming: blacks predominated in those areas where plantation agriculture prevailed, while whites predominated in the piedmont and mountain areas. Blacks and whites who worked at the same or similar jobs in mining, iron and steel plants, shipping, and services usually worked in segregated units, but not always. Observers frequently commented on seeing blacks and whites work side by side in the South but seldom in the North. Segregation in the South also gave black business people, entrepreneurs, and professionals opportunities to develop and serve all-black clienteles. Booker T. Washington was not merely courting his audience at the Atlanta Exposition when he asserted that Negroes had greater economic opportunities in the South than in the North in the 1890s. He was stating a fact.

Economic competition between blacks and whites was eased in other ways, to the disadvantage of blacks. Certain positions were reserved for whites only, especially the more skilled, better-paying ones and supervisory positions. Over time, black artisans lost out to white artisans, except in bricklaying and stone masonry. Trade unions lent Jim Crow a hand by making racially discriminatory uses of their apprenticeship rules. When black businessmen competed with white businessmen, they had serious handicaps. Lack of capital, credit, and training ensured that black-owned businesses would be small and especially vulnerable to economic fluctuations. Moreover, most black businesses served a low-income clientele, since most had a black clientele. Black physicians, dentists, and other professionals faced similar difficulties.

Blacks were excluded from one highly important manufacturing industry, cotton textiles. This was a de facto practice, not a de jure practice; only South Carolina passed a Jim Crow law for industry, in 1915, and then only for textiles. Worker insistence, more than anything else, accounted for this action. At the time textiles had an unusual labor force among industries: women, some of them quite young, made up approximately half the labor force in the industry. Many families worked as units. White textile workers grasped at the opportunity to portray Jim

Crow as a means to protect white womanhood. Attempts to deviate from strict segregation—even hints of such attempts—triggered strikes or threats of strikes and other protests.

This response discouraged textile company officials from hiring blacks, except in the most menial jobs, and thus from hiring those who might work for even lower wages. This did not, however, necessarily mean that the textile industry had to face inflated labor costs. (Wages and labor costs are not necessarily the same thing.) Had the industry attempted to force its white workers to work with blacks, it would have faced the heavy costs of strikes and of losing many or most of its more experienced workers. The industry probably would have encountered great difficulty recruiting other white workers and perhaps would have caused state and local governments to take negative action against the industry. Finally, the threat of black labor gave management a potent weapon for keeping its white workers in place, a weapon management did not hesitate to use. Jim Crow in textiles all but excluded blacks from the largest industrial employer in the South until the 1960s. Therefore, for more than a hundred years, blacks were excluded from one of the principal means of modest self-advancement available to the less advantaged in the Southeast.

THE BLACK WORLD

The American South had its own "twoness," a white world and a black world. Jim Crow reflected this "twoness," and exacerbated and perpetuated it. The existence of two worlds whose boundaries were marked by the physical characteristics— not necessarily the ancestry—of their inhabitants was not new in 1900, or even in 1860. But the depth and clarity of the divisions between the worlds were new.

Racial divisions became starkly simple. The "one drop" demarcation prevailed. Anyone with any African ancestry—"one drop of Negro blood"—was a

WOMEN'S BIBLE CLASS, COTTON MILL VILLAGE (South Carolina State Museum)

Negro, though he or she might be fair-skinned and blue-eyed. Thus by the early twentieth century such terms as *mulatto* fell into disuse, and American Negroes came generally to be thought of and to think of themselves as one people, no matter how dark or light they were. Some Negroes, however, did elect to "pass"— that is, to become accepted as white if their physical appearance made it possible for them to do so. Nor did Negroes always ignore their own variations in pigmentation: lighter skin continued to be more desirable among many Negroes.

Poverty, or perhaps more accurately relative deprivation, gave shape and substance to the black world. Occupational structure and the evidences and opportunities for self-improvement made this world very clear. Racial discrimination compounded by educational deficiencies and landlessness shaped the occupational structure among blacks in the South and limited their economic advancement. Employment opportunities, in turn, molded the world of the blacks in the South in decisive ways. Like southern whites, most southern blacks earned their living from farming, but they were much more likely than whites to be tenants, sharecroppers, or farm laborers. Proportionately fewer blacks than whites became professionals, merchants, or clerks. The numbers of black physicians, dentists, teachers, clergy, and lawyers were very small—especially lawyers, who were excluded from courtrooms. Eight in ten black professionals were teachers or ministers. After 1865, the number of black artisans declined. The overwhelming majority of blacks worked at jobs that required physical labor. A much higher percentage of black women worked outside the home than did white women. Here, need—sometimes desperate need—played its part. Because black women were more likely to be poor, more of them sought employment than did white women, more continued to do so after marriage and childbirth, and more remained employed for most of their lives. Bias played a hand, too. White women scorned domestic labor—cooking, cleaning, and laundering for others—as suitable only for blacks. More than eight in ten female domestics in the South in 1920 were black. Despite its low per capita income, the South had considerably more servants per household than any other region in the United States. In 1920, for instance, Atlanta had 249 female domestics for every 1,000 families, whereas Boston had 82, New York 74, and Chicago 68. Even white textile workers in the South employed blacks as domestics. Black poverty, in this instance, raised the standard of living, in noncash terms, of many whites by creating a large pool of cheap domestic help.

Despite numerous barriers, blacks made significant economic and social gains after 1865. Between 1865 and 1915, the number of blacks in the United States doubled while birth rates and mortality rates declined markedly. This fact indicated that, despite their poverty, the conditions of blacks' lives had improved after slavery. During the same time period, literacy rates among blacks rose from approximately 5 percent to over 50 percent. Income per capita among blacks probably more than doubled between 1866 and 1900. That rate exceeded the rate of increase for white incomes over the same years, but incomes of blacks remained well below those of whites—approximately 35 percent of incomes of whites in the nation. Moreover, had there been no racial discrimination, incomes for black Americans would have been 10 percent higher. The slave past, landlessness, and lower educational and skill levels, almost universal among blacks in 1865 and too persistent thereafter, probably account for much of the difference in incomes (and the

BLACK MOTHER AND SON, 1920s (South Carolinian
Library, University of South Carolina)

even greater difference in wealth) between blacks and whites in the South. Evidence suggests that blacks got about the same pay for comparable work, but blacks seldom got the better jobs.

Black gains after the Civil War came from several sources. No longer slaves, blacks commanded higher wages and had greater control over their labor and leisure. They used these advantages to improve their situations. They sought education for themselves and their children. In fact, through taxes and private giving and expenditures, blacks paid for a large part, possibly most, of the education they received, from elementary school through college. Blacks moved to areas that promised greater opportunities, and they worked and struggled. In 1910 the census reported that 71 percent of blacks over nine years of age in the United States had gainful employment, while 51 percent of whites did. Blacks created their own savings institutions, banks, realty companies, and insurance companies, which often grew out of various fraternal and religious bodies.

John Merrick, a Durham, North Carolina, barber-turned-entrepreneur, formed a group to take over a fraternal order and reorganize it into an insurance company. Eventually North Carolina Mutual would become the largest black business in the country. Alonzo Herndon, an Atlanta barber, founded the Atlanta Life Insurance Company in 1905; it became North Carolina Mutual's major competitor. Maggie Walker, the daughter of a former slave, founded the Penny Savings Bank in Richmond, her hometown. Under her presidency the bank prospered and later merged with other black banks to form the Consolidated Bank and Trust company. Walker also organized the Richmond Council of Negro Women. Its 1,400 members engaged in a variety of reform activities.

Negroes also joined in "buy black" campaigns in an effort to support black-owned businesses. Still, the great majority of black businesses remained very small—mom-and-pop grocery stores, pharmacies, and general merchandise stores. By 1910 some 218,000 blacks were part or full owners of nearly 15.7 million acres of southern farmland, worth more than $212 million. But there were six times as many white landowners. Their farms were valued at more than $3 billion and averaged twice as many acres as those owned by blacks. Moreover, such figures do not reflect differences in the values of farm buildings, livestock, and implements and machinery.

Maurice Evans, a South African who traveled extensively in the South and wrote about race relations there and in his native country, noted in *Black and White in the Southern States* (1915) that the "total advance of the negro people in material things since Emancipation has been indubitably very great." While Evans applauded this development, he saw it as potentially explosive. Evans saw black advances leading to competition with whites and then to conflicts and violent confrontation. Actually, that progression had already materialized. In the face of the competition in New South cities, the economic collapse of the 1890s, and the political turmoil of that decade, laissez-faire segregation failed. A dramatic increase in random racial violence took many forms, of which lynching was the most brutal and notorious. Jim Crow restored order, at a very high cost to blacks and some costs to whites.

Blacks had to accept the system of American apartheid because they had no alternative. Behind the barriers of Jim Crow they created their own world, dependent on whites yet independent of them. "Even in the midst of the brutalities and injustices of the . . . postbellum race systems, black men and women were able to find the means to sustain a far greater degree of self-pride and group cohesion than the system they lived under ever intended for them to be able to do." But blacks could not remain in their own world all the time. Most had to deal with whites on a daily basis and be ever attuned to them. Richard Wright, the black novelist, recalled that as part of his growing up he had to learn "how to watch white people, their every move, their expressions, and what they said or left unsaid." But he found that "it was utterly impossible for me to calculate, to scheme, to act, to plot all the time. I would remember to dissemble for short periods, then I would forget and act straight and human again." Wright left the South as soon as he was able to because he feared for his life. Yet, even as blacks put on an Uncle Tom face for whites, they derided whites in a variety of ways, especially in songs and in jokes.

"Boy. What are you doin' in here? Don't you know this is a white church?
"Boss, I only got sent here to mop up the floor.
"Well, that's all right then. But don't let me catch you prayin'."

INDUSTRIAL WORKERS IN THE NEW SOUTH

By 1900 the division between blacks and whites was only the most obvious division in the American South. As the new century began, more than 500,000 southerners earned their livings in manufacturing. Many of these people worked in small factories, but a majority worked in the larger factories that relied heavily on simple, repetitive, often hazardous and dirty labor, usually as machine tenders. In 1900 nearly 100,000 of these workers were in textiles. Large numbers would be found in iron and steel, lumber, and tobacco manufacturing.

Most of the industrial workers of the South came from farms; few came from Europe. The move from farm to factory required major changes. Most of these former farmers had controlled their daily work routines, determining when to start and stop work, and what tasks would be done when. The factories required them to work according to a new concept of time, time measured in hours and minutes, and under close supervision at assigned tasks.

Industrial workers usually lived in racially and occupationally segregated communities or neighborhoods. Very often they lived in company housing, and almost always near the workplace. The former farmers thus entered a different world. During the initial stages of this transition, many apparently maintained strong rural ties and moved back and forth between farm and factory. Later, apparently, most of them gave up agriculture permanently. Those who made the transition sensed they were crossing a chasm between two worlds, that something was dying even as something was beginning.

Ben Robertson, who wrote about his memories of the South Carolina upcountry in *Red Hills and Cotton,* remembered seeing cotton mill workers at the store on Saturday afternoon. Looking at their pale faces, the result of working indoors all the time, he felt "that they had been captured, that they were imprisoned, that they had given up being free." Robertson also recalled the terrible dilemma a landless farmer confronted when he weighed his chances of success on the farm and in the factory.

Tom Rampey had rented thirty acres on shares from Robertson's family for twenty years. When a chance to work at a nearby cotton mill presented itself, Rampey anguished in indecision, then discussed his alternatives with the Robertsons.

"I'm a landless man. As long as I stay with you, I have a house and I'll have something to eat, but what chance have I got to get ahead? What chance have I got ever to own any land of my own? . . . I could have money at the mill. . . . I ought to be able to save enough in no time to buy a few acres of my own—it oughtn't to take me long to save enough for that. . . . I want to improve my condition, . . . I want to educate my children. I want them to have things better than I have had them."

A few days later the Rampeys piled their things into a two-horse wagon and drove off. They moved into a house on the side of a steep hill at Cateechee Mill. . . . The whistle blew for them at half past four o'clock, and at six their work started. Six to six was their shift. It was a hard life for a family accustomed to the open, but Saturday was pay day—every Saturday. Sometimes on Sunday Mr. Tom would come back to see my Great-Aunt Narcissa at the Old House. He would eat dinner and my great-aunt would tell him he could move back if he cared to, and always this seemed to comfort him.

Finally one Sunday at Praters Baptist Church the preacher announced that Brother Tom Rampey and family desired to remove their letters of membership from Praters to Cateechee Mill Baptist Church. When the preacher asked the congregation what was their wish in this matter, my Uncle Philip moved that the request be granted. One of the Boldings seconded the motion. Thus did the Rampeys cut their last tie. They bought a new coal stove with their cash money. They bought an icebox, a car, a radio. Mr. Tom's oldest boy eventually was graduated from college.

The Tom Rampeys were legion, products of the markedly uneven rewards farmers in the South received. The federal censuses recorded the tale. In 1910, for instance, the South had more than half the nation's farmers but produced less than 30 percent of the nation's farm products. Southern farmers earned about 55 percent of the national average farm income. The value of farm implements, machinery, and livestock in the South was about 60 percent of the national average. Southern farmers used two-thirds of the total fertilizers applied by American farmers, a reflection of the continuing dominance of soil-depleting cotton. These figures did not reveal the great disparities within the South. In 1910, plantations with five or more tenants occupied 5 million acres in Alabama, Georgia, and Mississippi, and a study of some 200 of those plantations found they had fifty or more tenants each and averaged more than 4,200 acres worth $114,000.

Rising land values after 1900 proved a mixed blessing. As values doubled in the ten years after 1900, many farmers gained but many more joined the ranks of tenants. The number of tenant farms in the South increased 25 percent, to more than 1.5 million. Two-thirds of the tenant farmers were black. Farm size continued to decline, usually an indication of low productivity and low profitability. Thus the pattern of smaller farms that had set in after 1860 persisted. According to John L. Coulter, an agricultural expert employed by the Census Bureau, average farm size shrank from 321 acres in 1860 to 84 in 1910.

Tenancy, of course, does not automatically mean poverty. Renting land can be profitable, sometimes very profitable, for renter and landlord alike. Farm renters may, for example, find it to their advantage to use the capital they might have tied up in land to purchase better equipment and machinery. Generally, however, farm tenants in the South in 1910 rented or worked on shares because they had no other choice, not because they were trying to invest their assets as wisely as possible. Nearly half of all farm tenants in the South moved each year, seeking to improve their fortunes. Coulter believed that tenancy resulted in the "poor agriculture, exhausted soils, poor roads, decaying bridges, and unpainted houses" he saw in much of the South.

Factories and cities promised better things. From 1880 to 1900, the capital invested in manufacturing in the South quadrupled and the value of manufactured products tripled, then increased by 268 percent and 197 percent respectively during the next decade. The number of workers in manufacturing grew from 627,169 in 1900 to 1.01 million in 1910, to 1.3 million in 1920. At the same time, the population of the urban South rose from 3 million to 5.3 million, a 56 percent increase—a rate of urban growth that considerably exceeded the national rate.

UNIONS AND UNIONIZATION IN THE NEW SOUTH

The growing numbers of industrial workers clearly indicated a changing South, a South more like the rest of the nation. So did the growth of unionization in the South and the increasing conflict between labor and management. The Knights of Labor enjoyed impressive, but brief, success in its efforts to organize southern workers. The American Federation of Labor (AFL), founded in 1886, eventually enjoyed greater success than the Knights. Committed to trade unionism and eschewing the broad reform goals that the Knights had enunciated, the AFL effectively organized printers, building tradesmen, railroaders, and the skilled workers among the longshoremen. A number of AFL affiliates, including the International Brotherhood of Boiler Makers and the International Association of Machinists, had their origins in the South. The AFL unions usually segregated blacks into separate units or excluded them altogether, as did the railroad brotherhoods and Eugene V. Debs's American Railway Union.

As elsewhere in the United States, industrial unionism enjoyed little success in the South before the 1930s, whereas trade and railroad unions were very active. These patterns of unionization mirrored patterns in the rest of the nation. Of course, union members were fewer in the South than in the North, and so were the efforts to unionize; both reflected the smaller amount of industrialization and urbanization in the South. Coal miners, especially in Alabama, made serious efforts to organize as early as the later 1880s. Unionization among textile workers grew significantly around 1900, then subsided. In 1894 coal miners in the Birmingham region initiated a major strike in which black and white miners joined in a pitched battle against employers. Here the use of convict labor as strikebreakers and as a means of keeping wages low was a major issue. The miners also got involved in the political upheaval of the 1890s in Alabama and threw their support to Reuben Kolb, the Jeffersonian opponent of the Bourbon Democrats. Kolb's defeat and the defeat of this strike left bitter feelings and a demoralized union. Yet four years later, Alabama miners cast their lot with the national United Mine Workers (UMW); by 1902, more than 60 percent of Alabama miners were unionized. Then a major strike devastated the UMW in Alabama in 1908 and left a legacy of acute racial hostility in the coal regions. The UMW enjoyed more success in the Southwest, and before World War I the union experienced a more general revival in the whole South. The militant actions of miners in Tennessee had a decisive role in the abolition of the convict lease system there in 1902.

Efforts to unionize cotton mill workers in the South resulted in some victories, but local unions seldom survived encounters with determined mill owners, and those few locals that survived had no discernible impact on the industry. The Knights had a large organization in Augusta; elsewhere in Georgia, textile workers had joined the Knights, as they had done in South Carolina, North Carolina, and Alabama.

By 1895 the National Union of Textile Workers (NUTW), an AFL affiliate, began major organizing efforts in the South. Augusta and Columbus, Georgia; Columbia, South Carolina; Alamance and Greensboro, North Carolina; and Danville, Virginia, were the focal points of these campaigns. Initially the AFL acted to prevent the Socialist Trade and Labor Alliance, led by Daniel De Leon, from getting a foothold in the textile South. But the growth of southern textiles also played a hand. Leaders of textile labor unions in the North feared competition, especially the competition of a nonunionized and cheaper labor force in the South. In 1899 the NUTW issued fifty-four charters to new locals in the South. Labor newspapers in the South—among the important by-products of union activity in the region—claimed that the 500-member NUTW local at Columbia, South Carolina, was "the largest textile [local] union in the world." By 1900 the NUTW had 5,000 dues-paying members, most in the South, and a southerner for president. The NUTW and the AFL lobbied unsuccessfully for child labor legislation in the southern states. They also proved to be vulnerable to the strong counterattacks waged by southern mill owners, who managed to scuttle textile unions by the end of 1902.

As in the rest of the country, ethnic conflict marked and shaped labor relations in the South. In the industrial and mining regions of the Northeast and Midwest, for instance, there were sharp differences among Americans and native Europeans, as there were similar ethnic conflicts in the Plains, the mountain states, and the Far West. In the West, confrontations between whites and Asians were a major factor in successful efforts to limit Asian immigration severely or stop it entirely.

In the South, color had an immense impact on labor relations and occupations, whereas immigration, from either Europe or Asia, had almost no effect except in the coal and iron regions. Black and white workers formed alliances on several occasions in the 1880s and the 1890s. The Knights of Labor and the UMW demonstrated degrees of interracial solidarity that were unique for this era in the South or elsewhere, and indeed for many years to come in the South. Black and white Knights of Labor joined in the strikes against Jay Gould in 1885 and 1886. Black and white UMW members struck against coal operators in the Birmingham region in 1894. By 1902 the biracial union had the largest membership of any single union in the South. As subsequent events proved, however, the biracialism of the UMW was fragile.

Interracial cooperation among workers was not, however, limited to the Knights and the UMW. In 1892 a general strike called by an alliance of AFL unions in New Orleans involved 20,000 members of forty-two locals and virtually shut the city down for three days. It ended when the city's Board of Trade made concessions in regard to wages and hours but not in regard to union recognition or the closed shop (an agreement to hire only union members). The result conformed to the usual pattern of labor disputes of the era throughout the South and the nation. When employers made concessions—and they seldom did—they conceded points on narrow issues: wages, hours, working conditions. Employers almost never conceded on broader issues: recognition of a union as a collective bargaining agent or agreement to the closed shop.

Biracial solidarity among workers in the South also suffered setbacks. Racial divisions marred an 1894 strike in New Orleans. In 1908, Alabama coal miners divided along racial lines when they were confronted by mine owners and a state government determined to suppress their union even if they had to play to racial prejudice to do so. Jim Crow triumphed, erasing memories of interracial cooperation while erecting a segregationist tradition. The UMW declined sharply in Alabama, although the union did enjoy a revival in the state before World War I. The UMW, however, remained a strong force in Texas and Oklahoma and retained its biracial character there. The Brotherhood of Timber Workers also adopted a biracial strategy during its brief lifetime in the Southwest, 1910–1913.

The racial exclusivism that marked almost all of organized labor after 1900 created an atmosphere conducive to strikebreaking by blacks. Organized labor rather quickly came to associate blacks with strikebreaking, though unionists usually ignored their own role in creating the situation. Excluded from almost all unions, often desperate for work, and eager to improve their earnings, blacks did not turn away from offers of the jobs of striking white workers. They took such jobs with increasing frequency after 1910, especially in the North, where real or alleged strikebreaking by blacks contributed to a series of violent racial confrontations around World War I.

Even when employers did not use blacks as strikebreakers, they still could and did threaten to do so. Ironically, employers also appealed to white racial solidarity. These appeals gave employers an advantage over their white employees similar to the advantage white elitist politicians and their class allies enjoyed over their poorer white constituents. Less advantaged whites derived benefits—often more emotional than economic—from Jim Crow. But employers and white elitist politicians gained even more from a racially divided workforce and electorate.

New divisions among protestants

The Protestant churches, a collective cornerstone of the South, also reflected the growth of divisions in Dixie. So numerous and pervasive were the Baptists and the Methodists in the postbellum South that after color, form of baptism was the most common distinction among southerners. In addition to racial and baptismal distinctions, social and economic distinctions found more overt expression among the denominations and among churches of the same denomination. *"First Church," "Second Church," uptown church, mill church, country church* reflected a social and economic geography that was familiar to most southerners.

New and striking divisions among Protestants developed in the 1880s and became very obvious in the early twentieth century. The Holiness movement attracted numerous adherents, as did Pentecostalism (from Pentecost, the day when, according to the New Testament, the spirit of God descended on the early Christians) and the Church of Christ. Each has grown as a force in the lives of southerners since then.

Initially the Holiness movement and Pentecostalism had their origins in Methodism. Convinced that their church had become "lukewarm," too worldly, too formal, emotionally dead, and too much a church of "birthright" members instead of a church of members by conversion and conviction, Methodists, north and south, joined "a Great Holiness Revival." Initially hailed as a blessing, the revival erupted into bitter battles between Methodists who believed the Holiness movement had become "disruptive and unseemly" and those who believed they were following God's will. Eventually new denominations evolved: the Church of the Nazarene, the Assemblies of God, and other Pentecostal groups. Each stressed spirituality or being "born again," a rigid or perfectionist moral code, and doctrinal purity. Each of these groups preferred its ministers to be divinely "called" to preach and unsullied by much formal education, and often expected them to derive most of their income from nonministerial employment. These groups differed among themselves, sometimes very sharply, over issues of belief and church organization. The Pentecostals emphasized the "gifts of God," or such charismatic phenomena as faith healing; an aversion to medical treatment and care; glossolalia, or "speaking in tongues"; and the imminent end of the world and the return of Christ.

The available evidence suggests that these new religious groups had their greatest appeal for the poorest among industrial workers and poorer farmers in the South and elsewhere. One student of American religion has noted:

> Though sociological generalizations are risky, it is probably fair to say that the greater appeal [of these groups] . . . has been to the lower economic stratum, to those who, finding worldly goods denied them, have denied the world. At the same time they have affirmed a nobility of life which not only clearly distinguishes them from the world, but promises somehow to redeem elements of that world.

Ernest Troeltsch, a leading pioneer in the history of Christian social ethics, wrote some years ago:

> The really creative, church-forming religious movements are the work of the lower strata. Here only can one find that union of unimpaired imagination, simplicity in emotional life, unreflective character of thought, spontaneity of energy and vehement force of need, out of which an unconditional faith in divine revelation, the naiveté of complete surrender, and the intransigence of certitude can rise.

Economic and social factors seem to have set the stage for these developments in southern Protestantism. As the New South became a reality, as the economy diversified, as cities and towns grew, and as disparities between the successful and the unsuccessful became more obvious, Protestant churches reflected these developments. The disinherited or neglected, finding too little for themselves in the conventional churches, went elsewhere to find preachers who spoke in understandable terms. They found churches where they felt welcome and where they received assurances that they were purified, that they had greater virtue or the right relationship with God because they followed a stricter moral code, and that the inequities of this world would be suddenly and finally reversed. These new Protestant groups represented a blend of old religious ideas and sentiments with a particular set of social and economic factors. These groups reflected a recurring pattern in the history of Christianity, a pattern that earlier had produced the Anabaptists, Quakers, Methodists, and the Salvation Army, to name a few of the "churches of the disinherited."

The Churches of Christ had a history similar to that of the Pentecostals and the Holiness movement, but within a more traditional theological and biblical framework. Congregations within the Disciples of Christ denomination drew away from the Disciples over several issues, of which the use of instrumental music in worship was the most important stated issue. Unstated issues probably had greater weight: social and economic differences among the Disciples. This drawing away took explicit form by 1906. When the federal government took its religious census that year, the Churches of Christ asked to be enumerated separately from the Disciples. The new denomination enjoyed phenomenal growth, eventually becoming the most dynamic of the large denominations in the South. It has had its greatest success in Tennessee, Kentucky, Arkansas, Texas, and Oklahoma. The Churches of God found their largest following in Kentucky, Tennessee, Alabama, Georgia, North Carolina, and Florida; the Church of the Nazarene in Oklahoma and Texas as well as Arkansas and Tennessee; and the Assemblies of God in Arkansas, Texas, and Oklahoma.

The growth of these groups was paralleled by the growth in church membership. In 1890 perhaps one in three southerners, black and white, was a church member, an average that was lower than the national average. Since rural areas had fewer churches than urban areas, the South's lack of urbanization may explain why so many southerners were unchurched. After 1890, church membership in the South exceeded population growth, and churches became more diverse in their activities.

Personal salvation remained the predominant concern for most, but many urban churches became more institutional, developing institutions like Sunday schools, Bible classes, and missionary societies. Others became involved in the Social Gospel movement, the effort to apply the teachings of the Gospel to social issues. Those efforts ranged from expressions of concern about working conditions to issues of public piety—dancing, card playing, gambling, tobacco, and of course, alcohol.

POLITICAL DEMAGOGUES

Electoral politics in the late nineteenth and early twentieth centuries reflected the serious divisions in the South, divisions that found political expression even after the end of the depression of the 1890s, the demise of the Populist party, and the reentrenchment of the Democratic party throughout the South. The most obvious political expression of continuing group conflict was the profusion of political demagogues that the South produced in the early twentieth century. The demagogue was not a new phenomenon in the South—Ben Tillman had thrived in the 1890s in South Carolina, for instance—and the type continued to flourish in such latter-day versions as George Wallace of Alabama in the 1960s. Cole Blease succeeded Tillman in South Carolina in the early twentieth century. Mississippi produced first James K. Vardaman, then Theodore Bilbo; Georgia, Tom Watson; Tennessee, Fiddlin' Bob Taylor; Arkansas, Jeff Davis, who was variously described as "the Wild Ass of the Ozarks, the Tribune of Haybinders, a Karl Marx for Hillbillies."

Demagogue is too often a misleading political epithet or slur. Though these political leaders outraged many people with their vitriolic oratory and bizarre behavior, the epithet obscures their contributions to southern politics and what their existence and repeated successes at the polls meant. Their followings and their victories meant, among other things, that more conventional politics and politicians failed to meet the needs of many southerners. The demagogues were, as one historian has observed, "agrarian radicals [who] practiced a politics of catharsis and symbolic action." But their actions "probably inhibited radical change." They provided a voice, an emotional outlet, and symbols of success for the disinherited whites of the New South. Cotton mill workers felt so attached to Blease that they frequently wrote him to complain, especially about working conditions. Blease gave the mill hands a sense of importance, of having a political voice. In turn, cotton mill workers gave strong support to Blease at the polls.

Though some of the demagogues' contributions were concrete and noteworthy, it seemed at times that their major contribution was to the comic-opera aspects of southern politics. The demagogues flourished because the Dixie of the late nineteenth and the early twentieth centuries was deeply divided. The divisions were symptoms of the rapid social and economic change the South had experienced.

22
Southern Progressives

———— ❖ ————

aterialism, as Booker T. Washington suggested in 1895, had dramatically altered the South since 1880, and southerners began to realize that
they must bring some kind of order to their changed world. What kind
of order? Who would be its agents? Those questions were addressed by the men
and women of the progressive era.

Four Southern Progressives

James Kimble Vardaman, "the White Chief," served Mississippi as a legislator in the
1890s, then as governor (1904–1908) and U.S. senator (1913–1919). He was remembered more for his vitriolic racist demagoguery than for his political ideas and
achievements. Typical of white politicians of his day, he used Negrophobia to appeal
to voters. But he carried venomous racism further than most southern politicians.

Many of his contemporaries found his Negrophobic language and proposals
more than they could abide even in that day. Vardaman wanted to repeal the Fifteenth Amendment, modify the Fourteenth, and stop spending even the small
sums Mississippi spent for the education of "the black man" because "education
only makes the Negro dissatisfied with his lowly position in society." When President Theodore Roosevelt entertained Booker T. Washington at lunch at the White
House, the Mississippian favored the nation with his commentary:

> President Roosevelt takes this nigger bastard into his home, introduces him to his fam-
> ily and entertains him on terms of absolute social equality. He does more. He carries
> his daughter to another social function, where she and Washington ["the saddle-
> colored philosopher of Tuskeegee"] are to be among the special guest[s] of honor.

Was this not a presidential endorsement of the horror of horrors, interracial marriage?

Vardaman claimed he felt kindly toward blacks, that he wanted blacks to
prosper in their place. To do so blacks had to stay out of politics and had to accept
their subordinate social and economic position. As governor, Vardaman did sup-

JAMES K. VARDAMAN CAMPAIGNING (Courtesy of Mississippi Department of
Archives and History)

press racial violence, and some of his legislative program aided blacks, though
some of it certainly hurt them.

Vardaman's political power was rooted in his enormous popularity with the
small white farmers of Mississippi. Vardaman provided a catharsis, a symbol, and
something of a program for white farm families who had too little fertile land and
received meager earnings despite their efforts, who saw other Mississippi farmers
thrive (especially those in the delta), and who believed, not incorrectly, that prosperous farmers had an alliance with the railroads, banks, and the comfortable in
the towns against the interests of people like themselves. At a time when two in
three farmers and half of the white farmers were landless tenants and their ranks
were swelling, Vardaman's appeal is not much of a mystery. Small farmers
embraced a man who spurned the conventions of the established and successful
and who spoke the language of the small farmers, literally and figuratively.
Catching his spirit, they transformed the epithets *redneck* and *hillbilly* into badges
of honor. They displayed these badges on posters and banners at political rallies,
for instance, when they greeted Vardaman at Meridian as he stepped off a train in
his familiar white suit and white boots, a black broad-brimmed hat atop his
shoulder-length hair.

Vardaman's evolution as a politician was more conventional than his dress or
manner suggested. He early obtained a vehicle for himself and his views when he
became owner and editor of the *Greenwood Enterprise*, a step aided by the substantial inheritance of the widow he married. He entered politics as a party regular and

a partisan of the status quo in the 1890s—a Bourbon Democrat in Mississippi. His later break with the Bourbons can be attributed to personal ambition and a timely adjustment to changes in the politics of Mississippi. He sensed that he had little future among the regulars, since others had firm holds on higher rungs of the regular party ladder, and he became aware that the Bourbons had failed to respond adequately to the needs and fears of the majority of white voters in the state. Vardaman also took advantage of the opportunity presented by direct primaries, a new political device that made it easier to circumvent the power of the party establishment, which was based on control of party caucuses and conventions.

Vardaman broke with the Bourbons, then the old guard of Mississippi politics, and ran as a man of the people against the political establishment. Others did likewise at the time—for instance, Robert La Follette in Wisconsin, one of the patriarchs of the progressive movement.

Vardaman adopted many positions that were conventional for a progressive. He generally supported the concept of activist government, an attitude he showed even before he held public office. He was one of Greenwood's civic elite, who boosted the town and called for the expansion and improvement of public services. As governor he proposed measures to improve the judicial system; to obtain a more equitable tax system; to create a system for providing cheaper textbooks for schools; to secure better services for the mentally ill and incapacitated, the blind, the deaf and dumb, and those afflicted with tuberculosis; and to reform Mississippi's brutal, corrupt penal system. He moved to double appropriations for public education (for whites); to stiffen regulations and restraints on insurance companies, utilities, railroads, manufacturers, and large corporations; to create the office of agricultural commissioner; and to expand highway construction. He tried to obtain restrictions on child labor, state bank depositories for individuals and lower interest rates, and a state highway commission. Encouraged by Vardaman, the legislature passed Jim Crow laws for streetcars and a vagrancy law so harsh that it probably reduced many blacks to peonage. Employing his powers as governor, he led a campaign that effectively limited the spread of a yellow fever epidemic in 1905, a move that had no precedent in Mississippi. He used his office on perhaps nine occasions to halt lynchings, though he continued to uphold lynching "to defend the virtue" of white women. He directed a vigorous campaign against "whitecappers," groups who resembled the Ku Klux Klan and who used violence in southern Mississippi to force out black farm owners and tenants. Vardaman realized that whitecapping threatened the stability of the labor supply and discouraged businesses that wanted to operate in Mississippi. Even his opponents acknowledged that he was a good governor. In his autobiography, *Lanterns on the Levee*, William Alexander Percy, cousin of the novelist and essayist Walker Percy, reflected the attitudes of the elite toward those they dismissed as demagogues. He described Vardaman as "a kindly, vain demagogue unable to think, and given to emotions he considered noble. . . . a handsome, flamboyant figure of a man, immaculately overdressed, . . . [who] looked like a top-notch medicine man." Yet, Percy conceded, "He had made a good governor."

Later, as U.S. senator—an office he won after defeating Leroy Percy, father of William Alexander, in a bitter campaign—Vardaman followed his earlier course as a progressive Democrat. He also continued giving racist diatribes. For several years he toured much of the United States giving lectures, the most memorable of which was "The Impending Crisis!" The title of the lecture was an obvious imitation of Hinton R. Helper's antebellum alarm. The theme was vintage Vardaman: political equality for Negroes led to social equality and thence to interracial marriage; therefore, granting any political concessions to Negroes led inevitably to catastrophe. "Ambition in the negro is concreted in lust."

Edgar Gardner Murphy recoiled at the demagoguery of Vardaman and his kind. Murphy might have recoiled even more at the suggestion that he and the White Chief were fellow progressives. Born in Arkansas, educated at Sewanee (the University of the South) and at General Theological Seminary in New York, Murphy held several pastorates in the Episcopal church. He accepted a call to Montgomery, Alabama, in 1899, and there became involved in the Social Gospel movement. The Social Gospel, which evolved in response to the negative social ramifications of industrialization and urbanization—to brutalizing labor, growing disparities in income and wealth, and wretched urban conditions—emphasized the obligation of Christians to change social institutions and the social environment. Christianity, according to the Social Gospel, involved more than personal salvation, piety, and occasional gifts to the needy. The Social Gospel was on the cutting edge of a crucial shift in opinion about the human condition. Increasing numbers of people were coming to see environmental and social conditions as explanatory factors in the circumstances and behavior of human beings. People might have little education because they were poor, for example, not simply because they lacked motivation or ability.

Soon after he went to Montgomery, Murphy became aware of the plight of child laborers in the textile mills in Alabama. In an effort to restrict child labor, he founded the Alabama Child Labor Committee in 1900. Four years later he was the major figure in the founding of the National Child Labor Committee. By then he had resigned his pastorate and had become executive secretary of the Southern Education Board, which played an important role in the Southwide efforts to improve education in the early twentieth century.

Murphy also became involved in efforts to ameliorate the conditions of blacks in the South. He trod carefully here. He decried lynching but embraced Jim Crow. A thoroughgoing paternalist, Murphy rested his hopes for improving the conditions of blacks on the "better sort" of whites and on such means as industrial education. Predictably, Booker T. Washington and Tuskegee received lavish praise from Murphy. He feared that the racist demagoguery of the kind dispensed by Vardaman would enflame the white masses, and in his *Problems of the Present South* (1904) called upon the South "to do justice to the negro and to the more helpless elements of her industrial life." Whatever the biases he held in common with most of his generation, Murphy labored hard to implement his portion of the Social Gospel, an effort that may have been a factor in his early death.

Walter Hines Page joined Murphy in some of these efforts. Born in North Carolina in 1855, Page enjoyed a distinguished career as a journalist, editor, and publisher. While preparing for the Methodist ministry at Randolph-Macon College in Virginia, Page became a religious skeptic, a not unusual condition for educated Americans of his generation, who were heavily exposed to Darwinian thought and its ramifications. Page sought another calling. Two years of graduate study at John Hopkins University, then the most distinguished graduate institution in the United States, convinced him that scholarship was not his mission in life. Then he entered the newspaper business in North Carolina, and in 1886 left the South permanently to find greater opportunities in New York.

Page thus became a not uncommon southern figure, an expatriate who lectured the South on its deficiencies and proposed remedies. His lecterns eventually included at various times the *Atlantic Monthly,* the *Forum,* and *World's Work* and the publishing houses of Houghton Mifflin and Doubleday, Page. His early expatriate lectures in the form of weekly letters to the *State Chronicle* of Raleigh, North Carolina, reached a considerable audience and elicited mixed reactions. No doubt Page's argumentative style had something to do with those reactions. His "mummy" letter of February 1886 was long remembered. Upset by opposition in North Carolina to state-supported industrial education, a basic plank in the New South platform, Page wrote: "They don't want an Industrial School. That means a new idea, and a new idea is death to the supremacy of the mummies. Let 'em alone. The world must have some corner in it where men sleep and sleep and dream and dream and North Carolina is as good a spot for that as any." Opponents of innovation could simply ignore the reputation of North Carolina as "the laughingstock among the States," while "the most active and energetic men in North Carolina leave the state" and "bright and able men" drink themselves to death. "When every intellectual aspiration is discouraged, when all the avenues that lead to independent thought and to mental growth are closed, . . . there is absolutely no chance for the ambitious men of ability, proportionate to their ability." The "mummy" letter, one of Page's biographers says, "was the most controversial and . . . influential piece of writing that he ever produced." That letter and "The Forgotten Man," his noted address on education to the first class graduated from North Carolina's school for teachers, made Page's reputation as a leader in educational reform in the South. Page became part of the efforts of a group of journalists, politicians, activists, educators, and other professionals who prodded North Carolina to transform itself. They scored major successes in the early twentieth century, especially during the administration of Governor Charles B. Aycock and particularly in education.

Page also worked to reconcile North and South, to explain each to the other. Page saw himself as "the Southerner as American." In so doing, he embodied one side in the long debate about how distinctive the South was and is from the rest of the nation. It is a debate about whether southerners are first southern or first American—a debate that lies at the heart of the historical experience of the South and southerners.

In 1911 Page also helped initiate the campaign to get Woodrow Wilson elected president. The campaign led eventually to the return of the Democrats to the White House and, for a time, the restoration of southern Democrats to the front ranks of national leadership. Page's reward was the American ambassadorship to Great Britain, a position he held until shortly before his death in 1918. The southern expatriate went far from Cary, North Carolina, to financial success, to the forefront of journalism and publishing in New York and Boston, to leadership in reform and in sectional reconciliation, to the Court of St. James.

KATE BARNARD (Western History Collections, University of Oklahoma Library)

Kate Barnard did not go that far, but she went a long way in the border South. In 1907, voters in the new state of Oklahoma elected Barnard to be their first commissioner of charities and corrections, a position she held until 1915, when poor health forced her to retire from office. She came to the fore as progressivism, southern style, became a shaping force in Oklahoma.

Barnard was an "eighty-niner." Like thousands of other Oklahomans, she had joined in the Oklahoma "run" of 1889, the first of a series of runs for homesteads on lands that the federal government had declared open for settlement. Like many other people, her father had migrated to Oklahoma in order to reverse his fortunes. Many succeeded, but John Barnard did not. He soon gave up his homestead and moved to Oklahoma City, one of the "cities" instantly created in 1889.

The instant city soon developed old familiar patterns and problems. A "strange thing happened which opened my eyes to a new view of life," Kate Barnard remembered.

> The well-to-do people gradually moved out from the district around our home and the poor began to take possession of their dwellings. . . . out of these crowded

pest-ridden "homes" came the strangest children I ever saw—peaked and poor and thin and sallow . . . little children who drifted around, hungry, cold, uncared for, unloved. . . . I watched these children till my heart ached and I was compelled to cry out in their behalf.

A converted and deeply committed Catholic, Barnard felt prompted to act upon her Christian commitment. Barnard began a rapid transformation at thirty years of age, or twenty-six or -five or -three (somewhat uncharacteristically, Barnard followed the feminine convention of the day when asked her age). She started out in 1904 with private charities that practiced incidental relief—charities that took up occasional donations from the well-to-do and distributed them to the "deserving" poor. She quickly surmised that more than an occasional basket of food was required. She helped found the United Charities of Oklahoma City; then she turned to political and labor union activism. A local newspaper helped this transformation; the *Daily Oklahoman* paid Barnard's expenses for a nationwide tour to see how other cities dealt with the impoverished. Barnard met many of the leaders of the "social justice" faction of the progressive movement. She soon came to share their belief that poverty was a social problem, not a personal problem or the result of personal failings. Working closely with organized labor and other groups, Barnard helped draft a constitution for Oklahoma that incorporated much of this thinking.

Seemingly determined to cover every eventuality, the Oklahoma constitutional convention drafted a document of more than 50,000 words, "easily the world's longest constitution at the time." Reflecting the strong antimonopolistic views that prevailed in much of the United States and certainly in the South in 1907, the constitution devoted nearly one-fifth of its coverage to efforts to restrain the powers of the "trusts." The constitution established several graduated taxes, including one on incomes and another on corporations; restrictions on child labor; compulsory education; prohibition of contract labor and increased employer liability for occupational safety; an eight-hour day for miners and public employees; home rule for urban areas with at least 2,000 people; and a department of charities and corrections, whose elected commissioner could be a man or a woman. It was the only statewide office that carried that stipulation, which was intended to ensure that Kate Barnard would be its first occupant. Barnard received more votes than any other candidate in the state's first election—in which she could not vote because she was a woman.

The constitution also created a large number of elective offices, a reflection of the Populist legacy and the William Jennings Bryan tradition of progressivism. The constitution clearly reflected the southern background of many of its drafters and the people who had elected them to the constitutional convention. The constitution did not give women the vote. Opponents of women's suffrage sounded the familiar objections, including the assertion that suffrage for women would open the way to suffrage for blacks. The constitution did attempt to render Oklahoma a dry state. In an article that had to be ratified separately, the constitution prohibited the sale of alcoholic beverages except for medicinal purposes. Voters approved the article by an overwhelming vote, and available evidence indicates that the new state began its career in cold sobriety. More certain is the fact that the state clung to prohibition long after many Oklahomans ceased abstaining. Will Rogers, the beloved humorist, once claimed that his fellow Oklahomans would vote for a dry state "as long as they could stagger to the polls and keep it that way."

The new constitution would have disfranchised blacks and racially segregated schools and public transportation if the delegates to the constitutional convention had had their way. President Theodore Roosevelt objected to their efforts to put Jim Crow in the Oklahoma constitution and threatened to prevent Oklahoma from becoming a state if they went ahead with their plans. The apprentice state demurred and waited until it gained admission to the Union and had more freedom to follow its inclinations. The first legislature of the new state moved promptly to disfranchise blacks and to adopt Jim Crow in schools, transportation, and public facilities, although only 5 percent of the populace was black. Black disfranchisement enjoyed only limited success, in part because of a 1915 ruling of the U.S. Supreme Court against the state's blatantly discriminatory grandfather clause. The efforts of the Democrats to prevent blacks from voting persisted, because they believed that blacks provided the margin of victory for Republicans in elections in parts of the state. As in Tennessee and another border state, Kentucky, the Republican party was strong enough to present a continuing challenge to the Democrats in Oklahoma. Jim Crow in schools, transportation, and public facilities did become fixed, giving Oklahoma a distinctly southern quality in its race relations. Other aspects of Oklahoma contributed to the "southernness" of the state: the longtime dominance of the Democrats in the state, the power and numbers of evangelical Protestants, especially the Southern Baptists, and a farm-based economy that was beleaguered by overdependence on cotton and high rates of tenancy. The last was worsened after World War I by soil depletion and the advent of the boll weevil.

At its inception, Oklahoma embraced most of the advanced ideas of progressivism, southern style. Kate Barnard quickly discovered that the Sooner State could also beat a strategic retreat from some of the more advanced progressive positions. Almost immediately the state fell back from its antimonopolistic position because it feared that business would be driven from the state. Oklahoma thus discovered a crucial problem for modern reform movements in America: how to balance the perceived need to regulate business without raising fears— real, imagined, or cynically created—of hurting the economy. A midcourse quickly evolved in the new state: "business progressivism" gained sway, a progressivism that reflected the concerns and interests of the commercial-civic elites of businesspeople and professionals. Barnard and her allies, many from organized labor, immediately ran into strong opposition to implementing the restrictions on child labor that the state constitution called for. Only after Barnard led a strong lobbying effort in 1908 did the Oklahoma legislature pass, and the governor sign, a law to restrict child labor. It became a model for other states. Barnard also persuaded the state to adopt a series of penal reforms, including a juvenile court system, and to establish an institution for the "feebleminded." Impressed by her triumphs, Alexander McKelway of the National Child Labor Committee urged Woodrow Wilson to use her help in his 1912 presidential campaign because she was "the most consummate politician" in Oklahoma.

Exhausted and ill, Barnard did not run for reelection in 1914. She continued for some time to work with other "social justice" progressives, but she was never again as active as she had been. By 1922 she had departed Oklahoma, a symbol of the decline of her brand of progressivism and the advent of a "safer" brand.

PROGRESSIVISM, SOUTHERN STYLE

James K. Vardaman, Edgar Gardner Murphy, Walter Hines Page, and Kate Barnard make an unlikely quartet. Yet they illustrate the major characteristics, proclivities, assumptions, and achievements of southern progressivism. All accepted the cardinal principle of progressivism, the activist state. The diversity of this quartet also illustrates the diversity and diffuse nature of the progressives and their movement, which have so often baffled historians and others. Progressivism was propelled by a number of concerns that acquired intense urgency by the turn of the century: that the power of big business should be restricted; that industrialization's victims, especially women and children, should be aided and protected; and that services, like schools and public health agencies, had to be more efficient and more professional to meet pressing problems. Progressivism had both populist elements and elitist elements. Progressives supported some measures that enhanced individual liberty and others that limited individual liberty: liberalized divorce laws and women's suffrage on the one hand, prohibition and compulsory school attendance laws on the other. A person could be a progressive and be a Democrat or a Republican, or join a new party—the Progressive party, founded in 1912, or the Prohibitionist party, founded in the late nineteenth century.

Progressivism in the South drew upon an antimonopolistic tradition that had its origins as a political movement in the 1870s. That tradition received an enormous boost from Populism and the merger craze, which after 1895 produced business giants that were or seemed to be out of control. The power of the "trusts" caused apprehension throughout the South. As prices rose steeply after 1898, the power of U.S. Steel, of the Southern Railway and other major trunk lines, and even of the American Book Company, the "textbook trust" with which Vardaman warred, hardly was a phantom conjured up by politicians on the stump. Nor were local utilities and transportation companies that rendered indifferent or bad services at increasing costs to urbanites.

Progressivism in the South embraced antimonopolism at its height in 1907–1908. Jeff Davis fought a spectacular, if ineffectual, battle in Arkansas against outside companies. Governor Braxton Bragg Comer of Alabama warred with Milton H. Smith of the Louisville and Nashville Railroad until exhaustion forced a ceasefire. Texas passed the noted Robertson Act, which required out-of-state insurance companies to invest a percentage of their profits earned in Texas in the Lone Star State. Standard Oil lost its charter in Texas. In 1919 the state legislature gave the railroad commission power to regulate the oil industry. To the north, antimonopolism found a prominent place in Oklahoma's constitution. But antimonopolism soon subsided in the South, as elsewhere. The South needed capital too urgently to risk chasing it away.

Though progressivism in the South retained some of its Populist aspects, it came to have a more middle-class, urban quality. Populist ideology left its mark in the institutionalizing of direct democracy: primary elections, secret ballots, an increase in the number of elective offices, the initiative, referendum, and recall. Direct democracy had the ironic effect of increasing the power of interest groups at the expense of the power of political parties and the unorganized.

Progressivism dealt with a wide range of issues and left a substantial legacy. It left a much larger number of public agencies and public services, a much greater number of regulatory laws, and inevitably, substantially higher taxes. Between 1903 and 1922, state revenues in the South increased 400 percent. (Nationally, they increased 300 percent.) The south Atlantic states led the way with a fivefold rise; North Carolina led all the states with a sixfold rise. Progressivism attempted to ameliorate some of the harsher consequences of industrialization and urbanization. Prompted by humanitarian concerns, a direct and indirect result of the Social Gospel, progressivism was driven not only by an urge to exercise social control over a society seemingly threatened by deep divisions, but also by a "search for order" in an America that at the time was "a society of island communities." That society broke down under the twin forces of industrialization and urbanization. The United States could no longer rely primarily on local autonomy; Americans had to develop new approaches more appropriate to their needs. Turning from the personal, informal ways of the community, "Americans sought order through continuity and predictability," by creating new mechanisms and more centralized authority. Progressivism involved transformation, not revolution; reform of capitalism, not its rejection.

Southern progressivism mirrored its locale. It accepted the basic structure of race relations in the South. Some observers contend that among the earliest reforms of the progressives were disfranchisement of blacks and Jim Crow. From our perspective, such a contention appears to do violence to the concept of reform; but even greater evils might have been perpetrated in an era when racist orators appeared to know no limits and when the possibility of outright race war was not a fantasy of fanatics and the deranged. Moreover, turmoil during elections did seem to subside after the great majority of black men lost their voting rights. That loss significantly reduced the opportunities of white politicians to use the ballots of blacks for their own ends—to stay in power and protect their economic advantages and those of their allies. But blacks paid a high price for that change, and this was not the first or the last time whites in the South shifted the burden to the blacks. Moreover, as became very clear especially in the way public money was spent, without the vote blacks had even less opportunity to pressure public officials than they had had before.

Southern progressivism was almost exclusively a Democratic affair. The Populist-Republican fusion in North Carolina set some precedents in the 1890s, especially in education, that progressive Democrats followed. Tennessee Republicans took advantage of a split among Democrats over prohibition and a murdered leader, Edward W. Carmack, to get two terms in the governor's office. Tennessee Republicans elected one other governor during the era. Kentucky Republicans elected several. Republicans won seats in state legislatures, but not majorities. They won some congressional elections—consistently in a few places—and they won some local and county offices. Otherwise, the Democrats dominated elections in the South. Essentially, then, southern progressives worked through the

Democratic party. Progressivism was the product of bifactional politics, not partisan politics.

Southern progressives expressed their regionalism in other ways. So intense
and extensive was their interest in improving education (generally, for whites
only) that the movement to upgrade schools and universities in the South became known as "the education crusade." Prohibition received early, strong support in the South. Abolition of the convict lease system, a Southwide institution
with few imitations outside the region, became the most important of a series of
penal reforms. Women had an active role in progressivism, sometimes as leaders,
but they could not forget they were Southern Ladies. Indeed, feminine gentility
could be a weapon in dextrous hands. But those dextrous women could guide
only five southern states to ratify the Nineteenth Amendment, granting women
the right to vote.

Progressives in the South paid particular attention to public health, child
labor, and other issues of concern to working people. Tuberculosis, yellow fever,
typhoid, smallpox, pellagra, hookworm, and malaria were the leading threats to
life and health in the South in 1900. Within the United States by then, yellow fever,
pellagra, and malaria were major diseases only in the South. Malaria killed few of
its victims but contributed heavily to the chronic ill health of southerners. Tuberculosis took the most lives. Child labor, especially in the textile mills, became an
explosive issue and a scandal.

Finally, progressives remained loyal to the New South creed. Moreover, the
New South creed fit neatly with business progressivism, which stressed orderly
government and government services that facilitated the operations of private
business.

THE ROOTS OF SOUTHERN PROGRESSIVISM

The roots of southern progressivism were deep and extensive and intertwined
with the basic elements of the American South as the nineteenth century gave
way to the twentieth. Progressivism's growth and endurance throughout the
South and its appeal to so many people suggest that it developed in response to
widely perceived needs. Disarray was pervasive. The concrete achievements of
the New South—the growth of industry, transportation systems, and urban
areas—had brought blessings and unanticipated problems. The traditional response of passive government seemed woefully inadequate. The progressives believed that the power of the state was required to meet the problems of society as
they perceived and understood those problems. The progressives also directed
their attention to the needs of farmers and farming.

Progressivism did not develop in a vacuum of ideas. Though public funds
were short, southern Democrats after 1880 had generally been willing to use the
state to improve education, to provide some services to the needy, and to create
new agencies, such as state boards of health. Most Democratic leaders had long
been sensitive to the demands of farmers, who, after all, were the electoral majority. Lower tariffs, railroad regulation, currency inflation, and public services
for farmers consistently found favor among most Democratic politicians. Obvi-

ously, the agrarian unrest of the late nineteenth century indicated that many farmers felt that what Democratic leaders offered was not enough. Those feelings should not, however, leave the erroneous impression of callous disregard for southern farmers.

Conservation, a major concern of the progressives, also drew upon precedents from the late nineteenth century. The reputation of the Gilded Age for profit-driven exploitation of natural resources certainly was deserved. During the Gilded Age and the early twentieth century, extinctions or near-extinctions of major species occurred for the first time since the late Pleistocene epoch (a geological epoch that ended some 25,000 years ago). Victims included the whooping crane, cougar, timber wolf, red or Florida wolf, Carolina parakeet, and passenger pigeon. At the same time, whole forests fell to armies of loggers and to land-clearing farmers. Yet, drawing upon antebellum precedents, state legislatures passed laws to restrict fishing and hunting and to protect nongame animals, particularly birds. How effective these laws were is not clear. Changes in fashion may have done more to protect birds. Birds with spectacular plumage were safer after feathered hats became passé. Effective or not, these laws demonstrated that the Gilded Age South was not entirely indifferent to the environment.

Convinced that forests were also in danger of becoming things of the past, groups concerned about forest conservation proliferated dramatically in the 1890s. Their agitation led to the development of scientific forestry in the South. Support grew for the creation of federally owned forest preserves, support that helped secure federal legislation authorizing government land purchases in the Appalachians. Those purchases laid the foundation for what later became the Great Smoky Mountains National Park. Thus the Gilded Age South—including the Redeemers—left a more positive legacy for the progressives than has often been realized.

Progressivism also owed something to Populism, though how much varied from state to state. Like Populism, progressivism drew much of its motivation from a profound sense that the times were out of joint, especially in the 1890s. And some progressives had a strong Populist bent, which showed itself especially in the more rural-dominated states. In the case of Alabama, however, one historian concluded that progressivism and Populism were parallel developments in the 1890s: "Progressivism, the alternative to Populism, was a substantially different reaction by a separate set of men to the same enemy Populism faced—the dominant industrial wing of the Democratic Party." Progressivism in the South eventually ran a course far different from that which Populism envisioned. Developments in Alabama suggest rich insights into why their courses diverged so sharply. The Populists attempted to build a mass-based political movement. Their leaders were not among the state's elite, and they attempted to be spokesmen for the "dispossessed and powerless." The Populists focused their attention on modernizing agriculture and improving the position of farmers in the marketplace. They paid little attention to other sectors of the economy, though they were genuinely concerned about the plight of working people. The Alabama progressives, ambitious businesspeople, felt that "abolishing privilege was not enough." They believed that economic growth would increase equality of opportunity. That growth, they argued, depended on an increase in governmental services to stimulate development and help individuals take advantage of greater opportunities.

The aspirations of the progressives did not, of course, extend far toward the blacks. Nor did most progressives display great concern for working people. Progressivism remained close to those "tenets shared by comfortable Americans everywhere."

EDUCATIONAL REFORM

A substantial number of comfortable southerners did feel distressed about the state of education in their region in 1900. The "great educational awakening" began with the painful awareness of the woeful state of schooling in the South; then came vigorous publicizing of alarming facts, conferences, lobbying, and the involvement of philanthropists from outside the region. Remedies included substantial investments of money, large increases in public expenditures, expansion of public agencies, new laws, attempts to standardize, extensive use of experts, and the involvement of the universities of the region. Educational reform drew its breath from the urge of the "better elements" to uplift the lesser folk. It was a "mixture of paternalism and *noblesse oblige*." Educational reform reflected its local and state settings, and almost all the states of the South became heavily involved in it. Educational reform also stayed within the familiar confines of the New South, white supremacy, and male dominance.

Public education hardly existed outside the larger cities, and few of the many private academies were a significant improvement over the public schools.

> The public schools of the South at the opening of the century were for the most part miserably supported, poorly attended, wretchedly taught, and wholly inadequate for the education of the people. Far behind the rest of the country in nearly all respects, Southern education suffered from a greater lag than any other public institution in the region.

Perhaps 20 percent of whites and 50 percent of blacks were illiterate. In 1900 only two states in the South and border region—Texas and Oklahoma—spent as much as one-half the national average per pupil, $2.84. Alabama and North Carolina spent the least in the region, 50 cents. South Carolina followed at 67 cents; four others spent less than $1. These disparities represented years of fiscal tightfistedness, a legacy of the reaction to Reconstruction, the depressions of the 1870s and the 1890s, and harsh realities that defied quick remedies and determined efforts. The ratio of children to adults in the South was nearly double that in the rest of the nation. Those adults also had less to spend on schooling. Taxable wealth per school-aged child was five times greater in Massachusetts, for instance, than in North Carolina. The costs of education in the South were compounded by other demographic factors: population was less dense in many southern states than in the northern states, and the South's racial segregation required dual school systems and faculties and staffs.

Fewer than half of the school-aged children attended school in the South. Few schools stayed open as long as four months a year. Teachers generally earned less than $30 a month. Yet more men taught in the South than elsewhere, a clear and unfortunate indication that in 1900 job opportunities in the South lagged behind those in the rest of the nation. Still, it is easy to overlook important shifts in attitudes toward public education before 1900. Southern states significantly increased funding for public education after the depression of the 1870s ended. Kentucky, for instance, increased taxes substantially in 1881 and 1882 to raise money for public education. So did Georgia. In 1888 Georgia created a state property tax to raise money for a state school fund. Three years later the state legislature created the Georgia Institute of Technology, and state support for higher education gradually increased. Most of the southern states tried to improve public education by making changes in education administration and by increasing opportunities for teacher training. In 1900, however, the South still lagged far behind the rest of the nation in quality and funding of public education.

Having weathered the depression of the 1890s and the Populist challenge and buoyed by the easy victory in the Spanish-American War and the passing or defeat of an older generation of leaders, the South began an extensive, prolonged effort to overhaul public education. Initially a group of educators, journalists, and activists mounted a campaign of fact-finding, publicity, conferences, and lobbying. Northern philanthropists joined in, with substantial sums and quiet discretion.

Walter Hines Page played a strategic role in the early stages of the "educational awakening." He had long been interested in education reform. As editor of the *Forum* in the 1890s and later of *World's Work,* he had encouraged investigations into education. Page saw educational improvement as necessary if the New South were to be realized. In 1897 he delivered an address in Greensboro, North Carolina, which became a landmark. The "forgotten man," Page said, was the man who had not received an adequate education. Reflecting the progressives'

CELEBRATING EDUCATIONAL IMPROVEMENT, CONCORD, N.C. (North Carolina Collection, University of North Carolina Library at Chapel Hill)

penchant for facts and figures, Page claimed that failure to support education had cost North Carolina dearly. The steady emigration of Tarheels had exacted a heavy toll in lost talent. Those left behind paid a heavy personal price and were a millstone around the neck of the state.

> In 1890, twenty-six percent of the white persons of the State were unable to read or write. One in four was wholly forgotten. But illiteracy was not the worst of it; the worst of it was that the stationary social condition indicated by generations of illiteracy had long been the general condition. The forgotten man was content to stay forgotten.

Page's speech was the public capstone of a concerted effort to elevate schooling in North Carolina. The extraordinarily bitter, violent politics of North Carolina in the 1890s had obscured the emergence of a widely shared determination to improve educational opportunities in the state. Led by the new president of the University of North Carolina, Edwin A. Alderman, and Charles D. McIver, president of the recently opened North Carolina State Normal and Industrial School for Women (now the University of North Carolina at Greensboro), the campaign first succeeded in obtaining a more secure tax base for public education. Charles B. Aycock, governor from 1900 to 1904, and James Y. Joyner, long-time state superintendent of education, assumed command of a crusade for education that marked a turning point in the history of North Carolina. Newspapers in the state aided the impressive efforts. Similar developments occurred elsewhere in the South.

Coincidentally, aid came from the outside. Led by Robert C. Ogden, a wealthy New York businessman and supporter of Hampton Institute in Virginia, the Conference for Education in the South began in 1898. Initially concerned about education for blacks, the conference soon shifted its primary emphasis to whites. The Southern Education Board (SEB) evolved out of the conference in 1901, and the SEB became the major vehicle for publicity and lobbying for the education crusade. Edgar Gardner Murphy became the executive director of the SEB, which supported campaigns for educational reform in every southern state and ran a bureau that collected and disseminated information.

Other northern philanthropists provided critically needed assistance, another example of the not always welcome hand of outside reformers. John D. Rockefeller, Sr., gave $53 million from 1902 to 1909 through one of his organizations, the General Education Board (GEB). Rockefeller expressed a "special interest in education in the South." The SEB and GEB worked together closely; in fact, several individuals served on the boards of directors of both agencies.

Aided by funds from the GEB, the SEB distributed a steady stream of bulletins, documents, and reports; encouraged state campaigns; and sent out agents during a series of campaigns that extended for more than a decade. No one could entirely escape the crusaders; they turned up to speak at public gatherings of all sorts, from church meetings to barbecues. They relied on concentrated verbal blitzes reminiscent of revival meetings. Where the spoken word did not reach, the written word did, in newspapers and magazines fortified by the latest release from the SEB.

The southern states increased their total expenditures for public schools nearly 300 percent, from $21.4 million in 1900 to $57.2 million in 1910, then nearly tripled that sum to $156.3 million in 1920. (The increase in North Carolina exceeded 1,200 percent for the same years, from $950,000 to more than $12 million.) Illiteracy rates declined sharply, more so for whites than for blacks, an indication of the severe racial discrimination in the distribution of educational expenditures. The proportion of school-aged children enrolled in school increased significantly, as did the length of the school year and salaries for teachers. The ratio of pupils to teachers declined somewhat. By 1920, every southern state had adopted a compulsory education law. Schools, especially in urban areas, offered greater varieties of courses. Certification and administrative procedures diminished the power of local politicians to use local schools for patronage. That development lessened political pressures on teachers and school administrators. As they became more professional, they tended also to be more bureaucratic and insulated from the pressures of their constituencies. But neither they nor the schools were insulated from Jim Crow or from the efforts of powerful people in the state to determine the goals of education. Businesspeople, for instance, effectively pressed for schooling that was designed to produce "desirable" employees, though pupils often proved far less pliant than the champions of vocational education presumed. As late as 1940, every southern state spent far less on public education per pupil than other states spent, and not all the disparities can be explained by income differentials among the states. It is possible, however, that the disparities between expenditures per pupil might have been much less if comparisons are limited only to white pupils.

In almost every measurable category, however, the South continued to lag behind the rest of the nation. Jim Crow, dependency on cotton, and demographic factors still outweighed the efforts and successes of the education crusade. No state in the South or the border region except Oklahoma equaled or exceeded the national average for length of school term or for expenditures per pupil in 1920. All the states in the region trailed behind the national averages in daily attendance and literacy.

Lack of money constrained the impact of the education crusade. So did other factors, like local resistance to state or outside authorities. Modest funding limited the extension of teacher training, the implementation of new courses and curriculums, school consolidation, and the construction of new schools. State superintendents of education spent most of their time collecting statistics on education, and those were often unreliable. They generally lacked the funds and staff, and often the power, to do much else. Local officials resisted state officials and other education authorities as presumptuous intruders who threatened their power. In many communities, school administrators had one of the few good-paying positions. They, along with local school boards, also had considerable patronage. They hired and fired teachers and staff members. School consolidation was often the most important way to improve schools in rural areas and small towns, but consolidation could mean the loss of a prized possession and institution. After all, schools, along with churches, were the most important centers of community life and activity in the South.

For years, southern leaders deliberately discriminated against blacks in expenditures for education. From 1890 to 1930, for instance, Alabama increased the

SELECTED SCHOOL STATISTICS, 1900, 1920

	Average length of school term (in days)		School expenditures per capita/total population	
	1900	1920	1900	1920
United States	144.6	161.3	$ 2.84	$ 9.80
Alabama	78.3	123	.50	3.88
Arkansas	77.5	126	1.04	4.40
Florida	93	133	1.45	7.26
Georgia	112	145	.89	3.13
Kentucky	115.4	123	1.41	3.36
Louisiana	120	149	.82	6.32
Mississippi	105.1	140	.89	3.06
North Carolina	70.8	134	.50	4.75
Oklahoma	95.3	166	1.72	11.29
South Carolina	88.4	110	.67	3.94
Tennessee	96	133	.87	4.34
Texas	108.2	156	1.46	7.21
Virginia	119	147	1.07	5.62

SOURCE: Adapted from Dewey Grantham, *Southern Progressivism: The Reconciliation of Progress and Tradition* (Knoxville, Tenn.: University of Tennessee Press, 1983), p. 258.

gap between educational expenditures for blacks and whites. The width of the gap varied from area to area within the state, but every area spent at least twice as much for whites' schooling as for blacks'. In 1930 Lowndes County appropriated $53,525 for 975 white children and $48,786 for 10,039 black children. Similar patterns prevailed in Virginia, the Carolinas, and Georgia. In North Carolina, "for every $1.00 expended on a Negro child of school age, $3.22 was expended on the education of a white child of school age" in 1915. That same year the state superintendent of education in South Carolina asked, "Is it too much to hope for a minimum of $25 per white child and $5 per negro child?" South Carolina spent less for both in 1915, but at an even more lopsided ratio, 12.37 to 1. Some, but not much, of this imbalance was offset by the work of private philanthropies, the GEB and the Slater, Jeanes, and Peabody funds. Some of these funds antedated the education crusade. At great sacrifice, blacks also supported black education financially as individuals and through religious groups. The disparities could have been even worse. Hoping to spend even less on education for blacks, some southern leaders wanted to base appropriations on the taxes blacks paid. (In reality, taxes on blacks may have produced more revenue than was expended by state and local governments on education for blacks.) Vardaman took the most extreme position here: he wanted to eliminate public expenditures for black schools altogether. In this case, however, moderates held off the extremists.

The philanthropies, especially the GEB, tried to channel blacks into industrial and vocational education. They had a willing ally in Booker T. Washington. Such an approach fit the New South credo and the white view of the place of blacks.

AVERAGE MONTHLY SALARIES OF TEACHERS, GEORGIA ELEMENTARY SCHOOLS

	1901			1915	
White	1st Grade	$36.90	White men		$60.25
White	2nd Grade	28.11	White women		45.70
White	3rd Grade	22.33			
Black	1st Grade	25.60	Black men		30.14
Black	2nd Grade	26.00	Black women		21.69
Black	3rd Grade	16.30			

SOURCE: Louis R. Harlan, *Separate and Unequal: Public School Campaigns and Racism in the Southern Seaboard States 1901–1915* (New York: Atheneum, 1968), p. 245. Copyright © 1958 The University of North Carolina Press. Reprinted by permission.

AVERAGE ANNUAL SALARIES OF TEACHERS IN THE SOUTHERN SEABOARD STATES, 1911–1913

	Teachers		Salaries		Av. ann. salary	
State	White	Black	White	Black	White	Black
Va.	8,576	2,441	$2,767,365	$ 421,381	$322.69	$172.63
N.C.	8,716	2,875	1,715,994	340,856	196.83	118.59
S.C.	4,363	2,760	1,454,098	305,084	333.28	110.54
Ga.	9,053	4,052	2,884,580	483,622	318.63	119.35
Southern Seaboard	30,708	12,128	8,822,037	1,550,943	287.29	127.88

SOURCE: Harlan, *Separate and Unequal*, p. 257.

PER CAPITA EDUCATION EXPENDITURES FOR WHITE AND NEGRO IN SOUTHERN COUNTIES, 1916

County groups' % blacks in population	White teachers' salaries	Black teachers' salaries	Per capita white	Per capita black
Counties under 10%	$ 7,755,817	$ 325,579	$ 7.96	$7.23
Counties 10 to 25%	9,633,674	1,196,788	9.55	5.55
Counties 25 to 50%	12,572,666	2,265,945	11.11	3.19
Counties 50 to 75%	4,574,366	1,167,796	12.53	1.77
Counties 75% and over	888,759	359,800	22.22	1.78

SOURCE: Harlan, *Separate and Unequal*, p. 260.

Yet, as W. E. B. Du Bois and others contended, much of what was called industrial education was training in crafts that were becoming obsolete. Du Bois pleaded, without much success, for a broad education for more able blacks (his "talented tenth") who would provide leadership for the race. Not many whites had an interest in developing such leaders.

Interest in better education reached beyond secondary education. Well it might, given the unhappy state of colleges and universities in the South in 1900.

Few of them could meet the basic standards of the day for colleges—a four-year course in the liberal arts and sciences, a full-time faculty of at least six members, and a requirement that entering students have completed four years of high school. Most so-called colleges were no more than high schools. Funds for higher education were so limited that the annual income of Harvard University in 1901 exceeded the "total available income for the sixty-six colleges and universities of Virginia, North Carolina, South Carolina, Georgia, Alabama, Mississippi, and Arkansas." Several state universities received no state funds at all. Louisiana State University could receive no more than $10,000 from the state. The state constitution stipulated that sum, and it did not change until 1904, when the limit was raised to $15,000. Support for private education also lagged. In 1900 eighteen colleges and universities in the United States had endowments of $1.5 million or more. None was in the South. Only Tulane and Vanderbilt were among the thirty with endowments of at least $1 million. New York State had twice as much money for higher education as the entire South had.

The founding of the Southern Association of Colleges and Secondary Schools in 1895 signaled the determination of some southerners to improve this situation. Led by Chancellor James H. Kirkland of Vanderbilt University, the association set out to establish higher standards for scholarship, to codify differences between colleges and secondary schools, and to establish entrance requirements. Endowments increased to $12 million—a combination of gifts from the GEB and individuals. Some battles for academic freedom also were won. The efforts of sectarians to control higher education were blunted in some instances, and the effect of their attacks on institutions lessened. Higher education in the South, like that elsewhere in the United States, was becoming more secular or, at least, less explicitly religious. Vanderbilt established its independence from the Methodist College of Bishops. Trinity College (later Duke University) refused to dismiss Professor John Spencer Bassett after he called Booker T. Washington "the greatest man, save General Lee, born in the South in a hundred years" and not very subtly criticized white leaders who were "stirring up the fires of racial antipathy," a course he feared might lead "the country to an end which I dare not name." Bassett made his comments in the *South Atlantic Quarterly,* which he helped found in 1902. The quarterly, along with the *Sewanee Review* (founded in 1892), gave the South its first scholarly journals of real quality and continuing impact. Professor Andrew Shedd of Emory did not fare so well as Bassett. After he took mild exception to the racial orthodoxy of the South, Emory "accepted" his "resignation." Several years later, the college reinstated him.

Gains came slowly in academia. Eighteen years after its founding, the Southern Association counted only twenty-eight colleges and universities among its members, and only seven of them required four years of study for a baccalaureate degree. Despite improvements, serious deficiencies in financial support, facilities, library holdings, faculty, and student bodies remained. Even casual inspection revealed an abundance of institutions that were universities and colleges in name only. While some politicians led or at least encouraged the education crusade, others blundered. The worst incident occurred in Oklahoma. There the governor summarily and without explanation dismissed a fifth of the faculty of the University of Oklahoma in 1908. The university's president also was dispatched, along with his Harvard doctorate, to be replaced by a man with no academic degree at all.

HEALTH REFORMS

Matters of the body as well as the mind were high on the progressives' agenda. Indifference to water quality, garbage disposal, and sewerage services helped explain why tuberculosis, yellow fever, malaria, diphtheria, smallpox, and typhoid topped the lists of causes of chronic illnesses and death. The quality of medical services and health care, low incomes, undrained lowlands, and a hot, humid climate made matters worse. Average longevity—accurate figures are not available—was probably no more than fifty years.

This picture was altered significantly in the next twenty or so years, in large part because of the discovery that many of these diseases had bacterial origins. State and local boards of public health were reorganized or established; they became enforcers of quarantines, dispensers of vaccines and antitoxins, and providers of laboratory services and information. Improved water, sewerage, and garbage services made urban living safer. These things had a measurable effect: by 1920, longevity averaged slightly more than fifty-five years. Much remained to be done, of course, before the chronic diseases were reduced to minimal threats to life and health. At the same time, extensive draining of lowlands, such as those in the lower Mississippi basin, and spraying for mosquitoes reduced the impact of malaria and yellow fever. Outbreaks of both during the great Mississippi flood of 1927 underscored the tenuousness of the victory over these two. Still, nothing like the 20,000 deaths from yellow fever that occurred in 1878 in the Mississippi basin happened again. Sustained economic growth in the South after 1940 resulted in raised incomes and better health. Thereafter, the threats of bacteria-based diseases in the South were reduced to a minimum.

Medicine in the South followed other national patterns. Encouraged by the American Medical Association, which had reorganized itself along more professional lines in 1885, local medical societies focused on efforts to improve the training of medical personnel and the care patients received. These efforts resulted in the closing of some medical schools and improvements in others and the licensing of medical personnel. Licensing required a determination of what a physician was, what training was satisfactory, and what codes of ethical and professional behavior physicians should establish. This process of identification, development of professional codes, and certification or accreditation also took place among other professionals, such as lawyers, teachers, and engineers. While improvement of services provided much of the stimulus for this process, so did self-interest. Professionals thus got the power to limit access to their services—to reduce competition. Women, save for teachers, found the gates to the professions narrow indeed, and male professionals had markedly better earnings than women. Blacks, of course, also had limited prospects in the professions. Physicians also found other ways to protect their self-interest. For instance, the American Medical Association and other physicians' organizations in Florida opposed cooperative medical insurance programs. Physicians preferred the fee-for-service system, which became a critical, formative factor in American medicine in the twentieth century.

Issues of public health could and did cast an embarrassing light on the South. Predictably, some southerners reacted defensively to the news that the South was a hotbed of hookworm and pellagra. They saw the nefarious hand of medical carpetbaggers, and their suspicion was heightened by the association of the Rockefellers with a campaign to eradicate hookworm. In 1902 Dr. Charles Wardell Stiles, a New York–born, German-trained zoologist, announced, according to the *New York Sun,* that he might have found the "germ of laziness." The "discoverer of the hookworm disease" had found a scientific explanation for an infection that afflicted perhaps 40 percent of southerners, most of them white. At first southerners greeted Stiles's work with laughter. True enough, a lot of poor whites and blacks were known for their laziness, but how could a worm be a cause of that?

Hookworm, an intestinal parasite, can cause its host to suffer anemia, to be pale and suffer indigestion, cause developmental problems in children, create a general sense of weakness or fatigue, and produce melancholia. Combined with the nutritionally poor diet that most low-income southerners had in 1900 (and for some years thereafter), hookworm could have a very damaging, even fatal impact on its host. Hidden in the intestines and not striking with the noticeable swiftness of some other diseases, hookworm long persisted as an undetected scourge.

Beginning with a million-dollar gift from John D. Rockefeller, Sr., the Rockefeller Commission for the Eradication of Hookworm Disease spread its efforts out over much of the South. The efforts involved a combination of science and public education, administrative problems and innovations, evangelical fervor and public relations. The not always tactful Stiles was scorned as the Yankee "doctor of something else," not medicine. Bishop Warren A. Candler of Georgia, brother to pharmacist-turned-entrepreneur Asa G. Candler, founder of Coca-Cola, believed Rockefeller wanted to use the commission as a means to become a dominant force in southern education. Josephus Daniels, editor of the *Raleigh News and Observer,* a power among North Carolina Democrats and future secretary of the navy, wrote:

> Many of us in the South are getting tired of being exploited by advertisements that exaggerate conditions. . . . As to hookworm, this paper has accepted the statement of the widespread prevalence of that disease with many grains of allowance. Let us not canonize Standard Oil Rockefeller by putting laurels on his head because he seeks to buy the appreciation of the people whom he has been robbing for a quarter of a century.

Many southerners apparently felt otherwise about the commission. Walter Hines Page had helped connect Stiles with the people in charge of Rockefeller's philanthropies. Eradication of the disease involved delicate matters, most particularly the microscopic examination of samples of human feces and a campaign to persuade people without modern toilet facilities that they must construct, maintain, and use sanitary privies.

During the commission's five-year life, more than a million people were examined and some 440,000 people were treated. Another 254,000 received treatment elsewhere—no doubt a direct result of the work of the commission. The commission found infestation rates as high as 50 percent in North Carolina, 60 percent in

BLACK MIDWIFE, ABOUT 1935 (Courtesy Georgia Department of Archives and History)

Georgia, and 67 percent in South Carolina. So prevalent was the disease among cotton mill hands and their families that it was often referred to as "cotton mill anemia."

The commission did not eradicate hookworm in the South but it came close to doing so. Certainly it improved the health of many southerners. It significantly reduced the incidence of hookworm and suggested a nonproscriptive explanation for the gaunt appearance and widely reported "laziness" of a large number of southerners who deserved better and who knew that the way they felt was not "all in their heads." Moreover, the Sanitary Commission aided in the evolution of the public health movement in America. Its most important legacy in the South may have been the encouragement it gave to the development of state and local public health agencies. Finally, the commission laid the base for the Rockefeller Foundation and may have facilitated the campaign of Dr. Joseph Goldberger against pellagra, a disease that in the United States was found only in the South.

Goldberger, a Jewish immigrant from Hungary, had been reared in New York, where he received his medical training. As an employee of the U.S. Public Health Service he began his landmark research on pellagra in 1914, about the time some southerners became intensely concerned about the disease. That concern had mounted in tandem with the number of reported cases of pellagra, a relatively unknown condition before 1900. Between 1907 and 1911, eight states in the South reported 15,870 cases, with a death rate of nearly 40 percent. And things seemed to be getting worse.

Victims (pellagrins) developed a distinctive butterfly-shaped facial rash that caused a burning sensation, digestive disorders, dizziness, and depression. Some cases were mild; others were severe, often fatal. Pellagrins were often stigmatized and sometimes were isolated, like lepers. The stigma also marked the South, which became known as "the land of hookworm and pellagra."

Dr. Goldberger soon came to suspect that pellagra was the result of poor diet, that it was an affliction of the poor. His research led him to connect the disease with the diet of cornmeal, fatback (cheap cuts of pork), and molasses that so many poor whites and blacks in the South regularly consumed. Several obstacles hindered his work. Nutrition was a relatively new area of medical research. Other physicians clung to their belief that the disease was caused by bacteria. When Goldberger tried to alert the public and leaders in the South about the disease and its causes, many people regarded his efforts as one more attempt to stigmatize their region. Goldberger's reports about pellagra were dismissed as "malicious propaganda." Businesspeople worried about the effects of the reports on business interests, Florida that tourism would be adversely affected. Politicians talked about being made objects of scorn and charity. A number of state boards of health in the South denied that pellagra was a growing menace despite figures that indicated otherwise. Other public health officers in the region, however, concurred with Goldberger. Whatever its cause, pellagra was an urgent problem. Deaths from pellagra reached all-time highs in the South in the late 1920s, when some 200,000 cases were diagnosed.

The work on pellagra had struck the deep vein of southern defensiveness. That vein was the product of historical experience mixed with illusions and fears. Despite the anger that Goldberger's research elicited, his work had laid the base for the elimination of pellagra as a major threat to the health of southerners. That victory came, however, a quarter century after Dr. Goldberger began his research and more than a decade after his death in 1929. Scientists found a direct relationship between the disease and deficiencies in the consumption of nicotinic acid (vitamin B-12), deficiencies that could readily be corrected by the consumption of small amounts of eggs, meat, and green vegetables. In time the image and reality of the South as the "land of hookworm and pellagra" ended.

CHILD LABOR REFORM

Trouble and embarrassment struck the South from another quarter, this time from within the region, at least initially. Interest in child labor reform in the South began before 1900. In 1901, however, it got a major boost. That year Edgar Gardner Murphy led a group that founded the Alabama Child Labor Committee. The committee's statewide activities sparked a nationwide effort to restrict the amount of work children of fifteen or under could do in manufacturing and some other areas of employment. Murphy acted after he became aware that child laborers in Alabama cotton mills worked as many as seventy-two hours a week—six twelve-hour days with Sundays off—in dusty, noisy, often hot mills for 30 cents a day.

Murphy soon realized that child labor was a national as well as a regional issue. Child textile workers were common throughout the South. Of the more than 83,000 mill workers in 1900 in the principal southern textile states (Alabama, Georgia, and the Carolinas), nearly 30 percent (about 25,000) were ten to fifteen years of age. Many were six to nine years old. Children were commonly employed in all parts of the country. New England mills employed almost 11,000 workers under sixteen (6.7 percent of their workforce), and mills in the middle

Atlantic states used more than 4,300 (12.4 percent of their workforce). Glass-making in West Virginia and coal mining in Pennsylvania and southern Appalachia, two industries that caught the attention of the National Child Labor Committee (NCLC) because of their especially harsh and dangerous working conditions, employed substantial numbers of children in several states. In 1900 and 1910, more than 1.5 million children between the ages of ten and fifteen were gainfully employed in industry in the United States, though their proportion of all the gainfully employed had declined and would continue to do so. Most of the attention and concern about child labor centered on the textile industry in the South, in part because of the size of the industry and the numbers of minors it employed. Southern textile manufacturers and their allies saw more sinister motives for the spotlight in which they found themselves, and they were not entirely wrong.

The NCLC and several state child labor committees mounted strong campaigns to reduce or eliminate child labor from textiles and other industries. The NCLC had strong southern roots. Murphy initiated its founding and attracted some of the most prominent "social justice" progressives of the day to the committee. Alexander McKelway, a Presbyterian minister from North Carolina, directed NCLC activities in the South. Child labor reform ultimately involved major efforts at fact-finding and publicity. Lewis W. Hine left a valuable photographic record of child labor that helped establish his reputation as one of the giants of American photography. The federal government also contributed thorough studies of the employment and work lives of children and women.

By 1920 these activities brought concrete results. Each of the major textile states in the South had passed legislation to restrict child labor. North Carolina, for example, limited minors and women to sixty hours a week, no more than eleven hours in any day. All the states had compulsory school attendance laws, which varied in scope. Congress also had passed the Keating-Owen Act to restrict child labor, but the Supreme Court had declared it unconstitutional. Still, the NCLC could be pleased: child labor in southern textile mills had declined markedly. In 1919 the census reported that the proportions of mill workers under sixteen ranged from under 2 percent in Alabama to around 6 percent in the Carolinas.

The NCLC and its allies had overcome considerable opposition to get child labor laws passed. Restrictions on child labor involved complex issues and strong feelings. Child labor reform appeared to be a simple case of a struggle to protect the innocent and powerless from the greedy and powerful. Much more was involved, however, and it was not so morally unambiguous.

Child labor reform raised questions about the rights and powers of employers, of parents, and of children, and questions about where government ought to act or intrude. Should the state intervene on behalf of minors? If so, when and how? Child labor reform presented serious questions about law and its enforcement. If a parent swore that his or her child was of legal age or that the family was destitute and needed the labor of all in the family who could work, should public officials question or ignore such statements? The fact that many workers did not have birth certificates complicated matters. So did the obvious need of many families to increase their incomes if they were to survive.

Child labor reform aroused intense sectional feelings and defensiveness. Cotton manufacturers in the South claimed they needed the advantage of low wages if they were to compete against the more established mills of New England and the Middle Atlantic states. They argued that the survival of the industry in the South was critically important because it was a large source of the jobs their region desperately needed. They saw the devious, self-serving hand of northern textile manufacturers and organized labor behind the effort to limit child labor. In fact, the American Federation of Labor did oppose child labor as a threat to adult workers and to unions. The AFL was the original source of Murphy's information on child labor in Alabama and continued to supply data to him. He persuaded the AFL to remain in the background because he feared charges of outside interference.

In addition to triggering sectional feelings and defensiveness, which were particularly strong in this case because New England was once again perceived to be the main villain, child labor reform called into question the widely boasted achievements of the New South. Moreover, the movement besmudged the most advertised icon of the New South, the textile industry. Southern textile manufacturers and their supporters predictably, and not implausibly, claimed they were the soldiers in a second Civil War. They also employed less emotional and more specific arguments. They claimed, for instance, that the reformers exaggerated the drudgery of minors' work in their industry. Moreover, they correctly asserted that many parents wanted their children to work in the industry because they needed the money, and they noted that traditionally children had worked (and still did work) in agriculture and in family businesses.

The child labor issue thus revealed some of the unpleasant realities of the South's economy in the early twentieth century. Mill owners did exploit workers. They enjoyed high returns on their investment and should have been able to pay better wages. Still, even at the wages they did pay, the mills represented better opportunities than the farms the mill hands had left, where children also worked. For some years families survived and made modest economic and social gains by relying on the family wage system, or the pooling of family members' earnings in the mills. School was not a realistic alternative for many children, and probably was not a very desirable one. Education promised little to mill workers and their families in 1900. The education available to them was often woefully inadequate. And even if it had not been, they might very well have discounted it as not worth the costs. Given the jobs open to their children at that time, some mill families may have sensed that the costs of schooling were not worth bearing. Those costs sometimes included formal segregation in a separate school for "mill children" or informal segregation within a school. Over time mill workers did come to favor education for their children, but only after they were able to forgo the wages of young children and after they could see real economic and social benefits of education for their offspring. Such benefits became more obvious as the economy of the region continued to develop.

Mill workers had good reason to react coolly to child labor reformers. Child labor reform may have been essentially humanitarian, but it constituted a critical intrusion by outsiders in the lives of workers. Murphy defended such an intrusion on the grounds that the future of the children justified such action, for the sake of both the children and society in general. Murphy feared that the industry made mill hands "a fixed and semi-dependent class,—'once an operative, always an operative.' "

Child labor reformers carried a set of cultural assumptions to their crusade, and fears. A recent investigation concluded that child labor reform, at least in South Carolina, was rooted in cultural and political conflict. By 1900, as urbanization spread in South Carolina, an urban middle class emerged, composed primarily of business and professional families. These "town people" believed that "mill people" constituted a grave threat to their concept of a modern South Carolina, and, equally important, to white unity. The town people believed that mill people were isolated from modernization by their segregation in cotton mills and company-owned mill villages. Since approximately one-sixth of all whites in the state lived in those villages in 1905, the "mill problem"—a term and a notion conjured by the town people—was believed to be serious. What especially aroused the town people was the strong support mill hands gave to Cole Blease, a raucous demagogue who opposed modernization.

Alarmed at the growing division between the mill workers and the town people, the reformers (or progressives) wanted to use the powers of government to attack what they believed was their basic cause: the cultural isolation of the mill villager from the town. The reformers realized that industrialization was creating a factory class that lived and worked in segregation by occupation. The supposedly anachronistic culture that workers brought with them from the country, reformers believed, reinforced that segregation. Disinclined to blame mill owners for creating the mill problem, the reformers courted the owners, praised them for the jobs they created and whatever other benefits they provided, and generally ignored the continuing opposition by most owners to the reformers' programs. Most of the reformers' criticism "was directed, instead, at the operatives, above all at the mill family; the attitudes and habits of mill parents, perpetuated through their children, were threats to the social order, to be combated by using state power to obtain at least partial control over the upbringing of the mill child."

Southern legislatures also gave attention to other areas of labor reform. By 1920 most southern states had created at least rudimentary workers' compensation plans. Several had laws calling for mine and factory inspections and for limits on the number of hours women could work in manufacturing jobs. Most also prohibited night work for women and minors.

It is not clear how much effect these various labor laws had on labor practices. The laws restricting child labor and requiring school attendance had many loopholes and were not systematically enforced. Compulsory school-attendance laws, where they were enforced, probably had greater impact than child labor laws. Economic and technological changes had even more impact than the laws. Mill owners found that their increasing reliance on adult male workers, partly as a result of technological changes, made child labor less and less advantageous. Moreover, minors were simply not as able and reliable as more mature workers. Thus mill owners became less convinced that child labor was an important asset in their battles with northern textile companies and with their competitors in the South. Mill owners came to agree that more educated workers would benefit the industry and the South. At the same time, the reliance of the southern textile industry on the family labor system shifted. Around 1900, as dependence on child labor decreased sharply, a large number of women who previously had remained at home to keep house and tend to nearby vegetable gardens began to work in the mills. In a sense, they replaced their children, who now went to school. In doing so, these women took on a dual burden: they continued to run their homes, and they worked at physically exhausting jobs outside the home. They, too, became objects of the reformers' concern before World War I.

SOUTHERN LADIES

The image of southern women and the realities of their lives often differed, sometimes sharply, and not just among mill workers. This divergence existed before 1860 and became even greater afterward. The Civil War forced white women in the South to take on even greater responsibilities than they had assumed before the war. After the war, the deaths and severe disabilities of so many men, economic losses and disruptions, the ending of slavery, and then the evolution of a more industrial and urban South presented new burdens and new opportunities to women, white and black.

Immediately after the war, black men opposed fieldwork for black women. Apparently they felt that such work was not suitable for ladies. This was an opportunity for black men to assert their new freedom and control over their own lives and those of their wives and children, to act upon their notions about proper sex and family roles. Available evidence shows a sharp decline in the number of black women who worked in the fields. Whether or not that decline continued for a long time is not certain, but it is doubtful. The need to survive and the urge to get ahead very probably required black women in farm families to return to the fields eventually. White women among the thousands of poor families worked the land, too.

Economic realities prevailed over social assumptions. Poverty forced women out-of-doors or into new jobs in factories and cities and towns. Textiles provided the largest number of industrial jobs for white women. As late as 1890, one in two cotton mill operatives in the South (and New England and the Middle Atlantic States as well) were women. During the next three decades, the proportion of female mill hands declined, more in the South than in New England (to 38.2 and 42.9 percent, respectively, in 1920), but the number of women working in southern cotton mills grew to almost 78,000. Black women were much more likely to be gainfully employed than white women, native- or foreign-born, and black women found most of their employment in domestic service, an area few white women in the South entered. More than seven in ten black women who had nonagricultural employment were maids, cooks, or laundresses.

The Civil War and its aftermath created new opportunities for middle-class white women. Economic change subsequently reinforced these opportunities. Women became operators of farms and plantations and found greater outlets in writing and journalism. Like their male counterparts, most women writers found that they could attract more readers with sentimental stories and historical romances than with more realistic writing. Several women enjoyed success in newspaper work. Eliza Poitevent Nicholson, who became the editor of the *New Orleans Picayune*, was the most notable of these journalists. More well known was Elizabeth Meriwether Gilmer, who launched the first women's advice column in America in the *Picayune*.

More and more white women found employment as office workers, clerks in stores, and teachers. Teaching began its shift from male dominance to female dominance (numerically, at least) after Reconstruction. Later, during the education crusade of the early twentieth century, this trend accelerated. Women found some openings in other professions, but not very many. Some became proprietors of their businesses, most of which catered to women.

Black women had comparable experiences, though they faced even greater barriers than white women did. Maggie Walker succeeded as a banker in Richmond who served a black clientele. The most famous black woman entrepreneur was Madam C. J. Walker. Born on a Louisiana cotton plantation, an orphan at seven, a mother and widow at twenty, she built a national enterprise that made and sold hair products for African American women. The self-made millionaire became a philanthropist who supported black colleges and other causes.

Middle- and upper-class women found their greatest outlets in the various reform and mission groups that became involved in a wide range of activities—temperance, child labor reform, day nurseries, foreign and domestic missions, penal reform, education reform, health care and public health, industrial relations, race relations, women's suffrage. Many of these groups had counterparts among black women. As early as the 1870s, women in the South found new outlets for self-expression and vehicles for their concerns in the women's missionary societies of their churches, especially among the Baptists and Methodists. The Women's Home Mission Society of the Methodist Church, South, especially did not avoid controversial issues. Deeply concerned about family life, the society opposed child labor. Among other activities and concerns, the society also attempted to reduce racial tensions and eventually became involved in efforts to end lynching.

The Woman's Christian Temperance Union (WCTU) blossomed in the 1880s. It crossed denominational and sectional lines, had a substantial membership, and used its influence and lobbying powers for temperance and other issues. The abuse of alcohol was not a laughing matter, given its negative impact on individuals and families. Activists in the WCTU went beyond temperance to work for penal reform, maternal education, prenatal care, and shorter working hours. By the 1890s, women in the South had become involved in the club movement. Before 1910 every southern state had a state federation of women's clubs, and by that year all had joined the General Federation of Women's Clubs. The clubs had by then given themselves over to a wide range of reform activities. "One social concern led to another, and the social concerns inevitably led to politics." Few women got involved in the ways Kate Barnard did, but many became expert at lobbying legislatures and other political bodies. As Patty Blackburn Semple noted, the woman's club of Louisville treated politics as taboo, "but gradually we found that our efforts in behalf of civic improvements and the correcting of outrageous abuses were handicapped at every turn by politics."

The work of women in missionary societies, the WCTU, and women's clubs laid the necessary foundation for the politicization of women and their struggle to gain the vote. These experiences provided a form of higher education for women at a time when their opportunities for college or university training were severely limited. These activities provided crucially important opportunities for women to

NEW
        SOUTHERN
                    CITIZEN

OFFICIAL ORGAN OF
SOUTHERN STATES WOMAN'S SUFFRAGE CONFERENCE

Vol. 1. No. 1.   OCTOBER 1914

Votes for Women a Success
The Map Proves It

1913
Alaska

WHITE STATES: Full Suffrage SHADED STATES: Taxation, Bond or School Suffrage
DOTTED STATE: Presidential, Partial County and State, Municipal Suffrage
BLACK STATES: No Suffrage

Make the Southern States White

PRICE 5 Cents   NEW ORLEANS, LA.   50 Cents PER YEAR

THE FIRST ISSUE OF *NEW SOUTHERN CITIZEN* PROMOTING
WOMEN'S SUFFRAGE WITH RACIST APPEALS (Special Collections and
Archives, University of Kentucky Library)

learn to express their opinions and to organize and bring pressure. Women could
also strengthen their self-confidence and offset the psychological impact of the
ideal of the submissive Southern Lady. Still, the heritage of the submissive
woman persisted during the battle to secure the vote.

Woman suffragists and their male allies encountered strong opposition and
stirred deep emotions. Politicians worried about diminished power. Businessmen
saw women as too disposed to support measures they opposed. Liquor interests
saw a life-threatening link between women as voters and temperance. Some ministers criticized women's suffrage as against Scripture. Others saw socialism, foreign influences, and threats to domestic peace and marital harmony. Opponents
of women's suffrage correctly understood that women suffragists in the South,
and their male supporters, rejected the Southern Lady as a model, certainly that
part of the model that stressed submissiveness and the home as the only proper
place for women. Caroline Merrick, a bride at fifteen and later a Louisiana suf-

fragist, wrote in her memoirs: "I early ascertained that girls had a sphere wherein they were expected to remain and that the despotic hand of some man was continually lifted to keep them revolving in a certain prescribed and very restricted orbit." Eleanor Foster Comegys of Shreveport declared that she wanted "men to stop calling me a queen and treating me like an imbecile." She told her audience that she had "a head as well as a heart, common sense as well as intuition."

Suffragists believed the ballot symbolized equality of women with men and a necessary means for achieving many of the reforms they sought. For instance, they saw a connection between the right of women to vote and efforts to dismantle the double standard in sexual relations. They believed that the vote would help in battles against prostitution and in efforts to raise the age of consent, which remained very low in spite of numerous attempts to raise it. The Mississippi legislature may have been the most resistant: it refused to raise that state's age of consent (when a female may legally consent to sexual intercourse) above twelve.

Opponents of women's suffrage feared that it threatened "southern chivalry" and "southern civilization." They said that women should remain protected from the contamination of politics. They denounced suffragists as traitors to their region and the Lost Cause. Mildred Rutherford, a leader in the United Daughters of the Confederacy and in the National Association Opposed to Woman Suffrage, claimed that, "Woman's suffrage comes from the North and West and from women who do not believe in state's rights and who wish to see negro women using the ballot." Indifference compounded the suffragists' task. For whatever reasons, the majority of women in the South ignored the struggle over women's suffrage.

Just as important was Negrophobia. Opponents claimed that votes for women meant votes for black women. Supporters of women's suffrage employed Negrophobia in their own way: they pointed out that Jim Crow prevented black votes, male or female, from becoming a significant force in southern politics; thus, they argued, granting women the vote would have the happy effect of doubling the white electorate without greatly increasing the black vote. Some suffragists in the South, however, opposed amending the Constitution to grant women the vote. They preferred to have suffrage granted by each state, even if that procedure required many more years. Fearful of federal intervention, southerners, a northern suffragist remarked, "dreaded anything that called attention to the right of suffrage." Thus Laura Clay of Kentucky and Kate Gordon of Louisiana, two prominent suffragists, waged last-gasp battles against the ratification of the Nineteenth Amendment.

Most of the South resisted ratification, though the suffragists got a big boost from the surge of patriotic feelings during World War I and from the endorsement of the Nineteenth Amendment by President Woodrow Wilson, a southern-born Democrat. Wilson's endorsement may have influenced some southern Democrats in Congress, by far the strongest group of opponents to women's suffrage in Congress. Only five southern state legislatures ratified the amendment. Texas broke southern ranks first, becoming the ninth state in the Union to approve the amendment. Arkansas, Kentucky, and Oklahoma followed later. Last came Tennessee. Its approval on August 18, 1920, gave the amendment the required three-fourths vote for adoption. Tennessee did not achieve this distinction gracefully. Liquor lobbyists plied the legislature so freely that, according to reports, at various times during the fight over ratification none of the members of the lower chamber was sober. Opponents in the state senate tried to prevent a quorum by fleeing to Alabama. On the eve

of the 1920 elections, the object of this fright—the Southern Lady—continued her unfinished transition from pedestal to politics.

The South, even Southern Ladies, became a part of the progressive era before
1912. Activist government displaced passive government. Government agencies
proliferated. State and local budgets swelled, as did taxes. Regulations of business
increased—regulation of banking, insurance companies, railroads, and others.
Limitations on the labor of children and women were imposed, workers' compensation systems were created, and compulsory school-attendance laws were
passed. Professionals increased their role in the South, especially by making
human services more professional—medicine, dentistry, public health, law, social
work, and education. Professionals succeeded in imposing many of their standards on themselves and others. They formed national and regional organizations, such as the NCLC and the Southern Sociological Congress, in order to share
ideas and data and to lobby for their goals.

Women found a larger place for themselves in public life and in employment
than they had had before. Blacks enjoyed somewhat greater economic opportunities, but continued to find much of their private and public lives circumscribed by
the suffocating Jim Crow. The Democratic party remained dominant, but political
parties lost some of their impact to the growing power of other well-organized
groups. Urban elites held sway in the urban South.

PROHIBITION: THE NOBLE EXPERIMENT

Surging forward, then falling back, then surging again, prohibition eventually
conquered the South and won its endorsement for the Eighteenth Amendment.
Prohibition triumphed because, as one historian wrote, it "tied together most of
the reform strands of the progressive era and offered a simple, moral solution to
disturbing social ills." It afforded an opportunity to attack moral and political corruption. "It reaffirmed the evangelical ideals of southern Protestantism. It was
both a coercive reform with strong racial and class overtones and an expression of
social concern for those victimized by the South's new urbanization and industrialization." Enforcement of prohibition, however, proved to be far more difficult
than passing legislation to mandate it.

As a reform, prohibition failed so miserably that its adoption, against very
strong opposition, may, in hindsight, be puzzling. The liquor business—brewers,
vintners, distillers, and dealers—was one of the largest industries in the United
States in 1918 and a major source of government revenues. Others resisted prohibition as a dangerous expansion of governmental power, an unwelcome intrusion
into private life, and an attempt to destroy an age-old, pleasurable activity. Yet national prohibition received the required vote of two-thirds of both houses of Congress and the ratification votes of three-fourths of the state legislatures, thus becoming part of the Constitution.

Strong feelings associated with World War I gave the prohibition movement
its final needed thrust, but that thrust only added to what was obviously an enormous groundswell of support compounded of many elements. Most important
was the acute anxiety that the middle class felt about the growing power of big
business on the one hand and about the increasing unrest among industrial and

urban workers in the early twentieth century. The particulars behind this anxiety varied from place to place, from region to region. In an era when people had great anxieties about "trusts," the size of the liquor business made it vulnerable, and the business had an especially bad reputation for its close ties to saloons and to entrenched politicians, who resisted reformers' challenges to their lucrative domains. Several large brewers, including Anheuser-Busch, paid more than $290,000 in fines and costs for violating Texas election laws in 1910–1911.

Almost everywhere the saloon was castigated as corrupt and corrupting, extinguishable only by banning the production and sale of alcoholic beverages. Aside from most workers and some ethnic groups, few saw any of the saloon's virtues. Prohibitionists and supporters of temperance, if not of total abstinence, believed that saloons encouraged intemperance among the working class and that intemperance, in turn, encouraged unrest among workers.

Fears about recent immigrants fueled prohibition in the Northeast and the Middle West; in the South, the fears focused on blacks. The terrible Atlanta race riot of 1906 started when rumors about the rape of a white woman by a black man swept through white saloons. Texas prohibitionists also were hostile toward Mexicans, Chicanos, and German Americans, as were Florida prohibitionists toward Cubans, Italians, and Spaniards, most of whom then lived in Tampa. Battles between Texas prohibitionists (or "drys") and antiprohibitionists (or "wets") dominated politics, often dividing the Democrats into bitter factions. Several other southern states had similar factional feuds. Drys struggled with wets in Kentucky for years. They finally succeeded: prohibition came to the home of bourbon, where distilling was the leading manufacturing industry in the state.

Other motives energized prohibition: paternalism, the determination to create an orderly and efficient society, and genuine humanitarian concern that had deep religious roots. In a society where consumption of alcoholic beverages annually exceeded twenty gallons per capita, it is hardly surprising that many saw direct links between consumption of alcohol and grave personal and family problems, accidents at work and elsewhere, and crime and disease. Stimulated by the Social Gospel and often by revivalistic zeal, many embraced prohibition as the necessary means for achieving the Christian society they felt called upon to work for and believed was possible. Prohibition divided Christians, because Catholics were less likely to support the measure than were Protestants; Jews also resisted prohibition. Though prohibition involved using government to impose moral order, prohibitionists, like most progressives, had few qualms about using government to police personal behavior.

The prohibitionists promised too much. Prohibition did not open the gates to a "City on the Hill" or a "New Earth." The consumption of alcohol declined sharply for several years after the Eighteenth Amendment was implemented. Then the decline stopped and reversed. Laws against the making and selling of alcoholic beverages were violated flagrantly. Open saloons disappeared, only to be replaced by speakeasies. Bathtub gin and home brew became commonplace. Illegal trafficking in alcohol flourished, often enriching gangsters and other undesirables. Of the reforms of the progressives, whose legacy became a permanent part of the southern landscape, prohibition had the least impact. By the time Franklin Roosevelt, a New York progressive with important ties to the South, went to the White House, the nation was ready to repeal the Eighteenth Amendment and give up on its noble attempt to create a sober nation.

23

Restoration and Exile,

1912–1929

❖

World War I and the 1920s brought important changes to the South. But before war broke out, the South enjoyed a return to power in national politics such as it had not known since 1860. That return came in the wake of Woodrow Wilson's election to the presidency in 1912.

THE WILSON ADMINISTRATION

Three hundred thousand people looked on as Woodrow Wilson was sworn in as president of the United States on March 4, 1913. This crowd, the largest that had gathered for an inauguration up to that time, was an indication of the momentousness of Wilson's assumption of the presidency. Progressivism was at a high tide, the Democrats controlled both the White House and Congress for the first time since 1894, and Wilson was the first southern-born president since 1850.

It was purely coincidental that a former Confederate army officer, Chief Justice Edwin Douglass White, administered the oath to the new president, but the symbolism of the coincidence was not lost on the nation. The South, one observer wrote, "had come back to rule the Union." Carried away by the moment, another prematurely announced that "the return of the Democrats to power breaks down sectionalism."

The Wilson administration restored the South to a place in national politics that it had not enjoyed for more than half a century. From 1865 to 1912, no southerner or southern expatriate had been nominated for president or vice president by either major party. Few held cabinet or diplomatic posts. Only seven of thirty-one justices of the Supreme Court came from below the Mason-Dixon line. By contrast, southerners had occupied the White House for fifty of the seventy-two years from Washington to Lincoln, and they served for sixty of those years as chief justices of the nation's highest court. No wonder rebel yells and "Dixie" punctuated the inaugural festivities of 1913.

Wilson's road to the presidency ran through the South. Wilson thought of himself as rooted in the South, where he was born and reared. So were his most important initial supporters. Regional loyalties helped Wilson retain critically needed support during a difficult struggle to get his party's nomination. Then, aided by deep divisions among the Republicans during the 1912 presidential campaign, Wilson won a majority of electoral votes even though he won only 45 percent of the popular vote.

The Wilson presidency had a distinctly southern quality, as did the leadership of Congress, with which he worked closely. In general, Wilson's legislative proposals had strong support in the South. Some had their origins in the South. But the Wilson administration represented more than the triumph of Dixie. The Democrats' successes in elections and in their efforts to secure their legislative program in Washington were indicative of national developments.

The Democrats showed that their sentiments lay with progressivism. The forces of Populism, Bryanism, and progressivism had transformed them into something quite different from the Cleveland Democrats who had held sway in the late nineteenth century. This new generation of Democrats generally chose to follow the course of activist government. The Democrats passed the first significantly lower tariff since 1857, and the tariff legislation provided for a modest income tax, which opponents claimed was an attack on class and on the East by the South and West. The new banking system (the Federal Reserve System), which Congress created in 1913, answered some of the major complaints voiced by the South (and the West) in regard to the national banking acts. The old banking system, its critics said, was too centralized (in the Northeast), had too little government regulation, resulted in rigidities in the money supply, and failed to meet the credit needs of farmers. The Federal Reserve System, designed to answer these charges, was hailed by the South as a major victory. When the Democrats addressed the issue of monopoly, they chose what they believed was regulated competition (the Clayton Antitrust Act and the Federal Trade Commission Act).

Encouraged and sometimes led by southerners, Congress passed legislation to regulate the marketing and warehousing of cotton and created a federally sponsored farm land bank system, a system of extension education for farmers through county agents and land-grant colleges, and a program of federal aid for vocational education. The good roads movement, which enjoyed broad support in the South, reached a decisive milestone when the Federal Highways Act was passed.

The South also contributed to the dubious record of the Wilson administration on race relations. Wilson was not an extremist on race, but he permitted Jim Crow to flourish in official Washington. Numerous blacks lost positions in the civil service or were demoted. Racially segregated facilities became commonplace in public buildings. Such extremists as Ben Tillman of South Carolina and James K. Vardaman of Mississippi wanted even more than they got from the Wilson administration. But conscience, perhaps, and political expediency, certainly, stayed the hand of the president.

Democrats were aware that blacks, some of whom supported Democrats, voted in significant numbers in states like Illinois and New York as well as in the upper South and the border states. As the minority party, the Democrats needed every vote they could muster.

The president gave considerable ground to southern sentiments on race. He did not in other respects. With an eye to his reelection, Wilson endorsed labor legislation that received a cool or hostile reception from most southern leaders. In 1916 he lent his name to successful efforts to enact a federal child labor law (the Keating-Owen Act). Most of its opposition came from the southerners in Congress, especially those from the Southeast, where cotton mills were a major factor in the economy. A number of southern senators and congressmen did vote for the measure, however. Wilson also endorsed the Nineteenth Amendment, which gave women the right to vote—not a popular measure in the South, at least not among most men. Still, in the 1918 congressional election Republicans successfully attacked Wilson for allegedly being a captive of the South. They amassed a good deal of political capital with their claim that his wartime farm policy favored cotton more than other farm products, that sectional interests had won out over national interests during a national crisis. Such attacks helped the Republicans regain control of the Senate and the House of Representatives and set the stage for a Republican victory in the 1920 presidential election.

During their brief return to national political power, however, southerners in Congress figured prominently in the remarkable legislative record of the Wilson administration, most of which was enacted without the stimulus of an economic crisis or a war. As their support indicated, southern leaders (and their constituents) embraced activist government. "Progressivism, an amalgam of agrarian radicalism, business regulation, good government, and urban social justice reforms, became in the end a movement for positive government [which found] general acceptance." But this mixture of disparate elements could not survive the centrifugal forces loosed by World War I.

A DISRUPTED SOCIETY:
THE SOUTH DURING WORLD WAR I

In August 1914, World War I—or the Great War, as it was then called—enveloped Europe. The war soon made itself felt in the United States, first economically, then diplomatically, and finally militarily when Congress declared war on Germany in 1917. The war was a massive stimulant to the southern economy, and the resulting prosperity accelerated trends already set in motion before the conflict started. The town world continued to distance itself from the farm world. So many southerners joined the ongoing migration to towns and cities that the population patterns of the South of 1920 were markedly different from those of 1915. Many people, black and white, found life better at their destinations. These migrations also created and reflected social turmoil, which reverberated into the 1920s.

A powerful nationalism—100 percent Americanism—swept the nation. When the United States entered the war, local and state councils of defense directed the enormous wave of American nationalism that swept the South into voluntaristic efforts in support of the war effort. Unfortunately, and sometimes tragically, some of those energies spilled over into vigilantism, which was encouraged by the passage of espionage and sedition laws and by the policies and actions of public officials. For American radicals, the success of the Bolshevik revolution in Russia in 1917 made matters worse. Socialists and the less-numerous Communists became prime targets. Mounting antiradical sentiments among the public and repressive measures of government and private citizens combined with unprecedented farm prosperity to destroy the socialists, even in the Southwest, where they had had a strong following. The public also showed little tolerance for anyone they believed was lacking in patriotism, even the immensely popular Vardaman. The White Chief was hanged in effigy in Mississippi because of his opposition to the war; in 1918 he was soundly defeated in his attempt to be reelected to the U.S. Senate.

Vardaman's defeat removed one of the most outspoken, vitriolic Negro-phobes from the national scene. The war, however, had little impact on Negro-phobia in the South. Although the wartime surge of patriotism brought whites and blacks together in various efforts to support the war, Jim Crow remained intact. Racial animosities often worsened when the war stimulated social upheaval. As the ranks of the farm-to-town migrants swelled, competition for jobs, housing, and urban services grew. Blacks seemed to be rising out of their place.

The incidence of lynching, a bloody measure of the state of race relations, had been declining before the war, but that trend was reversed: the number of lynchings rose from sixty-seven in 1915 to eighty-three in 1919. No one, of course, counted the number of interracial confrontations between individuals or small groups. As returning black veterans discovered, not even the uniform of their country offered protection. Many whites were convinced that black servicemen had gotten "bad notions" from their experiences in the military and in Europe. Ten uniformed servicemen died at the hands of lynch mobs. And lynchings seemed to be getting even more grotesque: more black men were being burned alive.

Race riots erupted inside and outside the South. The first of a series of major racial conflicts broke out in East St. Louis, Illinois, and in Houston in 1917. The year 1919 was worse: Charleston, South Carolina; Longview, Texas; Washington, D.C.; Knoxville; Omaha; and Elaine, Arkansas. In all, twenty-five urban race riots occurred in a period of six months in 1919. Perhaps two hundred were killed; at least two-thirds of the victims were blacks. James Weldon Johnson, secretary of the National Association for the Advancement of Colored People (NAACP), called it the "red summer."

Two years later, Tulsa achieved the distinction of being the first American city to be attacked from the air. There a riot left thirty (many more, perhaps) dead and $1 million worth of property destroyed. Widespread looting and burning of black neighborhoods by whites caused most of the destruction. Some whites even used airplanes to strafe blacks and bomb them with dynamite. Tulsa blacks fought back, as blacks had done elsewhere during the race riots of the era. The poet Claude McKay spoke for blacks who risked their lives in defense of themselves and their dignity:

> If we must die, let it not be like hogs
> Hunted and penned in an inglorious spot,
> While round us bark the mad and hungry dogs,
> Making their mock at our accursed lot.

The fact that blacks had fought back, as the historian John Hope Franklin recalled of his boyhood, "had a great deal to do with eradicating the fear that a Negro boy growing up in Tulsa might have felt in the years following the riot."

Some southern blacks and whites reacted to these outbursts of racial violence by creating an interracial movement. Careful never to question or overtly threaten Jim Crow, the Commission on Interracial Cooperation worked to resolve grievances, to relieve tensions and prevent violence, and to change attitudes through education and interracial contacts. The NAACP, which grew rapidly in those years, used a somewhat different approach: it cautiously began to challenge Jim Crow in the courts and lobbied on behalf of Negroes.

World War I prompted other efforts at social reform. Social work programs experienced a major revitalization. The war also served as a catalyst for the prohibition movement. Amid these war-related activities, almost no one noticed "Colonel" William J. Simmons and his force of fourteen as they climbed to the top of Stone Mountain, outside Atlanta, in late 1915. There they gathered before an altar covered by an American flag, ignited a large cross, and resurrected the Ku Klux Klan—according to Simmons, "The World's Greatest Secret, Social, Patriotic, Fraternal Beneficiary Order." The Klan had only a small following until after the war ended. Colonel Simmons discovered that lighting a fiery cross on Stone Mountain was easier than attracting members and their dues. Energies that might have found expression through the Klan found more official outlets during World War I.

Though race relations seemed unchanged, southern blacks actually experienced profound changes in their lives during World War I. Some of those changes had begun before the war started. Sometime around 1910, the migrations of blacks from farms to cities in the South and North grew so large that it came to be called the Great Migration. It reached the proportions of a flood during World War I.

TULSA RACE RIOT, 1921 (Tulsa County Historical Society)

Blacks enjoyed unprecedented job opportunities. Faced with a smaller supply of labor, southern manufacturers, even textile manufacturers, employed increasing numbers of black workers. Northern industry also sought blacks as the war reduced the supply of unskilled European immigrants and coincidentally stimulated industrial expansion. Through labor recruiting and more often by word of mouth, newspapers, and magazines, blacks learned of opportunities in northern industries such as steel. Even at less than $2 a day for long, hard, and often dangerous work, jobs in steel mills looked better than work in cotton fields or occasional labor. While tighter labor markets provided a powerful pull on black (and white) migration, other factors provided strong pushes. First came the cotton crisis of 1914–1915, when World War I began; then came the boll weevil, which was eating its way eastward through cotton fields, and floods in the Deep South in 1915 and 1916. And there was the continuing hostility of southern whites.

Initially, whites welcomed the black exodus. But labor shortages soon caused some whites to reconsider and act to halt it. The fact that many of the migrants were skilled workers deepened these anxieties. Some communities, apparently convinced that southern blacks were not capable of making rational economic decisions and therefore that they were being enticed away by outside labor agents, tried to stop such recruiting activities. Montgomery prohibited labor recruiting altogether. Macon allowed recruiters to work if they had a license, which cost $25,000, and letters of commendation from local clergy, businessmen, and manufacturers. Other people were more direct: they prevented blacks from boarding northbound trains. Some white leaders did work to persuade their communities to be less hostile toward blacks.

But the exodus did not stop or even slow. So many people were leaving that railroads ran special trains. For the first time ever, the center of the black populace in America stopped moving southwestward and shifted northeastward. Perhaps 800,000 to 900,000 blacks departed; most went to urban industrial centers in the North and Midwest. The exodus got the attention of numerous observers. One investigator asked blacks detraining in Washington, D.C., why they had come north. He listed their explanations:

> Economic exploitation . . . insecurity of life . . . high mortgage rates, and the lack of credit for Negro farmers. "Jim Crow" . . . crop failures due to boll weevil and floods. Lack of employment. Poor school facilities . . . attraction of the North . . . letters from relatives and friends . . . labor demand of the North. Unfair treatment of sharecroppers and tenants . . . labor agents . . . travel . . . new locations.

As blacks left the South, they carried their culture and religion with them. One consequence was the appearance of jazz as a major form of musical expression in the nation as a whole in the late 1920s. Blacks, long a critical factor in southern politics, began to be a factor in northern politics as well. The significance of the latter development would be demonstrated in the 1930s.

GOOD TIMES: THE SOUTHERN ECONOMY AND WORLD WAR I

Like the social order, the economic order was shaken by World War I. Initially the war adversely affected the southern economy. The disruption in the sales of raw cotton, at a time when the cotton crop was the largest in history, plunged the South into a severe slump. Losses in 1914 totaled $500 million, about one-half the value of the crop. Major cotton exchanges closed and did not reopen for three months. Cotton prices fell below 10 cents a pound, generally considered to be the break-even price. Even at 5 cents a pound cotton found few buyers. Cotton went unpicked. Landowners released renters from contracts. Cut-offs of provisions left renters and croppers without food or supplies. The Red Cross, the U.S. Department of Agriculture, and other organizations gave food or money to the destitute and to local communities for relief purposes. For years thereafter, cotton farmers spoke about 1914 in somber tones as "that year."

Then, less than a year after cotton prices plummeted, they rose to 11 cents, then to nearly 20, then to nearly 36. From 1917 to 1919, the best years ever, cotton prices averaged 27 cents, well above increases in the cost of living. The latter year's crop sold for a record $2 billion. Negro tenants were reported to have "come to town with their pockets stuffed with paper money" to pay off debts and to buy. Landowners had to offer better-than-usual terms to prospective renters. "New houses, new barns, new roof paint, better roads, schoolhouses, churches, and better farm equipment" appeared in the countryside. Automobiles invaded the South. Prosperous landowners moved to new houses in town, complete with modern appliances and facilities, and commuted to their farm holdings in order to supervise renters and croppers.

SLOSS FURNACE, BIRMINGHAM, 1920s (Archives Department, Birmingham Public Library, Birmingham, Alabama)

The war-stimulated demand reached far beyond the cotton fields. Economic expansion stimulated such established industries as railroads, textiles, lumber, iron and steel, coal and oil, hydroelectric power, and tobacco manufacturing. The wartime boom spilled over into Appalachia, which hitherto had not been as affected by the forces of the New South as had other parts of the South. The economic surge that World War I had done so much to cause carried over into the 1920s in much of the South.

The military preparedness efforts of the federal government and then the nation's entry into the war altered the South and the lives of its inhabitants. Some southerners experienced the war very directly and personally. From farms, towns, and cities, from Virginia to Florida to Texas, 1 million men entered the armed forces. Many went far greater distances than they had ever gone before, even if they only went to a military training camp. Most of the boot camps were located in the South, where year-round training was more practical than in much of the rest of the country. (Cynics might, of course, think that weather was a lesser factor in the camps' location than the power of southern Democrats in Washington.) Some southerners went much farther—to Europe, to battle—and many did not return.

American blacks who fought in Europe fought with French units, because the American army refused to use blacks in combat. The army's attitude mirrored that of the white public. Larger proportions of blacks than whites were taken by the draft. Racial prejudice undoubtedly played a large part in these decisions. At the same time, local white citizens became quite uneasy when black trainees were located at nearby installations. Southern black soldiers received a wary, even violent welcome when they returned home.

A full accounting of the impact of the federal budget, which in current dollars grew 2,600 percent between 1916 and 1919, is probably not possible. Every southern state had at least one military installation or defense industry. Naval bases and shipyards ran along the coast southward from Hampton Roads, Virginia, to Charleston, around the Florida peninsula, and along the Gulf Coast to New Orleans and Texas. The powder and chemical industries expanded. The most important of these firms were Du Pont in eastern Virginia, the nucleus of what developed as Tennessee Eastman at Kingsport, Tennessee, and a dam and a nitrate plant at Muscle Shoals, Alabama. The last, which was not completed when the war ended, became the initial step in the massive Tennessee Valley Authority. By the late 1920s, Allied Chemical and other firms had followed Du Pont into eastern Virginia and helped make Hopewell the center of a burgeoning chemical industry. They lifted chemicals to second place in value added among industries in Virginia. Rayon, the first fiber to be conceived by artificial means (though from natural plant products), held a comparable position in Tennessee.

Chemicals were in the vanguard of an industrial development that grew rapidly during the war and continued growing afterward. Petroleum and petrochemicals, hydroelectric power, pulpwood and paper, furniture, tobacco manufacturing, and aluminum joined the ranks. So did iron and steel, though without the same vigor as the others. Real estate agents followed in their wake, finding most urban areas attractive, even intoxicating. Southern Appalachia and Florida especially drew investors. The boom in Appalachia antedated the war and had sufficient strength to last into the early 1920s. Florida, by contrast, experienced its greatest growth in the early and middle 1920s; so great was this growth that it became famous as the "Florida land boom." The demand for lumber and then for bituminous or soft coal seemed to turn Appalachia upside down during the generation that stretched from around 1900 to 1930. But demand for these products would not be sufficient to create sustained economic development in Appalachia and make it the promised land its boosters predicted. The Florida bubble burst in 1926, but the bonanza of the 1920s left some solid foundations for future development in the state. Finally, textiles, the flagship of industry in the South, thrived during the war, but not thereafter, a circumstance that had considerable significance for the industry, its workers, and the Southeast.

The war rescued the oil industry from excess capacity, which had devastated prices. Wartime demand caused an acute shortage and escalating prices. Overcapacity plagued the petroleum industry intermittently in the twentieth century, as it had earlier. A series of new oil fields, primarily in California, Oklahoma, and Texas, dramatically increased the amount of crude oil production in the country after 1900. Supply exceeded demand, though sales of petroleum products increased rapidly after 1900, largely as a result of the expanded use of fuel oil and gasoline for automobiles. The number of registered motor vehicles rose from about 79,000 in 1905 to 2.5 million by 1919. (The number reached 9.2 million by 1920, 26.7 million by 1930.) The demand for petroleum as an illuminant, however, declined sharply, displaced by electric lighting. By World War I, the United States produced almost 60 percent of the world's petroleum and exported nearly one-fourth of the oil it produced.

OIL BOOM, OKLAHOMA, 1920s (Archives and Manuscripts Division of the Oklahoma Historical Society)

New fields opened in Texas during the war, and in Louisiana, Oklahoma, and Arkansas after the war. The free-for-all atmosphere of new fields, wildcatters, instant towns, and even more instant fortunes (sometimes followed by instant bankruptcies) soon gave way to a more orderly world of substantial companies, then to the "majors"—the corporations that dominate the oil industry—and to oil refineries, networks of pipelines, and increasingly scientific and technical operations. In the 1920s, drilling for and piping natural gas, often to distant markets, became an important facet of the petroleum industry. So did petrochemicals.

Oil refineries and pipelines had greater permanence than did oil fields, especially new oil fields. Refinery workers were less transient than oil field workers, though many in both groups were highly skilled. Companies placed refineries near cities and major transportation facilities. Oil and gas fueled the rapid rise of Houston, Dallas, Fort Worth, Oklahoma City, and Tulsa as leading urban centers in the Southwest and lessened the dependence of each on cotton marketing as their principal source of income. Smaller towns that prospered with petroleum dotted the region: Ponca City and Bartlesville in Oklahoma; Wichita Falls, Amarillo, and Odessa in Texas; Lake Charles and Baton Rouge in Louisiana; and El Dorado and Smackover in Arkansas.

Electricity provided a growing portion of the energy used in the South. Using the power of dammed-up water (and readily accessible coal to generate steam power when it was needed), electric power companies grew rapidly along the rivers of the South. Generating capacity tripled in the South in the 1920s and by 1930 represented about 17 percent of the nation's capacity. Before the 1920s ended, large companies and outside investment characterized the electric power industry, and some companies had become household names—Alabama Power, Georgia Power, Gulf Power, Duke Power.

Southern forests continued to provide the raw materials for diverse industries. Lumber, turpentine, and rosins were well-established products. To them were added paper, pulpwood, furniture, and wood chemicals. High Point, North Carolina, became the center for furniture manufacturing in the South by 1922, and paper mills in the South produced half of the nation's paper by 1930. Rayon, made from cellulose, a wood by-product, introduced a new epoch in textiles. In North Carolina, Burlington Mills (now Burlington Industries) made a strong commitment to rayon and began its rise to the top of the world's textile industry.

Tobacco manufacturing expanded its strong base in North Carolina and Virginia. The war and changes in social habits that made cigarette smoking more acceptable provided enormous opportunities for an already substantial industry. Clever advertising and aggressive marketing were the weapons chosen by Reynolds Tobacco in 1913 to challenge the industry leader, the American Tobacco Company. Reynolds got the early lead in best-sellers with Camels. Liggett and Myers followed suit with Chesterfields. Then American, the largest of tobacco's Big Three, responded with Lucky Strikes. Cigarette consumption more than doubled during World War I. Thanks primarily to tobacco manufacturing, lumber and wood products, furniture making, and textiles, North Carolina became the most industrialized of the southern states by 1930. Georgia, also heavily industrialized, was the site of a growing beverage empire. As Americans doubled their consumption of carbonated drinks during the war, annual sales of Coca-Cola rose above $20 million; they exceeded $35 million before the end of the 1920s. Prohibition of alcoholic beverages may have helped stimulate these sales.

At the beginning of World War I, the Aluminum Company of America began large operations in Tennessee and North Carolina to manufacture aluminum and related products. The war gave some boost to the slow-growing iron and steel industry, centered in the Birmingham region. The faster growth continued after hostilities ceased. Southern steelmakers, most of whom were in Alabama, doubled their production of ingots by 1930, and the value added by steelworks and rolling mills had done likewise (from $15.6 million to $34.7 million). A parallel development was taking place in the coal industry. The demand for coal, one of the most plentiful minerals in the South, soared. Lesser-known ores and minerals were also being exploited, as phosphates had been for years. Many of those minerals came from southern Appalachia, which had only recently become a center of intense economic activity.

SOUTHERN APPALACHIA

Southern Appalachia runs north and east of northeastern Alabama, across northern Georgia and far northwestern South Carolina, through eastern Tennessee and western North Carolina, eastern Kentucky and western Virginia, and into southern West Virginia. (Though West Virginia is not generally considered a southern state, it has some southern characteristics, and some West Virginians, especially those in the lower part of the state, consider themselves to be southern.) Three mountain ranges compose southern Appalachia: the Blue Ridge, the Cumberland, and the Great Smoky. Not until 1870 did any railway line penetrate southern Appalachia. But before the century ended, the region had a rail network. The steel rails running to the rich natural resources of Appalachia carried a storm of change into the mountains.

Never static, southern Appalachia had been undergoing significant change before 1870. Despite its relative inaccessibility, it had felt the force of the Civil War, sometimes very directly. Then, after the war, this region of family farms, tiny communities, and small scattered towns began to feel the impact of a steady increase of population. Longer-established, better-off families took over more of the better plateau lands; others had to find land in more marginal areas. Sharp divisions based on wealth or the lack of it, however, did not exist yet. Mountaineers raised most of their own food, did some hunting and gathering, and traded by barter or with cash, sometimes for manufactured goods from outside the region. They worshiped, visited, and married within a setting bounded by familiar ridges and waters. Few were black, because slaves had been rare in the mountains. Almost all were Scots-Irish, Protestant, and overwhelmingly Baptist and Methodist.

Within a generation, a timber bonanza and then a coal bonanza shook the foundations of Appalachia. Coming by rail and then up along rivers, armies of lumberjacks cut into virgin forests. As the frenzy mounted, loggers cut over mountains. Companies, mostly from outside the region, bought up land in units of 10,000 acres. The holdings of the William M. Ritter Lumber Company, for instance, included nearly 200,000 acres in western North Carolina. There and in

SELLING OFF APPALACHIA (Courtesy of the Appalachian Photographic Archives, Alice Lloyd College)

eastern Tennessee, the Champion Company owned 420,000 acres, from which it got the raw material for wood pulp to make into paper. Champion built a complex that required a whole new town: the mill at Canton, North Carolina, had more than 7,000 people on its payroll before World War I and was the largest pulp and paper mill in the country by 1930.

It is probable that some 100,000 people worked in the southern Appalachian lumber industry during each of the boom years from 1890 to 1920. Lumber production in southern Appalachia peaked in 1909 at 8.5 million board feet (about 20 percent of the total production in the United States). Production declined thereafter despite greater reliance on heavy machinery in logging. By 1929, only 5.4 million board feet of lumber came from the region. As the number of timber workers fell by more than half, they had to look elsewhere for work. Some went to mining coal, bauxite, kaolin, and mica. Others turned to textiles, making up a small invasion force of mountaineers in the piedmont. Later, some textile companies reversed the process and set up plants in the mountains in order to take advantage of the low-wage labor force available there.

Coal began to be mined in southern Appalachia before 1890. Not until the late 1890s, however, did the industry show the rapid growth that was to characterize it until the mid-1920s. Bituminous coal from southern Appalachia had several advantages over its main competitor, the anthracite coal mined in the North. Most important, southern mountaineers worked for less than coal miners elsewhere in the United States, and the coal they mined was of better quality, more plentiful, and easier to extract. Costs to start mining were low, and small mines proliferated. Soon, however, profit margins narrowed, and large operators became dominant in the industry—and in the politics of the coal region.

A twentieth-century feudalism emerged. By-products of this development were legends and legendary figures, admixtures of fact and fiction and sordidness. John Calhoun Mayo taught school and moonlit as a land speculator. In less than a decade he acquired more than 500,000 acres of eastern Kentucky coal land. Mayo then combined forces with the Consolidated Coal Company, whose control extended over a million acres of southern Appalachia. Corporate giants entered the coal industry to assure themselves of steady supplies of the vital energy source: the J. P. Morgan interests, which included U.S. Steel and Southern Railway, International Harvester, Ford, and others.

Harlan County, Kentucky, began its legendary and often tragic career in coal in the early twentieth century. Rapid growth became runaway growth when wartime demand for coal soared. The population of Harlan also soared—from a prewar total of less than 11,000 to almost 65,000 in 1930. The populations of the neighboring coal counties, Pike and Perry, climbed rapidly, too: a twofold increase to more than 62,000 people in the first instance and a nearly fourfold increase to more than 42,000 in the second.

High earnings, especially in comparison with what could be earned from available alternatives, and plenty of work made coal mining very attractive to the mountaineers. The money also attracted European immigrants and southern blacks. Thousands became miners in spite of coal mining's well-deserved reputation as one of the most dangerous jobs in the country.

Because of the isolation and newness of most coal mining operations, coal companies frequently owned their own housing and even towns for miners and their families. Some firms provided good housing, stores, and a variety of educational and social services. Others provided only the crudest housing and little else. Not a few employed the only police officers in and around their operations. Control of the local police or the sheriff often came directly from control over local politicians or alliances with them. The industry generally did little to make its mines safer places to work. Probably 300 to 500 coal miners died each year in southern Appalachia.

No company could make adequate provision for the sharp decline in coal consumption in the late 1920s as alternate sources of energy gained favor. Even before the decline began, coal companies had mechanized and laid off miners to cut costs in order to meet intensifying competition from oil, gas, and hydroelectric power. The severe drop in demand for coal reinforced these effects. Company payrolls, hourly wages, and welfare programs shrank after 1923. Every third miner had lost his job by 1930. Protests, work stoppages, strikes, and unionization could not reverse the trend. The coal boom in southern Appalachia was over.

The coal boom and the lumber bonanza left environmental and human disarray. Although many companies had bought land outright, many others had purchased only the rights to the minerals beneath the surface of the soil or only the right to log the land. Lumber companies left landowners with denuded land and acute environmental problems. Coal companies tore up the land to get to the seams of coal. Landowners usually received less than $3 an acre for their land and even less legal protection. The terms of the land deeds were so broadly written and so generally interpreted to favor the companies that landowners were often owners in name only. Those who resisted the sale of rights to their land or of the land itself frequently lost their land through fraud, a method made easier by the inadequacy of public records and the lack of precise titles.

By 1930, mountaineers found that many fewer of them had land of any use for farming, and most were wage-dependent in a region where the number of jobs was shrinking. They had become poor subjects in an economy dominated by absentee owners and by the owners' local political allies. Many of the people of southern Appalachia were reduced to squeezing a living from their depleted farms and forests or seeking jobs outside the region. Some turned prohibition laws to their advantage; they became moonshiners. Others found employment in the growing tourist industry in such towns as Asheville, North Carolina. Others went to work on the Biltmore estate, where George Washington Vanderbilt had constructed an elegant 250-room château and where Pisgah National Forest began. Pisgah became the site of some of the earliest efforts in scientific forestry and conservation in the United States. By 1930, some of the larger lumber and forest product companies had become involved in conservation and reforestation, sometimes in cooperation with the U.S. Forestry Service. Appalachian natives often found the Forestry Service (and the Park Service) as economically and culturally imperious as others who came to the region. Like the lumber lords and coal barons, these agencies, and even self-described and often well-intentioned social and religious reformers, tarred Appalachia with the term *hillbilly*. A hillbilly was presumably backward, ignorant, lazy, and a quaint curiosity. The word underlined the social distance between Appalachia and the modernizing parts of the South, in particular the town world.

THE TOWN WORLD

The economic changes that World War I did so much to stimulate slowed in southern Appalachia in the early 1920s, but not in the towns and cities of the interior South outside of Appalachia. New Orleans remained the largest city in the South in 1930, but Houston was closing in fast, as was Dallas. Louisville, Atlanta, and Birmingham remained near the top in size, though none expanded so rapidly as the Texas cities. Memphis, San Antonio, and Richmond followed. Then came Oklahoma City, a newcomer. Behind it came Fort Worth, Nashville, Tulsa, Jacksonville, and Norfolk. Numerous substantial towns would become important cities in another decade or so.

Patterns in this urban growth became discernible. The piedmont continued to prosper from Richmond to Atlanta and Birmingham, though it was not certain then that Atlanta would eclipse the other two and become the urban hub of the Southeast. Smaller urban developments, spawned primarily by the textile industry, continued their expansion. Among eastern coastal locales, Norfolk and Jacksonville prospered, Charleston and Savannah did not. Situated on a fine natural harbor—the Atlantic Ocean—and the Atlantic Intracoastal Waterway, Norfolk became a major port, primarily for such bulk cargo as coal, lumber, and pulpwood. World War I brought a big boost to shipbuilding. Jacksonville, on the Atlantic and the St. John's River, grew as agriculture, manufacturing, and tourism developed in northern Florida. To the south, on the Gulf coast, Tampa based its economy on phosphate mining, cigar making, proximity to Florida's expanding citrus and truck farming, and developing industries in shipping and tourism. St. Petersburg, on the other side of Tampa Bay, relied much more heavily on tourism. On the Atlantic, Miami and Miami Beach grew out of sand, fertile imaginations, and the desire to be warm in the winter. Though development of the Gulf coast and the interior was hardly as spectacular or as well advertised as the Florida boom, urban growth increased steadily during the 1920s from New Orleans to Houston, up the Mississippi and some of its tributaries to Memphis, Shreveport, and Little Rock, and into the especially fast-growing oil regions of the Southwest. Nashville, Knoxville, and Chattanooga in Tennessee, Louisville, and Huntsville, Alabama, experienced steady growth in the upper central South and the Tennessee Valley.

In the 1920s the warm sun of southern Florida seemed to have addled the minds of the presumably sober. William Jennings Bryan became part of a public relations, sales, and land-speculation effort that resulted in a mushroom-like development of subdivisions. Some contained lavish homes that were reputed to be copies of Mediterranean styles but that one observer described as "the Bastard-Spanish-Moorish-Romanesque-Gothic-Renaissance-Bull-Market-Damn-the-Expense Style." Earlier, "snowbirds" had migrated south by rail and stayed at hotels and "tourist homes." Now they came by car, often using the new Dixie Highway, which ran from Michigan to Miami, and many bought homes. In 1926 disaster hit Florida. Fraud had a hand in it; so did gullibility and nature. Real estate salespeople sometimes made deceptive claims. More important, the land boom rested on an inadequate financial structure. The collapse left fortunes in ruins. Thousands of residents fled north. A hurricane struck six months after the financial bubble burst, destroying or damaging thousands of homes and leaving more than 400 people dead. Still, a foundation for future, bigger development had been laid—an expanded transportation and highway system and an extensive network of commercial buildings, residential developments, and new hotels. The 1920s was a benchmark in Florida's history. Thereafter, Florida would be less "southern" than it had been.

Cities in the South, like those elsewhere in the nation, offered more opportunities for social and economic mobility than rural areas, so they attracted growing numbers of newcomers. Those newcomers represented success and economic growth. They also presented problems: growing needs for water, sewerage, lighting, transportation, fire and police protection, some degree of regulation of social and economic activity, public health, pollution control, street construction and repair, and traffic control. Many of the cities applied similar solutions to similar problems. Most cities were dominated by civic elites. They came from upper-income groups, and they sought to fashion urban politics and policy. These elites varied in makeup to some degree, a reflection of the differences among cities. Where industry was more important—say in Birmingham, Dallas, Greensboro, or Macon—manufacturers had greater influence than in New Orleans, where banking and commercial interests had the upper hand. The civic elites marched in the front ranks of the urban boosters, lineal descendants of the New South advocates, but with a crucial difference. The civic elites of the twentieth century were also progressives—their New Southism had been shaped by the Social Gospel, the experience of the tumultuous 1890s, and the concern for order and professionalism so widely shared by the progressives. Moreover, they had more power to obtain the changes they sought than did the New South advocates.

The civic elites embraced vigorous growth and order at the same time, a course full of inherent contradictions. Many of the problems of urban order stemmed from the rapid growth that the elites generally hailed. Rapid urban expansion usually meant fast-growing populations (often with disproportionately large numbers of young male transients); housing shortages; inadequate services and facilities for education, fire and police protection, utilities, public transit, health, and the handicapped and the needy; and overtaxed systems of public streets.

The last problem was greatly compounded by automobiles, whose numbers grew geometrically during the 1920s. The horseless carriage brought with it a somber addition to the mortality statistics the government gathered and published: death by auto accident, a statistical category that grew at least as fast as the numbers of automobiles. Autos also contributed to air pollution, primarily by increasing the amount of dust in the air. (Most streets were unpaved.) The automobile, on the other hand, had a major multiplier effect on urban economies: sales agencies, service stations, parts stores, roadhouses, restaurants. It should also be remembered that horses and horse-drawn vehicles were not free of serious problems; they, too, were involved in accidents, and horses distributed pollutants of a particularly unsanitary kind. Prior to the extensive use of electricity and natural gas, the dust and exhaust from the coal furnaces then widely used in industry, businesses, offices, and homes gave some cities a dark-brown cast and caused discomfort and serious health problems.

From city to city, civic elites applied similar solutions—with varying success—to the problems they perceived and felt required attention. They chose means that were compatible with business progressivism, or what suited civic elites. The means they chose fit urban boosterism and growth and stressed efficiency, bureaucracy, and government by the "better elements." The urban leaders of the 1920s had precedents to draw on. Led by earlier civic elites, many cities and towns had changed their form of government from a large council with members elected by wards to a smaller council with members elected at large. This change further limited the political power of black voters, who had still exercised some power in local elections, and the power of others who were not part of the "better element" and might want policies that differed from those sought by civic elites. Those undesirable others included railroad workers, skilled tradesmen, and industrial workers. In 1912, for instance, Columbia, South Carolina, "reformed" its election laws to minimize the political power of its substantial body of railroad workers, many of whom were unionized, and of textile mill workers.

Galveston, Texas, became a model for the kind of urban reform civic elites wanted in the early twentieth century and continued to seek in the 1920s. Faced by rising debts and declining public services, Galveston business leaders had called for changes in the city government to make it more efficient and more responsive to what they believed were community-wide needs. Their calls went largely unheeded until September 1900, when the worst hurricane in the history of Galveston struck, leaving more than 6,000 dead and destroying large portions of the city. The city quickly adopted a commission form of government to deal with the crisis. Five commissioners presided over clearly defined departments and attempted to run Galveston like a modern corporation.

Galveston's commission form of government was widely publicized and carefully watched, and frequently was credited with the city's quick recovery from the hurricane. Probably no change in government could have kept Galveston among the leading cities in Texas. Memories of the hurricane, a long history of severe storms, and the dredging of the Houston Ship Channel (1912–1914) speeded Galveston's displacement by Houston as Texas's premier port. Moreover, the enthusiasm of urban leaders for commission government cooled after they determined that it created too wide a gap between responsibilities for governing and responsibilities for public services. Civic leaders found the city manager (an appointed professional or expert urban manager) form of urban government more to their liking. By World War I, many civic leaders had become strong supporters of that approach to city governance.

Accordingly, cities and towns in the 1920s increased their reliance on experts and paid agencies, often in a conscious effort to copy the management approach of large corporations. Appointed city managers presumably brought expertise to city management and supposedly made decisions in an atmosphere free of political pressure. The urban South in the 1920s also raised taxes and spent increasing amounts of money to pave streets, lay sewer lines, provide better water and sanitation services and more fire and police protection, and increase the amount and quality of public education.

Expenditures tended to reflect the biases and concerns of civic elites. Few black neighborhoods had paved streets or city water and sewers. White schools received more money than black schools—in Birmingham in 1911, for instance, nearly seven times more. Marked disparities prevailed in teacher pay and training, length of school year, physical facilities, and course offerings. Some southern cities did, however, include a new item in their expenditures for public education: high schools for blacks. Urban leaders spurned the idea of public housing; they believed that housing should be a function of the private sector of the economy. Similarly, they believed that private charities, not public agencies, should provide any relief needed. Services and facilities available for blacks in the urban South were poor, where they existed at all. Less advantaged whites tended to receive not much more than blacks. Elites could and did occasionally divide among themselves over important issues, such as what kinds of taxes were desirable or what kinds of business activity should be regulated. The fact that cities and towns in the South had less wealth and less revenue to spend than those elsewhere in the United States obviously shaped expenditure patterns.

Cities seemed to raise serious moral issues: vice, the sale and use of alcoholic beverages, the content and form of public entertainment, and the appropriate way to keep the Sabbath. Civic elites generally eschewed the use of government to police morals. Other groups, especially the clergy, often led efforts to force city officials to act on these matters. Some places censored books, movies, magazines, and theaters and even outlawed dance halls. Almost all had laws against prostitution, vice, and gambling. Sunday closing laws were common.

However, these laws were not consistently and vigorously enforced. Limitations of personnel and money contributed to the disparity between the written law and its application. More important was public indifference and even hostility to such laws, feelings that were most forcefully expressed in attitudes toward prohibition. The urban South had opposed prohibition in the first place and continued to do so after it was made part of the Constitution and put into effect. Saloons, of which there had been hundreds in the South (Memphis alone had more than 500), closed. So did open sales of packaged beer, wine, and liquor. Covert and not very covert forms of saloons and sales of alcoholic beverages started up and flourished. Charleston, South Carolina, spurned such subterfuges and defiantly sold and served alcohol publicly. Memphis remained wayward, largely untouched by sporadic attempts to purify the river city. William Faulkner wrote of Memphis as a den of iniquity that lured the natives of the region with temptations of forbidden but highly accessible evils. Yet "bossism" and entrenched political machines were apparently less prevalent in the cities in the South than elsewhere in the United States. The most notable of southern bosses was Edward H. "Boss" Crump, Jr., of Memphis. Crump developed an "easy" relationship with purveyors of booze and illicit activities. The Choctaw Club of New Orleans represented the political machine in its glory. By forming alliances throughout the state, the Choctaw Club wielded enormous power in Louisiana, as Crump did in Tennessee. At the same time, the South had many rural-oriented political machines. They were especially prevalent in the black-belt counties of the Deep South. The most famous, however, was in Virginia: the Byrd machine.

The urban South differed from the urban North in some important ways. Southern cities were smaller than northern cities, but after 1900 they grew three times faster. Southern cities and towns drew heavily on surrounding rural areas for much of their population growth. The urban South had fewer foreign-born residents, Catholics, and Jews and larger percentages of blacks. Whites in the urban South perceived blacks as a valuable but troublesome, even threatening presence. Blacks were believed to be valuable for the cheap labor the community required, but they were thought to be "irresponsible and unreliable" workers and inclined to antisocial behavior and crime.

"Most whites," a careful student of Birmingham has concluded,

> therefore favored frankly discriminatory law enforcement to render Negroes more available as a pool of cheap labor, to overcome their alleged unreliability as workers, and to curb their alleged criminal tendency. . . . The police, sheriff's deputies, and courts usually automatically accepted the word of any white man against that of any black.

Blacks were the main targets of vagrancy laws, chain gangs, and convict leasing. Chain gang members and leased convicts, 80 to 90 percent of whom were black, provided cheap labor for public works and private employers and occasionally served as strikebreakers. Their forced labor also reduced the costs of chronically underfunded penal systems.

Fewer cities and towns in the South relied on manufacturing as their principal economic activity, and the population density was lower in the urban South. Because urban areas developed later in the South than in the North, they felt the impact of the car in a more formative way. Cities and towns were more spread out and contained fewer high-rise buildings. Even southern ghettos differed from northern ones. Instead of tenements, urban copies of rural farm shacks were thrown up along railroad tracks, on the floodplains of rivers, and near factories. Blacks far outnumbered whites in southern slums. Labor unions in the South, generally smaller than their northern counterparts, also had lesser roles in urban politics.

Violence was much more common in the urban South than the urban North, if the available statistics on murder are any indication. Southerners, white and black, assaulted and murdered more often than northerners, white or black. The cities with the five highest homicide rates in the nation were located below the Mason-Dixon line—or, as a journalist wrote, "below the Smith and Wesson Line." Memphis led the nation with a homicide rate of 89 per 100,000 people in 1916, when the national average for cities was 9.2 per 100,000. Atlanta stood next (31), followed by New Orleans (25.6), Nashville (24.8), and Charleston (23.1). Apparently the homicide rate had been rising in southern cities since the first decade of the twentieth century, and the mayhem seems to have gotten worse in the 1920s and 1930s.

BUSINESS PROGRESSIVISM AND STATE GOVERNMENT

Progressivism became especially prominent in the state capitals in the 1920s. Stressing better education, good roads, and improved health services while downplaying regulation of business, especially regulation of labor-managment relations, southern state governments increased taxes and expenditures significantly. North Carolina led the way; in the process, the University of North Carolina became the leading university of the South, displacing the University of Virginia. The University of Texas and Duke University (formerly Trinity College, now renamed for its principal benefactor) also gained national reputations in the 1920s. The ranks of progressives among the governors of the South included Austin Peay in Tennessee, Thomas E. Kilby and Bibb Graves in Alabama, Cameron Morrison and Angus M. McLean in North Carolina, John E. Martineau in Arkansas, Huey Long in Louisiana, Harry Flood Byrd in Virginia, Pat Neff and Dan Moody in Texas, and Lamartine G. Hardaman in Georgia. The last three, however, were not able to achieve much. Prohibition divided Texas Democrats, crippled the forces of progressivism, and helped elect Miriam "Ma" Ferguson. She was the political stand-in for her husband, James E. Ferguson, who had been expelled from office in 1917 for corruption. In Georgia, progressives at the state level faced a hostile legislature and the forces of the popular Eugene Talmadge. A gifted manipulator of rural sentiments and prejudices, Talmadge became a major force in Georgia politics. Georgia's system of apportionment gave rural-based politicians like Talmadge electoral advantages (and power) against urban Georgia, particularly Atlanta. Almost everywhere in the South, malapportionment reinforced the power advantage of the rural counties and the county courthouse politicians against the urban South. Georgia, and possibly Virginia, was simply the obvious example of the disproportionate power the rural South enjoyed. As governor in the 1930s and 1940s, Talmadge provided more emotional release for disadvantaged whites than concrete programs for them or for the state. Despite his "country" image and bright-red suspenders, Talmadge pursued a status quo politics that many businesspeople found to their liking.

Louisiana's Huey Long (the "Kingfish") differed markedly from Georgia's Talmadge. A brilliant, enormously energetic lawyer from northern Louisiana, where Populism had once been strong, Long so effectively attacked corporations and entrenched power in his state that he was elected governor in 1928 when he was thirty-five years old. He had ready targets and ready tools. The latter included radio, a newly emerging means of mass communications, and a gift for riveting, outrageous oratory. His prime targets included lumber, sulfur, and oil and gas companies, which had formed alliances with large agricultural interests, sugar and cotton planters in particular. They worked closely with politicians who preferred the status quo. Established politicians remained established; taxes remained low; public services remained meager. Though Louisiana had very substantial natural resources (especially minerals), numerous prosperous farm operations, and the South's largest city and one of the nation's largest ports, the state had an appalling record of neglect of the needs of most of its citizens. For example, 40 percent of the native *white* males of twenty-five years of age had less than five years of schooling in *1940*; 15 percent had no schooling at all. In 1924, only 331 miles of the state's roads were paved.

As governor, Long boosted taxes on oil and other resources, a strategy that took advantage of Standard Oil's high visibility and unpopularity. Spurred by Long, the legislature went heavily into debt to pay for a greatly expanded list of public projects. A total of 3,754 miles of roads were paved by 1935. More than a hundred bridges were constructed—critical projects in a state laced with rivers, lakes, and bayous. Additions to public buildings included much-expanded facilities at Louisiana State University. Long got the legislature to provide free textbooks for all schoolchildren, public, private, and parochial. The last measure had broad appeal, not least among Louisiana's numerous Catholic voters.

In 1930 Long won election to the U.S. Senate, but chose to remain governor until 1932 to oversee his program and to secure a pliable successor in the statehouse. He created a statewide political machine that survived his death—by assassination in 1935—and divided the Louisiana Democratic party into bitter Long and anti-Long factions, the closest thing to two-party politics anywhere in the South until after World War II. Long increased taxes, state spending and indebtedness, corruption, and state programs, whose benefits reached many citizens. For all his anticorporate rhetoric, Long reached accommodations with business from which some businesses and the Kingfish personally benefited. Like his fellow business progressives, Long had a poor record on labor. He did little to improve workers' compensation. One popular myth about Louisiana politics had an element of truth: "Since Long, the people have the alternative of a venal administration with a dynamic program, or an honest, do-nothing administration belonging to the corporations."

Long kept a close watch and a heavy hand on state affairs even after he went to the Senate in 1932. There, the ever-energetic, hugely ambitious Louisianan

HUEY LONG AT A FOOTBALL GAME (Louisiana State Museum)

launched a successful, though short-lived, effort to become a major figure in national politics. Unlike other southern demagogues, Long avoided religious bigotry and usually eschewed race-baiting. He was also one of the few demagogues to deal with real issues—education, social services, regressive taxation, and entrenched corporations, though hardly with an even hand and usually with an eye to enhancing his own power.

Under Long, spending was increased for education for blacks and whites, but the gap between the two grew much wider. He took particular interest in Louisiana State University (LSU), and the university improved significantly. State services for the mentally and physically ill improved, but not as much as Long claimed. Long continued his state's tradition of gross neglect of the poor. His manic drive served a consuming need for power and attention. He attended to everything that fell within his purview, going as far as hiring and firing football coaches at LSU. By the time of his violent death in 1935, Long had become as close to a political dictator as the United States has ever had.

Most business progressives differed markedly from Long in their style and in the concerns they stressed, but they were not indifferent to the less fortunate. Every southern state but one had a public welfare agency by 1927, and Mississippi followed suit in 1934. Expenditures for public welfare increased dramatically. Obviously the Social Gospel was not dead, though it lost some of its force in the 1920s. Moreover, private philanthropic efforts were substantial. The Rosenwald Fund, the Milbank Memorial Fund, and especially the Rockefeller Foundation were the most notable. Between 1902 and 1947 the Rockefeller Foundation gave nearly $128 million to the southern states through its General Education Board and its International Health Board.

Despite steep increases in state revenues and expenditures in the 1920s, the southern states still lagged far behind the rest of the nation, taking in and spending only about one-half the national averages. Private giving could reduce these differentials only slightly. Serious, chronic deficiencies in health and education remained. Two measures of public health—the birth rate and the infant mortality rate—reflected the seriousness of these deficiencies. Southerners continued to have a higher birth rate than other Americans, and more of their infants died. In these categories the gaps between southern blacks and whites remained wide, and so did those between the rural and urban South.

By the 1920s the social and economic disparities within the town world became quite obvious. So did those between the town world and the farm world. Urbanites, especially the better off, illuminated their homes with electric lights, replaced their iceboxes with refrigerators, relied less and less on wood or coal for heating and cooking, and installed telephones. The prosperous had spacious homes with indoor plumbing on large, landscaped lots on tree-lined streets. Southern urbanites lived in more economically and racially segregated circumstances than ever before. The streetcar and automobile allowed people to live in racially and economically homogeneous neighborhoods at some distance from the places where they worked and traded.

Cities and towns reflected caste and class as never before. Whites might work closely with domestic (nearly always black) servants and have no close dealings with any other blacks. The wives of the prosperous managed their homes, joined clubs and societies, and often worked to improve their city and state and to help the less fortunate. Their husbands wore sober-looking three-piece suits, ties, and starched shirts to work in offices or stores. In larger urban areas, their children usually attended schools with their social and economic peers, then played with their peers in neighborhood parks or, possibly, at local country clubs. In smaller urban areas, the better off had to rely on well-known if less physically obvious means to define the boundaries of class and caste.

CAUSEWAY NEAR MOBILE ON OPENING DAY (Erik Overbey Collection, University of South Alabama Archives)

Clubs and churches also reflected the status of city dwellers. Catholics were not numerous and had little influence except in New Orleans, Mobile, and, surprisingly, Charleston and Savannah. Jews, who were strong in merchandising, were even fewer and were often excluded from clubs and some neighborhoods.

THE KU KLUX KLAN REBORN

Despite the predominance and power of white Anglo-Saxon Protestants in the cities and towns, the urban South in the 1920s developed a fortress mentality; southerners became almost hysterical about alien people and ideas. The social, economic, and political changes that came in the wake of World War I profoundly disturbed many Americans, north and south. That many of those changes were more apparent than real and that many were beneficial did little to soothe jangled nerves. Many southerners believed that foreigners and alien ideas constituted a grave threat to American values and even the very survival of the country. Aliens were vaguely defined to include immigrants, Catholics, Jews, blacks, communists, and socialists. Strange ideas were almost as vaguely defined: those that qualified included communism or bolshevism, socialism, modernist thought, evolution, science, and unconventional sexuality. Southerners were distressed by the recent tendency to be frank about sex and sexuality, the actual and apparent sexual freedom women seemed to have taken up during and after the war, and the demand of some women for changes in their roles both inside and outside their families.

Profound anxiety underlay the sudden growth of nativism, the Ku Klux Klan (KKK), and evangelical Protestantism. That anxiety was no less profound because some of its sources were more imagined than real. Few of the "new immigrants"— the great human tide that swept onto American shores from southern and eastern Europe between 1880 and 1920—settled in the South. In most places below the Mason-Dixon line the numbers of Catholics and Jews were insignificant. Even where they did congregate, their numbers did not compare with those in the urban North. Yet southern politicians increasingly became supporters of immigration restriction. Restrictionists finally won a major victory in 1917 and 1921, when Congress passed literacy requirements for immigrants and then severely reduced the number of immigrants the country would admit each year. Nativism in general and Anglo-Saxonism, its particular American variant, thrived in the South. Nativism was not, however, an altogether alien growth in the region. It found sustenance in the racism and war-stimulated patriotism of the region. Fear of domestic and foreign radicals soared during the war, especially with the success of the Bolsheviks in Russia.

The KKK benefited enormously from these circumstances and from rapid urbanization, among other factors. As southerners poured into the cities, they found uncertainties along with opportunities. Dependent on wages and salaries, often for the first time, and confronted by loss of individuality, often by unrealized expectations, and by a strange world, these people had very real needs that the Invisible Empire of the Ku Klux Klan seemed to serve.

In 1920 a catalyst emerged to spark the KKK's resurgence. Actually, two catalysts: Edward Young Clarke, a former newspaperman and salesman for fraternal organizations, and Elizabeth Tyler, a public relations expert and leader in the Republican party in Georgia. They owned and ran the Southern Publicity Association, a fund-raising agency whose accounts included the Theodore Roosevelt Memorial Fund, the Anti-Saloon League, and the Red Cross. They saw the commercial potential of the Klan and took it on as a client. Paid on the basis of the number of members they signed up, Clarke and Tyler organized a national network of recruiters, who also worked on commission. They enjoyed considerable success, but it was confined largely to the South until Congress lent an unwitting hand. Aroused by reports that the KKK was a secret, violent association, Congress held hearings. The result was helpful publicity. The head of the Klan, Colonel Simmons—colonel by courtesy of the Woodmen of the World, a fraternal order—was the star witness. Attired in Prince Albert coat, starched shirt, tie, and gold watch chain, he conveyed the image of respectability and 100 percent Americanism. Thereafter, Klan membership, which had been growing, soared to several million. So did profits—from initiation fees, dues, and sales of Klan regalia.

Approximately 40 percent of the Klan's membership at its peak in the early 1920s were southerners. Most of the members lived in urban areas. Some were prominent in their communities. Most were of the lower middle class. They represented a broad spectrum of occupations. Many were clergymen. Virtually every southern city or town that called itself a city had a vigorous local Klan. Of the larger cities, only New Orleans and Louisville did not. But even in the earliest days of its revival, the KKK faced opposition. Not all whites approved of the Klan or acquiesced in it. Such opposition, however, had little effect in the heyday of the reborn Klan.

The 1920s proved to offer an ideal environment for the growth of the Klan. The Klan offered much that southern (and many northern) whites seemed to need at the time: fraternity, idealism, secrecy, ritual and regalia, offices, a sense of self-importance, reform, and commitment to traditional moral values and sex roles. Only white Anglo-Saxon Protestant males could join. (Women were invited to join auxiliaries.) The Klan embraced evangelical Protestantism and biblical literalism. It espoused prohibition, attacked saloons, fought unions, favored immigration restriction, opposed the supposedly sweeping changes in sexual behavior and sex roles in the 1920s, and denounced political radicalism, prostitution, gambling, and the theory of evolution. Things foreign particularly incensed the Klan, as did deviations from isolationism: all non-WASPS, the League of Nations, and the World Court. The Klan thrived on anti-Catholicism, anti-Semitism, and antiradicalism, though the South had few Catholics, Jews, or radicals. Negrophobia played a secondary role, presumably because Jim Crow kept blacks so effectively "in their place." The Klan reserved its greatest alarm for the grave threats that they believed Catholics and the Pope represented for the United States. The "lure of the Klan," one scholar wrote, "was its anti-Catholicism and its promise . . . to bring Christian righteousness to society. . . . The Klan, in short, appeared to be doing what the Church talked about."

Reformism, according to a careful study of the Klan in the Southwest, was more instrumental than nativism in the manifestations of the Invisible Empire in Texas, Arkansas, Louisiana, and Oklahoma. The Klan in the Southwest became vigilante reformers who wanted to restore private and public morality that they believed had recently fallen apart. In a way, the Klan was correct when it called itself "progressive," but it was a backward-looking, xenophobic, and dangerous variant of progressivism.

To convey its message to the community, the Klan relied on intimidation and terrorism, although terrorism did not have the official sanction of the Klan's national leadership. The Klan conducted numerous masked demonstrations and parades, complete with fiery crosses, and it often resorted to violence. Klansmen flogged, branded, mutilated, beat, kidnapped, tarred, lynched, and otherwise murdered people they feared; for good measure they burned their houses.

Such atrocities contributed to the rapid fading of the Invisible Empire. More moderate members, including community leaders, abandoned an organization that attracted so many fanatics and sadists. Local and state governments turned against the KKK. The Klan was also damaged by internal dissension and power struggles, financial shenanigans, and the scandalous behavior of some of its officers. Finally, fear of the alien and the hysteria it triggered seemed to be subsiding by the mid-1920s.

By 1927, Klan membership in the South had plummeted from approximately 2 million in the early 1920s to somewhere around 50,000. At the same time, the Klan's political power virtually disappeared. It had elected or helped elect congressmen, U.S. senators in Oklahoma and Texas, and governors in Georgia and Louisiana as well as in Colorado, Ohio, Oregon, and Maine. The Klan had dominated Indiana politics for a time, and it had been a critical force in the nomination of the Democrat candidate for president in 1924. Four years later, the Klan could not stop Alfred E. Smith, governor of New York—Irish Catholic, opponent of prohibition, and a product of Tammany Hall and ethnic politics—from being nominated by the Democrats. Nor was the Klan very important in Smith's loss to Herbert Hoover in the 1928 election. However, the Klan might have had more staying power in the South in the 1920s if blacks had not been so thoroughly and systematically subordinated.

THE BLACK WORLD

Although Jim Crow circumscribed the world of black southerners, they found avenues of self-assertion in the 1920s that contributed to and shaped critical changes in that world. The migration of so many of them had the most far-reaching impact. Since a substantial proportion of the black migrants took a wide variety of skills with them, the South found itself in greater need of skilled workers than ever. Individually and collectively, blacks continued to build and maintain a world apart from whites. Even faithful servants remained distant. The black world became institutionalized: black churches, stores, banks, parks, libraries, picture shows, theaters, hospitals, drugstores, insurance organizations, and professionals—lawyers, ministers, realtors, clergy, teachers. Residential segregation was reinforced and sometimes caused by zoning laws and the availability of public transportation for people who could not afford an automobile. In urban areas especially, a new black elite developed to serve a black clientele. Ironically, this elite had a vested interest in Jim Crow, which ensured a steady though not very prosperous flow of black customers and clients.

Generally, however, blacks had fewer chances for employment or careers in the South and earned less after World War I ended. Blacks found fewer opportunities to work in services with a white clientele and in the building trades, where they had once been numerous. White-dominated labor unions acted to reduce job opportunities for blacks in railroading and most of the building trades. The International Longshoremen's Association, however, remained a stronghold for black workers, and in 1925 A. Philip Randolph started to organize railroad sleeping car porters, all of whom were black. Randolph later became a major figure in the civil rights movement. Blacks continued to make up much of the workforce in the iron and steel industry in Alabama, but they seldom held the better-paying skilled jobs. Studies of wages in Virginia in the 1920s confirmed what some observers had suspected: even if blacks did the same work as whites, they usually received less pay.

One of the more obvious ways for blacks to assert themselves was to join the NAACP. Many of the black elite, who formed the backbone of the organization, supported its efforts even though the NAACP's attacks on Jim Crow threatened the self-interest of many of them. Membership in the NAACP multiplied during and after World War I. This growth reflected changing circumstances within and without the organization. Even before Booker T. Washington's death in 1915, his power had waned along with the appeal of his passive approach to change. The war accelerated these shifts. Led by southern black expatriates such as James Weldon Johnson and Walter White and galvanized by the aggressive, forcefully argued rhetoric of the brilliant W. E. B. Du Bois, editor of *Crisis*, the main organ of the NAACP, the organization grew from fewer than 20 chapters (one in the South) to 300. More than half of the chapters were located in the South, as were almost half of the 88,000 members of the association.

The NAACP persistently sought relief by legal action and lobbying. In 1915 the NAACP succeeded in getting Oklahoma's grandfather clause declared unconstitutional. Two years later it obtained a federal court ruling against laws requiring residential segregation in municipalities. Neither decision, however, had any practical effect. Oklahoma passed legislation to evade the court's decision, and municipalities simply ignored the courts and continued to pass laws requiring residential segregation. In the latter instance, laws were probably unnecessary, because community pressures and economic realities made residential segregation virtually inevitable.

Most blacks remained beyond the reach of the NAACP; it appealed almost exclusively to the well educated and highly articulate. Marcus Garvey's Universal Negro Improvement Association, which flourished for a time during the early 1920s, had mass appeal, but it had few overt followers in the South. The "New Negro" movement of the latter 1920s had more effect, particularly on the campuses of black colleges. There students and their allies succeeded in replacing white administrators with black administrators. Residential neighborhoods around these campuses came to be favored by black elites.

After the racial turmoil of the World War I era waned, southern whites seemed not to perceive blacks as a serious threat. Neither the restiveness of blacks nor the NAACP caused whites to question the security of white supremacy. Certainly, little occurred from day to day in the 1920s to shake that sense of dominance. In 1928 the foremost southern historian and one of the leading scholars of the time, Ulrich B. Phillips, pronounced what seemed to be the final, definitive word on the relations of whites and blacks in the South: "the central theme of Southern history" was "a common resolve indomitably maintained" that the South "shall be and remain a white man's country."

THE WORLD OF THE FARM

Most southern farmers, black and white, lived a world away from the general prosperity of the towns in the 1920s. Gracie Turner, North Carolina sharecropper and mother of twelve, told an all too common story of farming in her childhood in the 1890s: the "most we cleared was $179 [a year]. . . . Most years it was fifty and sixty dollars." Although southern farmers did better in the 1920s than they did when Gracie Turner was a child, they did not do much better. As in the 1890s, farms in the South were too small, too undercapitalized, and too dependent on a limited range of cash crops. Studies have indicated that farm income generally rises as farms get larger. Unfortunately, southern farms seemed to be headed in the opposite direction. The number of agricultural units with less than fifty acres under cultivation increased, while the number of those with more than one hundred acres declined. Farm values for land and buildings averaged some $4,300 in the South and some $11,000 in the North, and comparative figures for livestock and machinery and tools revealed even greater contrasts. Southern farmhouses were much less likely than those in the North to have electric lights, running water, and indoor plumbing, and were much more likely to be located along unimproved dirt roads. The gap between the North and South narrowed, however, with respect to automobile ownership. Large numbers of even the poorest southern farmers owned cars.

Cotton was still the principal cash crop of the South; it provided the only cash income for 50 percent of all southern farmers. Tobacco, rice, and sugar were the other major cash crops. The proportion of investment in or income derived from livestock and poultry was still very small. The value of beef cattle, dairy herds, and poultry declined in the 1920s. Southern farmers did grow a wider range of crops than they had raised in the late nineteenth century. Citrus fruits continued to be critical in Florida, where their cultivation expanded rapidly during the 1920s. At the same time, citrus growing was introduced to the lower Rio Grande Valley in Texas. The growing of other fruits, especially apples and peaches in the Southeast, expanded, as did truck farming and peanut and pecan growing in various parts of the South. Soybeans made their first appearance on southern farms during the 1920s. Southern farmers raised more of their own food and probably ate better than they had done before, but agricultural diversification did not add much to farm incomes.

Cotton still reigned, if in a miserly fashion. No challenger or alternative was readily available. World War I left the basic structure of southern agriculture intact. Incomes from cotton followed a roller-coaster pattern after World War I, and cotton-dependent farmers were unable to avoid being hapless riders. Sharp declines in the price of cotton (and of tobacco as well) in 1920 and 1921 and the boll weevil took a heavy toll on farm incomes and welfare and forced many independent farmers to become renters and sharecroppers. Then higher cotton prices returned in the mid-1920s, and the boll weevil was largely contained. In 1925, cotton production almost equaled the record set in 1914, yet prices remained good. The following year farmers grew 18 million bales of cotton on 47 million acres, both records. This time prices fell—from 18 cents a pound in 1925 to 10 cents in 1927. Earnings from cotton declined by $500 million. The Great Depression arrived in the cotton fields—and thus in most of the rural South—two years before the stock market crashed in 1929.

The devastation was worst in the older cotton-growing areas, especially in the southeastern and south-central states. There farmers had plowed up more land than ever and used larger and larger amounts of fertilizer to squeeze better yields from their never overly rich and ever more eroded soils. They had done so, for one thing, to compete with farmers who grew cotton in the rich soils of northeastern Arkansas and the Mississippi-Yazoo delta, both of which had recently been drained and cleared, and with cotton growers in Texas and Oklahoma. The boll weevil had a much lesser impact on the western cotton belt. More important, farmers there could mechanize and cut labor costs much more easily than farmers in the older cotton-growing areas. Finally, all cotton farmers faced increasing competition from foreign-grown cotton and from synthetic fibers. One clear indication of the difficulties of cotton farmers in the late 1920s and of southern agriculture in general was the sudden increase in the incidence of pellagra, a disease that fed upon poor diets.

The census of 1930 presented a generally somber picture of the farm world of the South at the end of the 1920s. Between 1920 and 1930, the ranks of farm owners shrank by some 350,000. The ranks of sharecroppers swelled; those of tenants declined slightly. Approximately 60 percent of southern farm operators worked someone else's land. Rates of tenancy increased for whites and decreased for blacks. More than 155,000 whites became sharecroppers in the 1920s, but blacks still accounted for a little more than half of the 770,000 croppers in the region. As these figures represent heads of households only, perhaps 4 million southerners were sharecroppers in 1930. Too many people in the South tried to make a living at an occupation that yielded them little beyond bare subsistence.

Yet, tragically, the economy of the South could not absorb the multitudes who were leaving the land. There were not enough nonfarm jobs for them. Some 1.3 million blacks left the South during the 1920s. At the same time, about 1.5 million whites left the older parts of the South. Many of them went to the Southwest, where the population grew by nearly 900,000 people during the decade as petroleum propelled rapid economic expansion. Even that impressive growth and the growth of much of the urban South could not, however, prevent the region from suffering a decline in personal incomes. It was the first such decline for the South since 1870. No other region in American history has ever suffered a decade-long decline in per capita income. Some of that decline was probably the result of a birth rate higher than the national average and a higher proportion of children and young people who produced little or no income.

Migrating seemed to be the only alternative for many people. Politics offered little hope. Congress did pass legislation to improve marketing and encourage farm cooperatives. Late in the 1920s Congress even passed the McNary-Haugen plan in an effort to raise farm prices by reducing surpluses of agricultural commodities through government purchases of those surpluses. The government was either to hold the purchased commodities off the domestic market until prices rose above fixed levels or to sell them abroad. However, President Calvin Coolidge vetoed the measure in 1927, and when Congress passed a revised version in 1928, he vetoed that, too. Still, it is doubtful that the legislation would have helped much; McNary-Haugen made no provision for limiting what farmers produced. Very likely farm production would have continued to exceed effective demand. Government-imposed crop restrictions offered greater hope, but they were a political impossibility in the 1920s. Instead, there were the usual calls for voluntary restrictions, and the usual failures of farmers to heed them.

Southern farmers had no organized, effective voice, and they lacked strong political allies. Nothing like the Alliance or the Populists emerged. The Farmers' Educational and Cooperative Union (Farmers' Union), the nonpolitical successor to the Populists, was moribund several years before World War I. It had no successor. The farm bloc in Congress, composed of some southern Democrats and some northern and western farm-state Republicans, fought continuing, sometimes successful battles with Republican administrations in Washington in the 1920s. Their efforts, however, were inadequate to meet the crisis that thousands of farmers were experiencing. Even if farmers had been better organized, they would have had little chance to obtain legislation of the kind that might have aided the poorer farmers. The twenties were not the time for that—certainly not 1928.

THE END OF THE DECADE

In 1928 Republicans enjoyed their greatest political success in Dixie since Reconstruction. Noneconomic issues played a decisive part in that success. Alfred E. Smith, the Democratic nominee, carried too many liabilities for many southern whites. Not even the usual appeals to white supremacy could keep the South solidly Democratic. Seven southern states—Florida, Kentucky, North Carolina, Oklahoma, Tennessee, Texas, and Virginia—voted for Herbert Hoover, the Republican nominee. He ran well in traditionally Republican areas in the South and in the more prosperous urban areas that earlier had shown Republican leanings.

The Republicans continued to dominate the politics of the nation. The Wilson administrations and the Democratic Congress seemed now to be only an interlude, albeit a creative one, in a Republican era. Claims of a Democratic restoration or a South "come back to rule the nation" had been rendered hollow by subsequent events. Despite its electoral behavior in 1928, the South remained committed to the Democrats and white supremacy. Thus the South was politically isolated, part of a Democratic minority. The South's isolation had economic and cultural dimensions as well. Economically beleaguered despite the gains of the previous half century and still considered a cultural backwater despite evidence to the contrary, the South was the exile region of the nation.

Coincidentally, the distance between the farm world, including southern Appalachia, and the town world grew. It could be seen in the presence or absence of electric lights, running water, and paved streets, in diets, and in human expectations. Much of the urban South, especially the Southwest, enjoyed prosperity in the 1920s. There the events of World War I had altered the structure of the economy. Buoyed by the confidence generated by the material progress they perceived, the business progressives—small-scale copies of Herbert Hoover—embraced the "New Era" of the twenties and confidently looked to even better days.

Then the Great Depression struck. Suddenly the distance between the farm and the town shrank. In the wake of the worst economic collapse in American history, a major revolution in southern agriculture was launched, the Democrats became dominant in the nation's politics, the political isolation of the South ended, and white supremacy came under its severest challenge since the 1890s.

24

Religion and Culture in the New South

❖

The South was long perceived by observers within and without the region as
the "benighted South," a cultural and social backwater. The Scopes, or "monkey," trial, which occurred in 1925, underscored that reputation and helped
make the South, once again, the object of scorn and condescension. Ironically, even
as the trial was being held, revolutionary changes in the thought and literature of
the South were taking place. Perhaps the trial hastened those changes.

THE SCOPES TRIAL

The origins of the Scopes trial were innocent and not wholly peculiar to the South.
John Washington Butler did not set out in 1925 to become a catalyst for one of the
most famous trials in American history. Butler devoted most of his adult life to
tilling the 120 acres of a farm in Macon County, Tennessee, which had been in his
family for four generations. However, he was hardly a "simple farmer," whatever
that is. He had shown considerable skill at baseball when he was young, and he
passed on his fondness for music—and probably his talent for it—to his sons, who
formed a band. In time he went into politics. A very active, committed Christian,
John Butler worried about threats to the faithful and to people who might become
faithful if they could be protected from the lure of false doctrine. In particular, he
worried that Darwin's theory of evolution would undermine religious faith.

As a member of the Tennessee state legislature in 1925, he called for legislation to
forbid the teaching of evolution in any public school in the state. He drafted an

Act prohibiting the teaching of the Evolution Theory in all the Universities, Normals
[teachers' colleges] and all other public schools of Tennessee . . . [whereby] it shall be un-

608

lawful . . . to teach any theory that denies the story of the Divine Creation of man as taught in the Bible, and to teach instead that man has descended from a lower order of animals.

The Butler Act did not have wide support in the state. Substantial numbers of clergy and laity gave the measure strong vocal support, but they were not even a large minority. Opponents—including most but not all of the academics in the state as well as many of the state's cultural, business, and political leaders—either were indifferent to the measure or feared the power of its supporters. But legislators were not inclined to risk a vote that might be construed as a vote against God.

Similar fears gnawed at Governor Austin Peay. A progressive and one of Tennessee's best governors, Peay had managed a state debt crisis in the early 1920s, then persuaded the state to spend more money to improve highways, hospitals, and public schools and universities. The governor hesitated, then signed the bill. "This bill," he explained, "is a distinct protest against an irreligious tendency to exalt so-called science, and deny the Bible in some schools and quarters—a tendency fundamentally wrong and fatally mischievous in its effects on our children, our institutions and our country."

Americans in the 1920s, as the governor indicated, worried a great deal about their country and their institutions, about what they believed was a general decline in morals and values, and about what was happening to their children. John Butler was no hillbilly, and he was not alone in his unease. Still, not much was made initially of the Butler Act. Governor Peay said that he did not think the act would ever be enforced because schoolbooks in Tennessee contained nothing "with which this bill will interfere in the slightest manner." The governor's prediction might have proved correct if it had not been for the American Civil Liberties Union (ACLU).

Founded during World War I to protect the rights of pacifists, the ACLU expanded its concerns to civil and individual rights in general after the war. Having decided to test the constitutionality of the growing number of antievolution laws and policies being passed or implemented by state and local authorities in the 1920s, the ACLU published nationwide offers to pay the defense costs of anyone who wanted to challenge an antievolution law in the hope of getting such laws and policies declared unconstitutional. At that point John Thomas Scopes, a teacher in Tennessee, stepped forward, somewhat reluctantly. The twenty-four-year-old Scopes, a recent graduate of the University of Kentucky, taught science and coached football at a high school in Dayton, Tennessee. He did not particularly want to be arrested or to be the center of attention. Moreover, he thought that evolution and the biblical account of creation could easily be reconciled, and he knew that, contrary to what the governor said, Tennessee high school science teachers used a state-approved textbook that included a discussion of evolutionary theory.

Dayton was the small but prosperous seat of Rhea County, in the lowlands of southern Appalachia. Dayton had some 2,000 residents, several paved streets, municipally owned plants for electricity and water, and the range of Protestant churches usually found in a southern community, though about half the people in the town and the county were unchurched. It had a Progressive Club founded and run by community leaders with rising expectations for themselves and their community, perhaps 400 black residents who were thoroughly segregated, and no local Ku Klux Klan. Obviously Dayton was not an isolated, reactionary backwater. It had not, however, continued the growth it enjoyed in the late nineteenth century. It was increasingly overshadowed by Chattanooga, a city of more than 100,000 with a strong diverse economy, only forty miles or an hour and a half away.

Rhea County had a diverse economy, but it needed more diversity and greater growth. About half its residents farmed, most of them on holdings of fewer than 100 acres. Half the county's workforce found employment outside agriculture, in construction or mining or in sawmills, cotton mills, or knitting mills. Several hundred of them worked in the coal and iron mines operated by the Cumberland Coal Company under George Rappelyea, a thirty-one-year-old college-trained engineer from New York.

Rappelyea's position, background, and age were hardly likely to endear him to Rhea County natives. Still, he took an active part in the life of the town and served as superintendent of the Sunday school at the Methodist church. But he had an impolitic habit of expressing his opinions on such emotional topics as patriotism (he claimed to be a descendant of an American colonist who arrived in the New World in 1623) and evolution at two of Dayton's more important meeting places, the barbershop and Robinson's drugstore. The owner of the barbershop once bit Rappelyea during a dispute over evolution: the barber thought the engineer had called his family monkeys. Despite his less than winning ways, Rappelyea succeeded in convincing first local leaders and then Scopes that they ought to challenge the Butler Act.

Rappelyea persuaded the proprietor of Robinson's, who chaired the local school board, and the superintendent of the county schools that since Chattanooga's leaders had announced that they would drop their intended challenge to the Butler Act, Dayton ought to fill the void. No doubt the urge to put Dayton on the map made the leaders more receptive to Rappelyea's arguments. If so, they succeeded beyond their wildest expectations. Dayton became synonymous with the Scopes trial, or the monkey trial. John Scopes got part of his wish, too. Though the trial bore his name, he was shunted from center stage by more dramatic figures: H. L. Mencken, acid-tongued columnist, author, and literary critic with the *Baltimore Sun;* Clarence Darrow, the most famous trial attorney of his day; and William Jennings Bryan, former congressman, presidential candidate, and secretary of state.

Mencken saw the trial as a chance to display the South in all its backwardness and thus to defeat the opponents of freedom of thought and modern culture. Mencken's reporting of the trial, which he attended, and about Dayton and Tennessee reflected these motives and was, in some instances, distorted by this bias. He could, for example, have shown greater understanding of the serious religious and moral concerns of the antievolutionists. Mencken's reports went to much of the nation through the *Sun* and the wire services. Indeed, the trial and the town were besieged by the media. Other newspapers and magazines sent journalists, newsreel cameras whirred, radio announcers stood by their microphones to report the latest flash, and some members of the press even chartered an airplane to fly over Dayton, presumably to gain some perspective on the town.

Darrow happily volunteered to defend Scopes without charge. Long known as a defender of underdogs and dissidents and a profound religious skeptic, he found in the Scopes trial an unusual opportunity to defend personal and religious liberty and freedom of scientific inquiry. Like Mencken, he relished a chance to disturb the peace of the conventional world, and he shared Mencken's dislike of Bryan, though he had agreed with Bryan on many issues during Bryan's heyday as the foremost spokesman in American politics for the common people.

Bryan in the 1920s had assumed the role of major spokesman for biblical literalism, the belief that every word in the Bible was the literal word of God. Biblical literalists believed, for example, that what the Bible said about creation was what actually occurred: God made the world in six days, made Adam out of dust, and made Eve out of Adam's rib. Evolution and biblical literalism could not coexist. Bryan, predictably, became a major opponent of the theory of evolution. He genuinely believed, as did many others, that the teaching of evolutionary theory would undermine religious faith and consequently American society, which, as he saw it, was based on Christian faith, morals, and values. The nation—"man's last best hope"—was at risk. Bryan saw the Scopes trial as a duel to the death between religion and the theory of evolution. When the World's Christian Fundamentals Association asked Bryan to join the prosecution, he quickly agreed, and the prosecution welcomed him.

Bryan and Darrow occupied the center stage of the trial, sometimes sharing it with Judge John T. Raulston, over whose bench hung a banner that said, "Read Your Bible." The judge helped create and sustain an atmosphere that was more appropriate for a carnival than for a fair judicial hearing. Darrow correctly anticipated that even-handed justice was not to be dispensed. But he hoped that he could get the court to allow the case to be argued on broad constitutional grounds—freedom of speech and of religion. He wanted to air the need for unhindered scientific inquiry and to tackle the question of whether there was a conflict between science and Christianity. But Judge Raulston narrowed the issue to whether the state of Tennessee had the authority to pass the Butler Act and whether or not Scopes had broken that law. Once the judge ruled that indeed the state had that authority under the police powers guaranteed the states by the Constitution, the outcome of the trial was not in doubt, because Scopes readily admitted he had broken the law. The guilty verdict was anticlimactic when it came. Bryan and Darrow both had their moments during the trial, however.

Bryan told the court that the law was not the beginning of a broad attack on the freedom of speech and thought. Rather, the law reflected the concern of parents to protect their children's religious faith and welfare from such grave threats as evolutionism. Moreover, what children were taught should be determined by their parents and the majority of the community through local school boards, Bryan declared, not by school administrators, teachers, or outsiders with advanced academic degrees. Darrow decried the banning of evolution from the classroom as the first step toward the banning of books and newspapers, the setting of one religious group against another, and attempts to force one set of religious views on the holders of other views.

When Darrow managed to lure Bryan to the witness stand, the Great Commoner was more thoroughly routed than he could admit. Darrow led Bryan through a series of questions and answers that revealed how little he knew about biblical scholarship and history and how much he deviated from the biblical literalism he was supposed to accept and represent. But the best moments of the trial came from neither Darrow nor Bryan but from David Dudley Malone. "The truth," Malone said in his opening statement for the defense, "does not need the force of Government."

The trial attracted large crowds, food vendors, curio salesmen, and religious cranks. One man wore a sign proclaiming he was the world's leading authority on the Bible. Banners and exhibits urged all to read their Bible or be damned. Others had already given up, at least on Dayton. One woman was convinced that Dayton had "the mark of the beast." She took her children and fled to the surrounding mountains. "The thing is genuinely fabulous," Mencken exulted. "I have . . . enough material stored up to last me the rest of my life." By imposing "Baptist and Methodist barbarism," Mencken charged, the southern clergy had created a cultural vacuum and a fear of ideas. He referred to the people of Rhea County as "yokels," "morons," "hillbillies," and "peasants." He watched a nighttime Pentecostal revival outside Dayton and described the highly emotional service in unflattering detail and with little understanding of its meaning. Of course, many Daytonians also scorned such revivals of Pentecostals or "Holy Rollers." This scorn reflected a basic division in the South of the 1920s, a gap (sometimes a chasm) that reflected economic and social realities.

Mencken left the trial early. He had seen enough, he said, and he knew what the verdict would be. Scopes was found guilty and fined $100. The *Baltimore Sun* posted bond, and Scopes was free to go. He left Dayton and teaching, went to graduate school, and became a geologist for petroleum companies. The Tennessee Supreme Court saved the state's face when it reversed the verdict on a technicality. The court, however, upheld the constitutionality of the Butler Act. It was not repealed until 1967. George Rappelyea left for New Orleans. No doubt some of his former neighbors thought he had gone to Sodom. Rappelyea said he felt isolated in Dayton, a feeling that may have been reinforced by local law officials. After the trial started, they ticketed him three times in six days for speeding.

SPA BEACH IN ST. PETERSBURG, FLORIDA (*St. Petersburg Times*)

Save for Bryan, the other principals continued their lives as before. Judge Raulston, however, did not survive the next election; Rhea County voters retired him. Bryan died five days after the trial ended. His death was probably due to the diabetes from which he suffered, its effects exacerbated by the humid heat of July and the exertions of the trial. The trial itself so darkened the image of antievolutionism that it lost what momentum it had had before the monkey trial; it declined rapidly and remained largely quiescent until its post-1960 revival.

The trial powerfully reinforced the image of the benighted South. Revelations of the South's deficiencies poured forth through the media: reactionary fundamentalism, antievolutionism, prohibition, lynchings, chain gangs, debt peonage, forced labor in lumber and turpentine camps, the Ku Klux Klan, convict leasing, shootings, hookworm, pellagra, venereal diseases, dietary deficiencies, poor whites, degenerate white politicians, systematic repression of impoverished blacks, labor strife, repressive mill villages, poor schools, inferior colleges and universities, a void in intellectual life and activity, and a general reactionary attitude that numbed the mind. So negative was the image of the South, one distant observer recalled, that people just knew that the South could produce "nothing but fundamentalism and intolerance." Though the image of the benighted South was distorted and tended to obscure the genuinely positive accomplishments of the region, it contained a great deal of truth. And if the South was benighted, the religious heritage it had brought with it into the twentieth century had helped substantially to make it so.

THE RELIGIOUS HERITAGE OF THE TWENTIETH-CENTURY SOUTH

Possibly because of its preoccupation with the Lost Cause, the South was slow to feel the impact of the intellectual and scientific ideas that challenged established religious beliefs in the North after 1860. The theory of evolution, biblical criticism, and historical theology, to cite only three of the most important areas of intellectual and scientific investigation, presented revolutionary threats. Evolutionary theory appeared to reduce the biblical account of human origins to a perceptive, perhaps inspiring fable. Biblical criticism—the study of the Bible as literature and as a historical document—also seemed to raise serious doubts about the authority of the Bible, or at least about some of its passages and episodes. Historical theology suggested that basic Christian doctrines and beliefs, such as the second coming of Christ, were produced or shaped by particular historical settings. Eventually members of the clergy and the laity were forced to respond to evolutionary theory, biblical criticism, and historical theology, either by rejecting them altogether, by accommodating to them, or by abandoning Christian doctrine.

In the South, the most powerful and vocal response was rejection. Biblical literalism, in particular, became a very widely held position and a pervasive force. Literalists adhered to the letter of Scripture and frequently ignored the historical setting or context of Bible passages. Scripture interpreted as written, literalists maintained, provided the ultimate authority for true religion and moral values.

Biblical literalists are not the same thing as fundamentalists, though the two are commonly confused. Products of a long, complicated, and often highly disputatious process that involved Christians in every region of the country, the fundamentalists got their name from the publication of their basic beliefs in a series titled *The Fundamentals: A Testimony of the Truth* (1910–1913). Fundamentalists believe that true Christians accept certain basic beliefs: the virgin birth of Christ; his physical resurrection; the atonement (reparation) of Christ, who was sinless, for the sins of human beings by his acceptance of the crucifixion; the inerrancy of the Bible in every detail; and the imminent physical second coming of Christ. Most biblical literalists do not accept and stress all of these doctrinal positions of the fundamentalists, though they usually accept most of them. Finally, biblical literalism was considerably more influential than fundamentalism in the South of the 1920s. Fundamentalism has enjoyed much greater influence in the region since 1950. Clearly, both biblical literalists and fundamentalists reject the theory of evolution as well as most of biblical criticism and historical theology.

This rejection dates from the late nineteenth century. At that time southern Protestantism generally took an anti-intellectual and antiscientific posture. The Baptist and Methodist majority simply ignored or were largely unaware of the intellectual and scientific revolution going on around them. They concentrated their energies on evangelism, public piety, and internal disputes, all with considerable success. The ranks of the Baptists and the Methodists continued to expand despite internal divisions. The Baptists did so well that they became the leading denomination in the South in the early twentieth century. Baptists and Methodists alike became increasingly militant about public piety, or proper public behavior with respect to gambling and card playing, alcoholic beverages and tobacco, dancing and theatergoing. Self-interest caused modifications in the code of public piety, however. Carolinians, for instance, had a forgiving attitude toward the production and consumption of tobacco. Baptists divided sharply among themselves, especially over the Landmark issue. The Landmark Baptists claimed that they were the only true Baptists—and indeed the only true Christians—because they were directly descended from the original Christian church, the church of the New Testament. Eventually these particular divisions subsided. Obviously, they did not hinder the growth of the denomination and may have actually helped as various Baptist groups competed to attract followers.

Not all southern Protestants maintained an anti-intellectual and antiscientific stance in the late nineteenth century. The Presbyterians, better educated in general and more inclined to stress theology, were also more aware of the intellectual and scientific revolution of their times. The Presbyterians' theological orthodoxy, however, insulated them from the challenges of evolutionary theory, biblical criticism, and historical theology. Robert Lewis Dabney led the defenders of orthodoxy in religion as well as with respect to the Lost Cause. Having an "apparently inexhaustible reservoir of rancor," a Dabney biographer noted, he fought the "Yankee" (northern) Presbyterian church first from Union Seminary in Richmond, where he was professor of theology, then from Austin, where he was professor of moral philosophy at the University of Texas and where he helped found a Presbyterian seminary. Dabney figured prominently in one of the few instances in which evolutionary theory made a conspicuous entry into the citadels of southern Presbyterianism before 1900. James Woodrow, uncle of Woodrow Wilson and profes-

BAPTISM, COTTON MILL VILLAGE (South Carolina State Museum)

sor at the Presbyterian seminary in Columbia, South Carolina, indicated a willingness in 1884 to accept the theory of evolution. Dabney assumed a leading role in
the efforts to dismiss Woodrow, which led to his ouster in 1888. Thus Presbyterians in the South adopted a conservative position on evolution similar to that
taken by Presbyterians in the North.

On the whole, Episcopalians in the South devoted more of their energies to
disputes over forms of worship and to ensuring that their seminaries enjoyed intellectual freedom than they devoted to doctrine. Few Episcopalians knew about
William Porcher Du Bose. Soon after returning from service in the Civil War, Du
Bose joined the faculty at the University of the South at Sewanee, Tennessee, and
dedicated the rest of his life to rebuilding it and its seminary and to teaching and
writing about theology. Noted for his pastoral concern and his brilliance, Du Bose
was one of America's most gifted theologians.

Like the Episcopalians, the Lutherans and the Catholics had little to do with
the theological issues that preoccupied most of the other denominations in the
South. Since the South attracted few immigrants after 1860, Lutherans and
Catholics in the South, unlike those elsewhere in the country, did not face serious
internal divisions occasioned by the arrival of large numbers of new immigrants
in their churches. Southern Lutherans, in contrast to the Baptists, Methodists, and
Presbyterians, tended to stress unity with other American Lutherans. Catholics in
the South were preoccupied primarily by support of the "Americanists," those
who said the Catholic church in America had to assimilate with the dominant society and could do so without sacrificing its basic principles. Edward Fitzgerald,
the bishop of Little Rock, was one of only two bishops who voted against the doctrine of papal infallibility at the First Vatican Council in 1870. Almost all of the few

Quakers in the postbellum South lived in North Carolina. In the late nineteenth century, Quakers lost much of their distinctiveness as they began to model themselves on their evangelical Protestant neighbors. This adaptation may have saved the southern Quakers from extinction, but the sense of something lost tempered their pleasure at seeing their numbers increase. Some Quakers wondered if they had compromised too much.

Similar concerns troubled white evangelical Protestants in the late nineteenth century. Those concerns, which never involved questions about the morality of Jim Crow, led to major disruptions among the South's largest Protestant denominations, a major religious revival, and a surge of growth among Christian sects. Those disruptions left changes that still shape the religious landscape of the South. Most of these disruptions were related to the growing social and economic divisions that came in the wake of urbanization and industrialization. Churches and their congregations, the styles of their worship and practices, and their beliefs reflected the social and economic positions of the believers. Religious dissidents decried the "lukewarm" religion of "birthright" Christians, or those who had been born into their faith rather than converted to it. In order to appeal to the "plain people," some evangelists and their supporters called for more informal and emotional worship, simpler creeds, and ministers with less formal training and presumably more spirituality.

The Holiness movement and Pentecostalism, which reshaped much of religion in the South after the mid-1880s, were the primary products of the religious discontent and revivalism of the late nineteenth century. By the time of the Scopes trial, the Holiness movement and Pentecostalism had so thoroughly penetrated southern Appalachia that the region cannot have been so culturally isolated as it is often thought to have been. When the Holiness movement and Pentecostalism entered southern Appalachia, they became part of the most religiously diverse portion of the South. Baptists especially had long abounded there in numbers and in kinds, though few were Southern Baptist and very few were black. Southern Appalachia had few blacks of any kind. The small Protestant religious bodies in southern Appalachia stressed demonstrative worship and practice. When preachers were moved by the spirit, their highly charged sermons often seemed unintelligible, at least to the uninitiated. Speaking in tongues was common. Foot washing was not uncommon. A very few practiced snake handling as a demonstration of the power of faith. Music was central to the experience: gospel songs, not hymns, sung to a wide variety of instruments, but not organs. No wonder Mencken and many others found the religion of southern Appalachia strange, even outrageous, and too often missed the spiritual yearning that permeated it.

Most of these sects, which were hardly limited to southern Appalachia, had broadly democratic qualities. Governing structures were weak or nonexistent. Participation in decisions was wide. Some groups had women preachers. Some welcomed blacks as members of their congregations. Almost all stressed public piety and the need for continuing spiritual experiences. Most saw little connection between religion and political issues. They did not accept the Social Gospel. They did, however, stress concern and care for one another. In doing so, they met very real needs, especially in light of the straitened economic circumstances that prevailed in most of southern Appalachia. Not a few of their adherents believed that the Kingdom of God was at hand and that one must be prepared for its coming. Thus they stressed evangelism and revivalism. Unfortunately, many of these sects were xenophobic and fanatic, inclined to see "the mark of the beast" on places such as Dayton.

Evangelicalism and revivalism were part of the religious heritage of the twentieth-century South. As the South became more urban and less rural and agricultural, however, camp meetings declined in number and importance. In their place came "protracted meetings," series of revival services usually held in local churches and usually held at night to accommodate urban and industrial populations. The Methodist Sam Jones became the leading urban revivalist of the late nineteenth-century South after his conversion and the ending of his dependence on the bottle. Billy Sunday more or less followed in Jones's footsteps. The former baseball player made a number of forays into the South, though he carried on most of his work as an evangelist elsewhere. J. Frank Norris, Baptist evangelist, attracted so many worshipers to his church in Fort Worth that by the early 1930s it was the largest Baptist church in the world, with 8,000 members. Norris attacked evolution in his characteristically controversial way. In the 1920s he managed to rid Texas of at least six professors whom he accused of finding Darwin's theory reasonable. How many others Norris intimidated is uncertain. He may have had a hand, directly or indirectly, in persuading Governor Miriam Ferguson to censor biology textbooks. As head of Texas's state textbook commission, the governor imposed a policy of approving only texts that made no mention of evolution.

The religious heritage of the South was expressed also in the growth of educational institutions in the late nineteenth century and especially in the early twentieth century. Major denominations built or expanded colleges, universities, and seminaries. The seminaries reflected the growth of professionalism among the clergy. Being moved by the spirit was still of critical importance, but ministers were also expected to be educated. The number of Bible colleges and institutes expanded to give advanced training to people who felt called to church work and were not ready for or could not afford regular college, university, or seminary training. Bible colleges and institutes also promised to be safe havens for people who thought that secular academic institutions were unsafe for the faithful.

CULTURE IN THE POSTBELLUM SOUTH

If cultural heritages are measured by the quality and quantity of creative literature, music, and art produced by a society, the South inherited less culture than religion from the late nineteenth century. If the definition of cultural heritage is broadened to include folk arts, then the South's cultural heritage is much more substantial, particularly with respect to music and, to a lesser extent, such literary forms as folk stories and tall tales. But few people paid attention to the cultures of southern Appalachia, poorer whites in general, or southern blacks. Those who did attend to them often caricatured them, and those caricatures unfortunately received wide circulation and were accepted as realistic representations.

MARDI GRAS, MOBILE, ALABAMA, 1920s (Erik Overbey Collection, University of
South Alabama Archives)

Lack of money and concentrations of population contributed to the small
number and low quality of museums, galleries, concert halls, orchestras, theaters,
and dance and theatrical companies in the South. Other deficiencies, however,
had perhaps a greater negative impact on cultural institutions. The South lacked a
strong tradition of support for cultural activities, colleges and universities of high
quality, or a good system of public education. Moreover, the cultural institutions
that had existed before the Civil War often suffered grievously from wartime casualties and destruction and from loss of morale. During the war, book publishers, newspapers, magazines, and literary journals became impoverished or collapsed altogether. Few recovered after the war. The novelist William Gilmore
Simms lost his home and his library of 11,000 volumes. "I could wish," he told a
friend, "to have some books sent me. . . . I have had nothing to read for 4 years."
During the war and for some years afterward the arts had to be neglected while
more immediate needs were served. Finally, the Civil War and Reconstruction
constricted artistic imagination in the South, placing it in service first to the Lost
Cause, then to the romanticized Old South. At least both, especially the magnolia-
scented Old South, had the virtue of being highly marketable.

Writing was probably the strongest cultural enterprise in the South in the half
century or so after the Civil War. Yet, while the body of literature from the South
of the late nineteenth century was notable, it was not remarkable. Sidney Lanier
earned an honored place among poets, though the Georgian's poor health and his
need to make a living limited his output. When local-color literature became a

nationwide literary movement in the 1880s, southern authors were well received. Their acceptance reflected the growing reconciliation between South and North: in the immediate postbellum years, southern writers had not been welcomed by northern readers. Local-color writers tried to take selective verbal photographs. They stressed things that were peculiar to particular American regions: physical settings and the speech, dress, mannerisms, and thought patterns of the people of America's various regions. Antebellum plantation blacks, Louisiana Creoles, white mountaineers, and poor whites or "crackers," "rednecks," and "hillbillies" became staples of this literary genre. Of the local-colorists of the South, the most important were George Washington Cable, Thomas Nelson Page, Joel Chandler Harris, Mary Noailles Murfree, Kate Chopin, and above all, Mark Twain.

Cable's *Old Creole Days* (1879), about life among Louisiana's French-speaking people, was widely acclaimed as the best treatment of Creole life ever published. Vocal critics in Louisiana complained that Cable demeaned the Creoles by the indelicacy of his descriptions. When the New Orleans native and former Confederate officer continued to publish stories and novels about Creoles and Louisiana and dared to mention such matters as miscegenation, his Louisiana readers angrily joined in attacks against him. Deeply attached to the South but unable to ignore its worst features, Cable called for more equitable treatment of blacks in *The Silent South* (1885). Thereafter, made to feel thoroughly unwelcome by southerners who believed he had betrayed them, Cable left to spend the rest of his long writing career in New England.

Grace King was one of the New Orleans readers who believed that Cable had slandered the South in general and Creoles in particular. She set out to correct him. In her earliest work, "Monsieur Motte," a story she later expanded into a book, King told a complex tale whose primary focus was the roles played by black and white women. King made a career of writing. She read and was influenced by French realists, maintained close ties with leading literary circles in the North, and engaged in research in this country and in Europe. She produced short stories, novels, and serious works of southern history. Scholars have recently called attention to *Tales of a Time and Place* (1892) and *Balcony Stories* (1893), collections of her short stories, and several of her histories, including *Creole Families of New Orleans* (1921).

Thomas Nelson Page, unlike Cable, did not offend, at least not most of the readers of his day. Nor, unlike King, did he tell complex stories. Page's significance lay primarily in his fictional treatment of the Lost Cause. His novels enjoyed great popularity and gave the Lost Cause wide circulation both inside and outside the South. In such books as *In Ole Virginia* (1887) and *The Burial of the Guns* (1894), Page presented an overly romanticized version of antebellum plantation life. He established a formula that was and continues to be extraordinarily attractive to readers: idyllic plantations where chivalry reigned in a world of gentlemen planters, demure charming ladies, and happy faithful slaves. His plantation world only remotely resembled the real plantation world of the antebellum South. Still, readers north and south liked Page, no matter what the critics said, and fictional descendants of Page's historical romances continue to attract droves of readers. More than a generation of southern children learned about the Lost Cause from Page's *Two Little Confederates* (1888) and *Among the Camps* (1891).

More creative and lasting than the work of Thomas Nelson Page were *Uncle Remus: His Songs and Sayings* (1880) and *Nights with Uncle Remus* (1883). These ingenious tales, more than the simple stories for children they appeared to be, were the creations of Joel Chandler Harris, a Georgian who was born and reared in slim circumstances and worked his way up in journalism from printer's apprentice to columnist. Harris had a wonderful sense of the sights, sounds, and thoughts of middle Georgia towns and plantations. As the aged Uncle Remus told stories to a white child in a heavy dialect, he wondered out loud about the mysteries of life and reflected on what he had seen and experienced in his long years. Harris mixed humor, shrewd insight, and animal tales to create literature of memorable quality. The stories of the triumphs of the rabbit (Brer Rabbit) over the fox (Brer Fox) drew upon an African folk tradition carried to America by the slaves. Harris probably was unaware of this African element in his stories, but he was quite well aware that his animal fables reflected the view of southern blacks that the weak but clever could win out over the strong. It has been argued that Harris also envisioned the Uncle Remus tales as a device for challenging Jim Crow.

MARY JOHNSTON, POPULAR ROMANCE NOVELIST AND ACTIVE SUPPORTER OF WOMEN'S SUFFRAGE (Virginia State Library and Archives)

Mary Noailles Murfree (also known by one of her pseudonyms, Charles Egbert Craddock) drew heavily on her eastern Tennessee background and summer vacations in Tennessee's Cumberland Mountains to write a series of stories and mountain romances. *In the Tennessee Mountains* (1884) was so successful that her subsequent works had an instant market, and eventually she was able to drop her male pseudonyms. Unfortunately, like Page, she created stereotypes that lasted despite their distortions. She did not understand the folk culture of the mountains, the complexity of the life there, or the speech patterns of the region. She viewed the mountains from an outsider's perspective. Her mountaineers were simple, quaint folk caught in a physical environment that controlled their lives, and their dialect owed more to her imagination than to her ear.

Kate Chopin, "one of the acknowledged belles of St. Louis," is remembered best for her portrayal of Louisiana Creole life in *Bayou Folk* (1894) and *A Night in Acadie* (1897) and for *The Awakening* (1899). The last is a story about a married woman who leaves her businessman husband and two children and later has an affair. An especially well-crafted and beautifully written novel, *The Awakening* touched sensitive nerves, scandalized Chopin's contemporaries, and ended her writing career. Neither readers nor publishers welcomed Chopin's feminist themes or her probing of the realities of the Victorian patriarchal family and the supposed bliss of orderly domesticity. Chopin's writing reflected a deep sense of dissatisfaction that was all but inevitable among educated women confined to the role of Southern Lady in a time of social and intellectual ferment. Only recently has Kate Chopin received the acclaim she deserves.

Despite the role assigned them, a number of southern women had successful careers as writers. Most avoided the risks that Chopin took. Their careers attested to their talents and their hard work and to the lack of occupational alternatives available to educated gifted women. Most of these women, like comparable men writers, left little writing of enduring quality. Mary Johnston enjoyed the greatest commercial success. *To Have and to Hold* (1900), a historical romance about early Jamestown, Virginia, became a record-breaking best-seller and was twice made into a movie. Johnston, who supported herself and her sisters with her writings, embraced a number of causes including women's suffrage, compulsory education, and protective legislation for women and children. Her partially autobiographical suffrage novel *Hager* (1913) dwelled on a theme that preoccupied Johnston: the importance of economic independence for women. Deviating from the rampant racism of her day, Johnston attacked lynching in "Nemesis," a short story that *Century* published in 1923. A year later, in *The Slave Ship,* she portrayed slavery as evil.

Charles Chesnutt, the first important black fiction writer in America, wanted, like Kate Chopin, to use local-color writing to send a message that few wanted to hear. His unpopular purpose was to attack the notion of the blissful life on the antebellum plantation and to assert the humanity and rights of blacks. The North Carolina native used black narrators to tell stories that were intended to show that masters sought to make as much money as possible at the expense of their slaves, who lived lives of drudgery and fear. But most readers did not discover Chesnutt's intent because they were so charmed by the dialect stories in his most widely known work, *The Conjure Woman* (1899). His later work expressed his aims more bluntly and not so creatively, and his earlier success in attracting readers was not repeated. Critics took aim at his awkward plotting and melodramatic writing, but similar flaws did not prevent the Reverend Thomas Dixon's crudely white-supremacist novels (*The Leopard's Spots* [1902] and *The Clansman* [1905]) from being very successful. Sutton Elbert Griggs, a black minister in Texas, challenged Dixon in *The Hindered Hand* (1902), one of several novels that added a black perspective to southern fiction. Unfortunately, Griggs's artistic skill was no better than Dixon's, and he had far fewer readers.

Mark Twain grew up in Hannibal, Missouri, a town on the Mississippi, and first achieved literary fame in the 1860s as a local-colorist and humorist of the West. But his greatest work was based on the South. In *Life on the Mississippi* (published serially as "Old Times on the Mississippi" in 1875 and as a book in 1883), Twain wrote a loosely constructed memoir based on his experiences as a river pilot. Then he pushed local-color writing to previously untried depths in *Adventures of Huckleberry Finn* (1884), a classic of American literature that is regarded as Twain's greatest book. In *Huckleberry Finn* he set idyllic scenes peopled by simple innocents, detailed daily events with delicious humor, and then lured unsuspecting readers into dark, almost nightmarish scenes to explore lost innocence, violence, slavery, religion and the religious, government, and socioeconomic class.

On the whole, however, southern writers of the late nineteenth century adopted largely uncritical attitudes toward their region and its people. Moreover, southern writings of the period seldom indicate that their authors knew about recent trends in literature, though realism and naturalism were major literary movements well before the end of the century. Some of them, however, gave indications of change. The *Sewanee Review* and the *South Atlantic Quarterly* were vehicles for critical analyses of southern writing and more generally of the region and its condition. The *Review* was quartered at the University of the South in Sewanee, the *Quarterly* at Trinity College (Duke University after 1924), indications of the role some universities in the South would play as critics of the region.

Still, a stronger uncritical mentality persisted in the turn-of-the-century South. Wilbur Cash later described it as the "savage ideal," which he traced to attitudes that developed in the slave South and persisted thereafter. In *The Mind of the South* (1941) Cash described that ideal as one

> whereunder dissent and variety are completely suppressed and men become, in all their attitudes, professions, and actions, virtual replicas of one another. Tolerance, in sum, was pretty well extinguished all along the line, and conformity made a nearly universal law. Criticism, analysis, detachment, all those activities and attitudes so necessary to the healthy development of any civilization, every one of them took on the aspect of high and aggravated treason.

Southern writers stepped gingerly into the twentieth century, generally avoiding frontal assaults on their culture of the type that had been going on in the North for some years. Ellen Glasgow led the way, usually with muffled words. Glasgow witnessed the disorder and division of the New South from her upper-middle-class neighborhood in Richmond and then wrote about the disarray she saw as part of her attempt to create "a well-rounded social record of Virginia," though she wrote as much about her own personality and her own inner disarray as that of the world around her. Glasgow's work was one of the early forays into realism in southern lit-

erature. Eventually realism would become one of the hallmarks of southern literature and an elemental force in what is called the southern literary renaissance. The
best of her books include *Barren Ground* (1925), a novel about the meager rewards of
small farms and the heavy toll they exacted from the people who worked them, and
They Stooped to Folly: A Comedy of Morals (1929), a novel about the morals and manners of the upwardly mobile in New South Richmond. *The Sheltered Life* (1932) is a
masterly novel about the determination of tidewater Virginians to preserve their self-
image and their innocence while they steadfastly ignore realities.

James Branch Cabell, Glasgow's neighbor and friend, produced a large and
varied body of writing. They and other writers in Richmond at the time gave the
city a very active and productive literary group from the end of World War I to the
late 1920s and a national reputation as a literary center. During Cabell's early
years, gossip swirled around him. For that, his mother was largely responsible:
she divorced her husband. Proper ladies did not get divorced, or smoke cigarettes
and drink cocktails, as she did. After her lover, a cousin, was murdered, rumors
spread that Cabell had done the deed. Marriage at thirty-four apparently calmed
his life. Though he had been an active writer before, thereafter he became much
more industrious. He had the good fortune to have one of his books (*Jurgen*
[1919]) declared indecent in 1920 by the New York Society for the Suppression of
Vice. He and his publisher won in court while benefiting from the publicity. However, he never attracted the wide following that Glasgow did.

Cabell's writing confused and bewildered many people who attempted to
read it. He mixed realism, romanticism, and naturalism in a highly complex style.
At the heart of his work lay paradox or contradiction. Human beings need ideals
and dreams, yet such needs mislead the dreamers because they are unattainable.
He loved legend and myth and used both in his major work, the eighteen-volume
Biography of Manuel (1927–1930), which pulled together some of his earlier works
and expanded upon them in a work that ranged over seven centuries, from an
imaginary medieval land to contemporary Richmond. Late in his life he appeased
some people in his native city and state by paying his respects to General Robert
E. Lee and Virginia in *Let Me Lie* (1951). Even then, he could not resist a pun.
Cabell received enough critical acclaim, including that of Mencken, to have a
national reputation. Scholars, however, have generally neglected him; the complexity of Cabell's work may have deterred them.

The War Within

In 1917, when Mencken launched his famous attack on the South as the "Sahara of
the Bozart" (beaux arts), the best work of Glasgow and Cabell had not yet appeared, and no other southern authors of the stature they would achieve were
being published. Southern culture seemed locked in pious contemplation of the
Old South and in thrall to the uncritical mentality of the New South. Mencken offered his own explanation for the South's cultural torpor. The South, he said, had
fallen into cultural darkness after the Civil War because semiliterate Baptist and
Methodist clergymen had achieved dominance in southern religion, culture, and
politics. Mencken pictured the South as an "awe-inspiring blank" where "a poet

is now almost as rare as an oboe-player, a drypoint etcher or a metaphysician." Of "critics, . . . composers, painters, sculptors, architects, . . . there is not even a bad one between the Potomac mud-flats and the Gulf. Nor an historian . . . sociologist . . . philosopher . . . theologian . . . [or] scientist." Though Mencken's charges were exaggerated, they were largely valid.

Mencken's "Sahara of the Bozart" essay helped initiate a war within elite cultural circles in the South in the 1920s. When the smoke cleared around 1930, the Old South was no longer an object of unquestioning worship in intellectual and academic circles. Nor were the New South assurances of orderly progress toward a better life under the leadership of captains of industry accepted with only minor reservations. The war within helped produce the southern literary renaissance and southern regionalism, whose impact extended from the arts to economics and politics.

Mencken fired his barrage from the periphery of the South, Baltimore. Other critics shot from closer range. Gerald W. Johnson of the *Greensboro (N.C.) Daily News* produced a steady stream of clear, pointed editorials flavored by a "keen and relentless self-criticism" that Johnson believed the South desperately needed. In succeeding years, other journalists followed Johnson's lead. William Henry Skaggs, former mayor of Talladega and leader of Alabama's Populists, published *The Southern Oligarchy: An Appeal in Behalf of the Silent Masses of Our Country against the Despotic Rule of the Few* (1924). Skaggs let his fury get the best of him; it alienated readers who might have profited from his perceptive analysis and rich collection of data. That same year the historian Frank Tannenbaum, who was not a native of the region, explored the Klan, cotton mill workers and mill villages, and race relations in *Darker Phases of the South.*

Such attacks inspired others to race to the defense, a posture in which southerners all too often found themselves. Most defenders failed miserably. They hurled mud at Mencken in particular. He sneered his replies. Virginius Dabney of the *Richmond Times-Dispatch* offered a partially successful argument for the persistence of southern liberalism from Thomas Jefferson on in his *Liberalism in the South*. Reacting strongly to the Scopes trial, Edwin Mims, a Vanderbilt professor, attempted in *The Advancing South* to show that southerners who favored freedom of thought, self-criticism, and forward thinking were gaining ground on their opponents.

Dabney and Mims claimed too much, but they had a point. As should have been obvious even to casual observers, the South hardly had an exclusive hold on xenophobia in the United States during World War I and the years that followed. Nor was the South blindly attempting to restore the Old South. Whatever its limitations, the business progressivism that was predominant in the 1920s was not reactionary, though it was overly materialistic. And the reformist progressives remained active, though they were less vocal and less effective than they had been.

Stung by the surge of interracial violence during and immediately after World War I, small groups of southern whites and blacks had taken the small but bold step of forming the Commission on Interracial Cooperation in 1919. The commission contributed to efforts that eventually led to profound changes in southern race relations. The clergy, Mencken's favorite target, provided much of the leadership of the commission. Clergy also figured prominently in efforts to limit antievolutionism and then force it to retreat in every southern state.

KLAN PARADE, MONTGOMERY, ALABAMA, 1921 (Collection of the Alabama
State Department of Archives and History)

The Young Men's Christian Association (YMCA) and the Young Women's
Christian Association (YWCA) continued to pursue programs to study and relieve social problems. Women took particularly active parts in reform efforts in
the 1920s. Drawing upon experience and confidence gained from their work in
missionary societies, the Woman's Christian Temperance Union, women's clubs,
the YWCA, and the suffragist movement, women took on a wide range of issues:
maternal and infant health, child care and child labor, working women, industrial
relations, race relations and the conditions of blacks, and political reforms, especially the abolition of poll taxes. The YWCA directed particular attention to industrial relations. In addition to a program of legislation, the YWCA ran programs to
educate college women about industrial labor and held conferences for women
factory workers. Some of the women affiliated with the Southern School for
Women Workers in Industry later became labor union activists, while others became recognized authorities on industrial relations. In 1930 churchwomen from
the rural and small-town South, led by Jessie Daniel Ames, founded the Association of Southern Women for the Prevention of Lynching. The most lasting
achievement of women reformers in the 1920s may have been the part they
played in the effort to persuade business and political leaders as well as the public
that government had a continuing responsibility for public welfare.

Still, defenders of the culture of the South in the 1920s could win only skir-
mishes. Arts in the South, like much else in the elite culture of the region, remained
tied to the dead past. And the New South had a host of grave social, economic, and
political deficiencies. Elite culture in the South remained trapped in Victorianism as
late as the 1920s, long after cultural elites elsewhere in the country had embraced

"modernism." Not even Ellen Glasgow could bring herself fully, as she said, to "encounter reality." She remained a Victorian, though one in transition.

Victorianism assumed that the world was divided into separate compartments, the "civilized" and the "savage." Victorians believed that an educated, cultured upper class or cultural aristocracy presided over this bipolar world. The upper class was responsible for controlling the "savage" elements or "lower orders," whose ranks included the poor, factory workers, landless farmers, transients, the fallen, and similar sorts. The cultured "betters" could handle their formidable task because, Victorians assumed, the civilized were rational. Reason was the guiding force in the Victorian world. The civilized, at least civilized men, were presumed to be rational and able to control themselves and the world around them. Southern Victorianism had its peculiar regional twist. Slaveholding planters were still believed to have been a gentlemanly aristocracy who had held slaves, poor whites, and money-hungry Yankees in check until the defeat of the South in the Civil War. After the war, large landholders and New South industrializers and urbanizers assumed the role of the defeated slaveholding aristocracy and set the South on a progressive course.

Modernism assaulted the rock on which Victorianism was built. Drawing upon the insights of Darwinian biology and Freudian psychology, modernism rejected the idea that there was a sharp dichotomy between the civilized and the savage and the assumption that anyone was altogether rational. Thus the slave owner and the slave, the factory owner and factory worker shared a common humanity. Other major intellectual developments in the nineteenth century, such as Marxian social analysis and cultural anthropology, shaped and fueled the modernist inclination to analyze and to challenge basic institutions and practices.

Modernism sank deep roots in the South almost a generation after it had taken hold elsewhere in American culture. Once the South discovered it, it dealt mortal blows to piety toward the Old South and unquestioning praise for the New South. Nowhere was this changed state of affairs clearer than in the southern literary renaissance.

THE SOUTHERN LITERARY RENAISSANCE

Beginning in the 1920s, the quality, range, and quantity of southern literature soared; for the next forty years, the South dominated the American literary scene. The southern literary renaissance was so extensive that it is impossible here to do more than sketch its basic outlines and major figures. The most important writers of this renaissance were John Crowe Ransom, Allen Tate, Robert Penn Warren, Donald Davidson, Andrew Lytle, Caroline Gordon, Thomas Wolfe, William Faulkner, Cleanth Brooks, Katherine Anne Porter, Carson McCullers, Eudora Welty, Flannery O'Connor, and Tennessee Williams.

Ransom, Tate, Davidson, and Warren were part of a group called the Fugitives—from *The Fugitive*, a literary magazine they helped to start in 1922. Natives of Kentucky and Tennessee, they clustered in and around the English department of Vanderbilt University in Nashville, a city that could accurately boast of being a leader in higher education. The Fugitives became a very influential

group in American literary history. They wanted to break new ground in literature and, at least initially, to dissociate themselves from their region in general
and from its literary conventions. They found the worship of the Old South and
the hymns to the New South equally repellent. In their poetry and their literary
criticism, they stressed complexities in form, content, and language that appeared to be opaque and even completely meaningless to casual readers. They
succeeded wonderfully in their efforts to break new ground in literature. Eventually some of the Fugitives changed course and embraced their region, but not
with blind or stultifying affection.

In 1930 Ransom, Tate, and Warren, along with other southern authors and
academics, wrote *I'll Take My Stand: The South and the Agrarian Tradition.* Prompted
in part by their reaction to the Scopes trial, they called for a reassertion of past values to offset the materialism of the New South and the rationalism and skepticism
of Mencken and Darrow. Those past values, they contended, included religion
and faith, but they rejected the rigid religious stand taken by most evangelical
Protestants. Convinced that industrialization and urbanization undermined
human values and personal dignity, the Agrarians, as they came to be known,
called for a return to the land. Theirs was a perceptive if shortsighted view of the
South of their day—and a lament. As most of the people who worked the soil of
the South—something the Agrarians had not done—knew, the future of the great
majority of southerners did not lie in the land. But *I'll Take My Stand* was a striking
document and triggered wide debate about the nature and future of the region.
Thus the Agrarians helped reinforce and expand the growing self-awareness and
self-examination that were powerful forces in the South after the mid-1920s. They
served as catalysts, as Mencken and the Scopes trial had done.

Andrew Lytle, one of the contributors to *I'll Take My Stand,* became a major
novelist whose best work was about the central role of the family in the South. *The
Long Night* (1936) is set in the antebellum South and revolves around the powerful
force of family loyalty and blood revenge. Lytle's best novel, *The Velvet Horn*
(1957), traces the destruction that a family brings upon itself when, during Reconstruction, it withdraws into obsessive isolation. Lytle's memoir/chronicle, *A Wake
for the Living* (1975), has received high praise. Caroline Gordon, whose husband
was Allen Tate, was an Agrarian, though she was not a contributor to *I'll Take My
Stand.* Gordon used memories from her family and her region for material for several novels. *Penhally* (1931) is the story of an antebellum Kentucky dynasty that
disintegrates when it loses its sense of mutual dependence and its own destructive character flaws gain dominance. *None Shall Look Back* (1937) has been praised
as possibly the best southern novel ever written about the Civil War experience.

Some writers outside Agrarian circles also became part of the growing self-
examination of the region as part of their own maturation. Thomas Wolfe was
one of those. Wolfe's reputation rests essentially on *Look Homeward, Angel,* a
highly autobiographical novel about a young man's coming of age in Altamont,
North Carolina (the thinly disguised Asheville, Wolfe's home). Wolfe described
Asheville, the surrounding mountains, and the people in rich, evocative detail
that did not sharply differentiate fact from fiction. Many people in Asheville, but
not his family, resented the book, though it received wide critical and popular acclaim and made Wolfe famous. That resentment was understandable, given the

often unflattering portrayals in the novel. But too many readers missed a crucial point: though the book's protagonist was eager to get away from his hometown, he was anxious to take it with him, anxious not to lose his roots. Like the Agrarians, Wolfe could not or would not tear himself away from his southern past. Seven years after his masterpiece was published and Wolfe had become an international literary celebrity, Asheville welcomed him home with open arms. Death at thirty-seven ended a promising career.

The same year that *Look Homeward, Angel* appeared (1929), William Faulkner published *Sartoris*, the first of his Yoknapatawpha County novels, which were only a part, though a substantial part, of the writing he published between 1922 and 1962. Faulkner's fictional county and its inhabitants bore a strong resemblance to the rural counties and peoples, past and present, of Faulkner's home state, Mississippi. The county had old plantations in various states of repair, some still occupied by old families. Other families had left their plantations and moved to town to run stores, banks, and various businesses. Older families found themselves displaced by ambitious, driven seekers of money and power who had once

WILLIAM FAULKNER (The Bettmann Archive)

lived scruffier lives on the marginal lands of the county. Poorer whites farmed much of the county, some as landowners, most as renters. Below them were the white trash, who drifted about the county without visible means of support and only occasionally surfaced to be condescendingly noticed and dismissed. Blacks helped shape the life and texture of the county as farmers, farmworkers, domestics, and occasional laborers. They, Faulkner suggested, had a clearer understanding of the people and the life of Yoknapatawpha County than did most whites.

But Faulkner's Yoknapatawpha novels ranged far beyond history and social commentary. His writing has been called "southern Gothic" because it explores in depth the horrors of life: cancerous ambition, violence, self-destruction, mental incapacity, insanity, stunted lives, and poisonous race relations. He often used a convoluted, highly repetitive writing style. Faulkner was one of the most perceptive observers of the South and a literary genius. In 1950 he was awarded the Nobel Prize for literature. Throughout his work, he made extensive use of the region to which he was deeply attached, even while he exposed the dark, even demonic aspects of its people and its life.

Cleanth Brooks established himself as one of the foremost figures in modern literary criticism. His critical analysis of Faulkner is considered to be the best analysis of Faulkner ever done. Legions of colleges and high school students have been influenced by his textbooks about understanding and analyzing poetry, fiction, and drama. Katherine Anne Porter, a Texan, used materials drawn from the South and Southwest, a biting sardonic wit, and an extraordinarily economical style to create some of the finest short stories in American fiction. Carson McCullers also found material for her work close by—from places like Columbus, Georgia, where she grew up, and especially from personal relationships. The latter had a gothic quality like much of her writing. McCullers is best remembered for *The Heart Is a Lonely Hunter* (1940) and *The Member of the Wedding* (1946), which was adapted into a highly successful play and movie. Eudora Welty's exquisitely balanced, evocative novels and short stories have attracted a wide audience and much critical acclaim. *Delta Wedding,* set in her native Mississippi, is a subtle blend of memory, the sense of tradition, and divergent perspectives as a family prepares for a wedding on its plantation in 1923. Flannery O'Connor used rural middle Georgia as Welty used Mississippi for the settings and characters of her stories and novels. In *A Good Man Is Hard to Find* (1955) and *Everything That Rises Must Converge* (1965), collections of her stories, and in her novels, *Wise Blood* (1952) and *The Violent Bear It Away* (1960), O'Connor powerfully combined literary realism and a religious perspective that was consistently orthodox but expressed in unconventional terms. Tennessee Williams, born in Mississippi and reared in St. Louis, was one of the best playwrights America has produced. *The Glass Menagerie* (1944) and *A Streetcar Named Desire* (1947) are the best of a very substantial body of work.

Mencken's Sahara had blossomed. The blossoming was obvious as early as the late 1920s, and Mencken happily acknowledged the literary outburst, whose dimensions and duration neither he nor anyone else could have anticipated. Southern writers had deliberately and decisively broken with the Victorian genteel tradition and embraced modernism. In doing so, they cast a withering, introspective eye on the South without the sneers and caricatures of Mencken. They held that it was possible to examine one's region honestly and critically without being a traitor to one's homeland. Generally, that was a novel idea in the South in the 1920s, and not always a welcome one. Moreover, these writers helped set the stage for the conscious regional self-examination and the determination to change the South, which became major forces in the late 1920s and for years thereafter.

The critical attitudes of the 1920s carried over to blacks. The blacks in Faulkner's work were not the shuffling, aged, deferential but wise denizens of happy slave times. Nor were those in the writing of DuBose Heyward, Julia Peterkin, and Jean Toomer. Heyward caught the vibrancy and resilience of lower-class black life in Charleston, South Carolina, in *Porgy* (1925) and in Charleston and New York City in *Mamba's Daughters* (1929). Ira and George Gershwin used *Porgy* as the base for their opera *Porgy and Bess* (1929), a classic of American musical theater. Peterkin's work paralleled Heyward's. She tried to convey a faithful, moving picture of black life from what she knew from living on a plantation in the South Carolina low country. The heroine of Peterkin's *Scarlet Sister Mary* (1928) is interesting, combative, sensuous, and no simple heart-of-gold mammy. Her story won a Pulitzer prize for Peterkin.

Jean Toomer inspired his fellow black writers to explore their roots more fully and to express their feelings more candidly and less self-consciously. He is best remembered for *Cane* (1923), a collection of poems, vignettes, and stories. A native of Washington, D.C., Toomer was the grandson of P. B. S. Pinchback, who served as acting governor of Louisiana during Reconstruction. Visits to rural Georgia, where his family lived, gave Toomer much of the material and many of the ideas for *Cane*. Toomer's work fit with the New Negro movement and Harlem renaissance of the 1920s, which was centered in New York but reverberated throughout the South. One aspect of the Harlem renaissance that attracted a wide audience among blacks and whites was its music: jazz and blues. These African American creations are two of the most significant original and influential musical traditions ever created by Americans. (See chapter 28.)

SOUTHERN REGIONALISM IN THE 1920s AND 1930s

The Scopes trial had heightened the image of the benighted South, an isolated, stagnant cultural backwater. Whatever else one might have concluded about the South five years later, culturally it was alive. One aspect of that vitality was southern regionalism, or a deep commitment to regional self-examination and reform. Numerous southern writers and journalists, scholars, intellectuals, and activists became heavily involved in southern regionalism after the early 1920s. Never before had criticisms from within the South been so thorough and so sweeping. Southern regionalists defended their analyses as a necessary prelude to the change that the South needed to seek.

Southern regionalism found institutional support in the 1920s and 1930s in several universities, especially the University of North Carolina, which was then moving quickly to become a leading American university. Howard Washington Odum stood at the center of that development. He established or helped to establish the Department of Sociology, first of its kind in the South, the Institute for Research in the Social Sciences, the *Journal of Social Forces,* and the University of North Carolina Press, all of which became major forces in the South's self-examination.

The University of North Carolina Press published a steady stream of critical assessments of the South, some of which remain crucial to an understanding of the region. These works include, to name only a few, Rupert B. Vance's *Human Factors in Cotton Culture: A Study of the Social Geography of the American South* (1929) and *Human Geography of the South* (1932), Odum's *Southern Regions of the United States* (1936), Harriet L. Herring's *Welfare Work in Mill Villages* (1929), Arthur Franklin Raper's *Tragedy of Lynching* (1933) and *Preface to Peasantry* (1936), and *The Collapse of Cotton Tenancy* (1936) by Charles S. Johnson, Edwin Embree, and Will Alexander. Presiding over these and numerous other studies was the director of the University of North Carolina Press, William Terry Couch, who was only twenty-four when he took the job. Under him the press became the single most important means of bringing the work of the South's social critics before the public. During the interwar decades, the press became a major cultural force, a singular achievement for a university press. Couch also edited two valuable works: *Culture in the South* (1935), a model collection of essays on numerous facets of life and culture in the region, and *These Are Our Lives* (1939), a collection of oral histories of ordinary southerners and a pioneer among oral histories. The latter book grew out of Couch's strongly negative reaction to Erskine Caldwell's two best-selling novels, *Tobacco Road* (1932) and *God's Little Acre* (1933). Couch perceptively criticized their overdrawn picture of poor whites and the assumption that Caldwell's characters were typical southern whites. But Caldwell, a Georgian, was closer to the mark in his portrayal of the South's poorest whites than Couch acknowledged.

Caldwell later worked with the photographer Margaret Bourke-White to produce a famous photo-documentary on southern tenant farmers: *You Have Seen Their Faces* (1937). Widely praised now, though little noted at the time, was the Tennessean James Agee's study of white tenant farmers in Alabama, *Let Us Now Praise Famous Men* (1941), which included photographs by Walker Evans. Evans's work soon came to be recognized as classic, but the ironically titled book was a commercial failure, largely because of Agee's convoluted, introspective prose. In the 1960s, however, it was reissued to critical acclaim.

Other writers shared Erskine Caldwell's interest in southern industrial workers. The famous textile strike of 1929 in Gastonia particularly stimulated several "proletarian novelists," as they were called, to write novels with a social message about industrial workers. Unfortunately, the message overshadowed the plots and characters. They and numerous other writers who were part of the southern literary renaissance attacked southern racism. Their attacks were usually oblique, but not Lillian Smith's. In *Strange Fruit* (1944) Smith struck at southern racism's most sensitive nerve, interracial love. In this novel and by other means she took a forthright stance against Jim Crow. She was a rare person for her day: a native white southerner who openly and explicitly challenged the racial caste system of the South.

The most widely read and noted product of the self-examination encouraged by southern regionalism was Wilbur Cash's *Mind of the South*. More about the temperament and character of the South than about its mind, the book combined history, insight, and dazzling prose to argue that southerners, in the Old and New South, were inclined to rampant hedonism and Puritan guilt and disinclined to reflection and abstract thought. The South was

> proud, brave, honorable by its lights, courteous, personally generous, loyal, swift to act, often too swift, [and was characterized by] violence, intolerance, aversion and suspicion toward new ideas, an incapacity for analysis, . . . exaggerated individualism and a too narrow concept of social responsibility, attachment to fictions and false values, above all too great an attachment to racial values and a tendency to justify cruelty and injustice in the name of those values.

Cash's book enraged many readers, but it became a primer for southerners who were determined to shake the ghosts of the past and build a modern South. For a generation after its publication, it also had a unique influence on students of southern history.

The book came too late, however, to influence people who believed that the depression of the 1930s and the New Deal of President Franklin Roosevelt offered unusual opportunities to realize urgently needed changes in the South. Some of them were actively involved in the Roosevelt administration, in Congress, and elsewhere in shaping economic policy for the South. Their efforts and thinking were reflected in a major document of the 1930s, *Report of the Economic Conditions of the South*, which opened with the memorable statement: "The South [is] . . . the Nation's No. 1 economic problem." A number of these southern New Deal liberals formed an organization, the Southern Conference for Human Welfare (SCHW), in 1938 to work to transform the South. It attracted important political leaders, labor union activists, journalists, and academicians. "For the first time in the history of the region . . . the lonely Southern liberals met in great numbers—actually more than twelve hundred." Confronted by strong opposition and deeply troubled by internal divisions between liberals and radicals, the SCHW did more talking than acting. Its most important work was its campaign to abolish the poll tax. That campaign contributed to growing dissatisfaction with the tax, a major barrier to voting by low-income whites as well as blacks. Increasingly subject in the 1940s to charges that it was under communist influence and faced with declining interest, the SCHW disbanded in 1948.

The SCHW was also beset by allegations that it favored racial equality. Actually, it stepped lightly whenever it approached Jim Crow, though it did have a biracial membership, then a virtually unheard-of violation of racial etiquette. Few southern white liberals questioned Jim Crow. Instead, they supported efforts to rid the South of its worst racial excesses and to make "separate but equal" a reality—an advanced position at the time. Arthur Raper took exception to this approach. He described southern race relations in terms that accurately reflected its pathology and strongly implied that "separate but equal" did not and could not work. Raper assisted in a major study of race relations and the condition of American blacks that was published as *An American Dilemma: The Negro Problem and Modern Democracy*. Published in 1944, it is the single most important book ever written about American race relations, a source and stimulus for the civil rights revolution in the post–World War II South.

Blacks, of course, had long been critics of the South. The most important during the interwar decades was probably W. E. B. Du Bois. Certainly he was the most vocal. Returning to Atlanta University in 1934 after his long tenure as editor of *Crisis*, the journal of the National Association for the Advancement of Colored People, Du Bois resumed his career as scholar and teacher while remaining a vigorous critic of American race relations, of white supremacy and black subordination and submissiveness. In 1935 he published *Black Reconstruction in America*, an important revisionist interpretation of Reconstruction. Richard Wright, however, reached a wider audience. A survivor of poverty and blatant racial discrimination, Wright followed a migratory pattern not unlike that of other Mississippi blacks. He drifted to Memphis, got a series of jobs there when he was fifteen, and saved enough to move on to Chicago. He read whenever and whatever he could, caught on with the Federal Writers' Project, a New Deal program, and published his *Uncle Tom's Children* in 1938. Two years later came *Native Son*, his best work and the one that established his reputation as a major writer. Though it was set in Chicago, *Native Son* drew heavily on Wright's experiences in the South. In 1945 he used those experiences much more explicitly in *Black Boy: A Record of Childhood and Youth*, a blunt revelation of black life in the South. It suggested something that by the end of World War II would become increasingly obvious: blacks were no longer willing to submit to Jim Crow, and open challenges to the system were likely to increase.

GONE WITH THE WIND

The critical analyses of the southern literary renaissance and southern regionalism disturbed and often angered many southerners. Stark Young and Margaret Mitchell, for instance, reacted with memorable novels set in the plantation South. Young, one of the authors of *I'll Take My Stand*, used Mississippi legends and his family's history to reassert the values of the agrarian South in a very popular novel, *So Red the Rose* (1934). Similar motives prompted Mitchell, a former newspaper reporter and housewife. *Gone with the Wind*, published in 1936, enjoyed instant enormous success. Determined to show a South blissfully free of the grotesqueries described by Faulkner and Caldwell, Mitchell set her novel in the South of sumptuous antebellum cotton plantations, the Civil War, and Reconstruction. It combined historical fact and myth, powerful characters, and a compelling story of the South from antebellum splendor to crushing defeat to determined efforts to recover. The public, south and north, snapped up copies of *Gone with the Wind*. Within six months of its publication, a million copies were sold. Its sales now exceed 21 million. The cultural elite may have accepted modernism and cast aside the plantation myth, but not the mass public.

Gone with the Wind won a Pulitzer prize and was turned into the most successful movie ever produced and probably the most widely seen movie ever made. The novel and the movie, which had a lavish premiere in Atlanta in 1939, obviously struck a responsive note in a nation eager to recover from the Great Depression, its worst domestic crisis since the Civil War. That crisis did not end until the early 1940s, more than two years after World War II had begun. With the end of the Depression, the sense of the South as benighted faded. The loss of that sense was not, however, a product of economic change alone. It was also a product of conscious regional self-examination, determination to engage in major self-reform, and the southern literary renaissance, which had poured out its riches over more than two decades and would continue to do so for twenty more years.

Map Essay

The Changing South: People and Cotton

❖

Population changes in the South mirror the profound changes that have occurred in the region since the Civil War, especially since 1880. Initially, and for some years thereafter, the westward drift of the population of the South continued. Since 1900 the economic growth in the oil and gas states, in Florida, along the piedmont, in the Chesapeake Bay region, and in the resurgent urban centers of the Middle South, such as Nashville and Memphis, have reshaped the southern landscape into an area that is highly urban and sometimes metropolitan. As the population maps indicate, the South was much more prosperous after 1930 than it was before 1930. Strong economic growth continued in much of the region in the 1990s.

For many years, that prosperity did not include blacks, who over the years left the region in hopes of better opportunities and greater safety and personal dignity elsewhere. Black out-migration, then white in-migration after 1955 largely account for the South having proportionately fewer blacks today than at any time since the seventeenth century. However, since the mid-1970s, black out-migration has slowed and is now exceeded by black in-migration.

The prevalence of cotton in 1930 and its disappearance or decline to secondary importance in the rural South by 1959 also graphically reflect the transformation of the South since the Great Depression. Cotton is hardly the whole story of the South, or even of southern agriculture, but cotton is one telling barometer of the history of the South. The recent revival of cotton production in parts of the South is based upon capital intensive agriculture rather than the labor intensive agriculture that once prevailed in the South.

POPULATION OF SOUTHERN URBAN AREAS, 2000

Richmond ●
Norfolk ■
Raleigh
Greensboro ■
Charlotte ■
Greenville ■
Columbia ▲
Charleston ▲
Savannah ✦
Jacksonville ■
Orlando ■
Fort Lauderdale
Miami ●
Lexington ✦
Louisville ■
Knoxville ▲
Chattanooga
Atlanta ●
Nashville ■
Memphis
Birmingham
Montgomery ■
Mobile
Jackson
Little Rock ▲
Baton Rouge ▲
New Orleans ●
Tulsa ■
Oklahoma City ■
Dallas ●
Houston ●
Austin ■
San Antonio ■
El Paso ■

● 3,000,000 to 4,000,000
■ 1,000,000 to 2,000,000
▲ 500,000 to 900,000
✦ 200,000 to 480,000

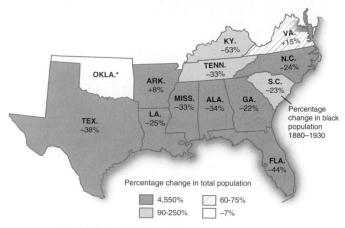

*Attained statehood in 1907; 1930 population was 2.4 million.

POPULATION CHANGES, 1880–1930

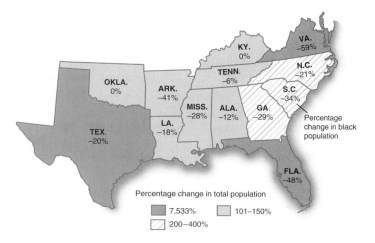

POPULATION CHANGES, 1930–1990

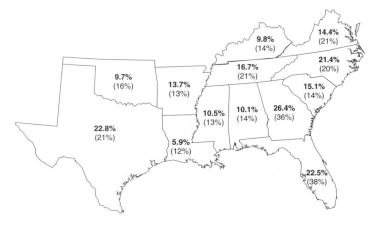

BLACK POPULATION CHANGES, 1990–2000

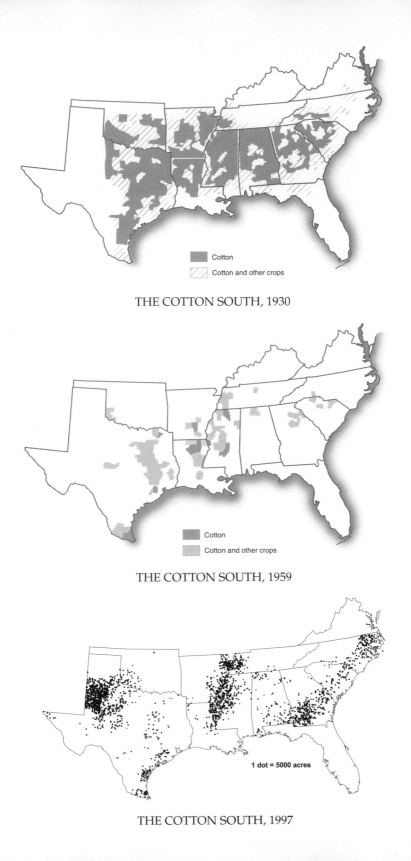

THE COTTON SOUTH, 1930

Cotton
Cotton and other crops

THE COTTON SOUTH, 1959

Cotton
Cotton and other crops

1 dot = 5000 acres

THE COTTON SOUTH, 1997

25

The Emergence of the Modern South, 1930–1945

❖

*I*n 1937, Brian and Mary Sue Smith left Portland, Texas, a town of perhaps 500 near Corpus Christi, after they lost their home and business during the Depression. They moved to Blanco County, fifty miles west of Austin, in the hill country of Texas. Though it had thin soil and slight rainfall, it "was the only place where land was cheap enough so we could buy a farm." The Smiths probably shook hands that year with twenty-eight-year-old Lyndon Baines Johnson, who was running for Congress in a special election. A man of great ambition and enormous energy, Johnson "pressed the flesh" with virtually every voter in Blanco County and with a majority of the other voters in the ten-county, 140-mile-wide Tenth Congressional District.

A lot more was involved here, however, than shaking hands and vote-getting. The Depression, which began in 1929, struck with such ferocity that it drove thousands back to the land. So many went back that the 1930s became the first decade in American history in which more people migrated to the countryside than to the cities. So desperate were people in the South that they fled to the land despite a 60 percent decline in farm incomes from 1929 to 1932.

Lyndon Johnson was desperate, too. Propelled by his ambition and his personal inclinations and circumstances, he left the hill country to pursue political power and personal fortune. Johnson went to Washington, D.C.—not to Austin, where his father had once been a prominent state legislator—in 1931. He had a job in Washington—in politics, which he loved, and away from the limited opportunities the hill country offered.

Johnson served as a secretary to a congressman (1931–1935), New Deal administrator (1935–1937), congressman (1937–1949), U.S. senator (1949–1960), vice president (1961–1963), and president (1963–1968). In 1964 he became only the second southerner to be elected president since 1848. Woodrow Wilson was the first, and Wilson initially achieved political prominence outside the South, when he was elected governor of New Jersey. Lyndon Johnson's political career and that of the modern South became intertwined; his career mirrored the evolution and transformation of the American South after the 1930s.

In 1937, however, Johnson concerned himself with present, not future, prospects. He told voters in the hill country what the New Deal had done for them and what it would do for them. The government, for instance, could help farmers obtain electricity, without which modern living and farming were impossible. That message must have struck a responsive note: in 1930 less than 5 percent of the farms in the South had electricity, compared with more than 14 percent nationally, 45 percent in New England, 33 percent in the middle Atlantic states, 22 percent in the Midwest, and 57 percent in the Pacific states. Fewer than 2 in 100 farms in Mississippi and fewer than 3 in 100 in Alabama, Arkansas, and Louisiana had electricity. Mary Sue Smith remembered that "moving from Portland into the Hill Country was like moving from the twentieth century back into the Middle Ages."

Russell Baker, author and noted columnist with the *New York Times*, recalled from his childhood in the settlement of Morrisonville in northern Virginia that

my mother and grandmother kept house very much as women did before the Civil War. Their lives were hard, endless, dirty labor. They had no electricity, gas, plumbing, or central heating. No refrigerator, no radio, no telephone, no automatic laundry, no vacuum cleaner. Lacking indoor toilets, they had to empty, scour, and fumigate each morning the noisome slop jars which sat in bedrooms during the night.

For baths, laundry, and dishwashing, they hauled buckets of water from a spring at the foot of a hill. To heat it, they chopped kindling to fire their wood stoves. They boiled laundry in tubs, scrubbed it on washboards until knuckles were raw, and wrung it out by hand. Ironing was a business of lifting heavy metal weights heated on the stove top.

They scrubbed floors on hands and knees, thrashed rugs with carpet beaters, killed and plucked their own chickens, baked bread and pastries, grew and canned their own vegetables, patched the family's clothing on treadle-operated sewing machines, deloused the chicken coops, preserved fruits, picked potato bugs and tomato worms to protect their garden crop, darned stockings, made jelly and relishes, rose before men to start the stove for breakfast and pack lunch pails, polished the chimneys of kerosene lamps, and even found time to tend the geraniums, hollyhocks, nasturtiums, dahlias, and peonies that grew around every house. By the end of a summer day a Morrisonville woman had toiled like a serf.

It should come as no surprise that the great majority of southerners eagerly embraced Franklin Roosevelt and the New Deal. Lyndon Johnson benefited from that embrace. Most people who went to the polls in 1937 had fresh, bitter memories of economic disaster and a federal government controlled by Republicans that in their eyes had done little to help a nation in distress. Cloaking himself in the mantle of Franklin Roosevelt and the New Deal, Johnson carried the Tenth District to become one of the youngest members of Congress and a member of the powerful Texas congressional delegation.

THE DEPRESSION AND THE SOUTH

The Great Depression was the worst economic crisis in American history. From 1929 to 1932, per capita incomes fell by 44 percent in the southern states; elsewhere in the United States they fell by 46 percent. Still, southerners made less than half of what Americans outside the South made. Since unemployment statistics for regions are inadequate for this time, it is impossible to determine whether jobs were harder to find in the South than elsewhere in the country. In the nation as a whole, unemployment rose from around 3 percent in 1929 to about 25 percent in 1932, and except for one year, it remained above 15 percent until 1940. Industrial production in the South declined by half. Ten thousand miles of rail lines were in the hands of receivers. By 1931 the Southern Railway owed the federal government $15 million for loans. Bankruptcy even threatened governments. Louisiana, South Carolina, and Arkansas defaulted on their debts. Most southern state and local governments survived only by making drastic cuts in their spending; by paying their employees in scrip, which without being discounted could be used to pay property taxes but nothing else; and by searching for new sources of revenue. The last effort led to general sales taxes, which became staples in the revenue policies of the South and which fell most heavily on the people least able to pay.

The state government of Tennessee had a brush with bankruptcy when the Nashville firm of Caldwell and Company, a large investment brokerage, collapsed. The fall of the "Morgan of the South" took $6.5 million from the state treasury and triggered a panic that swept away more than a hundred banks in seven states. In the five years after the Depression began, more than a third of the banks in the South failed altogether or disappeared in forced mergers, and 60 percent of the bank assets of the region (some $2.5 billion) were lost. Southern banking lost

BIRMINGHAM STEEL MILLS, 1936 (Library of Congress)

more heavily than banking elsewhere because the economy of the South was more vulnerable and its banks were more dependent on larger banks outside the region.

Numbers, however, cannot convey the human toll the Great Depression exacted. There is no way to calculate the costs of permanently impaired health, early death, shattered families, lost hopes, or the investments of lifetimes in farms, businesses, and homes that had been lost. The town world and the farm world were drawn together for a time by common adversity. According to the federal government, Birmingham was "probably the hardest hit city in the nation." An Alabama congressman stated in 1932 that of the 108,000 wage and salary earners in his district, which included the "Magic City" of the South, only 8,000 "have their normal incomes. At least 25,000 are altogether without work. Some of them have not had a stroke of work for more than 12 months." He reported that many farm owners could no longer furnish their tenants and croppers and were letting them go to provide for themselves wherever and however they could. "Any thought that there has been no starvation . . . is the rankest nonsense."

Relief workers estimated that of San Antonio's 280,000 residents, 88,000 were on relief. Of Houston's 380,000 residents, some 60,000 were on relief. It would have had more, but Houston officials, as one said, were "turning away as many Negroes as we can. We've got to, because of the mental attitude of the whites. We've been threatened with riots here." Mexican Americans probably received similar treatment from relief agencies in the South.

Economic distress, however, was not new to large numbers of southern farmers. They had struggled through hard times before, especially in the 1920s. "Well, we didn't know the difference in a depression," a Mississippi tenant farmer recalled, "except . . . what we would hear. It just increased the fear a little bit of maybe not being able to get any food at all. We was just living on the bare necessities anyhow." Many southerners had a far easier time. Ben Robertson remembered that "when the depression . . . hit us, we retrenched . . . we stayed at home and we did without. We lived on fried chicken and beef and turnip greens and sweet potatoes and string beans and cornbread and sweet milk . . . and we waited for the hard time to pass." As in the rest of the country, many people did not stay home. Large numbers of them became nomads. John Steinbeck's novel *The Grapes of Wrath* made some of the nomads famous: the 150,000 "Okies" (and "Arkies") who fled westward along U.S. Route 66 from the Mississippi Valley through Arkansas, Oklahoma, and northern Texas and finally on to California.

Others turned to direct action. In January 1931 some fifty farmers climbed on a truck owned by H. C. Coney, a white tenant farmer, and rode into England, Arkansas, to ask for food for their families. If politeness failed, they intended to take the food. When the Red Cross quickly rushed in relief, the "riot" ended. Several other Arkansas communities had similar experiences. Arkansas was particularly distressed because it was most adversely affected by the Southwide drought of 1930–1931. The severe drought was one of the worst in American history. In 1932 the Sharecroppers' Union, an organization of black farmers in Alabama, charged dues of a few cents. It "would back you up and fight your battles with you." That appealed to Ned Cobb. "Ever since I been in God's world, I've never had no rights, no voice in nothin that the white man didn't want me to have—

MIGRANT FAMILY IN THE OZARKS, 1930s (Library of Congress)

even been cut out of education, book learnin, been deprived of that." Cobb joined the organization. Later, without the help of the union—it was very weak and soon collapsed—he stood up to the sheriff's deputies who were confiscating the livestock of indebted farmers. Cobb survived the shootout that ensued—others did not—and spent the next twelve years in prison.

Labor unrest also became overt. Textile workers had engaged in work stoppages earlier, in the aftermath of World War I and toward the end of the 1920s when management moved aggressively to increase productivity. Efforts at increasing output per worker-hour usually took the forms of speedups and stretch-outs: management forced workers to work much faster and reduced the number of workers without reducing the amount of work required or increasing pay. Mill hands worked in unventilated rooms where the air was saturated by mechanical humidifiers while managers stood nearby and timed their work with stopwatches. "I had seen women, one of them my own daughter," one textile worker recalled, "going all day long in that unbearable heat with their clothes stuck to their bodies like they had been dipped in a pool of water." Such conditions triggered a series of walkouts in the late 1920s. The most celebrated of these strikes took place at Gastonia, North Carolina, in 1929. It attracted national attention, inspired a substantial body of literature, resulted in several deaths, and ended in emotional trials, miscarriages of justice, and the complete defeat of the union.

The American Federation of Labor (AFL) sought to take advantage of the unrest among southern textile workers by mounting an organizing campaign in 1930. Less than a year later, the AFL claimed more than a hundred new locals, including twenty-five in textiles, which were organized under the United Textile

Workers of America (UTW). But the organizing campaign sustained a crippling defeat at Danville, Virginia, when the UTW lost a four-month strike against the Dan River and Riverside cotton mills, where 4,000 workers walked out in September 1930. Neither the AFL nor the UTW had the human or financial resources to sustain that large a strike for more than a few weeks. The AFL also continued to demonstrate that it lacked the boldness such campaigns required and the commitment to organize industrial workers. The intransigence of the company and racial divisions also contributed to the defeat of the UTW at Danville. As a concession to white workers, the union excluded the few black workers at Dan River and Riverside. Blacks countered by crossing the picket lines.

Encouraged by local communists, cigar workers in Tampa marched to protest their plight. The action evoked a swift reaction. Local police and volunteers from the American Legion dispersed the march. When workers struck to protest this action, the cigar companies beat them handily and resumed their operations on a nonunion basis. Predictably, labor strife lasted longer and was more violent among the coal miners. More than 10,000 miners in Harlan County became involved. So did the sheriff's department, mine guards, and the National Guard. Seemingly everyone had a gun, and most used them. The "Battle of Evarts" left four dead. The United Mine Workers retreated from what they believed was a sure defeat for unionization. A communist-controlled union, the National Mine Workers Union, tried to fill the vacuum and was routed, in part by the miners themselves. Harlan became a subject of intense study and publicity as it joined Gastonia as a hallmark in the history of industrial relations in the South.

The Depression devastated the petroleum industry that was confronted with another of its periodic gluts. Oversupply got even worse in 1931 when the gigantic East Texas field began production. Prices fell from $1.30 a barrel for high-grade crude in 1930 to 10 cents a barrel in 1931 for East Texas crude. Despite the collapse of prices, producers pumped more oil. They feared they would lose oil to adjacent producers or market shares to oil companies in other regions. Desperate appeals to President Hoover for federal intervention brought no real relief. Governor Ross S. Sterling of Texas then dispatched the state militia to shut down the East Texas field, and the Texas legislature passed legislation to allow the state to prorate the amount of oil any well could produce. Oklahoma took similar action. Arrests and convictions of some of those who sold more than their quota of oil (or "hot oil") reinforced these actions. Thereafter, the oil glut ceased to be a critical problem.

Most southerners, however, avoided activism. Most of those who could vote expressed themselves through the ballot box. Once again the South gave its electoral votes to the Democratic presidential nominee in 1932. This time, however, there was a very significant difference. The solid South in 1932 found itself on the side of a large majority.

In THE DEMOCRATIC MAJORITY

The Great Depression transformed the political fortunes of the South. Economic disaster became political disaster for the Republicans. The Democratic party became the dominant party, a position it had not had since the 1850s. Southern Democrats consequently rose to unaccustomed power and prominence. They enjoyed important positions in the administrations of Franklin Roosevelt. Those administrations, however, which lasted from 1933 to 1945, never had the strong southern flavor those of Woodrow Wilson had had. With the exception of Senator James F. Byrnes of South Carolina, southern Democrats were not part of the inner circle at the White House. Vice President John Nance Garner's experience was typical. A Texas congressman who became speaker of the House, he lent southern balance to the Democratic ticket in 1932 and again in 1936, but he was not a close adviser of Roosevelt. Nor were the three cabinet members from the South.

The real power of the southern Democrats lay in Congress, where seniority allowed them to chair most of the committees and to serve as floor leaders in the Senate and the House. Using this congressional power base, the southern Democrats helped create and shape the New Deal. Some southern Democrats in Congress, however, opposed the New Deal from its earliest days, generally for doing too much, for spending too much. Meanwhile Huey Long, the most vocal southern critic of the New Deal, attacked it for not doing enough.

Initially, however, the president enjoyed almost undivided support from his party. For most Democrats (as for most Republicans), party loyalty was a powerful, persistent force. Extensive experience as a political minority reinforced party cohesion among the Democrats. So did the profound sense of economic and political crisis triggered by the Depression. Finally, Roosevelt had personal charisma and he employed it skillfully.

The Depression went on and on, and a sense of crisis could not be sustained indefinitely. Disenchantment with New Deal programs and proposals set in when full economic recovery was not forthcoming, though the worst of the Depression had passed, and the disenchantment deepened when times grew tougher in 1937–1938. Disagreements developed along sectional, rural and urban, and ideological lines. Convinced that low wages were a major asset for attracting the industrial investment the South so urgently wanted, southern leaders worked to obstruct efforts to close sectional wage differentials. As politicians from a predominantly rural region they supported measures that favored rural areas over more urbanized areas. They vigorously supported the landmark farm legislation of the New Deal designed to relieve agricultural distress, but they were often indifferent to or hostile toward relief of unemployed city dwellers. Fears of expanded federal powers and concerns about balanced budgets and rising governmental expenditures drove a number of southern leaders in Congress away from the New Deal. Southern Democrats accounted for about half of the party's anti–New Deal votes in the House of Representatives from 1933 to 1939 and almost one-third of such votes in the Senate. Other southerners in Congress remained vigorous New Dealers, sometimes outdistancing the president in pushing the New Deal leftward. Southern Democrats remained united, however, on race. White supremacy still stood as the cornerstone of the Democrats in Dixie, and the cornerstone seemed firmly in place in 1932, when Franklin Roosevelt was first elected.

Roosevelt's New Deal profoundly affected the lives of most Americans. The New Deal assumption that the federal government was responsible for the economic well-being of the country became a given in American politics and economics. For the first time the federal government gave direct relief to the unemployed and the needy, expanded its efforts to regulate and stabilize banking and finance, encouraged organized labor and collective bargaining, protected and stimulated private homeownership with government-supported loans, and created the social security system, which "brought government into the lives of people as nothing since the draft and the income tax."

THE NEW DEAL AND SOUTHERN AGRICULTURE

Two facets of the New Deal had particular impact on the South: its agricultural policies and its labor policies. The New Deal passed and implemented the most sweeping government farm program in American history. New Deal policies—reinforced by market forces—set the stage for an agricultural revolution in the South. By the end of the 1930s, the basis for more diverse, modern farming had been laid. The dawning of a new era in southern agriculture became evident in the fate of cotton. In a reversal of a history spanning more than 200 years, cotton acreage began a long-term decline.

Southern cotton farmers had struggled after World War I. Supply exceeded demand, and the situation was made worse by synthetic fibers and domestic and foreign competition in cotton growing. American manufacturers in the 1920s produced 120 million pounds of rayon annually. They tripled that output during the next decade. Farmers in California and Arizona became important cotton producers before 1930. Led by China, India, Brazil, and Egypt, foreign countries produced a growing share of the world's cotton supply, a development that reduced exports and prices for southern cotton farmers. Then the Depression sent shock waves into the already weakened foundations of the cotton kingdom.

For several years, however, the foundation remained secure—at least to the naked eye. During the long, hot summers from 1930 to 1935, the kingdom must have seemed permanent to the nearly 8 million southerners who were dependent on cotton. The wife of a white sharecropper told one of the dozens of writers (and scholars, journalists, and photographers) who examined and publicized the plight of the small farmer in the South during the 1930s: "We seem to move around in circles like the mule that pulls the syrup mill. We are never still, but we never get anywhere. For twenty-three long years we have begun each year with nothing and when we settled here in November we had the same." Three-fourths of all the farmers who produced less than $1,000 annually lived in the South. Fifty-five percent of southern farmers (60 percent of cotton farmers) were tenants, with little or no hope of ever owning their own land. It has been estimated that the ten principal cotton states of the South had 1.8 million tenant families, of whom 1.1 million were white. Tenants lived in virtual peonage in the cotton belt, in a "miserable panorama of unpainted shacks, rain-gullied fields, straggling fences, rattle-trap Fords, dirt poverty, disease, drudgery, and monotony that stretche[d] for a thousand miles." This harsh panorama did not end at the borders of the cotton kingdom; it ran on to the tobacco belt of the Southeast, to farms in the cutover pine and hardwood forests along the coastal plains, into Appalachia and the Ozarks, and to the dry, plowed-up grasslands of the western reaches of the South.

Yet as early as 1935 New Deal farm programs had initiated a process to re-shape this panorama and all the agriculture of the South. Then, enormously stimulated by World War II and postwar economic developments, the process resulted in the transformation of southern agriculture. In 1935 about 45 in 100 southerners farmed; in 1970 about 5 in 100 did. Farm output and methods underwent a similar transformation. By 1970 the average farm in the South was much larger, was heavily mechanized, was cultivated by scientific methods, and rather than grow cotton, was more likely to grow grains, livestock and poultry, fruits and vegetables, hays, soybeans, and trees for lumber, furniture, pulp, and paper.

The cornerstone of the New Deal's farm policy was the belief that raising farm incomes to parity (making them equal to or on a par with *real* farm incomes from 1909 to 1914 for most commodities, and from 1919 to 1929 for tobacco) should be the primary concern of the agricultural policy of the federal government. All other concerns were secondary. To raise farm incomes, the New Deal stressed a decrease in farm output and modernization of agricultural methods. The strategy was to encourage larger farms, mechanization and scientific farming, crop specialization, and production for cash. Other strategies might have been attempted; for instance, committing the necessary human and financial resources to develop smaller-scale, more self-sufficient farms, with less dependence on a cash crop. Whether this strategy would have worked will never be known. Political— and perhaps economic—realities precluded more than modest attempts at implementing such a strategy. The Resettlement Administration, later the Farm Security Administration, tried to rehabilitate small farmers. Neither agency had the financial or human resources to do much, and neither could match the power of the governmental and business interests that favored a big-farm strategy for agricultural recovery and reform.

To raise farm incomes by decreasing farm output and modernizing agriculture, the New Deal adopted an interventionist, sometimes contradictory policy that had mixed results and high human and financial costs. The haves gained more than the have-nots from government farm policies in the 1930s, as they have continued to do. Though this disparity was not the intended result, economic and political circumstances were more influential than intent in shaping the policy. Whether any farm program that could have been implemented would have significantly aided the majority of poor farmers, or even large numbers of them, is doubtful. Moreover, the better-off farmers had considerable advantages. They worked closely with and through the Department of Agriculture, local county farm agents, schools of agriculture in state universities, and such well-organized groups as the American Farm Bureau Federation. Probably the most influential person in the Agricultural Adjustment Administration was Oscar Johnson, a Mississippian who was the largest planter in the nation. The have-nots lacked personal resources and had few organizations or representatives to defend their interests.

The government assumed unprecedented powers to reduce farm output. In the past, farmers of most commodities had great difficulty altering their output in response to demand. Chronic surpluses and low farm incomes resulted. Given the large number of farmers and the dearth of their options, there was little likelihood that these surpluses would end without government intervention or a complete collapse of agriculture and the further spread of human misery.

Voluntary reduction programs had been repeatedly urged. Some had been attempted, but few had succeeded.

Now the New Deal forced or induced farmers to reduce output in return for government benefits. Benefits (implemented under the Agricultural Adjustment acts, the Bankhead Cotton Control Act, the Tobacco Control Act, and the Soil Conservation and Domestic Allotment Act) were based on reductions in the number of cultivated acres and in the production of the commodities covered by these programs (among them cotton, rice, wheat, hogs, dairy products, tobacco, sugar, peanuts, and cattle). Thus the larger the farm, the more benefits received. The hundreds of thousands of smaller farmers in the South got little. Nearly half the farmers in the South got less than $40 in benefit payments from the government in 1938, hardly enough to improve their standard of living. Such improvements were possible only if a farmer could take at least thirty to sixty acres out of production. Differences in benefits obtained could be startling. The British-owned Delta and Pine Land Company, in the Mississippi delta, got $114,480 for its 1933 crop reductions. The government could not have avoided such imbalances in benefits, however, given the program it adopted and its need for support from the bigger farmers in order to pass and implement that program.

New Deal farm credit programs drastically reduced the cost of money to farmers, provided, of course, that they were considered good risks. Not since the Civil War had southern farmers had such ready access to credit. Easier credit and benefit payments for crop and land reductions allowed farmers to make basic changes. Many did. They changed the kind and the quantities of the crops they grew; they took less fertile soils out of cultivation; and they relied less on sharecroppers, for whom they had year-round responsibilities, and more on day laborers. Farmers increased their investments in machinery, a major step toward capital-intensive agriculture and away from the labor-intensive agriculture that had long been characteristic of most of the South.

Southern farmers harvested 11 million fewer acres in 1939 than they had in 1929. More significantly, they decreased their harvested cotton acreage by 22 million acres (about 50 percent) and their cotton production by 277,700 bales (20 percent). They grew more corn, soybeans, peanuts, hay, wheat, and truck crops. Tobacco production remained virtually constant. Apparently tobacco was impervious to economic downturns, and it was bolstered by a special, particularly generous parity price (based on the higher 1920–1929 prices, as opposed to the more usual standard of 1910–1914).

The size of the farm population remained almost constant during the 1930s, or so it seemed. Actually, it grew by 500,000 from 1930 to 1935, then declined by a like number during the next five years. More significantly, the ranks of tenants and sharecroppers shrank by nearly 300,000 between 1930 and 1940. Many of the former tenants became day laborers on farms or, worse, could find only seasonal work, such as picking cotton.

New Deal farm programs had a large if unintentional hand in this process. The government encouraged landlords to sign agreements to divide and distribute benefit payments between themselves and their tenants in the same way they had divided crops in the past. A sharecropper working on "halves," for instance, should have received half of the benefit payment. Instead, many landlords kept

SOIL EROSION, ALABAMA, 1937 (Library of Congress)

the cash and reduced a tenant's debt by a like amount, or used the tenant's share of the benefits to pay bills the tenant owed to local merchants. Fraud sometimes compounded wrong. Landlords sometimes reduced their own land under cultivation but not that of their tenants, then claimed all of the benefit payments for themselves. Whatever happened, tenants had little or no recourse. Direct government payments to tenants would have required a more elaborate bureaucracy than even the New Deal farm programs developed and would have required the government to interpose itself between landowner and tenant. Landowners stood rigidly opposed to that policy because it would have threatened what one scholar has called "the traditional condition of sharecropper dependence," a condition that was often reinforced by the racial caste system. The general shift to more capital-intensive agriculture probably had an equally adverse effect on tenants and sharecroppers as well as on many small farm owners.

Reforestation and soil conservation programs permanently altered southern forests and lands. The New Deal reforested much of the South and launched the most comprehensive soil conservation effort ever to be undertaken there. The region had nearly two-thirds of the 150 million eroded acres in the United States. Severe erosion or loss of topsoil blighted every southern state. Virginia, for example, had lost the topsoil from 1.5 million acres; Alabama, from 4 million; Georgia, from 5 million; and Arkansas and Tennessee, from 3 million each. The Dust Bowl of 1934–1935, which came on the heels of the drought of 1930–1931, was the worst drought disaster in American history. Dust storms hit Oklahoma, Texas, and Arkansas especially hard and darkened skies as far as the Atlantic and Gulf coasts. Convinced that soil erosion was a major problem, Congress passed new soil conservation and reforestation legislation in 1935. During the next decade, the "plans [of the Soil Conservation Service] for land use, crop rotation, grasses, woodlands, contour plowing, terracing, strip cropping, ponds, drainage, and the planting of legumes like soybeans, kudzu, and lespedeza" were applied to 26.7 million acres in the South. That massive effort contributed significantly to the diversification of agriculture and the expansion of forest products in the South but not to the primary goal of New Deal farm policy, the reduction of output. Farmers removed their poorest land from cultivation while they cultivated their better lands more intensively. Yields per acre increased, and total farm output remained high.

New Deal relief programs, most of which took the form of work relief, provided some help for the landless and the small farm owners and also aided non-farmers in both the urban and the rural South. But the relief programs did not do nearly enough to alleviate the desperate circumstances poorer people experienced in the 1930s. The Federal Emergency Relief Administration (FERA) and the Public Works Administration, created by the Federal Emergency Relief Act in 1933, and other federal agencies provided relief to millions. In October 1933 more than 4 million people in the South were on relief, over 90 percent of which came from the federal government. By 1940, when most of the relief programs had ended, the combined expenditures of FERA, the Works Progress Administration (or WPA, which was later called the Works Projects Administration), and the Civil Works Administration reached nearly $2 billion in the South. Either inability or unwillingness kept the southern states from obtaining more federal funds to meet federal matching requirements. Whatever the reasons, the southern states received less for relief from the federal government than other states did, though the South had the greater need.

Millions found employment under these and other government programs, including the Civilian Conservation Corps (CCC), the Tennessee Valley Authority (TVA), and the National Youth Administration. Some people found work as teachers in financially devastated schools, in public health, in research, in surveying historical records, in libraries and archives, in writing state guidebooks and oral histories, and in drama, art, and music. Others found work building public housing, dams, schools, courthouses, playgrounds, privies, highways, and bridges, including the first bridge connecting the Florida Keys.

The Tennessee Valley Authority had striking scope. Constructing sixteen dams and related facilities in the Tennessee River basin by 1945, the TVA generated electricity for an area that had almost none, produced fertilizer for farmers, worked at regional planning, and reduced the incidence of malaria, an annual plague in the area. For the first time, much of the Tennessee River was navigable. There was a price for these benefits. Dammed waters covered thousands of acres of farms, numerous homes, and some communities. Those who were uprooted were seldom consulted; they were just told. The TVA's bureaucratic style angered many. In future years, that style badly damaged its reputation and even endangered its existence.

New Deal relief programs had ambiguous results. Those programs established crucial precedents and laid the basis for a transformation of social work in the United States, but the programs did little to alter the established order of the South. President Roosevelt asked for and Congress appropriated the funds for the largest relief measures in American history. The funds were dispensed as grants—

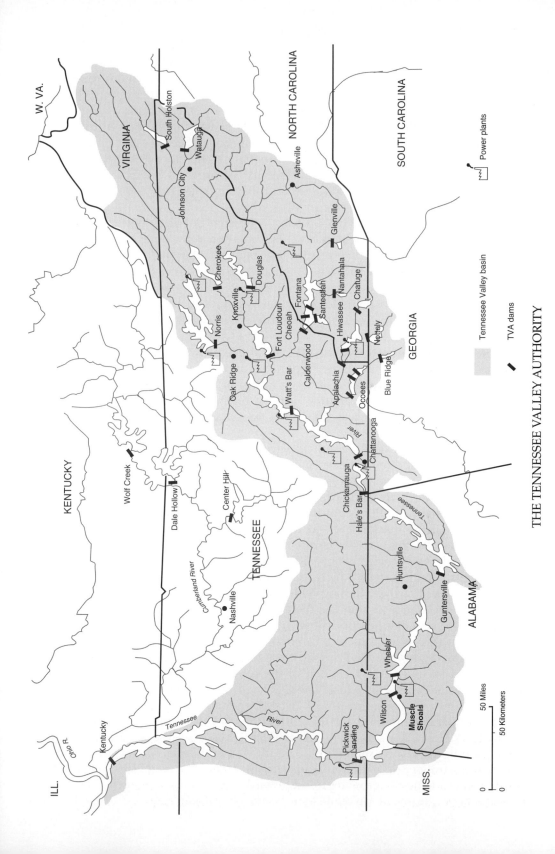

THE TENNESSEE VALLEY AUTHORITY

Power plants

Tennessee Valley basin

TVA dams

ILL.
Ohio R.
Kentucky
KENTUCKY
W. VA.
VIRGINIA
Wolf Creek
Dale Hollow
South Holston
Watauga
Johnson City
NORTH CAROLINA
Asheville
Glenville
Cherokee
Douglas
Norris
Knoxville
Fontana
Nantahala
Chatuge
Oak Ridge
Fort Loudoun
Cheoah
Santeetlah
Hiwassee
Nottely
Center Hill
Watt's Bar
Calderwood
Appalachia
Ocoees
Blue Ridge
GEORGIA
SOUTH CAROLINA
Cumberland River
Nashville
TENNESSEE
Chickamauga
Hale's Bar
Chattanooga
River
Tennessee
Huntsville
Wheeler
Guntersville
ALABAMA
Wilson
Muscle Shoals
Pickwick Landing
Tennessee
River
Kentucky
MISS.

0   50 Miles
0   50 Kilometers

not as loans, as under the Hoover administration—to state and local governments for distribution as direct relief to needy "unemployables" and as work relief for needy "employables," who were put to work on government projects. Those grants often required that federal funds be matched by state and local funds and that the administration of relief meet certain federal standards. This pattern continued and became fixed with the passage of the Social Security Act of 1935. In addition to its most important program, benefits for the elderly and for dependent survivors of deceased workers covered by the program, the Social Security Act included aid to dependent children and the blind and provisions for public health, maternal, and child-welfare services.

Even Virginia, then in the grasp of the tightfisted political oligarchy headed by Senator Harry F. Byrd, retreated from its commitment to "a negative policy on public services." A keen student of southern politics noted later that Byrd's Virginia, when faced with "an apparent demand . . . will grudgingly yield a bit here and there." As a result of the Depression and the New Deal, public assistance for the needy and pension benefits for the elderly became a fixed part of American public policy. The welfare agencies that they spawned at every level of government also became permanent.

New Deal relief efforts established crucial precedents, but they did little to alter the basic attitude "that many, if not most, of the destitute are undeserving," and those efforts contoured themselves to fit the farm season and Jim Crow. Programs for the needy too infrequently included rehabilitation. Finally, direct-relief and work-relief programs revealed the fault lines in the economy and the politics of the South.

Expenditures for relief programs followed the farm seasons: they rose during the winter months and fell in the spring. New Deal agencies often cut their work-relief rolls when the demand for farm labor increased, particularly at harvesttime. Agencies did differ with landlords over who should bear responsibility for tenants. Initially, many landlords got the agencies to assume that burden; later, the agencies shifted the burden back to the landlords. When they wanted to hire workers at low wages, landlords attacked relief programs as a threat to the farmer, though the agencies often paid less than prevailing wages in local communities. One landlord told a North Carolina welfare worker, "I don't like this welfare business. I can't do a thing with my niggers. They aren't beholden to me any more. They know you won't let them perish."

New Deal agencies seldom came into conflict with Jim Crow. Blacks had more trouble than whites getting direct or work relief, and they received less from the same programs. Blacks, who were much more likely than whites to be unemployed, received less than half of the relief funds, though they outnumbered whites on relief rolls 3 to 1. The CCC had racially segregated camps, disproportionately low enrollments of blacks, and no black supervisors. Later, under considerable pressure, the CCC altered its policies with respect to the last two matters. Public housing financed by federal money was segregated, but half of the total housing constructed in the South was for blacks. The Federal Housing Administration perpetuated and widened racial segregation in private housing, reinforcing the growing trend toward residential segregation. The TVA also followed the racial caste system. Some New Deal agencies did require certain percentages of blacks to be hired on federal construction projects. In doing so, they set precedents for racial hiring quotas for subsequent government programs.

Some New Deal programs discriminated unintentionally against blacks. When the industrial codes written under the National Recovery Administration (NRA), which was created by the National Industrial Recovery Act in 1933, raised manufacturing wages, thousands of blacks lost industrial jobs to whites. Already victimized by rising unemployment in domestic services and in agriculture, their principal sources for employment, blacks expressed their bitterness with the NRA by labeling it the "Negro Removal Administration." New Deal farm programs also victimized blacks. Disproportionately represented among sharecroppers and tenants, blacks suffered disproportionately from the crop-limitation efforts of the New Deal.

The New Deal did little to rehabilitate the rural poor, who paid high personal prices for the federal farm programs. Neither the Farm Security Administration (FSA) nor its predecessor, the Resettlement Administration, had enough money or staff to go beyond meager first steps toward resettlement communities, land use planning, and the transformation of more able tenants into landowning family farmers. The FSA, for example, made rehabilitation loans to only 15,000 farmers at a time when the number of tenant farmers in the southern states numbered nearly 2 million.

Despite the most sweeping government farm program in American history, much of southern agriculture in 1940 was still characterized by small cultivation units, too little diversification, low earnings, and poor living standards. On the average, farmers harvested fewer than thirty-five acres, and fewer than 10 percent had either a tractor or a truck. They had diversified their output modestly but had hardly increased their livestock holdings. Earnings remained low. Per capita *gross* annual earnings from 1924 to 1937 averaged $162 for farm people in Arkansas, Louisiana, Tennessee, Mississippi, Alabama, Georgia, and North and South Carolina. Earnings averaged $381 in the rest of the country. Living standards among farmers also had changed little by 1940. Too many families lived in poor housing without running water or any modern conveniences. A farm with a telephone or a radio was as uncommon as a farm with electricity or access to an adequate school or even a paved road.

Yet few families left the farm. They had little choice. So in 1940 southerners were still more dependent on farming than other Americans. More than twice as many people in the South (39 percent) farmed for a living as in the remainder of the United States (15 percent). Only a massive demand for labor could alter that situation—the kind of demand that would be generated by a major war.

Still, farming in the South had not remained static during the 1930s. Farmers grew more hay, corn, oats, and peanuts. Soybeans had become an important crop. Most significant, the amount of cotton acreage declined by one-half—a landmark in the history of the region. Major steps toward reforestation and better soil management had been taken. Other less dramatic but important changes had occurred. Like diversification, mechanization had increased somewhat, as had electrification, under the auspices of another New Deal agency, the Rural Electrification Administration (REA). About one-fifth of the farms in the region had electricity, an increase of 400 percent. The REA and the TVA accounted for most of this growth and laid the foundation for much greater expansion of rural electrification during and especially after World War II.

The Tenth Congressional District in Texas got electricity sooner than most. Thanks in large part to the explosive energies of Congressman Lyndon Johnson, electric power lines reached into distant corners of the district by 1940. Johnson had delivered on the promises he made Brian and Mary Sue Smith in 1937. He expected to be remembered at the polls, and he was; he easily won reelection to Congress in 1940.

THE NEW DEAL AND SOUTHERN INDUSTRY

Like agriculture, industry did not remain static during the 1930s. And again the New Deal—assisted by market forces—played a formative role. Industry recovered slowly but more rapidly in the South than in the rest of the nation because of the predominance of nondurable consumer goods in southern manufacturing. By the end of the 1930s, industrial output in the region had returned to the highs of 1929, and total wages had climbed to within 10 percent of the 1929 level.

Industry also became more diversified during the Depression decade. Chemicals and paper led the way. The chemical industry developed or expanded major facilities in Louisiana, especially at Baton Rouge, along the Gulf coast of Texas, at Hopewell, Virginia, and elsewhere. Innovations in chemical processing enlarged the range of paper products that could be made from the trees in southern forests, even from scrub pines and the waste from lumbering. Paper manufacturers invested $200 million in the South in the 1930s, locating plants in coastal areas that had long been economic backwaters.

Market forces, of course, had much to do with these and other changes that took place in the industrial South in the 1930s. So did the New Deal, directly and indirectly. Government spending poured enormous sums of money into a money-scarce economy. The Reconstruction Finance Corporation (RFC), for instance, lent funds to insolvent banks and financial institutions, insurance companies, and railroads. It also provided capital for government-owned corporations. Chaired by Texas millionaire Jesse Jones, a farm boy whose fortunes had soared with Houston's, the RFC dispensed more than $10 billion to the nation in the 1930s. Jones saw that the South got its share, perhaps more. Government-assisted hydroelectric power development and rural electrification expanded energy sources for industrial growth. The TVA was the largest of such efforts. Federally funded public works, especially highway construction, enhanced opportunities for economic development.

But the New Deal may have had its greatest impact on the industrial South by its labor policy. The New Deal raised wages, set maximum hours, and encouraged unionization and collective bargaining. The New Deal initiated these policies as early as 1933, when the National Industrial Recovery Act was passed. That law sanctioned business self-regulation in order to stabilize production and employment and to help the economy recover.

Protected from antitrust litigation by the new law, industry groups, such as cotton textile manufacturers, devised industry-wide codes that limited production in order to bring output more in line with demand, set prices, established maximum hours and minimum wages, and abolished child labor. Section 7(a) of the act guaranteed the right of workers "to organize and bargain collectively through representation of their own choosing." The nation's cotton textile manufacturers became the first to adopt such a code, acting speedily in the hope of restoring solvency to the industry. The seriousness of the industry's plight was indicated by the concessions southern manufacturers made on wages and hours. They accepted large reductions in regional differences in wages and a shorter workweek, advantages they had long valued. They agreed to a minimum wage of $12 for a forty-hour week. Elsewhere it was $13. They also accepted a two-shift operation limit (a total of 80 hours). But southern mill managers, as they demonstrated subsequently, made no concessions to unionization and collective bargaining.

The NRA code had an immediate and in some ways a lasting impact on cotton manufacturing in the South. Business improved markedly after the code was in place. So did workers' earnings—those of workers who kept their jobs. Confronted by higher labor costs, companies countered by laying off workers and increasing the productivity of those they kept. The stretch-out and the speedup reappeared or became more obvious. But these measures proved inadequate. After the initial surge, sales fell and inventories mounted. In December 1933 the NRA implemented a thirty-hour, two-shift workweek. The new limits remained in force for several months and reduced workers' earnings by a fourth. Manufacturers talked of reimposing the shorter week and cutting wages sometime in 1934. Workers responded by unionizing. By mid-1934 the UTW had more than 250,000 members, most of them in the South. Propelled by mounting frustration and anger over pay and working conditions, local union members initiated a general textile strike in Alabama and then persuaded the UTW to call a national strike for September.

The largest industrial strike in American history followed. During the months the strike lasted, perhaps 400,000 workers walked out from Alabama to Maine. Half the cotton mills in the South were shut down at one time or another. In some locales, every mill was closed. Workers divided among themselves; some of the divisions led to violence and bitter memories. At least ten strikers died in the South, two in New England. In general, government officials adopted promanagement positions. None went so far as Governor Eugene Talmadge of Georgia, who called out the state militia to arrest strikers and put them behind barbed wire at Fort McPherson in Atlanta. Reacting to Talmadge's "concentration camps" and other instances of harsh treatment of strikers, a prominent North Carolina Democrat expressed his concern for workers who were "forced in some mills to work long hours for compensation below proper sustenance. . . . It makes me sick to see soldiers beat them down, even when they make demands greater than the industry can stand in days of weak demand for their goods."

In 1934 cotton manufacturers could do little to meet demands to increase hours and wages, and their swollen inventories allowed them to wait out strikers. Workers were very vulnerable, as was the UTW. Workers had few resources, financial or otherwise, to wage a protracted struggle. Most lived in company housing; they could be—and often were—evicted for strike or union activities. The

WORKERS ON STRIKE IN ATLANTA DURING THE GENERAL TEXTILE
STRIKE OF 1934 (Bettmann Archives)

UTW also lacked the funds and staff to carry on a long strike, particularly one of
such unprecedented proportions.

The strike, which had begun with great enthusiasm, faltered in its second
week, staggered in its third, and fell apart within a month, though many union
members protested vigorously when national UTW officials called the strike off.
National leaders claimed the strike was a success because the Roosevelt administration created a committee to investigate labor conditions in the textile industry.
UTW activists in the South realized that this action afforded them no protection
against blacklisting. Aware that they had created union locals throughout the textile South and had even breached the color barrier by organizing separate locals
for black workers, the activists wanted to continue the strike in hopes of obtaining
a stronger position vis-à-vis management.

The union might have been more successful if it could have delayed the strike
until economic conditions improved. But, as one union leader noted, the "strike
was the result of an emotional wave that could not have been stopped by God
himself." For years thereafter, textile union officials and organizers heard about
the Great Strike. "The big argument all over the South was, 'Lord, we don't want
to get into that Union and have happen to us what they did to our mothers and
fathers in 1934.' "

More commonly, the Great Strike of 1934 faded from memory or was often
confused with the smaller but highly publicized Gastonia strike of 1929. The thorough blacklisting of strike leaders may have encouraged memory loss. Leaders
and their families were driven out of the industry and forced to leave their homes.
Families, many of whom were divided over the strike, often stopped talking
about it. Succeeding generations were more likely to hear that "outsiders"
brought the union in, caused trouble, and then absconded with union dues than

that southern mill hands had created one of the largest grassroots labor organizations in American history.

Bitter memories probably contributed to labor's limited success in organizing southern textile workers in the late 1930s, during World War II, and in the decades thereafter. That limited success contrasted with labor's triumphs elsewhere. From 1935 to 1945, organized labor enjoyed its greatest growth in American history. Membership among nonfarm workers rose from 3.6 million to 14.3 (38.5 percent of nonfarm workers). The South shared in that growth, though by the 1960s the proportion of southern workers who were organized was half the rate in the remainder of the nation, and the proportions of unionized workers in the South varied widely by industry.

Clearly, many workers in the South joined labor unions; clearly, most textile workers did not. The largest, most important manufacturing industry in the South was still largely nonunion. That left organized labor with a critical weakness in a major region in the United States. That weakness had broad implications for the economy and the political life of the South.

What is not so clear is why unions failed so dismally in the textile South. Several factors may account for this failure. The Great Strike of 1934 left bitter memories and damaged the credibility of unions and unionism among southern textile workers. Probably the most important factor was the nature of the textile industry—highly competitive, labor-intensive. Such an industry was bound to be especially hostile to organized labor. Unable to pass along increased labor costs to its customers, the besieged industry fought unionism by fair means and foul—and usually with success, even during the boom days of unionization.

The large pool of unskilled and semiskilled labor in the South gave management a great advantage. It could readily replace strikers and union activists. Moreover, the agricultural crisis of the 1930s and New Deal farm policies expanded that pool of labor. Other New Deal programs reduced the numbers of the unemployed, but not as quickly as their numbers were growing. Other factors may have contributed to the overall failure to unionize textiles in the South. Analysts have pointed to the dependence that life in mill villages supposedly created in workers, the otherworldly quality of much of the religious life of the workers, the cultural tradition of individualism and deference, the promanagement policies of government officials, the perceptions of union officials as outsiders, and the quality of textile union leadership in the 1930s.

The Great Strike may have left more than bitter memories and a dismal legacy for unionism. By reacting so strongly to cuts in their earnings in 1933 and 1934, textile workers may have helped ensure that the minimum wage and maximum hours established by the NRA became permanent standards, even after the U.S. Supreme Court declared that the NRA was unconstitutional. Most businesspeople welcomed the end of the NRA and its codes.

Southern employers had a special grievance against the NRA: it narrowed regional differences in wages. They assumed that smaller differences in wages, which remained even after the NRA had been abolished, weakened their competitive position in relation to New England textile firms. But the New England industry, burdened by lax management, old plants and machinery, and somewhat higher labor costs, continued its decline and virtually collapsed during the 1930s.

PERCENTAGE OF UNIONIZED WORKERS IN THE SOUTH, 1962, BY INDUSTRY

Industry	Percent
Primary metal	95
Petroleum and coal products	88
Transportation equipment	86
Rubber products	81
Paper and allied products	79
Electrical machinery and equipment	73
Tobacco products	72
Stone, clay, and glass products	65
Chemicals and allied products	62
Printing and publishing	61
Fabricated metal	54
Apparel	30
Furniture and fixtures	28
Lumber and wood products	27
Textile mill products	14

SOURCE: F. Ray Marshall, *Labor in the South* (Cambridge, Mass.: Harvard University Press, 1967), p. 317. Reprinted by permission of Harvard University Press.

Some of the larger of the New England companies moved south. In the decade after the Depression began, textile employment in New England declined to about 80,000 workers, a loss of some 40,000 jobs. Textile employment in the South grew by a comparable amount, to a total of more than 300,000 jobs. That growth was, of course, too small to accommodate the thousands of southerners who needed an alternative to farming. At the same time, bankruptcies and mergers significantly reduced the number of textile companies operating in the South. Still, the industry remained one of the most competitive in the country. It also faced what it believed was a grave challenge from a new source, Japan. Southern textile leaders acted as if they had sighted a typhoon. In alarm they turned to Washington and persuaded the government to restrict imports of Japanese textiles. They overreacted. Japanese textile manufacturers lacked the capacity to export much to the United States in the 1930s. We should note, however, that even the modest amount of textiles imported into this country exceeded exports of American textiles.

Southern employers had an even greater grievance with another legacy of the NRA. In 1935 Congress revived the collective bargaining portion of the NRA by passing the National Labor Relations (Wagner) Act. The Wagner Act probably had the effect of raising wages because it gave unions a powerful legal and psychological tool for getting and staying organized. The relationship between unionization and wages is often disputed. Numerous studies show clearly that organized and unorganized employees in the same industry have similar earnings. Therefore, some observers conclude that unionization has no impact on wages. But it is impossible to determine what the unorganized workers would earn if there were no pressure from unions. After World War II, for instance, the textile industry often increased wages and benefits for its workers as a preventive measure against unionization. Studies do show clearly that unions have often prevented cuts in their members' wages and thus have helped create a floor for wages.

New Deal assaults on low wages went beyond the NRA and the Wagner Act. The Fair Labor Standards Act (FLSA), passed by Congress in 1938, set maximum hours and minimum wages and forbade child labor. Again certain standards were put in place and established important precedents, though many workers did not initially enjoy the protection of the new law. Domestic workers and farm laborers were excluded, and some regional wage differentials were tolerated. To a large extent, these provisions represented concessions made to southern Democrats, without whose support the act could not have been passed. New Deal work-relief programs, especially the WPA, eventually adopted a policy similar to the minimum wage. For instance, the WPA initially based the wages it paid its workers on the wage rates that prevailed in the local area. By 1938 the WPA shifted from this "prevailing wage" policy to one that reduced regional wage differentials considerably.

CRACKS IN THE SOLID SOUTH

The legislative battle over the FLSA revealed the growing dissatisfaction of many southern Democrats with the New Deal, with Roosevelt, and with the national Democratic party. Southern Democrats had given Roosevelt and the New Deal, including the Wagner Act, strong support until 1936. The South had benefited considerably from the New Deal. Seemingly content, southern Democrats joined in the campaign to reelect the president and, coincidentally, accepted a major change in the nominating procedure for Democratic presidential candidates. During their 1936 national nominating convention, the Democrats repealed the requirement that their presidential nominee had to receive a two-thirds vote of the convention, a provision that had substantially enhanced the power of factions or sections, such as the South, in the nominating process. The rule had also resulted in deadlocked conventions. In 1924 the Democrats had sweltered through 103 ballots before they could choose a presidential candidate.

Party harmony at the 1936 Democratic convention lapsed at least once, however, for a few revealing minutes. South Carolina Senator Ellison D. "Cotton Ed" Smith walked out when a black minister stood to give an invocation. Later, during his campaign to be reelected to the Senate in 1938, Smith told and retold a carefully rehearsed version of the event. "[When a] slew-footed, blue-gummed, kinky-headed Senegambian . . . started praying, . . . I started walking, and as I . . . walked . . . it seemed to me that old John Calhoun leaned down from his mansion in the sky and whispered . . . you did right, Ed."

Smith's walkout showed how quickly southern Democrats could react to any challenge to their preconceptions. His actions also reflected a growing restiveness among southern Democrats who perceived their party becoming "northernized," urban, non-Protestant, and prolabor. Important southern Democrats began reluctantly to conclude that Roosevelt and the New Deal were converting the national

Democratic party into the party of northern liberalism. Their restiveness intensified markedly in late 1936, after Roosevelt had been reelected, when a number of unions affiliated with the Congress of Industrial Organizations (CIO) adopted the militant tactic of the sit-down strike. Instead of walking out when a strike was announced, workers stopped working and stayed where they were, blocking any effort to turn their machines over to strikebreakers. With food and other supplies brought by supporters and hauled up through the windows, they could stay there for weeks. The president remained aloof while others worried that the sit-ins constituted a massive assault on the sanctity of private property and the beginnings of a revolution. Prominent southern Democrats broke with President Roosevelt because of his failure to oppose the sit-down strikes.

That break widened in 1937, when the president attempted to overhaul the U.S. Supreme Court with his "Court-packing" plan. Fearful that the elderly conservatives on the Supreme Court were going to undo the New Deal, Roosevelt tried to alter the makeup of the Court by increasing the number of justices, or "packing" the Court. Southern opponents of the scheme had several motives. Most were inclined to the concepts of states rights and limited government. They saw the Supreme Court, largely secure from the winds of political change and shifts in public opinion, as a bulwark for such policies as Jim Crow. Finally, they used their opposition to the Court plan as an indirect means of expressing their growing reservations about particular New Deal programs and about Franklin Roosevelt. Those reservations grew and were more openly expressed as the country fell into the severe recession of 1937–1938, a slump that demonstrated that the "magic" of the New Deal recovery was ephemeral at best.

Most southern leaders liked the New Deal farm programs. New Deal relief programs and attacks on low wages, however, got a much more mixed reception. Southern political leaders knew that the human needs that relief programs addressed were real and that many workers' wages were far too low, but these New Deal programs created a dilemma for them. Recipients of relief, if they could and did vote, remembered the politician who supported relief measures. So did the beneficiaries of higher wages and shorter hours. But so did employers, who had very different interests and whose ranks included thousands of farmers.

New Deal policies also threatened the basic strategy the South used to industrialize and diversify its economy. The South had historically relied on a strategy of cheap labor, as measured in wages, for economic growth and development. Relief programs and laws establishing a minimum wage and maximum hours endangered this approach by raising the floor for wages, if only modestly in some instances, and by reducing labor's dependency on employers. Cotton Ed Smith attacked the FLSA as an attempt to raise wages in South Carolina to equal those of New England despite the lower living costs in South Carolina. "Why . . . don't some of these people call in God and tell Him that He must stop this thing of making one section more advantageous than another."

Southern leaders successfully defended some of their regional advantage in cheap labor. New Deal legislation and policy often favored the regional wage differential, though sometimes they narrowed it. Self-interest, of course, figured prominently in this battle. The South's low wages obviously benefited employers, some of whom were major forces in politics. Conversely, those wages harmed northern employers and organized workers, most of whom were outside the South.

But more than narrow self-interest was involved. Needing desperately to diversify its economy much more than it had already done, the South had little alternative in the 1930s to an emphasis on low wages, its greatest advantage as a region in its struggle for economic development. Southern leaders reacted hostilely to any real or imagined threat to this advantage. They included "damn yankees" in their indictments of labor unions. Northern competitors, so the argument went, encouraged attempts to organize southern workers in the hope of raising wages and thus undermining the South's most important competitive advantage. Predictably, the FLSA received strong support from labor unions and northern political and business leaders. It was, one observer declared, "a sectional bill disguised as a humanitarian reform."

Sectionalism reared its head in other economic matters. None got greater publicity than freight rates. Those rates, which were regulated by the Interstate Commerce Commission (ICC), favored the shipment of semiprocessed raw materials out of the South and the flow of manufactured goods into the region. Convinced that the South was being victimized by a domestic version of mercantilism designed to keep the southern economy in a subordinate or "colonial" position, southern leaders mounted a concerted attack to alter the rates. The actual economic impact of differential freight rates is hard to determine. Apparently they had some effect, but not as much as southern leaders claimed. Still the issue served a number of uses. It provided a means for venting sectional feelings and a way to put some of the blame for economic conditions in the South on others while deflecting attention from the serious internal economic weaknesses of the region. The struggle over freight rates also touched very deep emotions in the South, particularly its defensiveness vis-à-vis the rest of the nation and its sense that it was unfairly treated. Those emotions found expression in the parallel and widely held notion that the South was an economic colony of the North. Though the "colonial economy" concept had serious analytical deficiencies, it had a powerful appeal. After a five-year effort led by southern governors, the ICC altered the freight rate structure in 1939. The Southern Governors' Conference evolved from this struggle, a lasting product of the freight rate battles.

New Deal relief measures also stirred sectional feelings. These sentiments became more pronounced after 1936 as more southern Democrats began openly to criticize federal relief programs. Convinced, despite the serious recession of 1937–1938, that the worst of the Depression was over, they saw less need for such programs as the WPA than for a tax cut for business to stimulate economic activity. They worried about creating a welfare state and an expanded federal bureaucracy and about adding to the federal deficit. Southern Democrats believed, correctly, that more federal money went to the cities than to rural areas, and that the money was more likely to go to the North than to the South. Southern Democrats charged favoritism by the federal government but ignored offsetting factors. The South got more money from the federal government for agricultural programs than the North did, and because its incomes were lower, the South paid less in federal taxes. Race, as usual, also figured in the controversy over federal relief. Southern Democrats believed, again correctly, that federal relief efforts attracted black voters to the national Democratic party. They especially feared that northern Democrats would become too dependent on black voters. Conversely, southern Democrats thought that federal welfare measures would make blacks less dependent on whites for labor and therefore would cause wages to rise in the South and hurt southern employers, particularly farmers. State and local governments in the South kept welfare and relief payments well below levels that can be explained by their lack of revenues. This policy had a built-in risk: a shortage of needed unskilled, occasional labor might occur if people left the South to find more generous relief policies. It was widely believed that after World War II, when the South developed a very large surplus of unskilled labor, southern leaders consciously used niggardly welfare policies to encourage out-migration, especially among blacks.

Not all southern Democrats broke with the New Deal after 1936. The great majority of southerners who liked the New Deal were devoted to Franklin Roosevelt, the president they believed cared about them. Both Lister Hill of Alabama and Claude Pepper of Florida, for instance, strongly supported the New Deal, and both won Senate seats in 1938, Pepper for his second term. Alben Barkley of Kentucky, another New Deal loyalist, also won reelection with an assist from President Roosevelt. The president had less success with his highly publicized efforts to defeat two opponents in the Senate. Walter F. George of Georgia and Cotton Ed Smith had signed the "Conservative Manifesto," a document drafted and released in July 1938 by conservatives in the Senate. Of the ten signers, five were southern Democrats. The other three were Harry F. Byrd and Carter Glass of Virginia and Josiah W. Bailey of North Carolina. The manifesto called for tax reductions to encourage investment, a balanced budget, an end to sit-down strikes as a violation of private property and the right of workers to work, support of private enterprise, and "the vigorous maintenance of States' rights, home rule and local self-government."

Senators George and Smith won handily despite the president's campaign efforts against them. They were particularly effective at portraying the president as an intruder in the affairs of their states. Smith summoned up memories of federal intervention during Reconstruction. He claimed he was acting in the spirit of Wade Hampton and Robert E. Lee, and he repeatedly recited the story of his triumphant march out of the national Democratic convention in defense of white supremacy. After Smith won, a university professor wrote a colleague in South Carolina that he knew his friend was "rejoicing that States' rights, white supremacy, Bourbonism, low wages, long hours, and the right to ignorance, prejudice and superstition are no longer in jeopardy in S.C."

Although Roosevelt had not been completely routed in his efforts to align the Democratic party more closely with the New Deal, the defeats in Georgia and South Carolina were well publicized and were interpreted as indicating that southern Democrats who opposed the New Deal could be neither changed nor defeated. Thereafter, powerful southern Democrats appeared to work so closely with Republicans that a bipartisan coalition was thought to be a major force in American politics.

JIM CROW: AN UNCERTAIN FUTURE

The racial caste system faced growing though oblique challenges in the 1930s. Attacks came from several quarters, the most threatening from within the Democratic party, from blacks, and to a lesser degree, from southern whites. Those challenges became serious enough by 1940 to make the future of Jim Crow somewhat uncertain for the first time in the twentieth century.

That the Democratic party became a threat to Jim Crow was ironic. Since the Civil War the South had relied on that party to defend its peculiar system of race relations. The solid South's defenses faltered during the 1930s as black voters shifted their allegiance to the Democrats. This development was very important because the Great Migration had shifted large numbers of blacks to cities outside the South, and there they voted. In 1936 probably more than 70 percent of the blacks who went to the polls supported Franklin Roosevelt. They did so despite the very mixed blessings bestowed on them by the New Deal and despite Roosevelt's inconsistent support of their interests. Still, mixed blessings, inconsistencies, and all, the federal government did more for American blacks under Roosevelt than it had done since the Emancipation Proclamation and Reconstruction.

Convinced that the Republicans had ignored them for years and grateful to Roosevelt and the New Deal, blacks left the party of Abraham Lincoln in droves. They quickly made their presence felt in the Democratic party. In 1934 Chicago sent the first black Democrat to Congress, and black voters provided the margin for Democratic victories in Pennsylvania and Louisville, both Republican strongholds. The number of black faces at Democratic conventions increased, including some from Kentucky and West Virginia in 1936.

Roosevelt, who had not shown particular concern for blacks when he was governor of New York, had altered course as president. He had a "black cabinet"—blacks who held high-ranking (but noncabinet) positions in his administration. This group included Mary McLeod Bethune, founder and president of Bethune-Cookman College; the economist Robert C. Weaver, who in 1966 became the first black to hold an official cabinet post when Lyndon Johnson appointed him secretary of housing; and the political scientist Ralph Bunche, who won the Nobel Peace Prize in 1950 for his efforts as a U.S. mediator in the Middle East.

Roosevelt also appointed southern whites who by the standards of the day were liberals on racial issues. The most prominent were Will Alexander and Aubrey Williams. Formerly a Methodist minister with roots in Missouri and Tennessee, Alexander helped found the Commission on Interracial Cooperation and directed it for a long time. He worked under Roosevelt in the Resettlement Administration and then in the Farm Security Administration. Williams, an Alabamian, was a social worker who held positions with the WPA and the National Youth Administration. Alexander and Williams became two of the most forceful and persistent defenders of the rights and interests of blacks and the poor in general.

Williams worked closely at times with Eleanor Roosevelt. The president's wife publicly and repeatedly defended the rights of blacks and decried racial discrimination. In doing so, she attracted severe criticism from southern whites and the lasting devotion of blacks. The president shared her concerns, but he had to be more cautious because he had to work closely with powerful southern Democrats in Congress. Thus he refused to give federal antilynching bills his full endorsement because southern Democrats vigorously opposed such measures. Still, he did nothing to restrain his wife's activities on behalf of civil rights.

The president was caught in a dilemma that entrapped many American politicians. If they defended the rights of blacks, they risked offending whites, especially *but not only* in the South. If they failed to defend the rights of blacks, they risked offending blacks and losing their votes. Black votes in the South had been critically important to the Republicans after the Civil War. Black votes in the North became critically important to the Democrats when blacks switched to the party of Franklin Roosevelt. The number of black voters outside the South soared in the 1930s. Without blacks' shift in allegiance and their increasing eagerness to register and vote, the solid South would have remained secure for many more years, perhaps indefinitely.

Southern blacks also had a hand in shaking the foundations of the solid South during the 1930s—some by leaving, some by staying and becoming more active in politics. Perhaps 400,000 blacks left the South during the decade. Many became voters. At the same time, blacks who remained in the South became more active politically, especially in urban areas. Even modest increases in registering and voting had some impact, particularly in such border states as Kentucky, West Virginia, and Missouri. Black candidates won local offices in North Carolina in 1936, one in Raleigh and one in Durham. Public services for blacks improved in Miami and Tampa. Here and there, police and fire departments added blacks to their forces. Still, the scope of this new black political activism in the South was very limited. In 1940 only about 250,000 of the more than 4 million people in the old Confederate states who voted in the presidential election were black.

Still, whites worried. An official in Macon, Georgia, feared that "the ignorant class of white people we have got in Georgia" might form a political coalition with blacks. Happily, they were "violent nigger haters" who would probably be repelled by such an alliance. An official in Greenville, South Carolina, revealed that his county had been having "a lot of trouble about niggers registering." The "churches and preachers and the school and all kinds of organizations," a Charleston voter registrar explained, "are after them about their rights." A Montgomery registrar explained her reluctance to register blacks this way: "All niggers—educated and uneducated—have one idea back in their mind—that they want equality. . . . It is necessary to keep the Negro from voting, for voting would lead to social equality." Yet Montgomery leaders tolerated "token registration" by "the upper ranks of Negro society," since the white primary preserved white supremacy in politics. The Democratic party was, according to party officials, "a private party, like a social club . . . it is for white people."

The increases in political activism by blacks reflected some important changes among southern blacks—most of all, a lessening of their dependence on whites and their growth in self-confidence. The third generation of blacks who had never been slaves was coming of age. For the first time in their history, less than half the blacks in the South lived and worked on farms. Most had family members and friends who lived outside the South and were doing better. While black families in the South earned one-third to one-half what white families did, a tiny upper class of blacks had established itself, as had a slightly larger middle class, which included a growing number of professionals. Blacks had created and now sustained vigorous institutions—schools, churches, professional organizations, and fraternal orders. They had achieved much against terrible odds, and they wanted more.

So in the late 1930s the NAACP focused its attention on educational inequalities, one of the strongest of the deliberately constructed barriers against the efforts of blacks to improve themselves. The barriers they assaulted were high. In 1935–1936, the expenditures of ten southern states averaged $13.09 per black student and $37.87 per white student. (Nationally, expenditures per student averaged $67.88 in 1936.) Black teachers earned about 40 percent of what white teachers earned. High schools for blacks were still rare. No public institution in the South offered graduate or professional training for blacks.

Thanks in large part to the work of the NAACP, the gap between the salaries of black and white teachers was narrowed. Otherwise, the gap between expenditures for black and white education remained. The NAACP also succeeded in breaching Jim Crow in higher education, and at the same time reopened the issue of the constitutionality of "separate but equal" for the first time since 1896. The courts ordered law schools at the University of Maryland (1936) and the University of Missouri (1938) to admit black applicants because both states had provided law schools for whites but not for blacks and thus were in violation of the equal protection clause of the Fourteenth Amendment to the Constitution ("No State shall make or enforce any law which shall abridge the privileges or immunities of the citizens of the United States . . . ; nor deny to any person within its jurisdiction the equal protection of the laws"). In the Missouri case (*Missouri ex. rel. Gaines* v. *Canada*), the Supreme Court suggested for the first time that the "separate but equal" doctrine might not be secure. Although the Court found nothing legally wrong with the doctrine, it did imply that the courts ought to consider whether "separate but equal" was obtainable. If not, one could infer that "separate but equal" failed the equal protection clause and thus was unconstitutional.

Indeed, before the *Gaines* case the Court had shown a growing inclination, as one legal expert wrote, to use the due process clause for "protecting black men from oppressive and unequal treatment by whites." Beginning in 1925, the justices had ruled that defendants had a right to a trial free from an atmosphere of hysteria and intimidation. Then, in rulings involving the notorious Scottsboro rape case (1931), the court decided that due process in capital cases required that defendants have competent counsel and that the juries in such cases could not be selected by a process that systematically excluded blacks.

Another, more subtle indication that the foundation on which Jim Crow rested was becoming increasingly shaky can be seen in the behavior of southern whites. Subtle changes in attitudes were becoming apparent. Many southern whites, while accepting Jim Crow, rejected its more brutish versions and openly sought to do away with them. The numbers and the outspokenness of such people increased significantly during the 1930s. Just as important, they shifted their positions on Jim Crow. Some of them had their initiation in racial liberalism in the home mission societies of their churches, in the YMCA or YWCA, or in the Commission on Interracial Cooperation. In none of the interracial contacts or educational programs on race relations they sponsored did these organizations challenge racial segregation—probably the only reasonable course, given the times in which they operated. Still, the antilynching campaign organized by the Interracial Commission seems to have had a real impact. Encouraged by Will Alexander, then head of the commission, Jessie Daniel Ames launched the Association of Southern Women for the Prevention of Lynching (ASWPL) in 1930. The ASWPL's campaign undermined the principal justification for lynching: the defense of southern womanhood. Its members, 43,000 strong, succeeded in getting more public officials and leaders to take an open stand against lynching. At least one study indicates that those efforts had an impact. Happily, for whatever reasons, the incidence of lynchings in the South declined from 21 in 1930 to 5 in 1940 and remained very low thereafter.

The Southern Conference for Human Welfare (SCHW, 1938–1948) edged closer to an open break with Jim Crow. Composed of southern New Dealers and New Deal sympathizers, the SCHW drew politicians, journalists, academics, union leaders and activists, and reformers of various stripes, black and white. The SCHW's most concrete action was a vigorous but unsuccessful assault on the poll tax. That attack alarmed most southern politicians. According to Virginia Durr, the Birmingham native who led the anti-poll-tax campaign,

> Southern congressmen were just terrified of the race issue. They immediately translated the fight against the poll tax into the race issue. The Negro had no rights, couldn't vote, had no power whatever. The unions were coming South and some of them were integrated. White Southerners thought that getting rid of the poll tax would give all these people the right to vote—the unions and the Negroes and all these new labor people. The world would turn over. Cheap labor was the great selling point of the South. Every Southern state, every chamber of commerce, and every corporation thought the way to make the South prosperous was cheap labor.

When a delegation of white women tried to get a senator from the deep South to support repeal of the poll tax, Durr recalled that he exploded in anger: "I know what you women want—black men laying on you!"

Organized labor did represent a challenge to Jim Crow, though hardly a consistent challenge. Most of the unions affiliated with the AFL practiced Jim Crow, excluding blacks altogether or keeping them in the most menial positions. To protect the jobs of white members, the railroad brotherhoods had become virtually lily-white. Most of the black porters who worked the dining cars and sleeping cars on the railroads belonged to an AFL affiliate, the Brotherhood of Pullman Car Porters. The CIO, which was founded in 1937, welcomed black members and had some black officers—a factor in its rapid growth in some industries. Local CIO unions, however, frequently ignored the national union's biracial policy: racial discrimination and exclusion were not unusual in CIO locals in the South. Communist-led unions had long had a policy of desegregation, but as their following was small, that policy had little effect on blacks.

If the challenges to Jim Crow made its future less certain in 1940, they did no more than that. No one could have foreseen the enormous impact World War II would have on the racial caste system of the South, or on almost every aspect of southern life.

WORLD WAR II

World War II brought more rapid and greater change to the South than it had experienced since the Civil War. In 1945 the economy of the South differed significantly from that of 1940, Jim Crow was threatened, and the cracks in the solid South had become increasingly difficult to plaster over. Cotton, segregation, and one-party politics (Democratic, in this instance), the three pillars of the post-Reconstruction South, were in grave danger.

The war led the federal government to spend unprecedented sums in the region. It invested more than $7 billion on military bases and industrial plants in the South. Industry received another billion from private sources. Of the income payments in the region, which increased by 250 percent during the war, the federal government provided one-fourth. Thus the war, with its massive deficit spending, did what the New Deal could not do: it brought jobs, money, and renewed hope. Many southerners enjoyed prosperity for the first time in twenty years.

The South received a disproportionate share of military bases. Weather, readily available open spaces, and the power of southern congressional delegations probably accounted for that. After the war, many of those bases were expanded and made permanent. The prevalence of military personnel and retirees in the South since 1945 can be traced directly to World War II.

Still, the South received less than its share of government investment in war plants. Southern congressmen and senators charged regional discrimination, but it was historical circumstances rather than sectionalism that accounted for this disparity. Investment in war plants tended to go to places where industry was already strong. Production of military vehicles, for instance, was concentrated in the industrial Midwest, where automobile and truck production was well established. Still, the number of production workers in the South more than doubled, to almost 3 million.

Ordnance plants were closed after the war ended because few of them could be converted to other uses; but one ordnance operation became a permanent fixture. Built to process uranium for atomic bombs, Oak Ridge, a spin-off of TVA located near Knoxville, Tennessee, required 110,000 workers during its construction and 82,000 during its peak production period in 1945. Extractive industries received much heavier investments than did electrical machinery or vehicle manufacturing or steel and iron milling. Important, lasting investments were made in petrochemicals and other chemicals, oil pipelines, aluminum and tin milling, and shipyards and shipbuilding. Developments in shipbuilding were particularly noticeable, especially at Newport News and Norfolk, Charleston, Tampa, Mobile, Pascagoula, New Orleans, and Houston. These developments along the coast indicated a significant change in the geography of industrial and urban growth in the South. The coastal regions thus regained some of the ground they had lost to the interior after 1865. Similar though smaller developments occurred in aircraft

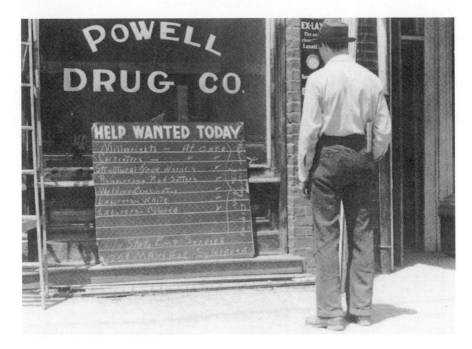

JOBS, WORLD WAR II (Library of Congress)

manufacturing. Areas along the Gulf coast received a disproportionate share of the new industrial capacity, with Texas leading the way by a wide margin, followed by Louisiana and Alabama.

Many of these gains remained in place after World War II. The industrial capacity of the region was estimated to have grown 40 percent; from 1939 to 1947, value added from the industry of the region soared from $3 billion to $10.7 billion. The ranks of production workers had grown by almost 50 percent during the same period, from 1.3 million to 2 million. Personal income in the South rose almost two and a half times in five years, from $13.6 billion to $32.1 billion. Per capita income increased from about 59 percent of the national average to 69 percent, the biggest gain the South had ever made. After the war personal income would continue to rise faster in the South than in the rest of the nation.

Some of the changes in the southern economy reflected deliberate policy choices by the federal government. The government continued its assault on low wages in the South by the way it implemented the Fair Labor Standards Act and through the National War Labor Board, a wartime agency. Washington's encouragement of unionization contributed to the substantial growth of organized labor in the South. Federal support may have made possible the organization of oil and chemical workers in the South during World War II. The Roosevelt administration selected the southwestern Gulf coast for the site of most of the production facilities of an important new industry, synthetic rubber, and the federal government financed the construction of those facilities. The growth of metal fabrication plants in the Southwest was also a result of conscious government policy, as was the development of aircraft manufacturing and shipbuilding in the South during the war. The Southwest—Texas, Louisiana, Oklahoma, and Arkansas—led all the regions of the United States in the growth of manufacturing during World War II.

At the same time, the Tennessee Valley Authority made a major change in course. Initially it had concentrated on generating electric power, controlling floods, improving river navigation, and producing fertilizer. These activities reflected the TVA's policy of moderate improvement of the economy and life of the region it served, rather than basic changes that might result in new industries and more and better-paying jobs. In 1942, however, the TVA began to seek new manufacturing industries for its region.

Tragically, little attention was given to the major victims of the federal government's assault on low wages: the people who for one reason or another were not qualified to hold jobs that paid better. They lost their jobs. As long as the war lasted, their plight was eased somewhat by opportunities to serve in the military and by a shortage of farm labor. After the war, they found themselves isolated from the new prosperity, from jobs, from any meaningful place in American society, south or north.

Willingly and unwillingly, perhaps one-fourth of the people in the South moved inside or outside the region. More than 4 million southerners served in the armed forces; more than 3 million left the rural South, a decline of more than 20 percent; 2 million blacks left the South altogether. At the same time, more than 6 million nonsoutherners invaded the region, most to serve in the military, some in civilian capacities. Unlike the invaders of the 1860s, they were friendly though not uncritical forces. Enemy prisoners of war joined the in-migration. Some 277,000 of the 372,000 captured Germans imprisoned in the United States were held in the South. German POWs praised the physical beauty of the South and reported the region to be generally prosperous. Nazis though they might be, however, they joined with American nonsoutherners in condemning the mistreatment of blacks. Conscripted as farm laborers, often as cotton pickers, many of the captured Germans developed a keen appreciation for the hard work blacks (and whites) did.

Civilians migrated to take advantage of the extraordinary employment opportunities the war created. They left agriculture, though farm wages doubled and even tripled during the war. Perhaps 4 million women were gainfully employed in the South in 1940; perhaps 5 million held jobs in 1945, and more of them were married, middle-aged, and mothers. Black women fled domestic service. Their flight may have prompted one of the more exotic rumors of the war. Despite the absence of any firm evidence, stories of "Eleanor [Roosevelt] Clubs" blossomed in profusion. These organizations of black domestics supposedly intended to place "a white woman in every kitchen." A jocular Tennessean observed that though white women in the South might not feel themselves personally threatened by Hitler, they "certainly recognized what a crisis the loss of a cook is."

Job seekers and military bases and industrial plants triggered unprecedented urban growth. Mobile's population nearly doubled. Public services faltered badly. Some schools operated in double shifts, and still classrooms were overcrowded. Waterless faucets were not uncommon, nor were queues outside movie theaters and diners. Virtually any enclosed space could be rented for housing. Crime, delinquency, and prostitution increased. Conditions in Norfolk became so bad that journalists nominated it for the title of "Our Worst War Town." Finally, after

WOMEN WELDERS, WORLD WAR II (Erik Overbey Collection, University of South Alabama Archives)

Congress investigated, the citizens of Norfolk made concerted efforts to deal with the problems.

People who stayed on the farm enjoyed good times, better than farmers in the South had enjoyed in a generation. Net farm income in the region tripled between 1940 and 1944, but the per capita net income of farmers in the South was still considerably less than that of other American farmers, $454 compared with $530. The number of mules decreased; the number of trucks, tractors, and automobiles increased. More farms had running water, telephones, and electricity. Electricity, which had reached fewer than one farm in five in the South in 1940, reached almost one in three in 1945. The Rural Electrification Administration and the Tennessee Valley Authority had much to do with that growth. The number of tenants and sharecroppers declined significantly and the number of farm owners expanded somewhat.

These changes reflected a crucial development in southern agriculture: the steady flow of large amounts of capital into farming and the marked decline in the availability of farm labor. That circumstance created an unusual need and an unusual opportunity. Southern farmers had to turn to less labor-intensive, more capital-intensive agriculture. More than ever before, they could afford to diversify and mechanize their operations. Peanut and soybean production doubled. The output of rice and sugarcane increased. Dairy farming, however, grew only modestly. Cattle and pig raising, as well as truck and fruit farming, grew faster, but not as much as had been predicted. Tobacco farmers, though they continued their largely unmechanized methods, had never had better times; the demand for tobacco, especially for cigarettes, soared, and so did prices.

Most farmers in the South still relied heavily on cotton, and that reliance persisted through World War II. About half of all farm income in the South came from cotton, which remained the principal cash crop of almost half the farmers in the region. During the war King Cotton rewarded them more generously than he had for a long time as cotton prices more than doubled. In response to wartime demand, American manufacturers absorbed almost all the cotton American farmers grew. Some southerners must have thought that the cotton South was returning to its best days.

But there were clear indications that cotton prosperity was going to be a wartime phenomenon for most growers and that the nature of cotton farming was continuing to undergo fundamental changes that had long-term implications. Carryovers—the unsold cotton carried over from one crop year to be sold in the next—provided a telling clue. Despite strong demand for cotton, the carryovers of cotton remained virtually unchanged from 1939 to 1945. Domestic demand was likely to decline after the war (as in fact it did). Renewed access to foreign markets would only partially offset this decline. Cotton growers also faced growing competition from foreign producers, primarily those in Brazil, China, and India, and from synthetic fibers, primarily rayon, but also nylon, a recently developed product. Total national output rose to as much as 10 million bales a year, but the amount of cotton acreage declined by more than 20 percent, from 22.8 million acres in 1939 to 17.6 in 1945. Yield per acre had risen significantly. A major factor in that increase was the continuation of cotton's westward march into heavily mechanized, irrigated lands in Texas, Arizona, and California. Moreover, even after 1943, when the government removed its restrictions on the number of acres that could be planted in cotton, total cotton acreage did not increase because of labor shortages and the availability of more profitable alternatives.

These developments, which had strong roots in the Depression and the New Deal, clearly indicated that Dixie was not necessarily the land of cotton. Another crucial development was graphically demonstrated by the International Harvester Company in the fall of 1944. While 2,500 people looked on at the Hopson Brothers Plantation outside Clarksdale, Mississippi, mechanical pickers harvested 1,000 pounds of cotton each an hour, about the amount that required fifty to sixty adult males to pick in the same time. Thus the threat of massive displacement confronted thousands of tenants, sharecroppers, and farmworkers. The prospect was particularly grim for blacks, because they were disproportionately represented in these groups. Mechanical cotton pickers were not so rapidly adopted in the postwar years as many people had anticipated, however. High purchasing and operating costs delayed adoption of the pickers.

Jim Crow faced more immediate threats during World War II. The most serious was a change in the attitudes of blacks. Howard Odum observed, "It was as if some universal message had come through to the great mass of negroes, urging them to dream new dreams and to protest against the old order." "By the way, Captain," a black sharecropper remarked to his employer soon after the attack on Pearl Harbor, "I hear the Japs done declared war on you white folks." Between 1940 and 1946 the NAACP grew from a membership of 50,556 in 355 branches to

JIM CROW MOVIE (Library of Congress)

nearly 450,000 in 1,073 branches: the NAACP had a grassroots following for the
first time in its history. Here and there blacks challenged segregation in public facilities. In 1944, at the invitation of the University of North Carolina Press, a group
of black leaders produced a collection of essays, *What the Negro Wants*. Although
the group represented a wide range of opinion, from conservative to radical, they
agreed unanimously that blacks wanted political and civil rights, equal educational and job opportunities, and equal access to public facilities—now. Their im-
patience was widely shared. A traveler in the South reported that blacks expressed "a sense of not belonging, and protest, sometimes not loud but deeply
felt." Blacks developed their own version of the widely popular *V*-for-victory
sign—double *V*, for victory abroad and at home.

Their wartime experiences demonstrated that this rendering of the signal was
all too appropriate. Perhaps 300,000 black men and women from the South served
in the armed forces, which were thoroughly segregated by race. Initially the
Marine Corps and the Army Air Corps (predecessor to the Air Force) excluded
blacks altogether. The United States Navy restricted blacks to menial capacities.
The United States Army allowed blacks to serve in a wider range of activities but
restricted the majority to menial positions. Proportionately fewer blacks became
officers, and they were limited to all-black units whose superior officers were
white. The Air Corps did eventually create a separate black unit of pilots, who
trained at Tuskegee Institute and then served in combat in Europe.

Military bases maintained racially separate and usually unequal facilities.
Separate and unequal treatment off the bases was, of course, routine in the South
and not rare elsewhere. Black and white military personnel fought each other—on
a few occasions with live ammunition. Blacks reported that white officers and

military police were often blatantly discriminatory and verbally and physically abusive. They complained even more about the civilian police they encountered off their bases. There were assaults and killings, some of which were never solved.

William H. Hastie, dean of the law school at Howard University and civilian aid to Secretary of War Henry L. Stimson, observed that "only the sensational cases of shootings, killings and rioting . . . attract public attention. But day by day the Negro soldier faces abuse and humiliation." The army, he contended in a letter to Secretary Stimson, had no comprehensive plan for dealing with this pervasive situation. The army investigated and reported, transferred individuals and occasionally court-martialed them, and sometimes shifted regiments to other stations. "The Army itself is busy with booklets, lectures and various devices of indoctrination, teaching our soldiers how to treat the peoples of India, the South Sea Islanders, the Arabs, everyone but their fellow American soldiers."

Blacks continued to receive separate and unequal treatment in civilian employment. Congress, marching steadily rightward, gutted federal relief programs faster than blacks could find jobs in a racially biased job market. Not until 1942 did that market grow enough to make even menial positions readily available for blacks, and only after 1943 were more skilled positions opened to blacks. In addition to carrying the burden of lower rates in literacy and skills, largely imposed by long years of racial discrimination, blacks had to overcome the discriminatory attitudes and practices of white employers and employees. A 1941 survey of defense contractors in Georgia revealed that 95 percent of their jobs were for whites only. The region's largest industry, textiles, maintained its policy of a virtually all-white workforce. Pressed by the federal government and a growing shortage of suitable white workers, shipbuilders in Mobile opened skilled and semiskilled positions to blacks in 1944. Their predominantly white workforce started a riot that ended only when military forces intervened. A compromise was subsequently struck. Several shipyards began working all-black and all-white crews. That arrangement gave blacks an opportunity to advance to better jobs. Trade unions usually maintained their Jim Crow traditions, but industrial unions continued to deviate somewhat from those traditions. Railroad brotherhoods in the South resisted all efforts at desegregation, despite considerable pressure from the federal government.

Even after job opportunities for blacks had improved, most blacks were still employed to do the heaviest, least desirable work. The legendary shipbuilder Andrew Jackson Higgins was a rarity. The New Orleans industrialist provided equal pay and work to blacks and whites and even worked cooperatively with unions. By the end of the war, black employment in manufacturing had grown so much that the number of black industrial workers equaled the pre-Depression number. Those gains, however, had a soft underpinning. Among the last hired, blacks were usually the first fired during postwar reconversion.

In fact, blacks seldom found effective allies in the federal government during the war. After a threatened mass march by blacks on Washington on the eve of the United States' entry into World War II seemed likely to materialize, President Roosevelt issued an executive order requiring nondiscrimination clauses in defense contracts and forbidding discrimination by defense contractors. To enforce these provisions the president established the Fair Employment Practices Commission

(FEPC), which walked softly and seldom carried even a small stick. It applied persuasion but would not touch its most formidable weapon, recommendations that defense contracts be canceled. The FEPC took no initiative in specific cases; it responded if someone complained, but people who complained risked retaliation. The president made some use of his patronage powers in an attempt to appease his black critics; for instance, he appointed Judge Hastie to the War Department to be a spokesman for blacks.

In 1944, however, the Supreme Court dealt white supremacy a major defeat. The Court ruled in *Smith* v. *Allwright* that the Texas white primary law violated the Fifteenth Amendment and was therefore unconstitutional. The upper South acquiesced in the decision, and the number of blacks in the upper South who registered to vote increased substantially in the ensuing decade. The impact of increased black voter registration was limited because blacks made up a small proportion of the registered voters in the upper South.

The lower South, where blacks made up a large proportion of the population, held its ground firmly on Jim Crow at the ballot box. Governor Olin Johnston of South Carolina even called the state legislature into special session to make the state Democratic party a private club, which could then set its own membership rules. The courts soon declared the new laws unconstitutional. Thereafter, South Carolina, like other southern states, used literacy tests and understanding clauses as its primary means of keeping blacks from exercising their rights as citizens. Southern whites seemed as determined to sustain white supremacy in 1940 or 1945 as they were in 1900. But a knowledgeable South Carolinian thought otherwise. "The Southerner's attitude," wrote John A. Rice in 1942, "is incredibly more humane than it was in the South I knew as a child."

Southern Democrats in Congress, however, resisted change. During World War II they helped dismantle some New Deal programs and blocked the expansion of others by making effective use of their strength in Congress. They had numbers (a strong, often united minority), seniority-based control of many congressional committees, the power of the filibuster in the Senate, and something approaching an informal alliance with congressional Republicans. So armed, the southern Democrats were able to defend most of the programs that southern farm owners wanted while virtually destroying the already enfeebled Farm Security Administration, whose programs were intended to aid landless farmers. It was replaced by the Farmers Home Corporation, which had reduced programs for tenant purchases of farms. The other liberal New Deal agencies—the WPA, the NYA, the CCC—were abolished.

When northern Democrats attempted to create a massive public housing program, southern Democrats emasculated the measure. In comparison with their northern colleagues, they had few urban constituents who would benefit from the program. Southern Democrats persisted in their strong opposition to organized labor; they pushed for legislation to forbid unions to make contributions to political campaigns or to strike during wartime. Southern Democrats eagerly joined those who denounced labor for the strikes that occurred during World War II. They seldom criticized employers for their part in some of these strikes. Southern state legislatures adopted a wide array of antiunion laws; the most popular were the so-called right-to-work laws, which outlawed collective bargaining agreements that required employees to join the union. And of course southern Democrats held firmly to Jim Crow. They successfully killed federal anti-poll-tax legislation. Fearing that blacks might find a back door to voting booths in the South, they eviscerated national legislation designed to allow soldiers to cast absentee ballots easily.

Southern Democrats also held firmly, though with growing doubts and discomfort, to the party of their fathers. Although their disagreements with President Roosevelt's domestic policies were sharp and very public, southern Democrats gave strong support to the president's foreign policy. That support was particularly important during the months of crisis between the start of World War II and the United States' entry into the war, and again when the president was working to establish the United Nations and to ensure American participation in that organization. They also supported the reelection of the president in 1944, as they had done in 1940, after some hesitation on both occasions. In 1944 they put pressure on Roosevelt to replace Vice President Henry A. Wallace, a New Deal liberal. In Wallace's place the president chose Senator Harry S Truman of Missouri, a border state with strong southern characteristics. The old balance of power between North and South in the Democratic party seemed to have been revived. That balance seemed even more secure when Truman succeeded Roosevelt. On April 12, 1945, as Roosevelt was sitting for a portrait in his cottage at Warm Springs, Georgia, he suddenly slumped over. Within minutes the man who so earnestly wanted to see a modern South was dead.

Five months later, on September 2, 1945, Japan surrendered. World War II was over, and a different world order was emerging. So was a different South, a modern South, where the three pillars of the prewar South were endangered or had started to crumble: Jim Crow, the solid South, and economic dependence on agriculture in general and cotton in particular. The Great Depression, the New Deal, and World War II had struck the region with elemental force. White southerners, at least those in seats of power, were shaken. A young newspaper reporter privately noted a year before the war ended that the South was "unhappy, restless, confused, embittered, torn by pressures steadily mounting. As far as the eye can see there is discontent and bitterness, faint intimations of a coming storm like a rising wind moving through tall grass."

Several months later, a South Carolina soldier sent an unintended warning that some of the storm clouds gathering over the South were being generated within the region. He had tried to vote as an absentee but found he could not do so because his state legislature refused to allow voters from his state to use ballots distributed through the armed forces. Legislators feared that blacks might use this means to obtain ballots.

Stung by the experience, the soldier wrote a letter of protest to his hometown newspaper. He declared that he was an "ardent Southerner" who was "always ready" to defend his state and the South. "But I can no longer hide the fact that actually I am ashamed of my state." He was distressed because, among other things, he had seen many southerners do poorly on examinations in the military because of their educational deficiencies. For that situation the South had itself to blame.

Yet often South Carolina leads the South in wailing about the injustices brought on us, such as high freight rates, or Elanor's medling [sic]. It's time we cleaned our own house, maybe if we did this, the yankees would quit trying to do it for us. . . . It seems to me that the average South Carolinian is so afraid that the negro will get ahead that he is willing to sacrifice his own rights just to make sure the negro won't have any. Are our fine Southerners afraid that if they meet the negro on equal terms, that they will be beaten?

The obsession of white southerners with maintaining their superior status and with keeping blacks in their place would drive away the outside business investment that the South wanted. "We can expect no prosperity as other states have it until we wise up to ourselves."

The soldier's letter at least suggested that Negrophobia, for some two hundred years the cornerstone of southern politics and society, rested on uncertain ground. The letter also suggested that the veterans of World War II were returning with different attitudes or more open minds. If so, then World War II had shaken Wilbur Cash's "savage ideal" and had helped prepare white southerners for the sweeping changes that transformed much of their world in the quarter century that followed the end of the war.

26

The End of Jim Crow

The Civil Rights Revolution

———— ❖ ————

Rosa Parks had worked all that Thursday in 1955 at her job as a seamstress in a Montgomery, Alabama, department store. Her feet hurt as she got on the 5:30 bus, which, like all Montgomery buses, was required by law to segregate black and white passengers. The first ten rows of seats on the buses were reserved for whites. Blacks sat behind those seats, or they stood. Blacks could not take empty seats in the other section if their own was filled, but whites could do so. If a white person did sit in the back, that row instantly became a white row and all the blacks seated in it had to move. Further, blacks had to pay their fares at the front door and then go out and enter again by the back door. The white bus drivers were often condescending, rude, and even abusive to black passengers. They sometimes drove off before blacks could board at the rear after paying their fares. Parks herself had once been physically thrown off a bus by a driver when she refused after paying her fare to disembark and re-board at the rear. Her clear recollections of that episode were stirred when she got on the bus that Thursday. The driver was the same one who had put her off the bus seven years before.

This bus quickly became crowded. When the white section was filled, a white man moved toward the row where Parks was seated. The driver ordered blacks in that row to give up their seats. Someone remembered that he used a familiar phrase: "Niggers, get back." Others moved, but Parks did not. Long an advocate of self-assertion in defense of one's rights, Parks had had enough. She was, as she said later, more than just physically tired. She was tired from "the accumulation of many years of oppression, of humiliation, of deprivation, and of just the attempt of those in power to make me feel less than a person—that is what it was designed to do." Too many times she had watched black parents instruct their children to stand on buses with empty seats, teaching them the lesson that they themselves had learned from Jim Crow—that they were of an inferior order of beings.

Asked if she intended to move, she simply said, "No." The driver left the bus and called the police. They came, arrested Parks, and took her to jail.

Rosa Parks had never before been arrested. A high school graduate who had attended Alabama State, she was a pillar of her church, was active in the Women's Political Council (WPC) of Montgomery, had served as secretary for the local NAACP chapter, and was working actively with the youth council of the local NAACP. The chapter president, E. D. Nixon, soon learned of her arrest and acted promptly to secure her release, with the assistance of a white lawyer, Clifford Durr. Then Nixon began to work with Parks to build a case to test the constitutionality of the law that required racial segregation on public transit in Montgomery, hoping the case might become a focal point for a protest movement.

The WPC also immediately grasped the larger significance of Parks's case. Frequent complaints about the bus system had usually been received politely by city officials, but had gone unheeded. Searching for a new, more effective strategy, the WPC developed the idea of a bus boycott. When Jo Ann Gibson Robinson, president of the WPC, learned of Parks's arrest, she recruited a colleague from the Alabama State faculty and two students. By Friday morning they had mimeographed 52,500 leaflets calling for a one-day boycott of the bus system on Monday, December 5, to protest the Parks case. They and others from the WPC distributed the leaflets to black Montgomery. Meanwhile, individuals and groups worked over the weekend to arrange for car pools and reduced-fare taxi services to get the boycotters to work and home again.

Then the anxious waiting began.

Robinson later recalled, "The suspense was almost unbearable, for no one was positively sure that taxi drivers would keep their promises, that private car owners would give absolute strangers a ride, that Negro bus riders would stay off the bus. And then there was the cold and the threat of rain."

The boycott proved to be amazingly effective. Black ridership on city buses dropped almost to zero. Monday night 5,000 to 6,000 people gathered at a church to celebrate and shouted their approval of a proposal to extend the boycott until they received better treatment on city buses. They chose the Reverend Dr. Martin Luther King, Jr., to lead them. Day after day Montgomery blacks endured the monetary and personal costs of relying on taxis, privately owned cars, and car pools. Some risked their jobs. Many gave nickels, dimes, and quarters to car pool drivers. A group of college students stayed out of school to drive boycotters. When King told a weary elderly woman that she ought to give up walking and go back to the buses, she refused. "Oh, no. I'm gonna walk till it's over." "But aren't your feet tired?" "Yes . . . but my soul is rested."

No one realized that the boycott would drag on for thirteen difficult, sometimes violent, months. No one could have anticipated that the Montgomery bus boycott would become a national and international event and that King would become the leading figure in a movement that was to transform the post–World War II South.

Rosa Parks's quiet rebellion was not an isolated event. Blacks, sometimes supported by a few whites, had been protesting Jim Crow individually and collectively since World War II. Circumstances more than personalities put Montgomery on the world stage. Montgomery showed how deep and widespread was the anger of blacks about Jim Crow, how tired they were of being kept "in their place." The Montgomery boycott, like the civil rights movement to which it contributed, was a grassroots movement.

JIM CROW AND THE TRUMAN ADMINISTRATION

The Montgomery boycott, of course, occurred within a larger context. World War II had eroded the ideas and attitudes that were vital underpinnings for the South's peculiar system of race relations. The gap between the claims and the practices of American democracy had become painfully obvious to most white Americans, even to some in the South, and utterly unacceptable to blacks. Racism—the assumption that one or another race is inherently superior—was losing its respectability. Physical and social scientists had destroyed its claims. Hitler had made it odious.

America's newly assumed role of world leader and Cold War competition made Jim Crow an unacceptable international liability. Communists kept up a steady stream of criticism of the treatment blacks received in the United States. As the world leader of democracy and a prime mover in the United Nations, the United States could not afford to ignore its commitment to equality. Jim Crow and that commitment coexisted awkwardly. Their coexistence became even more difficult as European colonies in Africa and Asia asserted and obtained their independence after 1945 and Third World nationalism became a force in international politics. Cold War considerations figured prominently in President Harry S Truman's conclusion that the federal government had to take steps to oppose segregation and racial discrimination.

So did domestic political considerations. Here American blacks assumed the initiative more forcefully and effectively than they ever had done before. Stronger economically and especially politically than at any other time in their three-hundred-year American experience, blacks after World War II could now make themselves heard. They could force American political leaders to become less evasive about racial discrimination and perhaps even to move against it.

A generation after the waves of black migration from the rural South had begun, the numbers of black voters in the North and border states made them a force to be reckoned with. For instance, the Truman administration concluded that it could not win the 1948 presidential election without attracting strong black support outside the South, even at the risk of infuriating the white South. Moreover, the president was said to have been stunned by NAACP reports of increased racial violence and lynchings and a new wave of Negrophobic literature.

However mixed his motives were, Truman was the first president since Lincoln to act forthrightly on behalf of black Americans. Truman created the Civil Rights Committee in 1947. Its fifteen members included corporate, labor, and academic leaders as well as two prominent blacks. Its final report, *To Secure These Rights,* became a landmark in civil rights history. The committee called for "the elimination of segregation based on race, color, creed, or national origin from American life." It urged passage of federal antilynching and anti-poll-tax legislation; an end to segregation and discrimination in the armed forces, in interstate

transportation, and in public services; and nondiscrimination in elections, education, and housing. To enforce these policies, the committee called for a fair employment practices act and asked that federal agencies charged with protecting
civil rights be enlarged and strengthened and that Congress make its grants-in-
aid to state and local governments dependent on nondiscrimination. State governments, the committee declared, ought to adopt similar policies and ought to
outlaw discrimination in public accommodations.

The report had little immediate effect. President Truman endorsed most of the
report in early 1948 in an address to Congress. Southern Democrats, who had
more than enough power to stall civil rights legislation in Congress, reacted with
such hostility that the president retreated on civil rights for a while. No consensus
for implementing any but the most modest proposals of the commission existed
in 1948 or for some years thereafter. Not until the mid-1960s did the necessary
consensus develop, and then only after the civil rights movement had forced the
issue.

None of the seventeen states that had Jim Crow laws and policies altered
course. Mounting disagreements among Democrats over major issues portended
a political civil war. Of these issues, civil rights was the most explosive. Truman,
who in 1948 was battling to get his party's nomination for the presidency, wavered as his party divided into warring factions. Truman finally acted decisively
in late July. By then the Democratic National Convention had endorsed most of
the recommendations in *To Secure These Rights* and had nominated Truman for reelection after a number of southern Democrats had bolted the party. The president
used his executive authority to order the gradual elimination of racial segregation
and discrimination in the armed forces and in federal employment. Thus began
the slow but steady decline of Jim Crow in the American armed forces. Racially
mixed units of American forces fought in the Korean War (1950–1953).

The coalition that had made the Democrats the dominant national party since
1930 splintered. Some left-wing Democrats departed to support Henry A. Wallace, the former vice president, who ran as the nominee of the hastily formed Progressive party. Much more important, then and thereafter, were the Dixiecrats.
When the Democratic party adopted a strongly worded civil rights plank in its
1948 platform, the Mississippi delegation and half of the Alabama delegates
walked out of the national convention. By prearrangement, they and other southerners met in Birmingham three days later to create the States' Rights party. The
States' Rights Democrats—or the Dixiecrats, as they were popularly known—
nominated Governor J. Strom Thurmond of South Carolina for president and
Governor Fielding Wright of Mississippi for vice president. A speaker at the Birmingham meeting caught the spirit of the occasion when he denounced President
Truman and his civil rights program as "threats to make Southerners into a mon-
grel, inferior race by forced intermingling with Negroes." Thurmond declared in
his acceptance speech: "There is [sic] not enough troops in the Army to force the
Southern people to break down segregation and admit the Negro race into our
theaters, into our swimming pools, into our homes, and into our churches."

The Dixiecrats believed that the national Democratic party had betrayed the
South, the region that had been most loyal to the party. Traditionally, the Democratic party's greatest asset in the South had been its ability to keep blacks in their

place and to prevent the federal government from intervening to alter that arrangement. That ability was clearly in jeopardy in 1948. The Republicans, however, were not an acceptable alternative for most southern whites in 1948. Traditional aversion to the Republican party and the strong civil rights stand that the national Republicans adopted in 1948 kept most southern Democrats from joining forces with the Republicans. Memories of the Depression and the New Deal may also have deterred some southern Democrats from switching parties.

The Thurmond-Wright slate carried four states—South Carolina, Alabama, Mississippi, and Louisiana—in all of which they ran under the official Democratic party label. The Dixiecrats did very well for a new third party, though they failed to achieve their goal of capturing enough electoral votes to force the election into the House of Representatives, where they might have been strong enough to engineer the election of a president more congenial to them. Loyalty to the traditional party of the region and the reluctance of most Democratic regulars to take the risk of deserting Truman counted heavily against the Dixiecrats.

However, Negrophobia or hostility toward any attempt to change Jim Crow significantly would in time dramatically change politics in the solid South. The year 1944 was the last time the Democrats captured all the electoral votes of the South. Joined with other forces—opposition to the economic policies of the national Democratic party and conservatives' reactions to the liberal policies of Democrats of the urban North—Negrophobia and defenses of Jim Crow dramatically transformed politics in the South and consequently those in the nation.

More immediately, the Democrats maintained an uneasy peace nationally. President Truman could do little about civil rights with the well-entrenched southern Democrats in Congress, and he tried little beyond ordering the military to desegregate. More energy was spent—with some success—in making compromises across sectional lines within the Democratic party in preparation for future elections. Thus neither the Congress nor the Truman administration did much to lend substance to the report of Truman's Civil Rights Committee or to the civil rights plank of the 1948 Democratic party platform. But the Supreme Court did. In 1950 the Court dealt racially segregated public education a major blow in a case that challenged the exclusion of blacks from a publicly supported law school.

THE SUPREME COURT AND "SEPARATE BUT EQUAL"

When Heman Sweatt, a World War II veteran, applied for admission to the law school at the University of Texas in February 1946, the state had 7,701 white lawyers and 23 black lawyers and no publicly supported law school for blacks. The university rejected Sweatt's application because he was black. Sweatt sued, asserting that his rejection violated the "separate but equal" doctrine. The state responded by establishing a separate law school for blacks. Sweatt's NAACP attorneys argued and a number of leading figures in legal education testified that the new school could not compare with that at the University of Texas. This approach reflected the NAACP's legal strategy of attacking the "separate but equal" doctrine by insisting on *real* equality. Some supporters, including Truman's attorney general, Tom Clark, a Texan, went much further. They filed *amicus curiae* (friend of the court) briefs challenging the constitutionality of the cornerstone of Jim Crow, *Plessy* v. *Ferguson*, the "separate but equal" decision of 1896. That decision, they said, violated the Fourteenth Amendment of the Constitution, and therefore the Court was obliged to declare the doctrine unconstitutional. Texas and eleven other states that filed *amicus* briefs countered with a defense of racial segregation as constitutional and with the assertion that the right of the states to abide by the traditions and preferences of their citizens in educational and racial matters was well established in law and in practice.

The Supreme Court ruled that the University of Texas had to admit Sweatt to its law school, but it did not declare "separate but equal" unconstitutional. It found the newly established law school for blacks to be unequal to that of the University of Texas because the latter had more faculty, students, course offerings, and opportunities to specialize, as well as a law review. "What is more important, the University of Texas Law School possesses to a far greater degree those qualities which are incapable of objective measurement but which make for greatness in a law school . . . to name but a few, . . . reputation of the faculty, experience of the administration, position and influence of the alumni, standing in the community, traditions and prestige." The new black law school could not possibly meet the "separate but equal" standard. "It is," the Court concluded, "difficult to believe that one who had a free choice between these law schools would consider the question close."

At the same time, the Supreme Court struck two more blows against Jim Crow. On grounds similar to those in the *Sweatt* decision, the Court ordered the University of Oklahoma to cease segregating George W. McLaurin, a black graduate student. Earlier the university had lost its legal battle to exclude McLaurin altogether. Then it attempted to segregate him within the university. When he attended a class, or studied in the library, he sat in an anteroom or alcove by himself. If he wished to eat in the cafeteria, he could do so only before or after whites ate there. The Court declared that since the restrictions imposed on McLaurin denied him an opportunity to study and learn equal to that accorded to white students, those restrictions violated the "separate but equal" constitutional standard. The Court also ruled that the Southern Railway violated the Constitution when it denied equal treatment to black passengers on its dining cars by restricting them to specific tables that were marked by signs and set apart by screens and barriers.

The *Atlanta Constitution* trumpeted that the *Sweatt* decision meant that " 'Separate but Equal' Still Stands." It stood, but on a very insecure foundation. How could the South meet the criteria set forth by the Court for law schools, medical schools, dental schools, engineering schools, graduate schools—all publicly supported educational institutions? The railway decision reinforced the Court's growing determination to refuse to sanction racial segregation on trains and buses that crossed state lines.

In the decade after the *Sweatt* decision, desegregation of higher education in the South increased substantially. The numbers grew from 200 blacks in twenty-one graduate and professional schools in 1950 to perhaps 2,000 in regular sessions and several thousand in summer sessions in 1954. By 1960, 131 previously segregated public institutions of higher education, fourteen of which had been all-black, had been desegregated. Most of them were graduate and professional schools. Perhaps 200 private colleges and universities had desegregated voluntarily. The Deep South, predictably, held out the longest, although Louisiana State University had lowered its racial barrier under a court order in 1950 and had more than 150 black students by 1953. Georgia admitted its first black student in 1961, but higher education in South Carolina, Alabama, and Mississippi remained completely segregated. The last two states would become stages for major civil rights confrontations in the 1960s.

Although racial barriers in interstate and intrastate public transportation had eroded, largely because of pressures from the federal government, those barriers held firm in most of the Deep South. Jim Crow remained intact in public education, but many people anticipated that this area would be the next and most explosive battleground in desegregation. Public school desegregation would become the most divisive domestic political issue in the twentieth-century United States.

The mood of the South after the Court's decisions expressed itself tellingly in two senatorial elections in 1950, then in the presidential election of 1952. Perceived as soft on segregation (and too close to organized labor), Florida's Senator Claude Pepper lost his reelection bid in a campaign loaded with racial overtones. Frank Graham's defeat in North Carolina had been an even greater shock. Graham had presided over the rise of the University of North Carolina to the front ranks in education in the South. Buttressed by his reputation as a great educator and his personal popularity, Graham carried a large lead from the first primary election in May into the runoff. Then came the Court's 1950 decisions on racial segregation. Graham's opponents quickly linked a vote for Graham with "your children sitting in Negro schools." Negrophobia spread like a prairie fire in North Carolina, from low-income and working-class whites who feared school desegregation and job competition from blacks to middle- and upper-income whites who wanted all-white schools. Labeled a "nigger lover," Graham watched his substantial lead disappear within days, and he lost his bid to return to the Senate. Like Pepper, Graham also suffered from his prolabor reputation. For many North Carolina voters he was simply too liberal.

The Democrats also suffered major defeats in the South in the 1952 presidential election. Four southern states—Virginia, Tennessee, Florida, and Texas—voted for Dwight D. Eisenhower, the successful Republican presidential candidate, as support for Eisenhower increased in the South to nearly 50 percent from about 35 percent four years earlier. Eisenhower's greatest strength came from traditionally Republican mountain areas and from urban areas where the economic policies of the national Democrats were very unpopular with middle- and upper-class voters. Counties with large black majorities and acute sensitivity to any changes along the color line also favored the Republican nominee.

More direct efforts to keep Jim Crow in place in public education were made in the early 1950s. Attempts to make "separate but equal" a fact, not a theory, increased markedly. Steps toward equalization had already been taken in teacher pay and in the provision of school buses and high schools for blacks. Large gaps remained, however. South Carolina, for example, tacitly acknowledged these gaps when it instituted a 3 percent sales tax in 1951 to fund a $75 million bond

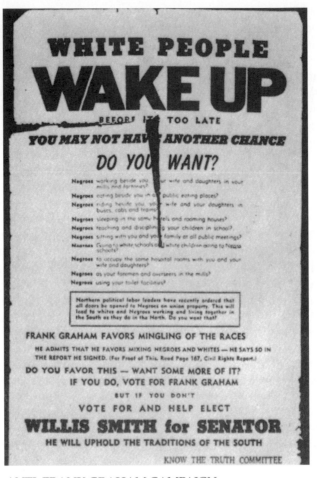

ANTI–FRANK GRAHAM CAMPAIGN
(The New York Public Library)

program designed to improve black schools. By 1952 the southern states spent 70 percent as much on education for blacks as for whites, up from 43 percent in 1940.

However, "separate but equal" was running a losing race. It was explicitly challenged in several court cases in 1952. Then in December of that year the Supreme Court heard arguments on several desegregation cases that collectively came to be known as *Brown* v. *Board of Education of Topeka*. After hearing arguments, then rearguments a year later, then extensively deliberating the cases, the Court unanimously declared on May 17, 1954, that "separate but equal" was unconstitutional, reversing *Plessy* v. *Ferguson*. "We conclude that in the field of public education that doctrine of 'separate but equal' has no place. Separate but equal facilities are inherently unequal." Justice Hugo Black, an Alabamian who was one of the first of the justices to conclude that *Plessy* was constitutionally indefensible, reportedly warned his colleagues when they were deciding on *Brown* that if they overturned *Plessy*, "it would mean the end of Southern liberalism for the time being. The Bilbos and the Talmadges would come even more to the fore. . . . The guys who talked nigger would be in charge, there would be riots, the Army might have to be called out." Still, Black "was determined to overrule it on principle." Justice Black's warnings ultimately proved correct. Almost everywhere in the South, *Brown* met strong resistance—blunt, overt opposition or deliberate evasion.

BROWN: *MASSIVE RESISTANCE, CALCULATED EVASION*

Overt opposition to school desegregation found expression in a variety of ways, including the revival of the Ku Klux Klan. In its third life, the Klan focused its anger on blacks and on school desegregation. Also born in the wake of *Brown* were white-collar or country-club segregationist groups. Peopled by local and regional elites, the Association of Citizens' Councils and such allies as the Virginia Defenders of State Sovereignty and Individual Liberties, the North Carolina Patriots, and the Georgia States' Rights Council formed a loose confederation, the Citizens' Councils of America (popularly known as the White Citizens' Councils). Numbering 250,000 members at their peak, the White Citizens' Councils had their greatest influence in the Deep South states of Louisiana, South Carolina, Mississippi, and Alabama. The councils exerted more influence than the Klan and, at least publicly, opposed the violence associated with the KKK. In Mississippi and Alabama the councils functioned as unelected governments for a time. Everywhere they could, they aggravated community anxieties and encouraged reprisals. Encouraged by local councils, businesspeople in several South Carolina communities used economic pressures to silence the NAACP and other dissenters. After the names of the black signers of petitions calling for school desegregation were published in local newspapers, signers lost their jobs, were evicted, could not get insurance policies renewed or receive credit, and had difficulties with their home mortgages. Soon the number of petitioners shrank. Some blacks retaliated by taking their business to other communities. Those actions and growing national pressure forced the councils to temper their use of economic boycotts. The White Citizens' Councils and other groups also founded and ran racially segregated schools, or "seg academies," designed to preserve racial separation in education.

The strongest forces of official opposition to *Brown* came from the Deep South and Virginia. Senator Harry F. Byrd of Virginia issued a call for "massive resistance," which became their rallying cry. Choosing a strategy of confrontation, they spurned the Supreme Court's invitation to present plans or suggestions for implementing *Brown*, and they attempted to barricade their schools against desegregation. Their bluntest tactic was their apparent willingness to abandon the public schools. In some instances, these states forbade the spending of public funds on integrated schools, repealed compulsory school attendance laws and provisions for public schools in state constitutions, and authorized the sale or lease of public school property and public aid to students attending private schools. To muffle dissent, steps were taken to weaken teachers' tenure. Several states made membership in the NAACP illegal for public school teachers. Some black teachers in South Carolina, for instance, lost their jobs and their pensions. One was Septima Poinsett Clark, who had a major influence on Martin Luther King.

The rest of the South adopted a less confrontational but no more conciliatory strategy on school desegregation. Such states as Tennessee, Texas, and Arkansas resisted passively and effectively, though in each state some schools were desegregated in areas where blacks made up small minorities. State leaders in North Carolina, led by Governor Luther Hodges, employed a school segregation strategy that permitted them to outflank both extreme segregationists who wanted to close the schools and integrationists. The North Carolina legislature passed laws permitting school districts to choose to desegregate or not. If they chose not to do so, they could then decide to close their schools. The state provided for financial aid for students to attend private schools if public schools in their districts were closed. North Carolina officials also initiated pupil assignment laws designed to minimize integration and encouraged blacks "voluntarily" to attend racially segregated schools. Thus the Tarheel State maintained its moderate image while effectively keeping Jim Crow in public education for a decade after *Brown.*

Such events as the Montgomery bus boycott added to the anxieties of those whites who were trying to preserve the racial caste system. Southern blacks had boycotted public transit systems earlier in the 1950s. In fact, some of the lessons blacks learned during a brief, unsuccessful bus boycott in Baton Rouge in 1953 were applied in Montgomery. Nor was the Montgomery demonstration the only one at the time. Tallahassee blacks conducted an even more effective boycott. But the charisma of Martin Luther King, Jr., and the adamant resistance of white segregationists in Montgomery drew the public spotlight to the city.

The Montgomery campaign also introduced a critical new element in the challenge to Jim Crow: the televised mass demonstration, which became a catalytic force in the early 1960s. Montgomery, as well as Baton Rouge and Tallahassee, revealed the extent of black discontent with segregation. Whites tried to claim that such protests were the result of "outside agitators," a few local malcontents who misled ordinary blacks, and even communists. The substantial size of the boycotts and their spontaneity belied these claims.

The Montgomery boycott received support from some local whites, and not just from those who considered their maids indispensable. White moderates walked or tiptoed an uncomfortable, often risky, even dangerous line between blacks and whites. Some lost customers; others received threats of business losses. A socially prominent architect in Montgomery whose racial moderation became known left after his clientele vanished. Virginia Durr's husband's law practice virtually evaporated. The Sunday school class Clifford Durr taught did evaporate. At one time a prominent attorney before he became a high-ranking official in the New Deal and then commissioner of the Federal Communications Commission, Durr struggled the rest of his life to make a living. Families were ostracized, sometimes threatened. At least two local churches—one Presbyterian, one Episcopal—hired police to bar blacks from services. When the Episcopal pastor objected, he was forced to leave. A white Lutheran clergyman shared a distinction with King and King's closest ally, Ralph Abernathy: each survived a bombing of his home.

The intransigence of the white leaders in Montgomery worsened the boycott. Initially the blacks in Montgomery had not sought an integrated bus system. They had asked for a more flexible version of segregated seating, such as the one already in place in Mobile and other southern cities; for the hiring of black drivers for routes that were heavily traveled by blacks; and for more courteous treatment by all drivers. White political leaders refused, although the bus company was willing to be more conciliatory. Black leaders then changed their demands: now they would settle for nothing less than a completely desegregated bus system. The final settlement came in November 1956, when the Supreme Court confirmed a lower court's decision, issued by Alabama federal judges Frank M. Johnson, Jr., and Richard T. Rives, that the Montgomery ordinance requiring racial segregation in public transit was unconstitutional. The Court based its decision on the Fourteenth Amendment and the precedent of *Brown*, thus widening the effect of *Brown* beyond public education.

The city of Montgomery exercised its last legal option and asked the Court to reconsider its decision. The Court refused. The decision became effective December 20. Early the next morning, Rosa Parks, E. D. Nixon, King, Abernathy, and Glen Smiley, a white, Texas-born civil rights activist, boarded a Montgomery bus at the front door and quietly took seats near the front. Photographers and cameramen recorded the event; it became a landmark in the demise of Jim Crow. Bitterness lingered, however. A major break in the racial caste system had occurred, but strong resistance remained. In the late 1950s Montgomery officials closed parks and a zoo to avoid integrating them and removed the seats from the public library after it was desegregated.

The situation in Montgomery did not, however, indicate what would happen if state or local officials chose to ignore or disobey a court order to desegregate. Would the federal government intervene to enforce the order? And if so, how? Events in 1956 were not reassuring for the champions of desegregation. In February 1956 Autherine Lucy won her three-year battle for admission to the University of Alabama. During Lucy's three-day academic career at Tuscaloosa, mobs rioted in protest. To quell the riots, state police expelled Lucy. The university's board of trustees made her expulsion permanent after she charged that the university administration had conspired with the mobs. "The lesson was clear," one analyst said. "Federal court orders could be forcibly nullified—provided that sufficient elements of the white power structure countenanced or encouraged it."

When another important element of the white power structure bluntly challenged *Brown* and the Supreme Court in March 1956, President Eisenhower said nothing. Nineteen of the 22 senators and 101 of the 128 congressmen from the former Confederate states signed the "Declaration of Constitutional Principles," or what was called the Southern Manifesto. It denounced *Brown* as a "clear abuse of judicial power," a threat to the rights of states and parents, and destructive of "the amicable relations between the Negro and white races." Tennessee's senators, Albert Gore and Estes Kefauver, refused to sign. By arrangement, the sponsors of the manifesto did not ask Lyndon Johnson of Texas, the majority leader in the Senate, to sign. None of the nonsigners in the Senate or the House came from the Deep South. Political considerations very probably prompted the manifesto and Eisenhower's silence: 1956 was an election year.

The failure of President Eisenhower to intervene on behalf of a flagrantly violated federal court order raised serious doubts about the civil rights policy of his administration. Eisenhower's position on civil rights was ambiguous. He had grave reservations about the *Brown* decision and he never publicly put the authority of his office or his person behind the decision by endorsing it, but he enforced *Brown* where he felt he had clear authority. On his orders, public schools and federal facilities in Washington, D.C., were quickly desegregated. He also pushed desegregation and nondiscrimination in the armed forces and in federal employment. Eisenhower's policy on civil rights was shaped by his conservative view of presidential and federal powers, by his belief that intervention would make race relations worse rather than better, and very probably by a lack of sensitivity in regard to the never-ending insults suffered by blacks. The failing was, of course, shared by the vast majority of American whites, north and south. Eisenhower also thought he could rely on quiet persuasion to get southern white leaders to make concessions. He obviously underestimated their intransigence.

Six months after the manifesto appeared, state officials in Texas explicitly refused to obey a federal court order to admit blacks to two all-white schools. Earlier, desegregation of public schools had gone smoothly in southwest Texas. Eastern Texas was another story. Part of the Old South with large black minorities, eastern Texas was a hostile setting for desegregation. Governor Allan Shivers revived the widely discredited pre–Civil War interposition doctrine—the concept that the federal government is not the sole judge of its powers and that the states may insert or interpose themselves between the federal government and individuals in the states. He used this doctrine along with the Texas Rangers to stop school desegregation in eastern Texas.

Growing hostility to *Brown* also led to not very subtle attempts to disfranchise blacks or to slow the significant increase in black voter registration that had been occurring since the white primary had been declared unconstitutional in 1944. Citizens' Council members advised some registered black voters to disfranchise themselves "voluntarily." By 1955 fifteen Mississippi counties had no black voters at all. Louisiana passed legislation in 1954 that allowed local officials to review the qualifications of registered voters and remove from voting rolls those deemed to be unqualified. Guided by a pamphlet, *Voter Qualification Laws in Louisiana—The Key to the Segregation Struggle,* registrars removed the names of more than 10,000 blacks from voter rolls.

In response to these and other developments, the Eisenhower administration and Congress passed the first federal civil rights legislation since 1875. The Civil Rights Act of 1957 provided for the creation of the Civil Rights Commission to investigate denials of voting rights and of equal protection of the laws, elevated the Civil Rights Section of the Justice Department to a division, and gave the Justice Department authority to intervene in voting rights cases. The legislation passed only after a compromise with southern congressional leaders diluted the measure. Majority Leader Lyndon Johnson's support was necessary for the bill's passage. Whatever prompted Johnson in this instance and in cleverly arranging to avoid signing the Southern Manifesto, he was keenly aware that no southern Democrat could cling adamantly to Jim Crow and ever be elected president. Other southerners in Congress from outside the Deep South—from Texas, Tennessee, Florida,

Kentucky, and Oklahoma—also supported the Civil Rights Act. Missouri, West Virginia, and Maryland, states with strong segregationist traditions, also supplied votes for the new legislation.

PUBLIC SCHOOL DESEGREGATION: LITTLE ROCK AND NEW ORLEANS

The most serious and highly publicized challenges to *Brown* in the 1950s did not, ironically, come from the Deep South. A number of school boards outside the Deep South adopted gradual, often token desegregation plans. Under these plans, very small numbers of black applicants were admitted to previously all-white schools, usually high schools. The school board of Little Rock, Arkansas, had such a plan. After opponents of the Little Rock plan lost their legal battle to stop it, school officials prepared to admit nine black students to Central High in September 1957.

Governor Orval Faubus, who was not known as an extreme segregationist, suddenly intervened to prevent desegregation. Claiming he was acting to prevent violence and was justified in doing so by the doctrine of interposition, Faubus dispatched the Arkansas National Guard to maintain order at Central High by preventing blacks from enrolling. Overnight Little Rock became a national news item. Court battles, negotiations, and protests went on for several weeks before they reached a climax. Faced with a federal injunction, Faubus withdrew the National Guard. A near riot and several days of disturbances followed. On September 24 President Eisenhower reluctantly federalized the Arkansas National Guard and sent units of the 101st Airborne Division to Little Rock to maintain order in and around Central High and to ensure the enforcement of the court order to desegregate the school. For the first time since Reconstruction, the federal government had used its military force on behalf of blacks. Also for the first time, Eisenhower had put the full force of his office behind *Brown*.

The paratroopers remained for two months. Elements of the National Guard stayed for the rest of the year. Black students lived through an awkward, difficult, and sometimes intimidating school year. In June, Ernest Green became Central's first black graduate. Twenty years later, Green, a lawyer, served as an undersecretary in the Labor Department for President Jimmy Carter.

But in September 1958, Little Rock closed all four of its high schools, black and white, and they stayed closed for that academic year. Authorized by recently passed state laws, Little Rock voted 19,470 to 7,561 to close the schools rather than integrate them. Clearly, most whites were expressing a deep commitment to segregation. They pointed to what they believed was the hypocrisy of northern whites, noting that blacks were often treated poorly outside the South and that many northern school systems were racially segregated. Whites resented the use of military force. Class complicated matters. Upper-income whites had less to lose than other whites. Most of the high school students from the more affluent homes attended newly opened Hall High, which, according to the original desegregation plan of the school board, was to remain all-white.

Sensitive to themselves as victims and insensitive to the victimization of blacks and their own role in that victimization, most whites in Little Rock fought to preserve Jim Crow in public education. Governor Faubus demonstrated the handsome political benefits that could accrue to militant opponents of *Brown*. He won reelection by a wide margin in 1958 and was reelected every two years thereafter until 1966, when he chose not to run again. State legislators joined Faubus's "massive resistance" campaign and in 1958 passed laws that allowed school officials to close public schools rather than desegregate them.

The Supreme Court ruled against the Arkansas school-closing legislation in September 1958, holding that the rights of black students "can neither be nullified openly and directly by state legislators or state executive officials nor nullified indirectly by them by evasive schemes for segregation." Still, public high schools in Little Rock stood empty during the 1958–1959 school year.

In August 1959 the high schools reopened. Four black students enrolled at Central High and Hall High. The action of federal courts and the forces of compromise had weakened the resolve to maintain segregation at all costs. Conscience and necessity had worked their way. The first factor is harder to document than the second. Fears about the adequacy of private education and about the children whose families who could not pay its costs outweighed fears of desegregated schools. As Little Rock's image as a progressive New South city shattered and, more to the point, as companies abruptly lost interest in locating facilities there, Little Rock's business leaders became more supportive of school desegregation. They also began quietly working with local black leaders to desegregate public facilities. A student of the Little Rock crisis saw "more than simply a desire for economic gain. . . . The emphasis on 'image' also reflected a desire to join, at last, the American mainstream."

Virginia also initially closed schools rather than desegregate them. Governor J. Lindsay Almond took the initiative; school systems under court orders to desegregate were closed by the governor in 1958. But the closings came to an end when the Virginia supreme court ruled that the state's school closing law was unconstitutional. The national media may well have influenced the situation. *Time* and the *New York Times* ran articles on "the lost class of '59." Edward R. Murrow and *CBS Reports* gave the issue extensive prime-time coverage. Only in Prince Edward County did schools stay closed to avoid desegregation. There the schools remained locked for five years, and white students received grants from county funds for their private school expenses.

In 1960 New Orleans provided the next major battleground when public schools there became the first in the Deep South to be required to integrate. Eight years after a suit to desegregate New Orleans public schools had been filed, U.S. District Court Judge J. Skelly Wright ordered the schools to drop their racial barriers. Turmoil followed as four black students enrolled in two all-white elementary schools in November 1960. A prominent Louisiana politician, Leander Perez, warned 5,000 protesters: "Don't wait for your daughter to be raped by these Congolese. Don't wait until the burr-heads are forced into your schools. Do something about it now." All the white students were quickly withdrawn from one of the schools. A small number stayed at the other. For weeks they and their parents were confronted daily by mobs that abused them verbally and physically. Local authorities provided no protection. Economic pressures were also applied. One nonboycotting white lost his job and could not find another. The parent of a black

BLACK FIRST-GRADER, NEW ORLEANS (AP/Wide World Photos)

student was also fired. His employer explained that he regretted firing him but had done so to placate customers who threatened to trade elsewhere if the employee was not dismissed. First white, then black teenagers rampaged through the streets. Called into special session by Governor Jimmie Davis, the state legislature resuscitated interposition to pass school-closing legislation and other measures designed to block desegregation.

Before the struggle reached a climax in early 1961, Judge Wright had issued injunctions or restraining orders against the governor, the legislature, the attorney general, the state superintendent of education, the National Guard, and the state police. Never had a judge gone so far to enforce a court order or to defend the supremacy of the federal government. Ninety percent of the people in New Orleans recognized the name of "that integration judge." Old friends avoided him and stopped speaking. He received numerous threats on his life. Federal marshals protected the judge at all times. The legislature gave a standing ovation to a coffin containing Wright's blackened effigy. But Wright persisted, and the forces of moderation and federal law finally prevailed.

Mob rule might have been avoided in New Orleans, which was not a typical Deep South city. Its ethnically diverse population gave the city a cosmopolitan character. Some public facilities had been quietly integrated before the crisis over the schools. Substantial numbers of blacks voted, and the move in the 1950s to disfranchise black voters in Louisiana largely bypassed New Orleans. However, race relations in the city were volatile. Serious racial violence had occurred there, and there were organized extremists among the segregationists in New Orleans.

Local and state leaders made matters worse, even when their intentions were not altogether obstructive. The school board acquiesced in desegregation only after a long legal battle. Then it made no effort to plan for desegregation until late in the day. The board chose to begin by desegregating two schools in lower-income neighborhoods, both of which had been long neglected by city officials. These neighborhoods felt they were being doubly victimized. And by desegregating only two schools, the board allowed extremists to concentrate their forces.

Mayor de Lesseps S. Morrison, a Democrat who aspired to higher office, carefully avoided offending the segregationists. He provided little public leadership during the turmoil and failed to order the police to disperse the mobs and restore order at the schools. Business leaders were divided or indifferent and caught in crosscurrents. As the televised "Battle of New Orleans" raged, the critically important tourist trade declined sharply. But moderates faced threats of economic retaliation and social ostracism. New Orleans' leaders had apparently learned little from events in Little Rock and Virginia. They failed to assert the kind of leadership that leaders in Atlanta and other southern cities demonstrated when their schools were desegregated. Politicians in Louisiana did learn from Faubus and others that resistance to school desegregation won favor with the majority of voters. At the state level, Louisiana had the best record of desegregation in higher education in the South. Yet the governor and the state legislature reacted with massive resistance to public school desegregation, going, as Governor Jimmie Davis said melodramatically, to the "last step before secession." Some church leaders in New Orleans publicly advocated desegregation and open schools. Other church leaders did the reverse. Most remained silent. Few of the laity heeded the admonitions of those clerics who advocated integration. The pronouncements of the local Catholic archbishop, for example, had little discernible effect.

Massive resistance failed in New Orleans, and unlike Little Rock, New Orleans desegregated its schools without federalized National Guard troops or the intervention of the United States Army. The Eisenhower administration made early and extensive use of federal marshals, something it had not done in Little Rock. The administration also sided with desegregationists in the courtroom. These actions suggested that the federal government was becoming more inclined to act in support of desegregation and in defense of the rights of black citizens. That inclination was also indicated by the passage of the Civil Rights Act of 1960. Though it was weak, the law did authorize federal judges to appoint referees to register qualified blacks who had been denied registration.

Desegregation of public schools provoked massive resistance or calculated evasion because it bluntly probed the most sensitive nerves of southern whites. Daily close contact among people of both sexes and races stirred the deepest phobias, and the contact was not necessarily limited to school hours. A prominent South Carolina journalist wrote in 1960:

The white Southerner's concern over race relations is in substantial measure a concern over sex relations. . . . Back of this preoccupation is a complex of reasons, both rational and irrational, which makes it impossible to raise the prospect of integration without raising the specter of interracial marriage, or of interracial sexual relations. Perhaps more than any other single factor, this apprehension has solidified white resistance to integration.

Integration of public schools also raised less personal but still powerful concerns. Education has long been closely linked with economic and social mobility. If integration threatened the quality of education, as many whites believed, then integration might jeopardize social and economic mobility. That was hardly a minor matter under any circumstances, and for southern whites who had only recently joined the American middle class it was a vital concern.

Southern whites genuinely believed that blacks were inferior. So did most other American whites. More than 300 years of discrimination and acculturation reinforced that view. Class complicated whites' assessment of blacks. Collectively blacks were poorer than whites, had poorer schooling and health, lower skills, less opportunity to enter the middle class. Almost entirely blocked from avenues to the middle class by barriers erected by whites, blacks had long had much less incentive than whites to pursue schooling for themselves or their children.

Schools and homeownership could easily become intertwined. Decisions to buy a home were often shaped by perceptions of the public schools in the area. The reputation of local schools, merited or not, could have a positive or negative effect on the largest single financial asset a family had. People often think of the school in their area as "theirs," a possession that, like their home, is regarded with affection, boasted of, and defended against real and imagined threats. Similar attachments dampened the enthusiasm of many blacks for school desegregation. Their schools were their cultural strongholds. Black schools elicited deep loyalties through histories of academic and athletic achievement. School officials reinforced such attachments by making significant improvements in public education for blacks in the 1950s. Desegregation held out the promise of a better education but involved the possible loss of one's school, of oneself in a white-dominated school, and of the daily comfort of being in a place where you were in the majority, where your color had little significance. More concretely, black teachers and school administrators could be and were displaced or discharged when schools were integrated. Thus, whereas Montgomery blacks had been united in their bus boycott, that unity evaporated when King and others pressed for desegregation of public schools.

Realizing the highly divisive implications of *Brown* and the great variety of conditions and circumstances prevailing in public school systems, the Supreme Court gave the lower courts wide discretion in deciding how and when schools should be desegregated. In its second *Brown* decision (1955), known as *Brown II*, the court stipulated only that desegregation should take place "with all deliberate speed." The federal judges primarily responsible for implementing *Brown* were district court judges in the South, most of whom were natives of their areas and were either openly hostile to *Brown* or quietly opposed to it. Most school boards and officials in the South had similar backgrounds and attitudes. Implementation also depended on the initiation of suits

by desegregationists, primarily blacks, which involved personal risks and considerable expense that often strained the limited resources of the NAACP and
its supporters. The result was prolonged delays.

School boards and school officials became accomplished at evading school
desegregation. Officials made artful uses of pupil-assignment laws and "freedom
of choice" desegregation plans to preserve segregation, either entirely or very
substantially. After 1965, "freedom of choice" became the favored means for evasion. School systems announced that their schools were open to all races and that
students and their parents were free to choose the schools they wished to attend.
Judge John J. Parker of the U.S. Circuit Court of Appeals had provided the legal
defense for pupil-assignment laws and "freedom of choice" plans. In *Briggs* v.
Elliott (1955), Parker had declared:

> Nothing in the Constitution or in the [*Brown*] decision of the Supreme Court takes
> away from the people the freedom to choose the schools they attend. The Constitution,
> in other words, does not require integration. It merely forbids discrimination. It does
> not forbid such discrimination as occurs as a result of voluntary action. It merely for-
> bids the use of governmental power to enforce segregation.

Not surprisingly, few blacks got assigned or chose to go to all-white or predominantly white schools. No whites got assigned or chose to go to black schools.

Blacks could be discouraged subtly or not so subtly from requesting transfers.
As one prominent Mississippi journalist wrote, "Most Negroes work for white
people in the South—and almost everywhere else. In a majority of instances a
white employer need only mention to his Negro employee that he is certain that
both agree that school segregation is the wisest course for all concerned." Harry
and Liza Briggs learned about such things. *Briggs* v. *Elliott* evolved in part from
their efforts to get their children admitted to the better, all-white public schools of
Clarendon County in the South Carolina low country. A navy veteran and father
of five, Briggs lost his job in a local service station and his credit at the bank. Liza
Briggs was fired from her job as a maid in a nearby motel.

Tokenism in school desegregation proved more effective and less risky and
disruptive than massive resistance. Dramatic conflicts such as those in Little Rock
and New Orleans were rare. Ten years after *Brown*, nearly 98 percent of blacks
attending public school went to all-black schools. Almost all black students who
attended previously all-white public schools lived in urban areas in the upper
South, in the Southwest, or in the border states. Jim Crow prevailed in public education a decade after the Supreme Court had declared "separate but equal"
unconstitutional.

In the face of tokenism in school desegregation, the persistence of Jim Crow
elsewhere in southern life, and the intransigence of whites, blacks became more
assertive and innovative in pursuit of their rights. They forced the federal government to take unprecedented steps. In doing so, they had an improbable ally: the
Fifth Circuit Court of Appeals, then sitting in New Orleans. The court became a
major force in establishing precedent-setting legal doctrines that helped implement the *Brown* v. *Board of Education* decision in the classroom, in politics, and in
the jury room. The court, which was dominated by Judges Elbert P. Tuttle, John
Minor Wisdom, John R. Brown, and Richard Taylor Rives, devised the legal basis

for forcing schools to take steps to end segregation speedily, for overcoming past discrimination through affirmative action, for making reapportionment more equitable, and for making it more likely that defendants would be tried before a jury of their peers. The impact of the court extended from jury boxes to schools to local governments, state legislatures, and congressional districts. In sum, the Fifth Circuit functioned like "an institutional equivalent of the civil rights movement."

THE CIVIL RIGHTS MOVEMENT

For several years after the *Brown* decision, assaults on Jim Crow focused on public schools, and most of these assaults occurred in courtrooms. However, significant challenges to segregation were also made through politics and organized protests. The latter evolved into the mass civil rights movement.

The voting power of Negroes had become important at several levels. By 1948 black voters had established their importance in close presidential elections as well as in some congressional elections and in state and local elections outside the South. By 1960 strong black support of John F. Kennedy in such key states as Illinois and Michigan played a significant role in his narrow defeat of Richard Nixon. Candidates in some nonsouthern states actively sought black voters. Thus civil rights legislation and attacks on Jim Crow often had Republican and Democratic support. Within the South itself, more than 25 percent of voting-age blacks had registered by 1960. Proportions ran considerably higher in the upper South (except in Virginia) than in the lower South. Blacks sometimes had enough votes to have a limited voice in local elections, and white leaders became more responsive to black constituents. More money was spent on black schools; recreational facilities for blacks were improved; cities hired a few blacks for their police forces; public transit systems were desegregated; occasionally Jim Crow signs over water fountains and on restroom doors disappeared. Here and there blacks won a few elected offices. Still, more than a decade after the publication of *To Secure These Rights* by the Truman administration, Jim Crow remained largely intact.

King and others, primarily black clergymen, had organized the Southern Christian Leadership Conference (SCLC) in 1958 to build on the gains made during the Montgomery boycott and to expand their civil rights efforts in other parts of the South and to other issues. A regional organization committed to desegregation and nondiscrimination, the SCLC struggled to find a feasible program and adequate financing. SCLC leaders expended most of their energies in the important but slow and difficult task of voter education and registration. The NAACP continued to confine most of its fight against segregation to the courtroom and to lobbying. The Congress of Racial Equality (CORE) was a direct-action group and lobby that had a small membership and was based in the North. The forces for desegregation appeared to be inadequate to the task. Jim Crow remained entrenched and apparently would remain so unless a more effective strategy could be devised.

Ezell Blair, Jr., Franklin McCain, Joseph McNeil, and David Richmond talked a lot about segregation during the fall of 1959, about, among other things, what King and the SCLC were doing. Then in February 1960 the four seventeen-year-old

SITTING IN, GREENSBORO, NORTH CAROLINA
(Bruce Roberts/Photo Researchers)

freshmen at all-black North Carolina A&T College in Greensboro decided to do something on their own. After arranging for the local newspapers to be informed, they went to a store in downtown Greensboro, made several purchases, and then went to the lunch counter and asked to be served. The store refused; it was following the customary policy of serving whites only at its lunch counter. The students remained seated. A policeman watched them closely. Two older white women praised their actions. Several others criticized them, including one older black woman. When the store closed, they got up and went back to their campus. Word spread. Twenty or so A&T students joined them the next day. A few white students from the University of North Carolina Women's College (now the coeducational University of North Carolina at Greensboro) joined in several days later. The sit-ins spread to other downtown stores, then to shopping centers. Crowds of white teenagers gathered to heckle. The demonstrators did not respond, even to physical abuse. By the following Saturday, hundreds of students were being confronted by gangs of white youths. After the stores were closed in an effort to dampen the explosive situation, a mass meeting of A&T students voted to halt demonstrations. It was the first of a series of demonstrations and racial confrontations that disrupted Greensboro for more than three years.

The Greensboro sit-ins came as a shock, at least to whites. North Carolina had a reputation as a progressive state, moderate on race relations. Greensboro was believed to be in the forefront of progress and moderation. It had removed some vestiges of Jim Crow in the early 1950s, and a black won a seat on the city council in 1951. Greensboro had been the first city in the South to announce it would comply with *Brown*, and in 1957 six black students enrolled in two previously all-white schools. Their numbers did not increase, however, and they met persistent harassment at school. Like other school systems in North Carolina, Greensboro's used recently passed school legislation to stifle desegregation while seeming to comply with *Brown*. Black parents who wanted their children to attend desegregated schools had to make their way through a bureaucratic maze, meet a complex set of criteria, and stand firm in an intimidating atmosphere—sometimes more. When two families succeeded in getting their children transferred to a previously all-white school, the school board then transferred all the white students, faculty, and staff out of the school.

Such measures stifled public school desegregation in North Carolina: the rate of integration in the state progressed to 0.026 percent by 1961. A Little Rock school official told a colleague in North Carolina: "You North Carolinians have devised one of the cleverest techniques of perpetuating segregation that we have seen." Yet the state maintained its moderate image by not openly engaging in the massive resistance practiced by its neighbors. Under Luther Hodges, widely praised as a moderate, North Carolina did pass legislation to allow local districts to close schools rather than desegregate. But none ever used that option.

Just as blacks found few places in Greensboro's white schools, they found few good places for employment or careers, though the city had a significant number of educated blacks. The tokenism of school desegregation, limited job and career opportunities, and other continuing evidences of racial prejudice and discrimination gave Greensboro's blacks a very different image of the city than most whites had. The contradictions between image and reality helped set the stage for the sit-ins.

When the Greensboro Four decided to take some action, they could not have anticipated that they would be giving impetus to a mass movement that would hasten the collapse of the South's racial caste system and have implications far beyond the South. A week after the first Greensboro demonstration, sit-ins started occurring elsewhere in North Carolina, then elsewhere in the South. By mid-April they were taking place in some sixty cities. Thousands of people were involved, mostly black college students. Small numbers of whites, usually students, joined in, as did faculty members at black colleges and a few local black leaders who were not academics. Protesters from twelve southern states met in Raleigh over Easter and formed the Student Nonviolent Coordinating Committee (SNCC, or "Snick"), which became a major force in the civil rights movement.

During the next five years, demonstrations and protests on behalf of the rights of blacks became familiar occurrences as blacks and their allies found that direct action was both necessary and effective. The sit-ins took place mostly in 1960 and 1961, then sporadically thereafter. Amazingly, there were few reported instances of violent confrontations between groups of blacks and whites. The protesters refused to be provoked. From the start, the sit-ins were "a movement of nonviolence . . . a Christian movement." John Lewis, a founder and chairman of SNCC who was elected to Congress in 1986 from an Atlanta district, said that nonviolence "became a way of life. You would put on your church-going clothes, Sunday clothes, and we took books and papers and did our homework at the lunch counter, just quiet and trying to be as dignified as possible."

LUNCH-COUNTER SIT-IN IN JACKSON, MISSISSIPPI, 1963
(AP/Wide World Photos)

Such conduct required discipline and courage. During a sit-in in Nashville, the manager of a hamburger stand locked demonstrators in and fumigated them, "the same thing that you use to fumigate for insects—the man just turned on this machine, and this huge foam covered the whole place. . . . He refused to let us out. We stayed in there, and finally the Nashville Fire Department came down, and they broke the window of the place." On another day in Nashville, hecklers cursed and spat on protesters as they sat stoically at a lunch counter, extinguished cigarettes on them, struck them, and jerked them off the stools. An elderly white woman intervened when a man threatened a young woman with battery acid. Another white bystander, perhaps a college student, forcibly disarmed another man who threatened to attack a demonstrator with a knife. Ann Moody was part of a group of black and white men and women protestors who in 1963 were dragged off stools in a store in Jackson, Mississippi, kicked, and carried or dragged out to the street. They returned immediately and sat quietly for three hours as they were taunted, smeared with food, and sprayed with paint. Police arrested hundreds of demonstrators—an estimated 3,600 in the first year alone—but few of their attackers. Sit-ins and their variant forms—pray-ins, stand-ins, sleep-ins, jail-ins, consumer boycotts—did not achieve dramatic results before 1964. Piecemeal desegregation over several years was the norm.

But despite the modest initial results, the sit-ins contributed significantly to the development of the direct-action strategy of the civil rights movement. Young people, especially college students, joined the movement en masse, supplying it with an army of volunteers willing to take serious risks and disinclined to compromise. They refined the tactics of nonviolent confrontation, learning how to alert the news media to dramatic events to come, causing businesses and communities to suffer economic losses and raising the specter of greater losses, distressing the image-conscious urban South, going to jail and refusing to leave, and remaining nonviolent despite provocations and assaults. They had taken the high ground in a moral crusade in a region (and a nation) deeply committed to religious values. The sit-ins escalated the process of forcing the white South to stifle or ignore its segregation-at-any-costs minority and retreat, however reluctantly, from Jim Crow. The sit-ins and SNCC also forced older black leaders to act more vigorously. Finally and crucially, pressures on the federal government to engage Jim Crow more directly and powerfully increased as the civil rights movement became more youthful and militant.

THE KENNEDY ADMINISTRATION AND CIVIL RIGHTS

The Kennedy administration faced mounting pressure from civil rights activists early in its inaugural year. Its first civil rights crisis passed quickly in January 1961. Georgia officials resisted a court order to integrate the University of Georgia by withholding funds from the university. But state officials suddenly reversed field and decided to desegregate the university rather than risk a showdown with the federal government and possibly more turmoil on the campus.

The next civil rights crisis was much more serious. In May, activists from CORE, joined by some from SNCC, started the "freedom rides," a move that put

SEPARATE WAITING ROOM (Library of Congress)

enormous pressure on President Kennedy and his advisers to act more decisively on behalf of civil rights. CORE freedom riders challenged racial segregation on interstate buses and in bus terminals. (The Supreme Court had ruled these forms of segregation unconstitutional in 1946 and 1960, respectively, but throughout the South both rulings were ignored.) Two busloads of black and white riders who had been trained in nonviolent tactics left Washington in early May for the South. The well-publicized journey proceeded uneventfully through Virginia and North Carolina. After some trouble in South Carolina, then none in Georgia, the buses entered Alabama. A mob near Anniston stopped one of the buses by shooting its tires out, then set it on fire. According to most accounts, the occupants were at first prevented from fleeing the burning bus. When they finally got out, they were beaten. Doctors and nurses at the local hospital refused to treat the injured. A caravan of armed blacks rescued the freedom riders after a white mob gathered at the hospital and it became apparent that law enforcement officials would not protect the demonstrators.

When the other bus reached the terminal in Birmingham, a planned assault began: white men beat the defenseless, unresisting freedom riders with baseball bats and chains for nearly fifteen minutes before the first police arrived on the scene. The next day CORE leaders agreed to a cooling-off period arranged by U.S. Attorney General Robert Kennedy in the hope of calming matters and perhaps achieving some compromise. The SNCC activists were convinced that Alabama leaders could not or would not make acceptable concessions, and they refused to stop the ride.

John Lewis and new volunteers from Nashville resumed the ride. James Farmer, executive director of CORE, reluctantly rejoined the ride, but Martin Luther King, Jr., declined an invitation to join, something SNCC activists long remembered. Heavily protected by state authorities on the road from Birmingham, they arrived at a suspiciously quiet bus station in Montgomery. Several hundred men "with ax handles, chains and everything else" soon appeared and attacked the riders. John Lewis later recalled lying on the ground while "the Attorney General of Alabama [was] serving this injunction . . . saying that it was unlawful for interracial groups to travel." Also badly hurt was John Siegenthaler, administrative assistant to Robert Kennedy, who had been sent to Alabama as an observer.

Two days later, another mob of angry whites gathered outside a black church in downtown Montgomery where a large gathering had assembled to support the freedom riders. Rampaging whites forced church doors open and charged in. Marshals, who had been dispatched by the Kennedy administration, pushed the attackers out and kept them precariously at bay. The possibility that the mob would burn the church while it was occupied by several hundred people was very real. Inside, King, the featured speaker of the evening, worked to calm the audience between urgent telephone conversations in which he explained the nature and gravity of the situation to Robert Kennedy. The state of Alabama finally took the decisive action Washington had been pleading for. Governor John Patterson declared martial law and sent 800 National Guard troops to the scene. They may have prevented the rioters from overwhelming the marshals and destroying the church and its occupants. By this time the story of the freedom rides was being featured prominently in the national and international news.

The rides soon began again, this time with heavy protection from the Alabama National Guard and, after crossing the state line, by the Mississippi National Guard. At Jackson, however, the freedom riders were arrested—for their own protection, claimed Governor Ross Barnett. After they refused to pay their fines, they served forty-day sentences in various Mississippi jails, including notorious Parchman Prison, where their stay was made as miserable as possible. Authorities denied the arrested freedom riders blankets and mattresses for their beds. Eventually some 300 riders served sentences. The freedom rides cost CORE more than $300,000 and nearly bankrupted the organization. Initially CORE had planned to use Gandhian tactics ("fill up the jails, as Gandhi did in India, fill them up to bursting if we had to.") in order to make segregation so expensive that southern leaders would conclude "that they no longer could afford it." That tactic did not succeed immediately, but the freedom rides achieved a great deal, perhaps as CORE had planned. Farmer wrote later that his organization had set out

> with the specific intention of creating a crisis. We were counting on the bigots in the South to do our work for us. We figured that the government would have to respond if we created a situation that was headline news all over the world, and affected the nation's image abroad. An international crisis, that was our strategy.

The Kennedy administration did respond, eventually, finding it could not ignore the crisis created by the intrepid band of bus riders. A week after the arrests in Jackson, Attorney General Robert Kennedy announced that he had asked the Interstate Commerce Commission to ban segregation in interstate travel, and the commission complied with the request that fall. Many communities defied the new regulation. The Kennedy administration also intervened in the crisis as a mediator, then as an advocate. Robert Kennedy pressed state and local officials to furnish protection for the riders and persuaded very reluctant bus companies to provide buses and drivers. The administration sent federal marshals and threatened to use even more force. Its sympathies clearly lay with the civil rights movement.

Still, President Kennedy temporized on civil rights. Narrowly elected, the president lacked a clear mandate to take a strong stand on politically divisive issues. Nor was there a clear national consensus on civil rights in the very early 1960s. Kennedy also had to be concerned about the southern Democrats, whose power in Congress could undermine his legislative program. The administration gave less attention to domestic policy than to foreign policy, especially relations with the (now-collapsed) Soviet Union. Other Cold War issues—Cuba and Vietnam—also received much attention from the Kennedy administration. Black votes and an election-eve endorsement by Martin Luther King, Sr., had been crucial to Kennedy's election, but the president did not meet personally with King, Jr., until nine months after his inauguration for fear of alienating southern Democrats.

The Kennedy administration did give blacks greater recognition in its appointments than its predecessor had done, and it privately urged southern political and business leaders to abandon segregation and racial discrimination. On the other hand, during its first eighteen months the administration acquiesced in the appointment of some archsegregationists to the lower federal courts in the South and ignored the advice of Vice President Lyndon Johnson about how to work with Congress to secure the passage of new civil rights legislation. Kennedy also selected Luther Hodges to be his secretary of commerce. As governor of North Carolina, Hodges had developed a "freedom of choice" strategy that effectively blocked public school desegregation in most of his state. The federal government did go to court and later used force to ensure the admission of James Meredith, a black army veteran and native of Mississippi, to the University of Mississippi. Tragically, two people were killed and many were injured in a riot that broke out as the university's first black student enrolled. Eight months later, the Kennedy administration symbolically would stand toe to toe with Governor George Wallace as the University of Alabama desegregated. The Kennedys also gave strong support to efforts to register black voters in the South. That these registration efforts could be made without highly publicized crises and politically awkward moments undoubtedly had appeal to the White House.

But civil rights leaders wanted greater and faster results than could be secured either in the courts or at the ballot box. To fight a long string of cases through the courts is a time-consuming, expensive process that is subject to a variety of limitations. For example, there was no federal law banning racial segregation in public accommodations and public facilities. Relief through the ballot box did not appear to be very promising, either. Few southern whites were willing to end segregation, and blacks lacked the necessary electoral power to defeat Jim Crow on their own. As late as 1962, less than 30 percent of voting-age blacks in the South were on the voting rolls. Poverty and defeatism contributed to low registration, as did fear, intimidation, evasion, violence, and state and local laws aimed at systematically limiting political participation by blacks. Of the means used to discourage blacks politically, economic intimidation and the poll tax were important, but "character," literacy, and "understanding" (of state constitutions) tests had the greatest impact. Gains in black voter registration were slow even though the Justice Department under Kennedy greatly increased its activities on voting rights cases. The Kennedy administration began to realize that its original strategy of working behind the scenes and stressing voter registration efforts by southern blacks was not very effective, that southern whites and their leaders remained largely intransigent or willing to make only minor concessions to blacks. Implicitly acknowledging the weaknesses of the Civil Rights acts of 1957 and 1960 and sensing the urgency of the civil rights issue, President Kennedy sent Congress his first major message on voting rights in February 1963 and two months later a proposal for new voting rights legislation. But by then militant civil rights leaders had conceived of and started a plan to force the federal government and the white South to do more.

BIRMINGHAM AND THE MARCH ON WASHINGTON

In early April, King and the SCLC implemented "Project C" (for Confrontation) in Birmingham. King hoped to force concessions from what had been called "the most segregated city in America" and to pressure the federal government into a more vigorous role on behalf of civil rights. The SCLC had chosen Birmingham deliberately. Its public safety commissioner, Eugene "Bull" Connor, seemed ideal for the sort of confrontation they had in mind. Connor was an intemperate, aggressive racist spoiling for a fight, and this was a fight he might welcome as an opportunity to further the political ambitions he apparently had. Earlier, at Albany, Georgia, the SCLC had learned that no confrontation was possible if law enforcement officials kept their tempers and avoided using excessive force. The civil rights demonstrations that King had helped lead in Albany had stalled because Chief Laurie Pritchett refused to be drawn into a dramatic confrontation. It was a critical defeat for King. The SCLC could not afford another Albany.

The SCLC launched an economic boycott against stores in downtown Birmingham in early April. They wanted the stores to desegregate their facilities (dressing rooms, restrooms, drinking fountains, lunch counters, and restaurants) and hire on a nondiscriminatory basis. The SCLC also asked the city to offer blacks equal employment opportunities in municipal jobs and to form a broad-based committee charged with extending desegregation beyond these first stages. Project C did not take hold, however, not even after King went to jail. While there he wrote his "Letter from Birmingham Jail" to local white clergymen in response to their criticisms of him and the SCLC. In what became one of the principal documents of the civil rights movement, King explained that other methods, including attempts at negotiation, had failed to dent segregation in Birmingham. He analyzed and justified the civil disobedience philosophy and tactics of the civil rights movement. He declared that blacks had waited long enough—"waited for more than 340 years for our constitutional and God given rights." And he criticized the white clergy for failing to lead efforts to end racial segregation.

> If I have said anything in this letter that is an overstatement of truth and is indicative of an unreasonable impatience, I beg you to forgive me. If I have said anything in this letter that is an understatement of the truth and is indicative of my having a patience that allows me to settle for anything less than brotherhood, I beg God to forgive me.

Soon freed from jail, King returned to a movement that seemed to be stalemated. He desperately sought some way to give it needed life and force the confrontation he believed the movement had to have. Finally, with grave reservations, King asked schoolchildren to march. Several thousand joined in. After several days of demonstrations, Connor rounded up 4,000 blacks, some of them children, in a city park and attacked them with high-pressure water hoses. Connor had also used clubs and police dogs on demonstrators. Blacks who had been bystanders entered the fray and fought police. A full-blown, bloody riot throughout Birmingham was a real possibility. News media gave the story extensive coverage. Millions read about it and watched on television as Birmingham policemen and firemen assaulted children and adults. A fortuitous development increased this exposure greatly: the networks had only recently inaugurated their half-hour national news programs. Andrew Young, an SCLC leader and later mayor of Atlanta, later explained:

> We were consciously using the mass media to try to get across to the nation what our message was. The movement was really about getting publicity for injustice. . . . The injustice was there under the surface and as long as it stayed below the surface, nobody was concerned about it. You had to bring it out into the open.

On May 10, black and white leaders, aided by officials of the Kennedy administration, announced a settlement that provided for desegregation of public facilities and lunch counters and for improvements in job opportunities for blacks. A biracial committee was created to deal with employment practices. The settlement broke the segregationist logjam in Birmingham, and the city started on a steady though uneven course toward desegregation. In Birmingham's wake there were demonstrations in perhaps 200 other southern cities and towns, many of which ended with agreements like the one reached in Birmingham. One scholar of civil rights declared, "More racial change came in these few months than occurred in three-quarters of a century."

It was not altogether a victory for King's aggressive nonviolent direct-action strategy. Violent encounters between blacks who were not associated with King and the Birmingham police and the Alabama Highway Patrol prompted Birmingham's less rigid segregationist leaders to compromise before matters got even worse. Rioting broke out after the bombing of the home of A. D. King, a brother of the SCLC leader. When King's motel room, which happened to be empty at the time, was also bombed, the rioting threatened to spread. President Kennedy federalized the Alabama National Guard to remove it from the control of Governor Wallace and stationed army troops near Birmingham. A month later the federal government defeated Wallace's attempt to keep the University of Alabama segregated. At Wallace's inauguration in January 1963 he had shouted, "Segregation now—segregation tomorrow—segregation forever!" and he had vowed to "stand in the schoolhouse door" to prevent the entry of black students. Now federal officials stepped past the governor to escort two black students to classes at Tuscaloosa. That night President Kennedy announced that he would soon send Congress new civil rights legislation. He became the first American president to give resounding support to civil rights for blacks.

> We preach freedom around the world, and we mean it. And we cherish our freedom here at home. But are we to say to the world—and much more importantly to each other—that this is the land of the free, except for the Negroes; that we have no second-class citizens, except Negroes; that we have no class or caste system, no ghettos, no master race, except with respect to Negroes. . . .
>
> We face, therefore, a moral crisis as a country and a people. It cannot be met by repressive police action. It cannot be left to increased demonstrations in the streets. It cannot be quieted by token moves or talk. It is a time to act in the Congress, in your state and local legislative body, and, above all, in all of our daily lives.

Only a few hours after the president spoke, a sniper shot Medgar Evers, field secretary of the NAACP in Mississippi, in the back as he got out of his car. Ripped open by the blast from a high-powered hunting rifle, Evers died in his front yard in Jackson as his wife and children tried to comfort him. Despite compelling evidence, two Mississippi juries in the 1960s refused to find Evers's alleged killer guilty of murder. Using additional testimony and prompted by changed circumstances in the state, the state of Mississippi obtained a guilty verdict of Evers's assassin in early 1994.

Evers was one of at least forty men, women, and children who between 1954 and 1970 lost their lives during the civil rights struggle. Many more people were victims of serious, often severe, beatings and intimidation. Some seventy churches, homes, and businesses were destroyed by bombings and fire.

The civil rights movement kept pressing throughout the summer and fall of 1963. Demonstrations in support of the movement were held all over the country. They reached a climax on August 28, when more than 200,000 marchers, about one-fourth of them white, marched in Washington. Movie stars appeared; so did many politicians and union leaders. Celebrities of the music world entertained as the throng gathered in front of the Lincoln Memorial. The audience joined in the singing. The theme song of the civil rights movement, "We Shall Overcome," rolled across the center of the nation's capital. Speeches went on into the afternoon. The crowd began to drift as the afternoon faded. Many people did not wait to hear King's memorable speech with its haunting repetitions of "I have a dream." Hazel Mangel Rivers, wife of a truck driver and mother of eight, twice jailed for demonstrating in Birmingham, her home, declared, "If I ever had any doubts before, they're gone now." She had paid $8, about a tenth of her husband's weekly pay, for a bus ticket to ride to Washington, the farthest north she had ever been. "When I get back there now I am going to do whatever needs to be done."

Opinion polls in mid-1963 indicated that most Americans believed that civil rights had become the nation's greatest domestic issue. The civil rights movement had succeeded in making segregation a critically important issue in the United States. However, President Kennedy's proposed civil rights legislation remained tied up in Congress, the result of a filibuster in the Senate led by James Eastland of Mississippi and Strom Thurmond of South Carolina. The emotional groundswell

MARCH ON WASHINGTON, 1963 (UPI/Bettmann Newsphotos)

that followed the tragic assassination of President Kennedy and the force and legislative skills of his successor, Lyndon Johnson, finally broke through the Senate.

Eight months after John Kennedy's death, Congress passed the Civil Rights Act of 1964, the most comprehensive and powerful law in support of racial equality ever enacted in the United States. It required that states apply the same "standards, practices, and procedures" to all persons who sought to register and vote and that literacy tests for voters must be administered on a nondiscriminatory basis. Racial segregation in public accommodations and public facilities was banned, the Civil Rights Commission was made permanent and given more power, the Equal Employment Opportunities Commission was established, and discrimination in employment because of "race, color, religion, sex, or national origin" was forbidden. The law forbade discrimination in any program that had federal assistance. Failure to comply with this provision could result in the withdrawal of funds. The Department of Health, Education, and Welfare was authorized to help school districts desegregate.

Less than a decade after Rosa Parks refused to give up her seat, the federal government had created the most powerful weapon for civil rights since the passage of the Fourteenth Amendment. The civil rights movement had played an indispensable role in these events. One of its principal and certainly best-known leaders, Martin Luther King, Jr., had been transformed from a local pastor into a national and international figure. He received the Nobel Peace Prize in December 1964. Southern blacks and their allies had undermined Jim Crow, one of the cornerstones of southern society since Reconstruction.

THE VOTING RIGHTS ACT

The Voting Rights Act of 1965 was designed to ensure that blacks could register and vote. By the mid-1960s, black voter registration had grown significantly in most of the South, but not in the black belt—not in places such as Dallas County, Alabama. There only 156 of the more than 15,000 voting-age blacks were registered. Using the authority granted it by the Civil Rights acts of 1957 and 1960, the Justice Department took the county to court in 1961, charging discrimination against blacks who attempted to register. The county delayed, evaded, and then allowed 71 more blacks (of 114 who had applied) to register. A federal district court judge in Alabama decided that the county was no longer discriminating against black registrants and ruled against the Justice Department. When SNCC started a voter registration drive in Dallas in 1963, the sheriff intimidated and harassed the organizers and the black citizens who applied to register. Would-be registrants also faced economic reprisals. Attempts to desegregate public facilities drew equally hostile responses in Dallas County. Though litigation was pursued more forcefully in Dallas County than anywhere else in the South, the number of black voters in the county failed to rise above 335.

In January 1965 King and SCLC opened a campaign to register black voters in the county. Working with SNCC, SCLC launched a series of demonstrations in Selma, the county seat. On Sunday afternoon, March 7, Alabama highway patrol troopers stopped a column of 600 people who had announced their intention to

SELMA MARCH, 1965 (Bruce Davidson/Magnum Photos)

march to Montgomery to protest. The officer in charge ordered the column to disperse within two minutes. The column remained in place. Perhaps a minute passed. The officer ordered the troopers to charge; they rushed forward with clubs, tear gas, and electric cattle prods. A posse numbering more than one hundred, many on horseback, joined in. Blacks fled in terror. Officers of the law pursued the demonstrators into their neighborhoods, even into their homes, repeatedly clubbing and stunning with the cattle prods those they could catch. Clusters of white spectators applauded and cheered. The Selma police intervened and finally persuaded the troopers and the posse to desist. Chief of Police Wilson Baker, with the full support of the mayor, had tried to contain Sheriff Jim Clark and the highway patrol. He feared that their tendency to resort to brutality when they dealt with black demonstrators would make Selma infamous. His fears were realized. Selma became a grim landmark in the history of the civil rights movement as millions watched the assault on television.

"Bloody Sunday" triggered a flurry of activity. President Johnson immediately gave first place to the new voting rights legislation his administration had been working on since the first of the year. On March 15 he addressed a joint session of Congress and made an urgent plea for his legislation. In his Texas drawl the president told Congress: "We have waited one hundred years and more and the time for waiting is gone. We *shall* overcome." Five days later, protected by a federal court order and the federalized Alabama National Guard, the Selma-to-Montgomery march resumed. It ended four days later at the state capital with 25,000 in attendance and millions watching on television.

In August the president signed the Voting Rights Act. Its provisions gave the attorney general the power to appoint federal examiners who would supervise voter registration in those states and voting districts that had literacy or other qualifying tests and where less than 50 percent of the residents of voting age were registered or had voted in 1964. This portion of the law was applied in parts or all of seven states—Virginia, the Carolinas, Georgia, Alabama, Mississippi, and Louisiana. The act provided for stiff penalties for interference with voting rights, abolished literacy requirements, forbade the creation of new voter qualifications unless they had been cleared by the Justice Department or by a federal court in the District of Columbia, and directed the Justice Department to test the constitutionality of poll taxes in state and local elections. (The Twenty-Fourth Amendment to the Constitution [1964] abolished poll taxes in federal elections.) Four states—Texas, Alabama, Mississippi, and Virginia—still had poll taxes for state and local elections. In 1966, in a case involving Virginia, the Supreme Court declared poll taxes in state elections unconstitutional.

Congress subsequently voted to extend the life of the Voting Rights Act and widened its coverage. In 1970 Congress altered the law to include cities and counties outside the South where literacy tests had been required, and lowered the voting age to eighteen. A year later the ratification of the Twenty-Sixth Amendment made the new voting age permanent and ensured its application to state and local elections. In 1975 Congress amended the act to protect the voting rights of American Indians, native Alaskans, Asian Americans, Americans of Spanish heritage, and illiterates. In 1982 Congress again strengthened and extended the Voting Rights Act. Shielded and encouraged by the federal government, black voter registration grew rapidly in the South. In 1964 an estimated 43 percent of voting-age blacks in the old Confederacy were registered. In 1968, 62 percent were registered. After that the proportion fluctuated, reaching 66 percent in 1984.

DISILLUSIONMENT

Less than a week after the Voting Rights Act became law, the country was shaken by a serious urban riot. More than ten days of rioting and looting left 34 dead, more than 1,000 injured, and $40 million in property damage in the Watts area of Los Angeles. Similar explosions took place in more than 100 cities in the next three years. Most of the riots occurred outside the South and often began innocently enough, perhaps when a white police officer stopped a black driver for speeding. The eruptions grew from deep cores of black resentment. Unemployment, for example: 30 percent of the employable residents of Watts had no jobs; or housing: residents lived crowded together in dilapidated housing because discrimination bottled up even financially able blacks in "their areas." Expectations had soared in the wake of the civil rights movement, but the realities of the lives of most blacks had not changed much, if at all. Opportunities for political participation had improved dramatically. So had educational opportunities. But job opportunities had not, at least not much. "Colored only" and "white only" signs were gone or were going. But lack of money kept many doors closed to the great majority of blacks. For blacks, the restrictions of caste had been greatly reduced, but for the majority, not the restrictions of class. Frustration turned to rage when blacks failed to find a starting place in the circular route to the American dream:

income—educational opportunity—educational achievement—upward mobility—income.

By 1968 the national consensus that had supported the assault on Jim Crow vanished, its disappearance hastened by the riots. But support for that assault never included a willingness to undertake a sustained, deliberate effort to close the gap in income between blacks and whites. Moreover, other points of strong resistance remained in the South. Whites accepted little more than tokenism in public school desegregation and not even tokenism in desegregation of private housing. Residential segregation remained intact. So did racially separate social worlds. In race relations, the South now closely resembled the rest of the nation.

The civil rights movement declined after 1965. Its white support waned. King split with Lyndon Johnson and attacked the United States' commitment to the war in Vietnam. The movement's never entirely harmonious factions split into warring camps. Different styles and aims, egos, generational divisions, and tactical disputes fueled the split. The movement's leaders disputed among themselves about black separatism versus racial integration, about how to attack the seemingly intractable problems of poverty, about whether to risk a break with Lyndon Johnson and openly oppose the war in Vietnam.

SNCC in particular reflected the growing sense of futility among civil rights leaders and many blacks. SNCC embraced black power, stridently demanding black control of the civil rights movement, openly challenging the intentions and abilities of older black leaders, and declaring that no "honky" (white) was to be trusted. Bitter experiences had shaped SNCC's attitudes. SNCC workers had attacked Jim Crow in its darkest, most resistant regions. Physically threatened, beaten, shot at, firebombed, even murdered, SNCC activists knew how deeply entrenched southern white hatred and resistance were. They saw blacks who attempted to register to vote lose their jobs, access to credit, and household utilities. SNCC volunteers, most of them middle-class college students, witnessed and experienced poverty and deplorable living and working conditions. The illiteracy and wretched education they found among rural blacks shocked them. A SNCC worker recalled a family with eleven children: "Seven of the children are school age, and not one . . . is in school because they have no money, no food, no clothes." Their house had "no paper or nothing on the walls and you can look at the ground through the floor and if you were not careful you will step in one of those holes and break your leg or ankle."

At the same time, SNCC lost all faith in the nation's white leaders. White liberals, particularly politicians such as John and Robert Kennedy and Lyndon Johnson, appeared all too ready to compromise the interests of blacks and appeared naive about the seriousness of black problems. Johnson infuriated SNCC and its allies in 1964 when he compromised at the Democratic National Convention with the regular Mississippi Democratic party, which was blatantly racist and often viciously discriminatory. Johnson refused to give his full support to the Mississippi Freedom Democratic party, which was biracial and had a grassroots following among Mississippi blacks. Federal law enforcement officials seemed indifferent and even hostile. SNCC frequently reported that agents of the Federal Bureau of Investigation stood by and took notes as blacks were beaten or crudely discriminated against. Perhaps SNCC should have had a greater appreciation for the legal limits under which federal officials worked. But when SNCC activists and others were being openly threatened and assaulted by whites who had the approval and even the active support of state and local law officers, they had an understandable tendency to forget that assault is a violation of state law but not of federal law.

With its call for radical change or perhaps revolution, black power had obvious appeal to many blacks (and some young whites, few of whom hailed from the South). Many young blacks in particular had concluded that the plight of blacks was hopeless short of revolutionary change. Black power also provided a way to express outrage, to strike out at "honkies," to intimidate *them* for a change. Stokely Carmichael, who became president of SNCC in 1966, urged blacks in Mississippi to reject the reform strategy of King:

> The only way we are going to stop them from whuppin' us is to take over. We've been saying freedom for six years and we ain't got nothin'. . . . The time for running has come to an end. . . . Black Power. It's time we stand up and take over; move on over, whitey, or we'll move on over you.

Black-power rhetoric was heady stuff. It had understandable appeal. It was also reckless, divisive, and rather silly. Black power was reckless because it suggested a racial civil war whose principal victims would have been blacks. Black power was divisive: it divided blacks among themselves and divided blacks and whites. Black power was silly when it talked of revolution: the means for revolution or radical change in the political and economic system of the United States did not exist.

Black power did contribute significantly to the self-image of blacks. Blacks took greater pride in their history and culture and resisted the idea that the price for desegregation and the end of racial discrimination was their becoming "white." But, ironically, this determination to preserve "blackness" and black institutions, such as black colleges and universities, strongly resembled the determination of white segregationists to preserve "whiteness" and white institutions.

The black-power movement was short-lived but important. More than anything else, it demonstrated the enormous difficulties the United States faced in trying to create an equitable society. Those difficulties preoccupied and often depressed Martin Luther King during the last three years of his life. Then an assassin's bullet stilled the clearest and most eloquent voice of the civil rights movement. King's death marked a climax in that movement and badly damaged the hopes the movement had stirred.

Extraordinarily high hopes had been required to sustain the civil rights movement in the face of continual verbal and physical abuse, even death. Those high hopes created unrealistic expectations of what could be achieved. Bitterly disappointed blacks, particularly young blacks, focused on what the movement had not done. Conversely, whites focused on what had been done. Almost everywhere in the South, and in a remarkably few years, Jim Crow was dead or dying. Whites added President Johnson's antipoverty program to the things they believed had been done for blacks, though whites also benefited from the "War on Poverty" and though Johnson's program was a limited war with a modest budget and short life. Such considerations, however, had little effect on the perceptions of whites.

Moreover, whites in the South after 1964 perceived a new and grave threat to their public schools. By various means, schools in the South had remained overwhelmingly segregated in spite of *Brown*. But that situation was changing. The percentage of black students enrolled in previously all-white schools increased to 7.5 in 1965, then to 12.5 in 1966. Pressures from the Johnson administration accounted for most of these increases. Acting with the authority of the 1964 Civil Rights Act, the Department of Health, Education, and Welfare (HEW) developed guidelines for school desegregation and then pushed their implementation. Also in 1966, the federal courts made a landmark ruling that greatly accelerated the desegregation of public schools.

THE END OF "FREEDOM OF CHOICE"

Declaring that "the clock has ticked the last tick on tokenism and delay in the name of 'deliberate speed,' " Circuit Court of Appeals Judge John Minor Wisdom fashioned a decision that was the most important judicial ruling on school integration since *Brown* v. *Board of Education* and *Briggs* v. *Elliott*. In *United States* v. *Jefferson County Board of Education* (1966), Wisdom, a native of Louisiana and a Republican appointed by President Eisenhower, set forth three principles. First, public school systems that had practiced de jure (by law) racial segregation had to do more than adopt nondiscriminatory policies. They had an affirmative duty to desegregate. Second, in doing so, they had to devise desegregation plans that followed HEW guidelines. Wisdom issued detailed instructions on such things as pupil assignments; the hiring, firing, and assignment of faculty and staff; and school bus systems. "Eradicating the vestiges of the dual system" was Wisdom's intention. School systems were free to choose from a variety of means to achieve this aim, but "the only school desegregation plan that meets constitutional standards is one that works." The third principle in *Jefferson* was compensatory justice: the remedies that schools instituted must constitute "the organized undoing of the effects of past segregation."

The Supreme Court accepted the *Jefferson* decision and expanded on it. Thus, after more than a decade as a passive agent in school desegregation, the Supreme Court ended "freedom of choice" as an option in school desegregation plans because it had left segregated schools largely in place. For instance, the board of education in the small rural county of New Kent, Virginia, kept its two schools completely segregated until 1965, when it adopted "freedom of choice" desegregation in order to continue to receive federal funds. No whites chose the black school; 115 blacks chose the white school. Eighty-five percent of the black students remained in the black school. This arrangement also required the county to bus students of both races across the county to attend the school of their choice. In a 1968 ruling the Court said the public schools in the South had the "affirmative duty to take whatever steps necessary to convert to a unitary system in which racial discrimination would be eliminated root and branch." These two decisions also had the effect of transferring the initiative for desegregation from blacks to white school boards.

The impact of the Johnson administration's support of school desegregation and these two court decisions appears to have been immediate. The Civil Rights

Commission reported that nearly a third of the black public school students in the South were attending schools with whites in 1968. "Deliberate speed" was dead. Its demise brought joy in some quarters in the South, outrage in others.

The 1968 presidential election accurately reflected the mood of the country that year: division and turmoil. It was an election in which the South would play a decisive role, one that reflected the profound changes that had occurred in southern politics. Of the many events that contributed to the turmoil in 1968, probably the most important were a war in Vietnam that seemed endless, a troubled economy, racial conflict, and a "cultural revolution" that shocked more than it transformed. The Democratic party fell into disarray. Less than four years after his overwhelming victory in November 1964, President Johnson announced that he would not seek reelection in 1968. After an acrimonious campaign, during which Senator Robert F. Kennedy was assassinated, and a chaotic national convention, the Democrats nominated Vice President Hubert H. Humphrey for president.

Humphrey lost by a narrow margin in popular votes (43.4 percent to 42.7) but by a wide margin (301 to 191) in the electoral college. Richard Nixon's victories in Virginia, the Carolinas, Florida, Kentucky, Tennessee, and Oklahoma figured heavily in his election. For the first time since 1876, electoral votes from the South had been critically important in electing a Republican president. Humphrey became the first Democratic presidential candidate in the twentieth century to win only one state in the South; he carried only Lyndon Johnson's home state of Texas.

Large numbers of white voters in the South rejected Humphrey but were not ready to vote for a Republican. Instead, they supported George Wallace, the Democratic governor of Alabama, who ran on the ticket of the American Independent party—the party for "the little man," the party that promised to "get the Federal Government out of the local schools." Like Thurmond in 1948, Wallace fell far short of his goal of denying either Nixon or Humphrey a majority of electoral votes and thus throwing the election into the House of Representatives, where the South might obtain concessions that Wallace hoped to dictate. "White backlash," hostility toward blacks and their demands, had drawn much of its energy from anger over school desegregation and had had much to do with the outcome of the election. The 1968 presidential election demonstrated that public school desegregation was the most divisive domestic political issue in twentieth-century America. Ramifications from school desegregation carried beyond 1968 into the 1990s.

To heighten the turmoil of the late 1960s, Martin Luther King, Jr., was assassinated in April 1968, while helping black garbage collectors in Memphis with their efforts to get better pay and working conditions. The murder of the nation's leading prophet of nonviolence triggered a wave of rioting, burning, and looting throughout the country. Thousands mourned King's death, which had occurred only a dozen years after the then-young Baptist minister reluctantly agreed to lead the Montgomery bus boycott.

Remarkable changes had taken place in the dozen years since Montgomery. Racial segregation in public facilities was dead. Barriers against registration and voting by blacks had been largely torn down, and the number of black officeholders was increasing. Blacks had greater access to schooling and jobs than ever before. After more than a decade of delay, evasion, and massive resistance, *Brown*

v. *Board of Education* was being implemented in the South. Black faces multiplied in classrooms, on athletic teams, among police and firefighters, behind counters in stores, at desks in government agencies, at front doors rather than back doors. A new etiquette for race relations evolved along with a greater sensitivity toward blacks. Politicians learned to solicit black votes. Sheriffs, police, and local courts treated blacks more evenhandedly.

Whites played critical if somewhat secondary roles in these remarkable changes. With rare exceptions, whites in the South—and elsewhere—had taken little initiative in the early stages of the assault on Jim Crow. Most whites had resisted change, often very aggressively, then accepted or acquiesced in desegregation and did so more quickly and quietly than almost everyone believed was possible. Demographics and economic change helped. The ratio of blacks to whites had declined in every southern state since 1900. In none were blacks a majority in 1960; in that year one in four people living in the South was black. Consequently, whites felt less threatened. Whites also enjoyed the greater security that post-1940 prosperity had brought with it. Still, few observers would have concurred with what Leslie Dunbar, the executive director of the Southern Regional Council, a pioneering biracial organization, predicted in 1961. Dunbar said that whites would fight desegregation because they felt duty-bound to defend their culture and their past, but they would accept desegregation rather quickly.

> Once the fight is decisively lost (the verdict has to be decisive), once the Negro has secured the right to vote, has gained admittance to a public library, has fought his way into a desegregated public school, has been permitted to sup at a lunch counter, the typical white Southerner will shrug his shoulders, resume his stride, and go on. He has, after all, shared a land with his black neighbors for a long while; he can manage well enough even if patterns change. There is now one less fight which history requires of him. He has done his ancestoral duty. He . . . can relax a bit more.

These remarkably perceptive comments suggest a more thorough transformation in race relations in the South than in fact has come about. Patterns of racial separation persist, most noticeably in social relations, but they are still very obvious also in public schools and in housing; and the persistence of separation has had major consequences, most obviously in the politics of the South—and of the nation. The pattern of race relations in the South has changed from conscious subordination of blacks to a less conscious but hardly accidental pattern of avoidance. Perhaps that was all that one realistically could have expected in a quarter of a century, but that was all that was achieved.

One facet of the civil rights movement often goes unnoticed. Southern whites were major beneficiaries of the movement. As race relations in the South began to resemble those in the rest of the United States, the South and southern whites were less stigmatized as backward and reactionary. If Jim Crow had remained in place, there would be no Sunbelt South.

27

The Modern South

————————— ❖ —————————

*L*ess than two weeks before the tumultuous 1968 presidential election ended, more than 16,000 people packed Madison Square Garden in New York to hear George Wallace, former governor of Alabama and third-party candidate for the presidency. "It was," as historian Dan Carter has written, "the largest indoor political gathering in New York City" since a 1936 speech by President Franklin Roosevelt in the Garden. The great majority of the audience got exactly what they wanted: a foot-stomping performance and Wallace's by now familiar angry rhetorical themes. The crowd included some members of the Ku Klux Klan, the Minute Men of America, and the American Nazi Party as well as a few anti-Wallace people. The last had been deliberately admitted into the carefully screened audience so that they could serve as willing fodder for Wallace's standard ploy of taunting and deriding opponents in his audiences.

Dime-store Confederate flags were in abundance. A band played "The Star-Spangled Banner," "Yankee Doodle Dandie," and "Dixie," and a priest gave the invocation. Wallace supporters and opponents, inside and outside the Garden, shouted epithets and shoved. Fists flew more than once. Some people were quickly taken away by New York City police, who maintained tight security in the Garden and in the surrounding streets. When Wallace came to the podium, spotlights swept the Garden, balloons cascaded from the rafters, and the audience exploded into a twenty-minute ovation. The five-foot, seven-inch, former bantam weight boxing champion of Alabama saluted and thrust his fist repeatedly as he strode back and forth.

When he finally spoke, he denounced former Vice President Richard Nixon and Vice President Hubert Humphrey, the Republican and Democratic nominees, as "unfit to govern in the next four years." He attacked the Supreme Court for its recent decisions on civil rights and the Johnson administration for its recent policy on civil rights and both of them for failing to take action against "left-wing intellectuals and Communist professors who advocate a victory for the Vietcong [Vietnamese Communists]." He claimed that the media were encouraging "rebellion in the streets" and were refusing to let "the people know what kind of support we have." Wallace skillfully mixed in jibes at the scattered groups of hecklers. "Hey there, sweetie," he said to one long-haired male protester. Then, after a pause, he added, "Oh, excuse me, I thought that you were a girl." He ended his speech with the assertion that he had "an excellent chance to carry the great Empire State of New York." A columnist for the *New Republic* wrote that the scene evoked the specter of Berlin in the 1930s.

Wallace did not carry the Empire State. He only got forty-six electoral votes (from Alabama, Arkansas, Georgia, Louisiana, and Mississippi), failing to achieve his goal of denying Nixon or Humphrey a majority of the electoral votes and forcing the election into the U.S. House of Representatives. Because he was more attractive to low-income whites, traditionally strong Democratic voters, than to other whites, Wallace probably hurt the Democrats more than the Republicans; Nixon won most of the South outside the Deep South, Humphrey, only Texas. Although the Alabamian was soundly defeated, he had mounted the most important third-party presidential race since Theodore Roosevelt ran as a Bull Mooser in 1912. Moreover, Wallace's impact on national politics extended far beyond 1968.

Southern Republicans, aroused from their long stagnation and expanding rapidly, were positioned to take the greatest advantage of the events and circumstances of the 1960s and Wallace's legacy. Southern Republicans synchronized with the booming economy of the South and the sweeping political changes in the region to emerge as the dominant party in the South. Southern Democrats initially embraced massive resistance as Wallace did, but then they moved, out of conviction or necessity, to accommodation with the growing political power of blacks. Ironically, one of the leaders of racial accommodation among Democrats became the first resident of Deep South to be elected president in almost 130 years. One hundred years after the disputed Hayes-Tilden election of 1876 and the end of Reconstruction, Americans chose James Earl "Jimmy" Carter of Plains, Georgia, to be the thirty-ninth president of the United States. Carter's electoral victory indicated that much had changed in the intervening decades.

Indeed, the South of 1976 bore only faint resemblance to the South of 1876. The overwhelmingly impoverished agrarian world of the 1870s had given way to a prosperous modern South of metropolitan complexes and cities, of diverse manufacturing and growing service industries, of agribusiness, retirement centers, and tourism. The 1870s elite of planters and their business and professional allies had been displaced by a more cosmopolitan elite whose base lay in the region's urban centers, in banking, insurance, law, manufacturing, services, and education.

Just as economic life in the South had been transformed, so had political life. Blacks had regained the vote and the access to public office that they had enjoyed in the 1870s, and this time their hold on both seemed more secure. The southern Democrats had moved from the politics of white supremacy to desegregation, even integration. By 1976 southern Democrats had forged an alliance of blacks and whites to meet the challenge of a revived Republican party in the South. The solid or one-party Democratic South was becoming a relic.

Another relic was Jim Crow. The rigid caste system of earlier days had collapsed, though more vestiges of it remained than many people cared to acknowledge. Even the humid heat of the long southern summers had been blunted, if not banished, by air-conditioning. Standing in the air-conditioned comfort of hotel rooms in Atlanta or Dallas, visiting corporate executives from Chicago or New York or Berlin or Tokyo could gaze out over a landscape of skyscrapers, freeways and interstate highways, franchise stores and eating places, suburban develop-ments, and shopping centers spilling over the horizon. Understandably, they might conclude that the South they saw was just like the rest of the United States, that the South was no longer clearly differentiated from the rest of the nation.

Striking distinctions remained, however, even if they were not so easily per-ceived as the economic backwardness, the one-party politics, and the racial caste system that once clearly delineated an older South. The South still had a disproportionate share of the nation's poor, undereducated, and unskilled. The South remained more Protestant—more Baptist, more Methodist—than the rest of the country, and less ethnically diverse, though it had the highest proportion of blacks. Southerners continued to talk with soft drawls, to attach more impor-tance to manners, to live at what appeared to be a slower pace, and to murder and assault one another more often than their fellow Americans. Southerners still maintained a peculiar attachment to their region, though they were usually aware of its deficiencies.

The South and southerners still had a distinctive identity a hundred years after Reconstruction, but that identity had lost some of its edge, had become murkier than at any time since the mid-eighteenth century. Historians and similar sorts had once been able to identify the South and southerners easily. By 1977, as Jimmy Carter prepared to enter the White House, that identification was no longer so straightforward. The task has become even more difficult in the inter-vening years. However, by 1977, it was not difficult to discern the growing power of the South in American politics. Ironically, Carter had defeated the man most re-sponsible for the southernization of American politics, George Wallace.

WALLACE AND NATIONAL POLITICS

Wallace's career in national politics began in an inauspicious place: Clio in Bar-bour County, Alabama. He had a hardscrabble childhood. His father failed as a cotton and cattle farmer, the victim of the sandy soil of Barbour County, the agri-cultural depression that beset much of the South after the mid-1920s, and alco-holism. Wallace had the means, barely, to attend the University of Alabama where he was an undergraduate, then a student in law school. Shortly after opening his law office, he was drafted into the armed forces and became a flight engineer in the Army Air Corps, where he saw combat.

After World War II ended, Wallace resumed his primary interest, politics. He won a seat in the Alabama House of Representatives in 1946, where he promptly vi-olated the unwritten rule that freshmen legislators deferred to their elders and quickly gained a reputation as a liberal spender, especially for education. He won election as a circuit judge in 1953. He finished second in the 1958 gubernatorial elec-tion, possibly because the successful candidate stressed his militant segregationist stance. The lesson of the 1958 race was not lost on the extraordinarily ambitious Clio native, who by Alabama standards was a moderate on race. When Wallace ran and won four years later (Alabama's governors were prevented from successive terms), he made the preservation of segregation his primary focus.

In his inaugural address, the new governor rehearsed the usual list of southern grievances against Yankees and the federal government, which included complaints about Reconstruction, the decisions of the Supreme Court on civil rights and on school prayer, and the use of federal troops during the desegregation of the University of Mississippi. He perceived the presence of Communists in high positions who had planted the seeds of godless government, and he reminded his audience of the recent turmoil in the Congo where Africans had massacred Europeans.

"From this day, we intend to take the offensive and carry our fight for freedom across the nation, wielding the balance of power we know we possess in the South. We . . . will determine in the next election who shall sit in the White House." Wallace reminded the audience that they were gathered at Montgomery, at "this Cradle of Confederacy, this very Heart of the Great Anglo-Saxon Southland. . . . In the name of the greatest people that have ever trod this earth, I draw the line in the dust and toss the gauntlet before the feet of tyranny . . . and I say . . . segregation now . . . segregation tomorrow . . . segregation forever." Someone in the audience may have caught the irony of Wallace's call to fight for freedom and his determination to preserve segregation. At the time, probably almost no one noticed Wallace's determination to carry his fight to maintain Jim Crow to the rest of the nation. The headlines of the day were dominated by President Kennedy's asking Congress for a massive tax cut and his warning to the Russians that if they did not adopt a more peaceful posture, the United States would build a larger nuclear arsenal than they could build.

Governor Wallace was obviously not the first southern white leader to pledge himself publicly to an all-out defense of segregation. At least two things set him apart from other "massive resistance" leaders. His driving ambition propelled him beyond a state or regional stage to a national stage. He had extraordinary skills as a demagogic orator who could relate viscerally with sympathetic listeners and could disarm protesters to his advantage. In spite of disparaging comments by some newspeople about his being a bantam-weight redneck who wore off-the-rack suits and slicked his hair down, Wallace quickly learned to handle the national media well, and even charm them.

Timing also aided Wallace. Growing numbers of Americans believed that the United States faced grave threats from abroad and massive domestic disarray. Domestic turmoil seemed, especially after mid-1965, to be spreading rapidly in the wake of the civil rights revolution, the anti–Vietnam War movement and protest demonstrations, the counterculture, real and imagined challenges to traditional values, a rising crime rate, and a series of violent urban riots. As blacks' incomes rose significantly in the early 1960s, the black exodus to better, often all-white neighborhoods and the suburbs increased significantly, a migration that unfortunately heightened tensions. As early as the 1964 presidential primaries, Wallace found fertile ground beyond the South for his message and his skills. The Alabama governor had surprisingly strong showings in primaries in Wisconsin, Indiana, and Maryland before his prospects faded. Wallace by 1964 had likely had what one perceptive observer called "a white, blinding vision: they all hate black people, all of them. They're all afraid of them. Great God! . . . They're all Southern! The whole United States is *Southern!*"

GOVERNOR WALLACE AND HIS
RUNNING MATE, GENERAL CURTIS E.
LEMAY AT MADISON SQUARE
GARDEN, 1968

By 1968, Wallace had learned to muffle his racism to a degree and to stress other issues that frequently, but not always, had subtle racial coloring. Before he arrived at Madison Square Garden in October, he had drawn large crowds in San Francisco, San Diego, Detroit, Cincinnati, and Baltimore as well as Boston, where 70,000 people filled the Boston Commons. Some observers from the gathering at the Garden explained why they favored Wallace. Someone needed to use force against "those college demonstrators and everything—everybody is against the country." Wallace opposed "them." He "says what he thinks." Many complained that "politicians" catered to blacks and other minorities. "All those giveaway programs, those welfare programs. They'd rather give them money then [sic] put them to work." "Look at your paycheck every week. That money they take out isn't going to the man who breaks his back—it goes to the man who stays in bed." Few explicitly mentioned blacks. One of those who did said, "Negroes move in and property values go down. And you lose your life savings. It's happening all over Brooklyn."

Wallace tapped swirling, barely submerged fears with his calls for "law and order," with his demands that antiwar protesters be suppressed, and with his promises to halt federal support of open housing and public school desegregation. Few observers believed his claim that he had "never . . made a speech that would reflect upon anyone regardless of their race, color, creed, or national origin." Running a campaign fueled by accumulated resentments and festering feelings of victimization, Wallace had little time for foreign policy in his presidential campaign. Like many other Americans, he called for victory in the war with Vietnam—without explaining either what he meant by victory or how it could be achieved.

Yet, even before Wallace's triumphant moment at Madison Square Garden, polls indicated that voter support for him was waning in the fall of 1968. Enthusiasm for

Wallace declined as voters worried about wasting their vote on a candidate who had little chance of winning. Organized labor effectively warned northern blue-collar workers of Alabama's (and the South's) low wages and hostility to unions. Wallace provided a means for expressing anger for many, but did they want him to lead the nation? He may have gained stature from his stand "in the schoolhouse door" at the University of Alabama in 1963, but events and televised images from the marches and violence of Birmingham and Selma must have shaken potential supporters. Too many of them remembered the lingering image of the tragic bombing of the Sixteenth Avenue Baptist Church in Birmingham in September 1963 that left four girls—two fourteen-year-olds, an eleven-year-old, and a ten-year-old—dead in their Sunday School. Wallace was too controversial, too hot, especially in an era when television dominated politics. Image was crucial, and television favored a cool image.

Wallace returned to presidential politics in 1972, this time as a Democrat. He swept the presidential primary in Florida, finished second in Wisconsin, and swept both Maryland and Michigan. But by the latter two contests, Wallace had been removed from the presidential race by a young, white, deranged assassin whose shots permanently disabled Wallace and left him wheelchair-bound the rest of his life. Wallace remained a public figure thereafter, but not a national political force. He made a brief, unsuccessful run at the presidency in 1976. Over time his attitudes changed or seemed to change, and so did his image. He made public apologies and asked for forgiveness. Eventually, he and many Alabama blacks embraced each other.

Although his political career was centered on racial issues from which he obtained his greatest political energy and appeal, Wallace was not an one-issue governor. As governor, Wallace vigorously pursued industrial development and stressed public education. His approach in these areas was similar to that of other Southern governors, but his programs had a more populist bent than did other governors' programs. Wallace's populism was reflected in his policies toward taxes. He also persuaded the legislature to provide free textbooks for public schools and to build trade schools and junior colleges. His populism contributed to his popularity or acceptance among Alabama voters, including black voters. Wallace was elected governor four times (five times, including the election of his first wife, Lurleen) from 1962 to 1982.

Ironically, he left a profound national legacy that was conservative. "George Wallace," as Dan Carter has written, "was not the first post-war figure to call for a return to 'traditional' American values. But the Alabama governor—more than any other political leader of his generation—was the alchemist of the new social conservatism as he compounded racial fear, anticommunism, cultural nostalgia, and traditional right-wing economics [low taxes and opposition to welfare spending] into a movement that laid the foundation for the conservative counterrevolution that reshaped American politics in the 1970s and 1980s." Southern Republicans took leading roles in that counterrevolution.

THE RISE OF THE SOUTHERN REPUBLICANS

By the last decades of the twentieth century, The Republican party had become a major force in the region. The Republican revival, which began shortly after World War II, received its initial stimulus from divisions among Democrats. Traditionally the Democratic party's greatest asset in the South had been its ability to keep blacks in their place and to prevent the federal government from intervening to alter that arrangement. By the 1940s, southern Democrats faced serious threats to their power to do either of these actions. Faced by the renomination of Harry Truman and the national Democratic party's endorsement of a strong civil rights plank in its platform, many voters fled. Traditional aversion to the Republican party and the strong civil rights stand that the Republicans had adopted in 1948 kept most angry southern Democrats from joining the Republicans. Those southern Democrats who broke with the national Democrats either retreated to the sidelines to wait out the election or became Dixiecrats.

Republican presidential fortunes improved dramatically in 1952. Except for Herbert Hoover in 1928, no Republican presidential nominee had done well in the South since Reconstruction. Dwight D. Eisenhower captured Virginia, Florida, Tennessee, Texas, and Oklahoma in 1952. To these states Eisenhower added Louisiana during his successful reelection campaign in 1956. The Democrats recaptured Texas and Louisiana when John F. Kennedy defeated Richard Nixon in 1960. The victories in those states were probably largely the result of Kennedy's choice of Lyndon Johnson of Texas, then Senate majority leader, as his vice presidential running mate. Johnson provided an urgently needed cohesive force for a divided Democratic party and strong regional appeal for southern voters. Johnson had been a cohesive force for the Democrats before. During the late 1950s he had stood midway between northern Democrats who wanted to abolish Jim Crow quickly and southern Democrats who adamantly opposed almost every facet of desegregation. A moderate on race, a politician who aspired to national office, and a master of political strategy, he realized that the Democratic party could not survive if it ignored the aspirations of blacks and tried to keep Jim Crow. Johnson, like a small but growing number of southern whites, seems to have believed that Jim Crow was immoral and was unworthy of a great nation, especially one that claimed to be a democracy and world leader.

Conversely, Johnson knew that an all-out government assault on Jim Crow would drive the great majority of southern Democrats out of the party, perhaps into the Republican party. Thus he adopted a convoluted course of action. He carefully and quietly avoided signing the Southern Manifesto in 1956. He orchestrated passage of the Civil Rights acts of 1957 and 1960. As weapons against Jim Crow, both measures had serious deficiencies, especially in their provisions for enforcement. Johnson was strongly criticized for that lack. Critics said he had so diluted the new laws to get them passed that they were civil rights laws in name only. Others, however, noted that Johnson's actions made passage of the laws possible, that they were the first of their kind since Reconstruction and thus constituted important precedents for stronger civil rights legislation in the future, and that the new laws were intended to be warning signals to the South.

Republican successes in the South from 1952 to 1960 had their basis in more than the collapse of Jim Crow and public school desegregation. The predominantly Anglo-Saxon Protestant South had more in common culturally with the national Republican party than with the national Democratic party that after 1900 had attracted large numbers of urban northerners who were Catholic and the products of the enormous wave of immigration from eastern and southern Europe after 1880. This cultural affinity became an important factor in political realignments once southern whites severed their ties with national Democrats. As has often occurred in shaping American party politics, religious and ethnic factors played an important role in the evolution of southern Republicanism.

Republican successes also reflected the economic and demographic changes that the region had been undergoing, especially since 1940. In the surge of post-1940 prosperity, the ranks of the urban middle class swelled. Professionals, managers, businesspeople, and corporate officials, most of whom were college educated, found the national Republican party more compatible with their views than the national Democratic party, which they perceived as too liberal, too inclined to support labor unions, and too disinclined to foster private business. Republicans had shown strength in the urban South before, as long ago as 1920. In the 1950s and thereafter, that strength was broader and more durable, in part because of precedent-setting court decisions on reapportionment, which shifted power from rural and center cities to suburbs.

Some of the Republican-leaning inhabitants of the new suburbs, with centrally air-conditioned and heated homes, expansive green lawns, second cars, private kindergartens, and dancing and music lessons for often reluctant offspring, were only a generation from farms, mines, and factories. Probably more came from second- and third-generation city families. Migrating "Yankees" added to the numbers of these two groups. As early as 1950, native whites born outside the South made up 30 percent of the white population of Florida. (No other southern state had as much as 15 percent until 1970.) Northern white migrants tended to concentrate in urban areas outside the Deep South, particularly in southern Florida, in northern Virginia, along the Chesapeake Bay, at Richmond, and in Dallas, Fort Worth, Houston, and San Antonio. Many of these newcomers had Republican ties or, like many of the other prosperous southern city dwellers, had only weak ties to the Democrats. Traditionally Republican areas—eastern Tennessee, western North Carolina and Virginia, portions of northern Alabama and northern Georgia, northeastern Oklahoma, northwestern Arkansas, the "German" counties in Texas—continued to vote Republican. That loyalty and the votes of the urban middle class accounted for the success of the Republican presidential candidates in the South in the late 1950s and early 1960s. Those successes ended in 1964 during Lyndon Johnson's reelection—but temporarily, as it turned out.

THE COLLAPSE OF THE SOLID SOUTH

The year 1964 marked a decisive turning point in the demise of the solid South, as it did also in the collapse of Jim Crow. In the decade or so after 1964, Democratic strength in the South declined precipitously while Republican fortunes rose rapidly. "The breadth of the Democratic collapse is staggering," two political scientists commented. "It would be difficult to find comparable instances in American political history of such a rapid and comprehensive desertion of an established majority party by an entire region."

Ironically, during the 1964 election the Democrats looked very strong in the region. Lyndon Johnson won the presidency in his own right in a landslide victory over Barry Goldwater, the Republican nominee. Johnson thus became only the second successful presidential candidate from one of the former Confederate states since Zachary Taylor. Johnson swept the border states and the upper South, areas where Republicans had been increasing in strength since World War II. The Democrats also made very strong showings in most of the congressional, state, and local elections in the South in 1964.

Many southerners, however, did not rejoice in Johnson's victory. Repelled by Johnson's embrace of civil rights, part of an evolving pattern of close ties between the national Democratic party and blacks, white voters in the Deep South flocked to the Republican candidate. Louisiana, Mississippi, Alabama, Georgia, and South Carolina joined Arizona, Goldwater's home state, as the only states that gave their electoral votes to the Republican senator. Goldwater's opposition to the *Brown* decision and to the Civil Rights Act of 1964 had great appeal in the South. He received 54 percent of the vote in Georgia, 59 percent in South Carolina, almost 69.5 percent in Alabama, and 87 percent in Mississippi to become the first Republican candidate to win those states since Reconstruction. Alabama also elected five Republicans to the House of Representatives, Georgia and Mississippi one each.

President Johnson's electoral triumph benefited as much from the candidacy of Goldwater as from his own appeal. A militant conservative, Goldwater alarmed moderates and liberals alike. They feared he would lead the United States into a wider, costlier war in Vietnam, risk nuclear confrontation with the Soviet Union, and undermine domestic programs many citizens thought were critically important. The senator had an unusual talent for triggering alarms. While campaigning in Florida, he convinced many elderly voters that he wanted to abandon social security; in Tennessee, he suggested that he wanted to sell the Tennessee Valley Authority to private investors.

But Goldwater attracted strong support in the Deep South, where race was the paramount issue. Convinced that the Republicans could not "get the Negro vote as a bloc" in 1964 and 1968, he had told a Republican audience in 1961 that they "ought to go hunting where the ducks are." Goldwater's assessment was based upon the fallacious notion that blacks after the 1930s voted only for Democrats. Eisenhower attracted large numbers of black voters, especially in 1952, and Nixon did well among black voters in some places in 1960. Moreover, congressional Republicans provided crucial votes and leadership in securing the passage of federal civil rights legislation.

Goldwater declared that school desegregation was "the responsibility of the states" and that he did not want his party to "assume it is the role of the federal government to enforce integration in the schools." The Arizona senator had opposed the *Brown* decision as an invasion of the rights of states and an overly broad interpretation of the constitutional powers of the Supreme Court. For similar reasons, Goldwater voted against the Civil Rights Act of 1964. By making him their candidate for president, the Republicans seemed openly to spurn black voters and the civil rights movement, and in some instances they did.

Conversely, the Democratic party under Kennedy and then Johnson had increasingly allied itself with the civil rights movement. That process had accelerated in 1963 as a result of the prolonged civil rights conflict in Birmingham, the march on Washington, and the nation's grief in the wake of the assassination of President Kennedy. Johnson now had the votes to push the Civil Rights Act through Congress, and he did so. The Texas Democrat had moved to embrace the civil rights movement and to ensure that blacks would be part of the winning political coalition he was constructing.

Segregationists eagerly joined the Goldwater forces and helped him win the Republican presidential nomination. They liked more than his stance on civil rights. His strongly conservative positions—for states rights, against communism, for reduced government spending on social programs and an increase in spending for the military—paralleled theirs. Most climbed on the Goldwater bandwagon so eagerly that they missed a subtle point. The senator had long believed that segregation was wrong. He differed with President Johnson, King, and others over means, not ends; over *how* segregation should be attacked, not over *whether* it should be attacked. Critics noted that Goldwater's chosen means—the states—were unlikely to dismantle Jim Crow, that his position on civil rights put him effectively, if unintentionally, in the segregationists' camp.

THE REPUBLICAN PARTY SECURES ITS PLACE IN DIXIE

The size of the Democratic victory in 1964 obscured most of the critical political changes that were occurring within the Republican party in the South. The nature of that party changed significantly. Before 1964 the Republican party in the South had been evolving by fits and starts from a party whose primary concern was the distribution of federal patronage to one that could beat the Democrats. That goal required a more vigorous organization, slates of viable candidates, and infusions of talent and money. Goldwater's candidacy stimulated this process, especially in the Deep South. Young, ambitious men and women embraced the Republican party as the party of the future. They could rise more rapidly there than in the Democratic party. They saw the Democratic party as entrenched, self-satisfied, and resistant to change, new ideas, and new people. Breaking away from the Democrats was a way to break from one's parents. Not a few of the young Goldwaterites were converted Democrats. Senator Strom Thurmond, the most successful politician in South Carolina's electoral history, also switched parties in 1964, bringing with him an important cadre of political activists.

Most of the Goldwaterites were ideological conservatives. Almost all of them opposed rapid desegregation; some were outright segregationists. One observer described the Goldwater, or "New Guard," Republicans in Tennessee as "prepared to exploit the older norms of white supremacy, laissez-faire, anti-unionism, and businessman Bourbonism." They were "politically inexperienced, but ideological and impatient with the supineness of the Old Guard," ready to employ "the hard sell, the grass roots drive, and the systematic organization which generated success in the business world" in pursuit of their political aims. The New Guard took over much of the Republican party structure and was ready to outorganize and outwork the Democrats, who were ill prepared for vigorous partisan battles after so many years of one-party politics. The New Guard Republicans were also ready to exploit racial divisions to their advantage.

Circumstances provided a strong stimulus for the growth of the Republican party in the South. Unrest grew in the South as the pace of public school desegregation quickened after 1964. Only two years after enjoying their greatest victories in the South since 1948, Democrats suffered defeats throughout the region in 1966. That year the Republicans in the South added a total of seven seats in the House of Representatives (though they lost two of their Alabama seats), elected a senator in Tennessee, reelected Thurmond as a Republican, elected governors in Florida and Arkansas, nearly won the governorship in Georgia, and almost doubled their seats in the state legislatures in the region. Voters thus swelled the ranks of the southern Republicans at the time that New Guard Republicans were taking over the leadership of the party.

As the New Guard pushed the Republican party to the right, it became whiter. Republican moderates and black Republicans found themselves shoved to the periphery or out of the party altogether. Ironically, moderates had been important in earlier Republican successes in the South. They had been prominent in the Eisenhower and Nixon campaigns. Some of those Republican moderates had been appointed to the bench by President Eisenhower—Judges Elbert P. Tuttle, John R. Brown, and John Minor Wisdom—and Judge Richard T. Rives, a Democrat appointed by President Harry Truman, led the Fifth Circuit Court of Appeals when that court became the foremost judicial force in the dismantling of Jim Crow. This judicial circuit, which then covered Texas, Louisiana, Mississippi, Alabama, Georgia, and Florida, made a series of landmark decisions in civil rights in the 1950s and 1960s.

Judge Frank M. Johnson, Jr., another Republican whom Eisenhower appointed, was also part of the judicial vanguard whose decisions undermined segregation and laid the foundation for sweeping political change in the South. Sitting on a special three-judge panel, Johnson and Rives formed the 2-to-1 majority that in 1956 declared unconstitutional the Montgomery ordinance requiring racial segregation on public transportation. They concluded that the ordinance violated the principle established by the Supreme Court in *Brown* v. *Board of Education* that "separate but equal" violated the Fourteenth Amendment. Judge Johnson later was involved in several dramatic confrontations with Governor George Wallace of Alabama over desegregation and civil rights demonstrations. Not all of Eisenhower's judicial appointees in the South were moderates, much less forces for desegregation. Judge Benjamin F. Cameron of the Fifth Circuit, an unbending segregationist, did his best to preserve Jim Crow, even if he had to ignore Supreme Court rulings to do so.

The Goldwaterites also carried the Republican party into the previously overwhelmingly Democratic black belt. John Grenier, an Alabama Republican who became a national party leader, later contended that the 1964 election gave the South a major voice in the national party. In the wake of Republican victories in the South and the growing weaknesses of the Republicans in the northeastern states, traditionally an area of Republican power, Grenier said, the South and the West had become the dominant regions in the national Republican party. These developments help explain the nominations of two Californians, Richard Nixon in 1968 and 1972 and Ronald Reagan in 1980 and 1984.

Certainly Republican presidential candidates have done well in the South since 1964. In 1968 Nixon carried Virginia, Tennessee, Oklahoma, and Florida, as Eisenhower had done, and added North Carolina and South Carolina. However, he lost Texas to Humphrey, the Democratic nominee, and Louisiana, Mississippi,

Alabama, and Georgia to George Wallace. When President Nixon ran for reelection in 1972 he swept the South, something a Republican had never done before.

In both 1968 and 1972, Nixon used a more subtle version of Goldwater's appeal to southern white voters. Nixon's "southern strategy" combined strong conservative positions on defense and on economic and social issues with obvious but not blunt appeals to the racial sentiments of whites. Nixon called for less government intervention in support of desegregation, and he said that the South ought to be given more time to adjust to the dramatic advances of desegregation from 1963 to 1968. Privately, Nixon was less subtle and more specific. To ensure his nomination in 1968, Nixon obtained the support of Senator Strom Thurmond by promising the South Carolinian that his administration would downplay school desegregation, appoint a southerner to the Supreme Court, and support a strong national defense.

When Nixon campaigned, he particularly criticized busing as a means of implementing school desegregation. He—and others—continued these attacks though they knew it was often impossible to desegregate schools without busing some students and that busing had in fact long been used to maintain segregated schools. He and his political advisers correctly sensed that the majority of both whites and blacks opposed busing. Hostility to school busing for desegregation stemmed from a complex array of ideas, feelings, fears, and sometimes misinformation. Moreover, this strong negative attitude created a large dilemma. Could school desegregation, which most people after 1970 said they favored or accepted, be achieved without busing, which most people said they opposed?

Busing aroused strong feelings because it undermined the concept of the neighborhood school, it had a strong impact on millions of families, it could be very expensive, and it raised issues of economic and social class. Busing raised all kinds of concerns, many of which were reasonable and some of which were not. Among those concerns were the safety of children, the expense of busing, and its effect on the education of children and the schedules of families, especially at a time when most adults were employed outside the home. Busing also seemed to be one more instance of the transfer of power over a basic institution to faceless judges and bureaucrats, who appeared to be moving students (and sometimes teachers) like pawns to meet racial quotas and seemed to order changes in desegregation plans every year. But the courts found that they had little choice about intervening in the running of public schools that had by law been racially segregated. The courts had an obligation to end racial segregation in public education. It had been declared unconstitutional, yet it persisted because most southern whites were determined to keep public schools racially segregated by covert or overt means, by legal or illegal means.

Opponents of school busing claimed that it would only cause resegregation of public schools because whites, who had more money than blacks, would put their children in private schools or move from urban districts to suburban districts. Many whites did in fact turn to private schools or move. But white flight was motivated by more than a desire to avoid integrated schools or busing. Suburbs provided newer, often more pleasant, usually safer, and frequently less costly housing than was available in many older urban areas. The flight to the suburbs reinforced the decline of central cities in the South as residential areas. Conversely, the decline of central cities reinforced the migration to the periphery.

Opponents of busing usually ignored facts that conflicted with their position. Busing had long been used to keep schools racially segregated, and long-distance busing was not uncommon. Some desegregation plans actually involved less travel for students and lower busing costs than did the transportation programs that some schools had in place before desegregation. Supporters of busing to facilitate desegregation rightly suspected that the real opposition often was not to busing per se but to school desegregation by any means.

The busing issue created a dilemma for the national Democratic party. In the 1960s the Democrats became the political leaders of the attack on Jim Crow and consequently led the political assault on segregated public education. In 1966 the courts (in *U.S.* v. *Jefferson County Board of Education*) ordered that school districts that had once been legally segregated by race must assume the initiative to desegregate and must have racially unitary school systems. To obey these judicial orders, school districts frequently had to bus large numbers of pupils considerable distances because of residential segregation. Residential segregation tended to be most pronounced in the large cities, where the majority of voters now lived. This set of circumstances led voters to associate the Democratic party with a highly unpopular policy. Southern Democrats tried to dissociate themselves from the party's position by decrying school busing.

Thus circumstances gave the Republicans a great political opportunity, particularly in the 1968 presidential election. Nixon quickly seized the opportunity, frequently denouncing busing and thereby simultaneously appealing to racial moderates and strong segregationists. The results at the polls in 1968 indicated that the southern strategy worked.

Once in office, President Nixon openly joined efforts to slow school desegregation. Moreover, southerners were appointed to high and very visible positions in the administration. Opposition in the Senate and the president's own ineptitude initially prevented him from putting a southerner on the Supreme Court. After two rejections, however, in 1971 the Senate confirmed Lewis F. Powell, Jr., of Virginia, Nixon's third nominee, for a seat on the Supreme Court. In 1972 Nixon's southern strategy helped him to capture the votes of people who had supported George Wallace in 1968 and to carry the entire South in a landslide victory. Republican successes in the South created a power base that had implications for national politics.

In the only presidential election since 1964 in which the Democrats did well in the South, Jimmy Carter carried eleven of thirteen southern states in 1976—all but Virginia and Oklahoma. The Democratic victory was short-lived. Carter had the misfortune to assume the presidency at an extraordinarily difficult time, when the United States was stumbling from one economic crisis to another and appeared to be impotent in international affairs. Four years later those problems remained, and Carter, one of the more intelligent presidents to serve this country, appeared to be confused and indecisive. The Iranian hostage crisis in particular emphasized the perceptions of America's—or at least of Carter's—weaknesses. Carter's inability to secure the release of Americans being held hostage by Islamic militants in Teheran seemed to be clear evidence that he lacked political skills. Then the president reacted too slowly to the growing rate of inflation that reached record levels. The luckless president, a self-proclaimed born-again Christian and a deeply religious person, was roundly condemned and sometimes crudely attacked by conservative Christians. They alleged that he encouraged homosexuals—whom they said were consciously sinning by adopting an "unnatural," ungodly way of life—to join his political coalition and his administration. They declared that in raising the Department of Education to a Cabinet level, Carter had dangerously enhanced the power of the federal government to intrude in family life, and they claimed that his foreign policies were directed toward one-world government, a violation of biblical sanctions. Public opinion polls showed that the "man from Plains" was one of the most unpopular presidents in this century. To virtually no one's surprise, he failed to win reelection.

When Carter lost to Ronald Reagan in 1980, he lost everywhere in the South except Georgia, his home state. President Reagan captured every southern state when he was reelected in 1984, as did George Bush during his successful 1988 presidential campaign. Carter's unpopularity abetted the emergence of a new "solid South," Republican style, at least in presidential politics. A striking indication of the new reality was the strength of President Bush's support in the South. He buried his opponent, Michael Dukakis, in Dixie by a margin of 58 percent of the vote to 42 percent, by far his largest margin of victory in any region. Elsewhere Bush won by about 52 percent to 48 percent.

In 1992 the Democratic ticket of Clinton-Gore regained some of the ground Democrats had lost in the South since the 1970s, winning Arkansas, Georgia, Kentucky, Louisiana, North Carolina, and Tennessee. However, in no southern state, with the possible exception of Arkansas, did the Clinton-Gore ticket get a majority of the white voters. Bill Clinton, a six-term governor of Arkansas, and Albert Gore, Jr., a congressman, then U.S. senator from Tennessee, were moderate southern Democrats who supported racial integration and who had been active in efforts to bridge the regional and ideological differences between northern and southern Democrats.

Though they had considerable political experience, both were comparatively young, having been born after World War II, and both share many of the attitudes of the generation that came of age in the 1960s. President Clinton actively opposed American involvement in the war in Vietnam, and he successfully avoided the draft—by dubious means. Vice President Gore served in the military in Vietnam but was not an enthusiastic supporter of the war. Thus, Clinton and Gore deviated from the southern tradition of strong support of the military. They did not deviate from the religious traditions of their home region: both were Southern Baptists. Neither religion nor regional origins, however, protected President Clinton from becoming unpopular in most of the white South, as the 1994 and 1996 elections made abundantly clear.

But Clinton remained particularly, almost singularly popular with blacks, something akin to being a "soul mate." The first black students who entered the formerly all-white law school at the University of Arkansas in the early 1970s (twenty years after the Supreme Court had declared in *Sweatt* v. *Painter* that racially segregated public graduate and professional schools were unconstitutional) called Clinton "Wonder Boy." One of the then-young law professor's students later remarked, "In the South at that time, whites would say one thing, but their deeds and words were often different . . . here comes a person where no matter what your relationship with him was, he was not prejudiced. He did not let race treat you different from anyone else. That's why we called him Wonder Boy.

PRESIDENT CLINTON AT A BLACK CHURCH

It was a miracle the way he was. He could have shunned black students politically. Fayetteville and northwest Arkansas was a white enclave. Wonder Boy Bill
did not waver in respect to his conduct with African Americans."

The 1994 and 1996 elections demonstrated how strong the Republicans especially had become in the South and how important that strength was to Republican power in the nation. In the South alone, the Republicans gained nineteen seats
in the U.S. House of Representatives and four seats in the U.S. Senate. This very
strong showing contributed significantly to their capturing control of both legislative bodies. Southern Republicans held numerous leadership positions in Congress. Speaker of the House Newt Gingrich of Georgia, for one, became a dominant force in legislative matters and a powerful figure in national politics.
Southern Republicans also had a majority of the region's governorships. In some
states the possibility of a new solid South—a Republican South—was real.

In addition to taking advantage of the demographic and economic factors
that favor them, the Republicans in many instances followed a path marked out
earlier by George Wallace, a renegade Democrat. The former four-time governor
of Alabama and defeated presidential candidate sounded themes in his campaigns that became elemental to American politics in the late twentieth century.
The angry populist from Alabama expressed bitter disaffection with the federal
government, fury over taxes on the middle class, and a visceral distaste for, in his
words, "pointy-headed intellectuals," "briefcase totin' bureaucrats," and "loose-
minded, high livin' liberals." Other politicians learned that they could win high
offices if they adopted Wallace's themes while muffling his overtly racist posture
and bulldog persona.

The Republicans also apparently benefited from the emergence of the Religious Right, a movement of Christian fundamentalists and evangelicals who are

political and economic conservatives. Led by conservative Protestant clergy, especially some of the televangelists, the Religious Right adopted the political activism of the civil rights movement in which, ironically, liberal clergymen were so prominent. Within the Religious Right, the most prominent organization has been the well-organized, well-financed Christian Coalition, founded by televangelist Pat Robertson of Virginia.

Concerned about what it believes is a marked decline in morals and values, the Coalition developed an agenda that goes well beyond its original primary concerns, that is, opposition to abortion and homosexuality. It wants to restore religion in the nation by, among other actions, displaying religious symbols such as Christmas scenes in public places and encouraging prayer or brief periods of meditation or silence in public schools. The Christian Coalition favors tax cuts, "school choice" as an alternative to public schools, and ending programs it considers tainted with liberalism, like the National Endowment for the Arts or the Corporation for Public Broadcasting. Praised as leaders in an urgently needed spiritual renaissance or damned as narrow-minded bigots, the Coalition became an important, grassroots-level political organization with a strong voice, particularly among Republicans. Although it failed to get former colonel Oliver North from Virginia elected to the Senate in 1994, the Coalition was credited with being an important, sometimes decisive factor in a number of congressional and state races.

THE TRANSFORMATION OF THE SOUTHERN DEMOCRATS

Just as the political terrain of the South has been transformed since World War II, so has the Democratic party in the South. The Democrats had to learn that not all white voters—other than eccentrics and mountaineers—were Democrats, that their power base in the black belt had been eroded, and that attracting and winning black voters was essential to survival. Initially the great majority of Democratic leaders sought to maintain their party's birthright as the party of white supremacy. White flight to the Republican party, the civil rights movement, and the weight of the courts and the federal government forced first a retreat, then the development of a new strategy. Some Democrats, such as Carter, welcomed the change. Most Democratic leaders changed because they had no choice; they either changed or lost.

Southern Democrats learned in the 1960s that many races could not be won without black votes. They learned they had to build political coalitions with black leaders and voters and support black candidates for office. In less than a decade after the Southern Manifesto appeared, the party of white supremacy in the South became biracial. The transition was not easy. There was open conflict, suspicion, and misunderstanding. (There still is.) White Democrats often found themselves caught between the need to satisfy the demands of blacks and anxieties about white flight. President Johnson and then Senator Hubert H. Humphrey, a long-time civil rights advocate, infuriated blacks when they refused to support the efforts of the predominantly black Freedom Democratic party of Mississippi to be seated as the state's official delegation at the Democratic National Convention in 1964. Fearing white backlash in Mississippi, Johnson and Humphrey refused to exclude the delegates of the regular Democratic party in Mississippi, though they were avowed segregationists and openly disloyal to the national party ticket.

Converts to biracial politics, however, eventually outnumbered unreconcilable segregationists. Herman Talmadge of Georgia was one of the more conspicuous converts. He had inherited the strong personal support of his father, Eugene, and had nurtured that support with racist rhetoric in successful gubernatorial and senatorial campaigns. A Supreme Court decision ruling unconstitutional the system by which Georgia managed to give greater weight to rural (white) votes than to votes in urban areas (where more blacks were registered to vote) and the Voting Rights Act of 1965 persuaded Herman Talmadge that he had to take a different tack. Senator Talmadge addressed a luncheon meeting of Atlanta's black leaders in 1966 and declared that "all candidates are going to solicit the votes of all Georgia citizens." Asked why he had not appeared before them five or six years earlier, Talmadge responded: "Five or six years ago, you didn't invite me." No one apparently said so at the time, but Talmadge probably sought the invitation. Political realities—like the growing number of black voters in Georgia—prompted dramatic changes in political calculations.

Democrats who openly favored racial moderation did very well in gubernatorial elections in 1970. The newly elected Democratic governors of Florida (Reuben Askew), Arkansas (Dale Bumpers), Georgia (Jimmy Carter), and South Carolina (John C. West) called for an end to segregation and racial discrimination. Republicans could, of course, also endorse racial moderation, as Linwood Holton of Virginia did. A "mountain Republican" from the state that once had led the "massive resistance" campaign against public school desegregation, and the first member of his party to be elected governor in Virginia in the twentieth century, Holton told his inaugural audience:

> Here in Virginia we must see that no citizen of the Commonwealth is excluded from full participation in both the blessings and responsibilities of our society because of his race. . . . As Virginia has been a model for so much else in America in the past, let us now endeavor to make today's Virginia a model in race relations. Let us, as Lincoln said, insist upon an open society "with malice toward none; charity for all."

Commentators hailed these governors as New South political leaders. Obviously the New South had retained its plasticity and its pleasing quality.

The limited involvement of southern blacks in politics changed dramatically after 1965. Black voter registration in the eleven former Confederate states increased from 1.5 million in 1960 to 2.7 in 1966, 3.4 in 1970, and 4.3 in 1980, and the percentage of the electorate that was black increased from 11 to 17 percent. There were some 2,600 black elected officials in these states in 1980, and nearly 4,400 in 1990, almost always where the majority of voters were black. Tuskegee, for instance, elected its first black mayor, Johnny Ford, in 1972. Other first-time black mayors—Birmingham's Richard Arrington, Atlanta's Maynard Jackson, Charlotte's Harvey Gantt, Richmond's Henry Marsh—were more conspicuous because they served much larger cities. Andrew Young, who had been one of King's closest advisers and a former Carter administration official, succeeded Jackson in 1982. John Lewis, former SNCC leader and militant civil rights activist, won a seat in Congress in 1986 when he defeated another prominent black civil rights figure, Julian Bond.

The growth of southern blacks' political power was impressive and unprecedented. But blacks were still a minority, albeit a franchised minority. Even with gains in black voter registration, 83 percent of the electorate in the former Confederate states were white. Moreover, the number of white voters in the South has grown faster since the 1960s than the number of black voters. Blacks have had their greatest political successes either when whites divided more or less evenly by party or candidate and blacks remained united or when blacks had majorities or near majorities. They are not a majority in any state. In only three states—Mississippi, South Carolina, and Louisiana—did blacks make up as much as 25 percent of the registered voters in 1984.

Other blunt realities have compounded the frustrations of the franchised minority. Most whites have refused to vote for black candidates. Consequently, blacks have difficulty winning elections in which they must attract more than a small number of white voters. Statewide races have proved to be especially difficult for black candidates. Only one black office seeker has won statewide elections in the South since Reconstruction: Virginia elected L. Douglas Wilder lieutenant governor in 1986, and in 1989 he was elected governor by a slim margin over an antiabortion Republican who was a very weak candidate. The Democratic party must attract black voters to survive but cannot appear to be a black party and do well. Conversely, the Republican party does not need to attract black voters to survive or even to do well in most elections. If the Republicans concede the votes of blacks to the Democrats, however, they will be in danger in any election in which Democrats attract a substantial portion of white voters. That is what happened when Carter swept most of the South in 1976. Southern Republicans have therefore dropped their once rather blatant racist appeals, though often only for more subtle versions. They have attempted to attract black voters with some success, especially middle-class blacks. Racial polarization along party lines, however, may be so strong a force that neither party can prevent it. In 1984 a political scientist from the South was invited by a businessman to switch to the Republican party: "Why don't you leave the niggers behind and come and join us?" Understandably, fears persist that the South's recently acquired two-party politics may become one party for blacks and one party for whites, a disquieting reminder of the past.

The 1980 and 1984 presidential elections reinforced those fears. Reagan got 61 percent of the white vote in 1980 and 70 percent in 1984. Eighty-nine percent of the black voters in 1980 supported Carter; 90 percent supported Walter Mondale, the Democratic nominee in 1984. Similar voting patterns appeared in the 1988 presidential election. But again, racial voting does not fully explain the success that the Republican party has enjoyed in the South since World War II. Ronald Reagan's enormous personal popularity accounted for some of this success in the 1980s. More broadly, Republicans have benefited greatly from the rise of a new urban middle class in the South and the economic distance the region has come since the desperate days of the Great Depression. The economic transformation of the region since World War II has played a large role in changing the politics of the South. Accompanying these economic developments has been the shift of political power in the South from the rural areas to the cities and suburbs, from the farm world to the town world and now to the metropolitan world.

The political power of the rural South—in particular, the power of black belt, county-seat politicians—fell rapidly in the 1960s. This decline had its beginnings earlier, largely in the massive migrations from rural to urban areas and the growth of the economic and political power of the cities. The courts hastened the political decline. In the process they broke new constitutional ground, setting new standards for representation in state legislatures, for state and local elections, and for the boundaries of political units.

The pivotal case for the courts involved political boundaries in Tuskegee, Alabama. Tuskegee typified the politics of the black belt. Blacks outnumbered whites about 4 to 1 (4,360 to 1,340), but whites controlled the politics of the town because very few blacks could vote. Intimidation, sometimes not very subtly applied, and paternalism kept blacks in their places. Tuskegee had what many whites in the South thought were "good race relations."

Tuskegee was not, however, a typical black belt town. It was the site of Booker T. Washington's Tuskegee Institute and a large Veterans Administration hospital that served black veterans exclusively. Tuskegee therefore had an unusually high proportion of well-educated blacks, so preventing blacks from registering was becoming increasingly difficult. To block access to the ballot box and to public office, white officials administered literacy and understanding tests. Officials found an unusually large number of people with masters' and doctoral degrees who became stupid or illiterate when they entered the voting registrar's office. Officials often complicated matters by applying arcane procedural rules arbitrarily and by making the time and place of voter registration as inconvenient and inconspicuous as possible. As elsewhere in the South, these devices had proved to be the most effective barriers to enfranchisement of blacks in the years since the end of the white primary.

When these barriers became increasingly difficult to maintain, Tuskegee whites asked the Alabama legislature for help. It obliged in 1957 by passing Alabama Act Number 140, creating new boundaries for the town. The legislature's new creation had twenty-eight sides, resembled "a stylized sea horse," and was artfully designed to include all the residences of the Tuskegee whites and to exclude almost all the residences of the Tuskegee blacks. The blacks countered by turning to the courts. Asserting that the new boundaries were an attempt to disfranchise them, the plaintiffs argued that the redistricting was unconstitutional. The lower courts refused to rule for the plaintiffs since the courts had traditionally held that setting political boundaries was a political issue and therefore not a matter to be reviewed or settled in the courts. "Courts," Supreme Court Justice Felix Frankfurter had declared in 1946, "ought not to enter this political thicket."

In 1960, however, the Supreme Court broke tradition and entered the "political thicket" in the case of *Gomillion* v. *Lightfoot*. It ruled that Alabama Act Number 140 was unconstitutional because it violated the equal protection clause of the Fourteenth Amendment and the Fifteenth Amendment, which states that no citizen's rights shall be "denied or abridged . . . on account of race, color, or previous condition of servitude." The Court also noted that the history of the Fifteenth Amendment indicated conclusively that the authors of the amendment had intended it to be a means to secure "the freedom of the slave race . . . from the oppression of those who had formerly exercised unlimited dominion over him."

In *Gomillion* the Court established new, crucial linkages between political representation and individual voting rights. It then strengthened those links in several important rulings in the 1960s. In *Baker* v. *Carr* (1962), a case that involved the failure of Tennessee to reapportion its legislature every ten years, as the state's constitution required, the Court declared that the federal courts had the authority and duty to consider the constitutionality of the apportionment of state legislatures. A year later, in *Gray* v. *Sanders,* the Court declared Georgia's county-unit system of apportioning votes in state primaries unconstitutional. Under that system, candidates had to obtain a majority of county units to win primaries. County units were assigned according to a formula that discriminated heavily against urban areas. The least populous 40 percent of the state's population had almost 60 percent of the county units. Fulton County (Atlanta) had 556,376 people in 1960 and six units, while small counties such as Chattahoochee (13,011) and Echols (1,876) had two units each. One vote in Chattahoochee had the same impact as fourteen in Fulton; one vote in Echols equaled ninety-nine in Fulton. The county-unit system also diluted the political impact of blacks in Georgia. Many rural counties had black majorities or large black minorities, but few blacks could vote there, whereas many urban blacks were registered voters.

Georgia's peculiar political institution permitted what V. O. Key, Jr., the noted political scientist, called the "rule of the rustics." Leaders of Georgia's rural white minority dominated the legislature and state offices and indulged themselves in what had long been a favorite Georgia pastime, attacking cities in general and Atlanta in particular. Eugene Talmadge had once been among the principal beneficiaries of this pastime. Affecting the image of a small farmer, the "Wild Man from Sugar Creek" mounted stumps, stands, steps, and backs of wagons all over Georgia, snapped his red galluses, and railed, especially against blacks. During a twenty-year period that ended in 1946, Talmadge ran in every state primary and was elected commissioner of agriculture three times and governor four times.

When it voided Georgia's county-unit system as a violation of the equal protection clause of the Fourteenth Amendment, the Court erected a new standard for apportionment and for redistricting political units—"one person, one vote." This decision, in conjunction with other factors, especially the civil rights movement and the Voting Rights Act of 1965, altered the basic structure of southern politics. Eugene Talmadge's son Herman joined other southern Democrats in shifting to biracial politics. The Republican party also found *Gray* v. *Sanders* useful in attacking apportionment measures written by Democratic legislatures. Thus blacks and southern Republicans have benefited the most from "one person, one vote." The principle has been applied widely outside the South, and Chicanos in the Southwest have taken particular advantage of it.

*T*HE SUNBELT

Like politics in the South after 1945, economic life has undergone a remarkable transformation. But like politics, the economy of the South also has unfortunate vestiges of the past. Personal income in the southern states grew more than 400 percent in real terms between 1945 and 1980. Thus, the post–World War II generation of southerners has had considerably more income than any previous generation of southerners ever had. Moreover, the gap in personal income between the South and the rest of the country narrowed after World War II. Per capita income increased from about one-half the national average in 1945 to two-thirds in 1960 to nearly nine-tenths in 1980, a ranking the South has not enjoyed since the firing started at Fort Sumter. The region that had been called the "Nation's No. 1" economic problem emerged almost magically as part of America's Sunbelt, that belt of warmth, newness, and prosperity stretching from the Chesapeake through the South, then westward to Arizona and California. Regional pride and self-confidence soared as thousands of southerners entered the middle class for the first time.

But distressing vestiges of the past lingered. Only Florida and Virginia were above the national average in per capita income in 1989; most southern states were not. Personal incomes in Texas, Oklahoma, and Louisiana declined sharply in the 1980s because of a recession in the petroleum industry, which is so important to those states. The gap between personal incomes in the South and those in the rest of the nation has remained about the same since the 1970s. Lower living costs reduced these differences but only to a degree, and lower living costs also meant that less was being spent for such services as health care and education. The South had 40 percent of America's poor though it had only 25 percent of its people. While impoverished whites outnumbered impoverished blacks in the region (8.3 million to 5.5 million), the proportion of blacks in that category far exceeded that of whites (49 percent to 12 percent). Poverty among blacks in 1993 remained especially pronounced in the Deep South, as did poverty among Hispanics in Texas, probably re-

PER CAPITA INCOME IN THE SOUTH, 1940–1989

State	1940	1950	1960	1970	1979	1989
Ala.	$278	$ 880	$1,493	$2,913	$5,894	$11,486
Ark.	254	825	1,376	2,869	5,614	10,520
Fla.	507	1,281	1,946	3,692	7,270	14,698
Ga.	336	1,034	1,637	3,318	6,402	13,631
Ky.	317	981	1,581	3,104	5,978	11,153
La.	360	1,120	1,662	3,068	6,430	10,635
Miss.	216	755	1,205	2,596	5,183	9,648
N.C.	323	1,037	1,558	3,218	6,133	12,885
Okla.	366	1,143	1,865	3,350	6,858	11,893
S.C.	301	893	1,372	2,963	5,886	11,897
Tenn.	334	994	1,544	3,082	6,213	12,255
Tex.	430	1,349	1,931	3,576	7,205	12,904
Va.	458	1,228	1,842	3,653	7,478	15,713
U.S.	592	1,496	2,216	3,943	7,298	14,420

SOURCE: U.S. Bureau of the Census, *Historical Statistics of the United States* (Washington, D.C., 1975), Pt. I, pp. 243–245; U.S. Bureau of the Census, *Statistical Abstracts, 1984* (Washington, D.C., 1984), p. 468; U.S. Bureau of the Census, *Statistical Abstracts, 1989* (Washington, D.C., 1989), p. 468.

MIAMI BEACH (Florida Department of Commerce, Division of Tourism)

flecting the low incomes earned by recent immigrants from Mexico. (Incomes among Hispanics in Arizona and California were also very low.)

There were other familiar disturbing patterns. As elsewhere in the United States, urban and particularly suburban areas were generally more prosperous than rural areas. Most of southern Appalachia had remained a distressed region. Personal incomes among its predominantly white populace were only 80 percent of the national average. Ratios in the Appalachian regions of Kentucky fell to as low as 63 percent, in Virginia to 71 percent. Similar low income patterns persisted in the Ozarks. Industrial workers still earned less and received less legal protection against unhealthful or dangerous working conditions than their counterparts elsewhere. The South still led the nation in infant and maternal deaths and trailed it in longevity of its inhabitants. Despite considerable advances, educational statistics still revealed serious deficiencies. Fewer people in the South had graduated from high school, and the South still spent less on education. The persistence of poverty and low incomes may help explain an aspect of voting behavior in the South. The percentage of voting-age people who have voted in presidential races has been declining since 1968, from 52 percent to 44 percent. (Outside the South, there were comparable developments: from 64 percent in 1968 to 51 percent in 1988.) Voter turnout has consistently been lower in the South, as low as 38 percent in South Carolina. Of course, turnout for nonpresidential elections is even lower than for presidential elections.

Wide differences in postwar economic change caused some observers to suggest a new geographical arrangement for the South: the outer South (the Chesapeake area, Florida, Texas, and Oklahoma); the middle South (the Carolinas, Georgia, and

EGLIN AIR FORCE BASE, FT. WALTON BEACH, FLORIDA

Louisiana); and the inner South (Arkansas, Mississippi, Alabama, Tennessee, and Kentucky). Marked postwar differences in economic growth rates, types of economic activity, occupational diversity, and urbanization justify this new economic geography. The outer South has experienced the greatest change. Military and defense spending during World War II had a particularly strong impact on the outer South, and during the Cold War the military-defense industry became a permanent fixture there. Among the benefits it brought were the expanded port facilities that were in place when the national economy became much more internationalized. A reciprocating chain reaction ensued: more international trade led to more international banking, trading, and services activities, which led to more economic growth in areas around ports. Since the 1950s, more than 40 percent of the people on military payrolls have resided in the South or close to its borders, most of them in the outer South. About 135,000 civilian employees of the Defense Department lived in the Chesapeake Bay region in 1980; 78,000 of them resided in metropolitan Washington and 40,000 in Norfolk–Newport News.

The outer South has been able to take particular advantage of the postwar economic trends: the expansion of financial, communications, and transportation services, the internationalization of trade, the shift away from manufacturing as the United States entered the postindustrial era, the boom in tourism and retirement, and the development and expansion of services that rely on sophisticated technology and communications. The value of the export-import trade reached $74 billion in the Gulf ports of Texas and Louisiana in 1982, and $27 billion in the Chesapeake ports. Such a large trade has had a substantial ripple effect, encouraging the growth of insurance companies, banks, law firms, and highly educated and skilled workforces. Northern Virginia, northern Florida, Houston, and Dallas–Fort Worth have led the region in high-tech development, well ahead of other important centers of this area of activity such as Atlanta; Huntsville, Alabama; Oak Ridge, Tennessee; Nashville; and Raleigh–Durham–Chapel Hill (the Research Triangle), North Carolina.

Oil and gas provided much of the economic growth and diversification in Texas and Oklahoma. Both, especially Texas, have petrochemical complexes, and recently both have found that boom-and-bust cycles still plague the oil and gas industry. Nor, as Louisiana has shown, do large reserves of oil and gas or a large petrochemical industry necessarily elevate a state's economy to the upper ranks of the region.

Much of the gap between the outer South and the middle South can be explained by the latter's greater dependence on manufacturing. Textile production has been and continues to be the leading industry in the middle South, though its preeminence is rapidly declining. More than 216,000 jobs in textiles—a 30 percent reduction—were lost between the mid-1970s and 1987. Similar declines, though smaller in absolute terms, occurred in tobacco, furniture, and wood products manufacturing. While manufacturing has become more diverse in the middle South, neither total manufacturing employment nor the real wages of industrial workers have increased. The middle South has less urban and metropolitan development than the outer South, despite the striking growth of Charlotte, Greensboro, Raleigh–Durham–Chapel Hill, Columbia, Charleston, Myrtle Beach, Baton Rouge, and most of all, Atlanta.

The inner South lags well behind its neighbors. Arkansas and Mississippi have been the least industrialized, least economically diversified of the southern states. Major industries in the inner South—aluminum, coal, and iron and steel—have suffered severe reverses. The new industries that have developed, such as the new manufacturing plants built by foreign and domestic automobile manufacturers, have not fully offset losses in older industries; nor have the activities at such high-tech centers as Huntsville, Nashville, and Oak Ridge. Only two cities in the inner South have been among the leaders in metropolitan growth in the South—Memphis and Nashville. Tennessee has generally had more economic success than its neighbors and may not belong in the inner South. In the 1980s Tennessee's population growth was modest, like that in the rest of the inner South, but Tennessee has considerably outpaced its neighbors in degree of urbanization, the growth and output of its manufacturing, and the success of its farmers.

Some of Tennessee's economic success may be attributed to the Tennessee Valley Authority, the largest effort at regional development in American history. But elsewhere in the inner South, not even the TVA has managed to overcome the problems that slowed economic growth. In fact, critics claimed that the rates the TVA charged for power nearly equaled those of private utilities; that it had overbuilt its generating capacity, especially its nuclear power plants; and that its heavy use of coal made it a major polluter in the region. Hope for economic expansion in some of the inner South rested in part on the Tennessee-Tombigbee Waterway, a $2 billion project completed in 1985 and designed to provide a cheaper means of transporting heavy cargo from the southern Appalachian states to Mobile and the Gulf coast by a canal system linking the Tennessee River to the Tombigbee River.

The Tennessee-Tombigbee Waterway is only one of the more recent examples of the adeptness with which southern leaders have pursued federal funds for their region since 1940. The ability of Congressman L. Mendel Rivers of South Carolina and Congressman Carl Vinson and Senator Richard Russell of Georgia to attract Defense Department dollars made them legendary figures. Where military spending has involved complex scientific and engineering work, it has tended to create new facilities and groups of scientists and engineers and to expand existing ones. The location of the army's Redstone arsenal at Huntsville, Alabama, for example, revived Huntsville and led to the creation of the University of Alabama at Huntsville. The National Aeronautics and Space Administration has had a similar impact along the Gulf coast, especially in Houston, where it is headquartered. In the last instance, the hand of Lyndon Johnson was very evident.

Before World War II the South did not seek federal funding as readily as other regions did. That situation changed after the war, especially after 1950. Southern leaders in politics and business adopted much more Whiggish attitudes: they, like the pre–Civil War Whigs, advocated certain kinds of government spending as a means of achieving economic growth. The modern Whigs found money in state and local treasuries to provide matching funds for interstate highways, airports, stadiums, and similar facilities that promised to stimulate the southern economy in ways they approved of. The advent of post–World War II Whigs to positions of power also indicated the decline of older leaders with ties to the black belt counties, county courthouses, local banks, and older manufacturing industries.

The expansion of airports and highways has had a profound effect on the geography of the South. Postwar highway construction, to which the Interstate Highway Act (1955) gave a massive stimulus, reinforced these developments, especially as trucks displaced railroads as the primary means for transporting freight. The horizontal growth pattern of the urban South has continued, geometrically in such cities as Houston, Atlanta, Charlotte, and Dallas. Atlanta may be the model for American cities of the future: metropolises with multiple centers or nuclei. In other instances, transportation systems have reinforced the dispersed pattern of manufacturing facilities in the South. Tourism and the retirement industry have been enormously stimulated by post–World War II developments in the transportation systems in the southern states as well as in air-conditioning. Chilled air also made some manufacturing and medical processes possible for the first time in the hot, humid South.

Long a staple of the region, tourism has been shaped by the limits of personal income and the availability of leisure time and adequate transportation. Well before the twentieth century, wealthy southerners sought relief from the heat by retreating to the mountains or the beaches. In the winter, privileged northerners sought warmth in the South. Horse racing and gambling frequently reinforced these impulses. Some also sought health resorts like Hot Springs, Arkansas.

Early tourism relied heavily upon waterborne transportation and animal power (for carriages and wagons). Railroads opened new tourist vistas after the 1880s. Travelers, once limited primarily to places like the Mississippi or Florida's lush semitropical rivers, could by the 1890s ride the Flagler rail system far into Florida. Trains also made the Appalachians (and, later, the Ozarks) more accessible, as well as numerous other interior areas. Automobiles and paved highways expanded that accessibility. Mass travel by air came after 1960.

The growth of the American middle class created a broader economic base for tourism as early as the 1920s. The post-1940 economic boom in the United States reinforced this economic base as millions traveled to beaches from Chesapeake Bay through the Carolinas and Florida, or along the Gulf coast from Alabama to Texas, or to the mountains of southern Appalachia and the Ozarks. After 1970, thousands of foreign travelers came, especially to Florida and New Orleans.

As the number swelled, tourism became a major industry and much more commercialized. Charleston provides some indication about how large the industry has become. By the 1980s, the South Carolina city was reported to be earning more than $450 million annually from visitors. Throughout the South, tourist cabins and camps were displaced by motels and fast-food facilities. Neither Colonial Williamsburg nor Vicksburg could escape commercialization. The Smokies seem to be groaning under the burden: the national park there may be the most heavily used of the national parks.

The tourist industry caters to a hodgepodge of tastes. There are recreational parks that offer themes like country music (Gatlinburg, Tennessee), ersatz Indians (Cherokee, North Carolina), and mountain rubes (L'il Abner in the Ozarks). Tourists can get closer to the real thing in country music by visiting the Grand Ole Opry in Nashville, though they would hardly escape commercialism. Or tourists can play miniature golf among life-size plastic dinosaurs, go to topless bars, or exercise on the hundreds of golf courses and tennis courts the region offers. The more sedate or adventurous may pursue fishing, hunting, white-water rafting, and rock climbing.

The region's attractions for retirees has generated a growing retirement industry. Air-conditioning, lower taxes, lower living costs, and more gentle winters have been the industry's primary assets. Florida has long been the prime haven in the South for retirees. Other states have attracted many retirees, and more are coming. Retired people have moved in large numbers into Texas's lower Rio Grande Valley, the Appalachians, and the Ozarks. More recently, many have settled along the coasts from Virginia through Georgia and along the Gulf coast.

Fiscal and budgetary policies in the South also have reflected Whiggish attitudes. Before World War II the South had higher corporate taxes than the rest of the nation; after the war, lower. On the other hand, most southern states have relied heavily on sales taxes, which weigh disproportionately on low-income groups. Moreover, state and local spending for social services is still generally lower in the South than elsewhere in the nation, though recently the pattern of expenditures for higher education has changed somewhat as leaders have concluded that quality in higher education and economic growth are closely connected.

"COTTON FIELDS NO MORE"

Whatever the relative economic position of the various parts of the South, one thing is clear: agriculture has undergone revolutionary change since 1940. When World War II began, more than 40 percent of southerners (15.6 million) farmed. Forty years later, only 3 to 4 percent (1.6 million) did. The number of farms had declined from 2.9 million to 949,000. The average size of farms, the value of farmland and buildings, and the value of their output had increased, often dramatically. Recent figures

AVERAGE NUMBER OF HARVESTED ACRES AND AVERAGE VALUE OF LAND, BUILDINGS, AND FARM PRODUCTS PER FARM IN THREE SOUTHERN STATES, 1940, 1978, AND 1987

	Acres			Land and buildings			Farm products		
	1940	1978	1987	1940	1978	1987	1939[a]	1978	1987
Fla.	27.0	93.1	98.8	$5,211	$351,646	$543,830	$1,494	$69,148	$119,033
Ala.	30.7	83.9	78.2	1,764	128,260	168,161	349	27,398	44,053
Va.	22.0	54.7	64.4	3,860	163,918	232,374	713	22,933	35,464

[a] Reported in 1940.

SOURCE: Gilberg C. Fite, *Cotton Fields No More: Southern Agriculture, 1865–1980* (Lexington, Ky., 1984), pp. 235–237; U.S. Bureau of the Census, *1987 Census of Agriculture* (Washington, D.C., 1987), Vol. I, Pt. 1, p. 1; Pt. 9, p. 1; Pt. 46, p. 1.

indicate that the decline in the number of farms in the South has continued, and at a faster rate than in the rest of the nation.

Clearly the volume of output per farm had soared. Comparable changes could be seen in the kinds of outputs produced. Beef cattle, poultry, soybeans, tobacco, and dairy products had become the leading farm products. Production of vegetables, fruits, and nuts had also increased, aided by improved transport and refrigeration. Some farmers added significantly to their incomes by selling off timber. However, nonfarmers, particularly large wood and paper products manufacturers, became the principal owners of timberlands in the South. Private corporations owned 133 million acres of southern forests, which by 1977 produced pulpwood for two-thirds of the paper manufactured in the United States and a fourth of the nation's yearly output of lumber. In no state was cotton the leading cash crop, though it ranked second in Texas and Mississippi. The land of cotton had come to look more like the land of soybeans, grass, cattle, and pine trees.

These radical changes resulted from the conjunction of numerous factors: mechanization; electrification; fertilizers; improved seeds; better control of pests, diseases, and weeds; better breeding stock; development of good pasture; removal of poor soils from production; the work of agricultural schools and extension services; greater attention to careful management; and more accessible credit, capital, and markets. Profits from current production (a large part of them generated by World War II), loans and payments from federal agencies and programs, and loans from commercial banks provided most of the capital and credit. People who were considered good credit risks got loans readily, but not marginal farmers, and they were legion. The process favored bigger farm owners over small farm owners, tenants, and sharecroppers. The most successful businesspeople were in agribusiness. Small towns stagnated. Most farmers became dependent on high-volume production, credit, and chemicals. The use of chemicals entailed unanticipated costs, which have been and often still are ignored. For instance, only after a long battle was the toxic chemical DDT banned in 1978. As a result of the post-1940 agricultural revolution in the South, a whole way of life disappeared in a generation: most family farms and almost all the tenants, sharecroppers, mules, and cotton gins. Networks of human relations—burdened though they were by racism, debt, and perennial disappointment—

collapsed. So did many wood-shack homes. Church pews emptied till the churches were abandoned. So were country schools and stores.

The agricultural revolution blessed many farmers and even more nonfarmers. Nonfarmers benefited from more, better, and cheaper farm products. Those farmers who were able to make the transition to modern, large-scale agriculture improved their incomes, sometimes dramatically. Some became wealthy. Their children, like Jimmy Carter, went to college, often the first members of their families to do so. They regularly shopped in places where they had seldom gone before, such as Columbus and Atlanta. Their involvement in community affairs went beyond their immediate locales. They joined civic clubs in nearby towns. Many worked with recently formed county and regional development boards and agencies to diversify declining rural economies and to offset the staggering loss of jobs created by the agricultural revolution in the South.

That revolution exacted a very high price in human terms, primarily from people who could not or did not make the transition to modern farming and who found inadequate employment opportunities even in the rapidly growing economy of the post-1940 South. In "one of the greatest movements of people in history to occur within a single generation," nearly 14 million southerners left the farms between 1940 and 1980, most of them for cities in the South and the North. In the 1950s and 1960s so many people climbed aboard northbound trains in the Carolinas clutching sacks of home-fried chicken for the journey that the trains came to be known as the Chicken-Bone Special. Thousands of these rural exiles found a better, though very different life. Thousands of others failed to find enough nonagricultural employment to raise themselves above the poverty level. Minimal skills and meager schooling limited many of them, especially those who were black—a disproportionate part of the South's displaced farm population.

Blacks also faced overt racial barriers in the job market until at least the mid-1960s. (Covert racial barriers have remained, though they appear to be coming down slowly.) Even where blacks found traditional nonfarm work, they were limited by lack of skills and inferior schooling. Racial preferences often precluded their rise to skilled or supervisory positions. Before the mid-1960s, white workers frequently joined with management to perpetuate racial discrimination. Strong worker sentiment in the textile industry, which was still largely nonunion, kept the workforce of that industry virtually all-white. There was, in fact, a good deal of evidence of a tacit agreement between white workers and management in textiles: if the workers kept unions out, management would keep blacks out. Only after labor shortages and pressures from the federal government forced management's hand did racial barriers begin to drop in the textile industry. In less than a decade the most racially segregated labor force in the South became one of the most desegregated.

During the post-1940 economic boom the number of nonagricultural jobs in the South more than tripled, from nearly 7.8 million in 1940 to 25.9 million in 1980; manufacturing employment almost doubled, from 1.9 million to 3.4 million. But the displaced farmers had to compete with more skilled and better-educated people. Most of their competitors came from southern towns and cities, though many of them were northerners who migrated southward after World War II. Modern air-conditioning encouraged this migration by easing the ordeal of

Dixie's hot, humid summers. By the 1960s the South had passed a major demographic landmark: for the first time in a century, in-migration exceeded out-
migration, though not among blacks. Then in the 1970s, for the first time since
Emancipation, more blacks moved into the South than moved out.

The post-1950s decline in America's heavy industries, traditionally the first
step up the social and economic ladder for impoverished farmers, compounded
the difficulties of rural exiles and their children, especially young males. Industrial decay came first in the North, then spread to the South in the 1970s. Industrial wages in the South remained low. Only in Louisiana, Kentucky, and Oklahoma were the average hourly earnings of industrial workers higher than the
$7.27 national average in 1980. In the most industrialized states of the South—
Virginia, the Carolinas, and Georgia—hourly earnings of industrial workers averaged less than $6. The South's most industrial state, North Carolina, had the low-
est industrial wages in the country. Its heavily industrialized neighbor, South Carolina, was a close second. The predominance of textiles probably explains that
statistic. The textile industry has traditionally paid low wages because it uses relatively unskilled workers, many of them women. The labor intensity of the highly
competitive textile industry has kept wages low. The weakness of labor unions in
the Carolinas also contributes to the low wages in manufacturing.

Workers in the South still tend to be less unionized than other American workers. Less than 10 percent of textile workers were unionized in the 1980s, despite numerous attempts to organize them. The largest of those efforts took place shortly
after World War II. Operation Dixie, whose primary target was textiles, lasted from
1946 to 1950, cost at least $5 million, and ended in almost complete failure.

The textile industry proved to be as subtle and resourceful as it was resistant.
The industry relied less on blunt intimidation than on public relations and on
timely pay raises and improvements in benefits. The industry also received encouragement from local and state governments, which saw labor unions as
threats to their efforts to attract industrial investors. Moreover, most southern
states had right-to-work laws, stipulating that workers could not be forced to join
a union in order to get or retain a job. Whether or not right-to-work laws actually
deterred unionization is a matter of dispute, though both labor and management
believed that they did. As late as the 1970s southern Democrats played major
roles in defeating federal legislation that they believed favored organized labor.
Labor leaders were convinced that President Carter had failed to act decisively to
get the Labor Reform Bill of 1978—a name its opponents disputed, of course—
passed by Congress. The bill was designed to make unionization easier by making the procedures stipulated by the National Labor Relations (or Wagner) Act
simpler and more quickly implemented.

In the face of massive, swift agricultural change and inadequate opportunities
off the farm, thousands of displaced farmers had few options. Most were landless
or became landless when farm costs increased rapidly after 1940. Black farm owners became virtually extinct. Some black and white farmers who managed to keep
their small holdings farmed part-time and did odd jobs, often in seasonal farm-
work. Over time, however, migrant labor took over much of the seasonal work.
Factory jobs, where they could be found in rural areas, tended to be low skill, low
pay, and unpredictable. Welfare provided minimal benefits and unwelcome

dependency. Welfare policy and practices encouraged out-migration. Southern states, more than most other states, had fewer resources to spend on welfare and proportionately more people who needed welfare. All the same, southern states were tightfisted in regard to the needy. In 1991, welfare payments to families in the United States averaged $394 a month; in Alabama they averaged $125, in Florida $267, and in Texas $166.

The civil rights revolution hastened the displacement of black farmers. As the traditional mode of white dominance and black subservience came under assault, personal relations between blacks and whites became more distant and white paternalism seemed to evaporate. A black farmer in Alabama remarked in 1967 that "them white folks got a lot more interested in machinery after the civil rights bill was passed." Government had little interest in the economic welfare of the displaced farmers. The plight of these people did not trigger federal or state programs or financial assistance that even remotely approximated their need.

Many rural counties in the South, especially in the black belt, Appalachia, and parts of the Ozarks, more closely resembled Third World countries than the Sunbelt. In such places as Greene County, Alabama, perhaps half the residents got government assistance in 1979. The civil rights revolution had made life better politically for the county's black majority but not economically. In an effort to improve things, the black-dominated county approved the opening of a dog track. It increased county revenues by nearly $2 million a year, but it did not create many jobs.

THE METROPOLITAN SOUTH

When farmers displaced by the South's agricultural revolution left their farms, many did not move far. So many black and white Mississippians moved to Memphis after World War II that it was called the "largest city in Mississippi." The migrants from the farms joined others from small towns in and outside the South to make southern cities among the fastest growing in America after 1940.

The urban South offered jobs. It also offered attractive services, recreational and cultural opportunities, and more desirable educational systems. Riding the wave of the post–World War II economic boom, the urban South worked feverishly to secure or expand the hallmarks of modernization: large airports, freeways, shopping malls, skyscrapers, major banks and other financial institutions, corporate headquarters, convention centers, museums, orchestras, restaurants and theaters, ballet and opera companies, sophisticated medical complexes, colleges and universities, and professional sports teams. The urban South also offered the possibility of living in an urban world that was leisurely, friendly, and mannerly, or claimed to be. Whatever the precise fit between possibility and actuality, southern cities have acted as magnets, as their growth since World War II clearly indicates. The growth of the metropolitan South reflects long-term patterns, with the upper South and the Southwest attracting larger numbers of new residents and experiencing faster economic growth. Atlanta, a Deep South state, stands out for its prosperity. It is really part of the piedmont.

Improvements in the quality and range of education offered in the South reflect the economic growth of the region and the large role urban areas played in

744 CHAPTER 27

POPULATION OF SOUTHERN METROPOLITAN AREAS, 1940–2000 (IN THOUSANDS)

Cities	1940*	1960	1970	1980	1990	2000**
Dallas/Ft. Worth	473	1,738	2,378	3,046	4,037	4,910
Houston	385	1,430	1,999	3,118	3,731	4,494
Atlanta	302	1,169	1,596	2,233	2,960	3,857
Tampa–St. Petersburg	169	772	1,106	1,614	2,068	2,278
Miami–Ft. Lauderdale	472	1,035	1,269	2,644	3,193	3,876
San Antonio	254	736	888	1,089	1,325	1,565
Charlotte	101	202	241	971	1,162	1,417
New Orleans	495	907	1,046	1,304	1,285	1,305
Nashville	167	597	699	851	985	1,172
Memphis	293	727	834	939	1,007	1,105
Jacksonville	173	530	622	722	907	1,056
Oklahoma City	204	512	719	861	959	1,046
Louisville	319	754	807	954	949	1,006
Richmond	193	462	548	761	866	961
Birmingham	268	747	767	815	840	915

*Urban only. Very large decennial increases in population may, to some degree, be the result of rapid annexations by cities or by changes in the Census Bureau's definition of a metropolitan area.

**Estimated populations.

Sources: U.S. Bureau of the Census, *Statistical Abstracts of the United States* (Washington, D.C.: 1942, 1962, 1982–1983, 1993); U.S. Bureau of Census website (for 2000).

it. The changes since the 1930s are striking. At that time the American Council on Education concluded that only seven universities in the entire South had departments that were qualified to offer doctoral degrees and that the South had only 42 of the 661 such departments in the nation. Only 2 of the 230 departments believed to have attained "eminence" were in the South. Collectively, primary and secondary schools in the South still were below national standards in 1980. But the gap had closed substantially. Moreover, many of these schools—public and private—met or exceeded national standards. The same could be said of postsecondary schools. Community colleges, technical colleges, and branch campuses of state universities had proliferated. Some professional schools had achieved national and even international distinction: the Texas Medical Center in Houston, the medical school at the University of Alabama in Birmingham, the Medical College Division of Virginia Commonwealth University, the law and medical schools at the University of Virginia, at Duke, Vanderbilt, and Emory, and the schools of engineering and architecture at Rice University. Among private universities, several had achieved high national ranking: Rice, Duke, Vanderbilt, Emory, Wake Forest, and Tulane. Three public universities had achieved similar status: the University of North Carolina, the University of Virginia, and the University of Texas. The University of Florida had almost joined that company by 1980. Colleges of distinction in the region include William and Mary, Washington and Lee, Richmond, Davidson, Wofford, Sewanee, Birmingham Southern, Millsaps, Rhodes, and Trinity. Every southern state had accredited graduate and professional programs in a wide range of fields.

The civil rights revolution contributed to the enhanced status of the universities and colleges of the South. Racial segregation had created a negative academic climate; in particular, it raised serious questions about academic freedom. Among the positive effects of desegregation are improved chances of attracting faculty and students from outside the region and a more open atmosphere on campuses. Yet desegregation has had a negative effect on traditionally all-black colleges and universities, like Fisk, Morehouse, and Howard, because many black students have chosen to enroll in formerly all-white schools. Many black faculty have taken a similar route.

Though obviously education in the South had improved markedly since World War II, serious concerns remained in 1980. Almost two-thirds of Americans who were twenty-five years of age or older had completed high school; but in only one southern state, Florida, was the proportion that high. The majority of southern states had fewer than six in ten high school graduates among that age group. Illiteracy also remained disproportionately high in the South. Southern states, despite great exertions, still spent considerably less for each school-age resident than most states outside the South. These facts disturbed government and business leaders because they had come to perceive a direct connection between continued economic growth on the one hand and educational achievement and the status of educational institutions on the other. State development boards, which had become sophisticated agencies for economic development, found that potential investors tended more than ever to shy away from places where schools were below their standards. It was no accident that a number of southern states made strong commitments in the 1980s to improve education. One of the striking developments of the postwar South is the amount of thought and energy poured into efforts to create jobs. Surely Henry Grady would have delighted in the sophistication of state and local efforts at economic development and the willingness of political leaders to pursue potential investors across the globe.

By 1980, however, and in some cases earlier, southerners discovered that the rapid economic and urban growth it had experienced had some major negative aspects. Not least was the fading of the more relaxed way of life that had long characterized the region. Most of the costs were more tangible: pollution, crime, personal violence, urban sprawl, traffic jams, commuting, overtaxed public services, blighted neighborhoods. White suburbs and, to a lesser extent, black suburbs proliferated around older urban cores where the less advantaged were trapped with little hope of leaving. These people were more likely to be black than white, more likely to be older, less educated, and less skilled.

To be sure, variations could be found in almost every southern city, sometimes reflecting its history or economic characteristics peculiar to itself. Miami had a large, prosperous Cuban community. Houston and San Antonio had large Chicano communities, portions of which had become middle class. Almost every southern city had "gentrified" neighborhoods, inner-city areas that had been reclaimed and refurbished by upper-middle-class professionals, and most southern cities had considerable black populations, more than cities elsewhere could claim. Among blacks there was a growing middle class, some of whom lived in racially desegregated neighborhoods. Still, southern cities were more racially segregated in 1980 than ever before. School desegregation had had a large part in that development as

MAJOR THOROUGHFARE, CHARLOTTE, N.C., 1970s (The Charlotte Observer)

whites had taken flight to suburbs, to all-white or nearly all-white school districts. As a result of that flight and the growth of enrollments in private schools, many public schools were becoming resegregated. Public schools in Little Rock, scene of the South's first major clash over public school desegregation, found themselves nearly as racially segregated as they had been in 1957. Similar trends could be seen outside the urban South. In many places no resegregation had occurred because the schools had never been desegregated to any significant degree. Race, however, was not the only reason that parents were turning away from public schools. Concern about quality of education, moral values, and religious beliefs prompted many parents to send their children to private schools, though they were costly. Unfortunately, these schools were all-white or virtually all-white. These trends in education clearly suggested that Jim Crow was not entirely dead and that some seemingly intractable class and racial differences between whites and blacks tended to persist.

As early as the 1970s, as the South entered its most expansive decade since the Civil War, observers had wondered if the urban South would repeat the mistakes of the urban North. Southern cities, one observer believed, had several advantages: they were smaller and generally younger, had less heavy industry, and had fewer areas that had decayed or had been abandoned. But two national trends threatened to erase these advantages: most of the jobs and most of the whites were in the suburbs, and the majority of blacks and the poor were concentrated in inner-city ghettos. Little that occurred in southern cities in the 1970s indicated that the path they had followed differed in any significant respect from the course taken by northern cities. Indeed, in the 1970s the differences between the South and the rest of the nation became so blurred that more than a few observers wondered if the South had lost its distinctiveness.

28

The Sunbelt South: No Eden in Dixie

❖

Since the earliest days of European settlement in North America, the historian Charles Roland remarked in 1970, people have been predicting that the American South "was just about to become the garden spot of the universe." Expectations, however, have repeatedly exceeded performance. "The South . . . has been, and remains today, a land becoming and not a land become—a garden spot that beckons only to recede like a mirage when approached. It is America's will-o'-the-wisp Eden."

As early as 1588, Thomas Hariot assured readers of *A Brief and True Report of the New Found Land of Virginia* that "the ayre there is so temperate and holsome, the soyle so fertile, . . . in short time . . . they may raise . . . those sortes of commodities which shall both enrich them selves, as also others that shall deale with them." Hariot's brief career as a colonist apparently did not dampen his spirits. The English mathematician, scientist, and preacher had been one of the 108 men who founded the first English colony in the New World. The colony lasted ten months. Disease, food shortages, and hostile Indians largely accounted for the short life of one of England's early attempts to create a great overseas empire.

Generations of boosters of the South have followed in Hariot's footsteps. Hopes—as well as judgments about the wholesomeness of the climate of the South, the fertility of its soil, and the extent of its natural resources—have repeatedly exceeded realities. In 1811 Thomas Jefferson foresaw an agrarian utopia in which the federal debt would be retired and modest taxes would generate enough revenue to pay for "canals, roads, schools, etc." The "farmer will see his government supported, his children educated, and the face of his country made a paradise."

Less than a decade after Jefferson retired from politics, new political voices endorsed the economic nationalism of Jefferson's fiercest enemy, Alexander

Hamilton. Henry Clay of Kentucky and John C. Calhoun of South Carolina called for a strong federal government, supported by the revenues produced by a high tariff, which would lead the way toward a strong, diverse American economy based on agriculture, commerce, and manufacturing. The result of this policy, Calhoun declared, would help American farmers, who made up the majority of the population of the United States and especially of the South. "The farmer," he predicted, "will find a ready market for his surplus produce; and what is almost of equal consequence, a certain and cheap supply of all his wants. His prosperity will diffuse itself to every class in the community."

The South, however, did not subscribe to Hamiltonian economic nationalism. It sought its fortunes instead in cotton, slavery, and free trade. Calhoun soon reversed his course. He rejected economic nationalism and the policy of a strong federal government, embraced states rights, and spent much of the remainder of his political life trying to devise some means to protect the interests of the South within the Union.

The economic success of the antebellum South, particularly the prosperity of the 1850s, seemed to justify the course the South had taken. In 1857 Senator James H. Hammond, a successor to Calhoun, declared, "Cotton is king." Confident of its economic strength, the South seceded three years later. It suffered massive military defeat, in part because of the gap between expectations generated by the cotton kingdom and its realities.

Boosterism, however, survived disunion and war. Even during the Civil War, at least early in the conflict, hope for southern self-sufficiency thrived. Another vision of southern prosperity was widely held in the North. According to that vision, slavery was the snake that had kept the South from being a garden of Eden. Once the snake was destroyed, "schools and churches will be multiplied under Northern inspiration and example, . . . industry, production, and intelligence will follow our arms, and when our forces withdraw instead of leaving a desolate country behind them, they will point to it as a blossoming and regenerated Eden." Similar smug thoughts provided much of the motivation and some of the policies of Radical Reconstruction.

After Reconstruction, the prophets of the New South called continually for southerners to make an Eden with their own hands. Of those prophets, Henry Grady of the *Atlanta Constitution* was the most prescient. Again and again Grady pleaded for economic diversification in the South, where

> is centered all that can please or prosper humankind. A perfect climate above a fertile soil, yields to the husbandman every product of the temperate zone. . . . There, are mountains stored with exhaustless treasures; forests, vast and primeval, and rivers that, tumbling or loitering, run wanton to the sea.

Few dissented from the pursuit of Eden in Dixie. Some religious folk had grave reservations about attempts to construct man-made Edens, but the religious dissidents were a small minority. The cultural elite provided a number of dissenters: Mark Twain, Ellen Glasgow, the Agrarians, Thomas Wolfe, and William Faulkner, to name only some of the most obvious. Stronger, more persistent voices in the 1920s and 1930s decried the gap between the realities of the New South and even a pale version of Eden. Their dissent found its most powerful vehicle in *Eco-*

nomic Conditions of the South. Written by the National Emergency Council, which President Franklin Roosevelt created, and published in 1938 as the nation was still mired in the worst economic crisis in American history, the report declared: "The Nation's No. 1 economic problem is the South." Like so many people before them, the council members believed that the South could do much better because it had good soils, a temperate climate, great quantities of water, and rich resources. "The paradox of the South is that while it is blessed by Nature with immense wealth, its people as a whole are the poorest in the country."

Soon after the report appeared, the South began three decades of economic growth unequaled in its history. By the early 1970s, the South was celebrating its place in the Sunbelt. By almost any conceivable measure, the South was far better off than it had been at the beginning of World War II. In 1940 southerners earned about half what other Americans earned, and the great majority of them made their living in dirty, physically arduous, and frequently hazardous work on farms and in factories, forests, and mines. Tuberculosis, hookworm, pellagra, and malnutrition were not uncommon in 1940. By 1970 each of these serious health problems had been very substantially reduced or nearly erased, and personal income had increased by more than 400 percent in *real* terms. But like most Americans, southerners made inadequate adjustments to their diets. Too many demurred from healthier diets to continue consuming what John Egerton calls "the major food groups in the South: sugar, salt, butter, eggs, cream, and bacon grease." Great improvements had also been made in housing, education, and leisure. By 1980, for the first time, the majority of white southerners had middle-class occupations. They indeed had much to celebrate.

Predictably, this economic growth came with a price. Family farms have become increasingly rare as farm size has continued to grow, and agriculture has become even more capital intensive and less labor intensive than it had been. When cotton growing staged a revival in the South in the 1990s, it came with the latest developments in scientific farming, heavy use of chemicals and clean-row agriculture, minimal use of labor, and heavy equipment, including costly, sophisticated cotton-picking machinery. Similar developments have occurred in tobacco-growing, though tobacco is still usually grown on small farms. It has remained an important crop in spite of health concerns, because tobacco is more profitable than other crops. Its manufacture remains highly profitable. Companies have offset the decline in domestic demand for cigarettes and other tobacco products by raising prices and expanding exports.

Swelling populations, especially in coastal areas, often encroach on critically needed ecological systems. Portions of southern Louisiana are notorious for the pollution that the petrochemical and oil-refining industries there have caused in the area. Low-income residents everywhere are more likely than other residents to be adversely affected by hazardous and unhealthy pollution. The Everglades are so damaged that slowing and reversing that damage will require massive expenditures of public money. Traffic congestion in metropolitan areas has turned commuting into daily two- and three-hour ordeals. Atlanta and Houston are among the ten most traffic-congested metropolitan areas in the country. Drawing on data from 1997, the *Atlanta Constitution* confirmed Atlantans' worst suspicions about congestion in their city. The data indicated that Atlantans annually lost 68 hours and $1,125 each because of snarled traffic and that Atlanta led the nation for the

longest daily commute, thirty-three miles per day. Coincidentally, rural areas in the
South continued to experience population declines, declines that were accelerated
by the expansion of the interstate highway system and the rapid evolution of interstate malls composed of motels, gas stations, fast-food outlets, and discount retailers. A few interstate exit areas boast of we-bare-all establishments that combined
"good food" and strippers.

THE VANISHING SOUTH?

The Sunbelt looked so much like the rest of postwar America that it provoked a
nagging question: had the South disappeared? The question had a bittersweet flavor. No one, for instance, lamented the end of the poverty of the 1930s or the disappearance of hookworm. Many whites mourned the passing of Jim Crow, but
most did not. Large numbers of southerners, white as well as black, rejoiced at the
ending of the racial caste system. But urban and industrial pollution unsettled
many people. The appearance of air-conditioning pleased nearly everyone, but
not the disappearance of front porches and front-porch culture. People went inside and watched television, which projected a homogenized national culture.

The boundaries of the South are no longer so clearly delineated. Yet certain
distinguishing features remain, among them regional speech patterns and food
habits, a concern for manners, and strong interest in tradition. The South has exported some of its tastes in food. Kentucky Fried Chicken has enjoyed considerable success outside Dixie. So, more recently, has Cajun cooking. Southern speech
patterns have received a more mixed reception. Southerners who are concerned
that they might sound slow or dumb are offered courses designed to erase their
accents. Conversely, southern girls are urged by "everybody north of Baltimore":
"Whatever you do, *don't* lose that lovely southern accent of yours."

Life may still take a slower pace in the South than in the rest of the country,
but in many parts of the region, the easy pace has become a thing of the past. The
population of the South remains blacker but less ethnically diverse than the rest of
the United States. However, the growing Chicano population of the Southwest is
rapidly altering the ethnic composition of such states as Texas. That change is also
increasing the size and importance of the Catholic population in parts of the
South. Similar developments have occurred in southern Florida. Thirty percent of
Texas's population is Hispanic, 15 percent of Florida's. Texas is now the second
most populous state in the nation, Florida, the fourth. Though other immigrant
groups have fewer numbers, they may, like Asian immigrants in Atlanta or northern Virginia, have greater impact than their numbers suggest. Students from Asia
have become integral parts of many graduate programs in southern universities.

*T*WO RELIGIONS: NORTH AND SOUTH?

Evangelical Protestantism still permeates the South, however, and since the 1950s,
fundamentalism and Pentecostalism, the hard and soft sides of evangelical
Protestantism, have been especially vigorous. They are also vigorous outside the

South, especially in parts of the Midwest and West. Southerners tend more than nonsoutherners to believe in God, to accept the Bible as literally true, and to belong to religious bodies and attend religious services. The religious hegemony of the Southern Baptists remains; since 1945 the numbers of Baptists in the South have steadily increased, and their conservatism strongly influences public and religious life in the South. Southern Baptists still resist the ordination of women and exclude them from boards of deacons, the ruling bodies of local churches. Disagreements over the role of women in the church and especially over biblical literalism have produced grave divisions among Southern Baptists.

The South has produced the leading Protestant evangelists of post–World War II America—Billy Graham, Oral Roberts, Jimmy Swaggart, Jerry Falwell, and Pat Robertson—and much of their following. Making especially effective use of radio and television, the "televangelists" have presented old-time religion in contemporary terms to large numbers of people looking for assurance in a rapidly changing world, a world that seems beyond the power of individuals to understand or to alter. The God of the evangelists is personal and accessible. Their message is personal, intense, immediate, and based on the Bible as the infallible, unambiguous authority. Graham has enjoyed the greatest and longest success of these evangelists. He has preached to more than 50 million people all over the world and has reached audiences through his books, newspaper columns, interviews, and films. Graham has also served as an unofficial, personal chaplain to American presidents. Perhaps ironically, he has been more effective outside the South than in it.

The influence of the televangelists has not been limited to religion. Following the example of the ministers who were active in the civil rights movement, some televangelists have become deeply involved in politics. They and their supporters have devoted themselves particularly to anticommunism, the restoration of prayer in public schools, and opposition to abortion, feminism, homosexuality, and pornography. Staunch defenders of the values they consider traditional, they favor censorship of schoolbooks and library books, the teaching of "creation science" as an alternative to evolution, and Christian schools and home schooling as alternatives to public schools. Since the great majority of the Christian schools operated by the televangelists were founded after the public schools began to be desegregated and since most of those schools have few black students, critics have denounced them as thinly disguised attempts to perpetuate racial segregation. In some instances such a criticism is unfair. In fact, several televangelists counseled moderation in interracial relations before that position was generally accepted among whites in the South.

Falwell and Robertson have been especially active in politics. Using his organization, the Moral Majority, which no longer exists, Falwell became a particularly vocal, vigorous supporter of the candidacy and presidency of Ronald Reagan. Robertson actively campaigned for the American presidency in 1988 and 1992. In doing so, he was following a course taken by Jesse Jackson, a black minister and civil rights leader. Television, the diverse directions taken by conservative Christian revivalists, and the unsettling effect of the rapid changes and disruptions that have marked American society since 1960 have greatly increased the impact of the southern-rooted evangelical revival. It has had much greater effect

REVEREND FALWELL AT THOMAS
RODD BAPTIST CHURCH

REVEREND FALWELL AND
PRESIDENT REAGAN

than the fundamentalist revival of the early decades of the last century. Thus Protestant evangelicalism has joined southern literature, jazz, blues, rock 'n' roll, and country music as a major means by which the South has shaped the nation's life and culture.

Defenders of the Protestant evangelists praise them for their efforts to bring people to God and to create a stable moral society. Critics say that the evangelists present an overly narrow, simplistic theology and espouse a religion that supports the status quo rather than one that provides a means to change it. Modern tel-evangelists extol the patriarchal family as divinely ordained even as increasing numbers of women work outside the home in order to meet their families' basic needs or to enable them to enjoy the material benefits of the modern South. At the 1980 White House Conference on Families called by President Jimmy Carter, evangelicals shattered the conference when they demanded that the conferees agree with their definition of what a family was—only persons who were related by blood, marriage, or adoption—and agree that the ideal basic unit was husband, wife, and children. Amid the turmoil at the conference about what was a legitimate family, there was little time to discuss abortion, gay rights, or the Equal Rights Amendment.

Intolerance has not, however, been one-sided. The opponents of the evangelicals have been too inclined to dismiss the often well-founded concerns of the evangelicals, for instance, their concerns about government interference in family life and in the schooling of children or about public policies that appear to be indifferent to or hostile toward the legitimate claims and concerns of religion. Evangelicals have too frequently been the targets of intellectual and cultural snobbery, often from those who know little about evangelical thinking and policy. The Fundamentalists and the Pentecostals have in the recent past grown rapidly while the more traditional denominations have experienced little growth. For instance, the Thomas Road Baptist Church, led by Dr. Falwell, has grown from less than 100 members to 22,000; has developed a wide range of programs and ministries, domestic and foreign; has built a broadcast network;

and has built Liberty University. Fundamentalism and Pentecostalism, have, however, also been divisive forces, as is indicated by the recent divisions in the Southern Baptist Convention over fundamentalism. Many Christians (and others) are also uncomfortable or repelled by the passion and zeal that some of the evangelicals, particularly the Christian Coalition, bring to politics.

These conflicts reflect profound theological differences among Christians that tend, broadly speaking, to fall along geographical lines. Bruce Bawer has suggested that in the United States there are

> two religions—the Church of Law, based in [but not limited solely to] the South, and the Church of Love, based in [but not limited solely to] the North—[that] differ on almost every big theological point:
> *Christian identity.* In the Church of Law's view, the only true Christians are those who evade God's wrath by subscribing to correct doctrine, heeding Jesus's "great commission" to evangelize. The Church of Love is generally loath to deny the name of Christian to anyone who claims it, and sees Christianity as a commitment to Jesus's "great commandment" to love God and one's neighbor.
> *Satan.* The Church of Law believes Satan is a real creature from whom only true Christians are protected. The Church of Love sees Satan as a metaphor for evil that exists in each person, Christian or not, which must be recognized and resisted.
> *The Bible.* The Church of Law reads the Bible literally and considers it the ultimate source of all truth. The Church of Love views the Bible as an inspired but human document that must be read with a critical understanding of its historical and cultural contexts. . . .
> The differences between the Church of Law and the Church of Love are so monumental that any reapprochement seems, at present, unimaginable.

Just as evangelical Protestantism has persisted in the modern South, so has physical violence. Southerners murder each other—usually a friend or family member—much more frequently than nonsoutherners do. Southerners own more guns than nonsoutherners do. Southerners are generally opposed to gun control laws. Southern men are more likely to hunt and to attach significance to hunting, an activity that is heavy with masculine overtones. Southerners more readily endorse corporal punishment from spanking to execution; the South also leads the nation in the percentage of people incarcerated in jails and prisons. Attacks on property and assaults associated with theft, however, have been more common outside the South, as have suicides.

For all its changes, the South remains committed to religion and physical force in every facet of life—in individual relationships, sports and leisure, and in public policy issues ranging from the discipline of children and criminals to foreign affairs. Asked in 1989 to explain why high school football games in Douglas County, Georgia, began with public prayer, a county attorney said that the prayer was intended "to add a solemn and dignified tone to the proceedings." The conjunction of prayer and football may express the continuing conflict in the southern mentality between piety and social control on the one hand and violence and unrestrained individualism on the other. Some observers have seen in this conflict a sort of battle of the sexes, a struggle between control, presumably a feminine attribute, and unfettered physicality, presumably a masculine characteristic. For longer than anyone can remember the Southern Lady has been expected to save the raucous South from itself.

OTHER FAITHS: SOUTHERN LITERATURE, FOOTBALL, AND ELVIS

Whether or not football games, have been microcosms of the southern mentality, they have been one of the prime products of southern high schools, colleges, and universities. Colleges and universities in the South have produced more players for the National Football League than have schools of any other region. The late Paul "Bear" Bryant, legendary football coach at the University of Alabama, attained the status of a religious icon. For many people, his most attractive attribute was that he was a winner, something the South desperately wanted. NASCAR stock car racing has produced similar "good ole boy" winners and icons, of whom Richard Petty is the most famous.

On the occasion of Coach Bryant's death in 1983, a grieving high-placed state official said (anonymously): "We are always at or near the bottom in virtually every category . . . dealing with income or education or life style. But Alabama football was always at or near the top. . . . Coach Bryant seemed to be the only one showing Alabama how to build and how to win." Thousands viewed his funeral cortege. Flags flew at half-mast as church bells tolled. The white columns of buildings were wrapped in black bands. Black streamers hung from car antennas. A miles-long procession followed the hearse from the church to the grave site.

Even as colleges and universities have sought to appease alumni with winning teams, they have won national recognition by improving themselves academically. More attuned to national and professional standards than they once were, the South's institutions of higher education have become strongholds of national and international culture. Few have remained academic outposts of regional culture, though the conduct of their students has often run counter to this trend. While these schools' broadened perspectives and gains in quality have generally been welcome, many southerners mourn a lessening of concern about local and regional problems, particularly in the universities.

Southern writers have continued to produce a large body of fine work that is read, studied, and treasured by thousands both within and outside the South. Mississippi's Eudora Welty has written steadily for some fifty years, and her works have been widely read and have received high praise from critics. Though less well known, Peter Taylor (*The Collected Stories of Peter Taylor* [1969]) has for forty years explored the conflict between the values of the southern small town and those of the big city. Taylor's most recent major work, however—*A Summons to Memphis* (1986)—is about family conflict and has no particular regional identity despite its title. Ralph Ellison's *Invisible Man* (1952) is a classic novel that combines complex forms and perspectives with African American folk devices that have a jazzlike quality. He takes his nameless black hero from the Jim Crow South to a still largely racially segregated, anonymous, bureaucratic New York City. William Styron went in the opposite direction, from New York to the South, in his widely praised *Lie Down in Darkness* (1951), a somber tale about individuals caught between two sets of traditional southern values.

Robert Penn Warren produced novels, essays, short stories, meditations, and poetry of lasting quality. *All the King's Men* (1946), based loosely on the life of

Huey Long of Louisiana, is a powerful novel about politics and power. Some of Warren's most recent poetry appeared in *Rumor Verified* (1981). Randall Jarrell and James Dickey are considered two major southern poets. Less and less of the work of major southern writers is clearly identifiable with the South. Anne Tyler's *Dinner at the Homesick Restaurant* (1982), a novel of disintegrating traditions and collapsing family structures, is set in her native Baltimore, but the story could have taken place almost anywhere. Though he used Tennessee as the setting for his *Orchard Keeper* (1969) and *Child of God* (1974), Cormac McCarthy is not regional in his graphic explorations of human depravity. Walker Percy used a thoroughly modern, almost pastless South to follow modern men who are searching for meaning and purpose: *The Moviegoer* (1960), *Love in the Ruins* (1971), and *Second Coming* (1980). The most creative literature of the South has lost most of its regional quality. It has become nationalized.

Two other major cultural products of the South have also developed national and international audiences: jazz and country music. Rooted in the music and folk traditions of, respectively, Africa and the British Isles, then filtered through history and shaped by changing technologies and commercial forces, jazz and country music and their lineal descendants have gained audiences all over the world.

Often hailed as America's greatest contribution to the art of music, jazz evolved in the nineteenth century from hymns, field shouts and work songs, black spirituals, and gospel music while using African elements in its beat and melody. Primarily but not solely a creation of American blacks, jazz evolved from barrelhouse music and ragtime. Jazz developed after the mid-nineteenth century through performances for audiences in juke joints, dance halls, bordellos, and nightclubs. Blues provided some of the characteristic notes and a lyrical tradition grounded in everyday life—work, poverty, love, sex, suffering, racial conflict, death. The Mississippi River basin was the home region, and Memphis and New Orleans the capitals, for this new music. By the 1920s, it had gained an increasingly wide hearing through concert halls and large popular audiences in the United States and abroad through radio and recordings. Movies, then television provided new vehicles. Jazz has undergone numerous permutations, including swing and big band, bop, progressive, and more, scatting away from its nitty-gritty roots to abstract, intellectual modes and themes. Since the 1950s, it may have scatted away from accessibility and popularity. There are recent indications, however, that jazz may regain a wide audience in the United States.

The list of star creators and performers from jazz is long and includes Scott Joplin, W. C. Handy, "Jelly Roll" Morton, Louis Armstrong, Duke Ellington, Count Basie, Benny Goodman, Dizzy Gillespie, Miles Davis, Dave Brubeck, Ella Fitzgerald, Ornette Coleman, Cecil Taylor, and Wynton Marsalis. George Gershwin wrote a symphonic jazz composition for *Rhapsody in Blue*, which premiered in 1924. A decade later, Gershwin produced a folk opera, *Porgy and Bess* (1935), from a story by the same name by Charlestonian DuBose Heyward. *Porgy and Bess*, the first opera composed by an American that achieved lasting international success, tells about life on Charleston's black margins. Its "Summertime," "It Ain't Necessarily So," and "I Got Plenty of Nuttin'" have been engraved in musical memory.

Country music originated in the folk music traditions of the British Isles. In the twentieth century, the country music style of the Southeast and the western

WYNTON MARSALIS (B. 1961), star trumpeter whose playing range extends from classical music to jazz (Reuters/Bettmann)

music style of the Southwest came together. Like jazz, country music has borrowed eclectically from a variety of sources including gospel music, a style in which black and white musical traditions have often intermingled. Folklorists were among the earliest fans of country music, which they discovered as they studied the folk life of Appalachia around 1900, but few beyond local audiences and practitioners initially shared their appreciation.

Country and western—simplified to country music—eventually gained wider audiences through commercialization and the mass media in the 1920s. Those people with claims to greater sophistication dismissed this music as "hick" and certainly would have dismissed the opening of the Grand Ole Opry in Nashville in the 1920s as a cultural event. The Opry would later become a national institution in the 1960s when Nashville became Music City, USA. Thereafter, not many could recall that Nashville had advertised itself as the "Athens of the South" and had erected its version of the Parthenon in the Tennessee city in 1896 to prove it.

Many of the stars of country music became household names: Jimmy Wells and the Texas Plowboys, the Carter Family, Jimmy Rodgers, Patsy Cline, Hank Williams, Sr., Johnny Cash, Loretta Lynn, Tammy Wynette, Charlie Pride, Willie Nelson, Dollie Parton, and more recently, Garth Brooks. Like jazz, country music has been shaped by changes in instrumentation and technology. Most important of these changes may be the development of electric instruments and the use of electronics. Bluegrass, a variant of country music, has remained more traditional

PATSY CLINE (1932–1963), singer who successfully
combined country and pop music (Country Music
Foundation, Library and Media Center)

in instrumentation and in choices of songs and styles. Deriving its name from a famous group, Bill Monroe and the Bluegrass Boys, bluegrass is usually identified
with Appalachia, but its roots are broader than this association suggests.

Racial lines were crossed in both jazz and country. Sometimes the lines were
blurred altogether, though country remains predominantly white people's music.
Bill Haley and the Comets, a white musical group, gained a national audience in
the 1950s for a newly emerging musical form, rock 'n' roll, later simply called
rock. It drew upon the blues, country, and gospel music, and, in Haley's hands,
softened resistance to black culture. Elvis Presley destroyed that resistance—at
least among young people seeking rebellion and a high-volume means for outrag-
ing their elders. Presley delivered raucous lyrics about love and youthful isolation
with a dynamic style that included suggestive body undulations. Then, the early
(some observers say the true) Elvis softened when he went "Hollywood." Mo-
town, a record company based in Detroit, with stars like Diana Ross and the

ELVIS PRESLEY (1935–1977; UPI/Bettmann)

Supremes, developed soul music, a very subdued version of rock that, like Presley's work, enjoyed great commercial success.

In the 1960s, Bob Dylan, a Minnesotan, combined rock and folk. He made famous the protest song "Blowin' in the Wind," which Pete Seeger, a political radical and "the patriarch of urban folk music," had written in the 1950s. Seeger, Dylan, and Joan Baez, another star of urban folk music, drew upon a music tradition whose greatest influence was Woodrow Wilson "Woody" Guthrie. An immensely talented performer and songwriter and a political radical, Guthrie vocalized the plight of the "Okie" migrants and the devastation of the Dust Bowl in the 1930s. He left a body of music that includes "This Land Is Your Land," "So Long, It's Been Good to Know You," and "Philadelphia Lawyer."

Also in the 1960s, the Beatles and the Rolling Stones, both from Great Britain, redirected rock toward black blues. The Beatles altered musical history with their

THE DIXIE CHICKS

album *Sgt. Pepper's Lonely Hearts Club Band*, which combined several musical traditions, including Oriental music, with rock. By then, rock was being heard
around the world. Like its progenitors, rock has reflected changing times and
moods as well as changing technology.

Rock, like urban folk music, picked up the themes of rebellion, sex, drugs,
and social protest associated with the late 1960s and early 1970s when the United
States became deeply divided over the war in Vietnam and was shaken by the
civil rights movement, new social mores, and a highly publicized counterculture.
The mood in rock music swung to alienation and confrontation with the Grateful
Dead, the Rolling Stones, the Doors, and others, including meteoric superstars
like Janis Joplin, Jimi Hendrix, and Jim Morrison.

Electronics and computers allowed a greatly expanded range of musical expression. Disco, then music videos, followed. This remarkable elasticity in musical

expression and form reflected the long tradition of experimentation and diverse roots that characterized jazz, country music, and rock. Some performers resist these trends. Nirvana and Pearl Jam, for instance, stress political themes and rely upon more traditional instrumentation. Mary Chapin Carpenter also draws upon the traditional, though she is an Ivy League graduate from New Jersey. Her musical influences include the legendary Oklahoma folk musician Woody Guthrie. The Dixie Chicks have developed their own mix of bluegrass, country, and pop music that has had remarkable success recently. The female trio, whose roots lie in Texas, have blended traditional and electronic instrumentation with their songs, some of which they wrote, to win major awards and, in one instance, to become a cause célèbre when they released "Goodbye Earl," a song about taking the ultimate revenge against an abusive husband. Reportedly, some male disc jockeys and radio programmers refused to play a song that so strongly resembled the themes of the movie *Thelma and Louise.*

These evolutions in music are a long way from the jazz of Louis Armstrong or the country music songs of Patsy Cline, both of which were clearly rooted in their region. Most of the music heard in the South today is hardly distinctive to the region, though it owes much to the rich musical heritage of the South.

Walker Percy's South may be the South of 2001—a region that is hardly distinguishable from the rest of the country. Perhaps the author-journalist John Egerton was right when he wrote in 1973 that "for good or ill, the South is just about over as a separate and distinct place." That assessment, however, appears to require that too much of the life and culture of the South be dismissed as peripheral and of little meaning. Moreover, it underestimates the stubborn determination of southerners to remain "southern" in the face of strong countervailing forces. That stubbornness takes many forms, some dubious, such as waving the Confederate flag, and some interminable, such as symposia on the South. That stubbornness also reflects the deep attachment of southern whites and blacks to their region.

PERSISTENT DIVISIONS: BLACK AND WHITE

Finally, more than a few vestiges of unhappier times cast shadows over the Sunbelt South and raise haunting memories of a past that is not altogether gone. Of those vestiges, the most troubling is the persistence of racial division, inadequacies in education and health, and poverty. Black and white southerners have long had much in common historically and culturally. They also share a profound sense that the South is their place and often have close, deep personal relationships with one another. Moreover, much of the South is more racially desegregated than the rest of America. But blacks and whites remain deeply divided about many matters and by their very different economic standings. Economic differences tend to reinforce racial divisions. In 1979, 45 percent of black families and 19 percent of white families in the South had annual incomes of less than $10,000; 77 percent of black families and 51 percent of white families, less than $20,000. The persistence of these disparities in income undoubtedly accounts for much of the disillusionment found among African Americans in the twenty-first century. Large numbers of whites have similar feelings about their failure to share in the material blessings of the modern South.

Attitudes and perceptions vary substantially between the races. Studies of attitudes among working-class white southerners and black southerners indicate sharp differences of opinion—about political terms like *conservative* and *liberal*, about political parties, and about groups, such as civil rights leaders or people on welfare. Some people had predicted that once Jim Crow had declined and politicians could no longer use blatant racist appeals to attract white voters while ignoring important economic issues, black and working-class white voters would form an alliance based on economic interests. Such an alliance is unlikely to materialize. Also, though public schools in the South are generally more desegregated than those outside the South, thousands of black and white students attend schools where there are few or no members of the other race. Resegregation has become widespread enough to occasion considerable comment.

Moreover, politicians have discovered that subtle and not so subtle racist appeals are effective with both blacks and whites. In 1980 Ronald Reagan launched his presidential campaign in Neshoba County, Mississippi. A small rural county in a state with only a handful of electoral votes seemed like a curious place to begin a presidential campaign. Probably not too many voters remembered Neshoba as a site of intense civil rights activity in the 1960s or as the place where three civil rights workers were beaten and murdered by a party of lynchers, whose ranks included officials of local law enforcement. Reagan did not mention James Chaney, Andrew Goodman, or Michael Schwerner, the civil rights movement, or the remarkable changes in race relations in Mississippi since the 1960s. Instead, he announced that he "believe[d] in states rights" and would work as president to "restore to states and local governments the powers that properly belong to them." Some observers saw this avowal of states rights as an attempt to reach Mississippi's and the South's white electorate through code words loaded with racial overtones. At the same time, much of Jesse Jackson's success—and lack of success—can be attributed to his being black.

Racial divisions were painfully obvious during and after the presidential election of 2000. More than 95 percent of the blacks who cast ballots voted for Albert Gore, Jr., then vice president and the Democratic nominee. In every southern state, President George W. Bush received a substantial majority of the white vote. Racial divisions were distressingly obvious during the emotional disputes over an accurate ballot count in Florida, a contest that only ended with an unprecedented decision by the U.S. Supreme Court. The 2000 election also demonstrated the power of the South in national politics and the power of Southern Republicans. Both Gore and Bush are native southerners, Gore from Tennessee, Bush from Texas. Republicans hold most of the region's congressional seats, and southern Republicans hold numerous key leadership posts in the House of Representatives and the Senate.

That the 2000 race also figures prominently in how southerners, black and white, perceive the past is hardly surprising. Nor is it surprising that public celebrations of history—in official holidays, monuments, or displays of flags—have repeatedly elicited volatile responses. As demonstrated by recent controversies over the public display of the Confederate flag, black southerners and white

GEORGE W. BUSH AND AL GORE, PRESIDENTIAL DEBATES, 2000

southerners have radically different perspectives about their shared history. Blacks see secession and the South's bid for independence from the Union as primarily motivated by the determination to maintain slavery. Conversely, most southern whites see secession and the war for southern independence as a noble cause, the Lost Cause, in which thousands of southerners sacrificed, fought, and died to preserve independence from a federal government that was intruding in their lives and threatening their well-being. They contend that states rights, not slavery, was the catalyst for secession. Most professional historians who have studied the issues have concluded that slavery was the trigger for secession and the Civil War that followed. Although states rights was a powerful part of southern ideology, the primary function of states rights during the antebellum era was to preserve slavery. Southerners abandoned states rights whenever doing so helped them maintain slavery.

The flag controversies have demonstrated that race can readily percolate from unexpected underground terrain. During the controversy about the Confederate flag being hung over the state capitol in South Carolina, a resident of the state declared that

> most white South Carolinians [do] not know the difference between Stonewall Jackson and Andrew Jackson . . . [and don't] care. What they care about is control. They see re-

moving the Confederate flag as another instance of the black minority forcing its will on the white majority. There is resentment over affirmative action, busing to achieve integration and other black-oriented legislation.

White southerners believe that they have little control over the federal government— government that they perceive as having acquiesced to black demands for more than 30 years, but they can control the flag issue. They have seized upon it with a passion that is at least as intense as the indignation of the black community. After all, for the state's black citizens, it is just one more battle in their long struggle for equality. Unfortunately, many of the white citizens have come to view it as the Alamo.

Low incomes could become a major political issue. Southerners, black and white, still earn less than their fellow Americans. As might be expected, education lags behind as well. Every state in the South falls below the national average in years of completed schooling. These deficiencies have persisted despite the very substantial efforts made to improve education since World War II, and they are deeply disturbing as the South enters the postindustrial era. Though much of the South gets high ratings as "an ideal place to live" and for a "good business climate," it still draws sharp criticism for its "climate for workers." Workers in the South earn less than most other American workers—even when the lower cost of living is taken into account—and have fewer benefits and less protection. One hundred and nine years after Henry Grady charmed a banquet audience in New York City with his talk of the New South, the wages of industrial workers in the South remain the lowest in the nation.

Even after more than fifty years of unequaled economic growth and improvements in the standard of living, the South is still "a land becoming and not a land become . . . America's will-o'-the-wisp Eden."

$\mathcal{B}$iographies

❖

Biographies of notable individuals provide much information and have considerable value. The following is an alphabetical listing (by subject) of biographies of many of the major figures in southern history. In appropriate instances more than one biography is cited. Published diaries, memoirs, and collections of letters are covered in the bibliographical essay.

Will Alexander
Wilma Dykeman and James Stokely, *Seeds of Southern Change: The Life of Will Alexander* (Chicago, 1962).

Jessie Daniel Ames
Jacquelyn Dowd Hall, *Revolt against Chivalry: Jessie Daniel Ames and the Women's Campaign against Lynching* (New York, 1979).

Joseph R. Anderson
Charles R. Dew, *Ironmaker to the Confederacy: Joseph R. Anderson and the Tredegar Ironworks* (New Haven, Conn., 1966).

Louis Armstrong
James L. Collier, *Louis Armstrong: An American Genius* (New York, 1983).

Pierre G. T. Beauregard
T. Harry Williams, *P. G. T. Beauregard: Napoleon in Gray* (Baton Rouge, La., 1955).

Mary McLeod Bethune
Rackham Holt, *Mary McLeod Bethune: A Biography* (Garden City, N.Y., 1964).

Theodore G. Bilbo
Chester M. Morgan, *Redneck Liberal: Theodore G. Bilbo and the New Deal* (Baton Rouge, La., 1985).

Hugo Black
Virginia Van der Veer Hamilton, *Hugo Black: The Alabama Years* (Baton Rouge, La., 1972).
Roger K. Newman, *Hugo Black: A Biography* (New York, 1994).

Braxton Bragg
Grady McWhiney and Judith L. Hallock, *Braxton Bragg and Confederate Defeat*, 2 vols. (New York and Tuscaloosa, Ala., 1969–1991).

John C. Breckinridge
William C. Davis, *Breckinridge: Statesman, Soldier, Symbol* (Baton Rouge, La., 1974).

Joseph E. Brown
    Joseph H. Parks, *Joseph E. Brown of Georgia* (Baton Rouge, La., 1977).
William G. Brownlow
    E. Merton Coulter, *William G. Brownlow: Fighting Parson of the Southern Highlands* (Knoxville, Tenn., 1991).
William Jennings Bryan
    Paul W. Glad, *The Trumpet Soundeth: William Jennings Bryan and His Democracy, 1896–1912* (Lincoln, Neb., 1960).
    Lawrence W. Levine, *Defender of the Faith: William Jennings Bryan; The Last Decade, 1915–1925* (New York, 1965).
George W. Bush
    Molly Ivins and Lou DuBose, *Shrub: The Short but Happy Political Life of George W. Bush* (New York, 2000).
    Bill Minutaglio, *First Son: George W. Bush and the Bush Family Dynasty* (New York, 2001).
Harry F. Byrd
    Ronald L. Heinemann, *Harry Byrd of Virginia* (Charlottesville, Va., 1996).
James F. Byrnes
    David Robertson, *Sly and Able: A Political Biography of James F. Byrnes* (New York, 1994).
Erskine Caldwell
    Dan B. Miller, *Erskine Caldwell: The Journey from Tobacco Road* (New York, 1994).
Asa Griggs Candler
    Charles H. Candler, *Asa Griggs Candler* (Atlanta, 1950).
Warren Akin Candler
    Alfred M. Pierce, *Giant against the Sky: The Life of Bishop Akin Candler* (New York, 1948).
Julian Carr
    Mena Webb, *Jule Carr: General without an Army* (Chapel Hill, N.C., 1987).
James Earl "Jimmy" Carter, Jr.
    Peter G. Bourne, *Jimmy Carter: A Comprehensive Biography from Plains to Postpresidency* (New York, 1997).
    Kenneth E. Morris, *Jimmy Carter: American Moralist* (Athens, Ga., 1996).
Wilbur J. Cash
    Bruce Clayton, *W. J. Cash: A Life* (Baton Rouge, La., 1991).
Mary Boykin Chesnut
    Elisabeth Muhlenfeld, *Mary Boykin Chesnut: A Biography* (Baton Rouge, La., 1981).
William J. "Bill" Clinton
    David Maraniss, *First in His Class: A Biography of Bill Clinton* (New York, 1995).
Theophilus E. "Bull" Connor
    William A. Nunnelley, *Bull Connor* (Tuscaloosa, Ala., 1990).
John J. Crittenden
    Albert D. Kirwan, *John J. Crittenden: The Struggle for the Union* (Lexington, Ky., 1962).
Edward H. "Boss" Crump
    William D. Miller, *Mr. Crump of Memphis* (Baton Rouge, La., 1964).
Joseph S. Cullinan
    John O. King, *Joseph Stephen Cullinan: A Study of Leadership in the Texas Petroleum Industry, 1897–1937* (Nashville, Tenn., 1970).

Jonathan Daniels
    Charles W. Eagles, *Jonathan Daniels and Race Relations: The Evolution of a Southern Liberal* (Knoxville, Tenn., 1982).
Jeff Davis
    Raymond Arsenault, *Wild Ass of the Ozarks: Jeff Davis and the Social Bases of Southern Politics* (Philadelphia, 1984).
Jefferson Davis
    William J. Cooper, Jr., *Jefferson Davis, American* (2000).
    William C. Davis, *Jefferson Davis: The Man and His Hour* (New York, 1991).
Joseph Davis
    Janet S. Hermann, *Joseph E. Davis: Pioneer Patriarch* (Jackson, Miss., 1990).
Francis W. Dawson
    E. Culpepper Clark, *Francis Warrington Dawson and the Politics of Restoration: South Carolina, 1874–1889* (University, Ala., 1980).
Thomas Dixon
    Raymond A. Cook, *Thomas Dixon* (New York, 1974).
Frederick Douglass
    William S. McFeely, *Frederick Douglass* (New York, 1990).
    Dickson J. Preston, *Young Frederick Douglass: The Maryland Years* (Baltimore, 1980).
W. E. B. DuBois
    David L. Lewis, *W. E. B. Du Bois: Biography of Race, 1868–1919* (New York, 1991).
    ——— , *W. E. B. DuBois: The Fight for Equality and the American Century, 1919–1963* (New York, 2000).
James B. Duke
    Robert F. Durden, *The Dukes of Durham, 1865–1929* (Durham, N.C., 1975).
Ralph Ellison
    Busby Mark, *Ralph Ellison* (Boston, 1991).
William Faulkner
    Joseph L. Blotner, *Faulkner: A Biography,* 2 vols. (New York, 1974).
    Joel Williamson, *William Faulkner and Southern History* (New York, 1993).
Rebecca L. Felton
    John E. Talmadge, *Rebecca Latimer Felton, Nine Stormy Decades* (Athens, Ga., 1960).
J. William Fulbright
    Randall Bennett Woods, *Fulbright* (New York, 1995).
Ellen Glasgow
    Julius R. Raper, *Without Shelter: The Early Career of Ellen Glasgow* (Baton Rouge, La., 1971).
John B. Gordon
    Ralph L. Eckert, *John Brown Gordon: Soldier, Southerner, American* (Baton Rouge, La., 1989).
Albert Gore, Jr.
    David Maraniss and Ellen Nakashima, *The Prince of Tennessee: The Rise of Al Gore* (New York, 2000).
Josiah Gorgas
    Frank E. Vandiver, *Ploughshares into Swords: Josiah Gorgas and Confederate Ordnance* (Austin, Tex., 1952).
Jay Gould
    Maury Klien, *The Life and Legend of Jay Gould* (1986).
Henry Grady
    Raymond B. Nixon, *Henry W. Grady: Spokesman of the New South* (New York, 1943).
Billy Graham
    William C. Martin, *A Prophet with Honor: The Billy Graham Story* (New York, 1991).

Frank P. Graham
    Warren Ashby, *Frank Porter Graham: A Southern Liberal* (Winston-Salem, N.C., 1980).
Joel Chandler Harris
    Paul M. Cousins, *Joel Chandler Harris: A Biography* (Baton Rouge, La., 1968).
William Hastie
    Gilbert Ware, *William Hastie: Grace under Pressure* (New York, 1984).
Rutherford B. Hayes
    Ari A. Hoogenboom, *Rutherford B. Hayes: Warrior and President* (Lawrence, Kans., 1995).
Andrew Jackson Higgins
    Jerry E. Strahan, *Andrew Jackson Higgins and the Boats That Won World War II* (Baton Rouge, La., 1994).
James S. Hogg
    Robert C. Cotner, *James Stephen Hogg: A Biography* (Austin, Tex., 1959).
William W. Holden
    William C. Harris, *William Woods Holden: Firebrand of North Carolina Politics* (Baton Rouge, La., 1987).
John B. Hood
    Richard M. McMurry, *John Bell Hood and the War for Southern Independence* (Lexington, Ky., 1982).
Thomas J. "Stonewall" Jackson
    Lenoir Chambers, *Stonewall Jackson*, 2 vols. (New York, 1959).
Andrew Johnson
    Hans L. Trefousse, *Andrew Johnson: A Biography* (New York, 1989).
Lyndon B. Johnson
    Robert A. Caro, *The Years of Lyndon Johnson*, 2 vols. to date (New York, 1982–   ).
    Robert Dallek, *Lone Star Rising: Lyndon Johnson and His Times, 1908–1960* (New York, 1991).
    ———— , *Flawed Giant: Lyndon Johnson and His Times, 1961–1973* (New York, 1998).
Albert S. Johnston
    Charles P. Roland, *Albert Sidney Johnston: Soldier of Three Republics* (Austin, Tex., 1964).
Joseph E. Johnston
    Craig L. Symonds, *Joseph E. Johnston: A Civil War Biography* (New York, 1992).
Mary Johnston
    C. Ronald Cella, *Mary Johnston* (Boston, 1981).
Olin D. Johnston
    John Ervin Huss, *Senator for the South: A Biography of Olin D. Johnston* (Garden City, N.Y., 1961).
Sam Jones
    Kathleen Minnix, *Laughter in the Amen Corner: The Life of Evangelist Sam Jones* (Athens, Ga., 1993).
Estes Kefauver
    Charles L. Fontenay, *Estes Kefauver: A Biography* (Knoxville, Tenn., 1980).
John F. Kennedy
    Herbert S. Parmet, *JFK: The Presidency of John F. Kennedy* (New York, 1983).
    Richard Reeves, *President Kennedy: Profile and Power* (New York, 1993).
Martin Luther King, Jr.
    David J. Garrow, *Bearing the Cross: Martin Luther King, Jr., and the Southern Christian Leadership Conference* (New York, 1986).
Edmund Kirby-Smith
    Joseph H. Parks, *General Edmund Kirby-Smith, C.S.A.* (Baton Rouge, La., 1954).

Seaman A. Knapp
 Joseph C. Bailey, *Seaman A. Knapp: Schoolmaster of American Agriculture* (New York, 1945).
Robert E. Lee
 Thomas L. Connelly, *The Marble Man: Robert E. Lee and His Image in American Society* (New York, 1977).
 Douglas S. Freeman, *Robert E. Lee*, 4 vols. (New York, 1934–1935).
 Emory M. Thomas, *Robert E. Lee: A Biography* (New York, 1995).
Abraham Lincoln
 David Herbert Donald, *Lincoln* (New York, 1995).
Huey P. Long
 William Ivy Hair, *The Kingfish and His Realm: The Life and Times of Huey P. Long* (Baton Rouge, La., 1991).
 T. Harry Williams, *Huey Long* (New York, 1969).
William Mahone
 Nelson M. Blake, *William Mahone of Virginia, Soldier and Political Insurgent* (Richmond, Va., 1935).
Thurgood Marshall
 Roger L. Goldman, *Thurgood Marshall: Justice for All* (New York, 1992).
Lucy R. Mason
 John A. Salmond, *Miss Lucy of the CIO: The Life and Times of Lucy Mason, 1882–1959* (Athens, Ga., 1988).
H. L. Mencken
 Fred C. Hobson, *Mencken: A Life* (New York, 1994).
Margaret Mitchell
 Darden A. Pyron, *Southern Daughter: The Life of Margaret Mitchell* (New York, 1991).
John Tyler Morgan
 Joseph A. Fry, *John Tyler Morgan and the Search for Southern Autonomy* (Knoxville, Tenn., 1992).
Edgar Gardner Murphy
 Hugh C. Bailey, *Edgar Gardner Murphy: Gentle Progressive* (Coral Gables, Fla., 1968).
Richard Nixon
 Stephen E. Ambrose, *Richard M. Nixon*, 3 vols. (New York, 1983–1989).
 Herbert S. Parmet, *Richard Nixon and His America* (Boston, 1990).
Flannery O'Connor
 Dorothy Walters, *Flannery O'Connor* (New York, 1973).
Thomas Nelson Page
 Theodore L. Gross, *Thomas Nelson Page* (New York, 1967).
Walter Hines Page
 John M. Cooper, *Walter Hines Page: The Southerner as American, 1855–1918* (Chapel Hill, N.C., 1977).
Walker Percy and William Alexander Percy
 Jay Tolson, *Pilgrim in the Ruins: A Life of Walker Percy* (New York, 1992).
 Bertram Wyatt-Brown, *The House of Percy: Honor, Melancholy, and Imagination in a Southern Family* (New York, 1994).
Leonidas L. Polk
 Stuart Noblin, *Leonidas LaFayette Polk: Agrarian Crusader* (Chapel Hill, N.C., 1949).
Elvis Presley
 Peter Guralnick, *Last Train to Memphis: The Rise of Elvis Presley* (Boston, 1994).
 Careless Love: The Unmaking of Elvis Presley (Boston, 1999)
A. Philip Randolph
 Paula F. Pfeffer, *A. Philip Randolph: Pioneer of the Civil Rights Movement* (Baton Rouge, La., 1990).

Ronald Reagan
  Lou Cannon, *President Reagan: The Role of a Lifetime* (New York, 1991).
Pat Robertson
  David E. Harrell, *Pat Robertson: A Personal, Religious, and Political Portrait* (San Francisco, 1987).
Franklin D. Roosevelt
  James M. Burns, *Franklin D. Roosevelt*, 2 vols. (New York, 1956–1970).
  Geoffrey C. Ward, *A First Class Temperament: The Emergence of Franklin Roosevelt* (New York, 1989).
Richard B. Russell
  Gilbert C. Fite, *Richard B. Russell, Jr., Senator from Georgia* (Chapel Hill, N.C., 1991).
Winfield Scott
  Charles W. Elliott, *Winfield Scott: The Soldier and the Man* (New York, 1937).
Hoke Smith
  Dewey W. Grantham, Jr., *Hoke Smith and the Politics of the New South* (Baton Rouge, La., 1958).
Lillian Smith
  Anne C. Loveland, *Lillian Smith, A Southerner Confronting the South: A Biography* (Baton Rouge, La., 1986).
Alexander H. Stephens
  Thomas E. Schott, *Alexander H. Stephens of Georgia: A Biography* (Baton Rouge, La., 1988).
Eugene Talmadge
  William Anderson, *The Wild Man from Sugar Creek: The Political Career of Eugene Talmadge* (Baton Rouge, La., 1975).
J. Strom Thurmond
  Nadine Cohodas, *Strom Thurmond and the Politics of Southern Change* (New York, 1993).
Benjamin R. Tillman
  Francis B. Simkins, *Pitchfork Ben Tillman, South Carolinian* (Baton Rouge, La., 1944).
Harry Truman
  Robert H. Ferrell, *Harry S. Truman: A Life* (Columbia, Mo., 1994).
  David G. McCullough, *Truman* (New York, 1992).
Henry McNeal Turner
  Stephen W. Angell, *Bishop Henry McNeal Turner and African-American Religion in the South* (Knoxville, Tenn., 1992).
Mark Twain [Samuel L. Clemens]
  Justin Kaplan, *Mark Twain and His World* (New York, 1974).
James K. Vardaman
  William F. Holmes, *The White Chief: James Kimble Vardaman* (Baton Rouge, La., 1978).
George C. Wallace
  Dan T. Carter, *The Politics of Rage: George Wallace, the Rise of the New Conservatism, and the Transformation of American Politics* (New York, 1995).
  Stephan Lesher, *George Wallace: American Populist* (Reading, Mass., 1994).
Robert Penn Warren
  John Burt, *Robert Penn Warren and American Idealism* (New Haven, Conn., 1988).
Booker T. Washington
  Louis R. Harlan, *Booker T. Washington*, 2 vols. (New York, 1972–1983).
Tom Watson
  C. Vann Woodard, *Tom Watson: Agrarian Rebel* (New York, 1938).
Henry Watterson
  Joseph F. Wall, *Henry Watterson: Reconstructed Rebel* (New York, 1956).

Aubrey W. Williams
    John A. Salmond, *A Southern Rebel: The Life and Times of Aubrey Willis Williams, 1890–1965* (Chapel Hill, N.C., 1983).
Woodrow Wilson
    Kendrick A. Clements, *Woodrow Wilson: World Statesman* (Boston, 1987).
    August Heckscher, *Woodrow Wilson* (New York, 1991).
    Arthur S. Link, *Woodrow Wilson*, 5 vols. (Princeton, N.J., 1947–1965).
Thomas Wolfe
    David Herbert Donald, *Look Homeward: A Life of Thomas Wolfe* (Boston, 1987).
Richard Wright
    Addison Gayle, *Richard Wright: Ordeal of a Native Son* (Garden City, N.Y., 1980).

Bibliographical Essay

❖

THE SOUTH SINCE 1865: GENERAL

The following four volumes of the ten-volume *History of the South* (Baton Rouge, La., 1947–   ), edited by Wendell Holmes Stephenson and E. Merton Coulter, are extremely useful to any serious student of the American South since 1865. E. Merton Coulter, *The South during Reconstruction, 1865–1877* (Baton Rouge, La., 1951), contains a wealth of information, but Coulter was too sympathetic toward southern whites and too hostile toward Republicans and what they were attempting to do. His treatment of blacks reflects the racial assumptions common among most whites in the South (and a great many in the North) in his day. C. Vann Woodward's *Origins of the New South, 1877–1913* (Baton Rouge, La., 1951), a landmark in the interpretation of southern history, represents a major shift in tone and interpretation. Spurning the racism and sectionalism that mars Coulter's book, Woodward concludes that southern political and economic leaders after 1865 did more to create the New South than did the Old South, the Civil War, or Reconstruction. George B. Tindall's *Emergence of the New South, 1913–1945* (Baton Rouge, La., 1967), is even more comprehensive than either the Coulter or the Woodward volume. It is a massive but clear synthesis of critical decades in the twentieth-century South. Numan V. Bartley's *The New South, 1945–1980* (Baton Rouge, La., 1995), covers the immense changes in the South in the quarter of a century since World War II. All four volumes contain very useful essays on sources. Two useful and suggestive publications are Edward L. Ayers, *The Promise of the New South: Life after Reconstruction* (New York, 1992); and Howard N. Rabinowitz, *The First New South, 1865–1920* (Arlington Heights, Ill., 1992). Charles P. Roland's *Improbable Era: The South since World War II* (Lexington, Ky., 1972); and David R. Goldfield's *Promised Land: The South since 1945* (Arlington Heights, Ill., 1987), are good syntheses of the South since World War II. A recently published history of the South is John B. Boles, *The South through Time: A History of an American Region* (Englewood Cliffs, N.J., 1995).

Of symposia on the South, there seems to be no end. Of particular merit and relevance for the South since 1865 are William T. Couch, ed., *Culture in the South* (Chapel Hill, N.C., 1935); and John C. McKinney and Edgar T. Thompson, eds., *The South in Continuity and*

Change (Durham, N.C., 1965). Several sources provide lists of recently published articles and books and recently completed dissertations. See *Writings in American History,* a publication of the American Historical Association; *America: History and Life;* and *Southern Exposure.* The *Journal of Southern History* and the *Journal of American History* periodically publish lists of recent publications and dissertations. Thomas D. Clark, ed., *Travels in the New South* (Norman, Okla., 1962), is very useful for finding firsthand accounts of the South since 1865. The South is, of course, the product of the interaction of people and a particular environment or set of environments over time. For a succinct, wise overview of that interaction, read Albert E. Cowdrey, *This Land, This South* (Lexington, Ky., 1983). More than most scholars, Walter Prescott Webb appreciated the significance of the changing environment that people confronted as they journeyed into the western reaches of the South. His *The Great Plains* (New York, 1931), is a compelling narrative, but be aware that some of Webb's perspectives were more suitable for an earlier generation.

RECONSTRUCTION

Reconstruction has proved to be one of the most difficult of terrains for historians to traverse. At one time most historians accepted the interpretation of William Dunning—for example, see his *Reconstruction, Political and Economic, 1865–1877* (New York, 1907)—who held that the white South knew it had been defeated, was willing to deal fairly with the former slaves, and wanted to rejoin the Union. But Radical Republicans spurned reconciliation, imposed Republican governments on the southern states, and enforced black suffrage with bayonets. Motivated by unreasoning hate, partisanship, and greed, the Republicans created "Black Republican" governments that were singularly corrupt and peopled by "unscrupulous carpetbaggers" from the North, "unprincipled southern white scalawags," and "ignorant freedmen." After a prolonged period of corruption and misrule, southern whites "redeemed" the South by overthrowing the Republican governments in the South and restoring home rule, or governments of themselves. Good government, Dunning assumed, could not include blacks, who supposedly lacked the capacity to govern or participate in governing.

The clearest, most concise refutation of Dunning is Kenneth M. Stampp's *Era of Reconstruction, 1865–1877* (New York, 1965). Most of the more recent general histories of the period reflect Stampp's influence. James M. McPherson's *Ordeal by Fire: The Civil War and Reconstruction* (New York, 1982), contains a brief but carefully balanced retelling of the Reconstruction story. Eric Foner's *Reconstruction: America's Unfinished Revolution, 1863–1877* (New York, 1988), part of the New American Nation series, is a comprehensive account based on copious research. Foner makes a compelling case for placing African Americans at center stage in the drama of Reconstruction. He has recently published *Freedom's Lawmakers* (rev. ed.; Baton Rouge, La., 1996), a biographical directory of African Americans who held public office in the South during Reconstruction.

Particularly useful for overviews of the period between the collapse of the Confederacy and the beginning of Reconstruction are Dan T. Carter, *When the War Was Over: The Failure of Self-Reconstruction in the South, 1865–1867* (Baton Rouge, La., 1985); and Michael Perman, *Reunion without Compromise: The South and Reconstruction, 1865–1868* (Cambridge, Eng., 1973). In *The Road to Redemption: Southern Politics, 1869–1879* (Chapel Hill, N.C., 1984), Perman traces political developments across the South from the start of Reconstruction to "redemption" and its impact on the configuration of politics in the New South.

A number of Reconstruction studies focus on individual states or regions, and some of them cover more than Reconstruction. These works include Stephen V. Ash, *Middle Tennessee Society Transformed, 1860–1870* (Baton Rouge, La., 1987); Horace Mann Bond, *Negro Education in Alabama: A Study in Cotton and Steel* (Washington, D.C., 1939); Alan Conway, *The Recon-*

struction of Georgia (Minneapolis, 1966); W. McKee Evans, *Ballots and Fence Rails: Reconstruction on the Lower Cape Fear* (Chapel Hill, N.C., 1967); Barbara Fields, *Slavery and Freedom on the Middle Ground: Maryland during the Nineteenth Century* (New Haven, Conn., 1985); William C. Harris, *Presidential Reconstruction in Mississippi* (Baton Rouge, La., 1967), and *The Day of the Carpetbagger: Republican Reconstruction in Mississippi* (Baton Rouge, La., 1979); Richard G. Lowe, *Republicans and Reconstruction in Virginia, 1856–1870* (Charlottesville, Va., 1991); Jack P. Maddex, Jr., *The Virginia Conservatives, 1867–1879: A Study in Reconstruction Politics* (Chapel Hill, N.C., 1970); Carl H. Moneyhon, *Republicanism in Reconstruction Texas* (Austin, Tex., 1980), and *The Impact of the Civil War and Reconstruction on Arkansas: Persistence in the Midst of Ruin* (Baton Rouge, La., 1994); William E. Parrish, *Missouri under Radical Rule, 1865–1870* (Columbia, Mo., 1965); Jerrell H. Shofner, *Nor Is It Over Yet: Florida in the Era of Reconstruction, 1863–1877* (Gainesville, Fla., 1974); Roger W. Shugg, *Origins of Class Struggle in Louisiana* (Baton Rouge, La., 1959); Joe G. Taylor, *Louisiana Reconstructed, 1863–1877* (Baton Rouge, La., 1974); George H. Thompson, *Arkansas and Reconstruction* (Port Washington, N.Y., 1976); and Ted Tunnell, *Crucible of Reconstruction: War, Radicalism, and Race in Louisiana, 1862–1877* (Baton Rouge, La., 1984). For a recent study of Reconstruction at the county level, see Barry A. Crouch, *The Freedmen's Bureau and Black Texans* (Austin, Tex., 1992).

Several topical studies about Reconstruction are important and useful: Martin Abbott, *The Freedmen's Bureau in South Carolina, 1865–1872* (Chapel Hill, N.C., 1967); Kenneth C. Barnes, *Who Killed John Clayton? Political Violence and the Emergence of the New South, 1861–1893* (Durham, N.C., 1998); George R. Bentley, *A History of the Freedmen's Bureau* (Philadelphia, 1955); Carol R. Bleser, *The Promised Land: The History of the South Carolina Land Commission, 1869–1890* (Columbia, S.C., 1969); Randolph B. Campbell, *Grass-Roots Reconstruction in Texas, 1865–1880* (Baton Rouge, La., 1997; Barry A. Crouch and Donaly E. Brice, *Cullen Montgomery Baker, Reconstruction Desperado* (Baton Rouge, La., 1997); Richard N. Current, *Those Terrible Carpetbaggers: A Reinterpretation* (New York, 1988); Edmund L. Drago, *Black Politicians and Reconstruction in Georgia: A Splendid Failure* (Baton Rouge, La., 1982); *Hurrah for Hampton: Black Red Shirts in South Carolina during Reconstruction* (Fayetteville, Ark., 1998); Randy Finley, *From Slavery to Uncertain Freedom: The Freedmen's Bureau in Arkansas, 1865–1869* (Fayetteville, Ark., 1996); Katharine L. Dvorak, *An African-American Exodus: The Segregation of the Southern Churches* (Brooklyn, N.Y., 1991); Richard Zuczek, *State of Rebellion: Reconstruction in South Carolina* (Columbia, S.C., 1997); Thomas Holt, *Black over White: Negro Political Leadership in South Carolina during Reconstruction* (Urbana, Ill., 1977); Michael L. Lanza, *Agrarianism and Reconstruction Politics: The Southern Homestead Act* (Baton Rouge, La., 1990); Peyton McCrary, *Abraham Lincoln and Race: The Louisiana Experiment* (Princeton, N.J., 1978); George R. Rable, *But There Was No Peace: The Role of Violence in the Politics of Reconstruction* (Athens, Ga., 1984); James E. Sefton, *The United States Army and Reconstruction, 1865–1877* (Baton Rouge, La., 1967); Mark W. Summers, *Railroads, Radical Reconstruction, and the Gospel of Prosperity: Aid under the Radical Republicans, 1865–1877* (Princeton, N.J., 1984); Allen W. Trelease, *White Terror: The Ku Klux Klan Conspiracy and Southern Reconstruction* (New York, 1974); Peter Wallenstein, *From Slave South to New South: Public Policy in Nineteenth Century Georgia* (Chapel Hill, N.C., 1987); Sarah W. Wiggins, *The Scalawag in Alabama Politics, 1865–1881* (University, Ala., 1977); Richard Zuczek, *State of Rebellion: Reconstruction in South Carolina* (Columbia, S.C., 1997).

Laura R. Edwards in *Gendered Strife and Confusion: The Political Culture of Reconstruction* (Urbana, Ill., 1997) presents a powerful argument for reconceptualizing Reconstruction as the struggle over how public life *and* private life will be organized in the wake of the defeat of secession and the end of slavery, and who will dominate that process. Peter W. Bardaglio deals with similar themes in *Reconstructing the Household: Families, Sex, and the Law in the Nineteenth-Century South* (Chapel Hill, N.C., 1995), tracing the story to the beginnings of the progressive movement.

AFTER SLAVERY: RACE AND LABOR IN THE AGRARIAN SOUTH

After the Civil War, southerners had to rebuild their economy and develop a new system of race relations and a labor system without slavery. The historians who have studied this difficult, highly complex process have produced a rich literature. Willie Lee Rose's landmark study, *Rehearsal for Reconstruction* (Indianapolis, 1964) is still valuable. James Roark, *Masters without Slaves* discusses the adjustment of slave masters to the loss of their slaves and the rapid decline of their economic and social status. Works on related topics include Louis Gerteis, *From Contraband to Freedman: Federal Policy toward Southern Blacks, 1861–1865* (Westport, Conn., 1973); C. Peter Ripley, *Slaves and Freedmen in Civil War Louisiana* (Baton Rouge, La., 1976); and Theodore Bratner Wilson, *The Black Codes of South* (University, Ala., 1966).

A number of books stress the adjustment of former slaves to emancipation and help us see that the South was a mutual creation of blacks and whites: Orville Vernon Burton, *In My Father's House Are Many Mansions* (Chapel Hill, N.C., 1985); Ronald L. F. Davis, *Good and Faithful Labor: From Slavery to Sharecropping in the Natchez District, 1860–1890* (Westport, Conn., 1982); Hermann Janet Sharp, *The Pursuit of a Dream* (New York, 1981); Peter Kolchin, *First Freedom: The Responses of Alabama's Blacks to Emancipation and Reconstruction* (Westport, Conn., 1972); Leon Litwack, *Been in the Storm So Long* (New York, 1979); Lawrence Powell, *New Masters: Northern Planters during the Civil War and Reconstruction* (New Haven, Conn., 1980); Michael Wayne, *The Reshaping of Plantation Society: The Natchez District, 1860–1880* (Baton Rouge, La., 1983); and Joel Williamson, *After Slavery: The Negro in South Carolina during Reconstruction, 1861–1877* (New York, 1965). Also see John B. Boles, *Black Southerners 1619–1869* (Lexington, Ky., 1983), for a good synthesis of recent scholarship.

Race relations in the post–Civil War South have long attracted the attention of historians. No one doubts that Jim Crow was firmly entrenched by around 1900, but historians disagree as to why and when Jim Crow was imposed. A good survey is C. Vann Woodward's *Strange Career of Jim Crow* (4th rev. ed; New York, 1974). Major contributions to an understanding of Jim Crow include John W. Cell, *The Highest Stage of White Supremacy: The Origins of Segregation in South Africa and the American South* (New York, 1982); George M. Fredrickson, *The Black Image in the White Mind; the Debate on Afro-American Character and Destiny, 1817-1914* (New York, 1971) and *White Supremacy: A Comparative Study in American and South African History* (New York, 1981). J. Morgan Kousser, *The Shaping of Southern Politics: Suffrage Restrictions and the Establishment of the One-Party South, 1880–1910* (New Haven, Conn., 1974); Howard N. Rabinowitz, *Race Relations in the Urban South, 1865–1890* (New York, 1978); and Joel Williamson, *The Crucible of Race: Black-White Relations in the American South since Emancipation* (New York, 1984). John Hope Franklin, *From Slavery to Freedom: A History of Negro Americans,* 7th ed. (New York, 1988); Jacqueline Jones, *Labor of Love, Labor of Sorrow: Black Women, Work, and the Family from Slavery to the Present* (New York, 1985); and August Meier and Elliott M. Rudwick, *From Plantation to Ghetto: An Interpretive History of American Negroes* (New York, 1966), should also be consulted. So should Eric Anderson, *Race and Politics in North Carolina, 1872–1901* (Baton Rouge, La., 1981); Joseph H. Cartwright, *The Triumph of Jim Crow: Tennessee Race Relations in the 1880s* (Knoxville, Tenn., 1976); H. Leon Prather, *We Have Taken a City: The Wilmington Massacre and Coup of 1898* (Rutherford, N.J., 1984); George B. Tindall, *South Carolina Negroes, 1877–1900* (Columbia, S.C., 1952); Vernon Lane Wharton, *The Negro in Mississippi, 1865–1890* (Chapel Hill, N.C., 1947); and Charles E. Wynes, *Race Relations in Virginia, 1870–1902* (Charlottesville, Va., 1961), as well as the fine two-volume biography of Booker T. Washington by Louis R. Harlan, *Booker T. Washington,* 2 vols. (New York, 1972–1983). John William Graves, in *Town and Country: Race Relations in an Urban-Rural Context, Arkansas, 1865–1905* (Fayetteville, Ark., 1990), reminds us that racial discrimination and Jim Crow were less rigid and less harsh in some parts of the South than in others.

The postbellum systems of labor relations and race relations were shaped by the economic and political alternatives available. The general histories of the South cited in the first section of this bibliographical essay are very helpful for understanding the economy, as are general histories of the United States and of the American economy. Two essays are particularly helpful: William N. Parker, "The South in the National Economy, 1865–1970," *Southern Economic Journal* 46 (1983): 7–27; and Harold D. Woodman, "Sequel to Slavery: The New History Views the Postbellum South," *Journal of Southern History* 43 (1977): 523–554. The title of Woodman's *New South: The Legal Foundations of Credit and Labor Relations in the Postbellum Agricultural South* (Baton Rouge, La., 1995) speaks for itself.

Gavin Wright's *Political Economy of the Cotton South* (New York, 1986) and *Old South, New South: Revolutions in the Southern Economy since the Civil War: Households, Markets and Wealth in the Nineteenth Century* (New York, 1978), are essential, as are Gilbert C. Fite, *Cotton Fields No More: Southern Agriculture, 1865–1980* (Lexington, Ky., 1984); and Harold D. Woodman, *King Cotton and His Retainers; Financing & Marketing the Cotton Crop of the South 1880–1925* (Lexington, Ky. 1968). Related important books include Robert L. Brandfon, *Cotton Kingdom of the New South: A History of the Yazoo Mississippi Delta from Reconstruction to the Twentieth Century* (Cambridge, Mass., 1967); Thomas D. Clark, *Pills, Petticoats, and Plows: The Southern Country Store* (New York, 1944); William Cohen, *At Freedom's Edge: Black Mobility and the Quest for Racial Control, 1861–1915* (Baton Rouge, La., 1991); Stephen DeCanio, *Agriculture in the Postbellum South* (Cambridge, Mass., 1974); Robert Higgs, *Competition and Coercion: Blacks in the American Economy, 1865–1914* (Chicago, 1980); Jay R. Mandle, *The Roots of Black Poverty: The Southern Plantation Economy after the Civil War* (Durham, N.C., 1975); Daniel A. Novak, *The Wheel of Servitude: Black Forced Labor after Slavery* (Lexington, Ky., 1978); Roger Ransom and Richard Sutch, *One Kind of Freedom: The Economic Consequences of Emancipation* (Cambridge, Eng., 1977); Joseph P. Reidy, *From Slavery to Agrarian Capitalism in the Cotton Plantation South: Central Georgia, 1800–1880* (Chapel Hill, N.C., 1992); Julie Saville, *The Work of Reconstruction: From Slave to Wage Laborer in South Carolina, 1860–1870* (New York, 1994); Mark V. Wetherington, *The New South Comes to Wiregrass Georgia, 1860–1910* (Knoxville, Tenn., 1994); and Harold D. Woodman, *New South, New Law: The Legal Foundations of Credit and Labor Relations in the Postbellum Agricultural South* (Baton Rouge, La., 1995). James C. Cobb's study of the Mississippi delta covers a broad time span and much more than agriculture: *The Most Southern Place on Earth: The Mississippi Delta and the Roots of Southern Identity* (New York, 1992). Also see Thad Sitton *From Can See to Can't: Texas Cotton Farmers on Southern Prairies* (Austin, Tex., 1997). In *Southern Paternalism and the American Welfare State: Economics, Politics, and Institutions in the South, 1865–1965,* (Cambridge, Eng., 1999) a book that is more suggestive than persuasive, Lee J. Alston and Joseph P. Ferrie argue that southern employers and politicians altered their policies on government welfare to suit their perceived labor needs, but their argument has considerable merit.

The term "colonial economy" aptly described much about the American South for a long time: a region that exported raw materials and imported manufactured goods, an economy with a surplus of minimally skilled labor that earned low wages and a shortage of skilled, high-wage labor. The exporter of manufactured goods, in this scenario, earned greater profits than the exporter of raw materials and had a more skilled, better paid workforce. Southern leaders and opinion makers after the Civil War asserted that the South's "colonial economy" was the product of a northern conspiracy to make the South a poor, dependent region. The concept appealed to the South's sense that it was the victim of a condescending North and allowed the South to attempt to shift blame for its being less prosperous than most of the rest of the nation.

The "colonial economy" concept is so analytically and historically flawed as to be worthless in assessing the causes of the South's economy lagging behind that of much of the nation. It assumes the existence of a northern conspiracy to make the South dependent without describing either the components or the workings of such a conspiracy. The concept also suggests that the South got nothing from the involvement of northerners in the economy of the South. Thus, it ignores the important role northern capital played in the emergence of the modern South, as well as the critical roles of skilled workers, engineers, and managers who moved into the South. Finally, the "colonial economy" concept obscures an unpleasant reality: the economy of the South was primarily the product of choices made by southerners. Arguably, southerners made the best choices available to them during the times in which they lived. They, not northerners, made the choices. Some of their crucial choices were made long before the Civil War and have had ramifications long after the bloody conflict. Southerners ultimately chose, for instance, to invest in slave-based, export-oriented agricultural products. The region reflected those decisions in critical ways long after Appomattox: a dispersed population with little urbanization, a small, but significant, industrial sector, minimal investments in developing an educated, skilled workforce, and a heavy dependence upon an abundance of low-paid workers. Undoubtedly, the South has periodically been the victim of a condescending North, but the economy of the region is largely a homemade product.

POLITICS IN THE NEW SOUTH: REDEEMERS, POPULISTS AND OTHER DISSIDENTS, AND PROGRESSIVES

Historians have debated whether the New South was very different from the Old South and whether the planter elite maintained political and economic power after the Civil War. Woodward contended in *Origins of the New South* that the Redeemers were "new men" who rejected agrarianism in favor of economic diversification. That view has been challenged or modified by a number of historians. Numan V. Bartley, "Another New South?" *Georgia Historical Quarterly* 65 (1981): 119–137; and James Tice Moore, "Redeemers Reconsidered: Change and Continuity in the Democratic South, 1870–1900," *Journal of Southern History* 44 (1978): 357–378, are good introductions to the debate. Dwight B. Billings, Jr., *Planters and the Making of a "New South": Class, Politics, and Development in North Carolina, 1865–1900* (Chapel Hill, N.C., 1979); and Jonathan Wiener, *Social Origins of the New South: Alabama, 1860–1880* (Baton Rouge, La., 1978), sharply challenge the "new men" thesis. Others modify it; they include William J. Cooper, Jr., *The Conservative Regime: South Carolina, 1877–1890* (Baltimore, 1968); Paul D. Escott, *Many Excellent People: Power and Privilege in North Carolina* (Chapel Hill, N.C., 1985); Jack Maddex, *Virginia Conservatives, 1867–1879; A Study in Reconstruction Politics* (Chapel Hill, N.C., 1970); and James Michael Russell, *Atlanta, 1847–1890: City Building in the Old South and the New (Baton Rouge, La., 1988)*. Woodward's argument receives strong support from David L. Carlton, *Mill and Town in South Carolina, 1880–1920* (Baton Rouge, La., 1982); and Michael Wayne, *Reshaping of Plantation Society* (Baton Rouge, La., 1983). The rhetoric and ideas of the New South boosters are explored in Paul M. Gaston, *The New South Creed: A Study in Southern Mythmaking* (New York, 1970).

By the end of Reconstruction, the solid, or Democratic, South was well established, though it had not yet reduced the Republicans or political independents to impotence. The place to begin reading about politics in the South after 1865 is V. O. Key, *Southern Politics in State and Nation* (New York, 1949). As Key and others have shown, the solid South had deep divisions throughout its history. Perhaps the most striking divisions occurred in the late nineteenth century, when disaffected farmers and their allies fueled an agrarian revolt that threatened the solid South for more than a decade. Theodore Saloutos, *Farmer Movements in the South, 1865–1933* (Berkeley and Los Angeles, 1960), provides a broad overview of that revolt. Other very useful studies include Steven Hahn, *The Roots of Southern Populism: Yeoman Farmers and the Transformation of the Georgia Upcountry, 1850–1890* (New York, 1983); William Ivy Hair, *Bourbonism and Agrarian Protest: Louisiana Politics, 1877–1900* (Baton Rouge, La., 1969); Roger L. Hart, *Redeemers, Bourbons, and Populists: Tennessee, 1870–1896* (Baton Rouge, La., 1975); Michael R. Hyman, *The Anti-Redeemers: Hill-Country Political Dissenters in the Lower South from Redemption to Populism* (Baton Rouge, La., 1990); Shawn Everett Kantor, *Politics and Property Rights: The Closing of the Open Range in the Postbellum South* (Chicago, 1998); Albert D. Kirwan, *Revolt of the Rednecks: Mississippi Politics, 1876–1925* (Lexington, Ky., 1951); Allen W. Moger, *Virginia: Bourbonism to Byrd, 1870–1925* (Charlottesville, Va., 1968); William Warren Rogers, *One-Gallused Rebellion: Agrarianism in Alabama, 1865–1896* (Baton Rouge, La., 1970); and Edward C. Williamson, *Florida Politics in the Gilded Age, 1877–1893* (Gainesville, Fla., 1976). Jane Dailey's *Before Jim Crow: The Politics of Race in Postemancipation Virginia* (Chapel Hill, N.C., 2000) explores how the Readjusters in Virginia made serious efforts to build a politically viable biracial coalition. On the awkward efforts of the national Republican party to build a party in the New South, see Vincent P. DeSantis, *Republicans Face the Southern Question: The New Departure Years, 1877–1897* (New York, 1969); and Stanley P. Hirschon, *Farewell to the Bloody Shirt: Northern Republicans and the Southern Negro, 1877–1893* (Bloomington, Ind., 1962). Michael Perman's *Struggle for Mastery: Disfranchisement in the South, 1888–1908* (Chapel Hill, N.C., 2001) is a newly published comprehensive analysis of the disfranchisement of blacks and poor whites that ensured the dominance of Democrats in the South.

John D. Hicks, *The Populist Revolt: A History of the Farmers' Alliance and the People's Party* (Minneapolis, 1931), is still the best place to get an overview of the Populists. Hicks has been challenged, most vigorously and successfully by Lawrence Goodwyn, *Democratic Promise: The Populist Movement in America* (New York, 1976). One need not accept Goodwyn's assertion that the Populists sought sweeping changes to be persuaded by his argument that southern Populism deserves more attention for its innovative thinking. Robert C. McMath, Jr., *Populism: A Social History* (New York, 1993), is the best synthesis and a fine overview of recent scholarship on Populism. Other good studies of southern Populism include Robert Durden, *The Climax of Populism: The Election of 1896* (Lexington, Ky., 1965); Gerald H. Gaither, *Blacks and the Populist Revolt: Ballots and Bigotry in the "New South"* (University, Ala., 1977); Sheldon Hackney, *Populism to Progressivism in Alabama* (Princeton, N.J., 1969); Robert C. McMath, Jr., *Populist Vanguard: A History of the Southern Farmers' Alliance* (Chapel Hill, N.C., 1975); Bruce Palmer, *"Man over Money": The Southern Populist Critique of American Capitalism* (Chapel Hill, N.C., 1980); Michael Schwartz, *Radical Protest and Social Structure: The Southern Farmers' Alliance and Cotton Tenancy, 1880–1890* (New York, 1976); and Barton C. Shaw, *The Wool-Hat Boys: Georgia's Populist Party* (Baton Rouge, La., 1984).

Some of the works listed previously in this section are also useful, directly or for background, in regard to the period from the progressive era through the 1920s. Dewey Grantham, *Southern Progressivism: The Reconciliation of Progress and Tradition* (Knoxville, Tenn., 1983), is a good overview. For general background, consult Arthur S. Link, *Woodrow Wilson and the Progressive Era* (New York, 1954). David Sarasohn argues in *The Party of Reform: Democrats in the Progressive Era* (Jackson, Miss., 1989), that the Democratic party, not the Republicans, led reform during the era of progressivism and that southern Democrats played leading roles in their party's reform efforts. The diversity of the politics of progressivism is reflected in some fine state studies. Danny Goble, *Progressive Oklahoma: The Making of a New Kind of State* (Norman, Okla., 1980); Lewis L. Gould, *Progressives and Prohibitionists: Texas Democrats in the Wilson Era* (Austin, Tex., 1973); David D. Lee, *Tennessee in*

Turmoil: Politics in the Volunteer State, 1920–1932 (Memphis, Tenn., 1979); Franklin D. Mitchell, *Embattled Democracy: Missouri Democratic Politics, 1919–1932* (Columbia, Mo., 1968); and Raymond H. Pulley, *Old Virginia Restored: An Interpretation of the Progressive Impulse, 1870–1930* (Charlottesville, Va., 1968), are particularly helpful. For a study that shows that the temperance and prohibition movements were much more than simple-minded efforts to legislate morality or reflections of ethnic and cultural conflicts, see Richard F. Hamm, *Shaping the Eighteenth Amendment: Temperance Reform, Legal Culture, and the Polity, 1880–1920* (Chapel Hill, N.C., 1995).

Other aspects of progressivism, such as city governance, women's rights, education, health, and labor reform, are dealt with in subsequent sections. Hugh C. Bailey, *Liberalism in the New South: Southern Social Reformers and the Progressive Movement* (Coral Gables, Fla., 1968); and Bruce Clayton, *The Savage Ideal: Intolerance and Intellectual Leadership in the South, 1880–1914* (Baltimore, 1972), are valuable guides to the narrowness of the progressives' mentality. For a better understanding of the political climate of those years, consult Charles C. Alexander, *The Ku Klux Klan in the Southwest* (Lexington, Ky., 1965); Kathleen M. Blee, *Women of the Klan: Racism and Gender in the 1920s* (Berkeley, Calif., 1991); David M. Chalmers, *Hooded Americanism: The First Century of the Ku Klux Klan, 1865–1965* (Garden City, N.Y., 1965); Willard B. Gatewood, Jr., *Preachers, Pedagogues, and Politicians: The Evolution Controversy in North Carolina, 1920–1927* (Chapel Hill, N.C., 1966); Kenneth T. Jackson, *The Ku Klux Klan in the City, 1915–1930* (New York, 1967); and Nancy K. MacLean, *Behind the Mask of Chivalry: The Making of the Second Ku Klux Klan* (New York, 1994). On southern Republicans during this era, see Paul D. Casdorph, *Republicans, Negroes, and Progressives in the South, 1912–1916* (University, Ala., 1981); Gordon B. McKinney, *Southern Mountain Republicans, 1865–1900: Politics and the Appalachian Community* (Chapel Hill, N.C., 1978); and Olive Hall Shadgett, *The Republican Party in Georgia: From Reconstruction through 1900* (Athens, Ga., 1964). On the socialists in the South, see Garin Burbank, *When Farmers Voted Red: The Gospel of Socialism in the Oklahoma Countryside, 1910–1924* (Norman, Okla., 1980); and James R. Green, *Grass-Roots Socialism: Radical Movements in the Southwest, 1895–1943* (Baton Rouge, La., 1978).

Finally, biographies are often useful for information on particular eras or developments in southern history as well as on individuals. Some of the most significant biographies are listed separately in the section on biographies. Those (by short title) and others are listed in this essay by topic. Arsenault, *Wild Ass of the Ozarks;* Blake, *William Mahone;* Cooper, *Walter Hines Page;* Cotner, *James Stephen Hogg;* Grantham, *Hoke Smith;* Holmes, *White Chief: James Kimble Vardaman;* Miller, *Mr. Crump of Memphis;* Noblin, *Leonidas LaFayette Polk;* Oliver H. Orr, Jr., *Charles Brantley Aycock* (Chapel Hill, N.C., 1961); Samuel Proctor, *Napoleon Bonaparte Broward: Florida's Fighting Democrat* (Gainesville, Fla., 1950); Simkins, *Pitchfork Ben Tillman;* Williams, *Huey Long;* and Woodward, *Tom Watson.* The generally sympathetic view of Huey Long found in Williams's *Long* is disputed by Hair, *Kingfish and His Realm;* and by Glen Jeansonne, *Messiah of the Masses: Huey P. Long and the Great Depression* (New York, 1993).

*F*ROM THE GREAT DEPRESSION AND THE NEW DEAL TO THE GREAT SOCIETY

For an overview of the New Deal, see William E. Leuchtenburg, *Franklin D. Roosevelt and the New Deal* (New York, 1963). Frank Freidel, *F.D.R. and the South* (Baton Rouge, La., 1965), provides useful background. Jordan A. Schwarz's *The New Dealers: Power Politics in the Age of Roosevelt* (New York, 1993), discusses how New Deal leaders thought they could use the power of the federal government to change the economies and raise the standards of living in the American South and the American West. Roger Biles's *The South and the New Deal* (Lexington, Ky., 1994), is a convenient summary. Economic and social conditions in the South on the eve of and during the Depression are discussed in a variety of sources. See especially Howard W. Odum, *Southern Regions of the United States* (Chapel Hill, N.C., 1936), a gold mine of statistical data; Twelve Southerners, *I'll Take My Stand* (New York, 1930); and Rupert B. Vance, *Human Factors in Cotton Culture* (Chapel Hill, N.C., 1929), and *Human Geography of the South* (Chapel Hill, N.C., 1932). Two anthologies of oral histories of ordinary southerners provide unique perspectives: William T. Couch, ed., *These Are Our Lives* (Chapel Hill, N.C., 1939); and Tom E. Terrill and Jerrold Hirsch, eds., *Such as Us: Southern Voices of the Thirties* (Chapel Hill, N.C., 1978). Also see James Agee and Walker Evans, *Let Us Now Praise Famous Men* (New York, 1941); Pete Daniel, *The Shadow of Slavery: Peonage in the South, 1901–1969* (Urbana, Ill., 1972); J. Wayne Flynt, *Dixie's Forgotten People: The South's Poor Whites* (Bloomington, Ind., 1979); Margaret Jarman Hagood, *Mothers of the South: Portraiture of the White Tenant Farm Woman* (Chapel Hill, N.C., 1939); H. L. Mitchell, *Mean Things Happening in This Land: The Life and Times of H. L. Mitchell* (Montclair, N.J., 1979); Arthur Raper, *Preface to Peasantry: A Tale of Two Black Belt Counties* (Chapel Hill, N.C., 1936); Raymond Wolters, *Negroes and the Great Depression: The Problem of Economic Recovery* (Westport, Conn., 1970); and Donald E. Worster, *Dust Bowl: The Southern Plains in the 1930s* (New York, 1979).

For a summary of the agricultural programs of the New Deal, see Theodore Saloutos, *The American Farmer and the New Deal* (Ames, Iowa, 1982). Important works on specific programs include Anthony J. Badger, *Prosperity: The New Deal, Tobacco, and North Carolina* (Chapel Hill, N.C., 1980); D. Clayton Brown, *Electricity for Rural America: The Fight for the REA* (Westport, Conn., 1980); Walter L. Creese, *TVA's Public Planning: The Vision, the Reality* (Knoxville, Tenn., 1990); Wilmon Henry Droze, *High Dams and Slack Waters: TVA Builds a River* (Baton Rouge, La., 1965); Nancy L. Grant, *TVA and Black Americans: Planning for the Status Quo* (Philadelphia, 1990); Preston J. Hubbard, *Origins of the TVA: The Muscle Shoals Controversy, 1920–1932* (Nashville, Tenn., 1961); Michael J. McDonald and John Muldowny, *TVA and the Dispossessed: The Resettlement of Population in the Norris Dam Area* (Knoxville, Tenn., 1982); and Thomas K. McGraw, *TVA and the Power Fight, 1933–1939* (Philadelphia, 1971). Thomas D. Clark, *The Greening of the South: The Recovery of Land and Forest* (Lexington, Ky., 1984), has a good deal of material on the New Deal's conservation and reforestation efforts. Of related interest are Jeffrey K. Stine's *Mixing the Waters: Environment, Politics, and the Tennessee-Tombigbee Waterway* (Akron, Ohio, 1993); and Lawrence J. Nelson, *King Cotton's Advocate: Oscar G. Johnston and the New Deal* (Knoxville, Tenn., 1998).

For the story of the New Deal's failure with respect to poorer farmers, see David Eugene Conrad, *The Forgotten Farmers: The Story of Sharecroppers in the New Deal* (Urbana, Ill., 1965); Donald H. Grubbs, *Cry from the Cotton: The Southern Tenant Farmers' Union and the New Deal* (Chapel Hill, N.C., 1971); and Paul E. Mertz, *New Deal Policy and Southern Rural Poverty* (Baton Rouge, La., 1978). For a study of another dissident farmer group, see Robin D. G. Kelley, *Hammer and Hoe: Alabama Communists during the Great Depression* (Chapel Hill, N.C., 1990). Three books include perceptive discussions of the impact of New Deal agricultural programs on the South: Pete Daniel, *Breaking the Land: The Transformation of Cotton, Tobacco, and Rice Cultures since 1880* (Urbana, Ill., 1985); Jack Temple Kirby, *Rural Worlds Lost: The American South, 1920–1960* (Baton Rouge, La., 1986); and Eldred E. Prince, *Long Green: The Rise and Fall of Tobacco in South Carolina* (Athens, Ga., 2001). A wide-ranging study of changes in the rural South since 1940 can be found in R. Douglas Hurt, ed., *The Rural South since World War II* (Baton Rouge, La., 1998). In *The Cotton Plantation in the South since the Civil War* (Baltimore, 1998), Charles S. Aiken presents a persuasive case that the cotton plantation has not disappeared but has been transformed.

James T. Patterson, *Congressional Conservatism and the New Deal: The Growth of the Conservative Coalition in Congress, 1933–1939* (Lexington, Ky., 1967), is important. Also see his *New Deal and the States: Federalism in Transition* (Princeton, N.J., 1969); and John Braeman, Robert H. Bremner, and David Brody, eds., *The New Deal: The State and Local Levels* (Columbus, Ohio, 1975). *Conservative Constraints: North Carolina and the New Deal* (Jackson, Miss., 1992), by Douglas Carl Abrams, tells how state and local opponents of the New Deal limited its impact. Several books discuss the New Deal in other states. Among them are Jack Irby Hayes, Jr., *South Carolina and the New Deal* (Columbia, S.C., 2001); Ronald L. Heineman, *Depression and New Deal in Virginia: The Enduring Dominion* (Charlottesville, Va., 1983); and John Dean Minton, *The New Deal in Tennessee, 1932–1938* (New York, 1979).

Again, biographies can be very useful. See Caro, *Years of Lyndon Johnson*; Dallek, *Lone Star Rising: Lyndon Johnson*; Eagles, *Jonathan Daniels*; Fite, *Richard B. Russell*; Hamilton, *Hugo Black*; John Robert Moore, *Senator Josiah William Bailey of North Carolina: A Political Biography* (Durham, N.C., 1968); Lionel V. Patenaude, *Texans, Politics, and the New Deal* (New York, 1983); and Robertson, *Sly and Able: . . . James F. Byrnes* (New York, 1994).

Efforts by southern liberals and radicals to change the South can be followed in Frank T. Adams, *James A. Dombrowski: An American Heretic, 1897–1983* (Knoxville, Tenn., 1992); Anthony P. Dunbar, *Against the Grain: Southern Radicals and Prophets, 1929–1959* (Charlottesville, Va., 1981); Dykeman and Stokely, *Seeds of Southern Change: The Life of Will Alexander*; Richard B. Henderson, *Maury Maverick: A Political Biography* (Austin, Tex., 1970); Holt, *Mary McLeod Bethune*; Thomas A. Krueger, *And Promises to Keep: The Southern Conference for Human Welfare, 1938–1948* (Nashville, Tenn., 1967); Robert Francis Martin, *Howard Kester and the Struggle for Social Justice* (Charlottesville, Va., 1991); Linda Reed, *Simple Decency and Common Sense: The Southern Conference Movement, 1938–1963* (Bloomington, Ind., 1991); and Salmond, *A Southern Rebel . . . Aubrey Willis Williams*, and *Miss Lucy of the CIO . . . Lucy Randolph Mason*. Julian M. Pleasants and Augustus M. Burns III, *Frank Porter Graham and the 1950 Senate Race in North Carolina* (Chapel Hill, N.C., 1990), shows how risky liberal stands on race or organized labor could be in the South, even for one of the giants of the region. In *Testing the New Deal: The General Textile Strike of 1934 in the American South* (Urbana, Ill., 2000), Janet Irons tells the story of the largest strike in the history of the American South (and one of the largest in American history) and the New Deal's inadequate response to this large, grassroots movement.

Race does not explain everything in the politics of the South, but it explains a great deal, as Key showed in his famed *Southern Politics*. Efforts to update Key's work have produced several useful books, including Jack Bass and Walter De Vries, *The Transformation of Southern Politics: Social Change and Economic Consequence since 1945* (New York, 1976); William Havard, ed., *The Changing Politics of the South* (Baton Rouge, La., 1972); and Alexander P. Lamis, *The Two-Party South* (Baton Rouge, La., 1984). Earl Black and Merle Black, *Politics and Society in the South* (Cambridge, Mass., 1987), is the best study of southern politics to appear since Key's book. In a sequel study, *The Vital South: How Presidents Are Elected* (Cambridge, Mass., 1992), the Blacks demonstrate how important the South has become in presidential politics.

For more recent political developments in the South, see Alexander P. Lamis, *Southern Politics in the 1990s* (Baton Rouge, La., 1999); and James M. Glaser, *Race, Campaign Politics, and the Realignment in the South* (New Haven, Conn., 1996); for one state, North Carolina, see Paul Luebke, *Tar Heel Politics 2000* (Chapel Hill, N.C., 1998). On the impact of conservative religious groups and contemporary politics in the South and beyond, consult William Martin, *With God on Our Side: The Rise of Religious Right in America* (New York, 1996); and Oran P. Smith, *The Rise of Baptist Republicanism* (New York, 1997). Nina J. Easton's *Gang of Five: The Leaders at the Center of the Conservative Crusade* (New York, 2000) is a breezy but revealing discussion of the key figures in the shift to conservatism in contemporary politics, a shift in which the South has played a critical role. Dan Carter's *Politics of Rage: George Wal-*

lace and *From George Wallace to Newt Gingrich: Race in the Conservative Counterrevolution, 1963–1994* (Baton Rouge, La., 1996) are essential to understanding this shift. Kari Frederickson, *The Dixiecrat Revolt and the End of the Solid South, 1932–1968* (Chapel Hill, N.C., 2001) provides some useful background.

Other valuable studies are Numan V. Bartley, *The Rise of Massive Resistance: Race and Politics in the South during the 1950s* (Baton Rouge, La., 1984), and *The Creation of Modern Georgia* (Athens, Ga., 1983); Earl Black, *Southern Governors and Civil Rights* (Cambridge, Mass., 1976); Bernard Cosman and Robert J. Huckshorn, *Republican Politics: The 1964 Campaign and Its Aftermath for the Party* (New York, 1968); Chandler Davidson, *Biracial Politics: Conflict and Coalition in the Biracial South* (Baton Rouge, La., 1972), and *Race and Class in Texas Politics* (Princeton, N.J., 1991); Steven F. Lawson, *In Pursuit of Power: Southern Blacks and Electoral Politics, 1965–1982* (New York, 1985); Neil R. McMillen, *The Citizens' Council: Resistance to the Second Reconstruction* (Urbana, Ill, 1971); Louis M. Seagull, *Southern Republicanism* (Cambridge, Mass., 1975); and George B. Tindall, *The Disruption of the Solid South* (New York, 1972). For a biography of Governor George Wallace of Alabama, the most charismatic leader of massive resistance who attracted considerable support throughout the South and beyond, look at Stephen Lesher, *George Wallace*, but be aware that it has been criticized for understating the blatant racism that characterized Wallace's politics for much of his career. Carter's *Politics of Rage* is the penetrating study that Wallace deserves and that has not been done before.

Other useful biographies and studies of important political leaders of the post–World War II South include Charles L. Fontenay, *Estes Kefauver: A Biography* (Knoxville, Tenn., 1980); Joseph Bruce Gorman, *Kefauver: A Political Biography* (New York, 1971); and J. Harvie Wilkinson III, *Harry Byrd and the Changing Face of Virginia Politics, 1945–1966* (Charlottesville, Va., 1968). On Jimmy Carter, see his *Keeping the Faith: Memoirs of a President* (New York, 1982) as well as Gary M. Fink, *Prelude to the Presidency: The Political Career of and Legislative Leadership Style of Governor Jimmy Carter* (Westport, Conn., 1980); Erwin C. Hargrove, *Jimmy Carter as President: Leadership and the Politics of the Public Good* (Baton Rouge, La., 1988); and Charles O. Jones, *The Trustee Presidency: Jimmy Carter and the United States Congress* (Baton Rouge, La., 1988). Also consult works cited in the biographies section.

Southerners, and especially southern leaders, did not restrict themselves to domestic politics alone, as the following works make clear: Alfred O. Hero, Jr., *The Southerner and World Affairs* (Baton Rouge, La., 1965); Charles O. Lerche, Jr., *The Uncertain South: Its Changing Patterns of Politics in Foreign Policy* (Chicago, 1964); and Tennant S. McWilliams, *The New South Faces the World: Foreign Affairs and the Southern Sense of Self, 1877–1950* (Baton Rouge, La., 1988).

Gunnar Myrdal's massive two-volume *American Dilemma: The Negro Problem and Modern Democracy* (New York, 1944), is still the most important book on race relations on the eve of World War II available. Two fine studies of Myrdal's book are Walter A. Jackson, *Gunnar Myrdal and America's Conscience: Social Engineering and Racial Liberalism, 1938–1987* (Chapel Hill, N.C., 1990); and David W. Southern, *Gunnar Myrdal and Black-White Relations: The Use and Abuse of "An American Dilemma"* (Baton Rouge, La., 1987). General histories of black Americans, such as John Hope Franklin, *From Slavery to Freedom*, and August Meier and Elliott Rudwick, *From Plantation to Ghetto*, ought to be consulted. Two important studies are Herbert G. Gutman, *The Black Family in Slavery and Freedom, 1750–1925* (New York, 1976); and Lawrence W. Levine, *Black Culture and Black Consciousness: Afro-American Folk Thought from Slavery to Freedom* (New York, 1977). Also see Willard B. Gatewood, *Aristocrats of Color: The Black Elite, 1880–1920* (Bloomington, Ind., 1990). Among the several studies of blacks in various states, see John Dittmer, *Black Georgia in the Progressive Era, 1900–1920* (Urbana, Ill., 1977); Lester C. Lamon, *Black Tennesseeans, 1900–1930* (Knoxville, Tenn., 1977); Neil R. McMillen, *Dark Journey: Black Mississippians in the Age of Jim Crow* (Urbana, Ill., 1989); and I. A. Newby,

Black Carolinians: A History of Blacks in South Carolina from 1895 to 1968 (Columbia, S.C., 1973). Among the published autobiographical works or memoirs of blacks, several are particularly good: W. E. B. Du Bois, *The Souls of Black Folk* (Chicago, 1903); Mamie Garvin Fields with Karen Fields, *Lemon Swamp and Other Places: A Carolina Memoir* (New York, 1983); Henry Louis Gates, Jr., *Colored People: A Memoir* (Knopf, 1994); Alex Haley, *The Autobiography of Malcolm X* (New York, 1965); John R. Oldfield, ed., *Civilization and Black Progress: Selected Writings of Alexander Crummell on the South* (Charlottesville, VA., 1995); Sarah Rice, *He Included Me: The Autobiography of Sarah Rice*, transcribed and edited by Louise Westling (Athens, Ga., 1989); Theodore Rosengartern, *All God's Dangers: The Life of Nate Shaw [Cole]* (New York, 1974); and Booker T. Washington, *Up from Slavery: An Autobiography* (New York, 1901). In addition to Du Bois's *Souls of Black Folk*, which is a classic, beautifully written and full of insights, his other autobiographical writings also contain many treasures. Also consult David Lewis' fine biography of DuBois, which is cited in the biographies section. For an examination of a black school, a crucial institution in the New South, see Vanessa Siddle Walker, *Their Highest Potential: An African American School Community in the Segregated South* (Chapel Hill, N.C., 1996).

There is no general history of the massive migration of blacks from the South. Daniel M. Johnson and Rex B. Campbell, *Black Migration in America: A Social Demographic History* (Durham, N.C., 1981), is too brief. More recent fine studies include James R. Grossman, *Land of Hope: Chicago, Black Southerners, and the Great Migration* (Chicago, 1989); Alferdteen Harrison, ed., *Black Exodus: The Great Migration from the American South* (Jackson, Miss., 1991); Carole Marks, *Farewell—We're Good and Gone: The Great Black Migration* (Bloomington, Ind., 1989); and Joe William Trotter, ed., *The Great Migration in Historical Perspective: New Dimensions of Race, Class, and Gender* (Bloomington, Ind., 1991). Two books deal with the 1870s migration of blacks to Kansas: Robert G. Athearn, *In Search of Canaan: Black Migration to Kansas, 1879–80* (Lawrence, Kans., 1978); and Nell Irvin Painter, *The Exodusters: Black Migration to Kansas after Reconstruction* (New York, 1976). Migration to Africa attracted the interest of some blacks. This is the subject of Edwin S. Redkey's *Exodus: Black Nationalism and Back-to-Africa Movements, 1890–1910* (New Haven, Conn., 1969). That interest was stirred again during World War I and especially during the 1920s by Marcus Garvey, who led the first mass black protest movement in America: E. David Cronon, *Black Moses: The Story of Marcus Garvey and the Universal Negro Improvement Association* (Madison, Wis., 1955); and Judith Stein, *The World of Marcus Garvey: Race and Class in Modern Society* (Baton Rouge, La., 1986).

Studies of race relations have generally tended to focus on particularly critical moments, such as the surge of Jim Crow legislation in the late nineteenth century, the wave of race riots after World War I, and the civil rights revolution. Arthur I. Waskow's *From Race Riot to Sit-in, 1919 and the 1960's: A Study in the Connections between Conflict and Violence* (Garden City, N.Y., 1966), is good general introduction. For a study of a specific riot, see Scott Ellsworth, *Death in a Promised Land: The Tulsa Race Riot of 1921* (Baton Rouge, La., 1982). Arthur F. Raper's *Tragedy of Lynching* (Chapel Hill, N.C., 1933), is still the best general treatment of that terrible practice. Two studies focus intensively on lynching in three states: W. Fitzhugh Brundage, *Lynching in the New South: Georgia and Virginia, 1880–1930* (Urbana, Ill., 1993); and George C. Wright, *Racial Violence in Kentucky, 1865–1940: Lynchings, Mob Rule, and "Legal Lynchings"* (Baton Rouge, La., 1990). Also see W. Fitzhugh Brundage, ed., *Under Sentence of Death: Lynching in the South* (Chapel Hill, N.C., 1997). Scholars have recently examined southern justice with, in some instances, particular emphasis on convict leasing and chain gangs: Alex Lichtenstein, *Twice the Work of Free Labor: The Political Economy of Convict Labor in the New South* (New York, 1996); Matthew J. Mancini, *One Dies, Get Another: Convict Leasing in the American South, 1866–1928* (Columbia, S.C., 1996); Martha M. Myers, *Race, Labor, and Punishment in the New South* (Columbus, Ohio, 1998); David M. Oshinsky, *"Worse Than Slavery": Parchman Farm and the Ordeal of Jim Crow Justice* (New York,

1996); and Stewart E. Tolnay and E. M. Beck, *A Festival of Violence: An Analysis of Southern Lynchings, 1882–1930* (Urbana, Ill., 1995). Karin A. Shapiro's *A New South Rebellion: The Battle against Convict Labor in the Tennessee Coalfields, 1871–1896* (Chapel Hill, N.C., 1998) tells how Tennessee coal miners were the flying wedge in an eventually successful effort to limit, then end convict leasing. In *The Color of Law: Race, Violence, and Justice in the Post–World War II South* (Chapel Hill, N.C., 1999), Gail Williams O'Brien shows that among the changes the war brought to the South was a shift from mob violence against blacks to confrontations between blacks and police.

Rich insights about race relations in the 1930s can be found in intensive studies done during that decade: Allison Davis, Burleigh B. Gardner, and Mary B. Gardner, *Deep South: A Social Anthropological Study of Caste and Class* (Chicago, 1941); John Dollard, *Caste and Class in a Southern Town* (New York, 1937); and Hortense Powdermaker, *After Freedom: A Cultural Study in the Deep South* (New York, 1939). Dan T. Carter's study of the notorious Scottsboro trial, *Scottsboro: A Tragedy of the American South* (rev. ed.; Baton Rouge, La., 1979); and James R. McGovern's discussion of a 1934 lynching, *Anatomy of a Lynching: The Killing of Claude Neal* (Baton Rouge, La., 1982), are full of insights. Also see James Goodman, *Stories of Scottsboro* (New York, 1994). Stephen J. Whitfield, *A Death in the Delta: The Story of Emmett Till* (Baltimore, 1988), tells the tragic story of the 1955 lynching of Emmett Till that shocked the country with its brutality and the refusal of Mississippi whites to convict the obviously guilty murderers. The Till lynching may have been a catalyst for the civil rights movement. Two murderous assaults on black communities (Kirven, Texas, and Rosewood, Florida) have been the subject of recent studies: Monte Akers, *Flames after Midnight: Murder, Vengeance, and the Desolation of a Texas Community* (Austin, Tex., 1999); and Michael D'Orso, *Like Judgment Day: The Ruin and Redemption of a Town Called Rosewood* (New York, 1996).

The best introduction to what blacks found in the American military during World War II and the Korean War is Richard M. Dalfiume, *Desegregation of the U.S. Armed Forces: Fighting on Two Fronts, 1939–1953* (Columbia, Mo., 1969). In gently nudging employers during World War II to hire black workers, the federal government tiptoed along the color line, but groundwork for greater challenges to Jim Crow was laid: see Merl E. Reed, *Seedtime for the Modern Civil Rights Movement: The President's Committee on Fair Employment Practice, 1941–1946* (Baton Rouge, La., 1991). Also see Harold P. Henderson, *The Divided Skies: Establishing Segregated Flight Training at Tuskegee, Alabama, 1934–1942* (Tuscaloosa, Ala., 1992).

THE CIVIL RIGHTS REVOLUTION

No general survey of the civil rights revolution is available, but see Adam Fairclough, *To Redeem the Soul of America: The Southern Christian Leadership Conference and Martin Luther King, Jr.* (Athens, Ga., 1987); David R. Goldfield, *Black White, and Southern: Race Relations and Southern Culture, 1940 to the Present* (Baton Rouge, La., 1990); Hugh Davis Graham, *The Civil Rights Era: Origins and Development of National Policy* (New York, 1990); Steven F. Lawson, *Running for Freedom: Civil Rights and Black Politics in America since 1941* (Philadelphia, 1991); Genna Rae McNeil, *Groundwork: Charles Hamilton Houston and the Struggle for Civil Rights* (Philadelphia, 1983); Aldon D. Morris, *The Origins of the Civil Rights Movement: Black Communities Organizing for Change* (New York, 1984); Harvard Sitkoff, *The Struggle for Black Equality, 1954–1980* (New York, 1981); Mark V. Tushnet, *The NAACP's Legal Strategy against Segregated Education, 1925–1950* (Chapel Hill, N.C., 1987); and Juan Williams, *Eyes on the Prize: America's Civil Rights Years, 1954–1965* (New York, 1987). Richard Kluger, *Simple Justice: The History of "Brown v. Board of Education" and Black America's Struggle for Equality* (New York, 1976), is valuable and compelling. The role of the courts, especially the federal courts, is discussed in Jack Bass, *Unlikely Heroes: The Dramatic Story of the Southern Judges of the Fifth Circuit Court Who Translated the Supreme Court's "Brown" Decision into a Revolution for Equality* (New York, 1981); J. Harvie Wilkinson III, *From "Brown" to "Bakke": The Supreme Court and School Integration, 1954–1978* (New York, 1979); Raymond Wolters, *The Burden of "Brown": Thirty Years of School Desegregation* (Knoxville, Tenn., 1984); and Tinsley E. Yarbrough, *Judge Frank Johnson and Human Rights in Alabama* (University, Ala., 1983). Bass and Yarbrough laud the judges. Wilkinson has reservations about the expansion of judicial authority in the school cases. Wolters is generally critical of the role of the courts in school desegregation.

Several books address the divergent ways liberals dealt with Jim Crow in the 1930s and 1940s. The most general of these works are John Egerton, *Speak Now against the Day: The Generation before the Civil Rights Movement in the South* (New York, 1994); Morton Sosna, *The Silent South: Southern Liberals and the Race Issue* (New York, 1977); and Patricia Sullivan, *Days of Hope: Race and Democracy in the New Deal Era* (Chapel Hill, N.C., 1996). Also see Anthony P. Dunbar, *Against the Grain: Southern Radicals and Prophets, 1929–1959* (Charlotteville, Va., 1981); Eagles, *Jonathan Daniels and Race Relations*; and John A. Salmond, *Southern Rebel: . . . Aubrey Willis Williams*; as well as John M. Glen's *Highlander: No Ordinary School, 1932–1962* (Lexington, Ky., 1988). Lillian Smith was one of the few southern whites who bluntly attacked Jim Crow: *Killers of the Dream* (New York, 1949). In the 1960s, James McBride Dabbs made an eloquent, ethically based attack upon race relations in his native region: *Who Speaks for the South?* (New York, 1964), while a fellow South Carolinian, William D. Workman, argued in *The Case for the South* (New York, 1960) against federal intervention in racial matters. The South should be left alone to deal with its own racial problems, Workman argued, but he was vague as to when and how the South ought to act. For similar arguments, see James J. Kilpatrick, *The Southern Case for School Segregation* (New York, 1962).

David J. Garrow and Taylor Branch have written extensive, rich studies of Martin Luther King, Jr., and the civil rights movement: Garrow, *Bearing the Cross*; and Branch, *Parting the Waters: America in the King Years, 1954–1963* (New York, 1988), and *Pillar of Fire: America in the King Years, 1963–65* (New York, 1998). Edited volumes of Martin Luther King's papers are beginning to appear: *Papers of Martin Luther King, Jr.*, ed. Clayborne Carson, 2 vols. to date (Berkeley, Calif., 1992–   ). Howell Raines, *My Soul Is Rested: Movement Days in the Deep South Remembered* (New York, 1983), conveys the emotion behind the movement and provides facts and insights that recognize not only the diversity of both the movement and its leadership but also the great risks many people took when they challenged Jim Crow. For the Student Nonviolent Coordinating Committee, see Clayborne Carson, *In Struggle: SNCC and the Black Awakening of the 1960s* (Cambridge, Mass., 1981). Of personal reminiscences of the civil rights movements, two of the best are Mary King, *Freedom Song: A Personal Story of the 1960s Civil Rights Movement* (New York, 1987); and Anne Moody, *Coming of Age in Mississippi* (New York, 1969).

The following are very useful for understanding particular events or groups: Charles T. Banner-Haley, *The Fruits of Integration: Black Middle-Class Ideology and Culture, 1960–1990* (Jackson, Miss., 1994); Catherine A. Barnes, *Journey from Jim Crow: The Desegregation of Southern Transit* (New York, 1983); David S. Cecelski, *Along Freedom Road: Hyde County, North Carolina, and the Fate of Black Schools in the South* (Baltimore, 1994); William H. Chafe, *Civilities and Civil Rights: Greensboro, North Carolina, and the Black Struggle for Freedom* (New York, 1981); David L. Chappell, *Inside Agitators: White Southerners in the Civil Rights Movement* (Baltimore, 1994); John Dittmer, *Local People: The Struggle for Civil Rights in Mississippi* (Urbana, Ill., 1994); David M. Douglas, *Reading, Writing, and Race: The Desegregation of the Charlotte Schools* (Chapel Hill, N.C., 1995); Alan Draper, *Conflicts of Interest: Organized Labor and the Civil Rights Movement in the South, 1954–1968* (Ithaca, N.Y., 1994); Glenn T. Eschew, *But for Birmingham: The Local and National Movements in the Civil Rights Struggle* (Chapel

Hill, N.C., 1997); Tony Allen Freyer, *The Little Rock Crisis: A Constitutional Interpretation* (Westport, Conn., 1984); David J. Garrow, *Protest at Selma: Martin Luther King, Jr., and the Voting Rights Act of 1965* (New Haven, Conn., 1978); Charles V. Hamilton, *The Bench and the Ballot: Southern Federal Judges and Black Voters* (New York, 1973); Fred Hobson, *But Now I See: The White Southern Racial Conversion Narrative* (Baton Rouge, La., 1999); Andrew M. Manis, *A Fire You Can't Put Out: The Civil Rights Life of Birmingham's Reverend Fred Shuttlesworth* (Tuscaloosa, Ala., 1999); Kay Mills, *This Little Light of Mine: The Life of Fannie Lou Hamer* (New York, 1993); Robert J. Norell, *Reaping the Whirlwind: The Civil Rights Movement in Tuskegee* (New York, 1985); William A. Nunnelley, *Bull Conner* (Tuscaloosa, Ala., 1990); Pfeffer, *A. Philip Randolph;* Jo Ann Gibson Robinson, *The Montgomery Bus Boycott and the Women Who Started It: The Memoirs of Jo Ann Gibson,* ed. with a foreword by David J. Garrow (Knoxville, Tenn., 1987); Cleveland Sellers with Robert Terrell, *The River of No Return: The Autobiography of a Black Militant and the Life and Death of SNCC* (New York, 1973); and J. Mills Thornton, "Challenge and Response in the Montgomery Bus Boycott of 1955–1956," *Alabama Review* 33 (1980): 163–235. The last study is extremely valuable. Full of insights is Melissa Fay Greene's reconstruction of people and events in a southern Georgia county that was reached by the civil rights revolution in the 1970s: *Praying for Sheetrock: A Work of Nonfiction* (New York, 1991). Elizabeth Jacoway and David R. Colburn, eds., *Southern Businessmen and Desegregation* (Baton Rouge, La., 1982), recounts the role businessmen played in encouraging acceptance of desegregation and their motives for doing so. Frank R. Parker does a detailed examination of the impact of the civil rights movement on politics in Mississippi: *Black Votes Count: Political Empowerment in Mississippi after 1965* (Chapel Hill, N.C., 1990). For a similar study of broader scope, see Chandler Davidson and Bernard Grofman, eds., *Quiet Revolution in the South: The Impact of the Voting Rights Act, 1965–1990* (Princeton, N.J., 1994).

Michael V. Namorato, ed., *Have We Overcome? Race Relations since "Brown"* (Jackson, Miss., 1979), is a reassessment of the civil rights movement. For an argument that economic and institutional factors are now more important than racial factors in determining the place and future of American blacks, see William Julius Wilson, *The Declining Significance of Race: Blacks and Changing American Institutions* (Chicago, 1978), and *The Truly Disadvantaged: The Inner City, the Under Class, and Public Policy* (Chicago, 1987). John Hope Franklin's *Race and History: Selected Essays, 1938–1988* (Baton Rouge, La., 1989) is a sober reflection about racism in American history by a highly respected historian.

To follow some of the recent debates about the civil rights revolution and its legacy, see Stephan and Abigail Thernstrom, *America in Black and White: One Nation, Indivisible* (New York, 1997); Abigail Thernstrom, *Who Votes?* (Cambridge, Mass., 1987); and J. Morgan Kousser, *Colorblind Injustice: Minority Voting Rights and the Undoing of the Second Reconstruction* (Chapel Hill, N.C., 1999). James Patterson has written a balanced, fair assessment of the *Brown* decision and its impact: *Brown v. Board of Education: A Civil Rights Milestone and Its Troubled Legacy* (New York, 2001).

WOMEN

Women in the South are a comparatively new area of historical study. The best place to start is Jacquelyn Dowd Hall and Anne Frior Scott, "Women in the South," in John B. Boles and Evelyn Thomas Nolen, eds., *Interpreting Southern History: Historiographical Essays in Honor of Sanford W. Higginbotham* (Baton Rouge, La., 1987). Several works of a general nature are important, especially Scott, *Southern Lady: From Pedestal to Politics 1830–1930* (Chicago, 1970); and Virginia Bernhard et al., eds., *Southern Women: Histories and Identities* (Columbia, Mo., 1992). To these add *Black Women in America: An Historical Encyclopedia* (Brooklyn, N.Y., 1993);

and Tera W. Hunter, *"To Joy My Freedom"*: *Southern Black Women's Lives and Labors after the Civil War* (Cambridge, Mass., 1997). Several other important works give some attention to the South: David M. Katzman, *Seven Days a Week: Women and Domestic Service in Industrializing America* (New York, 1978); Alice Kessler-Harris, *Out to Work: A History of Wage-Earning Women in the United States* (New York, 1982); and Barbara Mayer Wertheimer, *We Were There: The Story of Working Women in America* (New York, 1977). Carol Bleser, ed., *In Joy and Sorrow: Women, Family and Marriage in the Victorian South, 1830–1900* (New York, 1991) is a fine source of information and insights. Jacquelyn Hall's *Revolt against Chivalry: Jessie Daniel Ames and the Women's Campaign against Lynching* (New York, 1979) is a major contribution that focuses on women, feminism, religion, and social reform.

Women in the New South assumed leading roles in the churches, in social reform, and of course, in the drive to secure the vote for women. Eleanor Flexner, *Century of Struggle: The Woman's Rights Movement in the United States* (New York, 1979), provides a useful general introduction. Glenda Elizabeth Gilmore's *Gender and Jim Crow: Women and Politics in North Carolina, 1886–1920* (Chapel Hill, N.C., 1996) follows women as they stepped more boldly into the public sphere, even tentatively toward the racial barriers in that sphere. A. Elizabeth Taylor wrote extensively about the campaign for women's suffrage in articles and in *The Woman Suffrage Movement in Tennessee* (New York, 1957). Paul E. Fuller, *Laura Clay and the Women's Rights Movement* (Lexington, Ky., 1975), is about one of the South's leading suffragists. Mary Martha Thomas focuses on black and white women and reform in Alabama in *The New Woman in Alabama: Social Reforms and Suffrage, 1890–1920* (Tuscaloosa, Ala., 1992). Using collective biography, Marjorie Spruill Wheeler examined the leadership of the women's suffrage movement in the South in *New Women of the New South: The Leaders of the Woman Suffrage Movement in the Southern States* (New York, 1993). Three recent books add considerably to what we know about this movement: Elna C. Green, *Southern Strategies: Southern Women and the Woman Suffrage Question* (Chapel Hill, N.C., 1997); Rosalyn Terbor-Penn, *African American Women in the Struggle for the Vote, 1850–1920* (Bloomington, Ind., 1996); and Pamela Tyler, *Silk Stockings and Ballot Boxes: Women and Politics in New Orleans, 1920–1963* (Athens, Ga., 1996). Also see: Judith N. McArthur, *Creating the New Woman: The Rise of Southern Women's Progressive Culture in Texas, 1893–1918* (Urbana, Ill., 1998); and Anastatia Sims, *The Power of Femininity in the New South: Women's Organizations and Politics in North Carolina, 1880–1930* (Columbia, S.C., 1997). Paralleling the stiff opposition that women's suffrage faced in the South was the resistance against the attempt to put an equal rights provision in the federal Constitution by amendment. The story of the defeat of the amendment, primarily in one southern state, North Carolina, is told in Donald G. Mathews and Jane Sherron De Hart, *Sex, Gender, and the Politics of ERA: A State and the Nation* (New York, 1990).

The importance of women in religious groups and religiously based reform efforts is stressed in Jean E. Friedman, *The Enclosed Garden: Women and Community in the Evangelical South, 1830–1900* (Chapel Hill, N.C., 1985); Evelyn Brooks Higginbotham, *Righteous Discontent: The Women's Movement in the Baptist Church, 1880–1920* (Cambridge, Mass., 1993); John Patrick McDowell, *The Social Gospel in the South: The Woman's Home Mission Movement in the Methodist Episcopal Church* (Baton Rouge, La., 1982); and Cynthia Neverdon-Morton, *Afro-American Women of the South and the Advancement of the Race, 1895–1925* (Knoxville, Tenn., 1989).

Also see Daisy Bates, *The Long Shadow of Little Rock: A Memoir* (New York, 1962); Septima Poinsette Clark, *Echo in My Soul* (New York, 1962); Couch, *These Are Our Lives*; Virginia Foster Durr, *Outside the Magic Circle: The Autobiography of Virginia Foster Durr*, ed. Hollinger F. Barnard (University, Ala., 1985); Sara Evans, *Personal Politics: The Roots of Women's Liberation in the Civil Rights Movement and the New Left* (New York, 1979); Hagood, *Mothers of the South*; Jacquelyn Dowd Hall et al., *Like a Family: The Making of a South Carolina Mill World* (Chapel Hill, N.C., 1987); Gerda Lerner, ed., *Black Women in White America: A Documentary History* (New York, 1972); Loveland, *Lillian Smith*; Katharine Du Pre Lumpkin,

The Making of a Southerner (New York, 1947); Pauli Murray, *Proud Shoes: The Story of an American Family* (New York, 1956); Lucy Mason Randolph, *To Win These Rights: A Personal Story of the CIO in the South* (New York, 1952); Salmond, *Miss Lucy of the CIO;* Lillian Smith, *Killers of the Dream;* Terrill and Hirsch, *Such as Us;* and Ida B. Wells, *Crusade for Justice: The Autobiography of Ida B. Wells,* ed. Alfreda M. Duster (Chicago, 1970). More impressionistic but useful and sometimes amusing are Shirley Abbott, *Womenfolks: Growing Up Down South* (New Haven, Conn., 1983); Rosemary Daniell, *Fatal Flowers: On Sin, Sex, and Suicide in the Deep South* (New York, 1980); and Florence King, *Southern Ladies and Gentlemen* (New York, 1975). Two searing, wonderfully written memoirs are Rick Bragg, *All Over But the Shoutin'* (New York, 1997); and Mary Karr, *The Liars Club* (New York, 1995). Southern women novelists also provide important perceptions and perspectives. See Barbara Christian, *Black Women Novelists: The Development of a Tradition, 1892–1976* (Westport, Conn., 1976); Anne Goodwyn Jones, *Tomorrow Is Another Day: The Woman Writer in the South, 1859–1936* (Baton Rouge, La., 1981); and of course, the works of the novelists these books discuss.

Women have long been a critical part of the southern workforce, both at home and outside the home. Thus labor history is often also women's history. Women have also been leaders in efforts to improve working conditions and the lives of working people's families. In addition to the works cited in this section and some that are cited in the section on labor, useful material may be found in Julia Kirk Blackwelder, *Now Hiring: The Feminization of Work in the United States, 1900–1995* (College Station, Tex., 1997); Dolores E. Janiewski, *Sisterhood Denied: Race, Gender, and Class in a New South Community* (Philadelphia, 1985); Kathy Kahn, *Hillbilly Women* (Garden City, N.Y., 1981); Cathy L. McHugh, *Mill Family: The Labor System in the Southern Cotton Textile Industry, 1880–1915* (New York, 1986); and Rebecca Sharpless, *Fertile Ground, Narrow Choices: Women on Texas Cotton Farms, 1900–1940* (Chapel Hill, N.C., 1999). Mary Frederickson's study, *A Place to Speak Our Minds: The Southern School for Women Workers, 1927–1950* (Bloomington, Ind., 1990), casts new light on the relationship among middle-class women activists, women workers, and organized labor.

WORKERS AND INDUSTRIES

The amount of scholarly work on the history of labor in the South is not extensive, but it is growing. Even less is available about the history of industry, and that body of work is hardly growing. The best overview is James C. Cobb, *Industrialization and Southern Society, 1877–1984* (Lexington, Ky., 1984), but it is spotty—a reflection, in part, of the state of the literature. Cobb's *Selling of the South: The Southern Crusade for Industrial Development, 1936–1980* (Baton Rouge, La., 1982), is a lucid account of the region's pursuit of investors. Victor S. Clark, *The History of Manufactures in the United States,* 3 vols. (New York, 1929), is still useful, as are Harriet L. Herring, *Southern Industry and Regional Development* (Chapel Hill, N.C., 1940); and Broadus Mitchell and George S. Mitchell, *The Industrial Revolution in the South* (Baltimore, 1930).

Several books are very valuable as starting points on the economy of the South as a whole. They include Gavin Wright, *Political Economy of the Cotton South,* and *Old South, New South;* also see Melvin L. Greenhut and W. Tate Whitman, eds., *Essays in Southern Economic Development* (Chapel Hill, N.C., 1964); Calvin B. Hoover and B. U. Ratchford, *Economic Resources and Policies of the South* (New York, 1951); and William Hord Nicholls, *Southern Tradition and Regional Progress* (Chapel Hill, N.C., 1960). Government publications are very important sources for statistics and analytical studies. Also see the publications of the National Bureau of Economic Research. Very useful for grasping the larger picture of the economy of the South is William N. Parker, "The South in the National Economy, 1865–1970," *Southern Economic Journal* 46 (1983): 7–27.

Thoughtful, well-researched studies of business leaders and entrepreneurs in the New South are scarce. Students looking for good research topics should consider working in these areas. *James Bowron: The Autobiography of a New South Industrialist,* ed. Robert J. Norrell (Chapel Hill, N.C., 1991), offers rich insights.

The growth of the southern economy has been examined extensively. One of the most helpful works is Bernard L. Weinstein and Robert E. Firestine, *Regional Growth and Decline in the United States: The Rise of the Sunbelt and the Decline of the Northeast* (New York, 1978). Also helpful are the publications of the Southern Growth Policies Board, especially its overview of the economy of the South: *The Future of the South* (Research Triangle Park, N.C., 1981). The Southern Regional Council, whose activities include the publishing of studies of the contemporary South, continues to remind us of the shady spots in the Sunbelt. On the way southerners interact with the physical environment that they say they love, see Albert Cowdrey, *This Land, This South.* Nelson M. Blake, *Land into Water—Water into Land: A History of Water Management in Florida* (Tallahassee, Fla., 1980), is a sobering analysis of one specific environmental case.

Individual industries have received varying degrees of attention from scholars over the years. Two of the most glamorous industries, railroads and oil, have fared best. John Stover, *Railroads of the South, 1865–1900: A Study in Finance and Control* (Chapel Hill, N.C., 1955), is a good general introduction. The best history of an individual railroad company is Maury Klein, *The Richmond Terminal: A Study of Businessmen and Business Strategy* (Charlottesville, Va., 1970). Other fine studies of railroads in the South are James P. Baughman, *Charles Morgan and the Development of Southern Transportation* (Nashville, Tenn., 1968); and Allen W. Trelease, *North Carolina Railroad, 1849–1871, and the Modernization of North Carolina* (Chapel Hill, N.C., 1991). Among the several good books on the oil industry are Carl Coke Rister, *Oil! Titan of the Southwest* (Norman, Okla., 1949); John S. Spratt, *The Road to Spindletop: Economic Change in Texas, 1875–1901* (Dallas, Tex., 1955); and Harold F. Williamson et al., *The American Petroleum Industry,* 2 vols. (Evanston, Ill., 1957–1963). Arthur M. Johnson has written the basic study of pipelines, a vital aspect of the petroleum industry: *The Development of American Petroleum Pipelines: A Study in Private Enterprise and Public Policy, 1826–1906* (Ithaca, N.Y., 1956), and *Petroleum Pipelines and Public Policy, 1906–1959* (Cambridge, Mass., 1967). The tourist industry has received some attention from scholars. See, for example, Lynn Morrow and Linda Myers-Phinney, *Shepherd of the Hills Country: Tourism Transforms the Ozarks, 1880s–1930s* (Fayetteville, Ark., 1999).

Unfortunately, neither the coal nor the iron industry has attracted as much scholarly attention as the oil industry. Ethel M. Armes, *The Story of Coal and Iron in Alabama* (Salem, N.H., 1910), is useful in spite of its boosterism. Material can also be gleaned from H. H. Chapman et al., *The Iron and Steel Industries of the South* (University, Ala., 1955). But see W. David Lewis, *Sloss Furnaces and the Rise of the Birmingham District: An Industrial Epic* (Tuscaloosa, Ala., 1994), for a thorough, technologically oriented study of an important part of the metals industry in the South. On the decline of the coal industry after its years of expansion, see McAlister Coleman, *Men and Coal* (New York, 1943); and Malcolm H. Ross, *Machine Age in the Hills* (New York, 1933). The economic and social plight of Appalachia, partially the result of the decline of the coal industry, has received considerable attention. Harry Caudill has written extensively and passionately about that region. For instance, see his *Night Comes to the Cumberlands: A Biography of a Depressed Area* (Boston, 1963). Ronald D. Eller's fine historical study, *Miners, Millhands, and Mountaineers: Industrialization of the Appalachian South, 1880–1930* (Knoxville, Tenn., 1982), surveys economic development and exploitation in southern Appalachia. Eller also effectively undermines the notion that the people of Appalachia lived in naive simplicity in wooded mountains cut off from the rest of the nation. Other books on coal mining and life and politics in the Appalachian South include David Allen Corbin, *Life, Work, and Rebellion in the Coal Fields: The Southern West Virginia Miners, 1880–1922* (Urbana, Ill.,

1981); John Gaventa, *Power and Powerlessness: Quiescence and Rebellion in an Appalachian Valley* (New York, 1980); John W. Hevener, *Which Side Are You On? The Harlan County Miners, 1931–39* (Urbana, Ill., 1978); and Crandall A. Shifflett, *Coal Towns: Life, Work, and Culture in the Company Towns of Southern Appalachia, 1880–1960* (Knoxville, Tenn., 1991). The black minority in Appalachia has begun to receive scholarly attention: Ronald L. Lewis, *Black Coal Miners in America: Race, Class, and Community Conflict, 1780–1980* (Lexington, Ky., 1989); Joe William Trotter, *Coal, Class, Color: Blacks in Southern West Virginia, 1915–1932* (Urbana, Ill., 1990); and William Hobart Turner and Edward Cabell, eds., *Blacks in Appalachia* (Urbana, Ill., 1989). Durwood Dunn, *Cade's Cove: The Life and Death of a Southern Appalachian Community, 1818–1937* (Knoxville, Tenn., 1988), is a study of a once-successful farm area that was taken over by the National Park Service and tourists. Paul Salstrom has put the economy of Appalachia in a very broad time frame in *Appalachia's Path to Dependency: Rethinking a Region's Economic History, 1730–1940* (Lexington, Ky., 1994). Ronald Lewis's *Transforming the Appalachian Countryside: Railroads, Deforestation, and Social Change in West Virginia, 1880–1920* (Chapel Hill, N.C., 1998), is excellent. On moonshining, an often important economic and cultural phenomenon in Appalachia, see Wilbur R. Miller, *Revenuers and Moonshiners: Enforcing Federal Liquor Law in the Mountain South, 1865–1900* (Chapel Hill, N.C., 1991).

Several works on textiles are helpful. Broadus Mitchell's *Rise of the Cotton Mills of the South* (Baltimore, 1921), is valuable, though it lionizes the first generation of New South mill builders. Similar reservations apply to Holland Thompson, *From the Cotton Field to the Cotton Mill: A Study of the Industrial Transition in North Carolina* (New York, 1906). Melvin T. Copeland, *The Cotton Manufacturing Industry of the United States* (Cambridge, Mass., 1912), is also useful. Jack Blicksilver, *Cotton Manufacturing in the Southeast: An Historical Analysis* (Atlanta, 1959), brings the story up to more recent times but is brief. David Carlton's *Mill and Town* is a perceptive analysis of the early years of the textile industry and the reaction that followed the emergence of a large working class in the industrializing South. Louis Galambos's fine study, *Competition and Cooperation: The Emergence of a National Trade Association* (Baltimore, 1966), traces industry efforts from the 1890s to the 1930s to strike a balance between competition and cooperation. The best single company history is Robert S. Smith, *Mill on the Dan: A History of Dan River Mills, 1882–1950* (Durham, N.C., 1960).

Nannie May Tilley's excellent *Bright-Tobacco Industry, 1860–1929* (Chapel Hill, N.C., 1948), covers every aspect of bright leaf tobacco: its history, cultivation, and final processing into consumer products. For a similar fine study of sugar, see Joseph Carlyle Sitterson, *Sugar Country; The Cane Sugar Industry in the South, 1753–1950* (Lexington, Ky., 1953). Tilley also wrote a fine company history: *The R. J. Reynolds Tobacco Company* (Chapel Hill, N.C., 1985). More recently published histories of companies include Marvin Schwartz, *Tyson: From Farm to Market* (Fayetteville, Ark., 1991); and Sandra Stringer Vance and Roy V. Scott, *Wal-Mart: A History of Sam Walton's Retail Phenomenon* (New York, 1994). Randall L. Patton with David B. Parker, *Carpet Capital: The Rise of a New South Industry* (Athens, Ga., 1999) is a scholarly assessment of the carpet manufacturing industry in what became its primary location, Dalton, Georgia. Other than company- or industry-sponsored histories, little is to be found on such highly significant industries as banking, utilities, trucking, chemicals, and lumbering and forest products. Still, sponsored histories should not be completely ignored; some of them contain useful information. One book that definitely is not company- or industry-sponsored is *Barbarians at the Gate: The Fall of RJR Nabisco* (New York, 1990) by Bryan Burrough, a story of 1980s high finance, intrigue, and hubris that suggests the carpetbaggers struck again. Two recently published books are helpful: Germaine M. Reed, *Crusading for Chemistry: The Professional Career of Charles Holmes Herty* (Athens, Ga., 1995); and Richard A. Bartlett, *Troubled Waters: Champion International and the Pigeon River Controversy* (Knoxville, Tenn., 1995).

Durden's *Dukes of Durham* is a good study of one of the most powerful business families in the South. Two useful books on merchandising are Hugh G. Baker, *Rich's of Atlanta:*

The Story of a Store since 1867 (Atlanta, 1953); and LeGette Blythe, *William Henry Belk: Merchant of the South* (Chapel Hill, N.C., 1950). Unfortunately, we have no solid history of either Coca-Cola or Pepsi-Cola, two bubbling giants of the South.

General histories of the American worker and organized labor provide valuable direct and indirect data and perspectives on labor in the South. See, for instance, Ronald L. Filipelli, *Labor in the United States* (New York, 1984); and Robert H. Zieger, *American Workers, American Unions 1920–1985*, 2d ed. (Baltimore, 1994). David Brody's *Workers in Industrial America: Essays on the Twentieth-Century Struggle* (New York, 1980), provides useful insights. Christopher L. Tomlins, *The State and the Unions: Labor Relations, Law, and the Organized Labor Movement in America, 1880–1960* (New York, 1985), is a fine study of an important topic. F. Ray Marshall's *Labor in the South* (Cambridge, Mass., 1967), is a general study of organized labor in the South. Merl E. Reed, Leslie S. Hough, and Gary M. Fink, eds., *Southern Workers and Their Unions, 1880–1975* (Westport, Conn., 1981), is a collection of useful papers. So is Robert H. Zieger, ed., *Organized Labor in the Twentieth-Century South* (Knoxville, Tenn., 1991). Zieger's introduction is especially helpful; his essay on the historiography of southern textile workers is essential reading. Also see Zieger, ed., *Southern Labor in Transition* (Knoxville, Tenn., 1997). For a careful assessment of the importance of unions in contemporary America and a useful corrective to the unions-no-longer-serve-a-useful-purpose theme, see Richard D. Freeman and James L. Medoff, *What Do You Unions Do?* (New York, 1984). Cindy Hahamovitch treats a much-neglected area of labor history in *The Fruits of Their Labor: Atlantic Coast Farmworkers and the Making of Migrant Poverty, 1870–1945* (Chapel Hill, N.C., 1997), as do Neil Foley in *The White Scourge: Mexicans, Blacks, and Poor Whites in Texas Cotton Culture* (Berkeley, Calif., 1997); Emilio Zamora, *The World of the Mexican Worker in Texas* (College Station, Tex., 1993); and Arthur D. Murphy et al., eds., *Latino Workers in the Contemporary South* (Athens, Ga., 2001). These studies reflect a growing phenomenon in the South and in the rest of the United States—the importance of Hispanic labor.

Leon Fink, *Workingmen's Democracy: The Knights of Labor and American Politics* (Urbana, Ill., 1983); Melton Alonzo McLaurin, *Paternalism and Protest: Southern Cotton Mill Workers and Organized Labor, 1875–1905* (Westport, Conn., 1971), and *The Knights of Labor in the South* (Westport, Conn., 1978), deal with organized labor and worker protest in the South in the late nineteenth century. For a study of racial cooperation and conflict among workers in an important industrial state, see Robert D. Ward and William W. Rogers, *Labor Revolt in Alabama: The Great Strike of 1894* (Austin, Tex., 1965). For a similar story from New Orleans, see Eric Arnesen, *Waterfront Workers of New Orleans: Race, Class and Politics, 1863–1923* (New York, 1991). Ruth A. Allen also wrote about labor in Texas during these years: *Great Southwest Strike* (Austin, Tex., 1942), as well as *Chapters in the History of Organized Labor in Texas* (Austin, Tex., 1941), and *East Texas Lumber Workers, 1870–1950* (Austin, Tex., 1961). Henry M. McKiven, Jr., deals with many of these issues in *Iron and Steel: Class, Race, and Community in Birmingham, Alabama, 1875–1920* (Chapel Hill, N.C., 1995).

Child labor was at one time common in the South. On that topic consult Elizabeth H. Davidson, *Child Labor Legislation in the Southern Textile States* (Chapel Hill, N.C., 1931); Walter I. Trattner, *Crusade for the Children: A History of the National Child Labor Committee and Child Labor Reform in America* (Austin, Tex., 1970); and Stephen B. Wood, *Constitutional Politics in the Progressive Era* (Austin, Tex., 1968). David Carlton's *Mill and Town* discusses the motives behind child labor legislation and worker resistance to that legislation.

Perhaps because of their numbers, textile workers have received more attention than other workers in the South. Herbert J. Lahne, *The Cotton Mill Worker* (New York, 1944), is a valuable introduction. Jacquelyn Dowd Hall et al., *Like a Family*; and Allen Tullos, *Habits of Industry: White Culture and the Transformation of the Carolina Piedmont* (Chapel Hill, N.C., 1989), discuss the world the early textile workers came from and the world they helped to create. Also see the fine recent studies of I. A. Newby, *Plain Folk in the New South: Social*

Change and Cultural Persistence, 1880–1915 (Baton Rouge, La., 1989); and George Calvin Waldrep, *Southern Workers and the Search for Community: Spartanburg County, South Carolina* (Urbana, Ill., 2000). Cathy McHugh's *Mill Family* is a study of labor policy during the early years of the industry. Background to the labor strife that marked the industry in the 1920s and 1930s may be found in Irving Bernstein, *The Lean Years: A History of the American Worker, 1920–1933* (Boston, 1960); and George S. Mitchell, *Textile Unionism and the South* (Chapel Hill, N.C., 1931). Jeffrey Leiter, Michael D. Schulman, and Rhonda Zingraff, eds., *Hanging by a Thread: Social Change in Southern Textiles* (Ithaca, N.Y., 1991), deals with a wide range of topics, some in a cross-national context, and discusses some recent developments in the textile industry.

On the labor-management turmoil of the 1930s and on the labor policy of the New Deal, see Irving Bernstein, *Turbulent Years: A History of the American Worker, 1933–1941* (Boston, 1970), and *The Caring Society: The New Deal, the Worker, and the Great Depression—A History of the American Worker, 1933–1941* (Boston, 1985); James A. Hodges, *New Deal Labor Policy and the Southern Cotton Textile Industry, 1933–1941* (Knoxville, Tenn., 1985); and Liston Pope, *Millhands and Preachers: A Study of Gastonia* (New Haven, Conn., 1942). For a good firsthand account of a participant in the famous Gastonia strike of 1929, see Thomas Tippett, *When Southern Labor Stirs* (New York, 1931). John Salmond has written a history of the Gastonia strike: *Gastonia, 1929: The Story of the Loray Mill Strike* (Chapel Hill, N.C., 1995). The general textile strike of 1934 is carefully studied by Janet Irons in *Testing the New Deal*. On the change and decline of a major working-class institution in the South, read Harriet L. Herring, *Passing of the Mill Village: Revolution in a Southern Institution* (Chapel Hill, N.C., 1940). Barbara Griffith has written about Operation Dixie, organized labor's unsuccessful attempt to expand its base in the South: *The Crisis of American Labor: "Operation Dixie" and the Defeat of the CIO* (Philadelphia, 1988). Mimi Conway's *Rise Gonna Rise: A Portrait of Southern Textile Workers* (New York, 1979), is an interesting though journalistic account of the struggle to organize the J. P. Stevens mill at Roanoke Rapids, North Carolina, site of one battle in the long war between Stevens and organized labor. Robert Emil Botsch's *We Shall Not Overcome: Populism and Southern Blue-Collar Workers* (Chapel Hill, N.C., 1980), examines the possible emergence of a populistic black-white worker coalition in the contemporary South and concludes that there is little chance for such a coalition to develop and have an impact. In *The Fabric of Defeat: The Politics of South Carolina Millhands, 1910–1948* (Chapel Hill, N.C., 1948), Bryant Simon takes an innovative approach by asking why South Carolina textile workers, a sizable portion of the electorate, had relatively little political influence and what their primary political concerns were.

Among the valuable books on black labor are Philip S. Foner and Ronald L. Lewis, eds., *Black Workers: A Documentary History from Colonial Times to the Present* (Philadelphia, 1989); and Julius Jacobson, ed., *The Negro and the American Labor Movement* (Garden City, N.Y., 1968). For earlier years, see Gerald David Jaynes, *Branches without Roots: Genesis of the Black Working Class in the American South, 1862–1882* (New York, 1986); and Peter J. Rachleff, *Black Labor in the South: Richmond, Virginia, 1865–1890* (Philadelphia, 1984). William Hamilton Harris, *Keeping the Faith: A. Philip Randolph, Milton P. Webster, and the Brotherhood of Sleeping Car Porters, 1925–1937* (Urbana, Ill., 1977), deals with the first black union admitted to the American Federation of Labor and the men who created it. Randolph was the most important black labor leader in America and a major force in the civil rights movement. Nell Irvin Painter, *The Narrative of Hosea Hudson: His Life as a Negro Communist in the South* (Cambridge, Mass., 1979), is the story of another kind of black activist. Michael K. Honey, in *Southern Labor and Black Civil Rights: Organizing Memphis Workers* (Urbana, Ill., 1993), explores the mixture and admixture of race, class, and unionizing in the hub of the Mid-South, from the 1930s into the 1950s. Timothy Minchin has discussed the racial desegregation of industry in the South, an important but neglected part of the end of Jim Crow, in

Hiring the Black Worker: The Racial Integration of the Southern Textile Industry, 1960–1980 (Chapel Hill, N.C., 1999), and *The Color of Work: The Struggle for Civil Rights in the Southern Paper Industry* (Chapel Hill, N.C., 2001). Daniel Letwin's *The Challenge of Interracial Unionism: Alabama Coal Miners, 1878–1921* (Chapel Hill, N.C., 1998) is a subtle, revealing study. David R. Roediger's *The Wages of Whiteness: Race and the Making of the American Working Class* (New York, 1991) is a provocative analysis of the perceptions of work and race in America.

Information on workers and organized labor in the South can also be found in studies that are not specifically about the South: Melvyn Dubofsky, *We Shall Be All: A History of the Industrial Workers of the World* (Chicago, 1969); Walter Galenson, *The CIO Challenge to the AFL: A History of the American Labor Movement, 1935–1941* (Cambridge, Mass., 1960); Daniel Nelson, *American Rubber Workers and Organized Labor, 1900–1941* (Princeton, N.J., 1988); and Robert H. Zieger, *Rebuilding the Pulp and Paper Workers' Union, 1933–1941* (Knoxville, Tenn., 1984).

LIFE AND CULTURE IN THE CHANGING SOUTH

It is cooler in the South, at least inside. That critical change and its implications are examined in a must-read article by Raymond Arsenault, "The End of the Long Hot Summer: The Air Conditioner and Southern Culture," *Journal of Southern History* 50, no. 4 (Nov. 1984): 597–628. Focusing primarily on mass culture, Pete Daniel looks at change in the allegedly changeless 1950s in *Lost Revolutions: The South in the 1950s* (Chapel Hill, N.C., 2000). Ted Ownby narrows the place of his study to Mississippi and broadens its time frame in his innovative examination of consumerism: *American Dreams in Mississippi: Consumers, Poverty, and Culture, 1830–1993* (Chapel Hill, N.C., 1999).

Much of the change in the life and culture of the South since 1865 has taken place in the urban South, but urban history has been relatively neglected by historians of the South, and a good part of the scanty material available is to be found only in articles. *The City in Southern History* (Port Washington, N.Y., 1977), a collection of historiographical essays edited by Blaine Brownell and David Goldfield, is useful but dated. Goldfield has since published an overview of southern urban history—*Cotton Fields and Skyscrapers: Southern City and Region, 1607–1980* (rev. ed.; Baton Rouge, La., 1982)—which stresses the close ties between the South as a region and the character of its cities and contains a good bibliographical essay. For more recent urban studies, see Raymond A. Mohl, ed., *Search for the Sunbelt: Historical Perspectives on a Region* (Athens, Ga., 1993).

Older histories of southern cities—for instance, William D. Miller, *Memphis during the Progressive Era, 1900–1917* (Memphis, Tenn., 1957); and Joy L. Jackson, *New Orleans in the Gilded Age: Politics and Urban Progress, 1800–1896* (Baton Rouge, La., 1969)—are more descriptive than analytical, but they provide useful information. Much more analytical and suggestive are Carl V. Harris, *Political Power in Birmingham, 1871–1921* (Knoxville, Tenn., 1977); and Eugene J. Watts, *Social Bases of City Politics: Atlanta, 1865–1903* (Westport, Conn., 1978). Atlanta has received more serious scholarly attention than most other southern cities. The best biography of a southern mayor probably is Harold H. Martin, *William Henry Hartsfield: Mayor of Atlanta* (Athens, Ga., 1978). J. Michael Russell, *Atlanta*, covering 1847 to 1890, is very good. Howard L. Preston has examined Atlanta at a later time, when it was reshaped by the horseless carriage: *Automobile Age Atlanta: The Making of a Southern Metropolis, 1900–1935* (Athens, Ga., 1979). Scholars have also examined Nashville carefully. For instance, there are Don H. Doyle's studies of Nashville since 1880: *Nashville in the New South, 1880–1930* (Knoxville, Tenn., 1985), and *Nashville since the 1920s* (Knoxville, Tenn., 1985).

Michael Shirley traces the history of Winston-Salem, North Carolina, from its Moravian beginnings as Salem in 1765 to its evolution by the end of the nineteenth century into a community noted for its manufacturing and banking: *From Congregational Town to Industrial City: Culture and Change in a Southern Community* (New York, 1994). The impact of World War II on the urban South is well known, but one unusual instance of that impact is the subject of Charles W. Johnson and Charles O. Jackson, *City behind a Fence: Oak Ridge, Tennessee, 1942–1946* (Knoxville, Tenn., 1981).

Several historians have written fine monographs about particular aspects of southern urbanization. They include Ronald H. Bayor, *Race and the Shaping of Twentieth-Century Atlanta* (Chapel Hill, N.C., 1996); John W. Blassingame, *Black New Orleans, 1860–1880* (Chicago, 1973); Robert W. Ingalls, *Urban Vigilantes in the New South: Tampa, 1882–1936* (Knoxville, Tenn., 1988); and Howard Rabinowitz, *Race Relations in the Urban South.* Two very useful anthologies are Roger W. Lotchin, ed., *The Martial Metropolis: U.S. Cities in War and Peace* (New York, 1984); and David C. Perry and Alfred J. Watkins, eds., *The Rise of the Sunbelt Cities* (Beverly Hills, Calif., 1977). Some readers may dispute Carl Abbott's definition of the Sunbelt, but many will find his *New Urban America: Growth and Politics in Sunbelt Cities of the South* (Chapel Hill, N.C., 1981), informative and insightful.

There is no history of culture or religion in the South per se. The two most perceptive interpretations of the mind-set and values of the South are Wilbur Cash's *Mind of the South* (New York, 1941); and C. Vann Woodward's *Burden of Southern History* (Baton Rouge, La., 1960). Both are efforts to penetrate the paradoxes in the culture and religion of the South: extreme individualism coexisting with suffocating social conformity; egalitarianism with social stratification; paternalism with a ferocious sense of independence; sectional loyalism with fierce, unquestioning national patriotism; a one-party political tradition that disguised intense, ongoing political conflict and division; and deep religious and moral commitments with a blatantly discriminatory, dehumanizing racial caste system that was one of the cornerstones of southern life and politics.

Cash saw a continuing mind-set that survived the Civil War and persisted to his day. He contended that southerners did not think, they felt. They were romantics, rather than realists, and individualists who abhorred restraints, especially institutional restraints. Ironically, the masses were easily seduced by flamboyant rhetoric. They espoused personal independence, then loyally followed the lead of the political and economic elite of the region. The dominant white majority was obsessed by the large black minority. The region's pervasive evangelical Protestantism and the anguished coexistence of righteousness and guilt contorted the soul of the South. Michael O'Brien, in *Rethinking the South: Essays in Intellectual History* (Baltimore, 1988), argues, and demonstrates, that Cash was wrong and misled others when he created the notion that there was no serious intellectual activity in the South, Old or New. Bruce Clayton has published a biography of Cash: *W. J. Cash: A Life* (Baton Rouge, La., 1991). More evidence that Cash's life and his famous book continue to make others think and write can be found in the publication of two symposia on Cash: Bruce Clayton and Charles W. Eagles, eds., *The Mind of the South: Fifty Years After* (Jackson, Miss., 1992); and Paul D. Escott, *W. J. Cash and the Mind of the South* (Baton Rouge, La., 1992).

Woodward took a different tack from that of Cash. The burden of history, Woodward said, had shaped the South. Its experiences had made it different from the rest of the country: guilt for slavery and then Jim Crow; military defeat, occupation, and political reconstruction; and long-term poverty, relative to the rest of the country and the Western world. This burden has lost a good deal of its persuasive power in the last decade or so, but Woodward still offers a very perceptive approach to southern history.

Some historians have argued that the modern South has shaken off the burden of its past so completely that it is no longer distinct as a region. That is one theme of John Egerton's thoughtful book *The Americanization of Dixie: The Southernization of America* (New

York, 1974). As the title suggests, Egerton also sees the South "southernizing" the rest of the nation. Though a native of Dixie, Egerton does not think this process altogether good. The best answer to the contention that Dixie is dead is John Shelton Reed, *The Enduring South: Subcultural Persistence in Mass Society* (Lexington, Mass., 1972). When he carefully analyzed Gallup polls, Reed found that the South had retained a great deal of its regional distinctiveness. Reed has followed this work with *One South: An Ethnic Approach to Regional Culture* (Baton Rouge, La., 1982); *Southerners: The Social Psychology of Sectionalism* (Chapel Hill, N.C., 1983), *My Tears Spoiled My Aim, and Other Reflections on Southern Culture* (Columbia, Mo., 1993), and *Kicking Back: Further Dispatches from the South* (Columbia, Mo., 1995). Carl Degler in *Place over Time: The Continuity of Southern Distinctiveness* (Baton Rouge, La., 1977); and George B. Tindall in *The Ethnic Southerners* (Baton Rouge, La., 1976), also argue for southern distinctiveness, as do fifteen southerners in *Why the South Will Survive*, ed. Clyde N. Wilson (Athens, Ga., 1981). The last drew its inspiration from a famous collection of essays: *I'll Take My Stand: The South and the Agrarian Tradition by Twelve Southerners* (New York, 1930). A recently published, thoughtful examination of the agrarians is Mark G. Malvasi's *The Unregenerate South: The Agrarian Thought of John Crowe Ransom, Allen Tate, and Donald Davidson* (Baton Rouge, La., 1997). But before readers become so involved in the issue of southern regional identity that they perceive a second secession, they ought to remember that southerners are Americans. On that subject, a good reminder is Charles B. Sellers, Jr., ed., *The Southerner as American* (Chapel Hill, N.C., 1960). This debate has already been projected into the new century: Joe P. Dunn and Howard L. Preston, eds., *The Future South: A Historical Perspective for the Twenty-First Century* (Urbana, Ill., 1991). On the persistence of southern identity and its impact both inside and outside the South, see Peter Applebome, *Dixie Rising: How the South Is Shaping American Values, Politics, and Culture* (New York, 1996); and Tony Horwitz, *Confederates in the Attic: Dispatches from the Unfinished Civil War* (New York, 1998).

For guidance to the treasures created by writers of the South, consult Louis D. Rubin Jr. et al., eds., *History of Southern Literature*, which covers a very broad spectrum of materials and time. To understand fundamental changes in the literature of the South and in the assumptions of the elite culture of the region, Daniel Joseph Singal's *War Within: From Victorian to Modernist Thought in the South, 1919–1945* (Chapel Hill, N.C., 1982), is essential. Also see Fred Hobson, *The Southern Writer in the Postmodern World* (Athens, Ga., 1991); Richard H. King, *A Southern Renaissance: The Cultural Awakening of the American South, 1930–1955* (New York, 1980); and Michael O'Brien, *The Idea of the American South, 1920–1941* (Baltimore, 1979). Like others, historians have long found the work of William Faulkner an important vehicle for understanding the South. See, for instance, Joel Williamson, *William Faulkner and Southern History* (New York, 1993); Daniel Singal, *William Faulkner: The Making of a Modernist* (Chapel Hill, N.C., 1997); or *Writing the South: Ideas of an American Region* (Cambridge, Eng., 1986), by Richard Gray, an English scholar who explores Faulkner and other topics ranging from colonial Virginia to John C. Calhoun, to the New South, the Lost Cause, the Nashville Agrarians, Eudora Welty, and Walker Percy and the end of the distinctive South. Also see Bertram Wyatt-Brown, *The Literary Percys: Family History, Gender, and the Southern Imagination* (Athens, Ga., 1994), and *The House of Percy* (New York, 1994).

Evangelical Protestantism has permeated and shaped the South. For a general, thorough history of religion in America, see Sydney E. Ahlstrom, *A Religious History of the American People* (New Haven, Conn., 1972). Other very useful works of a general nature are Edwin S. Gaustad, *Historical Atlas of Religion in America* (rev. ed.; New York, 1976); and Samuel S. Hill, Jr., ed., *Encyclopedia of Religion in the South* (Macon, Ga., 1984). Two collections of essays are important: Charles R. Wilson, ed., *Religion in the South* (Jackson, Miss., 1985); and David Edwin Harrell, Jr., ed., *Varieties of Southern Evangelicalism* (Macon, Ga., 1981). Also see Samuel S. Hill, Jr., ed., *Religion and the Solid South* (Nashville, Tenn., 1972), and Hill, *The South and the North in American Religion* (Athens, Ga., 1980).

There are a number of studies of various denominations, black and white, Protestant and Catholic, by region, subregion, and state. Most are institutional in focus. Several histories that give special consideration to the social, economic, and political contexts within which particular denominations functioned demonstrate a shift away from an institutional focus: Mickey Crews, *The Church of God: A Social History* (Knoxville, Tenn., 1990); Clifford A. Grammich, Jr., *Local Baptists, Local Politics: Churches and Communities in the Middle and Upland South* (Knoxville, Tenn., 1999); David Harrell, *The Social Sources of Division in the Disciples of Christ, 1865–1900* (Atlanta, 1973); Paul Harvey, *Redeeming the South: Religious Cultures and Racial Identities among Southern Baptists, 1865–1925* (Chapel Hill, N.C., 1997); E. Eric Lincoln, *The Black Church in the African-American Experience* (Durham, N.C., 1990); Deborah Vansau McCauley, *Appalachian Mountain Religion, A History* (Urbana, Ill., 1995); William E. Montgomery, *Under Their Own Vine and Fig Tree: The African-American Church in the South, 1865–1900* (Baton Rouge, La., 1993); Jon Michael Spencer, *Black Hymnody: A Hymnological History of the African-American Church* (Knoxville, Tenn., 1992); Daniel W. Stowell, *Rebuilding Zion: The Religious Reconstruction of the South, 1863–1877* (New York, 1998); and Clarence E. Walker, *A Rock in a Weary Land: The African Methodist Episcopal Church during the Civil War and Reconstruction* (Baton Rouge, La., 1982). In recent years, the South's largest Christian denomination, the Southern Baptists, has been beset by inner turmoil and division. Among the recent writings about those difficulties, see Nancy Tatom Ammerman, ed., *Southern Baptists Observed: Multiple Perspectives on a Changing Denomination* (Knoxville, Tenn., 1993); Bill J. Leonard, *God's Last and Only Hope: The Fragmentation of the Southern Baptist Convention* (Grand Rapids, Mich., 1990); and David T. Morgan, *The New Crusades, the New Holy Land: Conflict in the Southern Baptist Convention, 1969–1991* (Tuscaloosa, Ala., 1996). Keith Harper's *The Quality of Mercy: Southern Baptists and Social Christianity, 1890–1920* (Tuscaloosa, Ala., 1996) effectively counters the assumption that Southern Baptists were indifferent to the Social Gospel.

Ronald Numbers has written a perceptive study of a major aspect of the controversy over evolution and religion: *The Creationists* (New York, 1992). Also see his *Darwinism Comes to America* (Cambridge, Mass., 1998). The issues that underlay the Scopes trial continue to attract attention and deservedly so: Edward J. Larson, *Summer for the Gods: The Scopes Trial and America's Continuing Debate over Science and Religion* (Cambridge, Mass., 1887); Jon H. Roberts, *Darwinism and the Divine in America* (Madison, Wis., 1998); and George Ernest Webb, *The Evolution Controversy in America* (Lexington, Ky., 1994). Ralph Luker has found that many Christians active in the Social Gospel movement in the late nineteenth and early twentieth centuries accepted the racism then in vogue and did not take issue with racial discrimination: *The Social Gospel in Black and White: American Racial Reform, 1885–1912* (Chapel Hill, N.C., 1991). Sandy D. Martin looks at a revealing facet of African American Christian life—the interest of African Americans in Christian missions to Africa—in *Black Baptists and African Missions: The Origins of a Movement, 1880–1915* (Macon, Ga., 1989).

Christian sects have been important in the history of the South, especially for the dispossessed, black and white. These sects have begun to receive the careful, sensitive attention they deserve. Consult the works of a general nature cited in this section as well as such books as Edith L. Blumhofer, *Restoring the Faith: The Assemblies of God, Pentecostalism, and American Culture* (Urbana, Ill., 1993); Thomas Burton, *Serpent-Handling Believers* (Knoxville, Tenn., 1993); David Harrell, *All Things Are Possible: The Healing and Charismatic Revivals in Modern America* (Bloomington, Ind., 1975), and *White Sects and Black Men* (Nashville, Tenn., 1971); W. J. Hollenweger, *The Pentecostals: The Charismatic Movement in the Churches* (Peabody, Mass., 1972); and Vinson Synan, *The Holiness-Pentecostal Movement in the United States* (Grand Rapids, Mich., 1971).

Jews, a small but important group of southerners, have been seriously studied by a number of people. Two useful collections of essays are good starting points: Leonard

Dinnerstein and Mary Palsson (Baton Rouge, La., 1973), joint comp., *Jews in the South* (Baton Rouge, La., 1973); and Nathan M. Kaganoff and Melvin I. Urofsky, eds., *"Turn to the South": Essays on Southern History* (Charlottesville, Va., 1979). Eli Evans, *The Provincials: A Personal History of Jews in the South* (New York, 1973), is valuable but unapologetically impressionistic. Other groups that have been or are somewhat outside southern ethnic and religious mainstreams have received little or no attention. Those groups include some that have had or are beginning to have a significant impact upon the South: Irish Americans; Quakers, or Friends; Greek Americans; Lebanese Americans, and especially Cuban Americans and Mexican Americans. German-Americans, however, have been studied rather extensively, as in Terry G. Jordan, *German Seed in Texas Soil: Immigrant Farmers in Nineteenth-Century Texas* (Austin, Tex., 1966); and Klaus Wust, *The Virginia Germans* (Charlottesville, Va., 1969). The early Italian, Cuban, and Spanish immigrants to Florida are the subjects of serious historical work: Garry Ross Mormino and George E. Pozzetta, *The Immigrant World of Ybor City: Italians and Their Latin Neighbors in Tampa, 1885–1985* (Urbana, Ill., 1985). On Cubans in Florida more generally, see Richard R. Fagen, *Cubans in Exile: Disaffection and the Revolution* (Stanford, Calif., 1968); Maria Cristina Garcia, *Havana U.S.A.: Cuban Exiles and Cuban Americans in South Florida, 1959–1994* (Los Angeles, 1996); Silvia Pedraza-Bailey, *Political and Economic Migrants: Cubans and Mexicans* (Austin, Tex., 1985); and Alejandro Portes, *Latin Journey: Cuban and Mexican Immigrants in the United States* (Berkeley, Calif., 1985). Finally, there is a fine study of Chinese Americans in Mississippi, modern-day manifestations of an attempt to import Chinese laborers to be farmworkers: James W. Loewen, *The Mississippi Chinese: Between Black and White* (Cambridge, Mass., 1971). It is also a somber reminder that racial and ethnic discrimination are more persistent than some of us like to believe.

The assumption that the South was (and is) a creation solely of black and white hands is being increasingly challenged by studies of Native Americans and of the Spanish colonial era. For the history of Native Americans in Oklahoma, see Angie Debo, *And Still the Waters Run* (New York, 1966). One example of growing scholarly attention to Hispanics is David Montejano's fine study, *Anglos and Mexicans in the Making of Texas, 1836–1986* (Austin, Tex., 1987). Arnoldo De Leon's essay, "Texas Mexicans: Twentieth-Century Interpretation," in *Texas through Time: Evolving Interpretations*, ed. Walter L. Buenger and Robert A. Calvert (College Station, Tex., 1991), is very helpful. So are others of the wide range of essays in the same volume. Also see De Leon's *They Called Them Greasers: Anglo Attitudes toward Mexicans in Texas, 1821–1900* (Austin, Tex., 1983).

Charles R. Wilson, *Baptized in Blood: The Religion of the Lost Cause, 1865–1920* (Athens, Ga., 1980), is a perceptive analysis of the Lost Cause as the civil religion of the postbellum South. Another fine study of the Lost Cause is Gaines Foster, *Ghosts of the Confederacy: Defeat, the Lost Cause, and the Emergence of the New South, 1865 to 1913* (New York, 1987). A provocative analysis of the patron saint of the Lost Cause is Connelly, *Marble Man: Robert E. Lee and His Image.* Charles R. Wilson explores different kinds of civil religion in *Judgment and Grace in Dixie: Southern Faiths from Faulkner to Elvis* (Athens, Ga., 1995), from the master of Yoknapatawpha County to legendary coach Bear Bryant and the star of Graceland.

Interpreters of religion in the South have too often been critics, emphasizing especially its indifference to social causes and reforms. Some sects are quiescent simply because they have rejected this world to focus on the next. Moreover, we are now aware that southern religious groups were active in issues such as prohibition and sabbath laws. But despite corrections provided by Ralph Luker's *Social Gospel in Black and White*, the charges are largely on target with respect to such highly sensitive issues as Jim Crow and the civil rights revolution, workers' rights and working conditions, women's rights, and poverty. Such blind spots have often been present among the faithful outside the South as well.

There are exceptions, of course, to all these observations. The black church and clergy were active in the civil rights movement and were the prime catalysts of the biggest social revolution in American history since emancipation. Many of the South's most outspoken and active dissidents have been motivated by their faith. Finally, one ought to remember that generalizations are necessary but they often distort and are very unfair. A book to ponder is James McBride Dabb's memoir: *Haunted by God* (Richmond, Va., 1972).

Education within the South must, of course, be placed within its national context first. Consult, for instance, R. Freeman Butts and Lawrence A. Cremin, *A History of Education in American Culture* (New York, 1953), for primary and secondary education; and Frederick Rudolph, *The American College and University: A History* (New York, 1962). Laurence R. Veysey, *The Emergence of the American University* (Chicago, 1965), is a very perceptive study of the governance of American colleges and universities. Much more needs to be done on the impact of desegregation, recent demographic shifts, conservative religion, increasing professionalism, and the federal government on education at all levels. For a study of the pernicious effects of Jim Crow on the education of blacks, see Louis R. Harlan, *Separate and Unequal: Public School Campaigns and Racism in the Southern Seaboard States, 1901–1915* (Chapel Hill, N.C., 1965). Robert A. Margo's carefully argued study of the impact of racial discrimination in spending for public education is convincing and highly relevant for the past and the present: *Race and Schooling in the South, 1880–1950: An Economic History* (Chicago, 1990). Lower-income whites also received unequal treatment in the public schools. In his *Mill and Town,* David Carlton convincingly demonstrates that students in mill schools received less financial support than did whites in other schools. J. Morgan Kousser arrived at similar conclusions in "Progressivism—For Middle-Class Whites Only: North Carolina Education, 1880–1910," *Journal of Southern History* 46 (May 1980): 169–194. For an assessment of the kind of resistance met by those progressives who wanted to reform public education, often in their own image, see William A. Link, *A Hard Country and a Lonely Place: Schooling, Society, and Reform in Rural Virginia, 1870–1920* (Chapel Hill, N.C., 1986). James L. Leloudis, *Schooling the New South: Pedagogy, Self, and Society in North Carolina, 1880–1920* (Chapel Hill, N.C., 1999) explores important themes in education in the New South.

There are numerous biographies of educators and histories of educational institutions and of the educational efforts of religious bodies. Older institutional histories include Daniel W. Hollis, *University of South Carolina,* 2 vols. (Columbia, S.C., 1951–1956); and Louis Round Wilson, *The University of North Carolina, 1900–1930: The Making of a Modern University* (Chapel Hill, N.C., 1957). Three fine studies are Paul K. Conkin, *Gone with the Ivy: A Biography of Vanderbilt University* (Knoxville, Tenn., 1985); Thomas G. Dyer, *The University of Georgia: A Bicentennial History, 1785–1985* (Athens, Ga., 1985); and Robert C. McMath et al., *Engineering the New South: Georgia Tech, 1885–1985* (Athens, Ga., 1985). More recent studies include Mark Taylor Dalhouse, *An Island in a Lake of Fire: Bob Jones University, Fundamentalism, and the Separatist Movement* (Athens, Ga., 1996); Robert Durden, *The Launching of Duke University, 1924–1949* (Durham, N.C., 1993); Cameron Fincher, *Historical Development of the University System of Georgia* (Athens, Ga., 1991); David Sansing, *Making Haste Slowly: The Troubled History of Higher Education in Mississippi* (Jackson, Miss., 1990); and Peter Wallenstein, *Virginia Tech, Land-Grant University, 1872–1997: A History of a School, a State, a Nation* (Blacksburg, Va., 1997). Edmund L. Drago has written about a noted black school: *Initiative, Paternalism, and Race Relations: Charleston's Avery Normal Institute* (Athens, Ga., 1990).

Most of life, of course, went on outside the halls of ivy. Too much of it went on in courtrooms and prisons. The most thoughtful recent examination of crime in the South is Edward Ayers, *Vengeance and Justice: Crime and Punishment in the Nineteenth-Century South* (New York, 1984). Though criticized for its statistical methodology, Sheldon Hackney's article on violence in the South is still essential for studying that grievous aspect of Dixie:

"Southern Violence," *American Historical Review* 74 (1969): 906–925. Mark Carlton wrote a history of Louisiana's penal system: *Politics and Punishment: The History of the Louisiana State Penal System* (Baton Rouge, La., 1971). William Lynwood Montell explores a more direct means of obtaining justice, or revenge, in *Killings: Folk Justice in the Upper South* (Lexington, Ky., 1986). Also see works cited on page 000.

Health and medicine have attracted the interest of too few historians. But the efforts of some historians have resulted in some very good work: Edward H. Beardsley, *A History of Neglect: Health Care for Blacks and Mill Workers in the Twentieth-Century South* (Knoxville, Tenn., 1987); Khaled J. Bloom, *The Mississippi Valley's Great Yellow Fever Epidemic of 1878* (Baton Rouge, La., 1993); John H. Ellis, *Yellow Fever and Public Health in the New South* (Lexington, Ky., 1992); Elizabeth Etheridge, *The Butterfly Caste: A Social History of Pellagra in the South* (Westport, Conn., 1972); John Ettling, *The Germ of Laziness: Rockefeller Philanthropy and Public Health in the New South* (Cambridge, Mass., 1981); James H. Jones, *Bad Blood: The Tuskegee Syphilis Experiment* (New York, 1981); Kenneth Kiple and Virginia Himmelsteib King, *Another Dimension to the Black Diaspora: Diet, Disease, and Racism* (Cambridge, Eng., 1981); and Edward J. Larson, *Sex, Race, and Science: Eugenics in the Deep South* (Baltimore, 1995). Natural disasters have been major elements in the history of the South. See, for example, Jay Barnes, *Florida's Hurricanes* (Chapel Hill, N.C., 1998).

Southerners, like other Americans, love sports. For general background, Benjamin G. Rader, *American Sports: From the Age of Folk Games to the Age of Spectators* (Englewood Cliffs, N.J., 1983), is useful. So is Allen Guttmann, *A Whole New Ball Game: An Interpretation of American Sports* (Chapel Hill., N.C., 1988); its bibliographical essay is virtually one of a kind. Most of the action in Jules Tygiel's *Baseball's Great Experiment* (New York, 1983), occurred outside the South, but the story of racial desegregation of baseball has significance for the modern South. For a perceptive assessment of the place of hunting in the South, consult Stuart A. Marks, *Southern Hunting in Black and White: Nature, History, and Rituals in a Carolina Community* (Princeton, N.J., 1991).

The music of the South, one of its greatest contributions to American and world culture and to general enjoyment, ought to receive more attention by historians. The following are useful and often very perceptive: William Ferris, *Blues from the Delta* (New York, 1979); Sheldon Harris, *Blues Who's Who: A Biographical Dictionary of Blues Singers* (New Rochelle, N.Y., 1979); Paul Kingsbury and Alan Axelrod, eds., *Country: The Music and the Musicians* (New York, 1988); Bill C. Malone, *Southern Music, American Music* (Lexington, Ky., 1979), and *Singing Cowboys and Musical Mountaineers: Southern Culture and the Roots of Country Music* (Athens, Ga., 1993); Jimmie N. Rogers, *The Country Music Message: All about Lovin' and Livin'* (Englewood Cliffs, N.J., 1983), and *The Country Music Message, Revisited* (Fayetteville, Ark., 1989); Jon Michael Spencer, *Blues and Evil* (Knoxville, Tenn., 1993); Brian Ward, *Just My Soul Responding: Rhythm and Blues, Black Consciousness, and Race Relations* (Chicago, 1998); and Martin Williams, *Jazz Heritage* (New York, 1985). Peter Guralnick's two-volume set, *Last Train to Memphis: The Rise of Elvis Presley* (Boston, 1994), and *Careless Love: The Unmaking of Elvis Presley* (Boston, 1999) is an excellent biography of the King of Graceland. Fortunately or unfortunately, moviemakers have paid the South a lot of attention. Two assessments of the results are Edward D. C. Campbell, *The Celluloid South: Hollywood and the Southern Myth* (Knoxville, Tenn., 1981); and Jack Temple Kirby, *Media-Made Dixie: The South in the American Imagination* (Baton Rouge, La., 1978).

Index

❖

Page numbers in bold refer to illustrations.